THE ROYAL HAMPSHIRE REGIMENT

The *River Clyde*

REGIMENTAL HISTORY

THE ROYAL HAMPSHIRE REGIMENT

VOLUME TWO

1914–1918

BY

C. T. ATKINSON

1952

PRINTED FOR THE REGIMENT BY

ROBERT MACLEHOSE & COMPANY LIMITED

THE UNIVERSITY PRESS GLASGOW

TO THE MEMORY OF
ALL MEMBERS OF THE ROYAL HAMPSHIRE REGIMENT
WHO HAVE FALLEN IN ITS SERVICE

AND OF

GENERAL SIR RICHARD C. B. HAKING
G.B.E., K.C.B., K.C.M.G.

COLONEL OF THE REGIMENT FROM 1924–1945
ON WHOSE INITIATIVE THE HISTORY
WAS WRITTEN

PREFACE

To try, over thirty years after the last events to be recorded, to put together an account of the share of a regiment of the Line in the war of 1914–1918 is to meet certain difficulties which would have been less serious had the attempt been made even ten years earlier. Time has made many gaps in the ranks of the survivors of that war, and not only are many who might have done much to supplement the available information no longer with us, but of those who are left many find that memories are getting dim, especially when it is a question of fixing accurately some doubtful detail. With others touch seems to have been lost, and though the compiler of this account has reason to be grateful to those who have been able to correct and expand the story, what help has been received only emphasizes how much more might have been obtained had more survivors been here to give it. A further loss is that during the war of 1939–1945 the Part II Daily Orders were destroyed in a ' blitz ', so that the very useful information contained in them has gone beyond recall. For things like changes in the officers with a battalion, dates and numbers of casualties, the award of honours, the arrival of drafts, the disposal of the officers and men of disbanded battalions, the Part II Orders would have been invaluable. Working through them was rather laborious work but, in other cases, it amply repaid the time spent on it and without their information many gaps must remain unfilled.

It is some compensation that the completion of the Official History provides much useful information about the main story of the campaigns in which the different battalions of the regiment took part. It should now be easier, with its help, to give a more correct and balanced picture of the background, to assess what the different campaigns and battles contributed to the ultimate result and to see what the whole was of which the regiment's achievements formed part. To keep the balance between that whole and the regiment's share is far from easy, there is always a danger of giving too much of the background and going into things which may seem to be outside the province of a regimental history. Still the opposite danger also exists, some regimental histories fail to show why certain sacrifices were demanded of individual units or what the reasons were for certain things which need explaining. A writer of a regimental history can be quite sure that whichever line he takes he cannot hope to please more than some of his readers, and perhaps it is better to insert than to omit.

The main sources for this account are the war diaries kept by the different battalions, supplemented to some extent by those of the brigades and Divisions in which they served, with the information contained in the regimental Journal. This last was particularly useful for 1914 and 1915 ; after that the exigencies of the censorship prevented it from being as definite and precise as it had been. After 1915 it contains few of the extracts from letters from the front which were so helpful for the retreat from Mons and for events up to the middle of 1915. The

' citations ' for the award of decorations are not very helpful when the date of an incident is not given and when it cannot even be certain with which battalion the recipient of an award was serving when he won his M.C. or D.C.M. Here the battalion diaries sometimes provide the answer, but by no means always. Two of the awards of the V.C. are not mentioned in the battalion diaries in which it might be expected to find them recorded. It is feared, therefore, that many gallant actions have not been recorded because they could not be dated with any accuracy.

The battalion diaries naturally enough vary greatly in their usefulness. Keeping them was hardly a matter of extreme urgency and clearly there were times of stress when more important things took up the attention of those responsible, when the diary was written up later on by someone who had not been in the action in which crippling losses had been incurred. It may also be that while the diaries were supposed to be kept in duplicate, the copy which has got to ' Records' has not been furnished with maps, orders and reports and other things which were attached to the top copy. But instead of complaining if some diaries fail to give any account of quite important engagements or to mention the names of officers killed and wounded in a major action, it is more reasonable to be grateful to those diary keepers who did insert these things and have provided much useful and detailed information. The diaries of the 1st Battalion for much of 1917 and 1918 and of the 2nd Battalion for a good part of 1916 and for 1917 may perhaps be mentioned as deserving of gratitude as having been very helpful. If there is some lack of proportion between the accounts of different operations it is because for some little information is to be had, whereas for other episodes the diaries are fuller and provide more of what the compiler needs.

I have occasion also to be grateful to several officers who have answered queries, sent me information and in particular to Mrs May for letting me see some most interesting and helpful letters from Captain H. W. M. May, which were of great assistance. Of published works Captain Bacon's *Wanderings of a Temporary Warrior* has been of great help and the short account of the 10th and 12th Battalions published in 1930 makes me wish that Major Cowland would have followed Captain Bacon's good example and written of those battalions at greater length. Of other regimental histories, Major Stacke's very detailed history of the Worcestershire Regiment has been very helpful for the doings of the 2nd Battalion and Captain Berkeley's account of the Rifle Brigade for those of the 1st Battalion, while for Salonica Colonel Jourdain's story of the 5th Connaught Rangers has been useful. It is odd that only one of the Divisions in which Hampshire battalions served has had its history written. The story of the Fourth Division is one which it is strange to find has not been tackled and among " New Army " Divisions the Forty-first had a record well worth telling. That of the Twenty-Ninth Division, which has been written, would have been more helpful if it had been more liberally furnished with maps and had it gone into certain episodes in rather fuller detail.

The cost of maps is so great and the need for them to illustrate the story is so imperative that I have provided a large number of more or less skeleton maps, in preference to a few really elaborate maps. Some of these are composite productions based on two or three sketches in diaries, and they do not claim to be more than diagrams in which I have tried to show really relevant features. If there are some discrepancies in spelling between maps and text this is partly because my authorities have varied considerably in the spelling they adopt, especially in those for the Macedonian, Mesopotamian and Palestine campaigns.

I have deliberately omitted initials except where officers of the same name might be confused ; this has been done to avoid the really large amount of space which the printing of initials in other cases would have taken up. Space also implies cost, for which reason the names of those who lost their lives have been omitted and no attempt has been made to provide a Roll of Officers for those who only held ' temporary ' commissions or for the Territorial Battalions. To produce them would also have greatly delayed the production of a work which has already been over long in labour. I have to thank Mr Holland of the Royal United Service Institution for his help in producing the list of Regular and Special Reserve officers which carry on from the lists in Volume I.

The Colonel of the Regiment has been very patient over the long time this volume has been in production. I owe him many thanks, as also to Major Jeffery, who has been unfailingly helpful in every way.

C. T. A.

Band Pouch Badge, 1887

CONTENTS

PAGE

PREFACE

CHAPTER

    I. LE CATEAU AND THE RETREAT — 3

    II. THE MARNE—THE AISNE—THE MOVE TO FLANDERS — 19

    III. THE FIGHT FOR THE CHANNEL PORTS—WINTER IN THE TRENCHES — 27

    IV. THE 2ND AND 3RD BATTALIONS—THE TERRITORIALS—EXPANSION — 41

    V. SECOND YPRES AND AFTER — 55

    VI. GALLIPOLI : THE LANDING—THE ADVANCE ON ACHI BABA — 69

    VII. GALLIPOLI (CONTINUED) THE STRUGGLE FOR KRITHIA — 82

    VIII. GALLIPOLI (CONTINUED) SARI BAIR AND SUVLA — 92

    IX. GALLIPOLI. THE FINAL STAGES—THE EVACUATION — 107

    X. THE TERRITORIALS IN INDIA—MESOPOTAMIA, 1915 — 117

    XI. FROM SECOND YPRES TO THE SOMME — 128

    XII. SALONICA, 1915–1916 — 141

    XIII. MESOPOTAMIA, 1916 — 157

    XIV. THE SOMME. THE OPENING PHASES — 169

    XV. THE SOMME (CONTINUED) — 179

    XVI. THE THIRD WINTER — 202

    XVII. ARRAS — 210

    XVIII. THE FLANDERS OFFENSIVE, MESSINES AND THIRD YPRES — 224

    XIX. THE FLANDERS OFFENSIVE, THIRD YPRES (CONTINUED) — 238

    XX. CAMBRAI — 251

    XXI. EGYPT AND PALESTINE, 1916–1917 — 263

    XXII. MESOPOTAMIA, 1917 — 274

    XXIII. SALONICA, 1917 — 288

    XXIV. PALESTINE, 1917 — 297

    XXV. THE FOURTH WINTER — 309

    XXVI. 1918 : I : THE MARCH OFFENSIVE — 318

    XXVII. 1918 : II : THE APRIL OFFENSIVE — 334

    XXVIII. 1918 : III : THE SUMMER MONTHS : THE 2/4TH ON THE MARNE — 346

    XXIX. 1918 : IV : THE RETURN TO THE ATTACK — 359

CHAPTER	PAGE
XXX. 1918 : V : THE FINAL ADVANCE	375
XXXI. MESOPOTAMIA AND PERSIA, 1918	397
XXXII. PALESTINE, 1918	407
XXXIII. SALONICA, 1918	416
XXXIV. AFTER THE ARMISTICE—DEMOBILIZATION	428
HONOURS AND AWARDS	448
ROLL OF OFFICERS	469
INDEX	481

PLATES

THE *River Clyde*	*frontispiece*
SECOND LIEUTENANT GEORGE RAYMOND DALLAS MOOR, V.C.	*facing page* 87
SECOND LIEUTENANT DENIS GEORGE WYLDBORE HEWITT, V.C.	,, 230
SECOND LIEUTENANT MONTAGUE SHADWORTH SEYMOUR MOORE, V.C.	,, 240

MAPS AND DIAGRAMS

	PAGE
THE LE CATEAU BATTLEFIELD	7
LE CATEAU—AUGUST 26TH, 1914	9
THE RETREAT FROM MONS, I, TO HAM	12
THE RETREAT FROM MONS, II, HAM TO BRIE COMTE ROBERT	21
THE AISNE	23
THE ADVANCE TO THE LYS	28
THE DEFENCE OF PLOEGSTEERT WOOD	30
POSITION AFTER THE LOSS OF THE BIRDCAGE, NOV. 7TH, 1914	36
SECOND YPRES, I, TO MAY 3RD	56
SECOND YPRES, II. AFTER MAY 3RD	60
THE INTERNATIONAL TRENCH	66
CAPE HELLES AND KRITHIA, TO MAY 8TH	70

PAGE

SEDD EL BAHR, APRIL 25TH–26TH, 1918   75

OPERATIONS MAY 8TH—JUNE 4TH   82

THE ATTACK OF JUNE 4TH, 1915   84

CAPE HELLES, POSITION, JULY, 1915   89

ATTACK OF AUGUST 6TH, 1915   94

CHUNUK BAIR, AUGUST 8TH—12TH, 1915   99

HILL 60, AUGUST 21ST, 1915   105

SUVLA   113

LOWER MESOPOTAMIA   118

THE AKAIKA CHANNEL, JULY 5TH, 1915   122

OPERATIONS, JULY 6TH–24TH, 1915   125

SALONICA   142

KOSTURINO, DEC. 7TH, 1915   145

OPERATIONS NORTH OF LAKE DOIRAN   147

OPERATIONS IN THE STRUMA VALLEY   150

THE DOIRAN FRONT   154

OPERATIONS FOR THE RELIEF OF KUT, JANUARY-APRIL, 1916   158

EL HANNA, JAN. 21ST, 1916   162

ATTACKS OF JULY 1ST AND SEPT. 3RD, 1916, ON THE BEAUMONT HAMEL—
    ANCRE FRONT   181

CAPTURE OF GINCHY : SEPT. 9TH, 1916   182

FLERS, SEPT. 15TH, 1916   187

ATTACK OF OCT. 7TH, 1916   191

ATTACK NEAR GUEUDECOURT, OCT., 1916   192

OPERATIONS EAST OF LES BOEUFS, OCT., 1916   197

THE SCHWABEN REDOUBT   198

ARRAS, APRIL–MAY 1917   210

POSITION TAKEN, APRIL 9TH, 1917   213

MONCHY, APRIL 1917   214

ROEUX, MAY 11TH–12TH, 1917   220

ATTACK OF JUNE 7TH, 1917   226

ATTACK OF JULY 31ST, 1917   228

ATTACK OF AUG. 16TH, 1917   234

ATTACK OF SEPT. 20TH, 1917   240

ATTACKS OF SEPT. 20TH AND 26TH, 1917   243

RAID OF JULY 26TH, 1917   245

ATTACK OF OCT. 4TH, 1917   246

ATTACK OF OCT. 9TH, 1917   249

THE CAMBRAI BATTLEFIELD   252

MASNIÈRES, NOV. 1917   254

ATTACK OF SIXTEENTH DIVISION, NOV. 20TH, 1917   258

CAMBRAI   261

GAZA ; MARCH 26–27TH AND APRIL 19TH, 1917   264

OPERATIONS FOR RECAPTURE OF KUT   274

THE HAI SALIENT, JAN.–FEB., 1917   277

THE SHUMRAN BEND, FEB. 23RD–24TH, 1917   281

THE DIALA VALLEY   284

POSITIONS HELD EAST OF LAKE DOIRAN   294

GAZA, NOV. 2ND, 1917   299

OPERATIONS FOR CAPTURE OF JUNCTION STATION, NOV. 1917   300

THE ADVANCE UPON JERUSALEM   302

OPERATIONS—THE COASTAL AREA, 1917–1918   306

OPERATIONS OF 11TH HAMPSHIRE. MARCH 21ST–24TH, 1918   320

MARCH 1918, OPERATIONS OF 15TH HAMPSHIRE   322

OPERATIONS OF 11TH HAMPSHIRE, MARCH 25TH–31ST, 1918   326

ATTACK OF MARCH 28TH, 1918   328

BATTLE OF THE LYS, APRIL 1918   336

PACAUT WOOD AND ROBECQ   338

PACAUT WOOD (NOT TO SCALE)   343

OPERATIONS OF TWENTY–NINTH DIVISION, JUNE–AUG., 1918   350

OPERATIONS ON THE ARDRE, JULY 20TH–29TH, 1918   354

OPERATIONS OF 2/4TH HAMPSHIRE, AUG. 24TH–28TH, 1918   362

THE DROCOURT–QUEANT LINE, AUG. 25TH—SEPT. 3RD, 1918   364

OPERATIONS OF 2ND HAMPSHIRE, SEPT. 1ST–4TH, 1918   368

OPERATIONS OF 15TH HAMPSHIRE, SEPT. 4TH, 1918   370

THE CAPTURE OF HAVRINCOURT, SEPT. 12TH, 1918   372

OPERATIONS OF 2/4TH HAMPSHIRE, SEPT., 27TH—OCT. 1ST, 1918   376

YPRES, SEPT. 28TH—30TH, 1918   379

	PAGE
Gheluwe, Oct. 2nd, 1918	381
The Advance across the Lys, 2nd and 15th Hampshire, October 1918	384
1st and 2/4th Battalions, Oct.—Nov., 1918	388
The Finish in Flanders	395
Operations of 1/4th Hampshire in Persia	398
Attack on Berukin, April 9th, 1918	410
Attack of Sept. 18th, 1918	414
The Roche Noire Salient, Sept. 1st–2nd, 1918	420
Operations North of Lake Doiran	424
North Russia	432

Drum Carrier Badge

BATTLE HONOURS

THE GREAT WAR

LE CATEAU

RETREAT FROM MONS

MARNE, 1914, 1918

AISNE, 1914

ARMENTIÈRES, 1914

YPRES, 1915, 1917, 1918

ST. JULIEN

FREZENBERG

BELLEWAARDE

SOMME, 1916, 1918

ALBERT, 1916

GUILLEMONT

GINCHY

FLERS-COURCELETTE

THIEPVAL

LE TRANSLOY

ANCRE HEIGHTS

ANCRE, 1916

ARRAS, 1917, 1918

VIMY, 1917

SCARPE, 1917, 1918

MESSINES, 1917

PILCKEM

LANGEMARCK, 1917

MENIN ROAD

POLYGON WOOD

BROODSEINDE

POELCAPPELLE

PASSCHENDAELE

CAMBRAI, 1917, 1918

ST. QUENTIN

BAPAUME, 1918

ROSIÈRES

LYS

ESTAIRES

HAZEBROUCK

BAILLEUL

KEMMEL

BÉTHUNE

TARDENOIS

DROCOURT-QUÉANT

HINDENBURG LINE

HAVRINCOURT

CANAL DU NORD

COURTRAI

SELLE

VALENCIENNES

SAMBRE

FRANCE & FLANDERS, 1914–18

ITALY, 1917–18

KOSTURINO

STRUMA

DOIRAN, 1917, 1918

MACEDONIA, ~~1914–18~~ 1915–18

HELLES

LANDING AT HELLES

KRITHIA

SUVLA

SARI BAIR   SHARON
LANDING AT SUVLA   PALESTINE, 1917–18
SCIMITAR HILL   ADEN
GALLIPOLI, 1915–16   SHAIBA
EGYPT, 1915–17   KUT AL AMARA, 1915–17
GAZA   TIGRIS, 1916
EL MUGHAR   BAGHDAD
NEBI SAMWIL   SHARQAT
JERUSALEM   MESOPOTAMIA, 1915–18
JAFFA   PERSIA, 1918–19
TELL 'ASUR   ARCHANGEL, 1919
MEGIDDO   • SIBERIA, 1918–19

Old Hampshire Title

THE HAMPSHIRE REGIMENT 1914–1919

CHAPTER I

LE CATEAU AND THE RETREAT

WHEN, in August 1914, the German violation of the Belgian neutrality, which the German Empire was pledged to defend, forced Great Britain into war to fulfil her treaty obligations, both Regular battalions of the Hampshire Regiment had spent nearly a year at the new stations to which the previous ' trooping season ' had transferred them. By shifting it from the Second Division to the Fourth [1] the 1st Battalion's move from Aldershot to Colchester had influenced its fortunes in the war far more than the 2nd's move from Mauritius to Bengal affected that battalion's doings, as the 1st Essex, who replaced the 2nd Hampshire at Mauritius, were actually in the same brigade of the Twenty-Ninth Division. The 1st Battalion's move meant that it missed Mons and the first great struggle in the Ypres Salient but fought at Le Cateau and helped in the stubborn defence of the British line in the Lys valley, that if not at Neuve Chapelle or Loos it was to be sorely tried in ' Second Ypres ', and that throughout the war its experiences were very different from those it would have met if still in the Second Division.

The gravity of the approaching crisis had hardly been generally appreciated in England before the Austrian ultimatum to Servia, news of which, appearing in the Sunday papers on July 26th, suddenly competed for seriousness with the grave developments in Ireland, on which most people's attention had till then been focused. The issue of orders on July 29th to adopt the ' precautionary period ' measures made it clear that the authorities were taking the gravest view of the situation, and therewith at all military stations preliminary preparations for mobilisation began to be put in hand.

The ' precautionary period ' measures included the recall of all those on leave and the manning of coast defences, the 1st Hampshire sending parties to Felixstowe and Purfleet. For political reasons actual orders for mobilisation were delayed as long as any faint chance of averting war remained, but meanwhile those actually with the Colours could be given medical examinations, equipment could be checked and other work got through before the great influx of Reservists [2] which followed quickly on the actual declaration of war on the evening of August 4th. Even before that Reservists had begun to report at the Depot, and on the Wednesday afternoon (August 8th) a large party left for Colchester under Captain Unwin, followed next day by another batch under Captain R.W. Harland ; amounting in all to 500 men. That left nearly as many to join the 3rd Battalion, whose mobilisation was completed by the evening of August 7th, so that it could leave for its war station at the Isle of Wight next

[1] The Fourth Division was commanded by Major General Snow and the 11th Brigade by Brigadier General Hunter-Weston. The 5th Brigade of the Second Division was under Brigadier General Haking.

[2] The Brigade and battalion War Diaries do not cover the period between mobilisation and the move overseas, and the unfortunate destruction by German air action of all the Part II Orders makes it impossible to supplement these gaps from this invaluable source.

day. Another 50 men from the Regular establishment of the Depot under Lt. Kent were also transferred to the 1st Battalion, which in turn sent back to the 3rd the few unfits and all those too young for service overseas.

The 11th Brigade's mobilisation was not impeded as was that of the 10th and 12th, which were sent off to York and Cromer as a precaution against a German raid. At Colchester the 11th was in position to meet a descent on Essex and did not therefore have to move, so all proceeded ' according to plan '. As the 1st Battalion had been at home nearly nine years most of the Reservists had done the bulk of their Colour service with the 2nd, so that many officers and N.C.O.s of the 1st, unless recently transferred from the 2nd, had seen little of them, but they fitted quickly into their places, while the fortnight that elapsed before the Fourth Division went overseas gave plenty of time for any unfamiliarity to pass off.

By August 17th the Special Reserve had taken over its coast defence duties, the Territorials had also been mobilised and their Divisions were at or on the way to their war-stations. The Fourth Division could therefore be relieved from its temporary role as the spear-head of the Home Defence Force and concentrated in readiness to follow the rest of the British Expeditionary Force overseas. August 18th found it assembling round Harrow, where its entrainment began on August 21st-22nd, the 1st Hampshire leaving soon after midnight and embarking at Southampton, headquarters and the right wing in the *Braemar Castle*, the left wing along with the Rifle Brigade in the *Cestrian.* Sailing before midday they were at Havre before midnight and before dawn had disembarked and moved out to a rest camp outside the town.

Before leaving Colchester orders had been received to find a Captain, a subaltern and 15 selected N.C.O.s to form a nucleus for the new ' Service Battalion ' which every regiment was to raise as part of the ' New Army ' of six Divisions, whose formation Lord Kitchener, now Secretary of State for War, had ordered. Captain Morley and Lt. K. A. Johnston were the officers detailed, along with 2nd Lts. Hudson and Waddington, recently appointed and due to take the next draft out to India, and to complete the war-establishment Captain Richards and Lt. Halls, home on leave from the 2nd Battalion, accompanied the 1st overseas, along with two Special Reservists, Lts. Rose and Griffiths.

The officers who went out to France were Colonel Jackson, Majors Hicks (2nd in command) and Barlow (O.C. C Company), Captains Palk (D), Baxter (B), Moore (A), Richards (A), Connellan (C), Perkins (Adjutant) [1] and Harland (B), Lts. Dolphin (B), im Thurn (D), Le Hunte (machine guns), Kent (A), Knocker (C), Halls (D), Edsell (transport), Cecil (A), Trimmer (C), Rose (C), and Griffiths (D), 2-Lts. Cowan (B), Sweet (C), Westmorland (D) and Nicholson (A) and Lt. and Qr. Mr. Hackett. Captain Williams (R.A.M.C.) accompanied the battalion as M.O., Captain R. D. Johnston being in charge of the first reinforcements. [2]

[1] He had just succeeded Captain Baxter, whose three years were up on August 6th.

[2] Besides the six Regular officers on the establishment of the 3rd Battalion, two Majors (Williams and Mackay) and three Captains were in Staff posts or at the Staff College, seven Captains were doing duty as Special Reserve or Territorial Adjutants, three Captains and seven subalterns were employed with the Egyptian Army or Colonial forces.

* Lt E·M·S Kent (A) K·I·A 26·8·14

The Fourth Division was not long at Havre. The B.E.F. was already in touch with the Germans at Mons, and before the whole Division had arrived in France entrainment had begun. Divisional Headquarters and the artillery were to detrain at Busigny, the 10th and 11th Brigades at Le Cateau and the 12th at Bertry. The 1st Hampshire entrained in the small hours of August 24th and after spending over 24 hours in the train, reached Le Cateau about 4 a.m. next day.[1] The men travelled uncomfortably, crowded in vehicles ' rather after the style of our guards' vans ' one officer wrote, but their discomfort did not prevent their being in high spirits. Detraining promptly the battalion had just time for a hurried breakfast before marching off N.W. to Solesmes, where the Division, or such of it as had arrived, was taking position to cover the B.E.F.'s retirement from Mons. It was very hot and the men, tired by the long journey, found a six miles march very trying.

Regimental officers and men naturally knew little even of the local situation, except that the ' B.E.F.' had been in action at Mons and was retiring Southward, while Sir John French's headquarters had left Le Cateau for a position further South. Of the miscarriage of the French counter stroke in Lorraine they knew nothing or of the unexpected strength of the German advance through Belgium, before which General Lanrezac's French Fifth Army was retiring, its retreat having been successfully covered by the British success in holding up von Kluck's First Army at Mons (August 23rd), after which the B.E.F. had itself to retire to avoid the envelopment which its stand had enabled Lanrezac to evade.

The Fourth Division's arrival at Le Cateau was the more timely because on that day Smith Dorrien's Second Corps and Haig's First had diverged, having to pass on either side of the great Forest of Mormal, while with von Kluck's Army bearing more SW. than South, the Second Corps was being followed by overwhelming forces ; indeed its situation would have been highly perilous had not the Fourth Division been there to cover its retirement and then prolong its line to the Westward.

Actually on August 25th the Fourth Division was not seriously engaged. The 11th Brigade's leading battalions, the 1st Somerset L.I. and 1st East Lancashire, were in position SE. of Solesmes quite early on, and the Hampshire's first orders were to support the E. Lancashire. Accordingly they dug in South of Solesmes about Bellevue Farm with the E. Lancashire on their right and the Somerset on the left, and awaited developments. C. Company was in advance of the rest just outside Solesmes. Heavy firing could be heard away to the Northward, and from parties of British troops who, mixed up with a flood of civilian refugees, were passing through the Fourth Division's line, a little news and rather more in the way of rumours could be picked up, but of the pursuing Germans next to nothing was to be seen. Captain Connellan took two platoons of C Company forward North of Solesmes to reconnoitre but merely met British cavalry, who reported that the Germans were keeping their distance.

[1] The battalion's first casualty occurred on the journey : the Adjutant's groom, trying to control his frightened charger in passing through a tunnel, was kicked out of the train and killed.

But until the rear-guards were through its line the Fourth Division had to retain its positions, the 10th Brigade S.W. of Solesmes, the 11th on its right and the 12th in reserve at Viesly. Early in the afternoon the Hampshire were moved Westward to Briastre where they remained till after dark, No. 15 Platoon from D Company under Lt. Halls being sent forward to a cross-roads North of Briastre on outpost.[1] Details of the Third Division were passing through and the enemy were shelling Solesmes, where towards dusk the Third Division's rear-guard became somewhat sharply engaged, the only time during the day when the Germans really came to grips with the British infantry. By 9 p.m. this rear-guard had been successfully withdrawn and the Fourth Division was free to fall back also. When the 11th Brigade's retirement started, A and D Companies under Major Hicks were left as rear-guard, two platoons of D Company under Lt. Halls being detailed as rear party in Briastre, while the brigade moved off SW. to the new position assigned to it. This was on the left of the Second Corps, whose line ran from Le Cateau Westward to Caudry and was to be continued by the Fourth Division from Fontaine au Pire to Wambaix on the rising ground North of the valley of the Warnelle brook. In this position the 11th Brigade was to be on the right, with the 12th on its left and the 10th in reserve across the Warnelle.

Moving off about 10.30 p.m. the Hampshire's rear-guard had to halt for a time, as the 10th Brigade was delayed ; it then had to toil along over a pavé road full of holes and ruts which a terrific thunderstorm late in the afternoon had left muddy. After their tiring journey and the intense heat and being drenched by the thunderstorm, while no supplies had been issued, all ranks were nearly exhausted, and on reaching the straggling village of Beauvois—Fontaine au Pire, in whose winding streets it was easy to go wrong in the dark, about 2 a.m., the men lay down in the streets to get what poor rest they could and eat a mouthful of biscuit. Here the rear party arrived about 3.30 a.m.; they had been attacked several times by cavalry patrols whom they had driven off each time. The battalion's rest was short enough, before dawn it was moving out NW. towards the position assigned to it further to the left. Parties of German cavalry were hovering about, so B Company with one of the Rifle Brigade were detailed to cover this move, and directly they got into line upon a ridge they came under artillery fire, B having several casualties.

Sir John French, in ordering the retirement from Mons, had originally intended to attempt a stand on the Le Cateau position. The rapid development of the German advance, its unexpected strength and the retreat of Lanrezac's Fifth Army on our right had made this impossible, and overnight G.H.Q. had ordered General Smith-Dorrien to continue the retreat as early as possible on August 26th. During the night information had come in, both about the Germans and about the British troops,[2] which convinced General Smith-Dorrien that to attempt to retreat as ordered would invite disaster and that he must stand and fight, in the hopes of inflicting such a check on the enemy that he would eventu-

---

[1] No. 15 made a road-block here ; perhaps the first made by the B.E.F.
[2] Some of the Third Division's rear-guard only reached the Le Cateau position about 4 a.m.

ally be able to disengage and withdraw in his own time. He had accordingly asked General Snow to place the Fourth Division under his orders and co-operate with the Second Corps in ' giving the enemy a wipe ', as Sir John Moore called it. General Snow had promptly agreed, but the news of his decision had barely reached his brigades before his infantry was already hard at it, keeping off the enemy's attacks.

The 11th Brigade's transport [1] was just starting off for the village of Ligny across the Warnelle ravine, when the German attack developed, and it had some difficulty in getting clear of Fontaine au Pire and suffered some loss, while about

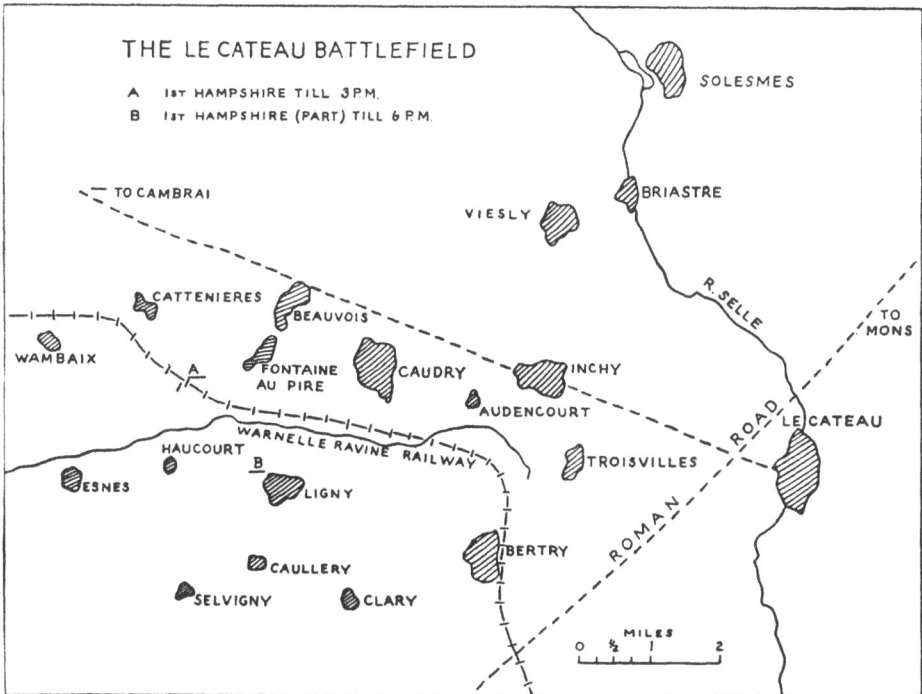

THE LE CATEAU BATTLEFIELD

A 1ST HAMPSHIRE TILL 3 P.M.
B 1ST HAMPSHIRE (PART) TILL 6 P.M.

this time the machine gun section got detached from the battalion but eventually took up position along with that of the Rifle Brigade on the South of the Warnelle ravine somewhere between Ligny and Haucourt. Here it was to remain in action till evening, getting several opportunities of opening fire with good effect at rather long range. Meanwhile the battalion was taking up its position roughly facing NW. towards Cattenières and astride a light railway running NW. Major Hicks had been able to carry out a hurried reconnaissance, and A and D were soon in position and were working hard with their ' grubbers ' [2] to throw up a little cover when the battalion came under machine gun and artillery fire.

[1] It could not accompany the battalion across country but some of the S.A.A. carts did reach the battalion's position and issued their ammunition, one being destroyed by a shell in getting away.
[2] The small entrenching tool then carried by the infantry.

The Fourth Division, or such portions of it as were coming into action, was engaging in battle at great disadvantage. The nicely adjusted organization of a British Division of all arms provided cavalry and cyclists for protective work, R.E. to direct working parties and supply skilled labour, R.A.M.C. to attend to the wounded, a Signal Company to provide its commander and his brigadiers with the means of controlling their commands. At Le Cateau the Fourth Division was unfortunately short of these vital elements and had not even the heavy battery of 60 pounders to supplement the fire of its 18 pounders and 4.5 inch howitzers. If the 12th Brigade, on the 11th's left, had most reason to regret the absence of the Divisional squadron and cyclists, who might have saved the heavy losses it suffered from having one battalion surprised in mass by machine guns, the Signal Company's absence [1] was probably on the whole the biggest handicap from which the Division suffered and was responsible for losses which with proper means of communication might have been averted.

The 11th Brigade, covered by its rear parties of the Hampshire and Rifle Brigade, took up its position without much delay or loss, the Hampshire on its left being separated from the 12th Brigade further West by a wide gap, but not too wide as to allow the enemy to advance into it, while again and again the battalion lent the 12th Brigade effective assistance by fire. Its line ran roughly along the crest of the ridge North of the Warnelle ravine, from which ridge the ground sloped slightly down to the Northward towards the high-road to Cambrai. The country, though under cultivation, largely with beet and clover, not yet harvested as other crops had been, was open, with few trees and hedges, and gave a fair field of fire, particularly to D Company, North of the railway, as the Germans[2] found when they tried to advance, British rifle-fire soon discouraging them and checking efforts to work round towards our left. Accordingly against the 11th Brigade they relied mainly on shell fire and machine guns and only very occasionally was the Fourth Division given targets like those by which the Second Corps had profited so much at Mons. Even so by the next morning many of the men proved to have had occasion to use up most of their ammunition.

After the brigade had taken up its position the covering parties were able to fall back. B Company had been quite sharply engaged and had several casualties. As they fell back one detachment had the satisfaction of wiping out a platoon of Jäger [3] who had incautiously emerged from Fontaine au Pire in pursuit. Half the company under Captain Baxter became separated from the rest and joined the Somerset, alongside whom they fought till that battalion had to retire on Ligny, Captain Baxter, whose party was about the last to retire,

---

[1] Being without the Brigade Signal Section, the Brigadier kept in touch with his forward troops by riding freely about : his charger having been shot under him he borrowed B. Company's charger which also was hit and with it were lost the company's Field Conduct Sheets in a wallet on the saddle.

[2] Dismounted cavalry in the early stages of the fight, infantry of the IVth Reserve Corps coming into action later.

[3] Jäger battalions were attached to the German Cavalry Divisions, whose fire-power they substantially augmented.

being badly wounded.[1] The rest of B under Captain Harland were now placed in reserve behind D, who had to endure the main ordeal of the German shell fire. The line here, on top of the ridge, was very much exposed, though a sunken lane leading down to the railway cutting gave the supports some shelter. However, Captain Connellan brought two platoons of C up to reinforce, and he and Captain Palk set a splendid example of leadership and coolness,[2] encouraging the men to

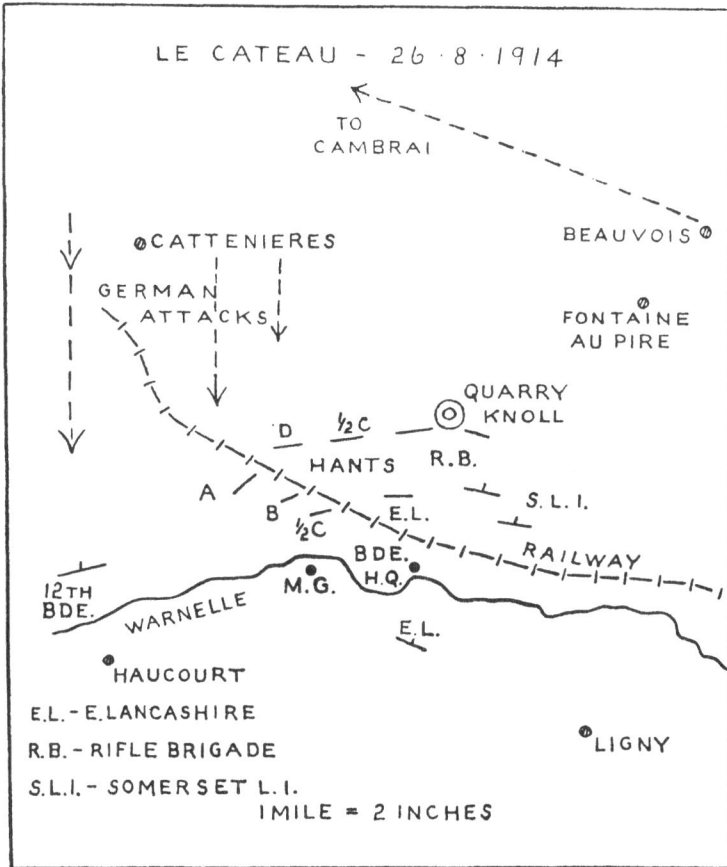

LE CATEAU - 26·8·1914

TO
CAMBRAI

●CATTENIERES   BEAUVOIS ●

GERMAN
ATTACKS   FONTAINE
                                 AU PIRE

                         QUARRY
                    D ½C ◎ KNOLL
                    HANTS   R.B.
              A /
              B   ½C   E.L.
                         BDE.●   RAILWAY
              12TH   M.G. H.Q.●
              BDE. WARNELLE   E.L.

              ●HAUCOURT

E.L. - E.LANCASHIRE

R.B. - RIFLE BRIGADE   ●LIGNY

S.L.I. - SOMERSET L.I.
              1 MILE = 2 INCHES

endure the ordeal and keeping them ready to take advantage of any targets which presented themselves. About 9 a.m. D had the satisfaction of seeing Germans coming forward in large masses. Reserving the fire of his left half-company till the enemy were quite close, Lt. Halls then opened rapid fire with great effect, the surviving Germans falling back to a ridge nearly 300 yards away, but after that few such targets were given again, and the Germans, apparently dismounted cavalry, merely maintained a desultory fire at a very respectful

[1] He got back to the dressing station at Ligny but was one of those who in the absence of the Division's ambulances were so unlucky as to fall into German hands.
[2] Captain Palk is said to have read Scott's *Marmion* aloud to his men.

range. South of the railway the left company (A) had rather better cover, thanks to sunken lanes, and its men dealt very effectively with efforts to creep forward along the line. Some Germans creeping up under cover got near enough to call out ' Retire ', which for the moment deceived a few men, but they gained little from their ruse.

On the Hampshire's left the 12th Brigade had recovered from the unfortunate opening of the battle, even the battalion which had been caught in quartercolumn had managed to extend along the shelter of a lane and had replied effectively to the machine-guns which had smitten it, and though about 9 a.m. the brigade had to retire across the Warnelle valley this movement was successfully carried out. In this two platoons of the Hampshire gave useful help ; pushing forward a little they got a good target in a battery which had unlimbered in the open near Cattenieres, shooting so effectively at a range of over 1200 yards that it was forced to limber up and get away. With the Germans chary of pressing home their attacks, the Hampshire, though prompt to take advantage of any targets, got but limited chances. The best marksmen of D Company were able to pick off some of the machine-gun crews and occasional officers who marked themselves out by carrying drawn swords, and the men were very steady and fired with good effect. One German machine gun was put out of action and the efforts of their infantry to cross the railway line or advance along it were effectively checked, while heavy as the shell fire was, much went high and our casualties were less than might have been expected from such a volume of fire. At one moment a battery got the range of the hedge along the railway cutting with disastrous results, Lt. Kent and 2/Lt. Cowan and several men being killed and many wounded, but this was luckily exceptional. Later on, however, when infantry were pressing forward against the 12th Brigade, now back between Ligny and Haucourt, parts of A and B Companies tried a counterattack to take this advance in flank, but their move drew down on them so fierce a storm of shrapnel that the Brigadier had to stop the advance and bring the men back to their line, several casualties having been suffered.

All through the morning the Fourth Division maintained its ground though more German batteries [1] had reinforced those of the Cavalry Divisions already in action in this quarter. With the 12th Brigade back across the Warnelle ravine and with the Third Division hard pressed to maintain its hold on Caudry, fully a mile to its right, the 11th Brigade's position was none too satisfactory, but any attempts of the German infantry to close with it were promptly checked, and if sometimes parties of our men were shelled out of their positions, these were soon re-occupied, the supports in the Warnelle ravine providing reinforcements.

Elsewhere the Fifth Division on the right was having an even harder time, being in a nasty salient under heavy enfilade artillery fire, and before 2 p.m. it had become clear that it could not hold on much longer. Its retirement necessarily involved that of the Third and Fourth Divisions, who could otherwise

---

[1] Those of the IVth Reserve Corps who had pushed on ahead of their infantry. These came into action later, early in the afternoon.

have held on,[1] as they were keeping their own opponents at bay, a counter-attack having recovered a large part of Caudry after that village had been evacuated by order. Somewhere about 3 p.m. General Hunter-Weston, seeing that his right flank was much exposed by the German lodgement in Caudry, while more German infantry were now moving up in his front,[2] ordered the 11th Brigade to retire across the ravine and re-form in front of Ligny. The Hampshire and East Lancashire were to go first, covered by the Rifle Brigade and such of the Somerset L. I. as were not already in the back position. As the Hampshire started to retire it seemed, as one officer wrote,[3] ' as if every gun and rifle in the German Army had opened fire ', but the movement was steadily carried out, the German infantry had been kept at too respectful a distance to press the retiring troops, who were soon in dead ground, though in mounting the slope towards Ligny they again came into view, whereupon the German gunners redoubled their efforts, inflicting more casualties, though with the men well extended the loss was not really heavy. When the rear-guard in turn fell back German infantry pushed forward, to be promptly checked by our guns. Renewing their effort a little later, they were met not only by our guns but by the rifles of such of the 11th Brigade as had reached Ligny and faced about there. Trying another advance they again failed in the face of our rapid fire and after that the 11th Brigade was left unmolested. It was, however, by this time rather split up ; companies and even platoons had got detached, and without the Signal Company the Divisional and Brigade commanders had found the controlling of the troops almost impossible. Consequently when, about 5 p.m., the 11th Brigade started to retire from the Ligny position, the orders failed to reach several parties and all its units were broken up into disconnected detachments, and though the Brigadier was able before long to collect a substantial body at Selvigny, many parties continued detached for some days.

About 300 Hampshire under Major Hicks, with whom were Captains Connellan, Moore and Richards and Lt. Dolphin, were still holding on at Ligny about 6 p.m., without any orders or any knowledge of the situation, when the Adjutant made his way back to order them to retire, the rest of the brigade having already moved off. As they left the village [4] it was very heavily shelled but otherwise the party was unmolested. Before long, touch was regained near Caullery with another party under Colonel Jackson, which had hung on even longer near Ligny, not retiring till 7 p.m.[5] From Caullery the battalion made its way across country, the road being blocked at Clery by troops of the Second Corps, and till nearly midnight the men tramped on, worn, weary and hungry. A halt was then called near Serain, where the main body of the brigade was near

---

[1] Captain Palk and his company were reported as being most reluctant to retire—they had not let any Germans get near them.

[2] Of the IVth Reserve Corps.

[3] Lt. E.J.W. Dolphin, for whose valuable letters I have to thank his brother, Colonel H. C. Dolphin.

[4] Most of the wounded of the brigade had been collected in the school at Ligny where the majority had to be left behind in the absence of the Division's ambulances.

[5] The Germans were not pressing them even then.

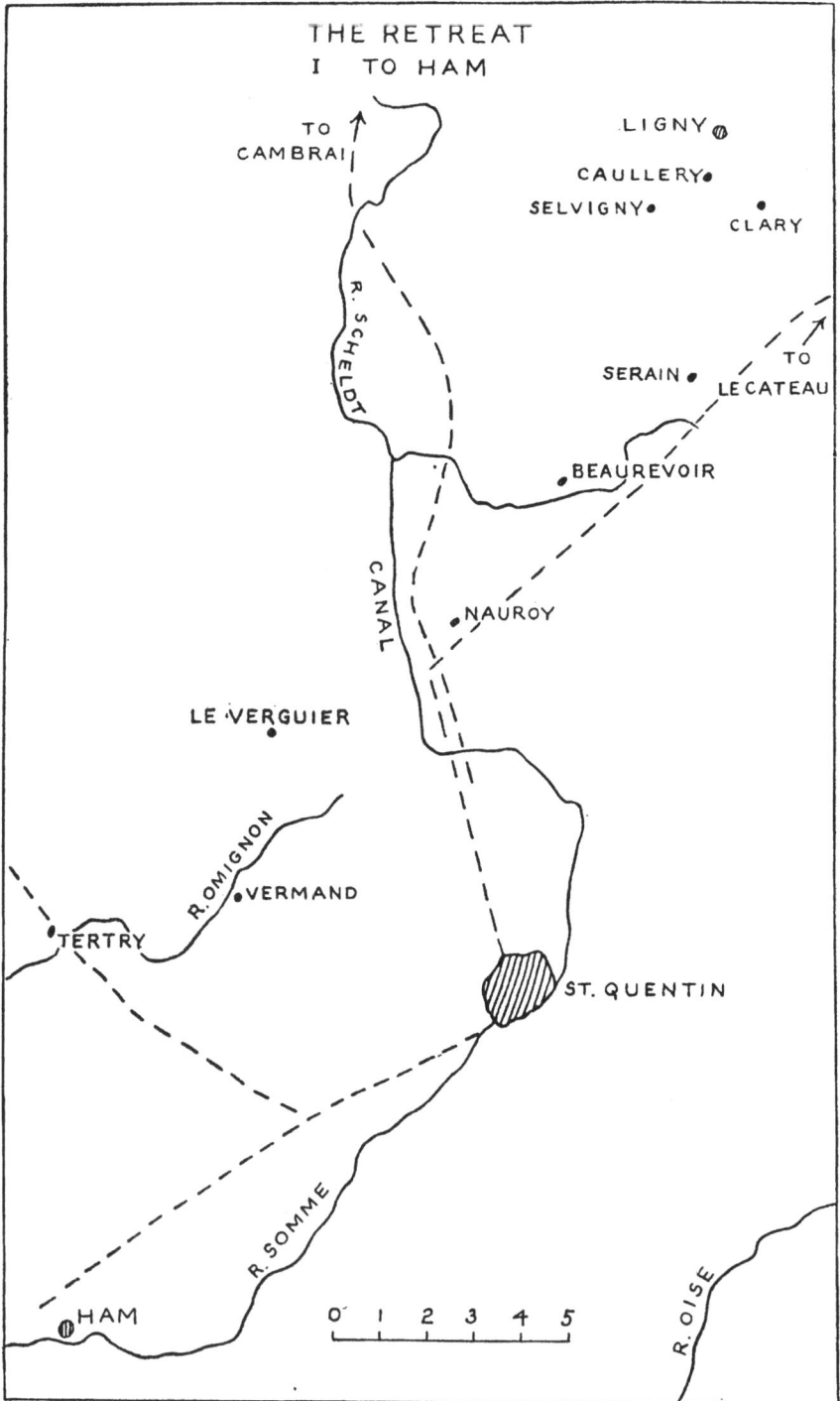

THE RETREAT
I   TO HAM

TO
CAMBRAI

LIGNY

CAULLERY

SELVIGNY

CLARY

R. SCHELDT

SERAIN

TO
LE CATEAU

BEAUREVOIR

CANAL

NAUROY

LE VERGUIER

R. OMIGNON

VERMAND

TERTRY

ST. QUENTIN

R. SOMME

0   1   2   3   4   5

HAM

R. OISE

at hand, and the weary men got a brief but welcome rest, before resuming the march about 2 a.m. The people of the place did what they could for them in providing bread and hot water for tea or soup. The retreat had so far been quite unmolested, the Germans, after the reception they had met, were in no mood to press forward in pursuit.[1]

Over 100 years had passed since the Thirty-Seventh had last been in action against a European enemy, and never since the Flanders campaign of 1794 had they been as severely tried or suffered so heavily. Their losses, when finally established, came to nearly 200. Lt. Kent and 2/Lt. Cowan had been killed, Captain Baxter, Lts. Rose, Halls, Griffith [2] and Le Hunte [3] were missing, with the M.O., Captain Williams, who had stayed behind with the badly wounded. Major Hicks, though continuing at duty, had been wounded, as had Lt. Cecil in leading a small counter-attack. Of other ranks 46 were killed and missing and 126 wounded, D Company having suffered the most severely.

However, the battalion with the rest of the brigade could congratulate itself in having maintained itself in one unfavourable position after another for ten hours and more, on having held its immediate opponents and punished them heavily and on having helped to foil their effort to envelope and corner the left wing of the B.E.F. Heavy as the British losses at Le Cateau were, the Fifth Division's losses in guns being specially serious, it may be claimed that at Le Cateau General Smith-Dorrien had achieved his main purpose ; his men had checked von Kluck's greatly superior force and hit it so hard that it made no serious attempt at pursuit and in consequence lost touch with the B.E.F. Moreover, as the German commander was confirmed in the erroneous conclusions he had formed about our movements, intentions and line of retreat, the stand at Le Cateau contributed appreciably to the foiling of the German effort to secure a ' knock-out ' victory. If for the moment the B.E.F. had to make a hurried and exhausting retreat, Le Cateau helped to secure it from molestation and was to yield no small harvest before many days were out.

Before dawn on August 27th such of the 11th Brigade as were together, including most of the Hampshire, were stumbling along Southward again, weary and hungry, moving across country by Beaurevoir to Nauroy, where they halted rather after 7 a.m. for such breakfast as was possible. About 9.30 the North Irish Horse, who were covering the position, reported that German

---

[1] They did not actually occupy Ligny till that morning, and a few Hampshire remained on outpost there all night without being molested ; but were mostly captured next morning.

[2] Originally reported killed.

[3] The machine-gun section, after remaining in position until dark, had then started to retire as all other troops near were doing. It had some difficulty in getting the limbers along a bad track but after a time met a Frenchman, who offered to guide it to Clery, where he said the English were concentrating. He may have been a German agent, for when the party, increased by stragglers to a dozen, reached Clery it was to run into the Germans in force and be taken. The two machine-guns, left for the time lying in a courtyard, were discovered there by a civilian, M. Fernaud Lerouf who concealed them so successfully that the Germans never found them. Eventually in 1921 the then Maire of Clery informed the local military authorities of the existence of these guns and Captain Le Hunte had the satisfaction of going to Clery to recover them for the regiment and express its thanks to M. Lerouf for their preservation : he had risked his life for it, as he would have been shot had they been discovered.

cavalry were approaching. The Brigadier not being on the spot at the moment, Colonel Jackson as senior officer present promptly sent the East Lancashire to take post East of the village and was preparing to post the Hampshire North of it when the Brigadier arrived and gave orders for the immediate resumption of the retreat. The troops were moving off when German guns opened fire at about 1000 yards range. The Brigadier thereupon directed Colonel Jackson to engage these guns and cover the retirement, to which end A Company of the Hampshire took post North and East of Nauroy and opened fire on the guns but was almost immediately fairly sharply engaged with cyclists and dismounted cavalry. This company, with about 50 details of all units whom the Brigadier had placed under Colonel Jackson, held on for some time, giving effective cover to the retirement of the main body. This, in moving across country to avoid the shell-fire, inevitably became split up again ; one large party, including most of the Hampshire under Major Barlow and guided by the Brigade Major, Captain Boyd, made its way by Le Verguier to Tertry. Major Hicks, still carrying on despite his wound, now took charge of about another 120 Hampshires with some details, having with him Lts. Knocker and Nicholson, and this party, having got away without much loss, eventually joined on to the tail of the Third Division, in whose company it reached Vermand that evening, having covered 25 miles in the day. Another 100 of the battalion under Captains Moore and Richards, most of whom had been part of the rear-guard and had been East of Nauroy, made their way back separately, getting across the St. Quentin Canal and joining some of the Rifle Brigade and East Lancashire under the Brigadier. Of the rest of the rear-guard the majority had become casualties and among them Colonel Jackson himself, who had the bad luck to be hit in the leg and disabled and had to be carried into the house of a curé, where he was found and taken by the enemy. It was hard on the battalion to lose so competent and trusted a C.O. and hard on an officer of his record and attainments to lose all chance of earning distinction in the war. Had he escaped he would in all probability have before long been removed from command of the battalion by promotion ; his good services in controlling his battalion at Le Cateau had been brought to notice by General Hunter-Weston, to be disabled and captured was a cruel misfortune.

Apart from this clash at Nauroy little was seen of the enemy all day and the different detachments plodded along unmolested. Supplies had been dumped at the road-side to be picked up as the troops passed by, while some lucky individuals were given eggs, coffee and apples by kindly farm-house people. All were terribly weary : one Hampshire subaltern, who was given a ride, found himself falling asleep in the saddle, though he managed not to fall off, and those men who were picked up in carts or lorries were likewise promptly asleep. Some got rides on gun-limbers and had to keep awake. The brigade's scattered detachments had remained separated all day, but at Ham, which they reached early on August 28th after starting from Vermand in the dark and covering ten miles, mostly in heavy rain, Major Hicks and his party found the Brigadier with Captains Moore and Richards and their men, and when, about 8 a.m., the march was again resumed most of the 11th Brigade was together again. Another long and trying march followed to Freniches, six miles short of Noyon, where after covering 15 miles on indifferent roads in great heat the brigade eventually halted, dead beat and very grateful to some R.A.M.C. who, having arrived there earlier, had prepared a hot meal for the later arrivals. Here also the Hampshire had the satisfaction of rejoining their transport which had got safely away.

It was a great relief next morning, after the first night's rest the Hampshire had known since leaving England, not to start off again at once. Apart from other reasons, it indicated that the B.E.F. had some freedom of choice in its actions and was not merely conforming to the enemy's moves. Regimental officers and men might be quite in the dark as to the general situation, this at least was some small encouragement. The Second Corps and the Fourth Division had by their exertions got clear away from the enemy, whose pursuit was being mistakenly directed Westward and SW. rather than following the Southward line of the British retreat, and so General Smith-Dorrien's men could get some of the rest they needed so badly. Their rest was broken into that afternoon by a sudden order to resume the march, but the roads were blocked with transport and little progress was made, the brigade eventually halting at Les Cloyes, where it spent the night in bivouac and where the Brigade Major's party, including Major Barlow and nearly 500 of the Hampshire, rejoined during the night, having made their way by Voyennes and Esmery-Hallon [1] to Sermaize, which they had reached on August 29th. Many individuals were still detached, some having attached themselves to other regiments, others having been given lifts in empty lorries and taken on well ahead,[2] but the Division was now largely re-assembled, having been rejoined by most of the units whose absence had cost it so much at Le Cateau.

The retreat was resumed about 6 a.m. next day (August 30th) with officers and men still in doubt about the situation, very weary and short of sleep but plodding doggedly on, getting occasional chances of supplementing their rations with fruit and eggs. Crossing the Aisne the Fourth Division reached Pierrefonds that evening, moved on Westward (next day) through the Forest of Compiegne, welcoming the shade on the hottest day yet, and halted at its SW. corner, covering St. Sauveur and Verberie. Here the battalion, posted East of St. Sauveur, had to picquet and obstruct roads leading NW. in which direction German cavalry were in evidence again, the picquets having a few brushes with their patrols. Major Hicks' wound had now forced him to retire to hospital, Major Barlow taking command.

While these days had seen the gap between the First and Second Corps virtually closed and the danger of their separation averted, since Le Cateau contact with the enemy had been almost lost, von Kluck's First Army having pushed on South Westward, and if our First Corps had had some clashes with Bülow's Second Army, these had not really impeded its Southward move. On August 29th Lanrezac's Army had attempted to check the German pursuit by standing at Guise, but this had not sufficed to do more than delay Bülow, and

[1] I.e. well West of the line taken by the rest of the brigade.
[2] These accounted for most of the stragglers who subsequently rejoined.

next day Lanrezac had to resume his retreat. His halt at Guise had, however, exposed him to envelopment should von Kluck's Army now wheel round to its left and, moving SE., fall on him before he could cross the Marne. This von Kluck was attempting and it was his cavalry advanced-guards that the Fourth Division's outposts had encountered on August 31st.

Sir John French's orders for September 1st prescribed for the Fourth Division and the 19th Brigade, now forming the Third Corps under Lt. General Pulteney, an early start for the area round Baron, ten miles South of Verberie. Many units of his Corps having reached their billets late on August 31st, General Pulteney had now to postpone his start, and the Hampshire outposts had not yet moved when about 6 a.m. cavalry [1] began pressing in on them. These they effectively kept at bay until, about 8 a.m. orders were received for the battalion and the East Lancashire on its left to fall back through the Rifle Brigade and Somerset, who were in a covering position on high ground in rear. As the Hampshire fell back, A Company furnishing a rear-guard, a company of the Somerset on their right rear gave the battalion useful help, being quite sharply engaged, while when the covering battalions retired in their turn C Company under Captain Connellan on a ridge at Vaucelle assisted the Somerset effectively, checking the Germans and then taking over the rear-guard. On getting away through a wood, the Hampshire's rear-guard rounded a corner to find dismounted cavalry in force only 200 yards away. These blazed away without much effect, the Hampshire replying with one 'area shoot' at a well-concealed enemy, while at another point some men under Lt. Dolphin lined a bank and had 'some very satisfactory shooting', with some hand to hand fighting in a turnip field. Orders reaching the detachment to retire, it did so, breaking off the engagement quite successfully. One party, with which were Captains Richards and Harland, Lt. Knocker and 2/Lt. Nicholson, now crossed an unfordable stream by means of a life-line formed by linking rifle-straps together for the non-swimmers. Increased by details from other units to nearly 150, this detachment made its way to Nery, passing close to the site of the morning's action there, and rejoined the battalion that evening at Rosieres. [2] Lt. Dolphin's party had also got away, crossing the same stream by using a fallen tree as their bridge.

'The Germans seemed to have suffered severely and did not press the pursuit' is the Somerset's account, and once the rearward movement had started it was not molested. Elsewhere all along the B.E.F.'s line, at Nery, Crepy en Valois and Villers Cotterets, our rear-guards had been more or less sharply engaged but had punished the Germans appreciably. One effect of these engagements was that von Kluck, having to his surprise encountered stiff resistance from the British, whom he had reckoned to be a negligible factor incapable of offering serious opposition, was distracted from his original plan. Instead of pressing on Eastward to fall on Lanrezac before he could cross the Marne, he swung his men round South to pursue the retiring B.E.F. but failed to

[1] The German 2nd Cavalry Division and the advanced troops of their IInd Corps.
[2] N.E. of Baron.

bring it to action, and when he resumed his Eastward move it was too late to intercept the French Fifth Army.[1]

That evening the Hampshire bivouacked at Rosieres [2] and got a really good meal, the more appreciated because it had been in preparation for some German cavalry, who had retired discreetly on their approach. They were glad also to rejoin their transport ; it had come under shell-fire, but Captain Hackett struck off across country and brought it through safely. Major Barlow had had the misfortune to be taken prisoner : going back through the forest to look for a missing company, he had run into German cavalry. Captain Palk therefore took command.[2]

Mere marching without any more fighting now followed ; the first day's march, still Southward and in stifling heat, brought the B.E.F. to the line Dammartin [3] (Third Corps)—Meaux, on the next it crossed the Marne, the Hampshire at Ligny, to get a welcome rest on September 4th, with a chance to wash and shave. That afternoon, however, the Hampshire were ordered to take up an outpost position near Couperey to cover the crossings of the Marne. An alarm that the enemy were bridging the river proved to be unfounded, but the battalion remained in readiness to dispute the passage till about 3.30 a.m. (September 5th) when it started off again. This early move was ordered partly to avoid hostile observation, partly to benefit by marching in the cool of the night and early morning.

As things turned out this had far-reaching consequences, as this move carried the B.E.F. to points SSE. of Paris, from Brie Comte Robert on the left (Third Corps) to Rozoy, well SW. of the line facing East which should have been taken up had General Joffre's orders for September 5th reached G.H.Q. in time for our march to be stopped and its direction altered. Could Joffre's orders have been carried out, the B.E.F. could have hardly avoided serious contact with the Germans directly it started forward on September 6th. What had happened was that von Kluck's effort to intercept Lanrezac and roll the French line up from its left had carried his Army SE., leaving on its flank the garrison of Paris with Maunoury's newly formed French Sixth Army and the B.E.F., the last not as incapable of an offensive as von Kluck seems still to have imagined. The would-be enveloper was thus lending himself to envelopment, and General Joffre, having substantially reinforced his left by reverting to the defensive in Lorraine and thus freeing many units for use elsewhere, was now in position to pass over to the offensive and fall on the weak flank-guard von Kluck had left facing Paris. Joffre's attack had actually started on September 5th, Maunoury's men advancing North of the Marne to engage Kluck's IVth Reserve Corps on the Ourcq, separated as it was by a substantial gap from the rest of his First Army. Realising its peril von Kluck had on September 6th to halt his advance and order his right and right centre, the IInd and IVth Corps,

---

[1] As the *Official History* (1914. I. p. 266) says, Kluck's Army had advanced ' under 10 miles and had not struck to any purpose either the French Fifth Army or the British '.

[2] This day's casualties only came to half-a-dozen.

[3] The Hampshire halted at this place.

to retrace their steps and recross the Marne, thereby opening a gap between them and his two remaining Corps, who were engaged South of Montmirail with the French Fifth Army, now under General Franchet d'Esperey.   Had the B.E.F. been where General Joffre wished it to be, the IInd and IVth Corps could hardly have carried out their move unimpeded but must have become engaged with the B.E.F. somewhere SW. of Coulomniers.

As it was, the early start had carried the B.E.F. well to the South and out of immediate contact with the enemy.   Its units had mostly reached their halting places [1] early in the day and were taking the opportunity to get a real rest and even a wash.   During the day most battalions and artillery brigades picked up their ' first reinforcements ', the Hampshire being joined by 52 men under Captain R. D. Johnston,[2] a much smaller reinforcement than most battalions received.   Their arrival was welcome, while the news that the retreat was over and that the B.E.F. was taking the offensive next day was even more cheering. If this meant fresh efforts and fresh exertions, at least the men would be going in the right direction.   The battalion had been marching almost continuously for nearly a fortnight, in which it had covered nearly 200 miles, often short of food, always short of rest and sleep, and the small number of sick and stragglers were a great testimony to the fitness, discipline and splendid spirit of the men.   It had been hard for regimental officers and men to understand why they were retiring before an enemy on whom they had inflicted substantial losses and whom they were ready to meet again.   A ' strategical retirement into the interior of the country ' may have been the only solution for the serious situation which had confronted the Allies after the unexpected strength developed by the German thrust through neutral Belgium and the failure of the French counterstroke in the Ardennes and Lorraine :   it was not easily appreciated by those who had to carry it out and to endure the toils and hardships of the ' Retreat from Mons '.   That retreat with all its exertions and difficulties had tested the the training, discipline and soldierly qualities of the British troops even more severely than their actual encounters with the enemy.   Those who emerged from it unshaken and undismayed, fully ready to turn and hit back effectively, had deserved well of their country and had more than sustained the regimental traditions and spirit which had helped appreciably in what they had accomplished.

[1] The Hampshire at Chevry, but with two companies on outpost to the NE. at Gretz, on the road to Tournan.

[2] Lt. J. F. Gwynn, R.A.M.C. had joined on the previous day to replace Captain Williams.

CHAPTER II

THE MARNE—THE AISNE—THE MOVE TO FLANDERS.

THE position in which the B.E.F. found itself on September 6th put its right ten miles too far West, while the Third Corps on its left was double that distance from its intended place, so that the first move had to be a wheel to the right, pivoting on the First Corps, which could not venture to push forward far until the Second and Third had come up into line on its left and were ready to support it. The advanced guards did indeed get into touch with German troops, those covering the move of von Kluck's IInd and IVth Corps back across the Marne, but they had to confine themselves to pushing these flank-guards back and were unable to press against their supports, still less to interfere with the main bodies beyond them. Rather after midday the Second and Third Corps came up into line with the First, the Third getting to Villeneuve le Comte, whence in the afternoon it advanced to Villiers sur Morin. The Hampshire had the satisfaction of seeing many signs of the hasty movement of the Germans, dead men, more dead horses and much evidence of damage, if they did not encounter the enemy. The B.E.F. was now in a position to advance NE. across the Grand Morin and Petit Morin into the gap now opening in the German line. This gap was widened during September 7th and 8th, when Maunoury's menace to von Kluck's right flank and rear brought the latter's two remaining Corps back Northwards across the Marne to join in the battle now developing on the Ourcq. This move uncovered the right flank of Bülow's Second Army, but, undervaluing once again the B.E.F.'s fighting capacities, von Kluck expected to check our advance with a screen of cavalry, reinforced by Jäger and cyclists with many machine-guns but quite inadequate, as it proved, for its task. The B.E.F., which had reached the Grand Morin on September 7th without meeting serious opposition, though the cavalry had several successful encounters, had quite stiff fighting next day, when its passage of the Petit Morin was stubbornly disputed, and some sharp actions resulted in our breaking through the enemy's lines at several points and inflicting quite substantial casualties.

The Third Corps on our left had met less opposition than the other two. On September 7th, the 11th Brigade had reached Montdenis beyond the Grand Morin after an exhausting march in great heat and very short of rations, and the next day's advance took it to Les Corbières. It was behind the leading brigades of its Division, which found the enemy in some strength at La Ferté sous Jouarre, where the Petit Morin joins the Marne. These brigades eventually crossed the Petit Morin and got into La Ferté, after some fighting, but the 11th did not come into action, and the Hampshire, who bivouacked at Les Corbières about 7 p.m. on high ground overlooking La Ferté, had a tiring day without firing a shot. Captains Palk and Moore having had to go sick, Captain Connellan took command, with temporary rank as Major.

The success of the First and Second Corps in forcing the passage of the Petit Morin and thrusting aside the opposing cavalry and Jäger was exploited next day (September 9th), when both Corps crossed the Marne unopposed at several several places above La Ferté sous Jouarre and established themselves on von Kluck's left rear, his whole Army being now across the Marne and closely engaged against Maunoury. Unluckily an inaccurate air-report of large columns moving NW. from Chateau Thierry caused the First Corps to halt just when another short advance promised to catch von Kluck's left at a great disadvantage. This unfortunate halt allowed von Kluck, now fully aware of his precarious situation, to break off his battle against Maunoury and thereby to extricate his army from its dangerous position, so that it got back across the Aisne, somewhat shaken and disorganized but with all its fighting formations intact ; it could therefore profit by the advantageous tactical position presented by the high ground on the right bank of the Aisne immediately East and West of Soissons, familiar as the Chemin des Dames ridge.

It may be idle to speculate on what might have happened had the B.E.F. closed with von Kluck on September 9th or if the night march of September 4th/5th had not prevented our engaging his main body in the act of retracing its steps Northwards across our front : still on the Aisne we fought at tactical disadvantages we should have escaped in either of the other situations, and even if we had had as heavy fighting and even more serious losses than we incurred in establishing ourselves across the Aisne, much more might well have been achieved.

September 9th did not bring the Third Corps, least of all the 1st Hampshire, much fighting, though the Germans were still hanging on to La Ferté sous Jouarre and were strongly posted North of the river. The Rifle Brigade were sent forward to clear up La Ferté, the Hampshire covering their advance from high ground to the SW., where they came under some fire from across the river, mainly snipers, and got occasional chances of replying. However the clearing of La Ferté took some time and not till late afternoon could the Hampshire move down into the town. Before this the 12th Brigade had got across at a lock some way upstream, whereupon the defenders of La Ferté, fearing to have their retreat cut off, had withdrawn. While they had destroyed the stone bridge, they had been in too great a hurry to put out of action the many rowing boats available, and in these the Hampshire and the East Lancashire began about 9 p.m. an unopposed passage.

B Company, now under Captain Harland, were the first Hampshire across, to find many wounded Germans but none to fight, and, covered by the screen B threw out, the rest were all across by 11 p.m., two men getting drowned in the process. There was no wasting time, by 2 a.m. (September 10th) the battalion was advancing again and before daylight had secured a line on high ground two miles to the Northward. But for one Uhlan patrol the only Germans encountered were dead or badly wounded and again the road-side was littered with the debris of their hasty retirement. The enemy was not standing on the order of his going, and the Third Corps, having been delayed at La Ferté, was slightly behind the Second and First, whose advanced-guards had sharp fighting with rear-guards, whom they handled quite severely besides capturing many

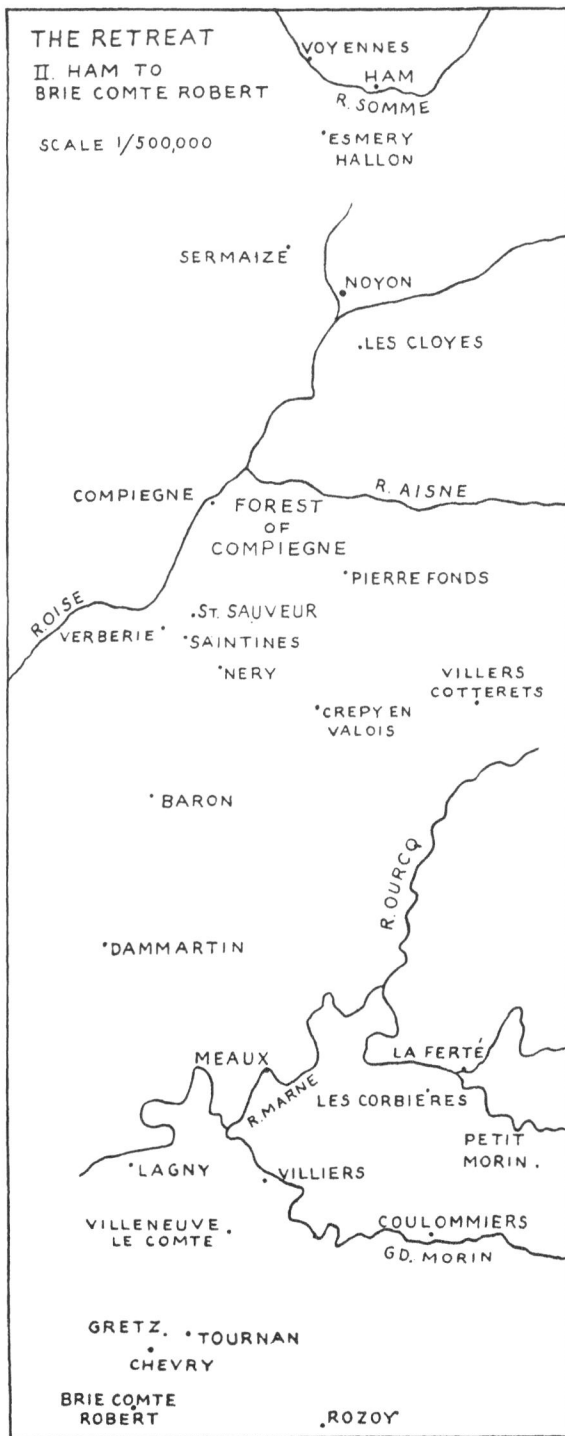

THE RETREAT
II. HAM TO
BRIE COMTE ROBERT

SCALE 1/500,000

VOYENNES
HAM
R. SOMME
ESMERY
HALLON

SERMAIZE
NOYON
.LES CLOYES

COMPIEGNE
R. AISNE
FOREST
OF
COMPIEGNE
PIERRE FONDS
ROISE
.St. SAUVEUR
VERBERIE SAINTINES
NERY
VILLERS
COTTERETS
CREPY EN
VALOIS

BARON

R. OURCQ

DAMMARTIN

MEAUX
LA FERTÉ
R. MARNE
LES CORBIERES
PETIT
MORIN.
LAGNY   VILLIERS
VILLENEUVE.   COULOMMIERS
LE COMTE
GD. MORIN

GRETZ. TOURNAN
CHEVRY
BRIE COMTE
ROBERT   ROZOY

stragglers, but neither on September 10th or 11th did the Hampshire come into conflict with the enemy. They toiled on, often through pelting rain and short of rations, cheered to be advancing and strengthened by a ' second reinforcement ' of 137 men under Captain Sandeman (3rd Battalion) who joined on September 9th.

September 12th brought the B.E.F. into contact with the enemy again, the First and Second Corps meeting opposition along the Vesle, a tributary which joins the Aisne near the bridge at Condé, where a spur of the high ground North of the river juts out almost to the bank. The Third Corps, whose line of advance was bringing it to the Aisne below Condé, did not meet this opposition, and by 3 p.m. its leading brigade, the 12th, had reached Septmonts, only three miles from the Aisne, and the Divisional cavalry, scouting ahead, were reconnoitring the bridges on its front, that at Venizel being found damaged but not destroyed. Brigadier-General Wilson, now commanding the Fourth Division as General Snow had been disabled by an accident, determined to see if this bridge could be used and detailed the 11th Brigade to attempt a crossing. Accordingly, about 10 p.m. the Hampshire, after three hours in billets at Septmonts, had to turn out and lead the way down to the river. As a preliminary Lts. im Thurn and Knocker were sent to reconnoitre the bridge, to find that though the main girders had been cut through, the reinforced concrete of the road-way offered a passage to men in single file. Lt. im Thurn thereupon cut the fuses of a charge of explosive which had apparently failed to work, an Uhlan patrol, which appeared while he was in the act of cutting the fuse, fortunately retiring without trying to interfere.

About midnight, therefore, the Hampshire started to lead the brigade across. It was a tedious business and tricky ; as one officer wrote, ' to cough on the bridge was to set the whole structure shaking ', while the ammunition carts had to be unloaded and taken across empty, their contents being carried over separately. The first men across formed a covering screen, but no German patrols troubled them, and by 3 a.m. (September 13th) General Hunter-Weston could order an advance towards the higher ground [1] beyond the two miles of water-meadows and flat ground immediately North of the river, the Hampshire in the centre making for Bucy le Long.

It was a daring move in the dark, over unreconnoitred ground, with no idea of what Germans were ahead or where they were, but its daring was fully justified. No opposition was encountered and after D Company (Captain Johnston) had found Bucy le Long unoccupied, the Hampshire reached the foot of the heights just as day was breaking : sweeping up them, the battalion established itself on the crest, German outposts, completely surprised, retiring in haste. A position was promptly taken up and entrenching begun, the Hampshire being around La Montagne Farm, with the Rifle Brigade and the Somerset on right and left respectively. The men were nearly dead beat, having marched over 30 miles since starting off on the 12th, but theirs was the only brigade of the B.E.F. across the Aisne.

[1] The ridge was about 300 feet up from the river.

Unluckily the position the Fourth Division had so enterprisingly secured had serious tactical defects, above all the difficulty of finding good artillery positions North of the river,[1] while the heights South of it were so far back that guns posted on them could not reach the German gun positions. Accordingly when, early on September 13th, the Germans started a heavy bombardment of the 11th Brigade's line, little reply could be made and the men could only hang on despite the shell-fire and do their best with their ' grubbers ' to im-

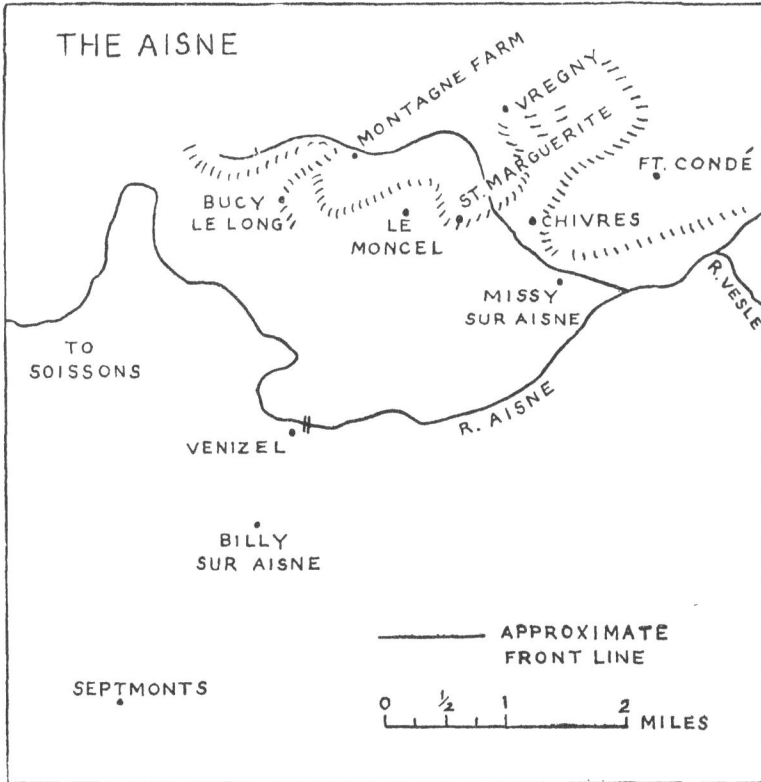

THE AISNE

prove their position. This lack of artillery support effectively forbade any advance by the Fourth Division or by the Fifth on its right, between it and the Condé spur, and though the Fifth Division with some help from the right brigade of the Fourth made several efforts the little ground gained was not worth the casualties, and during the three weeks the Hampshire spent on the Aisne no major advance was attempted, though a forward line was entrenched by night. Some wooded ground on their left front was a weak spot and at first a gap separated them from the Somerset L.I. This was filled on September 14th by two companies of the Dublins who assisted to drive off some enemy who were

---

[1] Some guns were eventually brought across and even found positions almost in the firing line, but the advantage in artillery positions was all with the Germans.

pushing forward, but after that the line remained virtually unchanged apart from readjustments between battalions, the Hampshire after spending four days at La Montagne side-stepping about a mile to the left.

The Hampshire's 'opposite numbers', part of the IInd Corps, showed little inclination to give them a chance to show their shooting powers by attacking. With all their advantages in numbers, in position and in artillery, the Germans here were singularly unenterprising. One officer wrote that 'but for sniping and occasional scrapping by outposts at night we have not had much infantry fighting. The Germans have made one or two disjointed attempts at attacking but have been beaten back each time.' On September 19th, for example, a wiring party was heavily fired on and this was followed by an attack, which was repulsed with only two casualties, including one man who ran his bayonet into his own nose. It was upstream of the Fourth Division's position that the critical fighting took place and that the timely arrival of German reinforcements only just forestalled the B.E.F.'s advance into the still open gap between the Ist and IInd German Armies and so prevented it making the Aisne what the Marne had just missed being, a decisive victory over the German right wing. The counterattacks which endeavoured to throw back into, and across, the Aisne the British troops established on the slopes of the Chemin des Dames did not extend below Condé, so the Fourth Division was denied the chance of hitting back effectively by which the First Corps and the Third Division profited.

To the 1st Hampshire the Aisne was therefore mainly notable as their introduction to that 'trench warfare' of which they were to have so much stern experience. For 'trench warfare' the British Army was but ill-equipped, all the apparatus it required, from periscopes onward, had to be improvised somehow and the technique and routine of this type of fighting painfully acquired. The Germans may not have expected the war to develop like this nor had they trained their troops for it, any more than we had, but being far better equipped for sieges they could utilise siege-warfare equipment for the new purpose. The 1st Hampshire in common with the whole B.E.F. had to learn the trade by experience. They busied themselves in consolidating systematically their position North of Bucy le Long, improving their trenches, connecting them, digging communication trenches leading back from the front line, putting up pointed stakes to serve as an obstacle, while they had to strip the neighbouring fields for wire. No Man's Land was open ground, under cultivation, but behind the front line there were woods and the steep slopes of the ridge contained caves, one 'weird and huge cave and quite romantic', it was said, gave quite good cover for battalion headquarters, another sheltering the reserve company. By night patrols pushed out towards the German trenches, here over 1000 yards away, and obtained much useful information, if encounters with hostile patrols were infrequent. Very occasionally a German patrol approached our trenches and gave our men something to shoot at; thus, early on October 1st, 'the first day of pheasant shooting', a patrol reported having 'bagged seven and half brace' of 'Pomeranian Grenadiers' at the cost of only one wounded, and on another occasion our machine guns got a chance when a haystack was set on fire and several Germans bolted from it. Our snipers also were busy. As one officer wrote ' we know when a German relief arrives, as they walk about on the sky-line but they don't do it a second time.' ' Things are pretty quiet here ' another wrote : ' we sometimes bag a German or two.' At first, before entrenching tools could be brought across so that the battalion was really well dug in, the shelling, which was often heavy, caused nearly all the casualties,[1] as our guns could not silence the German batteries which were mainly beyond their range. After that, with our position much improved, casualties decreased, while despite wet weather and the discomforts and bad conditions in the trenches fewer men went sick than might have been expected. Sleeping in the open, often on wet ground, with no chances of a change of clothing and the scantiest opportunities of washing, did not seem to disagree over much with the men's health, and once the retreat was over rations were plentiful and good. With the troops stationary in trenches, mails and parcels containing many ' comforts ' could be delivered regularly, while large supplies of clothing and equipment arrived, including two machine guns, and the battalion was soon pretty well refitted, though boots were slow to appear. Every new arrival commented on the extraordinary cheerfulness of the men and their endurance of the conditions. After a bit every-one got quite used to the shelling, which was largely ineffective, and life was developing into a regular routine. Two large drafts, amounting to 266 other ranks, many of them ' Section D ' Reservists, under Lts. Wade and Twining (3rd. Bn.) and 2/Lt. Gill [2] arrived before the end of September [3] and with them Major Parker, who had been commanding the new 10th (Service) Battalion, to take command, taking over from Major [4] Connellan who had been commanding for several days and doing admirably. Several vacancies among the subalterns were filled up by the promotion of N.C.O.s who had done good service in the field, including R.S.M. Fidler and C.S.M.s Coulter and Sprake.

Within a few days of the British reaching the Aisne it became evident that a deadlock was being established on that front. We had just failed to exploit our opportunity on the Marne but we had definitely foiled and thwarted the German effort at a ' knock-out ' blow on the Western front. A new phase in the operations was now developing : both the French and Germans trying to turn their opponents' uncovered Western flank. Each in turn prolonged the outer flank, the French extending their line Northward beyond the Oise to get round behind von Kluck's right. The Germans parried this threat by bringing troops across from their left and left centre, threatening in their turn to outflank the outflankers. They were still not without hopes of sweeping round the French left and with this were combining projects for seizing the almost uncovered ' Channel ports.' The ' Race to the Sea ', into which this developed, was going

[1] Up to September 18th 11 men were killed and Captain Richards, Lt. Westmorland and 54 men wounded. September 13th was the worst day.

[2] Newly commissioned from the R.M.C.

[3] The arrival of 20 ' stragglers ' is recorded on September 23rd, mainly foot-sore men who had fallen out during the retreat and had been given lifts in lorries. The battalion had fewer than any other in the brigade.

[4] Temporary rank.

on in the last fortnight of September and creating a new front line Northward from the Oise over the Somme into Flanders, so that it seemed possible that our line might gain touch with the Belgians, still in the occupation of Antwerp and of the Belgian coast line.   British reinforcements, a Seventh Division, mainly composed of troops withdrawn from South Africa and our Mediterranean garrisons, and the two Divisions which India was sending to Europe would soon be available, and it was desirable that all our troops should be together under our Commander-in-Chief.   Other considerations, mainly administrative, partly political, made it expedient to get the British forces on to the left flank again, instead of having them in the middle of the French line, and before the end of September it had been decided to relieve the B.E.F. by French troops and to transfer it to Flanders.

This move was begun by the Second Corps on October 1st, the Fourth Division extending to the right to take over the Fifth's trenches ; five nights later the Third Corps followed the Second, having been relieved by the French, the Hampshire, who had left their position North of Bucy le Long after dark on October 4th and crossed the Aisne at Venizel, bivouacked South of Ville Montoire ; starting off again at 1 a.m. they had reached Billy sur Ourcq before dawn. Five marches, mostly by night or in the late afternoon, in hopes of evading German air observation, then carried them Westward to the railway at Estreé St. Denis, where they entrained early on October 11th.   Journeying by Montdidier and Amiens they reached Wizernes about 10 p.m., detrained there and marched to billets at Oiselle two miles away.   Three weeks in the trenches had not been good preparation for marching, as it had been difficult to keep men properly exercised and many men's feet and boots had suffered from the mud and wet which so much rain had caused, some men indeed had to march in gym shoes and with bandaged feet, but the battalion was not much below establishment [1] and was very ready to give a good account of itself.

[1] Captains Beckett and Unwin and Lt. Prendergast (3rd Battalion) had joined just before the battalion left the Aisne, and Captain Cope and Lts. Standen, Morgan and Harrington (all 3rd Battalion) joined on October 11th, against which Captain Moore and 2/Lts. Sweet and Nicholson had been invalided home. Lt. Aitchison also joined in October.

CHAPTER III

THE FIGHT FOR THE CHANNEL PORTS
—WINTER IN THE TRENCHES.

THE B.E.F.'s move to Flanders had placed it on the left of General Maudhuy's Tenth Army, whose line extended Northward East of Arras and West of Lens almost to Bethune and the La Bassée canal.   When the B.E.F. reached Flanders the German right extended no further Northward, except that large bodies of cavalry, stiffened by Jäger and cyclists, were advancing Westward from Lille and SW. up the Lys valley, threatening to sweep away the thin screen of French cavalry and Territorials facing them on the line Bethune—Aire—St. Omer.   It was this cavalry that the Second and Third Corps were now to encounter, the Second astride the La Bassée canal but not reaching quite to the Lys, on whose left bank the Third, after detraining about St. Omer, would advance.   Ahead of them and between them and the great industrial area of Lille lay the Aubers Ridge, only a slight rise but sufficiently above the level of the low and rather water-logged Flanders plain to possess tactical and even strategical importance.

The Third Corps completed its concentration in time to advance on October 13th, the Second, which had started two days earlier, being already in conflict with the enemy.   The 11th Brigade had been taken in motor buses to Hondeghem on October 12th, a very bumpy journey being punctuated by many stops and some loss of direction and taking nearly five hours, time enough to have marched the 14 miles and been little more fatigued.   Next day, when the enemy were encountered at Meteren and driven back, the brigade was in reserve, and though about 9.30 p.m. the Hampshire were ordered forward to reinforce the 12th Brigade, they were not engaged.   Later on C Company came up between the 12th Brigade and the Sixth Division on its right, with whom a patrol under Captain Twining gained touch during the night, while the company covered a night advance by the Lancashire Fusiliers, who cleared Meteren, taking some prisoners,[1] thereby completing the previous day's work.   The next day (Oct. 14th) took the Hampshire forward to Bailleul ; they were advanced-guard to the Division but the only opposition came from cavalry patrols and cyclists, who were soon pushed back, a few prisoners being taken : the enemy apparently had been sharply punished at Meteren and had gone back behind the Lys.   The inhabitants' joy at being delivered from German brutalities found expression in their readiness to provide the troops with fruit and eggs and hot coffee at any moment.   The battalion spent most of October 15th on outpost, to the South of Bailleul, and it was dark before it received orders to push on to the Lys and occupy Nieppe.   It started forward therefore about 6 p.m. C Company leading and securing a covering position South of Nieppe, after which B Company (Captain Unwin) advanced direct upon the village to be received by machine-gun

---

[1] One was captured by C.

fire. They quickly established themselves in the village, however, having only a dozen casualties. Pressing on towards the bridge, Lt. Knocker's platoon found it strongly barricaded and came under machine-gun fire but escaped casualties, though Lt. Knocker was so unfortunate as to fall into a cesspit in avoiding the bullets. It was difficult to understand why the Division was not being directed to press forward more vigorously : the Germans did not seem to be in great strength and were retiring. Next day, (Oct. 16th) however, the Division secured the passages over the Lys at Pont de Nieppe and at Erquinghem, a little way upstream. At Pont de Nieppe C Company worked forward into a flanking position to cover the main advance by A and D ; this was also covered by the machine-guns, now under Lt. Wade, and after a 18 pr. had been brought forward and had demolished the barricade across the bridge with its first shot, the

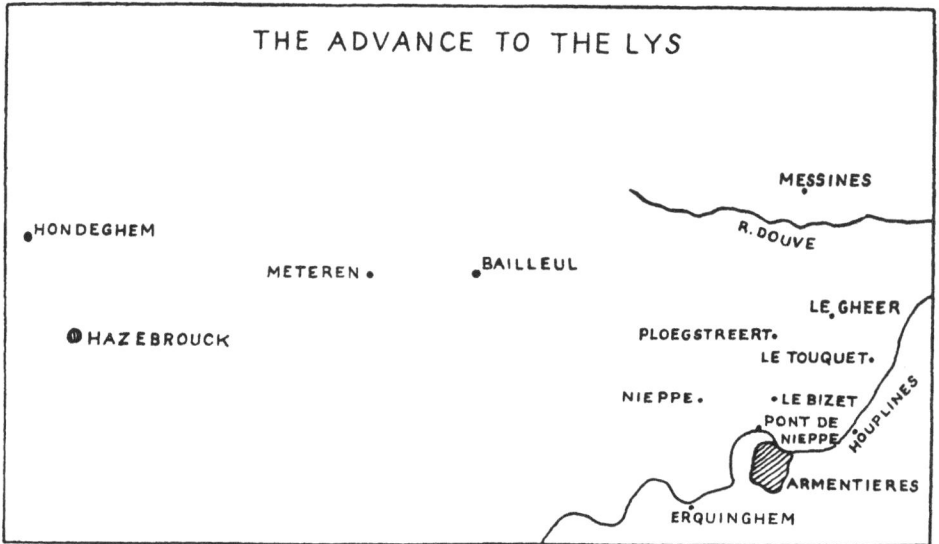

THE ADVANCE TO THE LYS

•HONDEGHEM

METEREN •   •BAILLEUL

⊕HAZEBROUCK

MESSINES
R. DOUVE

LE GHEER
PLOEGSTREERT.•
LE TOUQUET.•

NIEPPE.•   •LE BIZET
PONT DE
NIEPPE   HOUPLINES
ARMENTIERES
ERQUINGHEM

Germans retired hastily, assisted by 'five rounds rapid' from C. The Sixth Division on the right was also across, and during the day the cavalry gained touch with the Seventh Division, which, after a fruitless effort to help Antwerp, was now in front of Ypres and ready to co-operate in the main operations.

That evening found two companies of the Hampshire holding a forward line from Erquinghem along the railway to the Nieppe—Armentieres road, the other two being on the main road behind the left.

The next three days (October 17th—19th) the 11th Brigade spent in reserve, the 10th advancing through Armentieres to Houplines, while on its left the 12th reached a line East of Ploegsteert Wood ; the Hampshire, in Divisional reserve, came up to Armentieres on the 18th, waiting there next day. Some 'spy hunting' went on, parties searching the town for Germans in and out of uniform left behind to signal and get information, several being captured. The First Corps was now arriving from the Aisne and getting ready to advance beyond Ypres, to make what Sir John French optimistically hoped would be the successful out-flanking movement against the German right, but though to the Southward the Second Corps was established on the Aubers Ridge at Herlies, its right was meeting stiff opposition opposite La Bassée and it was only prudence to keep something in reserve. Already the B.E.F. was covering a front out of all pro-portion to its strength and its attacks had nothing behind them. That this imposed on the Germans and caused them to credit the B.E.F. with reserves it did not possess may be admitted, but when our offensive encountered opposition it could not overcome and we were thrown back upon an unprepared defensive, our long and thinly held line presented many weak spots and gaps.

This was evident when on October 20th the Germans, having been substanti-ally reinforced, passed to the offensive and thrust hard at both Second and Third Corps. Both had to give ground ; even if the Fourth Division slightly improved its position across the Lys, on its right the Sixth was thrust back and the Fourth had to prepare to see the counter-attack extended to its front. The 11th Brigade was held in reserve ' as long as possible ',[1] though a battalion had to be sent to help the hard-pressed Sixth Division. Of the Hampshire three companies were sent forward to entrench positions in support East of Armen-tieres ; in doing this they were heavily shelled and the casualties unfortunately included one of the battalion's mainstays, Major Connellan, now commanding C Company. He had given proof of his capacity when in temporary command on the Aisne and was much regretted.

October 21st brought no real relaxation of German pressure, though the heavy price their gains had cost them had taken some of the sting out of their attacks. Overnight General Hunter-Weston had been ordered to take all the available troops of his brigade to Le Gheer and Ploegsteert to support the hard-pressed left of the Division, but the Hampshire remained in Divisional reserve, having been detailed to be ready to help the Sixth Division, and they thus missed a share in the highly successful counter-attack by which their Brigadier restored the critical situation at Le Gheer where the Germans had broken through the 12th Brigade's front. About 10 a.m., however, A and C Companies under Captain Unwin were ordered up to Ploegsteert, to support the left of the Division's line against which the enemy were pressing. The rest of the battalion followed them in the evening, to be put into billets in Ploegsteert village and then turned out in the small hours (October 22nd) to relieve the King's Own, who had had a very hard, if successful, day at the Le Touquet cross-roads. This relief was not made easier by difficulties in finding the way and was not quite finished by daylight, when the Germans opened a heavy fire and started to advance against a trench which B Company was taking over from some of the 11th Hussars. Lt. Dolphin, however, rushed the leading men of his platoon up into the trenches in time to bring the German advance to a standstill by some accurate shooting and the German rifle-fire, though heavy, proved harmless and inflicted no casualties.

The Hampshire now started to improve their trenches and take any chances

[1] H.Q. Diary, Fourth Division.

offered by the Germans, whose line was about 700 yards away, too far for their snipers to do much damage. It was some satisfaction to see how heavily previous German attacks had been punished, the ground being covered with their dead. A and C Companies meanwhile were away to the left beyond Ploeg-steert Wood, between St. Yves and the Douve. Neither detachment was seriously troubled during the day and after dark both were relieved and drawn back into reserve at a chateau near Ploegsteert, where the battalion remained for

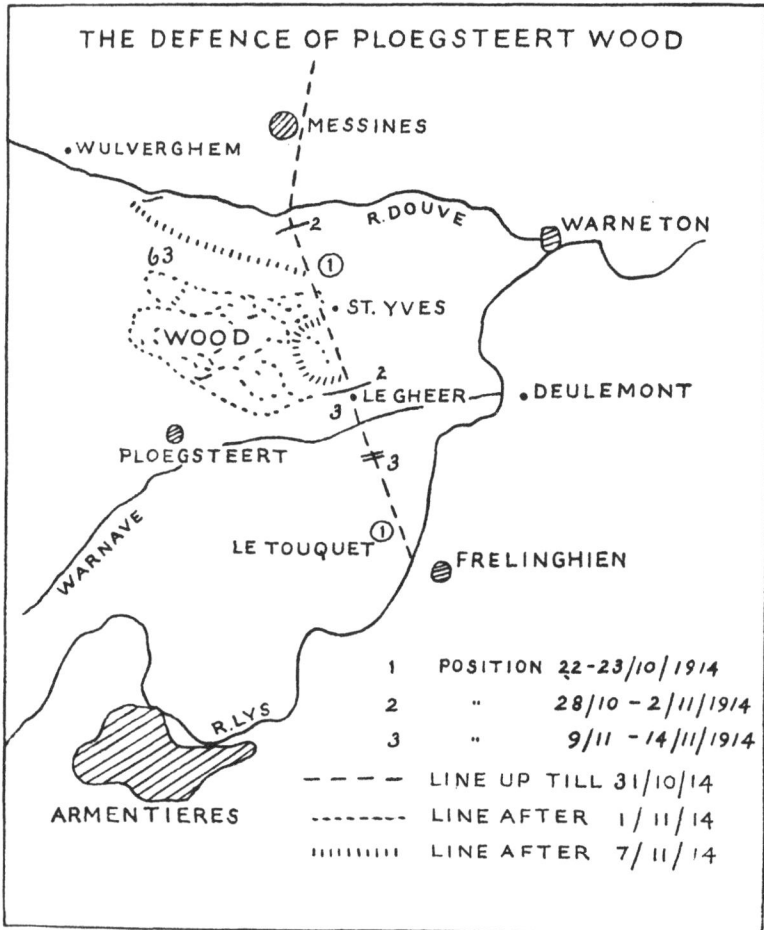

THE DEFENCE OF PLOEGSTEERT WOOD

1	POSITION	22-23/10/1914
2	"	28/10 - 2/11/1914
3	"	9/11 - 14/11/1914
- - - -	LINE UP TILL	31/10/14
--------	LINE AFTER	1/11/14
,,,,,,,,,	LINE AFTER	7/11/14

four days, digging a reserve line. The Division had meanwhile taken over more line on the right of the Lys and was thus extended over an eight miles frontage, thinly held and almost without reserves. Fortunately in its musketry the B.E.F. had still a substantial asset ; if the last Regular Reservists had before this time come out, the trained Special Reservists, now providing most of the drafts, had also learnt to shoot. Shortage of artillery ammunition, however, was forcing our guns to restrict their firing to the absolutely essential, making our chances more dependent than ever on our infantry's staunchness and good shooting, but in this we had something the enemy could not overcome.

But for persistent shell-fire the Fourth Division was not much troubled during the four days the 1st Hampshire spent in reserve at Ploegsteert. Something could therefore be done to improve the line, dig communication trenches and generally prepare to meet another thrust. Very heavy fighting had now developed East of Ypres, where the First Corps and the Seventh Division were deeply involved in their great defence of the Channel ports, while further South the Second Corps and the Lahore Division, just arrived from India, were almost as hard pressed, and though the Fourth Division only had to beat off several small attacks, especially against its right and centre, it could not expect much more of the comparative quiet it was experiencing.

On the evening of October 28th the Hampshire relieved the Somerset L.I. East of Ploegsteert Wood past St. Yves, their left (B Company) resting on the Douve and their right (A) reaching to Le Gheer. But for one platoon of A Company the whole battalion was in the firing line, over 2000 yards in length, which consisted mainly of separate trenches, not a continuous line, and was almost without communication trenches. The enemy's line was about 1100 yards away. The first day here passed quietly enough, but about 6 p.m. an attack developed on Le Gheer, in repulsing which the battalion was effectively assisted by the 68th and 88th Batteries, R.F.A. This was only the prelude to a tremendous bombardment, which started about 6.30 a.m. (Oct. 30th) and was maintained with varying intensity throughout the day. It was the heaviest the battalion had yet endured and the trenches and their garrisons suffered heavily, but the men held on unflinchingly and whenever German infantry attempted to advance our rifles were ready for them. About 7.30 a.m. the 11th Brigade reported one such unsuccessful attack and at 10.30 another had been repulsed. The most dangerous attack came about 4.30 p.m. when the Germans swarmed forward in masses, trusting perhaps to the failing light to handicap our shooting. ' They came on so thick you couldn't miss them ' one man wrote ' It was just like shooting rabbits on Shillingston Hill.' They were checked nearly everywhere, the right centre in a good position soon stopped them getting near but in our left centre dead ground helped them and they rushed an isolated trench, in advance of our line, to which Lt. Trimmer and No. 10 Platoon had been clinging with magnificent tenacity, taking a heavy toll of the attackers before being killed or taken almost to a man. The Hampshire lost another fine officer when Captain Harland was killed here, exposing himself gallantly to direct the defence, and the Germans, having overwhelmed the last survivors of No. 10,[1] threatened to break right through. They were prevented from exploiting their success, largely by 2/Lt. Fidler's platoon who, though attacked in flank and rear, disposed of the Germans who were breaking through and by the machine guns under Lt. Wade, while Captain [2] Aitchison, now commanding C, threw up a barricade across the end of the next trench and planted a machine gun to enfilade the

[1] A few wounded men were taken, the majority, including Lt. Trimmer, had been killed.
[2] Promoted October 21st.

captured trench. This foiled the effort to roll up our line from the left, and any Germans who ventured to advance across the open were promptly sent back to cover by our unfailing shooting,[1] while eventually Lt. Trimmer's trench was won back by the brigade reserve, two companies of the Somerset, who drove the Germans out, inflicting heavy casualties, to find practically all the original defenders dead at their posts. The battalion's tenacious gallantry was most warmly acknowledged by the Brigadier, who was loud in his praise of its stubborn defence. Several prisoners were taken, whose capture revealed the presence on the Third Corps' front of a fresh German Corps.

That night much of the line was re-dug, from which the battalion benefited next day, when the trenches were subjected to another tremendous bombardment, followed once again by an infantry attack. This time the enemy again reached the wire in front of our trenches but they were driven back without the brigade reserve being called upon ; they had suffered heavily, 75 of their dead being counted in front of one short trench only. A company of the Somersets had occupied the left centre trenches which C had been holding and assisted in the repulse, while the battalion's left was now covered by bringing the Inniskillings up from reserve. That evening a small patrol under Lt. im Thurn went forward some 200 yards and brought back trophies from an evacuated trench.

If the Fourth Division had managed to maintain its line intact, beyond its left across the Douve the Germans, attacking in greatly superior force, had driven our cavalry and some attached infantry units off the Messines ridge, the loss of which (November 1st) necessitated the flinging back of the Fourth Division's line along the Northern edge of Ploegsteert Wood, so that it presented a distinct salient at St. Yves, while the Hampshire's left could be enfiladed from the ridge. Could the Germans have exploited their capture of Messines by advancing Westward up the Douve, the Fourth Division's line would have become untenable, but this they failed to do, and the line which the Hampshire had managed to maintain on October 30th and 31st was to remain, save for one small loss of ground, virtually unchanged until the German offensive of April 1918 drove us back almost to the outskirts of Hazebrouck. It was only maintained after further stubborn resistance to renewed attacks. On November 1st and again next day the line was again heavily bombarded and infantry attacks again followed. Though suffering severely from the bombardment, the Hampshire were quite ready for the infantry and punished them heavily whenever they tried to take advantage of the shell-fire and advance. With infantry attacks our rifles could deal, even one particularly violent effort early on November 1st was repulsed without having to call on the brigade reserves. Next day (November 2nd) the Germans actually broke in, driving back a platoon of D, but they were soon expelled by about 40 men under Captains Unwin and Beckett, Lt. Prendergast and 2/Lt. Standen, who promptly counter-attacked and cleared them out, Captain Unwin being wounded but remaining at duty.[2]

---

[1] One man claimed to have fired 150 rounds, despite being wounded in the left hand.
[2] Lt. Standen also was wounded, more seriously.

Two platoons of B had reinforced D, whose right platoon, No. 14, had held stoutly on, while the left half company had supported the charge with most effective covering fire, catching the enemy as they rose to meet it.

The shell-fire was a more formidable ordeal, but the G.O.C. Fourth Division reported that the battalion's conduct under very heavy shelling had been excellent. The trial was indeed severe, the trenches had not yet been linked up into a continuous line and isolated detachments often found themselves under very heavy fire without any chance of help. Sergant Williamson, for example, held on most tenaciously with a few men in one isolated trench and maintained his position intact. But the Hampshire were weary and worn after enduring all this bombarding, and it was well that on the evening of November 2nd General Hunter-Weston could give them a well-earned and urgently needed relief. The Indian Corps had now taken over the front held by the Second, whose battered units after the briefest of rests were now thrown into the fight again at critical points, two being placed at the 11th Brigade's disposal. November 3rd therefore found the Hampshire resting in bivouac at Ploegsteert. Since going into the line on October 28th they had lost, besides Captain Harland and Lt. Trimmer, 46 men killed, 51 missing[1] and 121 wounded. Captains Unwin (at duty) and Johnston, Lts. Wade and Harrington [2] and 2/Lt. Standen had been wounded and during October the Quartermaster, Captain Hackett, and 40 men had gone to hospital.

In November 1914 to be ' relieved ' usually merely meant to be shifted to another point in the line, and on the evening of November 4th the battalion took over the trenches held by the East Lancashire on the Ploegsteert road at Le Gheer, B Company being in reserve and the rest in the firing line. This time the battalion had about half a mile to hold with well under a man a yard for the purpose. Two ' quiet ' days followed, with an attempt by Germans dressed in kilts to pass themselves off as Scottish Rifles, not very successfully, and then on November 7th came a fresh attack in force, advantage being taken of a mist to launch no less than eight battalions against the 11th Brigade. Against the Hampshire they made no impression ; ' we poured volleys into them ' writes one account ' and a long line of dead marked the position they had reached '. On the left in the Southern part of Ploegsteert Wood they broke through a weak and weary battalion of the Second Corps, fitter for a long spell in reserve than for the line, and a large party began advancing round the Hampshire's flank. However, this did not shake the battalion's hold on its line. Once again Sergeant Williamson and a small party held on firmly in an isolated trench, and A Company, recently relieved from the firing line, promptly counter-attacked. Headed by Captains Unwin and Dolphin,[3] they quickly cleared the intruders out, capturing an officer, though Captain Dolphin was killed, being shot as he went forward to receive the surrender of men who were calling out ' Don't shoot ' and pretending to be ready to give in. This reception effectively discouraged further German efforts at this point, and eventually the brigade reserves

---

[1] Many probably buried under demolished trenches.
[2] Died of wounds.
[3] He had just been promoted.

C   H.R. II.

recovered most of the lost ground except for some houses North of Le Gheer, the blunt salient thus left in our line, soon christened the ' Birdcage ', proving very troublesome thereafter.

The Hampshire's success had not beeen cheaply obtained, the casualties including Captain Dolphin and 34 men killed and missing and Captains Unwin (second time), and Aitchison and 2/Lt. Weston wounded with 20 men. Of the officers who had come out with the battalion only Captains Perkins and im Thurn [1] and Lt. Edsell now remained, though the campaign was well under three months old.

The attack of November 7th was the enemy's last serious venture against the Fourth Division. If the Germans, despite several efforts, maintained their hold on the ' Birdcage ', where the houses were sheltered by the wood from our artillery fire, even if ammunition had been available for demolishing them, they had had enough of attacking and did not repeat the experiment. Trench warfare conditions thus began some ten days sooner on the Fourth Division's front than in the Ypres Salient, where the German Guard had yet to make the supreme effort of November 11th which the remnant of the First Corps was to repulse so dramatically.

The Fourth Division's share in foiling the great German autumn offensive is apt to be overlooked, but attention should not be exclusively concentrated on the great struggle in the Ypres Salient to the extent of disregarding the achievement of the Second and Third Corps. They too had to struggle in most adverse conditions against very heavy odds, being at a great disadvantage as regards the volume of artillery support available, though so far as their limited means allowed our over-matched artillery shot extraordinarily effectively, earning the gratitude of our hard-pressed infantry : perhaps the attacks to be faced in this quarter, vigorous as they were, may have lacked just a little of the weight of numbers and thrust of those delivered against Ypres, but those two Corps and particularly the Fourth Division, had a much greater length of line to hold and this greatly enhanced the strain on them.

Those in the trenches in November 1914 may have hardly appreciated that the ' battle ' was over and that a stalemate was setting in. The 1st Hampshire continued in line at Le Gheer for a week after repulsing the attack of November 7th. The Germans, having evidently abandoned any idea of renewing their attacks, were busily improving their line, their working parties occasionally providing our rifles with good targets ; if shelling slackened, snipers were troublesome and caused most of our 30 casualties, which included four killed and two missing. We did some retaliatory sniping but were mainly occupied in working at the line, now becoming fairly strong, though bad weather severely impeded our efforts, trenches in that low-lying area rapidly becoming water-logged. Rain and mud greatly increased the strain of trench-warfare but despite all hardships and discomforts the men were extraordinarily cheerful, their patient endurance being really remarkable. ' The men are wonderful ' one

---

[1] Promoted Nov. 1st. besides him and Captain Aitchison, Lts. Venour and Wade had been promoted while most ' pre-war ' 2/Lts. had before this received a step.

company commander wrote, ' how they stick the wet and the cold with no sleep for days on end beats me.'

After three days out of the line, the battalion [1] then spent the last fortnight of November directly in front of Le Gheer and just North of its last trenches. Heavy rain had reduced the line to a dreadful state and hard as all worked it was difficult to produce much impression. Two companies were usually in front line, being relieved from support at regular intervals, the relief often taking several hours owing to communication trenches being so narrow and muddy and men going in ' loaded up like Tweedledum '. With the enemy so near nearly half the trench garrisons had to ' stand to ' all night, in hourly reliefs so that few got any real rest. Here also snipers were the chief trouble, causing another 20 casualties, nine fatal, while the Adjutant was wounded on November 18th when battalion headquarters was severely shelled, Captain im Thurn taking over his duties. The sick-rate was naturally high, Captain Cope (3rd Battalion), Lt. Edsell and 2/Lts. Coulter and Gill being sent to hospital with 92 men, while only 20 recovered sick returned to duty.

December brought little change. Our patrols were active, Lance Corporal Irish and Private Glasspool both distinguishing themselves by obtaining useful information about the enemy's defences, Glasspool locating a machine-gun.[2] Bad weather was more troublesome than the enemy, even constant pumping could not prevent the trenches from being flooded. They were continually caving in and needing revetting and even when temporarily free from water were knee-deep in slush. Some had to be abandoned and sandbag breastworks built up instead, while many experiments were made with bricks and wooden floors to keep men above the water level when in trenches. However, arrangements had now been made to give the men baths and clean clothes when they came out of trenches absolutely plastered with mud. Brewers' vats made excellent baths and ample supplies of clothing and ' comforts ' arrived regularly, supplementing the ample but rather monotonous rations. The clothing included ' some extraordinary fur garments with the fur outside ', ' one has only got to go on one's knees and growl to be like the bear in the pantomime ' one officer wrote. It was hard to be smart in such conditions. Considering the wetness of the trenches the sick-rate, 180 admissions to hospital in December, was hardly excessive, and the arrival of 260 men from the 3rd Battalion at the end of November went far to replenish the ranks. Major Hicks came back on December 12th and resumed command [3] and Captains Palk and Unwin also rejoined, while Captain Garsia, hitherto on duty as R.T.O., had joined on November 26th and taken over C Company. Several new subalterns appeared, of whom Lt. Smythe came from Sandhurst,[4] the others being from the 3rd Battalion, mostly Gazetted since August 4th but qualified to take their places in the field by a good deal of previous O.T.C. training.

---

[1] The Divisional Diary gives its strength on November 15th as eleven officers, no other battalion having as few, and 800 other ranks, two other battalions only being weaker.

[2] Both received the D.C.M.   [3] Promoted to temporary Lt. Colonel Nov. 29th.

[4] 2/Lts. Wyld (who was out with another regiment), Smythe and Gill, all commissioned from the R.M.C. in August, were promoted temporary Lts. in November.

The Birdcage was still a sore thorn in our flesh, its occupants could enfilade the left of the Hampshire line, which here formed a T, from 150 yards away, while it was too near our lines for our guns to range on it with any accuracy When therefore, in the middle of December, minor offensives were ordered at different points in our line to assist a French attack at Arras, the Fourth Division attempted to get rid of this constant cause of trouble, the Somerset

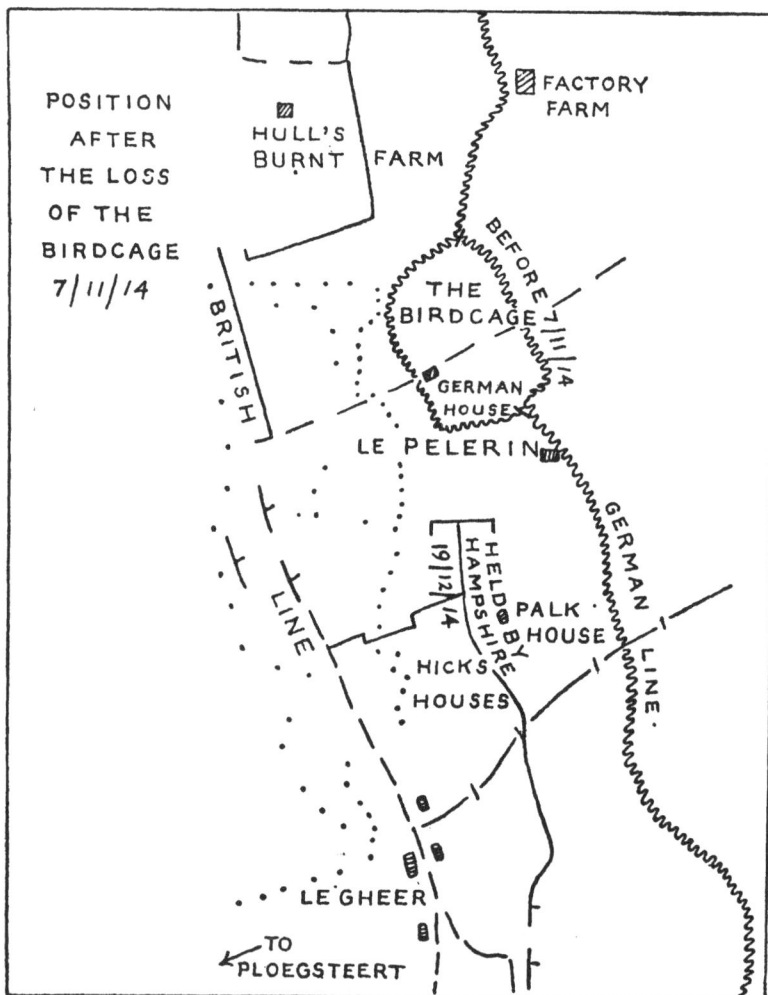

L. I. and Rifle Brigade being detailed for the attack, the Hampshire co-operating with fire and having a platoon of D company (Captain Palk) ready to dig in on the Rifle Brigade's right and connect the position captured with our main trench, now held by C Company (Captain Beckett).

Only a miserable allowance of ammunition was available, a mere 100 rounds for the howitzers, nothing like enough to give the attack a fair chance. Nevertheless, attacking at 2.30 p.m. on December 18th, the Rifle Brigade took the two nearest houses but could get no further, partly because our own shells fell short and caused several casualties. One Hampshire platoon caught several shells, but Captain Beckett steadied the men, setting a splendid example of coolness, and Sergeant Haydon backed him up well, C Company doing some effective shooting at Germans retiring from the forward houses, while the digging platoon under 2/Lt. Reeves got quickly to work, though the ground they had to entrench proved such a swamp that they soon had to come back. Unluckily, while directing machine-gun fire from our front trench, Major Parker was killed, the regiment thus losing yet another valued officer of much experience, ' a born leader ' who had commanded the battalion most successfully and was much missed by all ranks. In all, the Hampshire had 40 casualties, including Lt. Prendergast wounded and 15 men killed, and as the Rifle Brigade had over 70 casualties and only retained a small portion of their objective, the operation could hardly be reckoned very successful, though it was something to have ousted the German snipers from one coign of vantage. Both sides had by now constructed defences which could hardly be taken without a much larger ammunition expenditure than either could afford for a minor enterprise, and troops in trenches were now enjoying some respite from bombardment. Snipers, however, were very active : the flooding of the trenches which drove both sides to construct breastworks above ground naturally increased their opportunities, which neither side neglected, and of the battalion's 50 casualties in December, in addition to those of the 19th, snipers caused the majority, while ours claimed a good many hits, though the Saxons of the XIXth Corps, now facing the 11th Brigade, were not aggressive enough to offer many targets.

Trench mortars and hand grenades were now being brought into use, and with both the Germans were better prepared and better provided, while the British had to improvise, the ' jam-tin ' and the ' hair-brush ' patterns being among the earlier experiments, while if the ' drain-pipe ' brand of trench-mortar was as damaging to the enemy as it was dangerous to its crews, its use would have been amply justified.

The end of 1914 found the 1st Hampshire with only six officers present who had come out with the battalion in August, Lt. Colonel Hicks and Major Palk,[1] both of whom had rejoined, and Captains im Thurn and Knocker,[2] who had served continuously, as had 2/Lts. Fidler and Sprake, commissioned in October. Of original other ranks 366 were still present, the largest number in the brigade : 265 N.C.O.s and men had been killed or were missing, 390 had been wounded. Altogether eight officers had been killed, six were missing [3] and fifteen had been wounded.

The New Year brought the Hampshire little change. The Fourth Division's main problem was water, which the occupants of trenches in Ploegsteert Wood

---

[1] Promoted November. 20th.

[2] Captain Knocker had been off duty sick for a short time. He had been promoted temporarily on Nov. 15th

[3] All six were known to be prisoners of war.

had always with them, bale or pump as they would. A wet January ended with frost and snow, which went on into February and at any rate dried up the mud and reduced casualties, because with the communication trenches allowing of progress the temptation to risk crossing the open was less.

Spending hours in wet and muddy trenches was a constant cause of sickness, though from January extra rations, pea soup and more tea and sugar, were issued to men actually in the trenches. Though rheumatism and bronchitis were prevalent with a lot of ' trench feet ' and frost bite, for which new remedies had to be devised, pneumonia cases were remarkably few, and the admissions to hospital, 150 in January, 120 in February and 100 in March, were not as high as might have been feared.

Casualties in action came to Captain Knocker, who was hit by a sniper, and 11 men killed, Lt. Cecil,[1] 2/Lt. Lambert and 34 men wounded. That these were no higher was largely due to the steady improvement of the line, now showing the effect of all the hard work devoted to it. The men were becoming very expert at their work on the trenches, ' as good as R.E.'s ' one officer wrote. The houses behind the front line had become quite formidable ' strong points ', and though, as time wore on, the German shelling increased in volume it inflicted few casualties and did little damage to the defences, which were gradually becoming less uncomfortable as well as stronger. Conditions behind the lines also were being much improved, notably the arrangements for bathing and for providing dry clothing, and in February the arrival of a travelling kitchen or ' cooker ' was much appreciated.

Drafts came out in a fairly steady stream, though while some recovered sick came back straight from hospital in France, the majority of the sick and wounded were sent home, joining the 3rd Battalion on recovery. The drafts contained some re-enlisted old soldiers but now consisted largely of men enlisted since August 4th, good material if their musketry hardly reached ' mad minute ' standards, the trained men of the Special, as well as the Regular, Reserve being by now pretty well exhausted. Ten officers arrived in January, among them Captain Perkins and Lts. Cecil, K. A. Johnston, Capel, who had been with the Dorsets, and Wyld, who had been with the Bedfordshire. The R.M.C. was now turning out large batches after a shortened but intensified course, and the Special Reserve was well off for officer material, if many had to go overseas rather short of training. At the end of March the battalion had nine ' pre-war ' Regulars with it, the C.O., Major Palk and Captains Perkins and im Thurn having come out with it, together with eleven Regulars commissioned since August 4th, of whom 2/Lt. Sprake was acting Quartermaster, and eight Special Reservists, two of them attached from other regiments.

Opportunities of harrassing the enemy, though few, were not neglected, occasionally the machine-guns got at working parties while our snipers were always on the alert, but the enemy was not disposed to risk much.

Between the end of November and the re-opening of active operations with the British attack at Neuve Chapelle (March 10th) the Fourth Division's line

[1] Second time : he had rejoined on January 1st.

changed less and saw less activity than the rest of the front. Elsewhere, February saw much ' liveliness ', especially at Ypres, where the Fifth Corps [1] had relieved the French. On our right also, at Givenchy and Cuinchy astride the La Bassée canal, fighting had reached quite serious dimensions, both in December and in January, but the Fourth Division's opponents were content not to provoke it into an activity, which it, for its part, was in no position to initiate. The water-logged ground largely accounted for this, but the Division [2] had so long a front that it could not have collected the force required for a minor enterprise without weakening its defensive strength unduly. This inactivity gave its units a good chance to assimilate their drafts, while as they had more old hands to be a leaven to the new-comers, it was easier for the Fourth Division to maintain the old standards than for a Division even more depleted by constant serious fighting. The Division was to reap the benefit of this in the severe ordeal now close ahead of it.

A welcome sign of better things to come was the arrival in February of parties of the 7th Sherwood Foresters (North Midland Territorials) and of Canadians to be attached for instruction,[3] two companies of each going into the trenches at a time to be initiated into trench warfare by experienced old hands. This showed that at least some help was to be given to the much-tried ' Old Army ' and Special Reserve who had so long sustained their heavy burden without rest or relief. Every winter of the war may have its own title to have been the worst, weather conditions and increased German shell-fire, bombing behind the lines, the menace of the impending mass-attack, that of 1914–15 can at least claim to have imposed the most continuous strain with the fewest facilities for meeting it.

A re-arrangement of the Division's line and of the method of holding it, so that each battalion did six days in trenches and then six either in reserve or support,[4] was introduced early in March but made little difference, except that any new trenches the Hampshire had to take over fell distinctly short of their own high standards of cleanliness, comfort and defensibility. The Hampshire's line had been a real model of what trenches could be, its condition had won them much praise from the authorities and they had rightly prided themselves on their work. The enemy's shell-fire and sniping had both slackened off and our patrols found little trace of him in No Man's Land. From April 5th to 11th the battalion was in rest billets at Nieppe and then had its last spell in the Ploegsteert trenches, coming out on April 15th on being relieved by South Midland Territorials, under Brigadier General Nicholson, lately C.O. of the 2nd Battalion, some of whom the 11th Brigade had introduced to trench warfare earlier in the month. They were loud in their praise of the Hampshire trenches, ' the best and cleanest we have seen ', one account says, while a senior officer wrote of the vast improvement made in the lines ; ' where one used to have to

---

[1] It was mainly composed of Regulars who had been relieved from India and other stations overseas by Territorials, including both the original Wessex Division and its ' Second Line '.

[2] The London Rifle Brigade had joined the 11th Brigade, a picked Territorial battalion being attached to each brigade.

[3] Colonel Bewsher of the 10th Battalion was another visitor ' for instruction '.

[4] This had the advantage of having a complete battalion in reserve, not four separate companies.

crawl on one's knees one can stand upright in broad daylight.' The battalion now went back to Noote Boom near Bailleul. Here it spent a week, comfortably billetted in farms and well out of the line, carrying on general training, getting a little leave and doing some route-marching, badly needed after so long a spell in trenches. Several officers joined, including Major Humphery (3rd Battalion) and Captain Twining and Lt. Prendergast from hospital, with about 50 men. The battalion had been promised a longer rest, but on April 22nd the brigade was suddenly warned to be ready to move at short notice. The Germans had just attacked at Ypres, using the gas they were pledged not to employ and the collapse of the surprised French holding the Northern flank of the Salient had created a most dangerous situation.

CHAPTER IV

THE 2ND AND 3RD BATTALIONS—THE TERRITORIALS—
EXPANSION

AUGUST 1914 had found the British Regular Army better trained and organized than for any previous war and with the Special Reserve behind it to provide for draft-finding, while from the other branches of the old ' Auxiliary Forces ' a ' Home Defence ' force had been constructed which, whatever its deficiencies in numbers, equipment and training, was a great advance on any earlier ' second line of defence'. But these forces, even if India could to some extent supplement them and if the King's Dominions overseas contained considerable potential reserves of fine fighting material, were at best an inadequate contribution to the cause in which we and our allies had taken arms. The original B.E.F. had admittedly rendered invaluable services to that cause in the opening crisis of the war, but if we were to pull our weight and give our allies the support which, in our own interests no less than in fairness to them, was so urgently needed, the military forces of the Crown must be enormously expanded. It was a gigantic task, beset by every possible difficulty and obstacle, with little to forward it but the good-will and readiness to serve of the great majority of the King's subjects, and it is perhaps the greatest of Lord Kitchener's services that he determined that, despite almost overwhelming handicaps and hindrances, the tremendous expansion needed could be not only attempted but carried through. Vision and determination were both essential and fortunately he possessed both.

Of the measures he now set on foot two particularly affected the Hampshire Regiment, his decisions to raise the needed new forces on the basis of the old existing regiments, utilizing their great traditions and characters to help build up the new units and to set them standards to which to aspire, and to invite the Territorials, though specifically raised for Home Defence only, to undertake service overseas. By doing so they would relieve the Regular units in India and at Colonial stations who thus became available for the formation of new Regular Divisions, five of which eventually reinforced the original six, the 2nd Hampshire being allotted to the Twenty-Ninth Division, by no means the least in fame and achievement, if the last formed.

The 2nd Hampshire had had only eight months in India when war broke out. It was in the middle of the leave season, so several officers were at home, one, 2/Lt. Silk, was in Australia, and two, recently Gazetted, were due to join with the next draft, so the battalion was rather short of officers, though not much below establishment in other ranks. The Fifth (Mhow) Division, to which it belonged, not having been selected for employment either in France or in Mesopotamia, the battalion at first talked rather gloomily about ' being out of it ' and though on August 31st it was directed to leave Mhow at once for Bombay, this was merely to take over from the Sherwood Foresters, who were embarking for England. The battalion had received a very complimentary farewell from Major General Lloyd Payne, G.O.C. Mhow Division, praising its excellent conduct, smartness and manoeuvring and regretting its departure, but, though mobilised, the 2nd Hampshire remained at Colaba until the middle of November, when their own 7th Battalion relieved them and they also embarked. A variety of duties had kept them busy at Colaba, including the removal of ammunition from a ship on fire in the dockyard. Before leaving Bombay 20 N.C.O's and men had been detailed for service, some with ' Force D ' in Mesopotamia as signallers or with the Divisional Field Hospital, others for Base duty with the force proceeding to France, and ten picked N.C.O.s, among them Colour Sergeants Gawn and Wells, had been sent home for duty with ' New Army ' units. Another five, Sergeants Dalton and Moorse and Corporals Peckham, Ginn and Thorn, were commissioned into other regiments and five new 2nd Lieutenants, O'Brien, Parker, Lord, Howard and Hillis, were appointed to the regiment, three joining in time to embark in the *Gloucester Castle* on November 16th. In all 21 officers embarked, with 43 sergeants, 15 drummers and 816 rank and file, Lt. Smith and 24 other ranks being left to introduce the 7th Hampshire to the unfamiliar conditions of Indian service.

The voyage home, in company with many other transports, was uneventful, and on December 22nd the convoy reached Plymouth. A dozen N.C.O's and men, among them R.S.M. Holdway, had embarked with the battalion for Malta in September 1903 and had never been home on leave, while Major Leigh, Captains Addison, B. S. Parker and Reid and 22 men were still present but had not served with the battalion throughout the tour.

From Plymouth the battalion went to Romsey, where it was made very welcome, while the opportunity was taken to give most men short leave. Then on January 13th it moved to Stratford-on-Avon to join its Division, which was being collected in Warwickshire in preparation for active service. The 2nd Hampshire were allotted to the 88th Brigade, under Brigadier General Napier, and found themselves in company with the 4th Worcestershire, the 1st Essex, who had replaced them at Mauritius,[1] and the 5th Royal Scots, a fine Territorial battalion from Edinburgh. Several more officers joined, mostly from the 3rd Battalion, which supplied two drafts, one of them of 181 on January 31st, another of 50 on February 20th, to complete the battalion to establishment. Battalion and company training were carried on, as far as the difficulty of finding suitable manoeuvre ground allowed, and some musketry, while the Division's equipment was being completed. It was at first intended for France, but on the decision, eventually taken in March, to dispatch it to Gallipoli, several changes became necessary, mule transport having to be substituted for wheeled. However, this did not hold up mobilisation seriously and by March 20th the battalion left Warwick, whither it had moved a fortnight earlier, for Avonmouth, where it was to embark. Just previously, on March 12th, the

[1] Thus the Sixty-Seventh found themselves again serving alongside the 44th, who had stormed the Taku Forts along with them.

whole Division had passed in review of the King. It was a magnificent spectacle, a whole Division at war strength, the majority of its men seasoned soldiers of several years' service, the last formation provided by the Old Army, which had already suffered so severely and achieved so much.

In the various schemes for Army re-organisation brought forward in the ' Nineties ' and immediately after the South African war, the Militia had formed a substantial part of the field armies, leaving the work of draft-finding rather to the regimental depots, though during the South African war ' details ' of battalions on service were usually attached to the Militia battalions of their regiments when embodied.[1] In the scheme adopted in 1907 the Militia was converted into the Special Reserve, to be relegated to draft-finding and coast-defence duties and not to be invited to undertake the service overseas so many Militia battalions had seen between 1900 and 1902.

Accordingly upon the mobilisation order the 3rd Battalion, now under Lt. Colonel Powney, after assembling at Winchester upon August 7th, moved at once to the Isle of Wight to take up its war station at Parkhurst. It had only just been disembodied after its month's training at Christchurch, where it had encamped on the estate of Lord Malmesbury, a former officer of the battalion. Though much under establishment in men, many of the year's 200 recruits having already passed on to the Regular Army, it was well off for officers, both in numbers and experience, several of them having put in some years of training. On mobilisation it was joined by the surplus Reservists not required to complete the 1st Battalion to war establishment, nearly half the 950 who had reported being left to accompany the 3rd Battalion to ' the island ', while the ' details ' left behind by the 1st Battalion, ' young soldiers ', recruits in training and the very few found medically unfit, also joined it. On orders being issued to form a new ' Service ' battalion Major Parker and the other Regular officers with the 3rd Battalion, except the Adjutant, Captain Middleton, were posted to the new unit. But in their places came several ex-officers who had rejoined, with a flood of subalterns, nearly all with some training in the O.T.C., as well as several newly Gazetted Regular subalterns from Sandhurst.[2] Recruits rolled in as fast as the Depot could enrol them and do as much as was possible towards clothing and equipping them, though the influx was so large that any surplus supplies were soon exhausted and all sorts of makeshifts had to be adopted until the country's industries could get down to the prodigious task of fitting out a nation in arms.

The Depot had had nearly 1000 Reservists to deal with, some had even antici-pated the mobilisation order by reporting on the Tuesday, August 4th, before it was actually issued. On the 3rd Battalion leaving Winchester, Major Playfair (Reserve of Officers) assumed command at the Depot, with Major Bowker

[1] Cf. Vol. I, p. 393
[2] On September 10th thirty subalterns were with the battalion at Parkhurst, two-thirds of them Gazetted since August 4th.

(Reserve of Officers) as second in command, Captain Coddington becoming Adjutant, with Major Westmorland as District Recruiting Officer. Even with the demands of the ' New Armies ' for N.C.O.s of experience to help start the new units along the path they should take, a highly efficient staff could be maintained at the Depot, as any number of ex-N.C.O.s of the regiment hastened to re-enlist and do invaluable service. Not many of these veterans proved physically equal to the strain of active service overseas : trench warfare made demands on physical fitness which were beyond the older men, however willing and self-sacrificing, but these old soldiers did work of vital importance and the regiment and the country owed them a great debt. To many who took part in this attempt to expand the Regular Army into a force adequate to all that was at stake the task seemed almost insuperable, so great were the difficulties involved. That so large a measure of success was achieved was largely due to many who bore the heat and burden of the day at home, denied opportunities of active service but carrying on with the unending and arduous work of licking the new material into shape despite shortage of arms and equipment, even at times of absolute essentials, often in terribly overcrowded quarters with little room for training, and meanwhile having no small amount, especially in the early days, of defence work, patrolling the coast, digging trenches and keeping watch. Both the Depot and the 3rd Battalion did a good job of work and did it well.[1]

Draft finding began almost directly the 3rd Battalion settled down in ' the island '. The first drafts were composed of the surplus Reservists, with the ' details ' as they completed their training and qualified for the front ; but Special Reservists were soon finding their way overseas and long before the end of 1914 men enlisted since the outbreak of war were being included in the drafts. Lt. Sandeman [2] was the first Special Reserve Officer to go to the front, and by the time the 1st Battalion moved to Flanders Captains Cope and Twining and Lts. Lane, Harrington, Morgan and Prendergast and 2/Lts. Standen and Weston had all joined, while Captain Humphery had been attached to the Devons and Lt. Colebrook to the D.C.L.I. By October 440·men had already gone out in drafts, but their places were filled over and over again by the steady influx of recruits. On September 10th the battalion had 1600 men present, and soon afterwards its numbers passed the 2000 mark. It had taken over Albany Barracks at Parkhurst, which in peace-time held 700 officers and men, and to cope with the flood of new arrivals had to overflow into the criminal lunatics' ward at Parkhurst Prison, into which another 400 could be packed, the surplus being under canvas. The training was strenuous, though hampered by the shortage of weapons and equipment. Parades were a remarkable sight, every

---

[1] Besides those former officers who served either at the Depot or with a battalion of the regiment, many others were employed on various duties. Colonel Buckley was in charge of the Record Office at Hounslow, Colonel Munro on the Staff of the Eastern Command, Major A.C. Richards was a Railway Transport Officer, Major Tompson and Captain Kennedy Shaw were with the Remount Service, Captains Whitaker and Ennis were Recruiting Officers and Captain H.C. Dolphin served on the Lines of Communication in France.

[2] Promoted Captain in September, as was also Lt. Twining.

variety and combination of garments and head-gear, civilian and military. At the end of October 640 men could be turned over to a new ' Service ' battalion, the 13th, which for the time continued to share the 3rd's much over-crowded quarters. By this time convalescents from the 1st Battalion, officers and men, were joining the 3rd on discharge from hospital and were of great assistance in training the recruits. Despite the dispatch of 900 men to the 1st Battalion and the formation of the 13th, the 3rd ended the year with nearly 1400 men.[1]

The Territorial Force had been raised for home service only, though a few units had before August 1914 undertaken to serve overseas in case of war ; it was therefore asking a good deal of its members to present them within a few days of the outbreak of war with what was virtually a peremptory demand that that they should volunteer for the very service they had been repeatedly assured they would never be expected to undertake. The response of the Territorials to this none too tactfully presented request was a great tribute to their zeal and good sense. It was soon evident that an invasion of these islands was hardly to be apprehended : the German Navy was showing no disposition to try conclusions with our Grand Fleet, whom it was leaving in effective possession of that ' command of the sea ', which must be wrested from us before invasion could become a serious menace. It was clear therefore that Territorials were unlikely to find employment of the kind for which they had been raised. As was said on an earlier occasion[2] ' we are perfectly strong in point of home defence, our weakness lies in the want of Regular and offensive force'. To confine to home defence duties the large body of partially trained officers and men, many units of which had already reached a considerable proficiency, would have been a bad economy of force, and even if the Territorial Divisions were hardly ready yet, particularly as regards arms and equipment, as immediate reinforcements for the B.E.F., they were quite equal to relieving Regular units overseas to set them free to supplement the original B.E.F. In being asked to go out to India and undertake the duties of the Regulars normally stationed there, besides completing their war training, the Wessex Division was receiving a well-deserved tribute to its efficiency as well as undertaking work of the utmost value.

The four battalions in the Hampshire Territorial Brigade, of which Brigadier General G. H. Nicholson was in command, had duly assembled for their annual training at Bulford a week before the outbreak of war and were therefore already more than half mobilised. During the ' precautionary period ' detachments were found for guard duty at various key points, and on August 4th the brigade marched in to Salisbury and entrained for Portsmouth to take over the coast defences until they could be relieved by the Special Reserve units detailed for this task. Meanwhile at their respective battalion head-quarters every effort was being made to cope with the rush of recruits which was presenting itself and to complete mobilisation, no easy task, though willing helpers were plentiful.

[1] The highest figure it had reached was 2210 early in September.
[2] By David Dundas of the ' eighteen damned manoeuvres ' to Cornwallis in 1798.

Of the four battalions, the 4th and 7th were best off for officers, the 4th being three above establishment in subalterns, though one Captain short, and the 7th complete to establishment. The 5th lacked two Captains and four subalterns and the 6th five subalterns,[1] but all four had plenty of former officers with Volunteer and Territorial experience, many of whom now rejoined, though others went rather to the new Service battalions in hopes of getting sooner to the front. In other ranks again any shortage of establishment [2] was quickly made up by the re-enlistment of old members, including many who had just completed the four years for which they had engaged when the T.F. was formed.

By August 9th Special Reserve units had taken over the Portsmouth defences and the Hampshire Brigade could return to Bulford. It was here that the invitation to volunteer for foreign service was received and accepted by the great majority of officers and men. If a battalion could produce 600 volunteers it was to be accepted as a unit and brought up to an establishment of 1000 by recruiting,[3] those unable to undertake foreign service forming the nucleus of a ' Home Service ' battalion, on which the home defence duties should devolve and which should also provide drafts for the battalion abroad. All four soon produced the needed numbers. This meant some breaking up of companies and old associations, several officers and men being unable to pass the necessary medical tests for foreign service, while Colonel Naish of the 4th Battalion, being in Holy Orders, was at first refused ecclesiastical permission to go abroad. He was replaced in command of what now became the ' 1st Fourth ' by Lt. Colonel Bowker, who had retired as a Major in 1908, while Major Playfair took command of the 6th Battalion, Lt. Colonel Peters remaining with the 2nd/6th, as the Home Service units were soon re-named.[4]

The Wessex Division was so quick to form its ' Foreign Service ' units that on September 26th it was announced that it had been selected for service in India and that the Hampshire battalions would embark on October 9th. As they would replace Regular units in the Divisions already in existence in India, the Divisional and Brigade staffs did not accompany them but remained behind to take over the ' Second Line ' Division of Home Service units. These were to go into billets, the 2nd/4th (Lt. Colonel Naish) at Winchester, the 2nd/5th (Major Day) at Southampton, the 2nd/6th (Lt. Colonel Peters) at Petersfield and the 2nd/7th (Lt. Colonel Lord Montagu) at Bournemouth.[5] Before this the 2nd/5th had been sent at short notice to Lyndhurst to strike the camps of the Seventh Division, which had just gone overseas, and to guard the ordnance stores until they could be removed. This kept them in camp till nearly the end of October.

[1] The 8th (Isle of Wight Rifles) were three Captains and four subalterns short but had a supernumerary Major, the 9th (Cyclists) were one Captain and one subaltern short.

[2] The 4th was nearly 800 strong on mobilization, the 5th being down to 630, the 6th just under 700 and the 7th 760.

[3] They actually went out at an establishment of 800 other ranks.

[4] Lt. Colonel Burford-Hancock went out with the 5th and Lt. Colonel Parke with the 7th.

[5] The nucleus of the 2nd/7th consisted of about 400 of all ranks ; it was fortunate in that Captain Gribbon, the Adjutant, was left behind to train it. The Adjutants of the other battalions, Captain Barton (5th), Earle (5th), and Bowers (6th) accompanied their battalions to India.

The Territorials' voyage to India, though full of interest to all ranks, was not marked by any ' incident ', except for meeting large convoys of transports from India carrying some of the much needed reinforcements whom the Wessex Division was relieving. The *Emden* had not yet been ' liquidated ' but did not trouble the convoy which carried the Hampshires, though their closely packed ships gave [1] little chance of drill or exercise. A month after leaving England the convoy cast anchor at Bombay and the four battalions separated to their different destinations, Poona for the 4th, Allahabad for the 5th, Dinapore for the 6th and Colaba for the 7th. That battalion, as already stated, was actually relieving the 2nd Hampshire, whose band and drums played it into barracks, while the 2nd got a chance of seeing again many old friends, the senior N.C.O.s of the Territorials including many former Regulars.

Before the end of the year the ' Second Line ' Wessex formations were also invited to accept the overseas obligation and go out to India to relieve more Regulars. Though they were largely composed of recruits and as yet much handicapped in their training by lack of arms and equipment,[2] it showed that any amount of hard work had already been put in to make them fit to go over-seas. The invitation was no small compliment.

The decision to send the Second Wessex Division to India was taken before the end of November, and on December 12th the 2/4th, 2/5th and 2/7th left. The 2/5th were made up to 740 all told by a draft of 150 from the 2/6th, but the 2/4th and 2/7th had managed to reach the Indian establishment of 800 other ranks without drawing on other units. They were rather less time on the way out than their predecessors, the 2/4th reaching Karachi on January 11th and going to Quetta, the 2/5th reaching Bombay on January 4th and going to Secunderabad, whither the 2/7th, who landed on January 7th, followed them.

The 2/6th, after completing the 2/5th, had been reduced considerably below the establishment for service in India and was therefore retained at home, partly to produce drafts for the Territorials overseas, though ' Third Line ' formations for this purpose were also organized before long. A Provisional Battalion, of which Colonel Peters took command, was formed early in 1915 of Home Service men left behind by the different battalions, and this after a brief training was sent to Scotland for duty on coast defences, moving in May to the N.E. coast and performing similar duty at Blyth and neighbouring places. Originally ' the Hampshire Brigade Battalion ', then the 84th Provisional Battalion, it was finally renamed the 17th Hampshire.

The two Hampshire T.F. battalions not in the Wessex Division had not as yet left England. Their ' Special Service ' sections had been called out as early as July 25th, the 8th for duty on the coast of the Isle of Wight and the 9th to provide patrols along the South Coast. On mobilisation, the 8th concentrated at Sandown and took over the forts in the East of the island from the 4th Royal

---

[1] The 4th and 6th shared the 10,000 ton Cunarder *Ultonia*.

[2] Thus the rifles the 2nd/5th took out were condemned as unfit for use, and not till it was re-armed with the ' long ' rifles then discarded by the 1st/5th could the battalion get any proper musketry instruction.

Fusiliers, whom they also relieved of coast duties. Consequently the battalion was much split up, nearly 200 [1] men being on detachment, and not till September 9th could it be brought together as a battalion at Nunwell Park. Recruits flocked in and the battalion was soon above establishment, so that early in December a ' Reserve ' or ' Second Line ' unit could be organised, of which Lt. Colonel Wallace, formerly a Major in the Militia, took command as from December 5th, with Captain Grigg, formerly of the D.C.L.I., as Adjutant. Before this the original Adjutant, Captain Stone, had rejoined his own regiment, the Norfolk, and Captain Veasey had replaced him as Adjutant of the ' First Line ' unit, which by this time had been reconstituted with foreign service men only. It adopted the four company organization as from January 10th, but remained in the Isle of Wight on coast defence duty well into the New Year.

The 9th (Cyclist) Battalion [2] was not left long on the South Coast, on August 8th it was ordered to Lincolnshire, establishing its head-quarters at Louth and patrolling the coast from Grimsby to Skegness. A raid was looked upon as far from unlikely, and every night patrols maintained a vigilant watch from dark to dawn, constant alarms and rumours keeping them much on the alert. Like other T.F. units the 9th was invited to undertake overseas obligations, which it did, whereupon, as in other cases, a ' Second Line ' unit was formed,[3] Major A. B. Perkins becoming C.O., with Lt. Talbot-Ponsonby as Adjutant. This moved back by road to Portsmouth, arriving on October 1st. Its head-quarters were then established at Chichester, but two companies were detached to join the Plymouth garrison and another to Corfe Castle, while a fourth crossed over to Ventnor, where it was soon expanded into two companies, two more being formed at head-quarters before the end of the year to complete the 2/9th to eight companies.

Meanwhile the 1/9th had moved back to Sussex in October, taking over patrol and coastal duties, its head-quarters also being at Chichester.

Except for Lancashire, London and Yorkshire, Hampshire had more Territorials than any other county, and with the Navy drawing so largely upon it for recruits its resources were severely tried to provide its quota to the ' New Armies '. The First and Second New Armies, ' K 1 ' and ' K 2 ' as they were generally known, were composed of six Divisions apiece, organized by localities, except for a Light Division of Rifles and Light Infantry, each Regular regiment contributing one battalion [4] to each New Army. Both New Armies had three purely English Divisions, with eight battalions over, mainly from the Southern counties, who became ' Army troops ' and were attached to different Divisions for training. The ' K1 ' and ' K2 ' battalions of the Hampshire were among the Army Troops and were both attached to the Irish Divisions,[5] the Tenth and the Sixteenth.

---

[1] On mobilisation it mustered 25 officers and 540 other ranks, under Lt. Colonel Rhodes.
[2] Lt. Colonel Johnson was in command.   [3] It originally had five companies.
[4] Some Irish and Scottish and four battalion regiments raised more.
[5] The 10th Battalion started life at Winchester but moved to Dublin on Sept. 8th.

When it came to forming a Third New Army, ' K 3 ', authorised in September, no Scottish, Irish or Light Divisions were formed, only one Division reproducing those of ' K 1 ' and ' K 2 ', and the Hampshire battalion, the 12th, found itself in a Twenty-Sixth Division, composed mainly of regiments from the South and West of England with a Scottish brigade. In the Fourth New Army, formed in October from the battalions thrown off by the Special Reserve, the allotment to Divisions was in the main not local, though the Thirty-Second Division, to which the 13th Hampshire were assigned, came mainly from Southern counties.

Raising these ' New Armies ' naturally became more difficult with each addition, as the demand for instructors, for weapons, for clothing and for equipment of every kind became harder and harder to meet. For ' K 1 ' a satisfactory nucleus of trained instructors was available from the Regular officers serving with the Special Reserve and the two officers and 15 N.C.O.s which each Regular battalion left behind on going overseas. Thus the Hampshire made a good start, being fortunate in having Major Parker, promoted temporary Lt. Colonel on August 9th, to command them, together with Captains Morley and Black-Hawkins, Lts. Berkeley, Capel and K. A. Johnston and 2/Lts. Waddington and Hudson, these last four belonging properly to the 2nd Battalion. To these were soon added Captains Faith, who became Adjutant, and Savage from the Reserve of Officers, and Erle, who had only recently retired from the 3rd Battalion, with Captain McCormick of the 72nd Punjabis, formerly in the regiment and home from India on leave, and Major Pilleau, recently retired from the 105th Mahrattas. In Sergeant Major Saunders, appointed to be its Quartermaster, the 10th had a tower of strength and in its senior N.C.O.s [1] it was also very fortunate.

The many old members of the regiment who had rejoined included several N.C.O.s of experience, and the fine body of recruits who had been collected were better off for instructors than for weapons or equipment. The subalterns were a fine lot, nearly all with some O.T.C. training, considerably augmented during a month of intensive training in camps of instruction organized by the Senior Division of the O.T.C., which enabled them to take charge of their platoons directly they joined. This they did early in October after the battalion had left Dublin, where it had completed its formation, for Mullingar, where it was to spend the winter. It had overflowed the accommodation at Beggar's Bush Barracks, Dublin, 300 of its 1070 other ranks having to be under canvas, but a shift to Royal Barracks improved matters. Before the 10th left Dublin Lt. Colonel Parker had gone out to the 1st Battalion. He had started the new unit admirably and his departure was no small blow, but in Lt. Colonel Bewsher, who joined on October 10th, he had an able successor, under whose direction the battalion's training made as rapid progress as the difficulties of arming and equipping it would allow. There was no want of willingness or hard work and the battalion was made quite welcome at Mullingar, whither it was

[1] R.S.M. J. Smith, R.Q.M.S. W Barnes, C.S.M.s Whitaker, Groves, King and Parkinson, C.Q.M.S.s Goodall, Mills, Lewis and Barton, and O.R.S. Barratt.

soon followed by the 11th Battalion. This had come into existence at Dublin on September 14th. Command went to Colonel Kemmis, formerly of the King's Own,[1] with Major Robertson (late Connaught Rangers) as second in command, and Lt. Berkeley, who transferred from the 10th Battalion, as Adjutant, while several Regular N.C.O.s and P.S.I's whom the Territorials had left behind were posted to the battalion and did invaluable service.[2] Some of the new officers had previous service with Special Reserve or Territorials and its subalterns, like those of the 10th had mostly had some O.T.C. training or had been through the camps of instruction and were of the type required.

The 12th Battalion's first commander, Colonel Walker, came from the Indian Army, having commanded the 20th (Brownlow's) Punjabis. Majors Wombwell and Bazalgette were old officers of the 3rd Battalion, Major Rake had been in the 6th Hampshire, Captain Buckley had formerly held a commission in the regiment, Captain Church had been Sergeant-Major of the 3rd Battalion and Captain Stevens had retired from the West India Regiment. Lt. Persse, who became Adjutant, had served in South Africa with Brabant's Horse and the Imperial Yeomanry, so that the battalion started with several officers of some experience, while its N.C.O.s included over 20 old Regulars of the regiment. It was not long at Winchester, a first detachment, 250 strong, under Major Wombwell, leaving on September 30th for Codford in Wiltshire, where a camp was being formed. It found tents and blankets but no floor-boards, and in general the 12th had to rough it and make the best of even graver deficiencies in equipment than the 10th and 11th had had to face. Substantial detachments soon followed the first and the battalion was soon up to establishment. It was posted to the 79th Brigade, along with the 10th Devons, 8th D.C.L.I. and 7th Wiltshire, and soon settled down to a strenuous programme of training, much impeded as the autumn advanced by heavy rain, which reduced the camp site to a quagmire and eventually, after an ineffectual shift to higher and, for a brief time, drier ground, drove the brigade into billets in the middle of November, the 12th Hampshire going to Basingstoke, where they were warmly welcomed and were most comfortable. On the 2nd Battalion's arrival in England half a dozen of its N.C.O.s were attached to the 12th to assist in the instruction of young officers and N.C.O.s. For subalterns ' K 3 ' got rather fewer with any substantial O.T.C. training : ' K 1 ' and ' K 2 ' had absorbed nearly all who had not gone to the Special Reserve or Territorials, but before long a large number of young men of the right type began to appear from overseas, having come back from the Colonies or the Argentine to serve, a class who were just what was needed, rather older than those of ' K 1 ' and ' K 2 ', men who had already knocked about the world enough to face difficulties.

[1] He had commanded one of its Militia battalions in S. Africa.
[2] The Warrant Officers and Senior N.C.O.s were R.S.M. Simmonds, R.Q.M.S. Rendell and C.S.M.s Hopkins, Murdoch, Glasspool and Lambert, C.Q.M.S.s Hafles, Purnell, Weale, Gawn and Simms (O.R.S.)

The 13th Battalion, formed on October 31st from surplus officers and men of the 3rd, had for its original commander Major Thornton, another ex-officer of the Indian Army. In November, however, Major Crofts, who had retired from the regiment in 1907, was appointed to the command as Lt. Colonel. Hardly any of its officers had any previous connection with the regiment but it was also fortunate in getting a good many ex-N.C.O.s to give it a start. The battalions of the Fourth New Army, though allotted to Divisions, were left in the coast defences in which most of them had been formed, the intention being to move them in the spring to hutted camps at training centres.

Meanwhile a 14th (Service) Battalion had come into existence, raised at Portsmouth by a strong local committee, which undertook all responsibilities for the battalion until such time as it could be presented complete for inspection and approval by the Army authorities, who would then take it over. This was being done all over the country, largely by local authorities and committees, sometimes by bodies like the Church Lads' Brigade, and in the end produced eleven Divisions. The 14th Hampshire, originally allotted to the 121st Brigade in the Fortieth Division, were transferred to a newly-organized Thirty-Ninth in April 1915, but this was not brought together for training round Winchester till August, long before which the 14th Hampshire had been accepted by the War Office, having reached its establishment. The 14th's first C.O., Lt. Colonel Ramsbottom-Isherwood, formerly of the 3rd York and Lancaster, had been Gazetted to command it as far back as September 1st, 1914, and by April 1915 it was nearly complete with officers, its original second in command being Major O'Farrell, formerly of the 6th D.G., with Captain Finlay its first Adjutant.

With the 2nd Battalion home and likely before long to be at the front and in need of drafts, the 3rd Battalion's task did not grow any easier, though as the 1st Battalion spent the first quarter of 1915 in relative quiet, its demands for drafts were less insistent. However, over 200 men had to be found in January to complete the 2nd Battalion to war establishment, besides three drafts amounting to 150 for the 1st. At the end of January the 3rd Battalion moved to Gosport, with head-quarters in Fort Gomer and detachments at Forts Gillicker and Monckton, Calshot Castle, Horsea Island and Southampton Docks, Calshot being a seaplane depot and Horsea a wireless station with a lake where torpedoes were tested. Recruits continued to come in steadily and the battalion seemed likely to top the 2000 mark again, but the 2nd Battalion's heavy losses at Cape Helles and the 1st's casualties in its determined defence of Ypres caused nearly 600 men to be sent off in May, six officers going to Flanders and five with six from the 13th Battalion to Gallipoli. Lt. Tarrant also left to join the 1st Battalion, Captain Hackett, now convalescent, succeeding him. The battalion was fortunate in having the services of several convalescent officers from the B.E.F. who joined it on becoming fit for duty, their experience being most helpful in training the recruits. Another 300 men left for the Dardanelles at the end of June, 350 were sent off in July, with nearly 800 in September, 600 going to the 10th Battalion which had lost so heavily at Sari Bair. Nevertheless on

September 30th the 3rd Battalion had still 1926 men actually on parade and had touched 2903 of all ranks on the 12th, while up to December 31st 5247 men had been sent out with 124 officers.

Before the end of 1914 it was decided to add Pioneer battalions to the New Army Divisions, the 5th Royal Irish becoming the Pioneers of the Tenth Division, whereupon the 10th Hampshire replaced them in the 29th Brigade under Brigadier General Cooper, its other units being the 6th Royal Irish Rifles, 5th Connaught Rangers and 6th Leinster. In the Sixteenth Division the 11th Hampshire were chosen as the Pioneers and had therefore to acquire a sound knowledge of military engineering, while not neglecting their training as infantrymen, Pioneers being fighting soldiers as well as craftsmen.

March brought the 10th a move to the Curragh; they left Mullingar with the good wishes of the townspeople, with whom their relations had been of the friendliest, the excellent behaviour and exemplary discipline of both 10th and 11th Battalions having made a profound impression. They remained at the Curragh until early in May, confortably housed in huts, training hard. With most of the Division in the neighbourhood much more elaborate and advanced exercises could be undertaken and orders to go overseas were expected daily. On leaving Ireland, however, the Tenth Division did not go straight to France but to England to undergo final preparations for 'the front' round Basingstoke, so that the 10th Hampshire found themselves back in familiar country, while some strenuous Divisional training considerably extended their acquaintance with Berkshire and Surrey. The Division was now in the Aldershot Training Centre and battalions went in turn to the Ash ranges for intensive musketry, besides being initiated into bombing. An inspection by the King on May 28th and another by Lord Kitchener a few days later gave the Division an opportunity of showing what remarkable progress it had made in well under a year's training and that it was ready to go overseas.

Meanwhile its destination had been under much consideration. The virtual failure of the Allied Spring offensive in France had been mainly due to the inadequacy of the ammunition supply, and until far more ample quantities were available the resumption of our attack could not be contemplated. This added force to the arguments of those who urged that far-reaching advantages might be gained by exploiting the opening secured at Gallipoli by the gallantry of the Twenty-Ninth Division and the rest of the Mediterranean Expeditionary Force and that therefore the New Armies should be sent to Gallipoli. However, three ' K 1 ' Divisions had already crossed over to France before, on June 27th, the remaining three, the Tenth, Eleventh and Thirteenth, were warned to prepare for service in Gallipoli. The 10th Hampshire therefore found themselves preparing to assist the 2nd Battalion in its effort to reach Constantinople, instead of helping the 1st to expel the Germans from France and Belgium.

The change of destination meant much re-fitting and re-equipping, khaki drill clothing was issued and officers' chargers were withdrawn, helmets were fitted with Indian ' pagris ', and the inferior American leather equipment, already virtually worn out by three months' home service, was replaced by good English accoutrements. Battalion staffs and more particularly the Quartermasters had a hectic time, but by July 5th the leading units of the Division had started for Devonport to embark there. Drafts from the Sixteenth Division had brought units up to establishment.

Two companies of the 11th Battalion, A and B, had already quitted Mullingar before the 10th left, moving to Birr in February, the rest of the battalion soon after shifting to Moore Park, Kilworth. In March, ill-health forced Colonel Kemmis [1] to relinquish command, his successor being Lt. Colonel Crockett, formerly of the Leicestershire, who was already known to the battalion, being on the Divisional staff. To the general regret Major Robertson, the second in command, died in March, and several changes occurred among the officers, while those Regular N.C.O.s who were not re-enlistments for ' duration ' were recalled to the 3rd Battalion. The first week in April saw the battalion reunited at Moore Park, with which it was to become only too well acquainted, remaining there until, early in September, the Division crossed to England to complete its training in the Aldershot area.

After spending most of the winter comfortably housed at Basingstoke, the 12th Battalion had in March moved to Bathwick near Bath. If still short of up-to-date weapons and equipment, it had at least got proper uniforms and was presenting a greatly improved appearance. It had been inspected by the G.O.C., Southern Command, General Pitcairn Campbell, who was very well satisfied with its progress, while it was kept up to establishment by an excellent draft from the 3rd Battalion. It remained at Bathwick until early in May, when it moved to Sutton Veney near Warminster, where it found quite good and comfortable huts and ample ground for training. Major Rake and Captain Stevens left on medical grounds, Captain Church transferred to the Royal Sussex and Captain Buckley was given command of the 7th Leinster in the Sixteenth Division, their departure causing a considerable flow of promotion, and several new faces had appeared in the Officers' Mess before, in September, the Twenty-Sixth Division started to cross to France.

The Divisions of the Fourth New Army were to have been concentrated for training in the spring of 1915, but by then it had become abundantly clear that the difficulty of maintaining the strength of the forces in the field in modern war had been underestimated, trench-warfare with its perpetual contact and conflict causing a heavy drain, sometimes quite heavy, against which more provision must be made. The Special Reserve was being fully taxed to provide the Regular battalions with drafts and could not possibly cope with the demands the New Armies were bound to make. Accordingly ' K 4 ' battalions were converted into draft-finding, or ' Second Reserve ', units and the Divisional organization was abandoned, the Divisions of the Fifth New Army, mainly

---

[1] He made the battalion a much appreciated gift of eight bugles.

composed of the specially formed ' local ' units, being re-numbered.[1] Thus the 13th Hampshire, who had remained in the Isle of Wight after the 3rd had left in January but had crossed over in May to go into camp at Bovington near Wool, had now to settle down to their new duties and were soon sending out drafts almost as regularly as the 3rd Battalion. At Bovington the battalion had better facilities for training than when it had also had garrison and coast defence duties to discharge, good ranges were available and once effective rifles replaced its ' D.P. ' weapons considerable progress was made in musketry. Many officers [2] went off to the 2nd Battalion in the Dardanelles, to which theatre of war some six drafts had been dispatched before October. It was the first two drafts from the 13th Battalion that had the misfortune to be torpedoed on board the *Royal Edward*, sunk between Alexandria and Gallipoli on August 13th, only 26 out of the 250 [3] Hampshires on board being saved.

The 14th Battalion had meanwhile been taking shape steadily : during the early months of 1915 its establishment of officers was completed, while recruiting went well enough for the committee responsible for raising the battalion [4] to embark on forming another ' Portsmouth ' battalion, a 15th Hampshire, to the command of which Major O'Farrell was transferred as from April 20th 1915. As already mentioned the 14th had been allotted in December 1914 to the 121st Brigade of the original Fortieth Division,[5] but in April when the ' K 4 ' Divisions were broken up and the ' K 5 ' re-numbered, the 121st Brigade, in which were also three battalions of the Royal Sussex, the 11th, 12th and 13th (Southdown), was transferred to a new Thirty-Ninth Division and re-numbered as the 116th Brigade. The 15th was eventually allotted to the junior ' K ' Division, the Forty-First, which was not really organized until September 1915, though its formation had been authorised in April. Naturally these later formed ' New Army ' units were handicapped as regards trained personnel to instruct them, though before long wounded and invalided officers and men from overseas became available, but as regards equipment they were perhaps at a less disadvantage, as the country's industries were adjusting themselves to the situation and the necessary articles were being produced in some volume.

[1] Originally the Thirty-Seventh to Forty-Second they became the Thirtieth to Thirty-Fifth.
[2] The June Army List shows the 13th Battalion as having no less than 95 subalterns on its strength, a total which makes the 56 of the 3rd Battalion seem quite modest.
[3] 50 came from the 3rd Battalion.
[4] Unfortunately the records of this committee do not appear to have survived the air-raids on Portsmouth of 1940 and later.
[5] Re-numbered Thirty-Third in April 1915 and re-organised.

CHAPTER V

SECOND YPRES AND AFTER

THE winter of 1914–1915 had seen much greater activity in ' trench-warfare ' than was to prevail in later winters, when there was less harassing of the enemy and more inclination to avoid provoking retaliation without some very definite purpose ; strategically, however, it had been mainly a time of waiting and preparing and, apart from some heavy fighting in Champagne, neither side had attempted anything of more than local importance. The Allies were confidently hoping that a large scale offensive in the spring might recover much of the French territory in German hands, even if it did not achieve decisive victory. The Germans' decision to make their main effort in 1915 against the Russians must be attributed to their distrust of the ability of their Austrian partners to withstand further attacks, if left to their own resources, but after 1914, and particularly after Ypres, they may have felt disinclined to incur the costs of renewing the 1914 offensive against the enemies who had thwarted it and whose powers of resistance they had good reason to respect. The wisdom of their decision may be questioned. France had paid heavily for what she had achieved in 1914 and had used up much of her man-power, while British unreadiness for war was to be more conspicuous in 1915 than in 1914. The Old Army had accomplished more at Mons and Ypres than our augmented but ill-equipped forces could achieve in 1915 : we had virtually exhausted our trained reserves and available supplies ; the Territorials and the improvised New Armies were deficient in equipment and training and had to acquire experience and practice in actual warfare before they could fairly be asked to undertake a major offensive ; above all, the terrible shortage of ammunition, which crippled every British operation as well as handicapping our men dangerously even when merely holding the line, might have produced disaster had the enemy attacked our line in force. Fortunately for us he postponed his next major effort on the Western Front until 1916, by which time the British Armies in France, if hardly really ready even then for a major offensive, could lend the French substantial help by taking over more line and so setting troops free to reinforce Verdun. This they could not have done in 1915, and the Allies were fortunate that that year's one German offensive on the Western Front, which began with the gas attack at Ypres on April 22nd, was apparently undertaken more or less as an experiment and that the German supreme command was not prepared to take full advantage of its success and exploit it really vigorously. In resisting it the 1st Hampshire were to endure even severer trials than they had yet faced ; the stubbornness of the fight which they and the whole Fourth Division put up, along with the equally tried Fifth and Twenty-Seventh and Twenty-Eighth, may well have contributed to discourage the Germans from trying to develop the opening their disregard for another ' scrap of paper ' had secured them.

The gas attack (April 22nd) had completely surprised the French troops holding the Northern flank of the Ypres Salient, half Algerians, half Territorials.

Quite unprepared for this new form of attack, they gave way before it and their retreat uncovered the left flank of the Canadians, who had only just taken over from the French a very indifferent line roughly between the Gravenstafel–Passchendaele and the St. Julien–Poelcappelle roads. The Canadian reserves hastily threw back a line to cover their exposed flank, those of the Twenty-Seventh and Twenty-Eighth Divisions were hurried to their help and something of a front was patched up across the wide gap left by the French collapse. Further reinforcements followed, and on April 23rd the Germans made little further

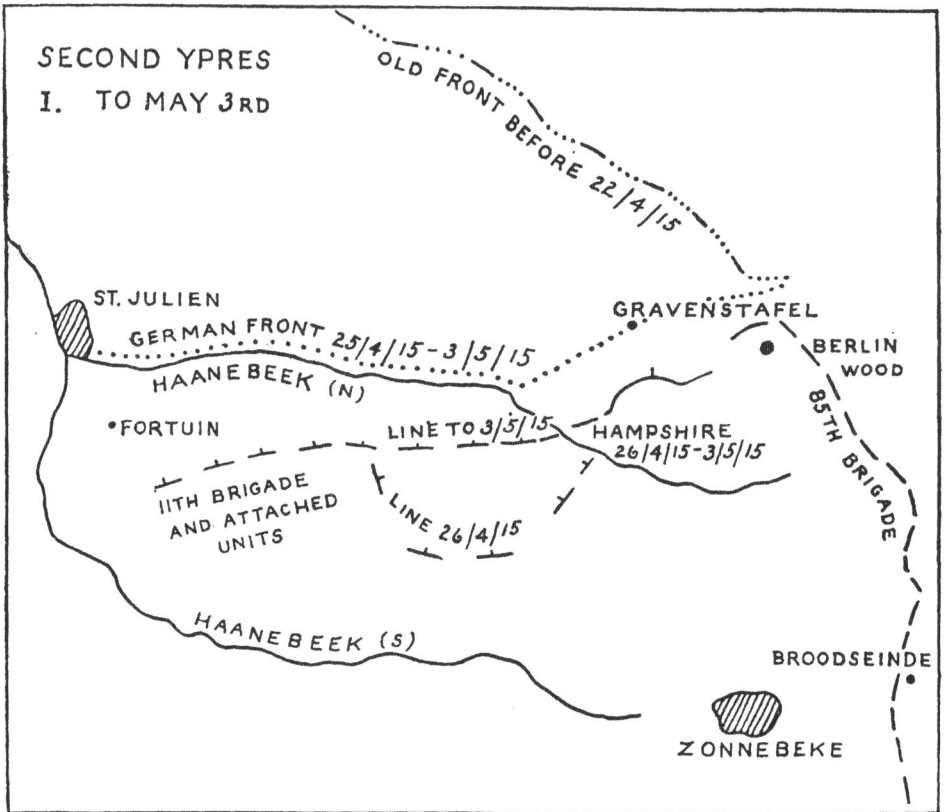

SECOND YPRES

I.   TO MAY 3RD

OLD FRONT BEFORE 22/4/15

ST. JULIEN

GERMAN FRONT 25/4/15 - 3/5/15

HAANEBEEK (N)

•FORTUIN

LINE TO 3/5/15

GRAVENSTAFEL

BERLIN WOOD

85TH BRIGADE

HAMPSHIRE 26/4/15-3/5/15

IITH BRIGADE AND ATTACHED UNITS

LINE 26/4/15

HAANEBEEK (S)

BROODSEINDE

ZONNEBEKE

progress, while some ground was secured by gallant but terribly expensive counter-attacks. But the German attack was now (April 24th) extended to the Canadian front and, despite their stubborn resistance, it drove them back from all but their extreme right, next to the Twenty-Eighth Division's left at Berlin Wood. St. Julien was lost, and though a fresh line was somehow formed behind it, this was a mere improvisation and hardly continuous. Meanwhile the 11th Brigade had been ordered to Ypres [1] and about mid-day (April 24th) the Hamp-

---

[1] The battalion was warned to be in readiness to move on the afternoon of April 22nd and had spent the next 24 hours in listening to the sounds of distant gun-fire before getting definite orders late on April 23rd.

shire entrained at Bailleul. The 10th Brigade had preceded the 11th and were already across the canal. Detraining at Poperinghe the Hampshire found the rumours about the gas attack confirmed by the sight of French and Algerian stragglers, victims of the gas and suffering greatly, while the chlorine could be smelt only too distinctly. However the brigade was merely placed in billets South of Poperinghe, thereby escaping a wet night in the open.

April 25th saw the 10th Brigade's splendid if unsuccessful attempt to recover St. Julien. If plenty of infantry were available, the artillery support, especially from heavy artillery, was quite inadequate, while had more guns been ready ammunition was sadly short. But the whole situation in the Salient was precarious; if St. Julien could not be recovered and with it more ground Westward towards the canal the position would become untenable, and the French were insistent on a prompt counter-attack even if their own contributions to recovering the lost ground lacked weight and vigour. That the 10th Brigade's counter-attack, made over ground it had not properly reconnoitred, failed to recover St. Julien is merely to say that it did not accomplish the impossible, but the line it established was to hold up the German advance in this direction until the evacuation, by order, of the old front of the Fifth Corps. But in the two miles' gap between the 10th Brigade's right and Berlin Wood the position was particularly dangerous. With their left flank ' in the air ', the few Canadians still holding on NW. of Berlin Wood could not maintain their ground and were forced back, leaving the 85th Brigade's left exposed, only some details and mixed parties hanging on to the Gravenstafel ridge on its left rear with, beyond them but some distance away, two weak battalions of the Twenty-Eighth Division. Meanwhile, early in the day, the 11th Brigade had moved up to Vlamertinghe and had been placed under General Bulfin, commanding the Twenty-Eighth Division, who decided to use it to relieve the scattered detachments between Berlin Wood and St. Julien, and fill the dangerous gap in our line. Some delay occurred, largely owing to the scrappy and conflicting reports received at the Division's head-quarters, before definite orders could be issued. Eventually about dusk the 11th Brigade moved forward across the canal to St. Jean. The move took them North of the outskirts of Ypres, which was being shelled, while wounded and stragglers were coming back and congesting the road. After a brief halt at St. Jean the Hampshire, who were leading, went on to Wieltje where Canadian guides were expected to meet them and direct them to their new position. No guides turned up and an exhausted Canadian Brigadier who appeared could only give a confused picture of the situation. Something had to be done without delay, and after an hour's wait the Brigadier [1] ordered Colonel Hicks to take the battalion forward to get in touch with the 85th Brigade and extend to its left, the rest of the 11th Brigade moving up to Fortuin, SE. of St. Julien, and extending Eastward from there towards the Hampshire.

On reaching the 85th Brigade's head-quarters at Verlorenhoek, discovered

[1] Br.-General Hasler, who had in February replaced General Hunter-Weston, promoted to command the Twenty-Ninth Division, of which the 2nd Hampshire formed part.

with some difficulty through a glimmer of light at the road side, Colonel Hicks found that its left battalion, the 3rd Royal Fusiliers, was completely ' in the air ', the Canadians hitherto covering it having been withdrawn, and that the telephone wire to the Fusiliers had been cut, so that the exact situation in the front line was very uncertain. Two signallers who were going up to repair the wire were therefore ordered to act as guides, and the Hampshire pushed on across country with only the vaguest ideas about the situation while the guides proved quite uncertain where they were going, though Verey lights and bursts of rifle and machine-gun fire ahead showed that the battalion was nearing the front. It was 2 a.m. by now, and with daylight not far off it was essential not to be caught in the open, in column of route complete with first-line transport, a fine target for the converging fire German guns could concentrate on the salient in our line.

On reaching a slight rise and knowing that he must by now be somewhere on the Royal Fusiliers' left flank and rear, Colonel Hicks halted the battalion and went forward with the company commanders to reconnoitre the position as far as the darkness would allow. A more unpleasant situation could hardly be imagined but Colonel Hicks did not hesitate. As an officer has written ,' he rose to the occasion as few men would. The odds against him were overwhelming. We should have been justified in retiring to the Zonnebeke ridge where trenches existed '. But Colonel Hicks had been sent up to fill a gap and meant to do it. Having found a line which seemed to give a fair field of fire and placed markers to show the frontages of the companies, he moved the men up into position and set them to work to dig in. His imperturbable coolness made a grand impression on all ; grave as the situation was he tackled it with calm and resolution and the men responded splendidly. ' It was ', as he himself has written, ' a race with dawn ' : the men were naturally tired but they knew how much depended on their being in good cover before daylight and they dug splendidly while luckily the earth was fairly soft.[1] Some old trenches facing North were discovered which could be utilised, and by good fortune the morning proved misty and gave the battalion another two hours of concealment.

While the digging was going on a large party was detected approaching our right. Calling out that they were Royal Fusiliers, they deceived and knocked out a too credulous patrol, but Captain Beckett was not to be caught and C Company quickly and effectively disposed of the intruders. A Company on the left fared worse : it had occupied some houses on the flank, but Germans, approaching in the mist, rushed them, drove the survivors of their garrison in on top of the men digging away at the trench and tried to roll up our line from the flank. A confused struggle followed. Captain Sandeman, a Special Reserve officer of ten years' service, was killed in rallying the men and preparing for a counter-attack and with him fell Captain Chapman (attached from the E. Surrey), but Lt. Le Marchant headed a party of bombers, among them Lance Corporals Field and Hare and Pte. Winter, and checked the rush, holding on at a traverse, and Sergeant Ley led a counter-attack which drove the enemy

---

[1] As there were only 25 shovels per company most men had to use their' grubbers '.

back and restored the situation. A barricade was thrown up and the flank secured.

By 7 a.m. the mist was lifting and the battalion found itself with its right, C. Company, facing N.E. towards Berlin Wood, 400 yards away, where the Royal Fusiliers' thrown back left faced NW.[1] D in the centre faced nearly due North, A, whose left was now thrown back, facing almost West. B was in a second line just over the crest of the ridge, with its left also thrown back. On this flank a wide gap separated the battalion from the next troops, a mixed detachment of the Twenty-Eighth Division South of the Fortuin–Mosselmarkt road. In the short time available the battalion had really provided itself with reasonably good cover.

It was to reap the benefit of its labours. Directly the mist really lifted, a most tremendous bombardment started, salvo after salvo of heavy shell descending upon its line in rapid succession ; shells at times were coming down at the rate of 50 a minute and that anyone survived was a marvel. The German tactics were to drench the ground with shells and then push infantry forward, thinking to take easy possession of a destroyed line ; but heavily as they shelled the Hampshire they did not shift them and any effort to advance was promptly checked. In places the Germans could get up close by using old trenches and saps, but they could not oust the Hampshire. Casualties, however, were heavy, nearly all from shell-fire, though 2/Lt. Walford was shot by a sniper. One serious loss was that of Captain Fidler,[2] who had returned from taking a platoon of B out to clear up the situation on our left and was hit when standing on the parapet to see that his men got quickly down into the trench. Commissioned from R.S.M. in October, he had done admirable service. The battalion was also nearly losing its head-quarters staff, who were buried when a shell hit the parapet nearby. Fortunately the soil was sandy and light and the C.O., whose head was not covered, so that he could call for help, was dug out unharmed, along with the Adjutant and the orderlies.

There had naturally been no time to do more than provide the minimum of cover, with no conveniences, the trenches were too narrow to let people pass along them easily, indeed there was hardly room to move. Conditions, even apart from the shelling, could hardly have been more uncomfortable or difficult.

All day the rain of projectiles went on, beating down incessantly, along the whole front, but the Hampshire stuck to their line, effectively preventing repeated efforts to turn the flank of the Royal Fusiliers or to penetrate into the wide gap on the left where the mixed detachment was hanging on beyond the Haanebeek. Casualties, however, came to over 150 ; 59 men killed and missing (probably buried), Lt. Watts and Lt. Le Marchant being among the 100 wounded. Captain Beckett's [3] coolness and gallantry were conspicuous and greatly encouraged the men, Lt. Wyld, whose company, C, had about the worst part of the line, set a splendid example, and the machine-gun officer, 2/Lt.

---

[1] Touch was established with them by a patrol under 2/Lt. Stevens.
[2] Just promoted to a Captaincy in the R. Warwickshire.
[3] He was awarded the D.S.O.

Holroyd (3rd. Bn.) did useful work with his guns, one of which could enfilade the nearest enemy from a forward sap, part of an old communication trench. He had the last surviving periscope, which proved of great use, and for a time his trench was the only part of the line in telephone connection with headquarters and the brigade. Despite everything the coolness and steadiness of the men was quite remarkable. Whenever the shelling slackened they stood to arms, ready to deal with any attacks and effectively checking some efforts to advance, the right of D Company and the left of C both getting opportunities.

Night brought a welcome relief from the bombardment but no relief from labour. It was only at night that movement and work were possible. The wounded had to be got back to the clearing stations, three miles and more away,

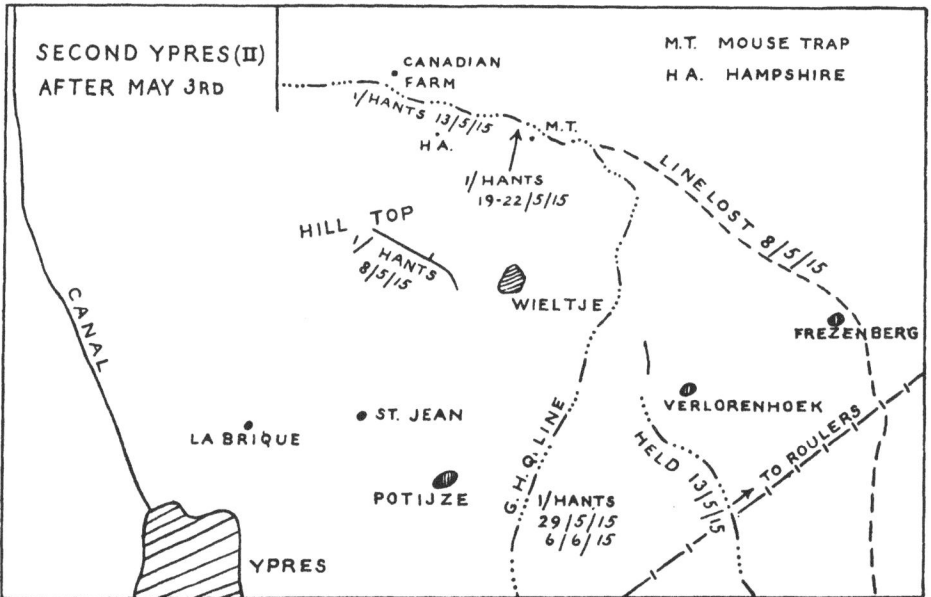

and that by stretcher bearers, no ambulances being able to get any nearer ; rations, water and ammunition had to be fetched over the same distance, much of the route being swept by fire, unaimed but none the less dangerous, the trenches had to be repaired, and they needed it, while a vigilant watch was necessarily kept against a night attack. By daylight on April 26th the line had been substantially improved and, though the bombardment continued all that day and the next four, it never reached the same intensity and the total casualties, 27 men killed and missing and 59 wounded, were little over half those of April 26th ; they included, however, another company commander, who could ill be spared, Captain Unwin, while Captain Beckett, who had again been conspicuous for good work, keeping his company steady under the heaviest fire, was wounded, as were Lt. Capel and 2/Lt. Weston. General Hasler having been killed early on April 28th, Colonel Hicks was away in charge of the brigade for three days, so Major Palk was commanding the battalion and setting a fine example of coolness and tenacity.

On the evening of April 27th two companies of the Durham L.I. (Territorials) were placed under Major Palk, who used them to extend his line to the left down to the Haanebeek, where good patrolling by Lt. Gill had helped to clear up the situation and gain touch with the troops who were now filling up the gap, and also to push out to the right. Two drafts, one of 25 and another of 143, who arrived on the 27th and 28th, were a welcome addition to the battalion's depleted ranks, while Lt. K. A Johnston rejoined from sick leave and took over A Company.

Meanwhile more counter-attacks had been made between St. Julien and the canal, in co-operation with the French and largely to comply with their wishes, but without appreciably improving the situation. Inadequate artillery support was again the main cause of our failures, while the Germans had had time to consolidate their positions and enjoyed great advantages in observation, besides having many more guns, and heavier guns at that, with ample ammunition. However, the position between Berlin Wood and St. Julien was much improved, the 11th Brigade relieving the details hitherto in the gap and establishing something like a continuous line, while the defence of the old Eastern face of the Salient remained unshaken, repulsing all attacks. The Germans were relying mainly on their artillery, and any efforts their infantry made to advance were promptly quashed, the Hampshire's machine-guns were well sited and quick to use any chance, Lance Corporal Collins doing some very effective shooting. Despite the shelling the trenches had been much improved and in consequence the casualties were much lower.

However, with the French unable to contribute effectively towards the recovery of the ground they had lost, the general situation remained very disadvantageous, and by April 29th it had been decided to evacuate the apex of the Salient and draw back to a more defensible line running Northward by Sanctuary Wood and East of Hooge to Frezenberg and thence N.W. by Mouse Trap Farm, NE. of Wieltje, to connect with the line now being consolidated on our left. Preparations for the withdrawal took some time and for another three days the 1st Hampshire had to hang on in their exposed position, maintaining it as best they could and keeping a sharp watch for any infantry advance. They owed much to the Transport Officer, 2/Lt. Hume, who never failed to keep them supplied with rations and ammunition despite many casualties among his men, horses and mules. The roads the transport had to follow were under constant fire and the men had great difficulty in controlling their frightened animals, but they stuck splendidly to their work with a determination which did them the greatest credit.

May 1st and 2nd saw the enemy's shell-fire increasing in intensity, adding another 50 to the battalion's casualty list, but though the enemy released gas against the 10th and 12th Brigades, the latter being now between the 10th's position and the canal, and followed this up with an infantry advance which was decisively repulsed, the gas was not extended to the 11th Brigade's frontage.

The 11th's trial was to come next day, when a bombardment of greater intensity than ever developed about day break and continued nearly all day. The Buffs, now holding the salient at Berlin Wood, got the worst of it, but the rain of shells on and behind the Hampshire's line was continuous enough, and it was a positive relief when, about 3 p.m., infantry began advancing to try to roll up the Buffs' line from the left. This gave the Hampshire's rifles and machine-guns the opportunity they had been awaiting, and their good use of it appreciably assisted the Buffs to repulse the attack, many Germans being shot down as they sought to enter the wood. The attack was renewed, however, after a fresh bombardment, and this time the Buffs, very much reduced, were driven back to support trenches behind Berlin Wood. On this the Germans turned their attention to the Hampshire, shelling their lines vigorously but ineffectually, and when the infantry attack at last developed C and D Companies and the machine-guns now got their real chance and profited by it most satisfactorily and effectively, the Germans being very decisively repulsed with heavy losses.[1] By 9 p.m. the bombardment had died down and the retirement, ordered earlier in the afternoon, could be started.

It was carried out by half battalions, the C.O., who had rejoined on Colonel Prowse of the Somerset L. I. taking over the brigade, started off with two companies at 10.30 p.m., leaving two under Major Palk to follow at midnight, a few picked men under Lt. Stevens [2] remaining a little longer to bluff the enemy into believing our line was still held. The German losses earlier in the day may have discouraged them ; close as they were in places to the British line, only about 50 yards away, they certainly did nothing to impede the move, which was carried out in excellent order, and, despite the crowded roads, there was no confusion. Only the very seriously wounded [3] had to be left behind, the machine-guns, entrenching tools and spare ammunition were all removed. Heavy rain made the move uncomfortable but helped to conceal it from the the enemy's aeroplanes, and by daylight the battalion was across the canal, halting near Elverdinghe about 5 a.m. to get some very welcome hot tea and a rest, which was soon disturbed, shell-fire making a move necessary. This time a well-wooded park gave shelter, a really warm day soon dried damp clothes, and nightfall found the battalion in bivouac two miles SW. of Elverdinghe, where it got a real rest, a change of clothing and a chance to wash and shave.

May 3rd added another 40 to the casualty list, Captain Twining being killed : this brought the total losses up to six officers and 116 other ranks killed and missing, among them some irreplaceable N.C.O.s, and five officers and 208 other ranks wounded. But the battalion's achievement had been one of outstanding merit, which earned it the well-deserved praise of the higher authorities from

[1] This attack seems to have been made mainly by the XXVIIth Reserve Corps which suffered heavily, as their regimental histories admit.

[2] He received the M.C., which was also awarded to Lt. Wyld.

[3] Captain Gwynne, the M.O., had done outstanding work during this time, always cheerful, helpful and untiring, while Corporal Turner, Lance Corporals Simms, Bone and Golding and Privates Brewer, Crawford, Cuffs, T. Smith and G. Williams all displayed great gallantry in attending to wounded men when under heavy fire.

the Commander-in-Chief downward. It could claim, as could the the whole 11th Brigade that, despite the scantiest artillery support, it had never lost a trench.[1] If the infantry attacks had not been pushed home with all the force and vigour of those it had withstood at ' Plugstreet ' Wood, the unceasing shelling had been terrible and the trials the battalion had had to face had tested discipline, endurance and training to the utmost. All who endured the ordeal could testify to the value of the example of calm and steadiness given by Colonel Hicks, ably seconded by Major Palk.

Only the briefest rest could be allowed to any unit engaged in ' Second Ypres '. The Germans, if rather cautious about following up our withdrawal, had soon brought their guns forward to renew their bombardment, and on May 8th after a tremendous shelling our new line was attacked in great force. The Fourth Division, which was on the left, having the 12th Brigade in line from Mouse Trap Farm to the junction with the French, escaped the main brunt of the attack, which fell on the Twenty-Eighth Division in the centre about Frezenberg. This was a weak spot ; our line was on a forward slope, exposed and overlooked ; the hastily dug defences were pretty well obliterated by the bombardment and the Germans, attacking in force, wrested a long stretch of our front line from the few surviving defenders. The 10th and 11th Brigades, both in reserve West of the canal, were called up to reinforce, the 10th counter-attacking with some success, while the 11th was mostly placed in second-line trenches, the Hampshire having their right at Wieltje Farm. They were heavily shelled and caught some machine-gun fire, mainly ' overs ' aimed at the front line, and had a dozen casualties, unfortunately including the C.O. who was hit when on his way to Brigade head-quarters. His wounds were very serious [2] and combined with enteric eventually proved fatal, to the great regret of the battalion. Colonel Hicks had had nearly 25 years service in the regiment and had been commanding the battalion for nearly six months, including its successful and tenacious defence in the Ypres Salient, an outstanding episode in its history and one in which his leadership and inspiring example had played a big part. He had left his mark on a battalion which owed him much.

After two days in second line the battalion, now again under Major Palk, moved up into the front line on May 10th, relieving the King's Own between Canadian (left) and Hampshire Farms. The line here faced North and, having been occupied for some days, was rather stronger than the lost trenches on the Frezenberg ridge, B Company in the centre benefitted by being on a reverse slope, with a section in an advanced post on the crest. Here the Hampshire were to have a hard week, including a really big attack on May 13th. They had been heavily shelled before that, and rifle grenades had been troublesome on May 12th till our trench-mortars, now passing beyond the experi-

---

[1] Besides the N.C.O.s and men already mentioned for good services, Sergeants Buller and Hardy were noted for their reconnaisance work, Sergeants Brown and Ley for services as platoon commanders, Sergeants Ormond and Wootten for coolness and good example under heavy fire and Sergeant Wright for taking messages under fire. Several men were also noted for repairing telephone wires under fire and for gallantry in action.

[2] His right leg was amputated above the knee.

mental stage and therefore less dangerous to those who handled them, replied effectively.

The bombardment on May 13th started with daylight. ' It *was* a shelling ' one officer wrote ' at one time the whole line of trench disappeared in a yellow cloud of smoke and the earth was absolutely rocking '. D Company on the right got the heaviest shelling, but eventually after nearly three hours the German guns lifted off the first line to the second and about 7 a.m. infantry began to advance. Before this the battalion had had to extend to its right, where the virtual annihilation of the Rifle Brigade's left platoon had left a gap near Mouse Trap Farm. No Man's Land was about 300 yards across but this was more than the attackers could cover in face of the rifles and machine-guns of the Hampshire and of the Somerset on their left flank. A few only reached the wire, to be shot down there. One forward trench held by D Company had to be abandoned after the garrison of 40 had been reduced to five, but even then Drummer Eldridge held on at a barricade across a communication trench up which Germans were trying to follow our men, refusing to retire till he had thrown all the bombs at hand, some 60. He was wounded but he kept the Germans at bay for half an hour, and then they went back.[1] Two further advances were repulsed, heavy casualties being inflicted on the attackers, and, to the disappointment of the defenders, who even stood up and challenged them to try again, the Germans abandoned the effort and let their gunners resume the bombardment, which raged on until nearly 2 p.m. when it gradually died away. After that, enemy trying to dig in on our front gave the battalion something to shoot at, but the infantry attacks were not renewed and though, away to the right, Mouse Trap Farm was for a time lost it was ultimately recovered. The day had cost the Hampshire 90 casualties, D Company being particularly hard hit, but once again the line had been maintained intact, and the German infantry attacks repulsed with loss. In the centre, where dismounted cavalry had replaced the Twenty-Eighth Division, we had again lost a long stretch of our front, but the Fourth regained such ground as it had had to evacuate, and, further to the right, the Twenty-Seventh, to which the Germans had recently transferred their attentions, was almost equally successful.

The Hampshire remained in front line until May 14th and were then back in the Divisional support line at View Farm : two drafts of 57 and 96 men respectively did something to replace the casualties, 60 killed and missing and Lt. Prendergast and 2/Lt. Holroyd and 107 men wounded, suffered since May 3rd. The battalion's next turn in front line was from May 19th to 22nd, just West of Mouse Trap Farm, but the fighting seemed to have died down and casualties only came to half-a-dozen. The battalion was back at rest near Pezelhoek when on May 24th the Germans started their final attempt to reach Ypres. This made a big dent in our centre, astride the Ypres–Roulers railway, but once again the gap was filled and a new line was patched up without the 11th Brigade doing more than move up to the Yser canal in readiness to reinforce.

[1] Drummer Eldridge, going out later to the evacuated trench, found it empty save for several wounded men whom he bandaged. He received the D.C.M. and the French Croix de Guerre.

May 27th found it in front line again, just East of Potijze. It had nearly a week here, the trenches were good, the weather fine and warm and the enemy had suspended his attacks and was not aggressive. The week's casualties were under 20, only three men being killed, while 2/Lt. Burge was wounded when on patrol. After three days in support at La Brique the battalion recrossed the canal again to its old billets near Poperinghe. If it had not quite finished with the Salient, ' Second Ypres ' was over.

' Second Ypres ' had been a hard and exhausting trial, the brunt of which had been borne by the ' Old Army ' Divisions, the Fourth, Fifth, Twenty-Seventh and Twenty-Eighth, who suffered over 41,000 of the 59,000 British casualties. Great credit is due to the Canadians for their splendid resistance in their ' baptism of fire ' to attacks backed by gas and by an overwhelming superiority in artillery and ammunition, but it should not be allowed to obscure the much severer and more prolonged strain which the ' Old Army ' units endured. All the Canadian infantry were out of the fighting line before May 1st and their 5,500 casualties were less by nearly 2000 than those of the least hard hit of the four ' Old Army ' Divisions. Heavy as our casualties were, and the loss of ground was in comparison a minor matter, we had again and again prevented the Germans from exploiting opportunities which, against a less determined and devoted defence, might have been turned to great advantage. Whatever th German purpose may have been, they had failed to drive us out of Ypres an so establish their claim to have completed the conquest of Belgium. ' Second Ypres ' has well been likened [1] to Inkerman, as a ' soldiers' battle ', enormously to the credit of the regimental officers and men who endured the strain and the shelling for over 30 days and stood up to the terrible new weapon against which no provision had been made, until in the end they brought the enemy's advance to a standstill. ' Second Ypres ' is an episode of which the Hampshire may well be proud, perhaps the severest strain to which the 1st Battalion was subjected in the whole war, if July 1st, 1916 was to cost it even more.

One satisfactory feature of May was that for the first time discharges from hospital, 104, nearly balanced admissions, 107 : drafts amounting to 266 men joined during the month with ten officers, including one ' pre-war ' Regular, of whom the battalion was now sadly short, Captain R. D. Johnston. Another 160 men joined the battalion on its arrival at Poperinghe, where it enjoyed several days of welcome rest, during which it was inspected by General Keir, to whose newly formed Sixth Corps [2] the Division had been transferred. This Corps had taken over the left of our line in the Salient, relieving the French East of the canal.

June 11th saw the Hampshire beginning their first spell in the new line, ' no health resort ' as one account says. As with most French trenches, the line did not conform to the British standards, especially as regards sanitation, and the battalion was kept busy if the enemy were unenterprising, apart from making much use of his very efficient trench mortars. The 1st Hampshire had two

---

[1] *Official History.* 1915. I p. 356.
[2] It was virtually the old Third Corps, as it consisted of the Fourth and Sixth Divisions.

spells in front line during June, from the 11th to 16th and from the 21st to 25th. Both were fairly quiet, patrols did some effective work, locating the enemy and finding targets for our guns when they had any shells to fire, and during the second tour a new forward trench was dug close to the enemy, A, now under Captain Garsia who had rejoined after a spell on the Staff, and B (Captain K. A. Johnston) doing the work, while a black night helped to conceal the diggers, whose work was warmly commended by the authorities. Casualties were light, 4 men killed and 38 wounded, together with Major Humphery (3rd Bn.), whose cheerfulness and unfailing coolness had been a great stand-by at Gravenstafel, Lt. Gill and 2/Lt. Beatty. Nearly 140 men went to hospital during the month, only 52 being discharged, but drafts numbering nearly 100 kept the battalion at a fairly good strength.

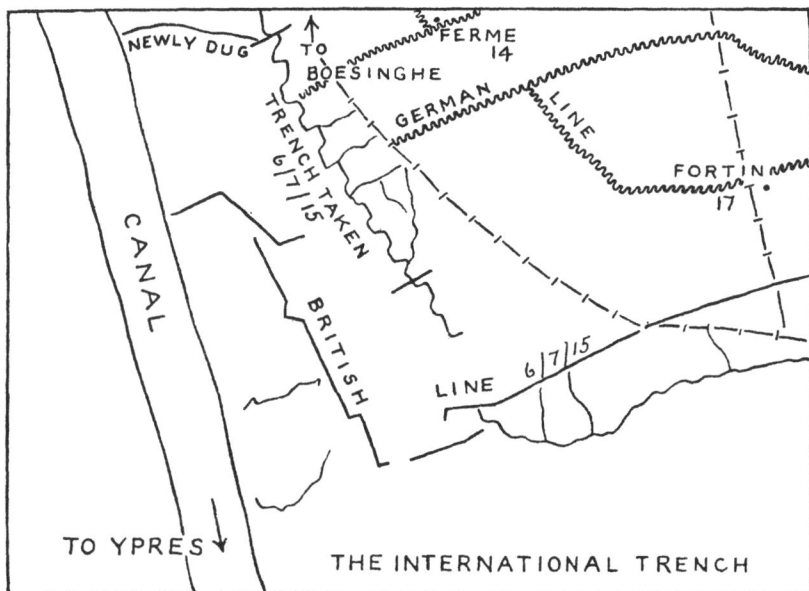

THE INTERNATIONAL TRENCH

At the Western end of the British line, which here ran North and South parallel to the canal for a short time and then turned Eastward, the French had lost about 300 yards of trench, now called ' the International Trench ' [1]: and the Second Army was anxious for its recovery which would improve our tactical position, while General Plumer also wanted to distract the enemy's attention from a larger operation soon to be undertaken at Hooge. The Fourth Division's commander, in view of the Division's recent losses and the shortage of really trained officers and men, was reluctant to attempt anything substantial, like the capture of the whole salient between Ferme 14 and Fortin 17, of which the ' International Trench ' formed the front. However, to meet the Army Commander's wishes he prepared an attack on this International Trench, to be

[1] At one point only a barricade separated the two sides.

carried out on July 6th by the Rifle Brigade, the Hampshire, who had just had another four days in front line (June 30th–July 4th) with 25 casualties,[1] mainly from shell-fire, being across the canal, in reserve.

The attackers, though losing heavily, carried their objective, capturing 30 prisoners, and then set to work consolidating under a heavy shell-fire, punctuated with infantry attacks, which were easily beaten off, and by bombing attacks on both ends of the line. To help deal with these the Hampshire bombing squad under 2/Lt. Stevens was sent up, while C and D Companies ' stood to ' in readiness. The Rifle Brigade, however, though hard pressed and suffering heavily from the German guns, held on stoutly to their gains with the help of the Somerset and of the Hampshire's bombers, among whom Sergeant Gledhill was prominent, while 2/Lt. Stevens as before did splendid work ; they had a very hard time, only five out of the 28 escaping unhurt, but they did not a little for the retention of the captured line, which was handed over that evening to the Lancashire Fusiliers. They in turn were hard pressed next day, when they were assisted in consolidating by working-parties from the Hampshire, whose machine-gunners also contributed effectively to repulse the most vigorous of the German efforts to recover their lost ground. But for the heavy losses inflicted on the Germans it might have been asked whether the capture of 300 yards of trenches had been worth 450 casualties. Of these nine killed and 2/Lts. Bradshaw and Stevens [2] and 25 men wounded belonged to the Hampshire.

After two more days in support the Hampshire on the night of July 8/9th relieved the Lancashire Fusiliers in the captured trenches, A and D Companies going into the front line and being heavily shelled and trench-mortared, while bombing duels went on all day. ' We had an awful time ' one officer wrote ' my company was in the worst place in the whole line and they shelled us the whole time.' But the battalion held the ground and took every chance of answering back and of improving the line. With the trenches much damaged and the parapet not bullet-proof casualties were heavy,[3] and to the general regret Captain Gwynne, who had given the battalion such devoted and efficient service as M.O. for nearly a year, was killed. He was right up in the front line and had dressed the wounds of several Lancashire Fusiliers, but hearing that a Rifle Brigade man, who had been badly wounded three days earlier, was lying out in a half-dug trench, he went forward to him and had just bandaged his wounds when he was hit in the head. ' One of the finest and bravest ' he had done splendid work and had endeared himself to all : his place was not to be easily filled.

Before being relieved next night, the Hampshire had had the satisfaction of catching and dispersing a party massing for an attack, which was thus effectively

---

[1] These included 2/Lt. d'Arcy, one of several officers recently posted to the battalion from the Artists' Rifles, now virtually an O.T.C.

[2] He died of his wounds : a particularly intrepid leader, always to the fore when a difficult job had to be tackled, he was a great loss to the battalion. He had received his commission in October, in recognition of fine work in the retreat from La Cateau. He was awarded the M.C., Gazetted after his death.

[3] 18 killed and 55 wounded.

nipped in the bud.   They now went right back to comfortable billets in farms round Watou, to enjoy their first fortnight of real rest since reaching France. They were visited by the Commander-in-Chief and by General Plumer, now commanding the Second Army, who congratulated them warmly on their fine work at Ypres and at the International Trench, for which they were also thanked in emphatic terms by their Brigadier who told them he had put them in to hold the trench because they had never lost a trench and he knew they would not lose this one.   Much refitting went on and several officers joined, including 2/Lts. Harding, lately R.S.M., and Diamond, lately R.Q.M.S., who both remained with the battalion though Gazetted to the Northumberland Fusiliers, while C.S.M. King now became R.S.M.   Major Perkins being away sick,[1] Lt. Hume was acting as Adjutant, Lt. Sprake succeeding him as Transport Officer on Lt. Tarrant coming out to be Quartermaster.

Meanwhile the wildest rumours were rife about the battalion's next move, the Dardanelles being a hot favourite.   Doubts were resolved when on July 23rd the battalion entrained for the South, where the newly-formed Third Army [2] was relieving the French on a fifteen mile frontage from Curlu on the Somme to Hebuterne.   Whatever the new front might prove to be like, nobody could believe it would not be preferable to ' the Salient '.

[1] Captain im Thurn was also sent home sick, he had been out since August 1914 and was the last ' original ' who had served continuously.
[2] Its headquarters were formed on July 13th.

CHAPTER VI

GALLIPOLI

THE LANDING—THE ADVANCE ON ACHI BABA

THE venture for which the 2nd Hampshire were embarking was a fine example of that ' doing things by halves ' for which Sir Walter Raleigh long ago and with good reason criticized Queen Elizabeth's handling of the war with Spain and of which British ministries have so frequently been guilty. An operation which, if anything ever did, called for the properly co-ordinated efforts of Army and Navy together, was started by the Navy alone, and only after its single-handed effort had failed, possibly by the narrowest of margins, was the Army called in to attempt a now almost hopeless task and try to retrieve the initial ill-success. Between the Navy's failure in the middle of March and the Army's belated arrival on the scene, the Turks and their German advisers had over a month to profit by the warning given them, and a well-prepared defensive was to await our troops and to make doubly difficult an enterprise which even with the advantage of surprise would have been none too easy. Even had the Navy postponed its attack till troops were available, the Germans might have persuaded the Turks to make adequate preparations against a highly probable contingency, but, had we not already shown our hand in March, the defenders might have been in doubt about the destination of the troops who were being collected in Egypt : the Dardanelles, if our most likely objective, was not the only one possible. If better planned and co-ordinated, our attack on the Dardanelles should have secured important results, while its object, the opening up of direct communications with our Russian allies, was one of such immense importance as to justify the diversion of a substantial effort from France to the Mediterranean. But the premature naval attack had thrown away the inestimable advantage of surprise. Our enemies, forewarned, were well prepared.

Leaving Warwick on March 28th the 2nd Hampshire embarked that day at Avonmouth, headquarters with W and X Companies on board the H.T. *Aragon,* Y and Z in the *Manitou,* the transport and machine-gun wagons travelling separately. Colonel Carrington-Smith was in command and Major Leigh senior Major. Majors Deane (W) and Beckwith (Z) and Captains Addison (Y) and Wymer (X) commanded the companies, Captain Reid was Adjutant and Lt. A. Smith Quartermaster. The other officers were Captains [1] B. S. Parker, Penn-Gaskell, Corner, Boxall, Day (Transport Officer), and Spencer-Smith, Lts. Rosser (machine-guns), C. R. Smith, Webb, Silk, White and Pakenham, 2/Lts. Gillett,[2] C. C. Harland,[2] G. R. D. Moor,[2] Howard, Lord and H. Parker, with R.S.M. Holdway and R.Q.M.S. Tyler : the embarkation strength in other ranks being 993.

---

[1] All Lieutenants down to Lt. Spencer-Smith had been promoted to Captain before the end of 1914, all pre-war 2nd Lieutenants becoming Lieutenants.
[2] Of the 3rd Battalion.

Sailing next day the Hampshire had a rather crowded and uncomfortable but uneventful journey, with much sea-sickness and rough weather. After calling at Malta, where some sick were landed, they reached Alexandria on April 2nd and had a week ashore, while the troops were being re-allotted to ships, these not having been loaded originally with a view to the tactical requirements of a landing. The opportunity was taken to get practice in boat work,

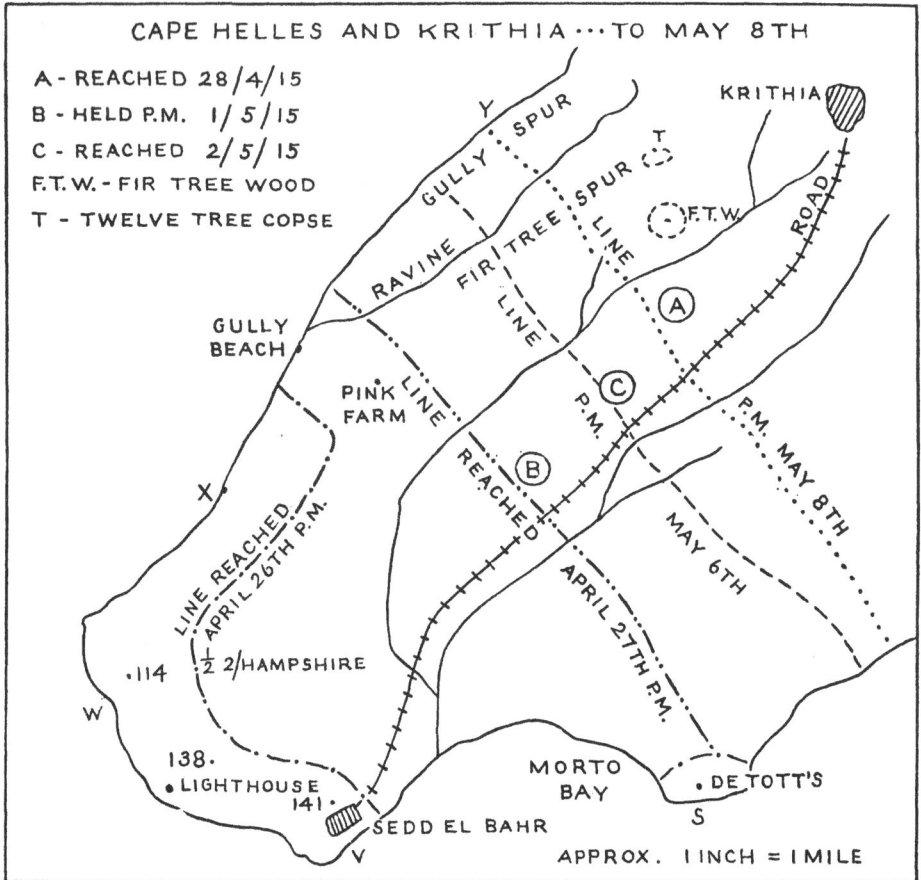

CAPE HELLES AND KRITHIA ⋯ TO MAY 8TH

A - REACHED 28/4/15
B - HELD P.M. 1/5/15
C - REACHED 2/5/15
F.T.W. - FIR TREE WOOD
T - TWELVE TREE COPSE

KRITHIA

GULLY SPUR
FIR TREE SPUR
RAVINE
GULLY BEACH
PINK FARM
T - TWELVE TREE COPSE
F.T.W.
ROAD
LINE
A
C
B
P.M.
LINE REACHED APRIL 26TH P.M.
114
½ 2/HAMPSHIRE
W
138.
LIGHTHOUSE
141
SEDD EL BAHR
V
REACHED
APRIL 27TH P.M.
MAY 6TH
P.M. MAY 8TH
MORTO BAY
DE TOTT'S
S
APPROX. I INCH = I MILE

for which more chances were given at Lemnos, the advanced base, whither the *Aragon* conveyed the battalion, arriving on April 13th.

Sir Ian Hamilton's plan of attack was rather elaborate. The Australians and New Zealanders were to land on the West coast of the Gallipoli peninsula about 14 miles from Cape Helles, where the Twenty-Ninth Division was to attempt to get ashore at five points, the most Easterly, at Morto Bay inside the mouth of the Straits, being nearly six miles by the coast from the most Westerly, Y Beach on the West coast. Meanwhile the French were landing on the Asiatic shore, mainly as a diversion. The Twenty-Ninth Division's main attack was being made at three beaches, X and W, NE. and SE. respectively of Tekke Burnu, the most Westerly point of the peninsula, and V, East of Cape Helles and close under the forts and village of Sedd el Bahr. The 86th (Fusilier) Brigade was to form a ' covering force ', to which the 2nd Hampshire, less two companies, were attached; this was to secure a line running roughly NW. from Sedd el Bahr to the cliffs above X beach, from which, after the landing of the main body, in which the remaining Hampshire companies under Major Leigh were included, an advance would be made to the dominating high ground of Achi Baba and the cliffs overlooking the Narrows.

It is easy to see now that the plan was over-optimistic; the covering force could hardly be expected both to secure the necessary foothold ashore and to play a major part in the subsequent advance; too small a reserve was left to exploit any opening that might be made; while the probability of serious casualties in getting ashore, a difficult task even in face of quite slight opposition, had hardly been appreciated; open boats crowded with men afford machine-guns and riflemen ideal targets and even a few well-placed and well-concealed defenders might do incalculable damage. These things perhaps should have been foreseen; what was less easy to foresee, without more experience, was the very limited support naval guns could give to troops ashore, that when accurate shelling of small targets like field or machine guns was needed the naval guns could not achieve it.

The covering force was making its biggest effort at V Beach. Three companies of the Dublin Fusiliers were to lead the way in ' tows ', each of four boats holding about 30 men apiece and hauled by steamboats. The Munsters, the last company of the Dublins and the headquarter wing of the Hampshire, with Y and Z Companies, were on board a collier, the *River Clyde*, which was to be run aground on the beach; ports had been cut in her sides to enable the men to get out quickly on to a steam hopper towed alongside her port side to provide a gangway ashore.

On April 24th headquarters and Y and Z Companies left Lemnos in the *Alaunia* for Tenedos, where they transferred to the *River Clyde*. The Hampshire were allotted to No. 3 hold, abaft the funnel and, as one account says, ' nicely placed to have it down on them should it get hit ', while the men were so tightly packed that movement and even sleep was impossible. Men were heavily laden, carrying 200 rounds, full packs, haversacks and three days' ' iron rations ', a total weight of 84 lbs. Shortly before midnight on April 24th the flotilla left for the peninsula, the movements being so timed that the ships and boats with the troops and their escorting warships should be off the landing places just before dawn.

At V Beach 300 yards of sand separate a steep cliff on the West, crowned by a fort, from the fort and village of Sedd el Bahr on another cliff to the East. A bank about five feet in height fringes the back of the sandy strip, beyond which the ground rises to a ridge about 100 feet up. Several lines of wire stretched across this rising ground, in which were several machine-guns and pom-poms in well-sited positions, hard to locate but covering the beach and all approaching it. These the naval bombardment, even with 12-inch guns, had been powerless to silence.

As the *River Clyde* [1] approached the shore she outstripped the tows and had to wait and let them get ahead, even so she had grounded 40 yards from the shore before the tows reached the beach. Almost immediately a devastating fire caught the crowded boats and within a few minutes terrible losses had been inflicted, many men being shot down before they could leave them, others were hit in the water, most of the wounded being drowned, and the few who survived to get ashore could only shelter behind the bank beyond the beach. Worse still, a hopper should have bridged the gap between the *River Clyde* and the shore, but it had swung away to port and failed to establish the connecting link, and the men had to jump out into shoulder-deep water and gave good targets as they slowly struggled shorewards. The *River Clyde's* captain, Commander Unwin, [2] managed to get three lighters in tow on her starboard side into position to make a bridge, giving the Munsters a chance to dash along the gangways towards the shore. So murderous and accurate was the fire, mainly machine-guns, that only a handful achieved their purpose and the gangways and lighters were soon crowded with dead and wounded, while after a sailor who was helping Commander Unwin to hold the lighters in position had been killed they drifted into deep water. A few men managed to wade ashore but after No. 9 Platoon of Y Company had lost its commander, Captain Boxall, [3] mortally wounded, and nearly 20 men in a gallant attempt to get ashore, Colonel Carrington-Smith, senior officer on board the *Clyde*, stopped further efforts as merely entailing useless sacrifice of life.

Meanwhile the battalion's machine-guns on board the *Clyde* under Lt. Rosser and some R.N.D. guns were trying hard to keep down the machine-gun fire and giving effective covering-fire to the men ashore, but the well-concealed Turkish guns were hard to locate and harder to silence.

The fleet sweepers with the bulk of the 88th Brigade were now approaching V Beach, and such few boats as had survived the first trip took off from one of them Brigadier General Napier himself, 50 men of W and X Companies of the Hampshire with Captains Wymer and Spencer-Smith and two platoons of the Worcestershire. On their coming alongside the *Clyde* they were hailed and warned that it was hopeless to try to get ashore. The Brigadier, however, would not be deterred and reached the hopper, only to be shot down along with Captain Costeker, his Brigade Major. [4] His death was a great loss: very much liked and respected, he had already gained a great hold on the brigade as a leader of great character and ability. Meanwhile the boats carrying the parties under Captains Wymer and Spencer-Smith were making a dash for the shore to starboard of the collier. A burst of fire met them, but they kept on and, jump-

---

[1] Lt. Colonel W. de L. Williams of the regiment, who was on the G.H.Q. staff, was on board and his account of the landing has been very helpful in compiling this chapter.

[2] The gallantry of the Naval officers and men who were acting as ' beach party ' here was outstanding, and all accounts from Hampshire eye-witnesses emphasize it.

[3] He was to have been the next Adjutant.

[4] This was rather before 11 a.m.

ing into fairly shallow water and scrambling along a projecting spit of rock, the two officers and two-thirds of their men [1] joined those Dublins and Munsters who were sheltering along the bank under the Sedd el Bahr cliffs. Here they were held up, and if the Turks never attempted to dislodge them they could only hang on with hardly a chance of a target: the stalemate was complete. The naval guns might pound away but they could not get at the machine-guns which dominated the situation.

It was while trying to locate the machine-guns that, about 3 p.m., Colonel Carrington-Smith was hit and killed. He was on the bridge of the *River Clyde* and had just marked down one machine-gun when he was hit. He had not been long with the 2nd Hampshire, he had won the confidence and respect of officers and men, and in him the regiment lost a most competent commander who might have gone far.

At the other beaches things had gone better: the Royal Fusiliers had landed almost unopposed at X and had eventually linked up with the Lancashire Fusiliers, who despite a far rougher passage had made good their landing at W. Reinforcements had followed the original attackers and about 10.30 Sir Ian Hamilton directed General Hunter-Weston to divert the rest of the 88th Brigade to W Beach, where accordingly the main body of W and X Companies under Major Leigh landed unopposed, pushing forward to fill a gap in the line which now stretched from the lighthouse near Cape Helles, which the Worcester-shire had taken, across by Hill 138 to Hill 114, where the W Beach troops had gained touch with the Royal Fusiliers. By the time this party was ashore the two redoubts on Hill 138 had been taken and the Hampshire merely filled a gap in the extended line of the Essex, North of Hill 138. Fighting had died down, if there were still Turks close in front of the line which we were entrenching. An advance from this line might have relieved the remnants hanging on to their precarious hold on V Beach, but the urgency of their situation does not seem to have been realised; the 86th Brigade's commander had been wounded and no senior officer was present to take charge and push on.

During the afternoon the fire on V Beach slackened and the sailors hauled the lighters connecting the collier with the shore back into position, whereupon the Munsters again tried a rush, only to awaken the Turkish machine-guns into renewed activity and be checked. Rather later three battleships gave the Turkish positions a fresh pounding, under cover of which a handful of Munsters and Hampshire tried to force an entrance into the Sedd el Bahr fort but without much success, having to shelter on the seaward face without getting in. Before it was dark, however, Major Beckwith went ashore to take over command and directed Captain Spencer-Smith and the 18 men left out of his 26 to push on into the fort and secure the exit from it to the North. Accompanied by some Dublins and Munsters, the party moved some way to the right, climbed the cliff, cutting many strands of barbed wire, and dashed into the fort, the Turks bolting before them. They then established themselves on the Northern face of the fort, where most of the walls were still standing, and under cover of

[1] Some 15 were hit.

this party, whose occupation of the fort prevented a counter-attack on that side, the remaining fighting troops from the *Clyde* crossed the gangways quite unhindered and brought welcome help to the survivors ashore. The wounded could now be succoured and removed and the troops sorted out and reorganized. To have attempted an immediate attack would have been futile, the exhausted survivors of the earlier attempts to land wanted a rest, and Major Beckwith had to arrange with Colonels Williams and Doughty-Wylie of the G.H.Q. Staff for a fresh naval bombardment before any further advance against Sedd el Bahr and the old castle could be attempted.

The Turks at V made no effort to impede our preparations, if patrols and scouts more than once approached the line further West in which W and X Companies were stationed and disturbed their rest, already rather broken into by the need for working parties to get rations, ammunition and water ashore. Few men had had a proper night's rest on the night before landing, and their fatigue and the need for unloading supplies largely explains the scanty progress made next day by the force covering W and X Beaches. Actually very few Turks were facing them, the defenders being apparently concentrated at Sedd el Bahr to resist our renewed attacks.

At V Beach two points had to be attacked, the fort and village of Sedd el Bahr on the East and the old castle on Hill 141 to the N.W. Nearly all the Hampshire had been collected on the Sedd el Bahr side. Before dawn Captain Spencer-Smith's party, who had held the ruins during the night, were withdrawn [1] to join the rest of the Hampshire on the top of the cliff. This detachment and the machine-guns could give covering fire to the main attack, some Hampshires under Captain Penn-Gaskell working through a gap which had been cut in the wire, were to attack West of the fort, the rest, together with some Munsters, after re-occupying the fort were to press forward against the village. These preparations were difficult to make in the dark, especially as many wounded had to be got away and a tangle of wire impeded movement.

Shortly before dawn (April 26th) the supporting ships opened fire again but directed their fire more against the village than against the fort. This led to some delay but eventually the attack went in, the fort being quickly cleared. In debouching beyond it by a narrow postern gate the troops came under accurate fire from trenches on the edge of the cliff and were checked. However, Major Beckwith soon had the advance going again and, headed by Captain Addison and by Captain Walford of the G.H.Q. staff, Y Company forced their way into the village, the machine-guns covering their advance. In the village they met desperate resistance; the Turks contested every house and had to be ousted with the bayonet from one after another. Some lay quiet, concealed in cellars or ruins, till our men had passed by and then fired into their backs. Machine-gun and rifle fire from Hill 141 was troublesome and, with the snipers very hard to dislodge, it took nearly three hours before the Hampshire finished clearing the village. Major Beckwith's gallantry and inspiring leadership were outstanding and made a tremendous impression on the men. It was largely due

[1] This was to let the naval guns bombard Sedd el Bahr.

to his leading that Sedd el Bahr was taken, he exposed himself recklessly and how he escaped being hit was a marvel. Captain Addison, who vied with him in leading the attack, was less fortunate, being killed by a bomb.

The fight for Sedd el Bahr finished with a charge against some trenches beyond the village, for which every available man had been collected, including Captain Spencer-Smith's party from the right. Major Beckwith himself headed the charge, brandishing an axe with which he had just cut a cable, leading, it was thought, to Kum Kale. This charge sent the surviving Turks flying,

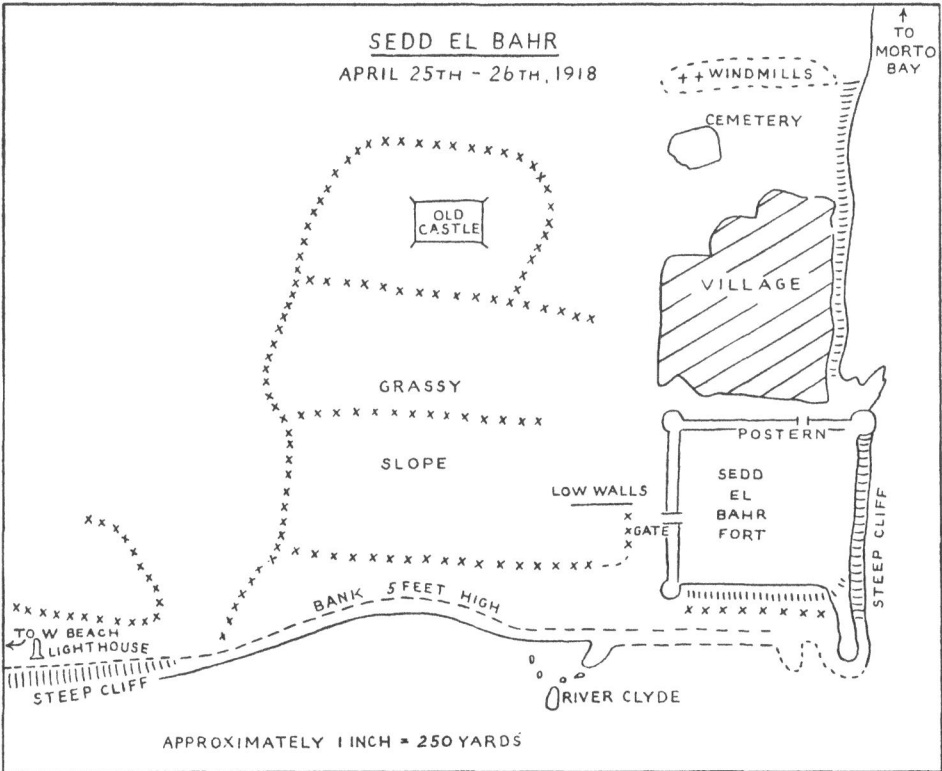

SEDD EL BAHR
APRIL 25TH – 26TH, 1918

APPROXIMATELY 1 INCH = 250 YARDS

several being shot down as they bolted. Pressing on, the Hampshire cleared a row of windmills on a hill overlooking Morto Bay and started to consolidate. Meanwhile, more to the left, where Colonel Williams had been organizing the attack, Dublins and Munsters with the two Hampshire platoons under Captain Penn-Gaskell were having hard fighting for the old castle: the enemy's resistance was obstinate and it took some time before the final attack could be launched. Enfilade fire from the village by which a Major of the Dublins was killed, had been troublesome, but about 2.30 p.m. Captain Penn-Gaskell could start the final charge which carried the position, when the surviving defenders, in making off Northward, gave good targets to the Hampshire's machine-guns with which Sergeant Jackson had been giving an effective covering fire. Touch was now gained with the troops at W. Beach and a continuous line was established from Sedd el Bahr to X Beach, Y and Z Companies being on the right on the cliff edge beyond Sedd el Bahr,[1] while W and X were well away to the left between Hills 138 and 114.

Sedd el Bahr had cost the Hampshire nearly 60 casualties, 2/Lts. Harland and Gillett being wounded. The fighting had been fierce, and if wisdom after the event suggests that the rest of the Division might have advanced at any time during the day without meeting serious opposition, the men were short of sleep and rest, water was short and the information available about the general position scanty and inaccurate.[2] The stubbornness of the opposition had concealed its weakness and, as things appeared at the time, it seemed reasonable to wait for the French, who only started to land late in the afternoon.

Fatigue and delays over landing supplies and getting the French ashore held things up on April 27th also. On enough French landing to relieve the troops at V Beach, Major Beckwith's wing moved across to rejoin the other companies, Major Leigh now taking command. Late in the afternoon an advance was begun, the troops crossing the saucer-like depression draining into Morto Bay and beginning to ascend the long slopes leading to Achi Baba. The French were on the right, the 88th Brigade in the centre, the 87th on the left and the 86th in reserve. Except for a little shell-fire the advance was unopposed, though a reconnoitring platoon of X, which carefully searched any vestige of cover, disposed of many snipers, some shamming dead.[3] After advancing about 200 yards a line was taken up running roughly Westward from the S.W.B's position at de Tott's Battery across to a point 500 yards beyond the mouth of the big ravine, later known as Gully Ravine, the Hampshire being astride the road leading to Krithia, with Z Company flung back on the left where the next battalion was some way in rear.

Once again, though no serious attack was made by the Turks during the night, several small advances, mostly against Z Company, being easily stopped, a rather disturbed night did not give the men much rest and most of them started the next day's advance hardly fit for strenuous work. However, the attack started quite well, the Turkish outposts falling back in disorder, and at first their shell-fire was negligible, if we had too few guns ashore to give really effective artillery support.

As the Essex on their left across the Krithia road had had to keep back level with the extreme left, the Hampshire had started nearly 600 yards ahead of them. Pushing straight ahead, with W and Z in the firing line and preceded by Lt. White's platoon of Z, the battalion made good progress and was soon ahead also of the Worcestershire on the right, whom the slowness of the French advance kept back. The thick scrub made the Turks hard to locate, and gullies

[1] The occupation of the windmill ridge meant that all the high ground overlooking V Beach was in our hands and the Turks were denied direct observation of it.

[2] Major Beckwith at Sedd el Bahr was quite unaware that the South Wales Borderers were at S Beach, a bare mile away.

[3] One account speaks of passing many dead Turks, apparently killed by the ships' fire.

and small ravines provided admirable natural cover, of which the enemy made good use. The men pressed on, however, and the leading platoon was under a mile from Krithia before the Turks were seen advancing to meet us. Lt. White's platoon now lined a low ridge and was soon reinforced by the rest of Z, W prolonging the line to the left, but with both flanks exposed to enfilade fire we could not get on.

About 11.30 a counter-attack in force checked the French, who fell back some way,[1] but the Hampshire machine-guns, well handled by Corporal Stone, helped to stop its progress. Without more artillery support, infantry could make little progress over the difficult country, but, while W and Z hung on stubbornly, Major Deane brought a party forward on the left and secured that flank, and eventually a determined advance brought the Worcestershire up level on the right, while rather later some Essex and Royal Scots got forward on the other flank. The machine-guns got some good targets at fairly long ranges and efforts to advance against the Hampshire met with little success, except where dead ground ahead of W Company gave cover. But Turkish reinforcements were arriving and ammunition began to run short. The Worcestershire in particular ran short and sent to ask the Hampshire if they could spare any. The 87th Brigade had also been checked, an effort by the much depleted 86th resulted in a handful of men reaching Fir Tree Wood, a little nearer Krithia than the Hampshire, but the general position remained unchanged. A gallant effort by W Company, led by Major Deane, reached a low crest line and our men carried two trenches, killing their occupants, but, on advancing again, they came under very heavy fire and could go no further, Major Deane being killed and half the company falling. The decisive episode was a counter-attack which drove the French right back. The Worcestershire, with their right exposed, had to give ground, and X Company had to conform. On the left also our troops were driven back and the Hampshire found themselves under fire from both flanks. With ammunition failing, despite untiring efforts by R.S.M. Holdway to replenish the pouches of the firing-line, and many men without water or rations, the position was untenable in face of the continuous Turkish pressure and their heavy fire, and eventually about 5 p.m. it was vacated by order, the troops falling back approximately to their starting line.[2] The machine-guns, assisted by those of the Royal Scots, covered the retirement effectively, but the day had been most exhausting and with everyone nearly dead beat it was not possible to get all the wounded away. The battalion's casualties had been heavy, 100 men killed and missing and 250 wounded. Besides Major Deane Lt. Pakenham had been killed. Major Beckwith, who had again led and rallied the men splendidly, was wounded, as were Captain Spencer-Smith and 2/Lts. Howard (mortally), Lord, Moor and Parker (mortally).

[1] R.S.M. Holdway, who was sent by Major Leigh with a message to the nearest French commander, expressed his opinion to that officer in no uncertain terms but without much result.

[2] On the extreme left the 87th Brigade had advanced nearly to Y Beach but had to be brought back during the night to straighten the line and avoid a salient. The line held that evening was to all intents that later known as the 'Eski' line.

With Captain Corner sick only a dozen officers and barely 500 rank and file remained fit for duty.

The Turks did not molest the retirement; they also had lost very heavily and had indeed been very near to giving way: accordingly the troops had an almost undisturbed night and a quiet day followed, spent in entrenching,[1] while Colonel Williams assumed temporary command of the 88th Brigade. Many wounded were now brought in, the Turkish failure to follow up having allowed most of those left behind to escape capture. About mid-day on April 30th the battalion was relieved by the French and went back to Morto Bay for the briefest of rests.

The failure to exploit our success in landing was most disappointing, but what the troops had achieved was an outstanding testimony to their gallantry and devotion, the regimental officers and men had made efforts which are beyond praise. The unhappy chance which so quickly had deprived the landing force of Brigadier General Napier, Colonel Carrington-Smith and so many other senior officers had been no small factor in the result, but it is hard to resist the conclusion that too much was expected of the men, that those who had forced a landing could hardly be expected also to exploit it immediately and that the plan was too ambitious for the force actually available. What the weakened and exhausted Twenty-Ninth could not accomplish, mainly because they had reached the limits of their physical powers, a fresh Division might well have achived, and Achi Baba might have been taken on April 28th. Spent force as the Twenty-Ninth Division was on that day, it was only by a narrow margin that the Turks had stopped its advance. It seems that they had put in their last available reserves.

The 2nd Hampshire had less than a day in reserve; by 4 a.m. (May 1st) they were relieving the Essex in the front line, between the track leading to Krithia (right) and the Kirte Dere or Krithia Nullah (left), the French were on their right and the combined Dublins and Munsters of the 86th Brigade on their left. That evening about 10 p.m. a heavy bombardment started followed an hour later by an attack in force.[2] Firing steadily with great effect, the Hampshire held up the attack, but the Turks broke through the 86th Brigade and pushed on nearly to the support line. Prompt counter-attacks by the Royal Fusiliers and Royal Scots restored the situation, but a small party penetrated to the Hampshire's support trench and someone, probably an English-speaking German, raised the cry ' All officers on the left '. Hurrying to the spot, Major Leigh and Captain Reid with two R.A. officers were shot down, and if the Turks were promptly wiped out to a man, it was little consolation to the Hampshire for the loss of an officer like Major Leigh, who had been doing magnificently and had inspired his men with affection as well as admiration and respect. His example and courage had been magnificent, he had exposed himself freely, ' always in the thick of things ' where he was most wanted, inspiring calm and confidence. Captain Reid, an admirable Adjutant, was also much missed.

[1] The discovery of a good spring of water just behind the battalion's trenches was most welcome
[2] The Turks had been reinforced and were putting in some 20 battalions.

But for the loss of two such invaluable officers, all the more felt after that of the C.O. and Major Deane, the Hampshire, now under Captain Wymer with Lt. Rosser as Adjutant, might have congratulated themselves on the night's work: they had held firm and never let the Turks get anywhere near, though the attacks were kept up until dawn and were pushed home, while the bodies whom daylight revealed lying thickly in our front bore witness to the accuracy of the battalion's fire, at least 400 could be counted within sight of its line. Elsewhere also the attacks had been repulsed, the Worcestershire from the support line having restored a nasty position on the right where some Senegalese had given way, while on the left the 87th Brigade had counter-attacked most successfully, carrying their line well forward and taking 120 prisoners, the 88th Brigade sending in another 100.

This encouraged those in command to order another general advance and at 10 a.m. (May 2nd) the Hampshire started forward. Heavy shrapnel fire met them almost at once but did not stop them, and they had covered nearly 1200 yards, capturing a good many Turks who were sheltering in holes and hollows, pinned to the ground by our fire, before they again found themselves ahead of the general line, especially on the right. Here [1] they held on till a French retirement completely uncovered their right and compelled them to fall back to the line from which they had advanced, no ground having been gained. Their casualties had been serious, 22 killed and missing, Lts. Smith, Webb, and Silk and 87 men wounded,[2] leaving them as the weakest unit in their brigade, little over 400 all told. But the enemy had lost heavily and the brigade had taken over 300 prisoners.

Three fairly quiet days followed, one in the trenches consolidating, two in reserve near Morto Bay, when for the first time since the landing a wash and a shave were possible, then on May 6th another advance was attempted. For this two fresh brigades were available, both recently arrived from Egypt, one of the Forty-Second (East Lancashire Territorial) Division and the 29th Indian Brigade. The 88th Brigade in the left centre [3] had to advance up a spur between the Krithia Nullah and Gully Ravine which was dotted with clumps of firs and consequently christened ' Fir Tree Spur '. Its aim was to capture Krithia and then to wheel round to the right and secure a position facing Achi Baba from the West, through which the 87th and Indian Brigades would deliver the final assault.

If the troops had started tired on April 28th they were little fresher now. Few officers or men had had any real rest since April 25th, few had had a change of clothes or many chances to wash. One officer wrote that ' officers and men have lived like animals, no blankets or kits, no clothes off at night, not even boots, feeding from hand to mouth and snatching sleep when we can '. Another wrote appreciatively of a wash in an empty oil tin, another described himself

[1] The Brigade diary puts them at Point 169 B., i.e. just South of Fir Tree Wood, but the squared map at first in use proved to be inaccurate and suggests further advances both on April 28th and May 2nd than were actually achieved. Sketch 12 is copied from a plan based on this map and is probably not accurate.
[2] Captain Wymer was also hit but remained at duty.
[3] The Hampshire were well to the left (North) of the line of their advance on May 2nd.

as ' filthy and black with dust and exposure '; ' we are not fed up but only tired ' was another summary. Luckily the weather had been fine, if cold enough at night to make men miss their blankets, though one letter speaks of being ' too sleepy to mind the cold '. Considering everything, the losses, the exertions and the fatigue, the general cheerfulness was amazing: like the B.E.F. in the Retreat from Mons the men seemed to be going on almost automatically and unquestioning.

In this fresh attempt (May 6th) the 88th Brigade had the Worcestershire on the right, then the Hampshire, with the Royal Fusiliers [1] beyond them, reaching to Gully Ravine. A screen of scouts headed the advance, which worked slowly forward for several hundred yards before opposition, largely from machine-guns in advanced posts, began to be serious. On neither flank were troops coming forward, the Lancashire Territorials could make little headway over the bare ground of Gully Spur, and though the French right made some progress their centre and left failed to get far. As before the artillery support was quite inadequate and the Turks, using the good natural cover, were hard to locate. Some of the 88th Brigade reached Fir Tree Wood but failed to clear it, and the line came to a halt about 500 yards from its starting line, with the Hampshire West of Fir Tree Wood; they and the Royal Fusiliers beyond them might have been able to get forward but that, being ahead of the troops on Gully Spur they were liable to be enfiladed from across the ravine. They could only dig in where they were to secure what ground had been gained. Casualties had not been heavy, the Hampshire returning six killed and 53 wounded but unluckily two more of the eight officers present were wounded, Captains B. S. Parker and Penn-Gaskell.[2]

The scanty success achieved on May 6th did not deter the higher command from renewing the attempt next day; though without more artillery support our tired infantry could hardly do much against a defence so well supplied with machine-guns. Once again the inability of the troops on Gully Spur to gain ground held back those East of Gully Ravine; neither the Royal Fusiliers, next the Ravine, nor the Hampshire could get on far, and further to the right Fir Tree Wood remained untaken, although the 87th Brigade had reinforced the attack, while the French also suffered heavily to little purpose.

However, the New Zealand Brigade and one Australian had been brought round to Cape Helles to reinforce the attack and May 8th saw yet another attempt to reach the objectives of May 6th. The New Zealanders, passing through the 88th Brigade, who remained in reserve, attacked up Fir Tree Spur, the 87th Brigade co-operating West of Gully Ravine. Advancing with great gallantry and determination, the New Zealanders could make little headway against a fire our bombardment had failed to subdue and were soon checked. After another bombardment they went forward again, with the 88th

---

[1] Attached from the temporarily broken up 86th Brigade.

[2] Those still unhit were Captains Wymer and Day, who had rejoined from the transport, and Rosser, Lt. White, the only subaltern still unhit, the Quartermaster and Captain Hodson (Reserve of Officers, attached).

in support and the Australians advancing on the right up the Krithia Spur. Once again the bombardment had been unsuccessful, the machine-guns were still unsubdued and the New Zealanders, despite another splendid effort, again came to a standstill.   The 88th Brigade struggled forward some little way despite a raking fire from well-concealed machine-guns, but it also was checked somewhere NW. of the still untaken Fir Tree Wood [1] and though it held on here till well into the night, before dawn it was ordered back.   The Hampshire had made another determined effort [2] which had cost them another 28, including Captain Hodson, killed and missing and Captain Day and 97 men wounded, leaving only four officers, Captains Wymer and Rosser, Lt. White and the Quartermaster, and 204 men, a remnant who badly needed the week's rest they were now given in a reserve position North of Sedd el Bahr, having been relieved by Australians.   In little over a fortnight three-quarters of the battalion had become casualties [3] and the survivors were for a time completely played out. It was wonderful that their gallant effort to accomplish a task altogether beyond the scope of one Division had come within reasonable distance of success.

[1] The precise positions are hard to locate owing to the inaccuracy of the maps in use at first. The map in the brigade diary would show that the battalion was in front of the North and South line through Fir Tree Wood, which seems too far.

[2] Lance Corporal Alexander did fine work, re-forming men and leading them forward to re-force an isolated advanced party. He received the D.C.M.

[3] Up to May 14th eleven officers had been killed, twelve wounded, and one invalided ; of other ranks killed, missing and died of wounds came to 198, wounded to 507. 2/Lieutenant Richards, killed on May 13th, had just received his commission.

CHAPTER VII

GALLIPOLI (continued)

THE STRUGGLE FOR KRITHIA

THE operations of May 6th to 8th ended a definite phase in the Gallipoli venture, the attempt to rush the defences at the Southern end of the peninsula and so assist the fleet to force its way through. That object had not been achieved, though if the Australian and New Zealand Corps had hardly enlarged the slender foothold originally obtained, at Cape Helles enough elbow-room had

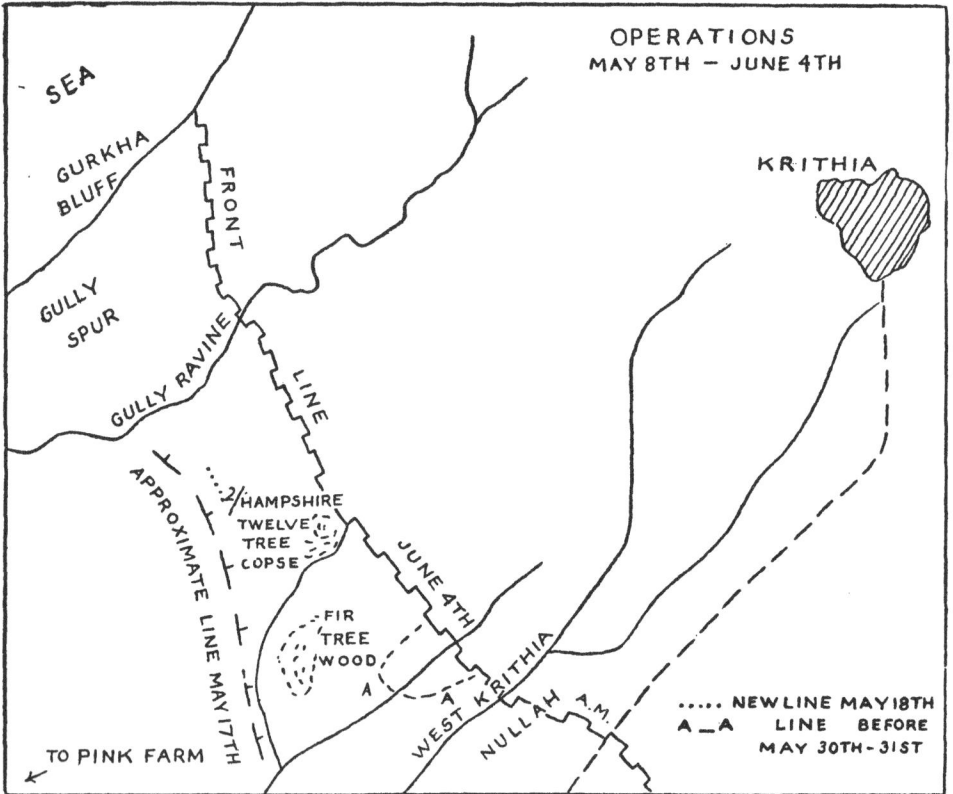

OPERATIONS
MAY 8TH — JUNE 4TH

been gained to allow of making preparations for another attempt whenever sufficient artillery and ammunition and substantial reinforcements should have reached the peninsula to warrant it. Why three months passed before these were forthcoming concerns rather the general history of the war than a regimental chronicle, which can hardly examine in detail the various strategical and political considerations concerned, even if ultimately they closely affected the fortunes of regimental officers and men; it is equally beyond its province to embark on a discussion of the conflicting claims of the Western Front and this subordinate operation, begun to assist the Navy but now developing into a major military venture. What the ' M.E.F. ' might have done on May 9th with half the guns, shells and men employed in that day's gallant failure to break the German lines in France can easily be conjectured; actually during the next three months it had to do its best to gain ground by local attacks against positions daily becoming more formidable, with but little additional artillery and ammunition, with drafts which hardly sufficed to replace the losses at the landing, let alone those incurred in the subsequent attacks, and with only one Division to reinforce the three who had already found their task beyond what could be reasonably expected of them.

These months therefore the 2nd Hampshire found both strenuous and exhausting ; with the elbow-room gained quite insufficient the troops in reserve, unless at Lemnos or Imbros, were always within range of the enemy's guns, and it was urgent to enlarge our territory and improve our tactical position.

When the 2nd Hampshire went back to a brief ' rest ' on May 10th their other ranks were up to 229, some convalescents having rejoined. During this ' rest ' 2/Lt. C. Harland rejoined from hospital and R.S.M. Holdway's well-deserved promotion to 2/Lieutenant increased officers present to six, while other ranks rose to 282, more convalescents reappearing. May 16th saw the battalion back in its old trenches 200 yards NW. of Fir Tree Wood, relieving the 127th (Manchester) Brigade of the Forty-Second Division.[1] The line was being advanced by sapping forward and then joining up the saps laterally: this was done mainly by night, while by day snipers usually remained at their forward ends. Once a new line had been linked up fresh saps were started, while on the night of May 17th/18th an advance of 100 yards was made over the open and a new line dug and joined to the old front. This was followed up by more successful sapping. Advantage was taken meanwhile of any targets the Turks offered and soon after the 88th Brigade returned to the line it had their snipers well under control. The Turks were being equally busy and constructed a formid-able-looking redoubt on a knoll on front of the Hampshire's left, about 150 yards away. This target was well plastered by our 60 pounders, and on May 24th the arrival of some trench mortars allowed us to bombard the enemy's front trenches very effectively. The whole Division was carrying on the same work with no small success, and May not only saw Fir Tree Wood made good but the line advanced 400 yards beyond it, while Twelve Tree Copse, some 600 yards North of it, was brought within our lines, the Hampshire's front line being within 300 yards of the Turks when they were relieved on May 25th. Further to the left a well-executed enterprise by the Indian Brigade had improved the position on Gully Spur, capturing a valuable bluff[2] above Y Beach, by which advance the flank of troops advancing up Fir Tree Spur was covered. These minor successes greatly encouraged the troops, whose determination and cheerful endurance of great discomforts was notable. When in reserve they could

---

[1] Captain Allen of the regiment was D.A.A. and Q.M.G. of this Division.
[2] Subsequently known as Gurkha Bluff.

indulge in excellent bathing, otherwise they were far worse off than the troops in France, where by this time troops out of the line were fairly comfortable. Never out of range of gun-fire, to which we could rarely reply, owing to the shortage of ammunition, they never faltered, put a good face on a bad situation and responded to every call.

This spell in trenches cost the 2nd Hampshire 18 killed and missing and 2/Lt. Holdway and 27 men wounded, but the Turkish accounts show clearly that their casualties during this period were heavier than ours. To balance our losses 46 men under 2/Lt. Lambert had arrived from the 3rd Battalion while

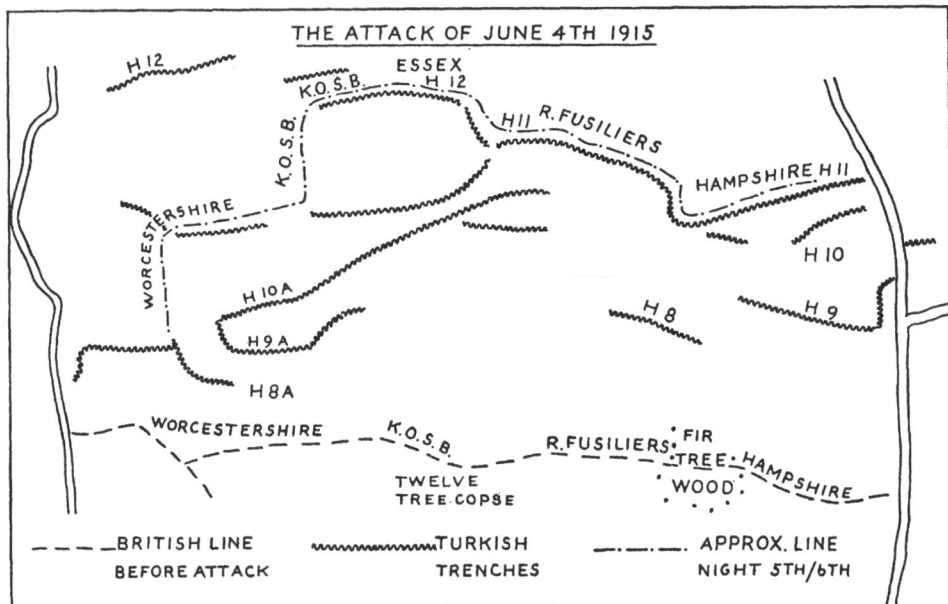

THE ATTACK OF JUNE 4TH 1915

———— BRITISH LINE BEFORE ATTACK   ‸‸‸‸‸‸‸‸ TURKISH TRENCHES   —·—·—· APPROX. LINE NIGHT 5TH/6TH

Lt. Webb, 2/Lt. G. R. D. Moor and 37 men rejoined from hospital, and by May 22nd other ranks had reached 334.

From May 25th to 30th the battalion was 'out' at Pink Farm a mile SW. of Fir Tree Wood. Here Captain Ford with 2/Lts. M.F. Cromie, N. Harland, C. Moor and Reeves joined from the 3rd Battalion with 48 men, and 200 of the 10th Manchester were attached for instruction. This instruction was rather impeded by calls for large 'fatigues', but as Pink Farm was within half a mile of Gully Beach bathing was possible.

May 30th saw the Hampshire back in reserve trenches about 2 miles SW. of Krithia. Colonel Williams had that morning taken command,[1] Brigadier General Doran having taken over the brigade. On the following evening X and Y Companies had to be put in on the 88th Brigade's right, SE. of Fir Tree Wood where the Forty-Second Division's advance had fallen behind the Twenty-Ninth's. This position they greatly improved by advancing by night and digging

[1] He was the fifth officer to command the battalion since April 25th.

a line of rifle pits across the gap, a very useful piece of work which was accomplished with only four casualties.

Preparations were now complete for another general attack to be made on June 4th, in which the 88th Brigade, to which the Royal Fusiliers and K.O.S.B. were attached, was advancing up Fir Tree Spur, with the 2nd Hampshire on the right, with thin flank on the Krithia Nullah, beyond which was the Forty-Second Division, on whose right a brigade of the R.N.D. and the French were also attacking. Fourteen officers of ' K 4 ' battalions [1] had arrived on June 1st and been attached to the battalion, so that though other ranks were little over 300 it was strong in officers. But after all the Twenty-Ninth Division had endured at and since the landing, another big attack asked much of its surviving officers and men.

The available artillery support was still sadly scanty, only four 60 pounders and eight howitzers altogether, while the ammunition allowance was far from adequate for the destruction of substantial defences, so the bombardment, which started at 8 a.m. could only be maintained at a slow rate until the last half-hour preceeding the infantry attack, which was to start at midday. The battalion's first objective, the Turkish first line, now marked on our maps as H.8 and H.9,[2] was to be assaulted by X (Captain Wymer) and Y (2/Lt. C. Harland), and at 12.15 p.m. W (Captain Evans) and Z (Lt. White) were to go through and attack the second line, H.10. The very minute that the bombardment stopped X and Y went forward splendidly, despite a very heavy fire, and were quickly into H.8 and H.9, capturing them with some 30 prisoners, including several officers, though both Captain Wymer and 2/Lt. Harland were hit. Sergeant Fisher, almost the first man to enter the Turkish line, seeing several Turks trying to creep away along a communication trench, pushed ahead, intercepted them and made them surrender.[3] Just before W and Z started to reinforce the leaders Lt. White was killed, but Captain Rosser took his place and, as ordered, the supporting companies went through the leaders, taking H.10 and the SE. end of H.11 beyond it. Both company commanders were wounded, but Lt. Lambert took over and led the advance to its objective. On the Hampshire's left the Royal Fusiliers and the K.O.S.B. had been checked by a redoubt facing Twelve Tree Copse and by H.9a, so that the Hampshire, being well ahead of them, had their left ' in the air '. The Forty-Second Division had also been held up, so Lt. Colonel Williams [4] decided not to press on but to consolidate what had been gained, good work being done by the machine-guns which their officer, 2/Lt. M. F. Cromie, brought forward ' in the nick of time ' as one account puts it ' to be instrumental in saving the situation'. Further to the left the Worcestershire had forged right ahead, taking part of H.12, while their leading men even reached H.14, within tantalizing

[1] Captain Evans of the 12th R. Warwickshire was an ex-Colour-Sergeant of the regiment.

[2] The trenches on Gully Spur were given serial numbers under J, those on Fir Tree Spur under H. and those on Krithia Spur under F.

[3] He received the D.C.M., also awarded to Sergeant Milne for conspicuous gallantry and good leading in the operations following the landing.

[4] He was wounded soon afterwards, 2/Lt. Cromie being killed.

nearness to Krithia, but unfortunately the attack up Gully Spur had not fared well and enfilade fire from across Gully Ravine prevented the Worcestershire exploiting their success. By 1.45 p.m., however, the Royal Fusiliers and K.O.S.B., having carried their redoubt despite heavy casualties and come up level with them, the Hampshire were reported as 'advancing again', and before 2.17 p.m. [1] H.12 had been secured all along the brigade's front,[2] while at 3.40 p.m. another advance was reported, the Hampshire actually reaching a fifth trench line before having to halt. If the French had failed and had thereby uncovered the R.N.D's right, the Forty-Second Division meanwhile had also got well forward, the Turks had lost heavily, few defences intervened between Krithia and our most advanced troops and, could a substantial portion of the Corps reserve [3] have now been put in to exploit the 88th Brigade's success, Krithia might have been secured. This was not done, and before long strong Turkish reinforcements were counter-attacking and exploiting their repulse of the French by driving in the R.N.D., whose retirement exposed the Forty-Second's right and in turn drove that Division back to its first objective, F.11 and the Vineyard,[4] which line it tried to maintain. The two most advanced of the five lines of trenches the Hampshire had over-run now become untenable, so at 6 p.m. they had by order to fall back to H.11, which with its continuation westward in H.12 the 88th Brigade was consolidating, and this line was successfully maintained.

The Hampshire's achievement had been notable, none the less that failures elsewhere prevented its exploitation, but the losses had been heavy. Of the battalion's own officers Lt. White and 2/Lt. M.F. Cromie had been killed, Colonel Williams, Captains Wymer and Rosser, 2/Lts. C. Harland, N. Harland and Lambert (mortally) were wounded, while those attached, Lt. Chilton (Argyll & Sutherlands) was killed, Lt. Malet was missing, Captains Evans and Bird and 2/Lt. McNair (all four R. Warwickshire) and Lts. Humbert and Phillips-Jones (both R. Berkshire) were wounded, last two mortally; of other ranks 56 were killed and missing and 95 wounded, out of about 300 in action. But the Turks had been heavily punished and the 88th Brigade could claim 250 prisoners.

Consolidation was little impeded that night or next day, though the guns did a little shooting to break up apparently impending counter-attacks. June 5th saw some small advances made on the left, and that evening the Hampshire shifted slightly to their right, keeping touch with the Forty-Second Division. Early next morning (June 6th) a heavy attack developed all along the 88th Brigade's front and beyond it to the right. Against the Hampshire the Turks made no headway, Sergeant Hanna doing most effective work with the machine-guns and breaking-up several attacks, and the battalion held firmly on, although it had to throw back its right, which the Forty-Second Division's loss of two trenches, G.11 and G.12,[5] had exposed. Confused fighting went on for some time

---

[1] Reported by the 88th Brigade at that hour.
[2] H.12 apparently proved to be not complete or continuous along the front attacked.
[3] The 87th Brigade and half the R.N.D.
[4] Just across the West Krithia Nullah to the right of the re-entrant marked on Sketch 14.
[5] Just across the West Krithia Nullah and in continuation of the right of H.11.

SECOND LIEUTENANT GEORGE RAYMOND DALLAS MOOR, V.C., M.C. AND BAR

Born on October 22nd, 1896 ; son of William Henry Moor (Auditor General, Transvaal, retired) and Mrs. Moor, and nephew of the late Sir Ralph Moor, formerly High Commissioner for Southern Nigeria. He was educated at Cheltenham College, commissioned into the 3rd Battalion The Hampshire Regiment in October 1914, and was granted a Regular Commission on August 1st, 1915.

After six months training in England and Egypt, he went with the 2nd Battalion to the Dardanelles, and was at the landing at V. Beach at Gallipoli.

His decoration was gazetted on July 24th, 1915, when he was only 18 years of age.

' For most conspicuous bravery and resource on June 6th, 1915, during operations South of Krithia, Dardanelles. When a detachment of a battalion on his left, which had lost all its officers, was rapidly retiring before a heavy Turkish attack, 2nd Lieutenant Moor immediately grasping the danger to the remainder of the line, dashed back some two hundred yards, stemmed the retirement, led back the men, and recaptured the lost trench. This young officer who only joined the Army in October, 1914, by his personal bravery and presence of mind saved a dangerous situation.'

He was invalided home soon afterwards suffering with dysentery. After recovering he joined the 1st Battalion, in France, and was badly wounded, in the arm. He returned to England, and —before regaining the use of his arm—was appointed A.D.C. to Major-General W. de L. Williams, C.B., C.M.G., D.S.O. (The Hampshire Regiment) in France, where he gained the M.C. and Bar. He died of influenza at Mouveaux on November 3rd, 1918.

Lieut-General Sir Beauvoir de Lisle, K.C.B., K.C.M.G., D.S.O., in a narrative of this action said: ' I have often quoted this young officer as being one of the bravest men I have met in this war.'

at this point, where our line was now a re-entrant, but the Hampshire were not shifted. On the other flank Turks outflanked the K.O.S.B's left and also broke in between them and the Royal Fusiliers, where a company of the Essex had come up into line; most of H.12 was lost and a disorganized mass of men was being pressed back against the Royal Fusiliers' left, where crowded and narrow trenches impeded any reorganization of the defence. The situation was becoming critical, officerless men were retreating in confusion when 2/Lt. G. R. D. Moor, left in temporary command of the battalion,[1] dashed across the open from the Hampshire's lines with a few men and stemmed the retirement by vigorous and forcible measures, actually shooting one or two panic-stricken fugitives. He did not stop here: having rallied and reorganized the men in a hollow, he led them back to the lost trench and cleared the Turks out, setting a magnificent example of bravery and resourcefulness which was most deservedly recognized by the battalion's first V.C.[2] since the Taku Forts.

Further to the left the Worcestershire had also held firmly on and, though no attempt was made to recover the salient formed by H.12, the line of H. 11 was secured, largely thanks to 2/Lt. Moor, and a renewed attack made about 6 p.m. was repulsed with heavy losses. In other ranks the Hampshire's losses, under 30 all told, were slight, while they had taken no small toll of the Turks, whose losses in the three days' fighting seem to have substantially exceeded the Allied casualties, though these came to over 6,000. But once again a big success had been missed, if by a narrow margin.

That evening 2/Lt. Moor had to be taken to Brigade headquarters, being completely exhausted, which left only the Quartermaster and three attached officers, Lts. Poole (Argyll & Sutherlands), who took command, Barrett (R. Warwickshire) and Manders (R. Berkshire), other ranks being down below 200. This remnant was relieved next afternoon and placed in support trenches, having its headquarters at Twelve Tree Copse. After three days here, during which Lt. Silk rejoined from hospital and took command, the battalion had four days' rest at Gully Beach. It was then in reserve trenches till June 19th, busily engaged on improving the line and digging communication trenches up to the new front in H.11 and burying the dead. On June 14th it welcomed Major Beckwith back, on whose arrival Lt. Silk took over the Adjutant's duties, and next day a draft from the 13th Battalion of 360 men with six officers [3] made its sadly attenuated ranks look quite full again.

From June 19th to 24th the battalion was 'at rest' on Y Beach, being persistently shelled by guns from across the Straits and having several casualties. The 88th Brigade then relieved the recently arrived 156th Brigade of the Fifty-

---

[1] Since June 4th Captain Mackay (A. & S. H.) and 2/Lt. Reeves had been killed and Captain Ellis (Suffolk) and 2/Lt. Cooper (Dorsets) wounded, while Captain Ford, Lt. Webb and 2/Lt. C. Moor were away sick.

[2] He was recommended for it by officers of the Royal Fusiliers who had watched his gallantry and determination. Lt. Colonel Williams, addressing the battalion before the attack, had expressed the hope that some one would win the V.C. for the battalion that day. 2/Lt. Moor was, it was said, the youngest winner of the V.C.

[3] Captains Bousfield, Pigott and Cowland, Lts. Morris, Sheffield and Luffmann.

Second (Lowland Territorial) Division who had been holding the Twenty-Ninth's right sector, the Hampshire taking over part of H.11, which they found much in need of repair. They quickly made the trench look very different and on June 25th had the satisfaction of getting good targets in wiring parties.

A fresh attack was about to be made by the 86th and 87th Brigades West of Gully Ravine and by the 156th East of it, with the 88th in support. To make room for the 156th Brigade the Hampshire moved back on June 26th to reserve trenches behind Twelve Tree Copse, where 30 recovered and wounded rejoined and with them Lt. Webb and 2/Lt. Lord, the latter taking over the Adjutant's duties.

This time more artillery support was available and when, at 11 a.m. on June 28th, the main attack went in, it was clear that West of Gully Ravine the bombardment had been most effective: the 87th Brigade carried its objectives with a fine rush, and the 86th and Indian Brigades, going through, pressed on and secured Fusilier Bluff, 1000 yards beyond the starting line, many prisoners being taken and the Turks heavily punished, while during the next few days, despite repeated efforts and heavy losses, they failed to regain any more than a very little of what had been wrested from them here. Unfortunately the ammunition had not sufficed for more than a most inadequate shelling of the H trenches, and though the Border Regiment stormed the Boomerang, a very troublesome redoubt on the Eastern edge of Gully Ravine, and the 156th Brigade's left and centre battalions took the Western half of H.12, further to the right another battalion was shot down wholesale by machine-guns on its right flank, so that, despite a gallant effort, it failed to reach its objectives. Counter-attacks were not slow to develop; the upper part of Gully Ravine provided a covered approach, and the troops in the captured Western portion of H.12 were soon hard pressed to hold on, let alone extend their gains, largely because the Turks were better off for bombs, a great asset in trench warfare, and if they lost heavily while they regained some ground, although the 88th Brigade put in the Essex and the 5th Royal Scots against the untaken Eastern half of H.12, [1] machine-guns in H.13 and H.14 to their right held them up.

Accordingly that evening the Hampshire were sent forward to take over the Western end of H.12. The trenches were terribly congested with dead and wounded, including many Turks, and about midnight, while the relief was still in progress, a sharp counter-attack developed, crowds of Turks pouring forward from Gully Ravine. This the Hampshire helped to repulse, though the Turks pressed the attack hard, only to be shot down in numbers. After this the relief could be continued and was completed before dawn, whereon the battalion set to work to consolidate and clear up the trenches and to dig a trench connecting the Eastern ends of our portions of H.12 and H.12a, these ends having been blocked by barricades.

This work the Hampshire carried on with considerable success for the next six days, besides getting some chances of killing enemy: the machine-guns for example co-operated most effectively on June 30th with the 87th Brigade

---

[1] H.12 seems to have been completed before this and another line, H.12a, dug in front of it.

in punishing a large party retreating from near Fusilier Bluff. On July 2nd W Company gained about 20 yards in H.12a. Further they could not go: rifle fire from the next trench behind and enfilade fire from a communication trench commanded a bend round which it proved impossible to advance, so a barricade was made. X also made about the same distance in H.12 and established another barricade, where also much bombing activity developed, while the battalion's machine-guns contributed very effectively to the decisive repulse of a most determined effort to recover the Fusilier Bluff position on July 2nd. ' We got two machine-guns on to them—that was quite enough ' wrote one

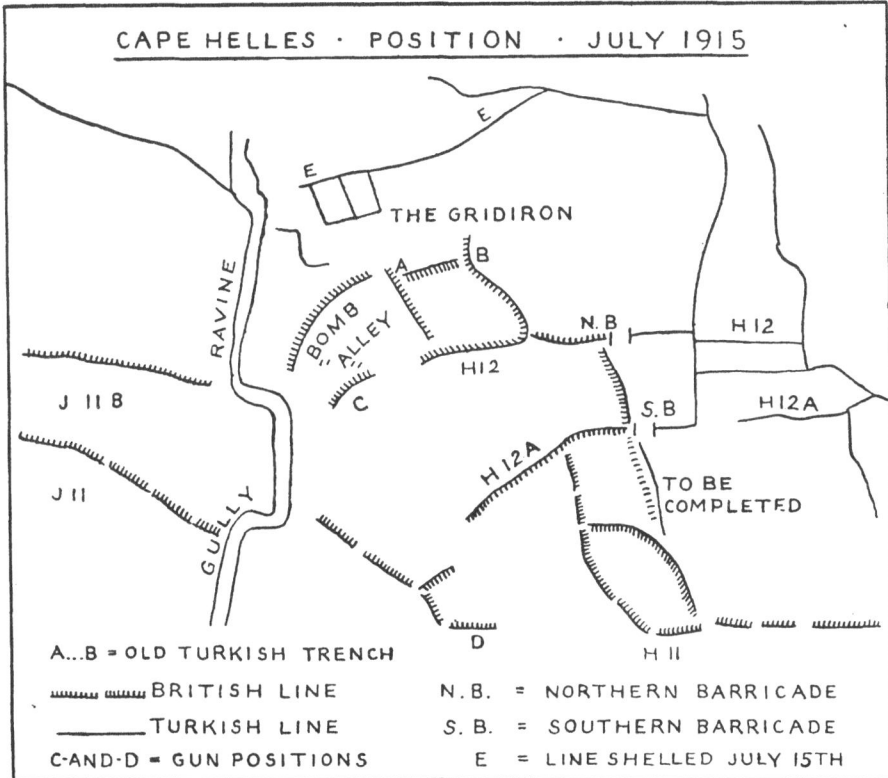

officer, and these days added substantially to the Turkish casualties, once again even heavier than the British. But the Hampshire were severely shelled, six days costing them 28 killed and missing and Captains Pigott and Cowland and 76 men wounded, and the strain was great. However, only three days' ' rest ' could be given them, spent at Y Beach, where dug-outs cut into the steep face of the cliff gave good shelter from the shelling from which ' rest ' areas at Cape Helles were never immune. Splendid sea bathing was some alleviation for all that had to be endured, discomforts of every kind and, what was even worse, the stench of the unburied corpses over which dense clouds of foul dust blew to and fro, the plague of flies which descended on every article of food, the shortage of water and that mainly brought from overseas in tanks and conveyed to the troops in petrol tins, the increasing heat, the lack of shade and shelter, the monotony of the rations, which could not be supplemented at canteens as in France. Diarrhoea and dysentry were rampant, the sick-rate was high and many not actually on the sick-list were in poor condition. It was some alleviation to hear rumours of substantial reinforcements, and with the whole Fifty-Second Division now present some of the more exhausted men could be given a real rest at Lemnos. Indeed the 2nd Hampshire were under orders for a spell there, when on July 7th they were ordered to relieve the S.W.B. astride Gully Ravine, holding H.12 and the Eastern end of J.11b, about 500 yards of front. Six officers of ' K 4 ' units [1] had joined with 20 convalescents, but the battalion remained much below establishment.

Holding these trenches proved strenuous. The trench just East of the Gully, ' Bomb Alley ', ran down to a barricade in the ravine, within bombing range of the enemy; 300 yards further to the East our holdings in H.12 and H12a [2] were blocked by barricades. Turkish snipers were troublesome, and from a knoll known as the Gridiron, they would shoot down Gully Ravine. Saps were started out towards it, and the Hampshire used trench mortars against the snipers to good purpose, besides improving the line appreciably. One useful achievement was the digging of a trench on the night of July 14th/15th across the open to get rid of a re-entrant in our line. This was done within 60 yards of the Turks but was not interrupted. ' It made a vast difference to a very shaky part of our line ' one officer wrote, while our machine-guns got some good targets and by simulating an intention to attack we induced Turkish machine-guns to give away their location and waste ammunition.

One feature of this spell in the trenches was the attachment for instruction first of a company of Argyll & Sutherlands of the 157th Brigade, whose arrival had completed the Fifty-Second Division, and then, much to everyone's interest, of the first instalment of the three ' New Army ' Divisions now reinforcing the M.E.F. This was a company of the 6th Loyal North Lancashire (Thirteenth Division) who, after 48 hours in the line, were relieved by one of the 6th East Lancashire. Their appearance was encouraging, it showed that the large reinforcements needed to carry the venture through to a definite success were at last coming out and that the hard-tried Twenty-Ninth Division was to be vigorously supported, while for the moment it was to get its much-needed and well-earned rest at Lemnos.

If July found the Twenty-Ninth Division too exhausted and spent for another serious offensive, one was attempted on July 15th by the Fifty-Second Division, the R.N.D. and the French. The 2nd Hampshire co-operated by keeping the trenches in their front under machine-gun fire, and on their immediate right the 86th Brigade's bombers tried to gain ground in H.12 and H.12a

---

[1] Captain Thomas, Lts. Falcon and Harding and 2/Lts. Armitage and Pearce (11th E. Surrey) and Lt. Hearnden (9th R.W.K.): Captain Day had also rejoined from hospital.

[2] The portions of these lines secured by the attack of June 28th were in advance of the line further to our right.

without much success. The main attack, gallantly pressed, after starting well failed to fulfil its promise, heavy losses were incurred and little more than the first objective was eventually consolidated; thus, as on June 4th and 28th, the strategical situation remained unaltered; if local advantages had been secured and rather more depth obtained behind our line, Krithia and Achi Baba were untaken. Such slender gains seemed hardly worth the casualties, 12,000 British and 6,000 French, incurred in these attacks, but there seems little doubt that the Turkish losses had been very much heavier. The recklessness with which they had thrown in mass after mass in counter-attacks had exposed them to be mown down wholesale: again and again they had virtually exhausted their reserves and on each occasion it looked as if, had another fresh Division been available and rather more artillery and ammunition, the Turkish resistance might have collapsed, but, as throughout the tragic story of Gallipoli, we had not secured ' the advantage of time and place, which ' as Drake tried unsuccessfully to explain to Queen Elizabeth ' in martial actions is half the victory ', reinforcements arrived too late and chances went a-begging. When early on July 17th [1] the 2nd Hampshire embarked at V Beach to follow the other battalions of the Division to Lemnos, a notable page had been added to the regimental annals. That, handicapped as it was from the start, the Twenty-Ninth Division [2] failed to reach Achi Baba and open the Straits to the Navy is not surprising, what is remarkable is that it went so near to achieving success. Sir John Fortescue has said that Albuera has a special place among battle honours, the same may with equal justice be said of ' Cape Helles '.

[1] Casualties in a ten days' spell in the lines came to 10 killed, Lt. Sheffield and 40 men wounded, Captain Parker, 2/Lt. G.R.D. Moor and 20 men had meanwhile rejoined.

[2] Now under Major General de Lisle, General Hunter-Weston having taken command of the Eighth Corps, comprising all our troops at Cape Helles.

CHAPTER VIII

GALLIPOLI (continued)

Sari Bair and Suvla

The troops now reinforcing the M.E.F. for the effort it was hoped would carry us to Constantinople included two Divisions in which the Hampshire were represented, the Tenth and the Fifty-Fourth (East Anglian Territorial), to which last the Isle of Wight Rifles had been posted in April, joining the 4th and 5th Norfolk and the 5th Suffolk in Brigadier General Brunker's 163rd Brigade [1] and replacing the 4th Suffolk, who had been among the picked Territorial battalions sent out to France in 1914.

The 10th Battalion had had nearly two months in Hampshire before embarking at Liverpool on July 6th in the *Transylvania*. The transport under Lt. Scott was left to follow later, Lt. Lowy being placed in charge of such details as did not accompany the battalion, while several surplus subalterns went off to the 13th Battalion. The *Transylvania* was terribly crowded, the 6th R. Irish Rifles being also on board, giving little space for the exercise needed to keep men fit, while great vigilance had to be maintained on account of submarines. None appeared, and after brief calls at Gibraltar and Malta the *Transylvania* reached Alexandria on July 17th, disembarked company storemen and base kits and went on to Mudros, where the battalion landed on July 26th to make the acquaintance of the dust, the flies, the thirst—the allowance of rather tepid water was only a gallon a day—and the diarrhoea which were the chief features of residence on Lemnos. Incessant ' fatigues ' severely limited the chances of training and made it difficult to recover the condition and fitness which the cramped conditions of the voyage had naturally impaired.

With three fresh Divisions at his disposal and two more following them, Sir Ian Hamilton could at last attempt a major operation. For this the cramped space available at Cape Helles afforded nothing like enough room, apart from other unfavourable aspects of the tactical situation, but although the Australian and New Zealand Corps had been unable to enlarge appreciably its rather precarious original foothold, that quarter offered more chance of developing an attack. Now that sufficient force was available, an attempt to break out on its Northern flank in hopes of securing the dominating Sari Bair ridge could be combined with a fresh landing further North in Suvla Bay, where conditions seemed to invite a surprise attack. The Turks appeared to have only a few troops in this area, so a prompt advance might secure the ridge running from · North to South on the Eastward edge of the Suvla plain. This, it was hoped, would not only secure the new base to be established in Suvla Bay but would cover the flank of the Sari Bair attack and appreciably improve its chances. The Turks had no reinforcements within easy reach of Suvla, our persistent

---

[1] The 162nd Brigade was under Brigadier General de Winton, formerly C.O. of the 1st Hampshire.

attacks from Cape Helles had attracted their reserves to Krithia and Achi Baba, and the new venture's prospects seemed promising enough, even if its planners had been rather optimistic and had certainly underestimated the practical difficulties of negotiating the rugged and virtually unknown slopes of Sari Bair. They certainly asked rather much of the inexperienced ' New Army ' battalions in their ' baptism of fire ': while unfortunately the Australians and New Zealanders, after being so long cooped up in their cramped position, were mostly verging on ' staleness ' and lacked something of their old dash and fire, never more needed than in this new attack over such difficult ground.

For the attack on Sari Bair General Birdwood's Australians and New Zealanders were being reinforced by the 29th Brigade, the Thirteenth Division and the 29th Indian Brigade, while the Eleventh Division with the rest of the Tenth were alloted to the Suvla landing and were to be reinforced by the Fifty-Third and Fifty-Fourth Divisions. Accordingly the 10th Hampshire embarked on the afternoon of August 5th on board the small vessels which served as ferries between the islands and the peninsula and started off in time to approach the shore under cover of darkness. Major Morley, Captain Hudson, 2/Lt. Calderwood and 150 men had been left at Mudros as a 'first reinforcement', rather 'robbing Peter to pay Paul'. All ranks were wearing thin khaki drill with patches of coloured cloth sewn on their helmets as distinguishing marks, the Hampshire's patch being claret and yellow. All were heavily laden, three days' rations having been issued, and the boats were so closely packed that movement was virtually impossible. Except for occasional snipers there was no firing and the men were soon transferred to lighters, from which they landed just at daybreak (August 6th), to be hurried off up Shrapnel Gully and hidden away from Turkish observation and fire in the shelters excavated in its sides. Movement by daylight had to be carefully restricted: it was essential that the Turks should not discover that five additional brigades were being concentrated in General Birdwood's narrow area, and both Staff and troops deserve much credit for the successful accomplishment of this difficult task.

The advance against Sari Bair and the landing at Suvla were to be started after dark on August 6th. To distract the enemy's attention and keep him from reinforcing the crucial point, subsidiary attacks were to be made, by the Australians' right at Lone Pine and by the Eighth Corps at Cape Helles. The Lone Pine attack merely affected the Hampshire because it drew down heavy retaliatory shelling on the whole of General Birdwood's position which cost the 10th Battalion a dozen wounded, the Cape Helles attack was to involve the 2nd in the worst of all its experiences at Gallipoli.

The 2nd Hampshire had landed at Lemnos about 10 a.m., July 17th, to find a welcome draft of 300 men awaiting them. These came mainly from other regiments, notably the Oxford and Bucks L.I., but the officers with them, Captain Popham, Lt. Pigott and 2/Lts. Gawn and Nalder, came from the 3rd and 13th Battalions. 2/Lt. C. Moor also rejoined from hospital, and companies could now be reorganized with four platoons apiece, each platoon having an officer: Captains B. S. Parker (W) and Day (Z) and Lts. Webb (X) and Lord (Y), commanded the companies, while Lt. Poole acted as Adjutant.   Other ranks now stood at 732 and officers, including the M.O., Captain Levi, an Australian, at 24.

The 2nd should have had a full fortnight at Lemnos, where, if conditions were far from ideal, a dusty camp site, no canteen or means of supplementing the monotonous rations, except by purchase at exorbitant rates from the inhabitants, and few amenities, they were out even of sound of shelling.   However, an alarm of an intended Turkish attack cut the Division's rest short, and on July 28th the 2nd Hampshire were back at Cape Helles, being in brigade

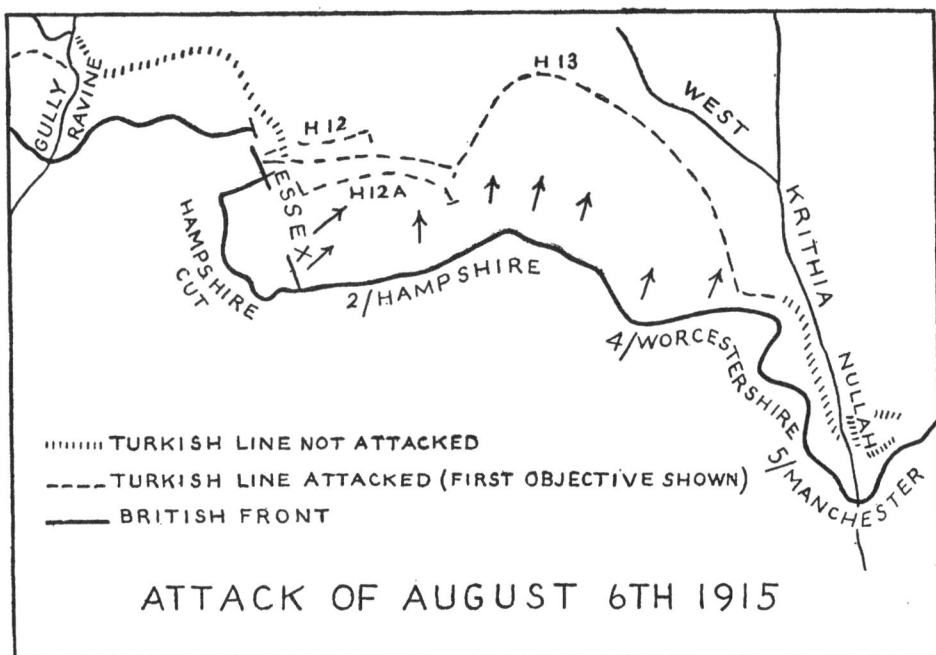

TURKISH LINE NOT ATTACKED
TURKISH LINE ATTACKED (FIRST OBJECTIVE SHOWN)
BRITISH FRONT

ATTACK OF AUGUST 6TH 1915

reserve at Gully Beach, mainly occupied in road making.   Two officers [1] and 110 men now joined, and with Captain C. B. Pigott, Lt. Sheffield and 16 men returning from hospital the battalion was stronger than it had been since the landing.   Unluckily on August 1st Colonel Beckwith was nastily wounded in the hand, and while he was in the C.C.S. having a shattered finger amputated, a shell, hitting the cliff above, brought down a lot of it, burying him just as he had come round from the anaesthetic.   He was nearly suffocated and very badly hurt and had to be shipped off to hospital, Captain Parker taking command.

After five days in the reserve line the 88th Brigade took over the right sub-section of the Divisional line, East of Gully Ravine, in readiness for another

[1] Lt. Mercer and 2/Lt .Mann.

attempt on its old objectives, H.12a, H.12 and H.13, on August 6th, the Forty-Second Division being ready to exploit any success by attacking next day beyond the Krithia Nullah. The Turkish position had been considerably strengthened since our last attack, and the Hampshire had the nastiest piece of the work, for their left had to tackle a formidable redoubt while their right and centre had nearly 300 yards of open to cross to reach H.13, here a re-entrant, whereas on their flanks the Worcestershire (right) and the Essex (left) had shorter distances to cover and the Essex could also attack from the flank, from Hampshire Cut.

The assaulting troops were in position by 8 a.m. (August 6th) but had to wait for six hours before the bombardment started. As again the artillery support was utterly inadequate: General Davies, who had just arrived from France to take over the Eighth Corps [1] from General Hunter-Weston, invalided, was quite horrified to see how very far it fell short of the Western Front standard, low as that was in 1915, and the volume and vigour of the Turkish reply showed that they were unpleasantly ready for the attack and augured ill for its chances. After an hour's deliberate bombardment by a handful of heavy guns, the field guns took up the tale and for 30 minutes plastered the objective as vigorously as their scanty ammunition would allow: then at 3.50 p.m. the infantry went forward with the utmost dash and gallantry, the Hampshire attacking in four waves. A low crest fifty yards from our line was crossed almost without loss but then machine-guns opened up on all sides and mowed the attackers down wholesale before many of them had got any way across No Man's Land, some guns across the Krithia Nullah on our right being particularly deadly. Our guns could do nothing to subdue their fire and under it the attack soon withered away. The Hampshire suffered terribly, above all in losing Captain Parker, who fell in leading the advance of the second line, and with him two other ' originals ', Captain Day and Lt. Webb, both previously wounded but back at duty, and 2/Lt. Gawn, who had won the D.C.M. in Somaliland, while 2/Lt. C. Moor fell on the Turkish parapet, which a very few of the leading waves seem to have reached. The supports lost as heavily as the leaders but pressed forward with equal determination, and some men, among them Lt. Morris and some of Z Company's second wave, entered the Turkish lines and established themselves in H.12a, some apparently even reaching H.13. Too few to maintain their foothold, they were overcome by numbers, though Sergeant Sinsbury held on for some time to a sap with a few men and, when they were bombed out, he covered their retirement with great skill and resource.[2] Rather more Worcestershire got in and held out till dark, while a fair number of Essex from Hampshire Cut established themselves in H.12 and eventually managed to retain a tiny corner, but within a few minutes the attack had come to a complete standstill, the unhit survivors lying out among the dead and wounded, pinned to the ground by the machine-guns and

---

[1] The troops at Cape Helles, those at Suvla forming a Ninth.
[2] He was awarded the D.C.M., which was also given to Private Hampton for carrying a message across ground swept by heavy fire.

unable to move until darkness let them and the more slightly wounded crawl back. It had been the worst day in the whole story of Cape Helles.

Inadequate artillery support had once again led to a heavy sacrifice of lives to little purpose. Nothing had been gained locally and even if the Turks had been distracted from the main attack at Suvla, its unavailing gallantry had left the 88th Brigade a wreck, the Hampshire having lost eighteen officers and 224 other ranks [1] killed and missing. Of their own officers, besides those already mentioned, Captain Popham, Lts. Sheffield and L. B. Piggott, 2/Lts. Derry [2] and Nalder were killed and of those attached Captain Thomas, Lts. Barrett, Falcon, Harding and Hearnden and 2/Lts. Armitage and Pearce also fell, an eloquent testimony to the devoted gallantry with which the attack had been led. The M.O., Captain Levi, after working strenuously all night, was killed next morning by a shell which hit the dressing station and also killed C.Q.M.S. Fisher and wounded R.Q.M.S. Smith, C.Q.M.S. Giles and several men, Captain Pigott and 2/Lt. F. R. Mann and 210 men were wounded. This left the battalion with only the Quartermaster, Lts. Lord, Manders (R. Berkshire) and Poole (A. & S.H.), and 2/Lt. G. R. D. Moor and about 400 other ranks. [3] *Photograph page 11, Jan 16*

During the night any wounded who could be reached were brought in, [4] and *Jbui* then the 86th Brigade relieved the 88th and the surviving Hampshires made their way back to Gully Beach, where they were warmly congratulated on their gallantry by General de Lisle and reorganized in two companies. Little rest could be given to the brigade: shattered as it was, it had on August 14th to take over the line again from the 86th. Things had gone wrong at Suvla, and though Sir Ian Hamilton had deliberately refrained from using the Twenty-Ninth Division in that attack because he had already asked so much of it and wished, if possible, to spare it, [5] he had now to employ the 'Old Guard' of the M.E.F. in a last-minute effort to retrieve the situation.

Before this both the 8th and 10th Hampshire had been heavily engaged, though neither actually went into action till the situation had been jeopardised beyond recall. The plan for the attack on Sari Bair involved the preliminary seizure of covering positions by flanking columns to protect the main advance in the centre, but in the intricate and difficult country to be traversed, virtually a terra incognita to all concerned, delays and loss of direction, with some want of determination and enterprise in the handling of one assaulting column, meant that Chunuk Bair, which should have been secured, was not occupied, and though next day, (August 8th) a belated lodgement was made on this all-important point, sufficient Turkish reinforcements had arrived to prevent our consolidating, let alone expanding, our precarious foothold. On the left of the line errors over the positions reached and the fatigue of the troops equally pre-

[1] Corrected figures. The Worcestershire's losses were even heavier.
[2] Just joined from the Ceylon Planters Rifle Corps.
[3] Lt. Mercer had gone sick.
[4] A party of volunteers went up next day to make a fresh search of No Man's Land, but by then all survivors had been brought in.
[5] I had this from Sir Ian Hamilton himself.

vented our securing the positions we wanted, and the plans for August 8th had to be modified. Even then the 2/6th Gurkhas established themselves on Hill Q, beyond Chunuk Bair, and had they been supported promptly and in force their achievement might have been exploited. Most of the Thirteenth Division had before this been thrown in to support or relieve the Australians and New Zealanders who had opened the move, and the evening of August 8th found only four battalions, two of Brigadier General Baldwin's 38th Brigade with the 10th Hampshire and the 6th R. Irish Rifles, available for a last effort to gain the ridge. These were now to advance up the Chailak Dere, one of the many gullies leading up to Chunuk Bair, and to come in on the left of the New Zealanders and the other troops who were clinging on at Chunuk Bair.

The 10th Hampshire meanwhile had spent the early hours of August 7th in a futile move up another gully North of Russell's Top, only to be sent back again to Shrapnel Gully and to spend the day there inactively, hearing all sorts of rumours. Starting off again about 10 a.m. next day they filed along the great sap running Northward up the coast to the Fisherman's Hut, where they remained until evening. Advancing again, they found the seaward end of the Chailak Dere being shelled and so had to rush across in small parties and then to struggle in single file along the narrow gully, choked with wounded making their way down it. Progress was slow and tiring, touch was hard to keep, halts and delays were frequent, and the column had barely settled down in a bivouac before, about 10 p.m., orders were received to push on. The guides then went wrong and led the column to the foot of a precipice. This meant turning round and retracing the route, doubly difficult in the dark and in the congested narrow space, and though General Baldwin eventually found a track leading across to the left into the Aghyl Dere, by 5 a.m. (August 9th), when the troops on Chunuk Bair (right) and on Hill Q (left) should have started an advance, his column was not up in its place to join in. Accordingly no advance was attempted on the right, and though the Gurkhas pressed forward and even established themselves on the crest of Hill Q, for want of support they were driven back, to hang on just below.

By the time (6 a.m.) that Baldwin's battalions could start their advance, moving just North of Rhododendron Spur, the main approach to Chunuk Bair, the Turks were ready and well placed. The East Lancashire, who were leading, were soon checked and the Irish Rifles could not get any further, The Hampshire accordingly halted about 600 yards West of ' the Farm ' [1], a building in a patch of cultivation, and stayed there till, about 9 a.m., Colonel Bewsher was ordered to fill a gap between the Irish Rifles and the New Zealanders on Chunuk Bair and Rhododendron Spur. For this purpose Major Pilleau, with A Company and half D, now went forward up a gully SW. of the Farm;[2] at its head, however, they came under heavy fire, mainly machine-guns with some shrapnel, and could advance no further. Accordingly they established themselves in the best positions to be found and before long obtained touch with the New Zealanders on their right. Major Pilleau was wounded but, after being bandaged, rejoined the detachment.

---

[1] About 80 D. 6 on plan.   [2] 80. F. 7.

Meanwhile Lts. Grellier and Williams had taken another party to support the East Lancashire nearer the Farm, and about 2 p.m. Captain Hicks took half B Company to reinforce the New Zealanders on Rhododendron Spur but was sent back as the Brigadier was unable to use the party, which thus incurred a good many casualties and was quite exhausted to no purpose before it got back to battalion head-quarters. Eventually after dark half B [1] was placed on the left of Major Pilleau's men, who were digging in along the ridge at the head of their gully, while C Company also moved forward and linked up with the Irish Rifles.[2] This left only a small reserve with battalion head-quarters, one machine-gun being put in front and the other well forward up the hill. Further to the left a vigorous counter-attack against our troops on Damakjelik Bair had been repulsed with heavy losses, but no forward move could be developed on that flank to assist the troops on the bare slopes of Chunuk Bair. They had to lie out, exposed without shelter to a scorching sun, with a mere mouthful of water, while every attempt to advance or move instantly drew fire, and as the troops had little to fire at, their own casualties, though not heavy, were the more noticeable.

No more counter-attacks were attempted during the night, but with dawn (August 10th) the Turks came forward in great force, pressing hardest against the troops on Chunuk Bair and driving them back upon Rhododendron Spur. One attack on the Irish Rifles was caught in flank by the Hampshire's fire and stopped, but the attack soon spread to Major Pilleau's men, who found their right flank exposed but held on stoutly for some time [3] until a specially vigorous attack dislodged No. I platoon and drove them back down hill, Lt. Cheesman being killed. The survivors rallied on B Company, who had been getting good targets in Turks moving across a cornfield below them, but meanwhile other Turks had got in between the New Zealanders and D Company, outflanking D and driving it back. However, as the Turks did not follow up their success, Captain Shone took two platoons [4] forward to try to regain D.s trenches. They reached them, but in insufficient strength to maintain the ground, and were forced back, Captain Shone being wounded and Sergeant Barber killed, while about 8.45 a.m. Captain Hicks, finding B's advanced position untenable, had also to fall back towards battalion head-quarters; A Company, with Lt. Hellyer the only officer unhit, had likewise to quit its now exposed forward position. Before this Captain Black-Hawkins had taken the reserve [5] forward to reinforce the left, which also was being hard pressed, where he was before long hit and killed, setting his men a fine example, and Colonel Bewsher himself had been wounded. He had been bandaged up and was starting off for the beach when a wounded N.C.O. came in, declaring that no officers were left unhurt in the firing line. The Colonel therefore went forward, to find that General Baldwin had

---

[1] Two platoons, VI and VII, were away on fatigue.

[2] Some of A seem to have become detached and were further to the left, but the exact localities are hard to fix accurately. The Irish Rifles seem to have been to the left (North) of the Farm.

[3] Major Pilleau was apparently killed about this time, leading a counter-attack : he had already been wounded again.

[4] Apparently Nos. VI and VII platoons, who had rejoined.   [5] Apparently the rest of D.

been killed, that General Cooper, who had reached 38th Brigade headquarters, had been wounded and that he was the senior officer left. He therefore re-mained near the Farm, where the line was now held by C Company with some Irish Rifles on the left and a few of the 38th Brigade. Only one machine-gun was left but the line was holding on, though the enemy were pressing hard. Their attacks had now extended further to the left and after the survivors of Major Pilleau's party and Captain Hicks and the remnant of his men had been driven in, it was clear that the Farm plateau could not be held without grave risk of its defenders being surrounded, so Colonel Bewsher now ordered them to fall back and re-form on the next ridge, Cheshire Ridge.[1] This was done and the

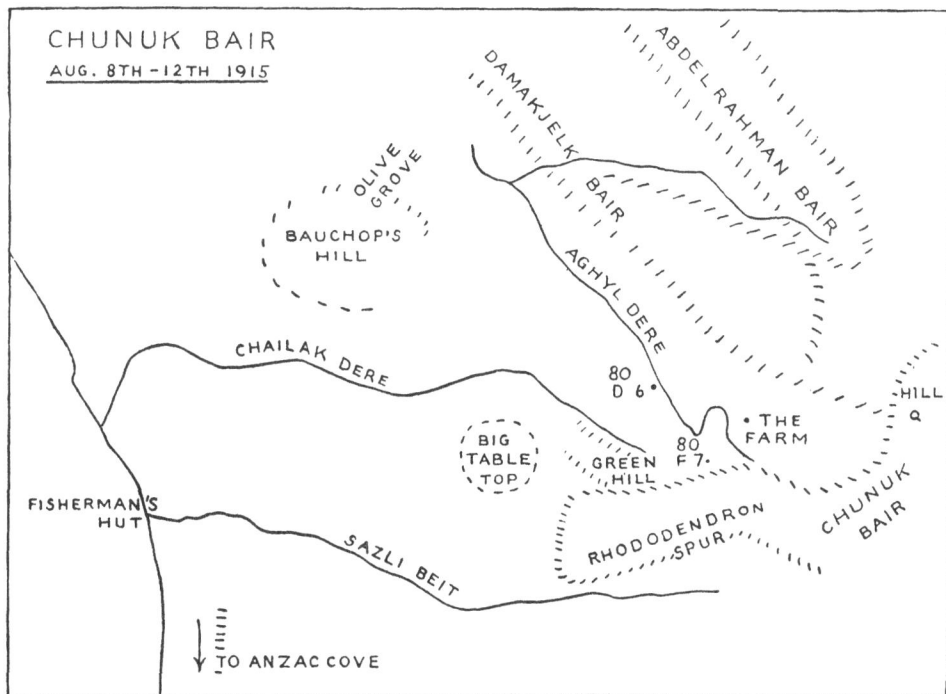

CHUNUK BAIR
AUG. 8TH – 12TH 1915

DAMAKJELIK
ABDEL RAHMAN BAIR
OLIVE GROVE
BAUCHOP'S HILL
BAIR
AGHYL DERE
CHAILAK DERE
80 D 6
HILL Q
BIG TABLE TOP
GREEN HILL
80 F 7
THE FARM
FISHERMAN'S HUT
SAZLI BEIT
RHODODENDRON SPUR
CHUNUK BAIR
TO ANZAC COVE

men were rallied and actually made a gallant but hopeless attempt to advance. However, Cheshire Ridge was held and the Turks checked. Not only was this position secured, touch was eventually obtained with the troops still holding on to the slopes of Rhododendron Spur. Further to the left also the Turks were held and a line maintained running North down the Damakjelik Spur. Colonel Bewsher [2] had now been ordered back to hospital by a senior Staff officer and, with Captain Hicks also wounded, only Lt. Hellyer and the Quartermaster were left unhurt. As far as could be ascertained Major Pilleau, Captains Savage, Black-Hawkins and Hayes, Lts. Bell, Cheesman and Williams and 2/Lts. S. A. Smith, Whalley and Morse were killed or missing. Other ranks killed and

[1] Marked on some maps as Green Hill.   [2] He subsequently received the D.S.O.

missing came to 155, with 276 wounded. Besides the C.O. and Captain Hicks, Captains Faith and Shone, Lts. Clement, Griffiths and Tanner and 2/Lts. de Gaury, Dupree, German, Parry, Grellier and Whittome had been wounded.[1]

The fight which the battalion had put up was greatly to its credit: its Brigadier wrote that its resistance had saved the situation on the right and enabled the next brigade to withstand the pressure: he had always, he said, had a high opinion of the battalion and its fighting had fully justified him.

To so depleted a battalion the arrival on August 10th of the ' first reinforcement ' was very welcome. This party had left Lemnos on the previous evening, arrived at Anzac Cove about 1 a.m., landed and moved by the Anzac Sap to the Fisherman's Hut, to find the beach crowded with wounded. They were then sent on up the Chailak Dere to 29th Brigade H.Q. on Cheshire Ridge, which they reached about 4 p.m. after a tiring march. Here Major Morley got orders to collect the battalion, two parties being eventually discovered still in line, one of 80 under Sergeant Lewis and a smaller one further to the front under Lt. Hellyer. All told some 280 were present, but the battalion was very short not only of officers but of N.C.O's, nearly all the seniors having been hit. It was now ordered back to a small valley in rear, where the only available water was a well, which was under continuous rifle and machine-gun fire, so directly it was dark the men were turned to construct a covered approach to it. Rocky ground and the exhaustion of all ranks made this very difficult and with 100 men required as a burial party, few got any rest. Here the battalion remained for three days, working away at the sap despite all difficulties and several casualties. Some stragglers [2] had turned up and some re-organization was now possible, Lt. Saunders, a tower of strength in this emergency, indefatigable and resourceful, combined the Adjutant's duties with his own, and the men were sorted out into four weak companies.

August 14th brought a move, not into reserve to rest, but back in the firing line to relieve Gurkhas at the upper end of Damakjelik Bair, the spur beyond the Aghyl Dere. It was a bad position, being enfiladed and overlooked from Abdelrahman Bair, a spur of the Chunuk Bair ridge, while our line formed a salient; moreover in that hard and rocky soil trench-digging had been difficult and the trenches in places were under 3 feet deep; to obtain any cover breastworks and sangars had to be built up and the battalion had many casualties before it could subdue the enemy's snipers. It held this line for six days, improving the defences and communications and burying the nearest of the many dead who littered the ground in front. The position was always under fire, mainly machine-gun, which at times developed into a regular ' hate ' of considerable intensity, and between sickness and casualties the battalion was nearly 80 weaker before it was relieved on August 20th and given its first night's real rest for nearly a fortnight. This merely meant that another effort was to be demanded of it, part of an eleventh hour snatch at the success which had eluded us at Suvla.

---

[1] Captain Waddington, the Brigade machine-gun officer, was also wounded.

[2] In that intricate and little-known country many men had naturally got detached.

If the failure at Sari Bair may partly be put down to the poor physical state of such experienced soldiers as were employed, many of the inexperienced men who landed here and at Suvla were suffering from the diarrhoea and similar complaints which had fastened on them soon after reaching the Eastern Mediterranean. An equally serious handicap was that while these new troops ' knew what they ought to do, they did not know how to do it ',[1] they were being required to race on their trial trip, but at Suvla the root of the failure to develope a splendid opening and to exploit surprise must lie at the door of Corps and Divisional headquarters; where energy, initiative and promptitude in appreciating the situation and the urgent value of time were so conspicuously lacking. By the time the Fifty-Fourth Division's infantry were ashore the chance of success was already almost lost. The vital Anafarta hills and the ridge running Northward from them to the Kiretch Tepe ridge along the coast were firmly held by the Turks in some strength, and the artillery ashore was quite insufficient support for an attack on their position, strong in itself and already partially entrenched.

The Isle of Wight Rifles, on joining the Fifty-Fourth Division in April, had first found quarters at Bury St. Edmunds but soon moved to Watford, round which the Division was being concentrated. Here they spent two months, largely notable for the arrival of some fine and very lively transport mules from South America, and in July the Division started for Gallipoli, the battalion [2] being among the 8,000 troops carried by the great Cunarder *Aquitania* which sailed from Liverpool on July 30th and reached Lemnos inside a week. The 8th did not land but were transferred almost at once to smaller vessels for transport to Suvla Bay, where they disembarked on August 9th. A ' first reinforcement ' of four officers and 180 men under Captain Fardell having been left at Mudros, only 25 officers and 750 other ranks were present.

Sir Ian Hamilton was intending to keep the Fifty-Fourth Division together and not throw it into action piece-meal, as other reinforcements had been, but when its first battalions landed they found Ninth Corps head-quarters greatly agitated about a gap between the Tenth Division's right on the Kiretch Tepe Ridge and the left of the Eleventh and Fifty-Third, now much intermingled, which did not extend much beyond Sulajik in the plain. Accordingly, despite G.H.Q's intentions, several units of the Fifty-Fourth Division were hurried forward into this gap and among them the 8th Hampshire, who found themselves on outpost [3] with the very vaguest idea of the ground, of the situation and of what was expected of them.

Being uninformed of this G.H.Q. sent orders next morning (August 11th) that the Fifty-Fourth Division should push forward that evening to the foot-

---

[1] A company commander of the Eleventh Division.

[2] Colonel Rhodes was in command and had with him Majors Lewes and Veasey (Adjt.), Captains C. and D. W. Ratsey, Ellery, Holmes-Gore, Fardell, Marsh and Loader, Lts. Read, Pittis, Young-James, Seeley and Curtis, 2/Lts. Bartlett, Brannon, Sutton, S. G. Ratsey, Kingdom, Murphy, Shelton, Latham, Watson, Fox, F. C. Raymond and Weeding and Lt. and Quartermaster Giddens. Captain G. Raymond (R.A.M.C.) was M.O.

[3] Apparently just East of Point 28.

hills of the Tekke Tepe ridge in readiness to attack at dawn. Against this the Ninth Corps protested, but the operation was merely postponed 24 hours and on the afternoon of August 12th the 163rd Brigade started forward, its objective being some huts about a mile ahead of its outpost line..

Since August 10th the troops had been sorted out and brigades got together, but little opportunity had offered for becoming better acquainted with the lie of the land and the enemy's dispositions. Immediately ahead lay open grazing land, dotted with a few scattered trees and patches of cultivation, with some ditches and hedges. Beyond this scrub extended to the foothills, which it covered.

The 163rd Brigade had three battalions in front line, the Isle of Wight Rifles being in the centre between the 5th Norfolk (right) and 5th Suffolk (left) with the 4th Norfolk in support behind the left. An 18 pounder battery, two mountain batteries and some naval guns were to provide artillery support, but, like the infantry, the gunners had little idea of the enemy's dispositions and without more definite targets could give little help.

Starting off at 4.40 p.m. the brigade at first made fair progress, though directly it moved machine-guns from the left inflicted many casualties, while from the other flank came shrapnel fire. The troops pushed on, however, meeting no very great opposition,[1] but casualties mounted up, the supporting artillery being quite unable to subdue the flanking fire, and before long the battalions were losing touch and the brigade's line had become disconnected. Most of the 5th Norfolk, carrying with them some Hampshire, diverged to the right and lost touch, many of them penetrating deep through the scrub into the Turkish position, where they were overwhelmed, their bodies being discovered half a mile beyond the front line, after the armistice.[2] The Hampshire, with their flank uncovered, pushed on about 1000 yards over ground which grew worse with scrub as they got further on, until the machine-guns on the left eventually halted them near the Anafarta Ova wells. Here along a ditch the leading men established themselves: but being only a handful they could not maintain their ground and had to retire, rallying in a sunken track some way back, where about 800 of all units of the brigade were eventually collected, with others further back on the left, where the 4th Norfolk were entrenching. Here they hung on until the evening of August 14th, consolidating the position as far as possible when short of tools and in rather hard ground, despite persistent sniping, to which the men endeavoured to reply. On the right touch had been gained with the Fifty-Third Division, but the left was open. An attempted Turkish advance on August 14th gave the 8th Hampshire's machine-guns under Lt. Pittis a chance to do some effective shooting in repulsing an effort to outflank the left, and that evening the 5th Essex arrived to relieve the battalion, which withdrew to its original position near Point 28.[3] It had been a hard trial

[1] The rifle fire was mainly from long range, if there were snipers in the scrub, whom the brigade pushed back as it went forward.

[2] Some Hampshire were among them.

[3] Major Veasey (Adjutant), Lieutenant Pittis and R.S.M. Bryant were mentioned in dispatches, Lieutenant Pittis being subsequently awarded the M.C., while Captain Raymond, the Medical Officer, who had worked untiringly, was also ' mentioned '.

for inexperienced troops, especially when so little artillery support was available. Casualties now proved to have amounted to nearly half those in action, Major Lewes, Captains Holmes-Gore, C and D. W. Ratsey and Loader, Lts. Young-James and 2/Lts. Raymond and Watson and 150 men had been killed or were missing, Lt. Sutton and 140 men being wounded. Practically all those returned as ' missing ' must have been killed, though about 20 turned up later among the wounded in hospital, having got detached and been rescued by other units. The 5th Norfolk had suffered even more heavily, but the brigade, though for the moment incapable of another offensive, was on the evening of August 16th ordered to take over trenches on the Kiretch Tepe Sirt ridge behind the Tenth Division. That Division had on the previous day attempted to advance along that ridge, while on its right the 162nd Brigade had attacked Kidney Hill, from which had come the flanking fire which had been mainly responsible for checking the 163rd Brigade's attack. In directing this attack Brigadier General de Winton had been very seriously wounded and though, thanks largely to his leadership and example,[1] some ground had been gained, it had been impossible to retain it and these days' operations had added another 2,000 to our casualties without any appreciable improvement in our position, even if the Turkish losses may have been nearly as heavy.

By August 15th the great attack had virtually failed: if the British had extended substantially the area they occupied they were no nearer to having attained their objective, tactically or strategically; the ground gained was not worth a fraction of their heavy casualties and even at Suvla their reserve positions were, as at Helles, still within range of the Turkish guns. The great reinforcement had shot its bolt, and the question now arose whether more troops should be thrown in, if they could be found, or whether failure should be admitted and the enterprise abandoned, if indeed the troops could be re-embarked without disastrous losses.

However, Sir Ian Hamilton's optimism was not quite quenched. He had given General de Lisle command of the Ninth Corps and, as already mentioned he now decided after all to call on the Twenty-Ninth Division to snatch success out of failure at the eleventh hour. Accordingly on August 17th the 87th Brigade reached Suvla, being followed in turn by the 86th and 88th.

After two days in the H trenches the 2nd Hampshire had moved across Gully Ravine on August 16th to take over the front line beyond Fusilier Bluff. Lts. Silk and C. Harland had rejoined from hospital, Lt. Silk taking command, but 250 men from the 3rd and 13th Battalions who should have reinforced the 2nd had most unfortunately been lost through the torpedoing on August 13th of their transport, the *Royal Edward*, only about 30 surviving. Then, late on August 19th, the battalion was relieved and moved back down Gully Ravine, to go on next day to V Beach and embark there, only arriving at Suvla after day-break (August 21st) and having to disembark under shell-fire, which fortunately proved innocuous.

---

[1] He subsequently received the C.M.G.

This new attack involved an attempt by the Twenty-Ninth Division, advancing from Chocolate Hill, to capture Scimitar Hill and Hill 112 South of it, while the Eleventh on their right advanced by Hetman Chair and Aire Kavak against the 'W Hills', with the Tenth, in which dismounted Yeomanry just arrived from Egypt had replaced the 29th Brigade, forming a reserve. Simultaneously, a composite force from General Birdwood's Corps under the New Zealanders' Brigadier, General Russell, was to assault the strongly held Hill 60, at the seaward end of the spur facing Damakjelik Bair. Could this hill be carried it was hoped to push forward to Susak Kuyu wells NW. of it and gain touch with the Eleventh Division further North. This composite force included the 10th Hampshire, now up to five officers and 330 men,[1] who were to cross the Kaiajik Dere [2] to our right of Hill 60 and nearer the inland end of the spur.

The main attack started at 3 p.m. on August 21st, but once again the utterly inadequate artillery support proved the decisive factor. The Turks were well dug in, and their numerous and well-sited machine-guns could not be subdued by the British guns, too few and including naval guns whose armour-piercing projectiles were ill-suited for bombarding trenches which were none too accurately located. Both Eleventh and Twenty-Ninth Divisions attacked with great determination, but while on both flanks a little ground was gained, by the 34th Brigade at Azmak Dere and by the 87th on Scimitar Hill, in the main the attack was held up and, during the night, even the slender gains had to be relinquished, a proposal to put in the 88th Brigade being fortunately rejected. It could have achieved nothing except add to our losses.

The Hampshire meanwhile had merely advanced in open order across the Salt Lake, now virtually dry, to reserve trenches behind Chocolate Hill. Though shelled during this advance, they escaped with one casualty, Lt. C. Harland being hit in the leg, but while digging in they caught more shell-fire and had over 20 more casualties. On the following evening the battalion shifted to its left to One Tree Gully, the 88th Brigade having relieved the Fifty-Fourth Division and taken over the line just South of Kiretch Tepe Sirt. The battalion now welcomed back Captain Spencer-Smith, who took command with the rank of Major, and with him came 180 men and four officers, including Captain Lane and Lt. Collett of the 3rd Battalion, followed shortly by another 40 men under Lt. Swayne (13th Battalion). Lts. Silk and Poole now had to go to hospital, Lt. Lord taking over duty as Adjutant. After a week here, during which snipers on the higher ground in front and on the left flank proved troublesome but did not cause many casualties, while a bad line was much improved, the brigade was relieved and went off to Imbros for a well-earned rest.

Unlike the 2nd Battalion, the 10th Hampshire had been heavily engaged on August 21st. The position they had to attack was unpleasantly strong and where they were crossing the ravine it could be enfiladed from higher up on Abdelrahman Bair. Hill 60 itself was being attacked by the 5th Connaught Rangers and some New Zealand Mounted Rifles, the Hampshire being in support,

---

[1] More details had rejoined.   [2] Between the Hill 60 spur and Damakjelik Bair.

while on the right two Australian battalions were attacking. The assault was timed for 3.30 p.m., but, as always at Gallipoli, too little artillery was available for a really effective preparation and the half an hour's bombardment only served to give warning of the coming attack.

Consequently, when the Australians went forward, they met so fierce a fire that they were soon brought to a standstill, their leading lines being nearly

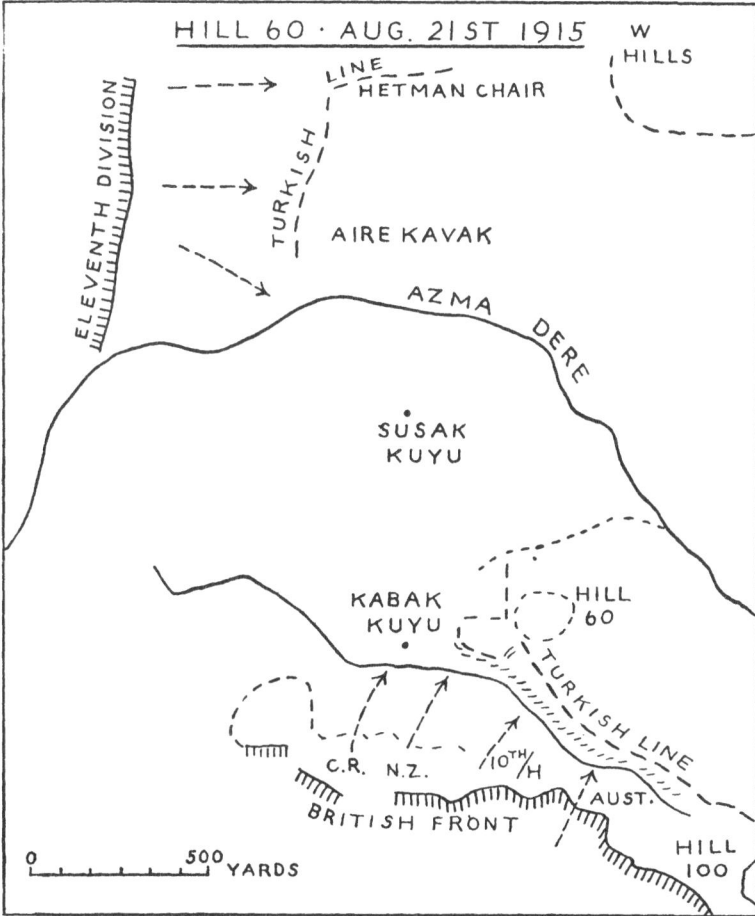

wiped out; though the New Zealanders fared better, making a lodgement in the enemy's lines. Major Morley, bringing the Hampshire forward in support [1] found that the danger point was the passage of a flat-topped ridge which was completely exposed to artillery and machine-gun fire from our right. However, it was essential to support the few New Zealanders visible in the Turkish trenches, who were trying to extend their hold by bombing, and accordingly he sent C

[1] They were in four lines C (Captain Hudson) in front, then D (Lt. Calderwood), then A and B (Captain Hellyer).

Company forward. They had to cross one gully and then the flat-topped ridge before reaching some shelter at the foot of the rise to the Turkish line. On the flat ridge a hail of fire bowled most of them over, hardly any getting across or reaching the captured position. D followed, only to fare as badly, Lt. Calderwood being killed, while to make matters worse the scrub took fire, though luckily the wind blew the flames away from where most of the wounded were lying. Advancing in their turn A Company met as fierce a fire and were checked, Captain Hellyer being very badly wounded.[1] Coming forward with B Company, Major Morley himself was hit and, realizing the hopelessness of crossing the ridge at this point, on handing over to Lt. Saunders, he told him to take B down the gully and try to cross at a less exposed spot. Meanwhile the Connaught Rangers had reached Hill 60, and though its summit remained in Turkish hands they had secured two valuable wells at Kabak Kuyu at its foot. On reporting to General Russell Lt. Saunders was ordered to bring his men up on the left of the position gained. Taking advantage of the cover of a sunken road, they reached the point indicated and got touch with the Gurkhas on the left who had secured the wells at Susak Kuyu to the North West. Here Captain Hudson and the survivors of the other companies rejoined them after dark and eventually, on being relieved by the Indian Brigade, the Hampshire went back to 29th Brigade head-quarters in S.W.B. Gully on Damakjelik Bair.

The attack had hit them hard, with another 43 killed and missing and 110 wounded. This reduced the battalion to well under 200 all told, Captain Hudson and Lt. Saunders being the only officers, and left it quite unfit for the moment for anything more than finding various fatigues for Brigade Head-quarters.[2]

The unsuccessful attack of August 21st was the last offensive effort of the Gallipoli venture, after that only local attacks were made for the improvement of the line. Before another advance could be attempted substantial reinforcements must be provided, over and above the drafts needed to bring the existing forces up to establishment and to relieve the many men who were carrying on though debilitated and really unfit for hard work. Moreover without far more artillery and ammunition it would be futile to send more troops, and even then the slender foothold already gained would hardly provide enough space for the artillery and reinforcements needed. Reluctant as were the higher authorities, both on the spot and at home, to admit it, the necessity of evacuation was making itself increasingly clear as the weeks passed on. Over four months were to elapse before that evacuation was to be successfully completed and, if long before that one Hampshire battalion had left Gallipoli, the other two had still much to endure there.

---

[1] He died of his wounds.

[2] Lt. Saunders was 'mentioned' in Sir Ian Hamilton's dispatches describing the Suvla and Anzac operations and received a well-deserved M.C. Captain Hudson was also 'mentioned', as were C.S.M. Sturges, Lance Sergeant Bowers, Privates Biddlecombe, Dyer, Moxham and Shaw, Sturges, Bowers and Biddlecombe received the D.C.M.

CHAPTER IX

GALLIPOLI

The Final Stages—The Evacuation

REGIMENTAL officers and men serving on the Gallipoli peninsula in the autumn of 1915 were naturally not aware of the course of the discussions about the future of the expedition which followed the check of August 21st., still they could hardly fail to realize that sooner or later something must be done to break down the existing stalemate, and they could form their own opinions as to the prospects, about which few can have been very optimistic. If the majority were quite ready to deal with a Turkish offensive, which would have given them a chance of getting their own back, there could be little question that tactically the Turks had the advantage, that conditions on the peninsula were most unpleasant and trying and largely responsible for a high sick-rate, with dysentery and diarrhoea as substantial contributors, that such amenities as troops in France enjoyed when ' resting ' were unknown even on the islands, whose one attraction was being out of range of the Turkish guns, that merely to maintain our position meant hard and monotonous work with little tangible result, while an ascendancy over the enemy in sniping, in bombing, in patrolling and in other activities of trench warfare, took some establishing. It was impossible not to be depressed by the failure of the great effort from which so much had been hoped: if those chiefly responsible for the miscarriage at Suvla had been replaced by more energetic and more inspiring commanders, the harm they had done was not easily eradicated and some of the more inexperienced and less well-trained units were slow to recover their former standards. Hardly a battalion in the M.E.F. but had suffered heavily and lost most of those who had made and trained it, many indeed needed to be virtually re-made. If the Twenty-Ninth Division, despite all it had endured, was quick to give others a lead and morally had little lee-way to make up, even it was weak and terribly short of experienced officers and N.C.O.s, so that the return of any ' original ', was an event of note and a good draft from a 3rd Battalion, imbued with the regimental traditions and spirit, worth much more than its mere numbers. The War Office, more perhaps from accident and necessity than from design, was terribly apt to reinforce battalions with officers and men from other regiments, though few of these had been long enough with their proper unit to feel themselves strangers in another.

The three Hampshire battalions in the M.E.F. were to go their own individual ways without meeting. The Twenty-Ninth Division had just taken over, at the end of August, the sector North of Sulajik, the left centre of the Suvla position, the spot where a Turkish counter-attack had fewest natural obstacles to meet and could most easily penetrate to the vital beach area. The Tenth Division, which had moved down off Kiretch Tepe Sirt for the attack on August 21st, remained in the Chocolate Hill sector until transferred to Salonica early in

October, while the Fifty-Fourth, which had replaced the Tenth astride Kiretch Tepe Sirt, moved to General Birdwood's command early in September to allow of the Thirteenth Division joining the Ninth Corps, to which it properly belonged. This brought the 8th Hampshire to the Rhododendron Spur—Damakjelik Bair sector, where the 10th had undergone its strenuous initiation to active service. Thus the paths of the three battalions did not cross.

The Twenty-Ninth Division's sector offered more opportunities than the others for minor tactical enterprises. The line here needed much improving, detached posts and trenches had to be joined up, communications improved and the line made habitable as well as defensible, and after that a wide and uneven No Man's Land, with many gullies, nullahs and hillocks, challenged our troops to push forward and establish advanced posts out of which a new line could be constructed. It gave chances also to snipers and the Twenty-Ninth Division had no intention of leaving the enemy alone.

The 2nd Hampshire had just a week at Imbros, really resting. The weather was good, the men got plenty of bathing and were refitted. Returning to Suvla on September 7th, they found 34 men from the 3rd Battalion awaiting them and next day took over from the Munster Fusiliers some excellent trenches on the Division's right, some two miles West of Anafarta Sagir. Saps were now pushed forward and, when far enough out, were joined up as an advanced line and meanwhile served as good sniping posts. Patrols were active; one which ran into a Turkish outpost on the night of September 17/18th had four men wounded, but thanks to good work and resourcefulness all four were brought safely in to our lines; on another occasion Corporal Nunn distinguished himself greatly by skilful handling of a covering party when a ditch in front of our line was being cleared, while other patrols located Turkish posts accurately so that our machine-guns could be turned on to them. One feature of the month was the attachment to the battalion for instruction of parties of the Royal Newfoundland Regiment and of the 2/1st London (T.F.), both these battalions having been attached to the 88th Brigade. Our snipers on balance had much the best of the exchanges, the month's casualties despite much shelling only coming to 20, five being killed. Diarrhoea, dysentery and other ailments sent three officers [1] and 133 other ranks to hospital, and although 80 men under 2/Lt. Bircham joined on September 29th, the battalion ended the month with only 12 officers and 564 other ranks.

After nearly four weeks in front line the 2nd Hampshire went back on October 4th to a reserve line, a mile in rear, consisting chiefly of dug-outs. This did not take them beyond the range of the Turkish guns, which did their best to discourage cleanliness by persistently shelling bathing parties. However, a week here, mainly spent in working on communication trenches, only cost the battalion one killed and two wounded. It then took over the Division's extreme left, on the rocky lower slopes of Kiretch Tepe Sirt, where digging was very difficult, indeed blasting was needed to get down any depth, so that sand-

[1] Captain Lane (3rd Battalion), 2/Lts. G. R. D. Moor and N. R. Gill.

bags had to be extensively used. It was as bad a piece of line as the battalion had yet met, and with the snipers opposite very active and enjoying the advantage of higher ground, hard work was needed to establish a satisfactory ascendancy. This was done, rifle grenades being also used effectively, while the battalion's patrols scored several successes and the month's casualties only came to eight killed and 32 wounded, though once again sickness caused many admissions to hospital, 137, including four officers. Against that drafts amounting to 138 men joined, another 80 returning from hospital, with ten officers, four attached from the 5th Royal Scots, who now had to leave the brigade [1] as their reserve unit could not produce the drafts they needed. Of these Lt. Kingsley Darling took over Z Company. From October 30th to November 6th the battalion was again in brigade reserve and then relieved the Essex in the right of the brigade sector. Here a ruined cottage, converted into a bullet-proof blockhouse, was a great centre of activity, Turkish bombers were inclined to be active, but the Hampshire replied effectively with rifle-grenades and with bombs from a catapult [2] with a range of 170 yards, besides dispersing wiring and working parties with rifle fire or rifle grenades. In common with the rest of the Twenty-Ninth Division they were not going to let the Turks have the best of things, and they effectively discouraged any attempt to attack our lines.

The weather was now turning colder and bathing had been given up, but the sudden change which produced the terrible blizzard of November 28th to 30th was hardly expected. Luckily for the 2nd Hampshire they had gone into reserve on the 20th, their occupations now including the removal to the beach of all surplus trench stores, a step distinctly suggestive of evacuation. Being on rather higher ground they escaped the worst of the blizzard, though even so they suffered considerably from the combination of the torrents of rain, the piercing wind and the intense cold, and three officers and over 100 men had to be sent to hospital in three days. They now had to find parties to occupy the key points in the 86th Brigade's line, among them the block-house, ' Dublin Castle '. The 86th had suffered particularly severely, its trenches being sub-merged by the flood of icy-cold water which poured down from the higher slopes, filling every depression, drowning several men and carrying away arms, equipment and food. After the flood had subsided, the Hampshire found many corpses [3] in the trenches, men who had been drowned or frozen, with any amount of material to be salvaged. The battalions in front line were virtually out of action, but fortunately the Turks, if on higher ground, were worse clothed and worse fed than our men and suffered even more from exposure to the bitter cold. At one time 170 Hampshires were holding the 86th Brigade's entire front, some 1,200 yards long, but the Turks were incapable of attacking, and in moving about behind their wrecked trenches they gave good targets to the Hampshires' rifles and machine-guns, not to mention the bomb-throwing

---

[1] The Newfoundland Regiment replaced them.
[2] One, accurately directed by the Adjutant, pitched within a yard of one sniper's loophole from which there was no more firing.
[3] Some Turks as well as British, washed down from their lines.

catapult. But the main need was to get the mud out of the trenches, recover the arms and equipment submerged under it, repair the parapet and clear the communication trenches. A return to fine weather early in December was very welcome and not only cheered up the troops after the bitter cold and wet of the previous week but allowed much of the preliminary work before evacuation to be pushed on, while the arrival within five days of four drafts amounting in all to 270 restored the battalion to a good strength, more than balancing the 207 admissions to hospital of November, and provided additional labour for working parties.

The evacuation was a triumph of care, forethought and organization. Intermediate lines of defence were prepared between the front line and the beach, the routes to be taken by the different parties were most carefully selected and marked out: all trench stores and weapons that could be got off were taken down to the beach and embarked, and yet all the while no hint of what was in preparation had to be given to the Turks. The front line had therefore to appear to be fully manned, snipers and machine-gunners continued to harass the enemy and all evacuating was done under cover of darkness.

For the 2nd Hampshire the first big step was their occupation on December 13th of the 86th Brigade's whole firing line. Three companies took over, X remaining behind at Hill 10, a key point in the line to be held after the evacuation of the front line, as it provided an upper tier of trenches from which men could fire over the front line. Next day the 86th Brigade embarked.[1] Then on the 16th packs, officers' valises and everything removable were sent down to the beach. Meanwhile normal activities were pursued in the front line, damaged parapets were repaired and trenches drained, snipers continued to be active, and any patrols which ventured to approach our line were promptly received with rifle-fire and driven back. If any suspicions had been aroused by the assembly of more ships than usual at Imbros, they were assuaged by the appearance of our lines and the activity of our trench garrisons.[2] At 6.45 p.m. on December 18th five officers and over 300 men [3] moved out of line and quietly filed back to the beach, leaving 275 of all ranks behind. These carried on as usual, except that all sniping was stopped for three hours and then suddenly resumed, a move calculated to make the Turks think that a cessation of sniping was a trap to lure him into an unwise advance. Another 100 of all ranks left the front line at 5 a.m. (Dec. 19th) for Essex Ravine, 1000 yards back, where they spent the day in readiness to reinforce the second line, 30 men and two machine-guns taking post at Hill 10. This left under 150 men to hold the 1200 yards frontage. These made as much show as possible, moving about and firing from different points: it was an anxious time, had the Turks realized what was happening and attacked, the tiny parties still on shore would have stood little chance. But the precautions had been sufficient, the Turks, deceived perhaps by the activity of our snipers, evinced no suspicion of anything unusual being afoot, gradually the day wore uneventfully on, and with evening the Essex Ravine

---

[1] The 87th had been sent round in October to reinforce the three weak Divisions at Cape Helles.
[2] Cf. *Gallipoli*, II. 459.   [3] These included X Company from Hill 10.

party could embark, followed about 11.15 p.m. by battalion head-quarters, who had left the front at 7.45 p.m. Another 20 moved off at 10.15 p.m. picking up the Hill 10 party on their way. Forty picked men under Lt. Cuddon [1], one to every thirty yards, were left in the front line but moved at 1.30 a.m. (December 20th), having first lighted candles which had been prepared with fuses and detonators so as to let off fixed rifles to imitate snipers, even after the line had been evacuated. As this last party made its way towards the beach they could hear these shots and the Turks replying, while sounds of wiring suggested that the Turk was improving his defences in anticipation of attack. Not a shell was fired as these rear parties filed down the communication trenches, all being aboard by 3 a.m. The night had been wonderfully still, the sea was quite smooth and the moon if anything too bright, and the actual embarkation went off quite quietly and quickly, motor lighters taking the men out to the larger ships. The Turk had been magnificently and completely hood-winked, and a difficult task,[2] which even the optimistic had calculated must involve at least 25% of casualties, had been accomplished without loss of life and with less sacrifice of stores and guns than had been expected, thanks to careful planning and well-disciplined execution. German critics have themselves hailed it as a ' masterpiece ', something till then quite unprecedented.

Neither the 8th nor the 10th Hampshire had seen anything of the evacuation: the 10th having quitted the peninsula at the end of September and the 8th early in December.

The 10th, a mere remnant after their fight for Hill 60 and the wells, had spent nearly all September on beach duties. Lt. Dupree, the first wounded officer to return, had rejoined on August 23rd, Lt. Clement soon following, and the arrival on September 9th of 134 men from the 3rd Battalion, many of them old Regulars, including a sprinkling of transfers from the cavalry, was very welcome as it increased the number available for the numerous ' fatigues '. A few officers also joined, Major Colquhoun of the Leinsters assuming command on September 25th. Shell-fire caused a dozen casualties, including four killed, while Captain Hudson and over 80 men had to go to hospital, dysentery and other bowel complaints being prevalent, and when on September 30th, the battalion embarked for Mudros, ' other ranks ' barely mustered 300, very few recovered sick and wounded having rejoined. At Mudros it found drafts from the 3rd and 13th Battalions, amounting to 117, with whom was Lt. Nicholson of the 1st Battalion, who relieved Lt. Saunders of the Adjutant's duties he had been discharging in addition to his own labours as Quartermaster.

This move proved to be no ordinary relief to give the battalion a chance to get rested and refitted, though it needed both. The changed situation in the Balkans had led to the decision to dispatch British and French troops, among them the Tenth Division, to assist the hard-pressed Servians.

[1] 7th Queen's, he had joined in November, being given a regular commission in the Regiment in June 1916.
[2] The evacuation of the ' Anzac ' position had been equally successful.

The 10th Hampshire who left Gallipoli for this new venture were very different from the battalion which had embarked in July so full of hope and promise. To have made so fine a unit in so brief a time had been an achievement greatly to the credit both of instructors and instructed. It was one of the worst features of the tragedy of Gallipoli that so many units of that great company, the ' First Hundred Thousand ', should have been shattered and broken in an attempt to accomplish a task which, as can be seen now, was from the first fraught with the greatest difficulties. The 10th Hampshire had been put into the fight when the chances of success had all but vanished: they had made a fine effort and had shown themselves worthy members of the regiment, to whose record their effort had added no mean page, even if the phrase to be applied to it is that in which every stage of the Gallipoli campaign from April 25th onward may be summarized, ' too late '.[1]

The 8th Hampshire had had two days on the Kiretch Tepe Ridge, being persistently sniped from the slopes above them and finding the snipers hard to subdue. Their losses here included Lts. Bartlett and Latham and though the ' first reinforcements ' had rejoined, nearly 100 men had gone to hospital besides their 300 casualties. A spell at Lala Baba, in reserve, which allowed of bathing, was a welcome change and from there the battalion shifted to its new sector.

When the Fifty-Fourth Division reached ' Anzac ' its battalions were all much below establishment, several having suffered heavy casualties, while sickness had hit its unacclimatized men hard. Fortunately, if a renewal of our offensive was out of the question, the Turks also had suffered too heavily to be anxious to risk incurring more losses in trying to recover their lost ground, and the Fifty-Fourth found its new positions fairly well consolidated. Consequently the three months the 8th Hampshire spent in this sector passed uneventfully, though maintaining and improving their line kept them fully occupied. They were at first posted on Hill 60, where the smell of the unburied bodies between the lines was very offensive. There was some activity here, bombing and sniping, but the position remained unchanged. From the middle of September, being very weak, little over 400 strong, they were attached to the 161st (Essex) Brigade, in exchange for the stronger 7th Essex, as their own brigade, who were holding the Hill 60 sector, needed reinforcing and a fresh effort to secure the rest of that important tactical feature was under contemplation. The 161st Brigade's sector was further to the right, on the Southern side of the Kaiajik Dere and opposite Hill 100, another post which Turkish industry had converted into a veritable fortress. Few drafts appeared and a steady drain of sick to hospital left the brigade so weak that the mere maintenance of the line put a considerable strain on those present A man who got one full night's sleep a week could reckon himself lucky, and with rations monotonous, water hardly sufficient for washing and shaving, no real rest even when in reserve and constant hard work with many ' fatigues ', the troops were

---

[1] In Sir Ian Hamilton's dispatches, published on January 6th, 1916, Lt. Colonel Bewsher, Captain Hicks, R.S.M. Smith and C.S.M. Groves (killed in action) were ' mentioned '.

not well off. Most of the brigade's line was beyond bombing range of the enemy and despite occasional shelling, casualties were few, the 30 which the 8th recorded in September being mostly suffered at Hill 60 [1] early in the month, while in October and November, hardly any are recorded, though in November 2/Lts. Pavey and Reeve were wounded when out on patrol.

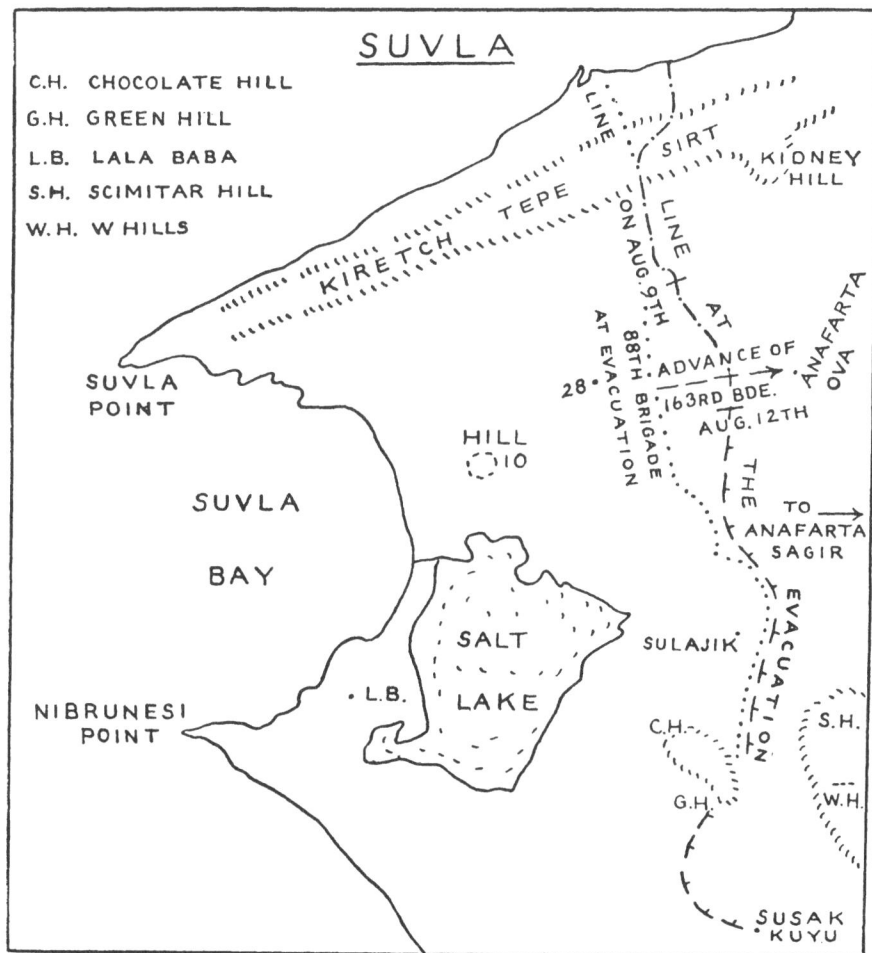

An issue of serge clothing in the middle of October was welcome, as the weather was getting colder and the khaki drill shirts and shorts, appropriate enough in August, were no longer adequate, but little occurred to vary the regular routine.

Colonel Rhodes had to go to hospital on September 10th, Captain Ellery taking command, but he also went sick in the middle of October when Captain

[1] 2/Lt. Fox, who remained at Hill 60 as bombing officer, did excellent work until wounded on October 21st and eventually received the M.C.

H   H.R. II.

Marsh took over. A dozen subalterns, mostly from the 8th Wiltshire, reported for duty and 40 men rejoined from hospital, Lt. Brannon also returning. Clashes with the enemy were infrequent: our snipers, though constantly on the look-out, got few chances, though Sergeant Halsey scored several successes, for which and for good work on patrol he was awarded the D.C.M., while a catapult bomb-thrower was occasionally used to good effect. Incidents of note were few, the enemy were unenterprising and, with evacuation becoming daily more probable, nothing was to be gained by an attack, which, even if it might improve the tactical situation, could not affect the strategical deadlock.

The great November blizzard was perhaps less felt at Anzac than at Suvla. Being high up in the hills the 161st Brigade escaped the flooding from which troops in the lower ground suffered so severely, and if the cold and the wet produced several cases of frost-bite the Division's sick rate did not leap up so alarmingly after it, as did that of some Divisions at Suvla.

The Fifty-Fourth Division had indeed received orders to move before the blizzard, which found the 8th Hampshire in reserve at ' Hatfield Park ', expecting orders to embark. These were cancelled and not until December 3rd did the battalion leave the peninsula, reaching Mudros next day and rejoining its own brigade when that in turn reached the islands. After ten days in camp it embarked on December 15th in H.M.S. *Victorious* for Alexandria, where it arrived on December 19th, going to Sidi Bishr camp. The infantry of the Division had left the peninsula nearly 60% below establishment, but its artillery and other units which had not accompanied it to Gallipoli were now to rejoin, and the whole Division was to be re-united and its infantry brought up to establishment.

Suvla and Anzac had been evacuated: would it be possible to repeat the feat at Cape Helles with the Turk and his German mentor on the look-out for its repetition. Now that the factor of surprise had been eliminated the difficulties would be greater, but there was also the consideration that after all the British might retain possession of Cape Helles. Naval reasons made it desirable, to assist the fleet to maintain a blockade of the Straits, while some believed that evacuation would be so difficult that retention would be the lesser evil. The Turk might well be in doubt, but evacuation here was clearly going to be even more difficult than getting away from Anzac and Suvla and it would require the best troops at General Birdwood's [1] disposal. The Divisions composing the Eighth Corps were much below establishment and in urgent need of relief, and once again it was to the Twenty-Ninth Division that those in command turned to carry out the second evacuation.[2]

Much to their surprise therefore the 2nd Hampshire had hardly landed at Imbros before they had to re-embark and on the evening of December 22nd they found themselves landing at W Beach. Only the later parties to embark were with battalion head-quarters, the first and larger detachment having gone

[1] He was now in command, Sir Charles Monro, who had succeeded Sir Ian Hamilton in October, having returned to France.
[2] The Thirteenth Division was also sent to Cape Helles.

on to Mudros and not rejoining till December 25th. The 86th Brigade, now commanded by Brigadier General Williams [1], had already joined the 87th, and the Division was holding the line between Gully Ravine and the Krithia Nullahs, ground only too familiar to the survivors of August 6th. A new firing line had been formed between the barricades in H.12 and H.12a and the front trenches were dry, if some of the communication trenches were nearly knee-deep in mud.

Their first few days at Cape Helles the 2nd Hampshire spent in reserve, fully occupied in clearing the communication trenches and improving the Eski Line, now the line to be held to cover the evacuation. This line they took over on December 31st, sending their machine-gunners and picked bombers up to reinforce the Essex in front line between the two branches of the Krithia Nullah, to the right of their old position. Major Spencer-Smith was still in command, with Captain Lord as Adjutant and Captain Jones (Y), Lts. Cuddon (W) and Darling (X) and 2/Lt. Bircham (Z), commanding companies, Lt. Smith, the Quartermaster, had gone to hospital in November, he had long out-stayed all the others present on April 25th, if some had rejoined.

These bombers had a lively time. The front line had been captured in a recent local attack by the Fifty-Second Division and, being much knocked about, wanted much consolidating, while three saps, really parts of Turkish communication trenches, were to be connected into a new firing line. This work had to be carried on within bombing range, the enemy being in places only ten yards off and bombing away vigorously, though our reply seemed much more effective; his guns also were active, though luckily their fire was not very accurate. It was the more important to push on with the new firing line in order to conceal from the Turk our approaching withdrawal, preparations for which were being steadily pushed forward. Altogether the battalion's last turn in the Cape Helles trenches was distinctly ' lively ' and it was lucky to escape with many fewer casualties than the volume and vigour of the enemy's bombing and bombarding might have caused. These included 2/Lt. Lambourne, mortally wounded on January 5th, the last of the many officers [2] the 2nd Hampshire had lost at Gallipoli.

It was really rather remarkable that the Turks, who can hardly have failed realize that we were likely to evacuate Cape Helles also, should not have tried to catch us in the act and drive us into the sea. Their abstention perhaps indicated a reluctance to risk the reception we should give. Their one tentative attempt was certainly not encouraging to them. Heavy shelling on January 7th seemed to indicate a coming attack, for which Turks could be seen to be collecting, but opposite the Hampshire they could not be induced to leave their trenches, and a rather feeble attempt against the Thirteenth Division on our left was speedily and effectively discouraged.

Next day (January 8th) was ' Z ' day for the final evacuation. The programme adopted at Suvla was repeated: parties withdrawing according to a carefully arranged schedule. Of the Hampshire Z Company from the Eski Line

---

[1] He commanded it until promoted in April 1917 to command the Thirtieth Division.
[2] In all 26, apart from 13 attached officers : the 8th Battalion lost ten and the 10th twelve.

led off directly it was dark, followed by X from the Redoubt Line. At 8 p.m. 160 of all ranks, including battalion headquarters, left the firing line for W Beach, leaving 80 men, mainly bombers, under Captain Jones to hold the firing line for another four hours. Just before this party was due to leave the Turks started bombing our sap-heads and our men had to return bomb for bomb. This they did so successfully that the Turks stopped bombing in time for this rear-guard to quit the firing line just before midnight as arranged.

The actual embarkation was more difficult than at Suvla: the sea was getting up, one lighter in which the Hampshire should have embarked was damaged and could not be used and it was touch and go whether the last parties could get away. However, once again good discipline, careful arrangements and a strict adherence to programme surmounted the difficulties, and eventually all were on board, the last Hampshire embarking in a destroyer, already uncomfortably crowded, which carried them to Imbros. Luckily the Turks had never realized what was happening, their shelling, though fairly heavy, was desultory and only when all were on board was our departure announced by a big ammunition dump blowing up, followed by other explosions which set fire to all the stores which had been left behind. Then their guns opened up in style and blazed away, merely wasting their ammunition on destroying stores which might have been very useful to them. As from Suvla and Anzac we had got away from Cape Helles almost without losing a man: once again a stupendous task had been accomplished with amazing success. As at Suvla the 2nd Hampshire had been selected for the most difficult and dangerous part of the operation and had carried it out most successfully.

'Wars are not won by evacuations', however successful, and highly satis-factory as was the M.E.F's safe extrication from the Gallipoli peninsula, the abandonment of the enterprise was an admission of failure. In that enterprise the regimental officers and men of the Twenty-Ninth Division had made a name for their Division which stands high in the records of our Army, and 'Landing at Helles' and 'Suvla' very properly appear among the ten battle-honours for 1914–1918 on the regiment's King's Colours. In the story of the Sixty-Seventh 'Landing at Helles' may well rank with 'Barrosa'.

CHAPTER X

THE TERRITORIALS IN INDIA—MESOPOTAMIA—1915

THE seven Hampshire Territorial battalions who had gone out to India all started with much the same experiences: they had to become acclimatized, to accommodate themselves to the very unfamiliar conditions of Indian service and to complete their training. Of this last the three Second Line units naturally were most in need, but the others had been somewhat disorganized by the changes of personnel caused by the reorganization into Foreign Service and Home Service units and they contained many recruits, even if many ex-Territorials and old Volunteers had rejoined. All were short of equipment, being issued with anything but the latest pattern of rifle, and the officers and senior N.C.O's had a task of much difficulty, especially as the subalterns were mainly newly commissioned. Some battalions were fortunate in going to Frontier stations like Quetta, to which the 2/4th were posted, and Rawal Pindi, whither the 1/4th moved from Poona in January, where they found themselves alongside some of the few Regular battalions remaining in India. Others were lucky to have detachments from those units attached to them as instructors [1] and benefitted enormously from their help, while nearly all battalions included some sprinkling of ex-Regulars of the regiment who had served in India and from whose knowledge of the country and its ways the uninitiated benefitted greatly. All soon settled down to the new conditions and duties,[2] but training was impeded by the need to make substantial detachments, the 1/6th sent several companies from Dinapore to Dum Dum and the 1/5th at Allahabad had to find detachments for duty at Benares and Cawnpore, while before long battalions were having to find men for the multifarious 'employments' for which skilled men were needed, and another and, in the end quite substantial, drain developed in the commissioning of many N.C.O's and men, some in the Indian Reserve of Officers, whose demands were continually increasing, others going home to take 'New Army' commissions. Many men quite suitable for commissions but lacking the qualifications for selection for the earliest formed 'Service' battalions, which could not at once absorb all those who came forward, had enlisted rather than wait about until further additions to the Army found them vacancies, and it was not long before many of these were wanted for bigger responsibilities than those of a Private or Lance Corporal. On the whole the health of the Territorials was better than might have been expected from as large a body of unacclimatized [3] and inexperienced men, many of them young, though some time elapsed before drafts from home were forthcoming to balance the wastage.

---

[1] The 2/5th at Secunderabad, for example, owed much to a most helpful party of the 1st Royal Sussex, the 2/7th to the 2nd North Staffordshire and the 2/4th at Quetta to the Somerset L. I.

[2] Captain Bacon's *Wanderings of a Temporary Warrior* gives a most interesting account of the experiences of the Territorials in India. It has been most helpful.

[3] At one time nearly 100 of the 2/4th were suffering from defective heart action, caused by hard work in an atmosphere as rarified as that of Quetta, but these men soon became fit again.

Before long another substantial drain developed, drafts being wanted for the British units in Mesopotamia, whither the Sixth Indian Division had been sent in October. In the major campaign into which the operations in that country were to develope, several Hampshire battalions saw some very varied active service, extending as far afield as Persia and the Trans-Caspian, while the 1/4th had the distinction of being the first Territorial battalion to be selected for service there.

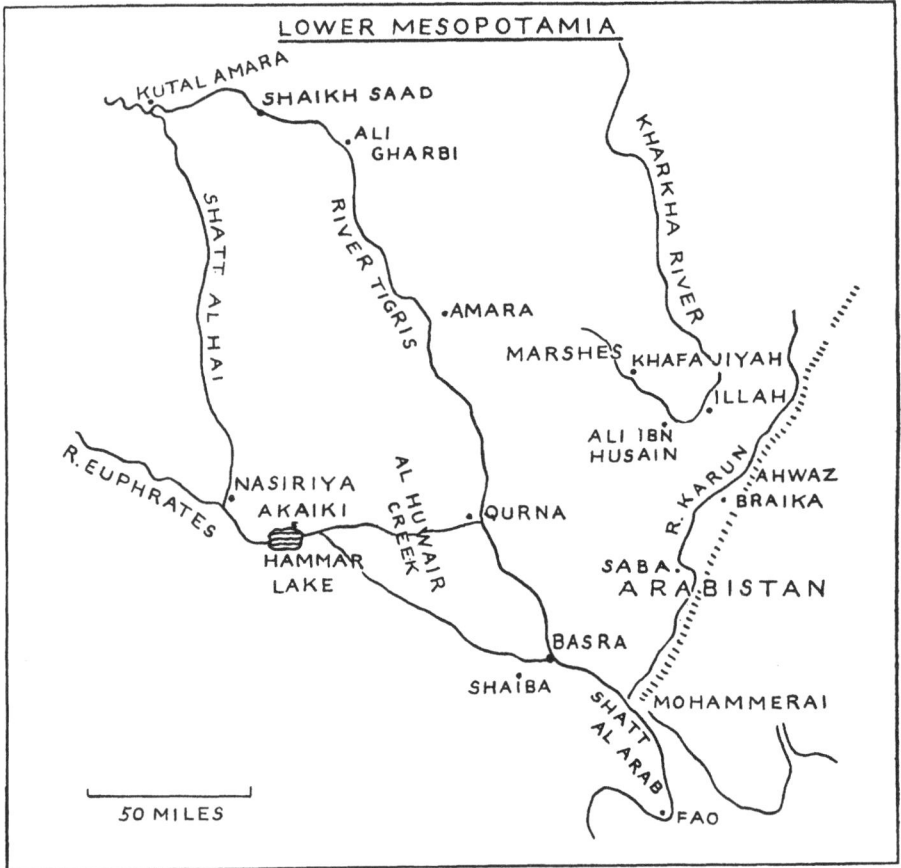

The campaigns in Mesopotamia provide an excellent example of the difficulties of confining a ' side-show ' to its original purpose, even if that has been purely defensive and indeed necessary to prevent an enemy from attacking some vulnerable point. Once Turkey had come into the war we could not ignore the danger of her developing, under German guidance, an attack from Mesopotamia upon the Persian oil-fields, all-important to our oil-burning Navy, or fomenting trouble on the inflammable North West Frontier, and it is hard to criticize the dispatch of a force to the Persian Gulf to secure the oil supplies.

But, once Basra and Qurna had been occupied, the local tactical and strategical advantages of a further advance, first to Amara, then to the junction of the Tigris and the Shatt al Hai at Kut, even to Baghdad, began to be urged. It could be argued that to halt at Qurna would allow the Turks to counter-attack, at their own time and convenience, that our adoption of a defensive attitude would discourage those Arabs who might otherwise be inclined to take our side. It was easier to lay down the principle that our object was merely to achieve security than to agree upon the exact method of attaining that end and no more. Anyhow in January another brigade had been ordered to reinforce the original Division, and hardly had it arrived before the development of trouble in Arabistan threatened the pipe-line from the Ahwaz oil-fields and made further reinforcements necessary, whereupon a 33rd Brigade was mobilized with the 1/4th Hampshire as its British battalion.

The 1/4th had had not quite two months with the Second Indian Division at Pindi, when they received on March 7th orders to mobilize at once. No mobilization scheme had been worked out, but with welcome help from the Adjutant and staff of the 2nd North Staffordshire all was soon in train. Machine-guns were received from the 114th Mahrattas at Jhelum, new rifles were issued, the necessary stores and equipment drawn: by 6 p.m. on March 9th mobilization could be reported as virtually complete, and next evening 31 officers and 790 other ranks entrained for Karachi.[1]

Four days took the battalion to Basra, where it was established in camp at Makina Masus, in a palm grove cut up into small islands by deep ditches. For the moment the ground was dry and conditions not unpleasant, the days being not unbearably hot and the nights cool. The duty here consisted mainly of finding many guards, picquets and night outposts, with occasional escorts to convoys going out to Shaiba, five miles West of Basra, where a substantial force was posted in readiness to meet an advance down the Euphrates. This meant hard work, toiling through mud and water, but before long much of the intervening country became flooded and supplies had to be sent up in ' bellums '[2], the escort also travelling by water. One party engaged in this duty under 2/Lts. E. A. Burrell and Rutherford had a miniature naval battle, being attacked by Turks in bellums, but it soon drove the attackers off by rifle-fire, without suffering any casualties.

The first detachment more actively employed was one of 25 men under Lt. Forbes detailed to man the *Sulimi*, one of the steamers employed in the ' Euphrates Blockade ' and operating against the communications of the Turkish force which was concentrating on that river and evidently intending to attack. A machine-gun section under Sergeant Raynbird on board the *Shushan*, another of the flotilla, was also very active and had several encounters with the enemy.

---

[1] Lt. Colonel Bowker was in command, the other officers being Majors Footner and W. B. Stilwell, Captains Barton (Adjutant), Brandon, G. P. Burrell, Foster, Page-Roberts, Parsons, Reeks, Simmons and Spinney, Lts. Cooper, Forbes, Harris, Lester-Garland, Macrae, Naish, Osborne and J. G. Stilwell 2/Lts. Andrews, Bucknill, G. A. Burrell, H. A. Burrelll, Capes, Chitty, Cowan, Lacey, and Rutherford and Lt. and Qr. Mr. Buckingham with Captain Jones, R.A.M.C.

[2] Country sailing boats which might be as large as 75 tons.

In April the Turkish counter-attack developed and was effectively defeated in a hard-fought engagement at Shaiba (April 12th–14th). The Hampshire had no part in this, though held in readiness to reinforce, but they were busy after the battle in helping to get our wounded down from Shaiba and in guarding the numerous prisoners captured, while the *Shushan* took part in pursuing the enemy, capturing and destroying many mahailas [1] and other country sailing craft which formed their transport. Several hostile Arab villages were destroyed and an effective control of the water-way was established, while valuable information was acquired about its navigation. Lt. Forbes' party was away till the middle of May, the machine-gunners remaining on board the *Shushan* for another three weeks.[2]

With this attack defeated, General Nixon, now commanding in Mesopotamia, could resume the offensive and undertake operations in Arabistan against the forces menacing the pipe-line, and on April 25th the 4th Hampshire were ordered to embark for Ahwaz. Disembarking at Saba on the Karun river on the evening of April 27th, the battalion marched upstream to Braika, 16 miles below Ahwaz. It had now been transferred to the 30th Brigade under Major-General Melliss, which moved forward NW. on May 1st to Ali Ibn Husain on the old bed of the Kharkha river. The heat was now great, frequent dust storms were a great inconvenience, while occasional heavy rain slowed down the marching over the loose soil and impeded operations. Advancing again on May 6th, in hopes of bringing the enemy to action and assisting the operations General Nixon was now developing from Qurna, the troops reached the Kharkha at Illah next day. Here the river was 250 yards wide and in full flood,[3] and its passage was no easy matter, as the bridging material available was quite insufficient. It was effected, however, the Hampshire manning pontoons and rowing them across, and then, on May 13th, the main body moved forward NW., leaving the Hampshire and other troops to protect the crossing place, assist to construct a flying-bridge and cover the arrival of supplies. They were kept busy and with the heat increasing, supplies short—it was an unattractive country, bare where not swamp and marsh—the sick rate soon began rising. On May 15th half the battalion had a long and trying march escorting a convoy to Khafajiyah, 15 miles down the Kharkha, to which the main body had advanced, engaging and punishing the enemy very successfully. Various punitive operations were now undertaken against the local Arabs, the Hampshire providing an escort for the guns during the burning of one big village.

By May 17th the battalion was concentrated at Illah, whence it moved back on the 19th to Ahwaz, marching 18 miles in great heat, to embark there next day and regain Basra on May 21st. Some very fatiguing operations involving much hard work with little shelter and scanty rations without the satisfaction of a fight had sent 60 men to hospital. But they had achieved their object, most of the troops employed could now return to Basra and Qurna, and General

---

[1] Another type of country river craft.   [2] They had two casualties.
[3] Private Woods distinguished himself by a gallant effort to rescue two sepoys who were in danger of drowning.

Nixon could undertake the attack, generally known as ' Townshend's Regatta ' on the Turkish positions North of Qurna. In these, largely conducted by water, the troops advancing through the marshes in bellums, Lt. Macrae and 16 men of the Hampshire joined Sergeant Raynbird and the machine-gun section already aboard the *Shushan*, and Lt. Osborne and 30 men were on board the river steamer *P.7*, the battalion itself remaining at Basra. It was feeling the effects of its hard work in Arabistan and of the increasing heat, many more men going sick, while several died.

In the highly successful attack of May 31st the *Shushan* and another steamer were detailed to advance by the Al Huwain creek, which joins the Euphrates above Qurna, and to demonstrate against the enemy's right flank, but some ' friendly ' Arabs, who should have co-operated, did not prove too eager to fight, while difficulties over navigation prevented the steamers getting into really effective range. Still the attack diverted the attention of the Arabs who might otherwise have seriously impeded the main attack. This was completely successful, the Turkish advanced positions were captured with very few casualties and next morning's advance found the main position behind evacuated, the Turks having retired in disorder upstream. Thereupon the river flotilla started off in pursuit, half-a-dozen Hampshire in H.M.S. *Comet* [1] sharing in the amazing adventure which culminated in the unopposed occupation of Amara (June 4th) by some 40 men. This handful not only received the surrender of several hundreds of Turks, but disarmed them, put them on board boats for conveyance downstream and policed the town, discouraging looting by shooting down any Arabs seen making off with plunder. Early on June 4th the arrival of the leading party of the 16th Brigade made the situation secure.

The party on board the *P.7* had had less excitement, merely escorting captured Turks downstream to Basra. They made two journeys on this errand and one upstream to Amara to bring back more prisoners and sick, before rejoining the battalion on June 9th. By this time the climate and particularly the moist heat was making itself felt, sick in hospital were up to 180 by June 16th, half a dozen men had died, mainly from heat-stroke, and on June 17th 84 men were invalided to India. With others detailed for various employments, under 300 other ranks and 16 officers were available when on June 24th the battalion was detailed to join the force about to advance up the Euphrates to Nasiriya.

This advance was aimed at securing the greater part of the Basra vilayet (district) against another counter-attack down the Euphrates and at making an impression on the local Arabs. As a first step it was essential to secure the navigation of the channels leading into the Hammar Lake from Sukash Shuyukh where the main stream of the Euphrates divides into several branches. The most navigable, the Akaika channel, was known to be blocked by a dam just above the lake, but no other channel could be used by vessels of any draught and there was no alternative to forcing its passage.

For this expedition the 30th Brigade, still including the 4th Hampshire, had

[1] General Townshend himself was also on board.

been selected, two batteries, half the 48th Pioneers and other details being attached to it. The force was carried in a most miscellaneous flotilla, stern-wheelers like the *Shushan*, armed launches, tugs, rafts, mahailas and bellums. The larger vessels could not cross the shallow Hammar Lake and this reduced considerably the artillery support available.

Contrary to expectations, no opposition was offered at the dam, through which a passage, large enough for the stern-wheelers, was blasted, though such was the force of the water rushing through the narrow opening that large parties had to haul on hawsers to get the vessels through, 150 men on one hawser, and

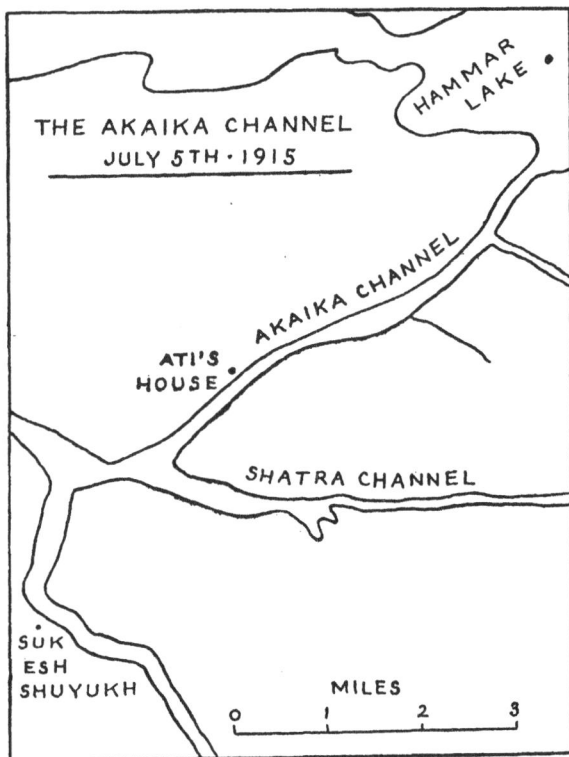

THE AKAIKA CHANNEL
JULY 5TH · 1915

HAMMAR LAKE

AKAIKA CHANNEL

ATI'S HOUSE

SHATRA CHANNEL

SUK ESH SHUYUKH

MILES
0   1   2   3

even then it was difficult enough. The *Blosse Lynch*, in which the 4th Hampshire had embarked, only got through on July 2nd after one failure, and not till July 4th was the whole flotilla through, so that an advance could be made.

The enemy were posted on both banks of the Akaika channel above a tower, known as Ati's House, on the left bank. They were hard to locate in the thick date-plantations, themselves no small obstacle, even when not intersected by ditches and channels. Landings were made on both banks on July 4th, but little progress was made and before daybreak (July 5th) the Hampshire, till then held in reserve, were landed on the right bank to reinforce the 2/7th Gurkhas, who were held up along the Shatra channel, which leaves the Akaika some way above Ati's House. After crossing this Shatra channel they were to advance towards the main stream of the Euphrates, while another column advanced on the left bank of the Akaika channel. The Shatra channel, however, was deep and broad, while the Arabs were well posted and too well concealed to give many targets and, like the Gurkhas, the Hampshire could not get across but had to hang on for several hours, taking advantage of any targets they got [1] until, the left bank advance having proved successful, some 48th Pioneers could be sent over to cross the Shatra some way to the left of the Hampshire. The Hampshire were then withdrawn from the firing line to follow them, and, crossing the creek in small boats, which took them two hours, worked along it to take in flank the stockade from behind which the enemy had been holding them up. On their advance it was evacuated, and by this time the troops beyond the Akaika had not only cleared the enemy out but had crossed the Euphrates and captured two guns, so that the flotilla could push on up the river.

This success had cost the British 100 casualties, the Hampshire losing Lt. Macrae, a pre-war subaltern, and three men killed and Lt. Lester-Garland and four men wounded, but with all units so much below establishment it was clear that reinforcements would be required if Nasiriya was to be taken. Accordingly at the Asani Bend, ten miles below that town, General Gorringe [2] decided to halt and await reinforcements before pushing on. Careful reconnaissances, including one in a ' masheuf ' (native boat) over the flooded area on the Turkish right, now showed that the enemy were strongly posted some way upstream, at the Majinina creek on the right bank and between the Atabiya and Maiyadiya creeks on the left, having several guns. During the next fortnight gradual advances up the right bank took us nearly to the Umm as Sabiyan creek, where on July 13th the Hampshire took over from the 24th Punjabis. They had moved upstream in a barge, which got stuck on the mud, attracting a heavy fire as soon as daylight revealed it to the Turks. It was set on fire, but the fire was promptly put out by a small guard who had been left on board. The battalion's trenches were also heavily shelled, but they had been well dug and its casualties only came to half-a-dozen. Meanwhile the 76th Punjabis had pushed forward another 1,200 yards and had their right on the river at Sixteen Palms. This line the Hampshire took over next evening and held for 24 hours, improving and consolidating it despite heavy fire and so intense a heat that 15 men collapsed with heat-stroke, one dying. From July 16th to 23rd the battalion was back in support trenches near Umm as Sabiyan and then moved up to Sixteen Palms in readiness to attack next day (July 24th), when it and the 2/7th Gurkhas were to assault the Majinina creek trenches as soon as the left bank attack came up level with their positions.

The artillery opened fire at 5 a.m. and half an hour later the left bank attack started and, going well, gradually captured the trenches below the Maiyadiya creek. Thereupon, at 7.8 a.m., General Melliss ordered the Hampshire and 2/7th Gurkhas forward, Nos. 2 and 4 forming the Hampshire's firing line under

[1] Private Elkins got the D.C.M. for returning to the steamer under heavy fire for ammunition.
[2] G.O.C. Twelfth Division to which the 30th Brigade belonged, who was in command.

Captain Burrell, with No. 1 (Major Stillwell) in support and the 2/7th Gurkhas on the left, No. 3 (Captain Parsons) being on board a barge carrying material for bridging the Majinina creek, which was believed to be unfordable.

Directly the advance started a heavy fire was opened, but the men pushed forward well and covered about 200 yards before halting to return the fire. High grass made it difficult to fire while lying down, so the troops pressed on and by 7.30 a.m. had reached the creek. Here they halted to let the barge be got into place, which was eventually accomplished about 8 a.m., when the survivors of No. 3, who had had 20 casualties among 35 men, landed on the far bank and took up position to cover the construction of the bridges. Before this Lt. Colonel Bowker had been hit and disabled, Major Stilwell taking over, and the battalion had suffered a grievous loss, the Adjutant, Captain Barton, being killed.

By this time the Gurkhas and Hampshires were all mixed up in the firing line, and as the creek had unexpectedly proved fordable the men waded across, formed under cover of the far bank and, dashing forward across a second and smaller creek, were quickly into the enemy's front trenches. Privates Hill, Verrall and Player were much to the fore in the assault, Hill and Player being first into the trenches, while Verrall fell just before reaching them. Lance Corporal Snow also used his machine-gun effectively throughout the attack, firing steadily and carefully and continuing in action although wounded till a shell disabled his gun.[1] A few Turks held out on the flanks of the position carried, but they were quickly dislodged by enfilade fire and went off at top speed, pursued by the Gurkhas, the Hampshire halting by order to consolidate the position captured and to cover a machine-gun battery now in position there. Five guns had been taken in these trenches with 100 prisoners and, with the left bank attack also a complete success, the Turks were soon in flight, Nasiriya being occupied without further opposition.

Reduced, mainly by sickness, to 150 of all ranks before the attack, the 4th Hampshire had really suffered very severely in losing Captains Barton and Simmons and nine men killed and Colonel Bowker, Captain Parsons, Lt. Osborne [2] and 34 men wounded, leaving Major Stilwell, Captain Burrell, Lt. Forbes, who took over as Adjutant, and 2/Lt. Bucknill as the only officers unhit. But the battalion's work was warmly praised by General Melliss and the D.S.O. awarded to Major Stilwell, the M.C's given to Captain Burrell, Lt. Forbes and 2/Lt. Bucknill and the four D.C.M's [3] were some indication of the approval of the authorities. Captain Barton, a most popular and efficient Adjutant, had done much for the battalion and was greatly missed.

Beyond Nasiriya there was no intention of advancing, the Turks had been well and truly beaten, nearly 1,000 being taken with 15 guns, and with another 2,000 casualties there was nothing much left of them, while the Arabs had been given reason to be respectful. Only a small force was required up the Euphrates, but though the rest of the 30th Brigade returned downstream, the mere handful

---

[1] All four received the D.C.M.   [2] He died of his wounds.
[3] Besides these Lt. Colonel Bowker and Lt. Osborne were mentioned in dispatches.

left of the 4th Hampshire remained at Nasiriya till the middle of August. They were encamped in a date plantation which gave some shelter but was rather airless; plenty of vegetables and fresh meat could be obtained and as little work was required, the men got some relief after their strenuous exertions. On July 26th they took part in a ceremonial parade when the Union Jack was hoisted over the Turkish barracks, after which the battalion was congratulated by General Melliss for its assault on the Turkish defences. The battalion was then

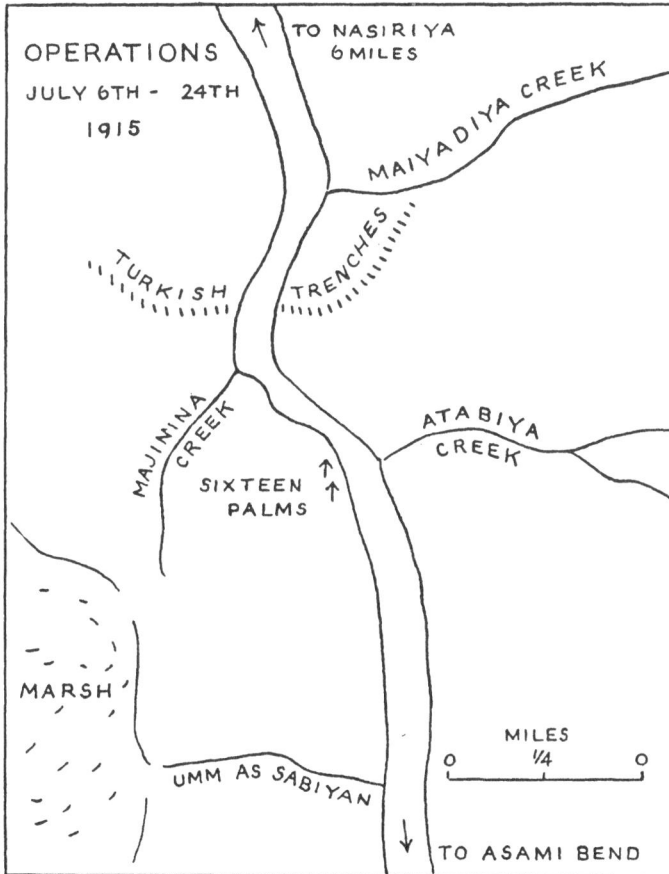

OPERATIONS
JULY 6TH - 24TH
1915

TO NASIRIYA
6 MILES

MAIYADIYA CREEK

TRENCHES

TURKISH

MAJININA CREEK

SIXTEEN
PALMS

ATABIYA
CREEK

MARSH

UMM AS SABIYAN

MILES
0   ¼   0

TO ASAMI BEND

sent back to Qurna, one large barge accommodating all present. The voyage downstream was adventurous, the steamer which was towing the barge lost the channel and grounded, remaining firmly fixed. However, another steamer which was aground nearby was eventually got off and took the battalion's barge in tow. Passing down the Akaika channel the steamer had to cross the bar leading to the Hammar Lake stern first, as steering bow first, was impossible. Lt. Forbes, knowing the lake, successfully piloted the steamer across its shallows, a task quite beyond her Arab captain, and on August 23rd Qurna was reached. Here the battalion transhipped to the steamer *Malamir*, which carried it up the bending Tigris to Amara, where eight officers and 167 men landed, another 25 having been left sick at Qurna. Captain Floyd of the Norfolk had joined and taken over the Adjutant's duties.

Too weak for active employment, the 4th Hampshire now began a spell of ' line of communication ' duties at Amara, which kept it out of both Townshend's success at Kut (September 28th) and his ill-fated advance on Baghdad, which took him and the Sixth Division to the Pyrrhic victory at Ctesiphon (November 22nd). Not till nearly the end of November did any Hampshire quit Amara, the headquarters wing being then ordered up to Kut. Before this the battalion's scanty numbers had been substantially replenished by the arrival on September 1st of 200 men from Hampshire Territorial battalions in India. With these were Lts. Needham (5th), Palmer (6th) and Padmore (1/7th), and 2/Lt. Vernon (2/7th); 2/Lt. Bucknill and 25 of the battalion's own men also rejoined, and the battalion could be reorganized as four companies and more machine-gunners and signallers trained. The new arrivals were a fine lot, their healthy appearance contrasting notably with that of those who had endured a summer in Mesopotamia, and with the increased numbers the camp and garrison duties were not too heavy. It was getting cooler now, at nights ' British warms ' and jerseys were being worn and it was possible to play football. Rations were good, the Tigris teemed with fish, eggs could be got and milk, if poor, was plentiful. The men's health was in consequence much improved.

The battalion had been inspected both by General Nixon, G.O.C. ' Force D ', and by General Townshend, under whose command it had been at Rawal Pindi, both being very complimentary about its achievements.

Another substantial reinforcement arrived at the end of October, when Captains Brandon and Reeks, Lt. E. A. Burrell and 2/Lts. Andrews and Lacy and 82 men rejoined from sick leave in India,[1] and Captain North, Lts. Butler, Elton and Jensen and 2/Lts. Fine and Wyles of the 2/4th joined with 237 men from that battalion. Thanks to this, when on November 24th headquarters and two companies were ordered to embark at once for Kut, they could produce 14 officers and 302 other ranks. Major Footner was in command and with him were the Adjutant, Captains Foster and Reeks and the M.O., Captain Jones. Major Stilwell remained in command of B and C Companies at Amara.

The battalions in India had meanwhile carried on their routine of duties without having anything very special to chronicle.[2] The ordinary routine gave most men a turn at hill stations during the ' hot weather ', the four-company organization was adopted and training went steadily on. The 2/4th had some lifelike training in Frontier warfare with the Quetta Division, now under General Grover, which was to stand them in good stead later on, in Palestine,

---

[1] Major Footner and Captain Foster rejoined a little later.

[2] Without the Part II Records it is impossible to check the many changes in personnel which occurred, or to note many other details they would have supplied. ' War Diaries ' were only begun when battalions were ordered on active service.

and most battalions were put through strenuous ' Kitchener tests ', though some suffered from being split up, having to make detachments for ' internal security ' purposes, particularly the 2/5th and 1/6th, while the 2/5th had to find a company for duty at Fort St. George at Madras. Numbers available for duty were considerably reduced by the drafts required for Mesopotamia, the 2/4th having to send off 250 of their best men to the 1/4th in October, but before the end of 1915 wastage was being replaced from the ' Third Line ' units which had been formed at home. Thus the 1/5th got a good draft in November and 50 men joined the 1/7th about the same time. Less wastage was caused by sickness than might have been expected, but skilled men were always being taken away for employments of different characters, from munition making to driving motors, and the claims did not decline. One change occurred among the C.O's, Lord Montagu becoming Director of Motor Transport in India in April 1915, whereon Major Gott took command of the 2/7th.

CHAPTER XI
FROM SECOND YPRES TO THE SOMME

THE formation of a British Third Army in the summer of 1915 had been made possible by the arrival of substantial reinforcements. By the end of January the original six Divisions had been doubled by the addition of the Indian Corps and of the Seventh, Eighth, Twenty-Seventh and Twenty-Eighth Divisions. Six Territorial Divisions and the Canadians had followed during the spring, allowing a third Division to be added to each Corps, and in May ' K 1 ' had begun to appear, though the Tenth Division's diversion to the Dardanelles and the replacement in ' K 2 ' of the Sixteenth Division by the Thirty-Seventh postponed the appearance in France of any Hampshire Service battalion till ' K 3 ' came out in September, and as even then within five weeks the Twenty-Sixth Division was transferred to Salonica, and with it the 12th Hampshire, the 1st Battalion remained as the regiment's sole representative on the Western Front until nearly the end of the year, as it was late in December before the Sixteenth and with it the 11th Hampshire appeared. Moreover, as the Fourth Division's new front lay outside the area of the ' Loos ' offensive and remained ' quiet ' throughout the winter and spring, even the 1st Battalion had only minor activities to record for nearly a year.

This new front[1] lay NE. of Amiens and stretched from the Ancre near Hamel Northward. The 1st Hampshire made the acquaintance of its extreme right after dark on July 29th, when they relieved the 62me Infanterie in trenches just North of Hamel. They had detrained at Doullens on July 24th, had been inspected next day by their new Army Commander, General Monro, and had then moved forward to Engelbelmer in readiness to take over. A small draft with three officers had just arrived from the 3rd Battalion and the battalion was fairly strong in officers. The relief was easily accomplished, despite some difficulties over language, without any interference from the enemy, and the battalion could take stock of its new surroundings. These were very different from the damp and breastworks of ' Plugstreet ' Wood and free from the unattractive features of the Salient. The front line was on a ridge, from which the ground sloped down forward towards the enemy's line and on the right to the Ancre, though it was overlooked from high ground across the river, near Thiepval. The trenches were cut deep into chalk and loam, which in fine weather required little revetting and had allowed deep and capacious dugouts to be constructed, in which bunks and even arm-chairs were available. From the fighting point of view the trenches left more to be desired, in places the parapet was hardly bullet-proof, evidently neither side here had been inclined to disturb their opponents into unnecessary activity, but this was soon put right. Good communication trenches permitted access to the front line by day, and to the battalion's satisfaction hot meals could be supplied even in that line, as the ' cookers ' could be safely brought far enough forward to allow of this. Battalion head-

[1] Cf. Sketch 24 (p. 181).

quarters were comfortably housed in Hamel, with good swimming within easy reach, and officers and men could congratulate themselves on a degree of comfort never encountered ' in the line ' anywhere else. If the French standards of cleanliness and sanitation were hardly satisfactory, the battalion put in a lot of work on its billets and did much to clean them and clear things up.

Apart from having better trenches and more amenities behind the line, the battalion found itself faced across a ' No Man's Land ' about 250 yards wide with an unobtrusive enemy, who might indulge in a little shelling on most days but did not do much sniping and rarely patrolled. The area had seen heavy fighting in 1914, during the ' Race for the Sea ', but since then neither side had attempted to alter the situation and both had very much left their opposite numbers alone. If the British were slightly more active than either allies or enemies, especially about patrolling, the serious shell shortage so acutely felt both by the B.E.F. and in the Mediterranean precluded major activities, though if the enemy started a bombardment our guns were usually prompt in retaliating and as effective as the limits of the ammunition supply allowed.

However, the 1st Hampshire were hardly idle. The 11th Brigade promptly started digging a new line along a railway embankment, 150 yards nearer the enemy, but the large working parties employed were not seriously impeded. Our patrols were active and the Hampshire's, which were quick to find their way about No Man's Land, showed considerable enterprise in locating the enemy and indicating targets for our guns' none too plentiful ammunition, while the battalion's snipers gradually established a definite ascendancy over their opposite numbers and made the most of the occasional targets offered them. The Ancre's banks were swampy and it took some time to discover the best line to follow in these marshes.[1] Several encounters occurred near a large ruined mill, which both sides were in the habit of visiting but which neither tried to occupy permanently. On August 28th 2/Lt. May and two men, one a gamekeeper in civil life, who had waded and swum through the marshes to avoid approaching the mill by the only track, reached the buildings and were examining them when they were attacked by a German patrol of several times their numbers. However, they promptly attacked the enemy, apparently inflicting some casualties, under cover of which they made good their escape.[2] Another patrol had captured two prisoners a few days earlier, while some unusually inquisitive Germans had ventured near enough to our line to be fired at and dispersed, so that the battalion could congratulate itself on the situation ' between the lines '.

Occasionally the German guns became active. On August 28th trench-mortars and howitzers bombarded one of our posts vigorously until the 37th Battery R.F.A. retaliated so effectively that they stopped firing, while our trench-mortars also helped to ' give the Germans back all we had got '. Two other ' hates ' caused several casualties, and between August 26th and September 2nd the battalion had six killed, including an excellent N.C.O., Sergeant

---

[1] 2/Lt. May, who had come home from Canada to serve, found the mosquitos of these marshes quite as active as the Canadian.
[2] Their enterprise was warmly praised by the Brigadier, B. General Brown.

Jackson, and 20 wounded. This was much above the average; if the August casualties reached 35, including nine killed and 2/Lt. Dale wounded, the next four months only saw nine men killed and 27 wounded; nearly all by artillery fire. In the colder winter months men did three nights in front line, followed by three in close support, so that the amount of night work was reduced and with it the sick-rate, but even so admissions to hospital caused a considerable drain, 240 in five months, while various ' employments ' absorbed a substantial number so that, though nearly 100 reinforcements arrived and about as many men returned from hospital, those available for duty tended to decline. Still the end of December found the battalion with just over 800 other ranks available. Among the officers who joined or re-joined were Majors Middleton [1] and Moore, who became Brigade M.G. officer, Captain Edsell and Lt. Westmorland, but Major Perkins was posted to the staff of the Mediterranean Expeditionary Force, Major Middleton replacing him as second in command. During most of the autumn Captains R. D. and K. A. Johnston, Smythe and Wyld were commanding the companies.

Outstanding incidents were few. Parties of ' New Army ' Divisions were attached for instruction, notably some from the Thirty-Sixth (Ulster) Division. During ' Loos ' our bombers were active and we frequently opened rapid fire as if we were going to attack. Something more might have been attempted had it seemed that the Germans had substantially weakened their trench garrisons to meet the Loos offensive, but their reply showed that this had not happened. Moreover their position was too strong to warrant any local attack without far more artillery support than was available. Occasional ' hates ', in which trench-mortars were largely used, did some damage to our trenches without inflicting much loss, and we retaliated effectively, making good use of rifle-grenades, while some excitement was caused in September by two deserters, Alsatians, coming over to give themselves up. The autumn was wet, heavy rain brought new problems of maintenance, especially in draining the trenches, which tended to dissolve into liquid mud and ' went like a lump of sugar in a cup of warm water ', so that much revetting was necessary and an issue of ' waders ' had to be made, while the fall of the leaves exposed things which the foliage had concealed, whereupon brushwood screens had to be put up. During October patrols from A and D Companies met and scattered German patrols very successfully and Lt. Hillis [2] twice penetrated well beyond the Mill and obtained useful information, while Lts. Goodford and May, Sergeants New and Squibb, Lance Corporals Dollery and Morris and Privates Levy, Simcock and Upson were also ' brought to notice ' for patrol activities. An advanced post had been established quite close to the Mill, so that that spot was much easier to approach and at night we usually had men posted in the gateway to wait for

[1] He had been relieved as Adjutant of the 3rd Battalion by Captain Aitchison, the latter having recovered from his wounds. In September all Captains of 15 years service and upward were promoted to Major, the promotion extending to Captain Symes, who was still with the Egyptian Army, as was also Captain Mills. ' Pre-war ' subalterns, if not already Captains, had been promoted to temporary rank, as had several Gazetted since the outbreak of war.

[2] Transferred to a Service battalion of the Irish Rifles as Adjutant in December.

any inquisitive Germans. One misty morning in November gave the battalion a chance: the mist suddenly cleared, exposing to view some 20 Germans on the top of their parapet, and the good target thus offered before they realized their peril was not missed. If the very wet weather made life in the trenches most unpleasant, parcels with every variety of comforts and extra food were arriving regularly from home and were very welcome, and when out of the line men could reckon on being able to get cleaned and to be really very comfortable. Things were better than they had been at ' Plugstreet '.

Meanwhile another battalion of the regiment had reached France. The 12th had spent the summer at Sutton Veney, where its Division was completing its training despite considerable difficulties over equipment, a matter of ' first formed, first equipped '; if the reserve supplies had hardly sufficed for ' K 1 ', ' K 2 ' and ' K 3 ' fared progressively worse, and for many months they had to put up with makeshifts and improvisations, the R.A. being especially handicapped. Many changes, both in officers and other ranks occurred: several veterans who had done good service in helping to form the battalion and in inculcating in its ex-civilians the ideas and standards of disciplined soldiers could not meet the medical requirements for active service and had to be replaced, mainly from the 13th Battalion. Despite all its difficulties before going overseas the 12th had reached a good level all round, though it was a bare twelve months since its formation had been authorized.

Leaving Sutton Veney early on September 20th the 12th Hampshire [1] had an uneventful passage from Southampton to Havre, landing early on the 26th and entraining for Longeau, whence three marches took them to Gentelles near Amiens. On the way they were inspected by Sir Charles Monro, to whose Third Army their Division had been allotted, and again, just as they reached Gentelles, by their Corps commander, Lt. General H. F. M. Wilson,[2] G.O.C. Twelfth Corps. After ten days training and route-marching at Gentelles, the battalion moved to Cachy on October 8th to be initiated into trench warfare by the Twenty-Seventh Division,[3] head-quarters with C and D Companies being instructed by the 3rd/60th, A and B, under the second in command, Major Bazalgette, by the 2nd K.S.L.I. No casualties were suffered during this ' inoculation ', after which the battalion returned to Gentelles for further training, including a strenuous two days' tactical exercise (October 15th/16th) which tested fitness severely, the battalion's mere handful of stragglers testifying to its fitness. Just before this Lt. Colonel Majendie of the 60th had replaced Colonel Walker, who had done so much to make the battalion and train it on sound lines but, like other officers of his seniority, could hardly be expected to be physically equal to the exacting strain of trench-warfare, especially in winter, severe enough even for much younger men.

[1] 30 officers and 883 other ranks. Unfortunately the battalion's diary does not detail the officers and the destruction of the Part II Orders makes it impossible to give their names.

[2] Formerly G.O.C. Fourth Division.

[3] Then in line South of the Somme, the Third Army having taken over more line.

A move to Cardonette on October 21st brought no change in occupations and after a week the battalion moved on to Chipilly, for further instruction under the Fifth Division, in line just North of the Somme. Before it could go into the line its Division was selected for transfer to Salonica, and accordingly the 12th marched back to Beaucourt, where they spent a week, preparing for the move, which involved some re-equipment, the transport exchanging its horses for mules, and then, on November 11th, 29 officers and 845 men entrained at Longeau for Marseilles. There the battalion embarked in the S.S. *Canada* along with the 79th Brigade head-quarters, sailing for Alexandria on November 15th.

The 12th Battalion's departure for Salonica left the 1st as again the only Hampshires in France, but just before the end of 1915 the 11th arrived and doubled the regiment's representation. The Sixteenth Division's training had been much retarded, not till late in August could it leave Kilworth Camp for Aldershot and the final stages of its preparation. Eventually December found the Division reported as fit to go overseas, and on December 18th the 11th Hampshire, who had been quartered at Pirbright, crossed from Southampton to Havre, going on by train to Chocques, whence they marched to Noeux les Mines. Lt. Colonel Crockett now had Major G. H. Earle [1] as his second in command, Captain Berkeley as Adjutant and Lt. Davies as Quartermaster. Majors Palmer and Bell [2] and Captains Hazard [3] and Andrews commanded the companies, with Captains Stacke, Bland, Powell and Thyne under them and no less than 21 subalterns.

The 11th's first work was to erect huts for other units of the Division, with some road-making and boring wells, while though the Division did not go into the trenches till well into the New Year, parties of the 11th were sent up before that to assist the Forty-Seventh Division in wiring and entrenching.

Shortly before the end of 1915 Sir John French's final dispatch had been published, which 'mentioned' Captains Wyld and and Hume, 2/Lts. Dale, Goodford, Harding, May, Rodocanachi (3rd Battalion, attached O.B.L.I.), M.T. Smith, Stevens and Ward (attached M.G. School) C.Q.M.S. Wheeler and Sergeants Ley and Price, together with Lt. General Haking, Brigadier General Nicholson and Captain Garsia, all three on the staff. The 'New Year Honours' brought General Haking the K.C.B., Brigadier Generals Nicholson and de Winton the C.B. and C.M.G. respectively, Captains Garsia, Hume and Wyld and 2/Lts. Goodford, Harding and M. T. Smith the M.C., while Colour Sergeant Shearing, Sergeants Budden and Ley and Privates Eldridge and Harden were awarded the D.C.M.

The New Year, which saw the 11th Hampshire start their apprenticeship

---

[1] From the 3rd Battalion, which he had rejoined early in 1914 after serving in the Inniskilling Dragoons.

[2] A Winchester master and an O.T.C. officer.

[3] One of several former officers of the Volunteer battalions who had rejoined.

to war, brought little change to the 1st Battalion, but before the end of the first quarter of 1916 two more battalions of the regiment had reached France, the 2nd arriving from Egypt in March, in which month the 14th also came out, while the 15th followed in May, so that when 'the Somme' started on July 1st five Hampshire battalions were on the Western Front, a number never exceeded during the war.

The 1st Battalion continued on the Hamel front all January, but being 'out' on January 4th it escaped one heavy bombardment which almost obliterated the right company's usual trenches. These it had to re-dig when next in the line and in doing so dug out an East Lancashire private, who had survived under a pile of debris for six days and was not seriously damaged. Much attention was now being paid to instruction in bombing, and another feature of the period was the issue of 'tin hats', shrapnel-proof steel helmets, with which all ranks were soon provided. In an encounter on January 21st near the Mill in the Ancre marshes [1] the battalion had the misfortune to lose 2/Lt. Wilde, who had been very successful in patrolling, another of his party being reported as missing, though two others who were wounded succeeded in escaping, but several successes for the battalion's snipers afforded some compensation, while its patrols continued their activities with good results, one under 2/Lt. May [2] having a satisfactory brush near 'the Ravine' on January 23rd, using a rifle grenade most effectively. Several fresh subalterns were warmly welcomed, the battalion being so short of officers that 'duties' were becoming rather burdensome.

February 5th saw the battalion beginning its first long rest since reaching France. This was in billets at Beauval, far enough back to be merely reminded of the war by the sound of distant gunfire. After ten days here it moved to Lucheux, having to cover twelve miles in heavy rain. Here the billets were good and the people cordial, and the battalion could settle down to a programme of training, which was about equally impeded by bad weather, 'real winter' with much snow and very cold, and by the difficulty of finding ground not under cultivation which could be used for field exercises and for football and athletic sports. A move to Beaudicourt followed early in March, a month marked by a Brigade Assault at Arms and a Horse Show, the battalion winning the former and doing quite well in the Horse Show. Several drafts joined, with Captain Bonham Carter of the 3rd Battalion who had served in South Africa with the 1st Volunteer Service Company and had more recently seen more fighting in East Africa,[3] but Colonel Palk had to go to hospital, Major Middleton taking over command. Towards the end of March the Fourth Division went into the line again South of Arras [4] where the battalion was at first employed

[1] The Third Army's frontage had been reduced since the departure of the Twelfth Corps to Salonica but now extended Eastward across the Ancre to the Somme.

[2] He was awarded the M.C. in June, primarily for his good work on patrol.

[3] He was well over 40 but stood the strain better than some younger men.

[4] On the frontage recently taken over from the French, to set troops free to reinforce the defenders of Verdun.

on second-line trenches (A Company), road-mending (B and C) and wood-cutting and hurdle-making (D). This seemed to many hardly the best use for a fine fighting battalion, but labour for such work was scarce and the state of the roads a serious handicap to the development of offensive plans. Several officers now took the chance to visit the 2nd Battalion, recently arrived from Egypt and in billets nearby at Louvencourt. Then in the last week of April the battalion returned to the front line, this time East of Fonquevillers, where it found that heavy rain had turned the trenches into a mass of sticky yellow mud, while the enemy were inclined to be busy, using rifle-grenades and trench-mortars freely, to which our machine-guns replied, often very effectively. The rain had reduced some communication trenches to mere drains and the line needed a lot of work. Casualties were not numerous, barely a dozen, but the officers were very unlucky, Captain Westmorland was hit by a sniper on April 29th when taking ranges and in the same week three, Lt. V. C. Smith and 2/Lts. Sims and Swettenham, were wounded by shell-fire.

This spell in trenches was very short, the Division being ' out ' nearly all May, training. The Hampshire were constantly on the move, once or twice in great heat,[1] and sampled a great variety of places, Auteuil (May 3rd–6th), Longuevilliers (May 6th–14th), Yvrencheux (14th–21st), where the brigade rehearsed its part in the coming attack over ground similar to its intended objective, and finally Bertrancourt (May 23rd–June 10th), where the battalion was employed in digging assembly trenches. On May 18th Lt. Colonel Palk rejoined, Lt. Colonel Middleton transferring to the 2nd Battalion.

On June 11th the battalion left Bertrancourt for Beauval, had three days rest there and then moved to Beausant and Mailly, putting in some final work on the assembly trenches, mainly carried on at night, and practising the attack. From June 26th to 29th it was in front line NW. of Beaumont Hamel and then, after a very brief spell ' out ' for final preparations, moved up again on the evening of June 30th in readiness for the assault. It had been a little dis-couraging that, despite the deluge of shell to which the German lines had been subjected, the discharge of smoke on the Division's front, after four days' bombardment, aimed at drawing the German fire, had produced so vigorous a reply from machine-guns and artillery as to make it doubtful if, after all, the bombardment had been as effective as the higher authorities calculated.

Meanwhile the 11th Battalion had come in for some fairly lively times. The Loos sector, behind which their Division was concentrated, was far from ' quiet ', the Forty-Seventh Division, though much below establishment, was holding a long frontage and welcomed the 11th's assistance, C and D Companies under Major Earle going up on January 11th to relieve its Pioneers. This party had plenty of hard work and suffered several casualties, and on January 22nd the battalion undertook its first minor operation, a detachment under 2/Lt. Donni-thorne assisting to consolidate a new crater near the Double Crassier, SE. of

---

[1] On one march of 15 miles some men of other regiments died, but the Hampshire came through well, with the least number of men falling out in the brigade.

Loos. Directly our mine went up the Pioneers dashed forward and started work, though under heavy fire, redoubled when German flares went up and the men showed up clearly against the white chalk thrown up by the explosion. They stuck to their task, however, encouraged and directed effectively by 2/Lt. Donnithorne who, though wounded, refused to go back till all the other wounded had been succoured and the work had been done.[1]

The 11th's total casualties for January came to three killed and 44 wounded, including shell-shock cases, while their work was much commended by the Forty-Seventh Division, whose G.O.C., on the battalion being relieved on January 10th, warmly praised its steadiness under fire, its good discipline and its hard work.

Until the middle of March the battalion was ' out ', mainly working in quarries or under the Forest Control. An epidemic of measles sent many men and several subalterns to hospital, but the February casualties were little over 20, including 2/Lt. Tollemache wounded. A spell in March at Mazingarbe under the Fifteenth Division was chiefly notable for snow and generally bad weather, but good work was done and the line much improved.

Early in April the Sixteenth Division took over the Northern portion of the Loos salient and the 11th Hampshire reverted to its command. But under whatever Division they were the Pioneers were always busy, some in the front line, others on communication trenches and rear areas. One piece of work which earned special praise was the virtual reconstruction of Railway Alley, a communication trench running North of Loos to the front near Chalk Pit Wood. Casualties, though frequent, were never heavy, and some small drafts with several officers from the 13th Battalion filled up the gaps, caused more by sickness and various ' employments ' than in action. April 27th brought an intense bombardment of our Hulluch and Chalk Pit Wood sectors, followed up by the release of gas and an attack in some force. Several parties entered our lines only to be promptly counter-attacked and driven out, while the corpses visible in No Man's Land testified to the efficiency of our counter-bombardment and rifle and machine-gun fire, but repairing the badly damaged trenches gave the 11th strenuous work. A renewed gas-attack two days later caused heavy casualties, but this time the Germans never reached our trenches, while they suffered severely from their own weapon when a shift of wind carried the gas back over their lines. This gave the 11th more damage to repair under harassing machine-gun fire, while on the night of May 1st/2nd bombers who had forced an entrance into our lines gave a wiring-party under Captain Hazard the chance to help in driving them out, Captain Hazard's successful leading of his bombers and recovery of the lost ground earning him the M.C., the second awarded to the 11th.

The middle of May brought the battalion a shift, into the defences of Loos, from which detachments went forward to work in the front line. Outstanding incidents were few, though both sides did some raiding, but in this quarter no major operations were projected and we merely sought to keep our line intact

[1] He was awarded the battalion's first M.C.

and harass the enemy, so as to prevent him thinning his line. Casualties, seven killed and missing and 2/Lt. Pearce and 21 men wounded, were not heavy, considering how much was done and the enemy's increasing activity with rifle-grenades and aerial torpedoes.

June the 11th spent in the Loos salient. Thunderstorms and heavy rain produced much mud and impeded work and casualties were heavier than in May, Captain Wellsted, the first officer of the 11th to lose his life, being killed on June 29th when the Germans bombarded our lines and back areas vigorously, the Quartermaster, Lt. Davies, being slightly wounded. This may have been in retaliation for a successful raid two days previously by the 7th Leinster, following mine explosions at Harrison's and Hart's Craters near the Double Crassier. Consolidating the new craters gave the 11th plenty of work, and then, on June 30th, the First Division attacked near the Double Crassier to distract the enemy's attention from the opening of our offensive on the Somme, and the 11th stood to, ready to help consolidate any gains, while their machine-guns supported the attack, whose failure left the 11th with nothing to consolidate.

The 2nd Battalion meanwhile had reached Alexandria on January 13th and on landing was dispatched to Suez. Under 600 all told had left Gallipoli, but reinforcements amounting to over 450, including nearly 200 of the battalion's own convalescents, brought numbers up to establishment, so that companies could be re-formed with four platoons. Sixteen new officers appeared, among them Lt. Arnell, who had left the battalion in South Africa in 1910 as a Sergeant to join the Rhodesian Police and had recently seen active service in German South West Africa. At Suez much-needed refitting and re-equipping was possible, with some company training, and nearly 160 men were given instruction as 'grenadiers'. The last week of February saw the battalion employed on the Shaluffa defences across the Canal, but by then the threat of a Turkish attack in force on Egypt and the Canal had virtually vanished. If the Turks had held us at Gallipoli, the achievement had fairly crippled them and their heavy losses had left them incapable of developing their expected counter-offensive. If they managed to reinforce Mesopotamia and clinched their hold on the beleagured Kut, against Egypt they were impotent, and it was soon evident that the large force available there could be safely reduced, the Twenty-Ninth Division being among the first formations to be transferred to France, where German pressure on Verdun was making it urgent that the British Armies should take over more line to allow of the French troops thus set free reinforcing the hard pressed defence. March 15th found the 2nd Hampshire at sea again, Marseilles being reached on March 21st. Several attached officers had rejoined their own units, among them Captain Kingsley-Darling and Lt. Cowan. Major Spencer-Smith was still in command and Captain Lord Adjutant, Lt. Cornish was Machine-gun officer, Captain Cardy Transport officer, 2/Lt. Miller was officiating as Quartermaster and Captains Cuddon (W), Arnell (X), Jones (Y), and Field (Z) commanded the companies. R.S.M. Tyler and R.Q.M.S. Sumner were among the very few present at 'the landing' who had never been away from the battalion, others being Orderly Room Sergeant Thompson, Sergeant-Cook Holman, Sergeant-Shoemaker Crease, Sergeant-Drummer Holman, C.S.M's Bird and Salmon, C.Q.M.S. Penney and Sergeants Norris, Ghell and Woolford.

The Twenty-Ninth Division was now allotted to the Third Army, joining the Fourth Division in the Eighth Corps [1] under its old G.O.C., General Hunter-Weston, so that both Regular Hampshire battalions were close together, though by March 1916 'pre-wars' still with either battalion were but a handful, if many others who had enlisted since August 1914 had already served in both battalions. The 2nd Battalion's first quarters were at Vauchelles les Quesnoy, whence it moved early in April to Louvencourt. Much re-equipping was necessary, with instruction in gas-drill, a new feature to troops from Gallipoli, and other training. Leave to England was given as freely as possible and the battalion welcomed back the Quartermaster, in time to be present along with Major Spencer-Smith and the Adjutant at a dinner given by General Hunter-Weston on April 25th to the officers who had been at 'the landing'.

The 2nd Hampshire were in Divisional reserve at Mailly-Maillet from April 13th to 23rd and then took over the line opposite Beaumont-Hamel. The trenches were in bad condition after heavy rain, but things were generally 'quiet' and less rifle ammunition was expended than at Gallipoli, though opportunities of hampering and harassing the enemy with rifle and machine-gun fire were not neglected, several German working parties being dispersed.[2] while their 'minenwerfer' were successfully discouraged. An attempted raid under 2/Lt. Saunders on April 29th near Mary Redan found the enemy on the alert and lining their parapet in strength: the raiders nevertheless, using a Bangalore torpedo and finishing off the last two feet of the wire with hand-cutters, got within bombing range, but they could not force their way in and had to retire after throwing their bombs. An effort to cut them off was checked by our machine-guns and by Corporal Lark, who covered the retirement most effectively, while some Germans who started crawling forward as though to counter-attack were caught by Lewis gun fire and driven back. Our casualties were one man killed and two wounded, both of whom 2/Lt. Saunders brought in to our line, going back into No Man's Land for the second man. Two nights later a raid on one of our saps was beaten back, and when, after a sharp but brief bombardment, the Germans collected for another attempt, they were effectively dispersed by our fire, our casualties being only three killed and five wounded. Much useful information about the enemy's defences and the work in progress was obtained by our patrols and passed on to the artillery.

From May 3rd to 18th the battalion was out of the line and had ten days in Corps reserve before going back to the firing line at Mary Redan on May 18th. Lt. Colonel Middleton joined on the 21st and took command and a dozen officers

---

[1] Holding the frontage from the Ancre Northward.

[2] Thus on the night of April 25th enemy were heard hammering stakes into some ' dead ground near one of our sap heads, so a Lewis gun was taken forward to the end of our sap and the work came to a quick conclusion.

arrived, mainly from the 3rd Battalion, while drafts amounting to 120 filled up the ranks. Until May 28th the 2nd remained in front line, having a quiet time though our patrols were active; our snipers now scored several successes, reducing the German snipers almost to inactivity, while good work was done on communication trenches. From May 28th to June 6th the battalion was in Divisional support at Mailly-Maillet and then had a week at Louvencourt, practising the attack over ground marked out to resemble the trenches to be assaulted. Eight quiet days on its old front opposite Mary Redan followed, after which it went back to Louvencourt for final preparations. Seven officers and about 100 men joined during June and, with only 30 casualties, 40 officers [1] and 950 other ranks were available for the big attack, in which the 88th Brigade was to be in reserve.

As late-formed a Division as the Thirty-Ninth had naturally had to wait for weapons and equipment, and in consequence its training had been much retarded. The Division had not been brought together until October 1915 when it was assembled round Winchester, and even after that one infantry brigade had been reconstituted.[2] A move to Witley followed in November, and there the Division remained till ordered in February 1916 to mobilize. Shortly before this the infantry had fired their musketry course at Aldershot, having only just previously received Service rifles. Many changes had occurred among the personnel [3] and the 14th Hampshire who went overseas differed considerably from the original battalion. Lt. Colonel Hickie (Royal Fusiliers), who had taken over from Colonel Ramsbottom-Isherwood in January, was in command, with Major Furley as senior Major and Captain Finlay [4] as Adjutant.

Leaving Witley on March 5th, the battalion crossed that night from Southampton to Havre and went on up country by train to a concentration area round Blaringhen. Its Division had been allotted to the First Army and received its initiation to war under the 23rd Brigade in a sector which no Hampshires had yet visited, at Laventie, opposite the Aubers ridge.

The 14th Hampshire were unlucky in their first experience in the trenches, as all C Company's kit and rations was destroyed by a heavy bombardment and 2/Lt. Langdon was mortally wounded. After undergoing the usual introductory process the battalion was first put into the line on its own at Givenchy on April 14th, and for several months it did duty here or South of the La Bassée Canal at Cuinchy or further North at Festubert, going usually to Riez du Vinage or Annequin when 'out'. This part of the front was less unattractive in the spring and early summer than when autumn and winter rains reduced much of it to swamps, in which flooded trenches had to be replaced by breast-

[1] Captains Cuddon (W), Arnell (X), Jones (Y) and Massey (Z) were commanding the companies, none of which had less than six subalterns : orders had, however, been issued that only 25 officers were to take part in any attack.

[2] Eventually one brigade was left behind and replaced by four Territorial battalions already in France. The composition of the 116th Brigade was not changed.

[3] Here also the loss of the Part II Orders is much to be regretted. The diary does not detail the officers who went out with the battalion.

[4] Formerly of the Leinster.

works and isolated ' island ' posts.[1] Mining activity had left the drier ground at Givenchy a tangle of craters and was still going on, the 14th losing Lt. ~~G. L.~~ Y. L. Ellis and C.S.M. Graham in a mine explosion on May 28th. The battalion made its first raid at Cuinchy on June 7th, when a party under Lt. Ashmore, effectively covered by another under 2/Lt. Fairlie-Cunninghame, got into the German trenches and did some useful bombing, driving the trench garrison back some way and inflicting several casualties, only five of the 20 raiders being wounded. Before this Lts. Moxley, ~~Y. P.~~ Ellis and Ashmore had all carried out patrols with considerable success and several N.C.O.s and men were commended by the Brigadier [2] for good work on patrol and in wiring. Several drafts from the 13th and 16th [3] Battalions kept the ranks fairly full, though casualties were rather heavy for a ' quiet ' part of the front, the total up to June 30th coming to 24 killed and 42 wounded, including 2/Lt. F. C. H. Gilbert, killed in April on his first day in the trenches, apart from those suffered on June 30th, when the 12th and 13th Royal Sussex attacked the Boar's Head, a salient East of Richebourg St. Vaast, A Company of the Hampshire holding part of our original front, while the other three were in readiness to exploit success.

This attack was another of the diversionary operations undertaken to assist the opening of the ' Somme '. The attackers carried their first objective, but their losses were heavy and the attack provoked an immediate retaliation which prevented consolidation, let alone exploitation, and eventually drove the survivors of the assaulting battalions back to our lines, which meanwhile had been heavily bombarded, the 14th having early 50 casualties, including Lt. Allen and 2/Lt. Sangster wounded and eight men killed. Several men did good work in bringing in the wounded, Sergeants Byrne, Gibbons and Lee and Corporal Midlam making rescues in broad daylight.

The 15th Battalion reached France two months after the 14th. Like the Thirty-Ninth, the Forty-First Division had had to contend against many difficulties in training, and not till it was collected in the Aldershot area in October [4] 1915 and received short Lee Enfields, Mark III, with proper equipment for training signallers and other specialists, could very serious progress be made. In Major General Lawford, formerly a brigadier in the Seventh Division, the Forty-First was fortunate in its G.O.C.: he worked it hard but developed no small degree of efficiency, and after the Division was concentrated during February in Aldershot itself for final training, progress was rapid. Lt. Colonel Malone, who had taken command in September 1915, when Colonel O'Farrell went to the 16th Battalion, vacated command in February, being succeeded by

[1] Corporal King distinguished himself by crossing over in broad daylight to one of these islands ' to bandage two wounded men.

[2] Brigadier General M. L. Hornby.

[3] Formed in September 1915 from the reserves of the 14th and 15th, Lt. Colonel O'Farrell taking command : like the 13th it was a draft-finding unit, becoming part of the Training Reserve early in 1917.

[4] The battalion had spent most of 1915 at Portsmouth, moving first to Witley in Surrey and then into barracks at Aldershot.

Lt. Colonel Harvey, formerly of the O.B.L.I., but in April he also retired, being replaced by Lt. Colonel Cary-Bernard of the Wiltshire who had gone out with the B.E.F. in August 1914. A most competent and efficient commander, he did much to ' make ' the 15th, which was to earn a fine reputation under his command.

Before the end of April the Division[1] was ready for service overseas, and after an inspection by the King on April 26th departure was not long delayed, the 122nd Brigade crossing to Havre on May 1st. Its destination was the Hazebrouck area, the 15th Hampshire going first to Meteren. From May 10th to 27th parties were sent to the Ninth Division for their preliminary dose of trench warfare, one party which was attached to the 11th Royal Scots coming in for a violent bombardment. This was followed by a raid, some enemy entering our line to be promptly expelled without reaching their apparent objective, the shaft of one of our mines. The Hampshire party took its share in repulsing this attack, Captain Amery and 2/Lts. Afriat and Pearse being commended for their coolness and resource, and was lucky in escaping with under a dozen casualties.

After a short spell in reserve the brigade took over on May 30th trenches in ' Plugstreet Wood ' of which the 1st Hampshire had seen so much in the ' first winter '. Its line turned West at the NE. angle of the wood and in places had been pushed slightly forward since 1915. The Division promptly started to harass the enemy, using rifle-grenades fairly freely and being active in patrolling and small raids. Lts. Gates and Peterson, who were soon prominent in patrolling, had one narrow escape from capture but got back all right, and the battalion had the best of several minor encounters, notably on June 23rd when a patrol under Sergeant Learey met ten Germans close to the enemy's wire, knocked out several with bombs and brought in all its own wounded. The battalion's snipers and machine-gunners scored several successes, and then on June 30th the 15th tried its first raid; three parties under Lts. James and Gates and Sergeant Green leaving our trenches after the enemy's lines had been drenched with gas. One party got within bombing range and threw its bombs, apparently with good effect, but the others were hampered by our own gas and could not get in, and eventually the raiders had to return, having had eight casualties. Lt. Gates, after seeing his men back into our trenches, returned into No Man's Land with Corporal Murden and Private Parris to bring back Sergeant Green's body from close to the enemy's wire and, despite heavy machine-gun fire, recovered it.[2] The raid provoked violent retaliation and the day's casualties came to nearly 40, including ten killed, but still it had apparently achieved its purpose in drawing the enemy's attention and making them apprehensive of an attack and the Divisional commander congratulated the battalion warmly on its spirited effort.

[1] The 15th was in the 122nd Brigade (B. General Towsey) along with the 12th E. Surrey, 16th R. W. Kent and 18th K. R. R. C.
[2] Lt. Gates received the M.C. and the two men the M.M.

CHAPTER XII

SALONICA, 1915–1916

To the decision to abandon the Gallipoli enterprise the development of a new drain on the Allies' military resources had contributed appreciably: assistance had to be sent to Servia. The transfer to Salonica of the Tenth Division and nearly half the French contingent may not have materially affected the tactical situation at Gallipoli, but any chance of the substantial reinforcement necessary for a renewed effort to force the Straits was rendered most unlikely when a big effort was required to succour the junior partner in the alliance, who had done so well in beating off the first attacks of the Austrians in the autumn of 1914 but was now threatened with an attack in greater force, directed by Germans and combined with a flank attack in strength from Bulgaria.

The renewed offensive against Servia had been made possible by the Austro-German successes in Poland against Russia, which, together with our failure to achieve a real success at the Dardanelles, had decided Bulgaria to join the Central Powers. The Servians had been quite unable to resist the double attack, while the Bulgarian advance not only took them in flank and rear but interposed between them and the Allied troops who landed at Salonica early in October, too late, as it proved, to gain touch with them. Overwhelmed and outnumbered, the Servian armies were pressed Southward and Westward and driven to the desperate expedient of crossing the mountains of Albania and Montenegro in the hope of being taken off by Allied vessels should they reach the shores of the Adriatic. This object a substantial portion eventually achieved after desperate efforts and great sufferings, while the Allied advance from Salonica had distracted the Bulgarians sufficiently to prevent their cutting off the Southern wing of the retreating Servians. This work, however, fell mainly on the French, who were able to push three Divisions up the Vardar, where during November they had quite heavy fighting.

Into the tangled story of the Allied relations with Greece and Servia and of the projects and counter-projects for additional Allied action in the Mediterranean, a regimental chronicle need not plunge. Whatever the verdict on the political and strategical considerations which decided the British government to send troops to Salonica, they affected the Hampshire Regiment because not only was the 10th Hampshire transferred from Gallipoli to Macedonia but the four British Divisions sent from France to the new theatre of operations included the Twenty-Sixth and with it the 12th Hampshire. That Division, however, did not reach Macedonia till the Servians were nearing the Adriatic, while what with the trouble caused by the very doubtful Allied relations with Greece and delays over providing transport and equipment, the Tenth Division never reached the front until the French had been driven back down the Vardar. All it could do was to take over a line from the NW. corner of Lake Doiran to Kosturino, on the right of that of which the French were seeking to stand.

The 10th Hampshire had reached Mudros barely 300 strong, and even the reinforcements awaiting them there had not brought them within 50% of establishment, but on October 4th no less than 520 men appeared, mainly transfers from the Bedfordshire and the East Surrey. With them came ten subalterns, including Lt. Lowy left behind with the details when the 10th started for Gallipoli, and when, on October 5th, the battalion embarked again, sharing the H.T. *Clan Macgillivry* with the Royal Irish and the Connaught Rangers, it mustered 19 officers and 947 other ranks. Major Colquhoun had rejoined the Leinster but Captain Lyster of that regiment had replaced him.

The *Clan Macgillivry* was terribly overcrowded, carrying 2,000 men when intended for 1,200, but the voyage was soon over and the evening of October

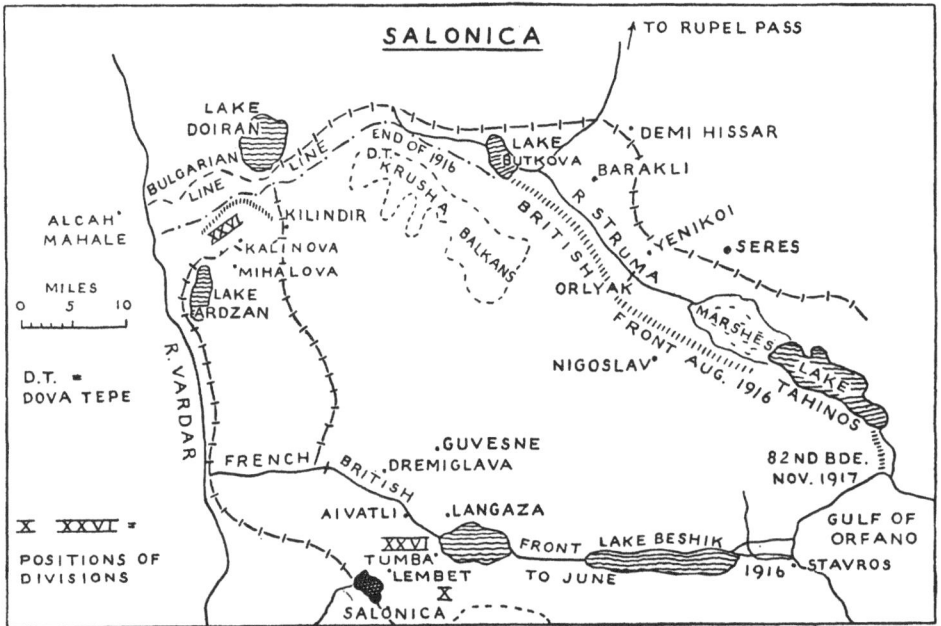

6th found the 10th encamping 2½ miles outside Salonica. Only a few tents were available: heavy rain had turned the clay soil into mud, and the constant fatigues impeded training and made it difficult for officers to get their companies and platoons into shape. Moreover as the Division's transport had been left in England it had to make shift with that of another Division: its own artillery had been likewise replaced by any brigades available in Egypt: great shortages of essential equipment existed and could not be quickly made good, and when at last the Division advanced it was far from ready for service, being still short of numbers and equipment. Meanwhile route marches were attempted, with a brigade field day and other instruction in open warfare, the bare and rocky hills, intersected by gullies and with steep gradients, providing useful preparation for what was actually in store. Bad weather did not make things easier and many men went sick, the ' effective strength ' on October 31st being down to 860, though 35 men under Lt. Scott had rejoined with the battalion transport on October 25th. Early in November Major Scully of the Royal Irish replaced Captain Lyster, while on November 14th 2/Lt. Grellier rejoined on recovery from his Sari Bair wounds. The next day brought orders to move and, that afternoon, 20 officers and 859 other ranks entrained for Doiran, where the battalion arrived early next morning, to encamp SE. of Doiran Town, across the Servian–Greek frontier and near enough to the lake to let the men wash in it.

Two days later the 10th moved forward by Causli to Tatarli, where they were in Divisional reserve, finding two companies to prepare a defensive line on Crete Simonet, a ridge North of Tatarli. They remained here until November 29th, during which time Major Beckett arrived from England and took over command, having recovered from the wounds he had received at Ypres. The weather had turned very cold, with much snow and rain, and the troops in front line, many of them none too well off for clothes and others still affected by their experiences at Gallipoli, went sick in such numbers that the Hampshire and Connaught Rangers had to be lent to the 30th Brigade to allow its two most depleted units to be brought back into reserve and given a chance to recover.

The battalion now found itself on the Dorsale des Cinq Arbres, a rocky ridge North of Kajarli, formerly occupied by the French, whose siting of the trenches excited much criticism. ' So badly sited originally that little could be made of them ' is one account.[1] The line was on a forward slope, exposed to the enemy on higher ground across a valley, and rocky ground made satisfactory defences hard to construct, especially as work had to be carried on in full view of the enemy and under fire. The wiring of the line was very imperfect, but no more wire was available, while not enough tools were to be had. Snow and frost increased the strain on officers and men, to provide hot food was almost impossible, everything had to be carried up to the line by hand over steep ground slippery with ice, and the men were very severely tried. On December 2nd 20 men went sick with frost-bite and, when it thawed, the trenches filled with slush, while foggy weather concealed the enemy's movements and meant that extra vigilance in patrolling was necessary. The Bulgarians, who were collecting in force opposite the Division, contented themselves at first with shelling our line, sometimes quite heavily, while their snipers tried to draw our fire and make our men disclose our positions, without much success, though our artillery replied, apparently to some good purpose, while advantage was taken of any targets the enemy might present; thus on the evening of December 4th parties were seen collecting in front of the Connaught Rangers' right, as if to attack, but a heavy and accurate fire soon discouraged this.[2]

[1] *The History of the Connaught Rangers* by Colonel H. F. N. Jourdain, which gives the best and fullest account of these operations and of the hardships endured.

[2] It was intended to evacuate the position on December 12th, and as the 10th and the Rangers had already had a week on end in the line it was proposed to relieve them on the 6th for two days but to bring them back for the evacuation. In view of the exertions involved in the journey to and fro, including a stiff climb on the return, Colonel Beckett and the Rangers' C.O. preferred to stick it out.

The 30th Brigade's line was none too satisfactory, its right formed a salient, being liable to be enfiladed. The key to the position was Rocky Peak, a detached hill SW. of Ormanli, held by two companies of the 31st Brigade, who continued the Division's line to the Hampshire's right, facing almost East. This Rocky Peak was attacked in force on December 6th, when the enemy entered our trenches but was driven out by a counter-attack. This attack was not pressed home on the 30th Brigade's front, though the line had been subjected to heavy shelling and rifle fire, but our rifles got targets in parties which pushed forward and tried to collect in the gullies and ravines in our front. Here dead ground gave them cover, but beyond this cover they failed to advance and during the night our patrols found plenty of evidence of the effectiveness of the 30th Brigade's reply.[1]

Early on December 7th the attack was resumed and in greater force. The shelling was very heavy and before long infantry were pressing forward also. The fog helped them considerably, and they made good use of the dead ground in which they were collecting and which prevented the British guns from giving the infantry really effective support, though our men were able to use their rifles to good effect and kept the enemy at bay. The Bulgarian guns proved very effective, gradually demolishing the ill-sited trenches of the Hampshire and of the Rangers and making their position untenable, while the loss of Rocky Peak, which this time was not retaken, allowed mountain guns and machine-guns to enfilade the position from the right. Up till then the Rangers had been inflicting very heavy casualties on the enemy, and if the Hampshire were rather less favoured by opportunities, they did not neglect what they got. An artillery officer in describing the action wrote with enthusiasm of the battalion's stubborn resistance. Some 7th R.D.F. had reinforced the Hampshire's right and were soon absorbed into the firing line, but the pressure steadily increased, the Bulgarians were in great force and their heavy losses did not deter their efforts to advance. Eventually about 2 p.m. the Hampshire's left company and, according to one account, the Rangers' right company also had to be withdrawn from their virtually demolished forward trenches to get some shelter behind the crest. This move was unfortunately mistaken by the next company of the Hampshire for the beginning of an ordered retirement, to which it conformed, going right back to Crete Simonet, where the 6th R.D.F. of the Divisional reserve were manning the rear position.[2] Here the company rallied but its retirement had left a gap in the line, which could not be re-established, and the Bulgarians pressed forward, coming to close quarters. A general retirement now became necessary and, covered by Colonel Beckett[3] and a party mainly from battalion head-quarters, it was effected in fairly good order, first to Crete Rivet, where the battalion took post on the right of the 7th R.D.F., and then

---

[1] The Connaught Rangers' *History* speaks of Bulgarian prisoners admitting to heavy losses on December 6th.

[2] What exactly happened is obscure : the accounts are most conflicting.

[3] The Brigadier's report emphasizes his good work in getting the bulk of the battalion back. Major Scully, 2/Lt. Grellier and Privates Flaxman and Payne were also brought to notice ' for good services '.

back to Crete Simonet. Meanwhile some of the left company had not gone back any further and along with the Rangers held on for some considerable time longer, until eventually they could not maintain their now quite isolated position. On the Crete Simonet line the Hampshire and the 6th and 7th R.D.F. made a successful stand, with the 31st and 29th Brigades on their right prolonging the line North of Tatarli towards Lake Doiran. On the left were

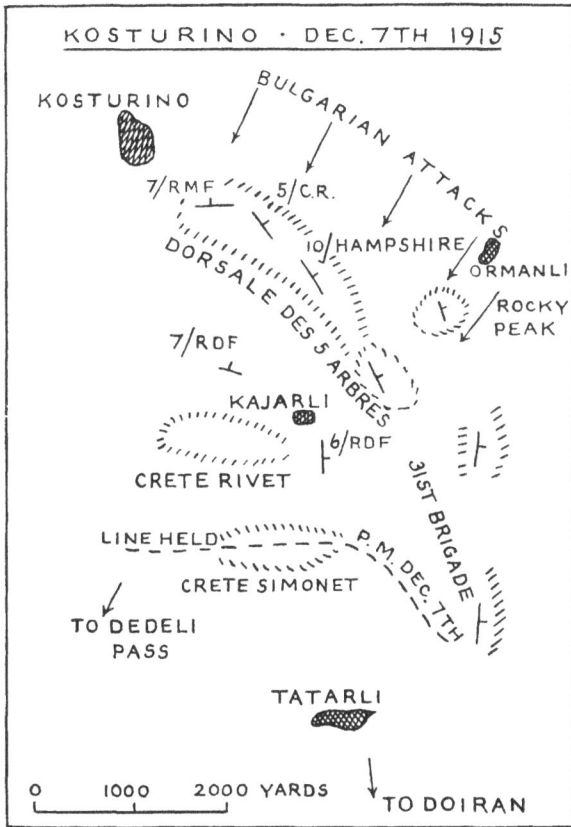

the Rangers, with whom were some 40 Hampshires,[1] and the 7th R.M.F. were covering the Dedeli Pass, with the French beyond them.

If the front line had been lost its capture had evidently cost the Bulgarians dear, as they showed no disposition to press our retreating troops: indeed by daybreak next morning they had not even advanced to Crete Rivet, which two companies of the 6th R.D.F. reoccupied and held for several hours, repulsing several advances, while the troops on Crete Simonet maintained their position until dark. They might have held on longer but that the enemy broke in between two battalions of the 31st Brigade further to the right, and to its

---

[1] From the left company.

retirement the 30th had to conform, though just as it started to go its rear-guard had the satisfaction of beating off a Bulgarian advance by rapid fire. The evening's retirement, which was unmolested, took the Division no further back than the Kara Bail ridge, which the 29th Brigade and a recently arrived brigade of the Twenty-Second Division were holding, the 10th Hampshire, still under the 30th Brigade, being placed on the left, towards the Dedeli Pass. All ranks were very tired, having had no food for two days, while most men had lost packs and great-coats, but Colonel Beckett had the battalion well in hand and an issue of rations helped to put a better complection on the situation, especially as the Bulgarians made no attempt to follow up their success or to try another attack, rather to the disappointment of the Tenth Division, the Hampshire being reported as in excellent spirits despite all their difficulties and the bad weather. It was intensely cold and the men's cheerfulness and behaviour deserved the greatest praise.

After two bitterly cold but quiet days, practically untroubled by the enemy, a fresh retirement was ordered on December 10th, the Hampshire being directed to Doiran station. One officer and 20 men from each battalion remained behind to conceal the move from the enemy, should he prove more inquisitive than of late. Before daybreak on December 11th the battalion started off. The move was unmolested, though much delayed by the roads being crowded with French troops and transport, who should have been further West, but before midday the Hampshire were South of Doiran station and once more under their own Brigadier. The losses could now be ascertained, killed and missing, mainly the latter, came to 183,[1] wounded to two officers [2] and 86 men, which with those already evacuated sick reduced officers to 16 and other ranks to 480.

As before the enemy had not pressed the retreat. The little rear parties had only seen a few scouts and had got safely away. It seemed as though the Bulgarians did not mean to cross the Greek frontier, behind which the Allies had now withdrawn, and though positions were taken up in readiness to deal with an advance, the 29th Brigade being West of Doiran station, the force was to be withdrawn to Salonica as soon as possible. The brigade had to spend two more cold and trying days on outpost, many were in rags, what clothes they had were soaked with rain and mist and all ranks were nearly exhausted. However, the 30th Brigade started the entraining, the 29th following on December 15th, when the 10th Hampshire marched back to Kilindir, to entrain there, and reached Salonica next morning.

Despite the failure to assist the Servians the Allies had no intention of quitting Macedonia, if they were content to adopt a defensive position covering Salonica. Of this the British took the Eastern portion, extending from just West of Salonica to Stavros on the Gulf of Orfano. Of their 50 miles of front two lakes, Langaza and Beshik, accounted for nearly half, and while three Divisions were allotted to the thirteen miles West of Lake Langaza, one was

---

[1] Of the missing 44 were known to have been wounded. A good many were later reported as prisoners of war.
[2] 2/Lts. Lowy and White.

considered enough for the eight between the lakes together with the four at their seaward end.   The Tenth Division was selected to hold these two sectors, the Twenty-Sixth being originally posted just West of Lake Langaza, from Tumba to Aivatli.

The Tenth Division had got back to Salonica much weakened, by sickness even more than by battle casualties, and in great need of refitting.   It could be given only ten days for this before having to take up its new line, the 29th

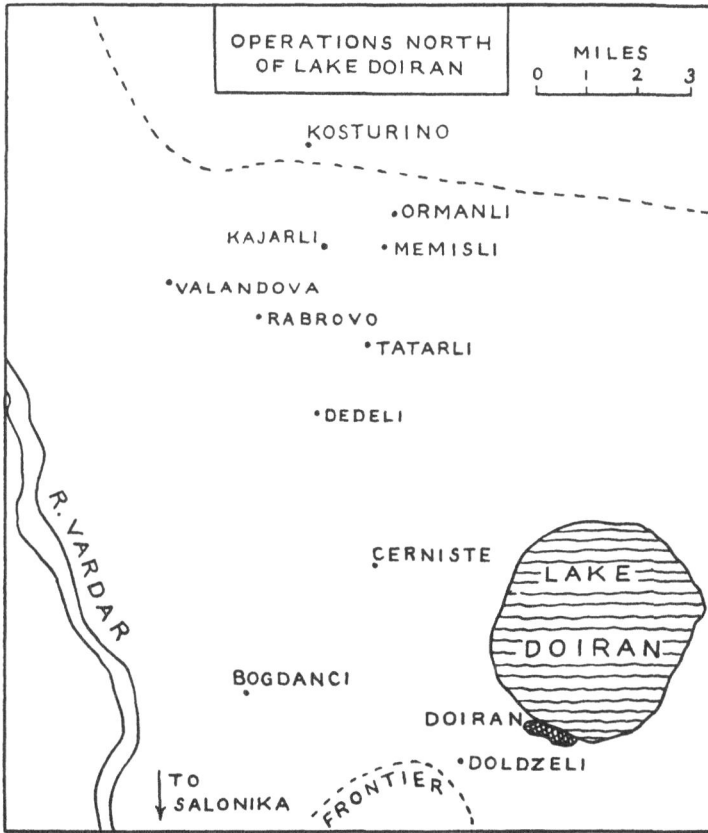

OPERATIONS NORTH
OF LAKE DOIRAN

MILES
0   1   2   3

KOSTURINO

•ORMANLI

KAJARLI•   •MEMISLI

•VALANDOVA

•RABROVO

•TATARLI

•DEDELI

ÇERNISTE   LAKE

DOIRAN

BOGDANCI

DOIRAN

•DOLDZELI

TO
SALONIKA   FRONTIER

R. VARDAR

Brigade being sent by sea to take over the portion between Lake Beshik and Stavros, where it landed on December 29th, the Hampshire having their left flank on the lake.   They were here just over a month, improving the defences as much as a shortage of tools and their scanty numbers would permit.   This last defect was to some extent remedied by the arrival of seven subalterns and 145 men on January 12th, while some stragglers re-appeared, and with returns from hospital, among them Lt. Dupree, other ranks reached 680 by the end of the month.   The weather was none too good, with snow and the piercing ' Vardar ' wind, which penetrated even goatskins, but the men worked well and before long the defences were far enough advanced to be held by reduced garrisons.

Accordingly, early in February the Division could be relieved by the Twenty-Seventh and brought back to Salonica, where it was placed in reserve on the Ortiach plateau, SE. of Salonica, and could settle down to a programme of training, varied by quarrying, road-making and preparing a second line of defence. This was to occupy it for the next four months, during which Captains Faith and Hicks rejoined. Captain Davies of the Royal Warwickshire had joined in February as second in command, Major Scully having transferred to the Connaught Rangers. Several other officers joined, including Captain Cowland, who had been in France with the 1st Battalion and at Gallipoli with the 2nd, while drafts brought its numbers well up above 700, though as the weather warmed up the climate began to take its toll of the unacclimatized. In April the battalion was converted to pack-transport, which caused many men to make the better acquaintance of the mule, while slouch hats were issued, giving the battalion something of the appearance of Australians. Some quite strenuous brigade manoeuvres during April included much picqueting of hills and other training in hill warfare.

The 12th Hampshire, who had reached Salonica on November 25th, after ten days at sea, were undergoing very similar experiences meanwhile, digging, wiring, road-making and training keeping them busy enough, with more training and route marching and less digging as the defences grew stronger. Incidents were few. The battalion was at Lembet Camp most of December, moved forward on the 20th to take over Langaza village as an advanced post and thereafter until June was either forward at Langaza or back in support or reserve in the Lembet valley. The work on the defences was heavy, the ground was rocky, and with hardly any explosives to assist the men's picks and shovels what they accomplished when so ill-equipped did them no little credit. The War Diary makes rather monotonous reading. The usual record runs ' Work on trenches —musketry—various fatigues ' with an occasional ' Battalion exercise in hills —picqueting in advance '.

Various changes occurred, mainly through invalidings, with some promotions and transfers. Lt. Colonel Majendie returned to the 60th in June to command the 4th Battalion, being replaced by Major Baker of the Royal Fusiliers, who soon returned to his own regiment, when Major Tweedie of the Gloucestershire took over but transferred to the 12th Lancashire Fusiliers in July, command then passing to Major Koebel of the North Staffordshire. Before this the battalion had shifted early in June to Dremiglava, NW. of Langaza, moving after a fortnight to another camp at Summerhill but without much change in its occupations. With the weather getting hotter sickness increased, though only in the Struma valley was malaria much in evidence.

The first half of 1916, eventful enough on other fronts, passed uneventfully at Salonica. If an Allied offensive in this quarter had ever been contemplated ' Verdun ' put an end to it. Most of the troops evacuated from Gallipoli had to be hurried from Egypt to France, one Division was rushed off to Mesopotamia to succour the beleaguered garrison of Kut, and though the expected Turkish offensive against the Suez Canal never developed Egypt could not be denuded of troops, and those at Salonica remained too few for a major offensive but uneconomically numerous when immobilized by merely facing an enemy who showed no inclination to attack. General Sarrail, the French Commander-in-Chief at Salonica, may have entertained ideas of an offensive; all that happened was that the French established an outpost line on the near side of the Greco-Servian frontier, two British brigades, the 7th Mounted and one of the Twenty-Second Division, being sent forward in April to assist in watching the enemy. The French then brought their main forces forward, taking post from the Vardar Eastward, South of Lake Doiran and into the Struma valley, but though the Twenty-Second Division moved forward (May) to assist them neither the Tenth nor Twenty-Sixth left the Salonica defences.

If it was not desirable to have so many troops idle in Macedonia, at best giving occupation only to Bulgarians who were unlikely to be used anywhere else, many considerations, tactical, administrative and strategical, were against an Allied offensive from Salonica. Still the French would never have agreed to withdraw the troops for use elsewhere or that the British should withdraw and leave the campaign to France to run, even if such a proposal would have been politically acceptable.

At the end of May, Germans and Bulgarians suddenly advanced into the Struma valley, quite unopposed by the Greeks, and thereby, to some extent, forced the hand of the British Commander-in-Chief, General Milne, who now used the Tenth Division to relieve the Twenty-Sixth between Tumba and Aivatli, the Twenty-Sixth moving West and forming an Army Reserve. General Sarrail now announced his intention to adopt an offensive, whatever the British did, and this led to General Milne's agreeing to take over the Allied line from the mouth of the Struma virtually to Lake Doiran. The Tenth Division accordingly advanced to the Struma, early in June, the Twenty-Sixth remaining in the old defence line until the end of July. It then took over the left of the Twelfth Corps' front from Kilindir to just North of Lake Ardzan, the whole British force having now come forward, though East of Lake Doiran French troops interposed between the Twelfth Corps and the Sixteenth in the Struma valley. Roumania seemed now on the point of joining the Allies, in which event the forces at Salonica would be undertaking offensive operations to assist their new ally.

When eventually, towards the end of August, Roumania did take up arms, the Allied offensive was delivered West of the Vardar, with the re-fitted Servian army having the hardest fighting: the British, both on the Doiran and Struma fronts, confined themselves to distracting the enemy by raids and local attacks, some quite considerable affairs, which involved no small aggregate of casualties besides inflicting heavy losses on the Bulgarians. Neither 10th nor 12th Hampshire, however, was required to undertake anything substantial.

When in June its long inactivity had ended, the Tenth Division had advanced from the Ortiach plateau towards the Struma, taking the Seres road. The weather was very hot and the heavily-laden men, still on winter-scale equipment, suffered severely, many falling out exhausted and one dying. On the Division relieving the French between Lakes Tahinos and Butkova (June 11th) the Hampshire were at first in reserve but then took over the Orlyak Bridge defences from the Connaught Rangers. Much work was required here, particularly in wiring, and with the river falling the banks had to be patrolled and posts established at the fords. Fruit, vegetables and eggs could be obtained and the countryside was still green and more attractive than Gallipoli, while the river gave good bathing and shelters of branches covered with waterproof sheets and blankets kept off the sun. Mosquitoes were rampant, so quinine was now a regular daily issue, but nevertheless admissions to hospital were increasing and

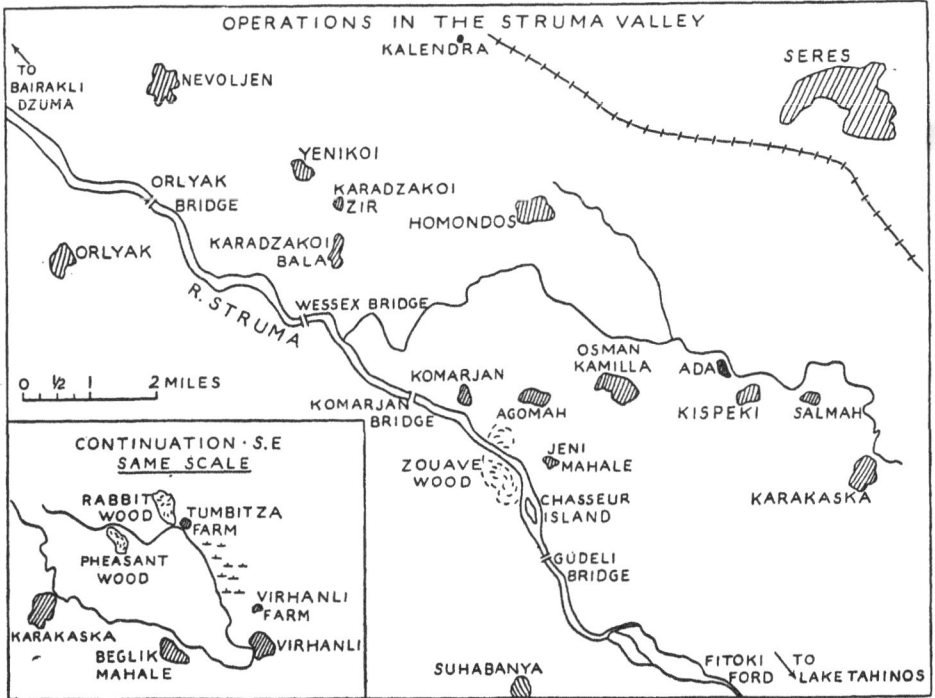

when, after four weeks in this position, the 10th moved back into reserve (July 19th), other ranks fit for duty were down to 440, a fall of over 100 men in three weeks. The battalion now moved back by Aivatli to Dremiglava, the whole Division having been withdrawn into reserve, much reduced in numbers by its brief sojourn in the malaria-infested Struma valley. Major Garsia, who had been attached to the Servian army, now joined, becoming second in command, while any remaining wheeled transport was exchanged for pack. With no drafts and returns from hospital far below admissions, the battalion could only produce one company of reasonable size, after finding all the specialists required,[1] and

[1] These were given on June 4th as bombers 9, Lewis gunners 32, scouts 16, signallers 16, transport 110.

though it had 604 other ranks nominally effective it could only parade 349 when inspected on August 9th by the Divisional Commander, Major General Longley. The other units of the brigade being no stronger, a 29th Composite Battalion was formed on August 21st, each battalion contributing one company, the Hampshire finding the head-quarters under Lt. Colonel Beckett with Major Garsia as second in command and Captain Nicholson as Adjutant, Major Davies commanding the Hampshire company [1] with Captain Clement as his second in command.

This battalion now moved forward again to the Struma [2] and on August 27th relieved the French between Komarjan Bridge and Zouave Wood, three miles downstream. An attack being expected, great vigilance was maintained and many patrols were sent out, one having a successful brush with the enemy near Komarjan, while much useful information about the enemy's dispositions was obtained. The Bulgarians did not attack, and it was the British who took the offensive, the Sixteenth Corps undertaking several raids and local attacks aimed at keeping its opposite numbers from reinforcing the front further West which was being more seriously attacked.

These actions gave the Hampshire their first real clash with the enemy since Kosturino, as the 29th Composite Battalion was to attack the villages of Komarjan and Jeni Mahale on September 15th. On the right two and a half companies under Major Garsia, crossing in rafts to Chasseur Island, made for Jeni Mahale and, well supported by the artillery, worked steadily forward despite the enemy's fire. Having got within 100 yards of the village they assaulted and carried it, the enemy offering a poor resistance and being quickly ousted, to open a heavy fire from Agomah, North of the village. A line was taken up just outside Jeni Mahale in readiness for a counter-attack; none was attempted and, after holding on for about an hour, the detachment withdrew quite unimpeded and in good order, bringing away all its few wounded.

Meanwhile the rest of the battalion under Lt. Colonel Beckett had been equally successful at Komarjan. Assisted by a good barrage from field guns and the brigade machine-gun company, the attackers pressed forward despite heavy fire from front and flanks and cleared the village, taking over 20 prisoners. Here also no counter-attack followed, though heavy fire was maintained on the captured position and the right flank had to be reinforced by Lewis guns from the left. At 7 p.m., as arranged, the troops began falling back and duly recrossed the river at Zouave Ford. The total casualties came to just over 20. less than the prisoners alone, Lt. Tanner, who was among the half-dozen killed, being the only Hampshire casualty.

The Composite Battalion was now in camp for several days, during which the Irish Rifles and Leinster companies were withdrawn, sufficient reinforcements having arrived to allow their battalions to provide independent wings, while on the arrival of seven officers and 112 men from the details at Dremiglava

---

[1] Details not required for the battalion remained at Dremiglava under Captain Faith, who, however, left in September to become Camp Commandant on the L of C, being promoted to Major.

[2] The Tenth Division was coming into line again.

the Hampshire formed a second company, under Captain Grellier, as did the Rangers also. Major Garsia now left the battalion to join the staff of the Twenty-Sixth Division.

To improve his position and to distract the enemy General Briggs [1] was now preparing a really substantial operation, aiming at securing possession of the villages of Karadzakoi Bala, Karadzakoi Zir and Yenikoi, opposite Orlyak. The first two were to be attacked by the 81st Brigade (Twenty-Seventh Division), after which the 30th was to tackle Yenikoi. The 29th Brigade was to cover the flanks, the Composite Battalion protecting the 81st Brigade's right rear by crossing at Wessex Bridge downstream of the main passage and working forward along a nullah which entered the Struma rather lower down.

The attack was delivered early on September 30th, a foggy night having helped to cover the passage and assembly. The bombardment started at 5.45 a.m., half an hour later the infantry advanced and despite stubborn opposition carried Karadzakoi Bala, taking nearly 100 prisoners. The Composite Battalion, which had already crossed the river and collected in a wood, then pushed forward along a sunken road and, having got touch with the 81st Brigade, began to consolidate a line facing SE. and leading back to the river. Beyond a little shelling the enemy did not interfere with the work and by the early afternoon a good line had been dug. Meanwhile Karadzakoi Zir had given more trouble and was only taken after a first effort had been checked. Violent counter-attacks followed, the Bulgarians displaying great determination, coming on again after their first repulse and being only beaten off with some difficulty and after suffering very heavily. The counter-attacks, which went on at intervals for three days, did not extend to the Composite Battalion's front, and it merely continued its consolidation despite the shelling and some rather wild and innocuous rifle fire. It was relieved on October 2nd and moved over to the left, to be in reserve to the 30th Brigade, who next day (October 3rd) attacked and with some difficulty mastered and held Yenikoi against determined counter-attacks. The Composite Battalion had merely found carrying parties and afterwards entrenched a line running back from Yenikoi to the Struma, again being shelled but escaping almost without casualties.

This line was not attacked. The Bulgarians, whose repeated attacks had been heavily punished,[2] had to leave us in possession of the captured villages along with Nevoljen, NW. of Yenikoi, and now retired on a wide front, going back nearly four miles to the foot of the hills. The action had certainly left them depressed and not disposed to try conclusions with the British again.

The Composite Battalion was next placed in line between Yenikoi and Karadzakoi Zir, where it reverted to the orders of its own brigade, and on October 10th on more details coming up from Dremiglava the Rangers and Hampshire resumed their independent formations, though only two companies,

[1] G.O.C. Sixteenth Corps.
[2] Apart from 350 prisoners the dead actually buried considerably exceeded the 1150 British casualties.

Y (Captain Grellier) and X (Captain Clement) could be formed.[1] For the next fortnight the 10th continued in the same line, finding a strong outpost to occupy Kalendra Wood across the Doiran–Constantinople railway, beyond which line the Bulgarians had been drawn back. With the enemy some way off, things had quietened down, apart from some shelling and occasional patrol encounters, and though on October 31st the Twenty-Eighth Division attacked Barakli Dzuma with great success,the 29th Brigade merely covered its right flank and the Hampshire were not seriously engaged, being in reserve until the attacking troops fell back, when the battalion occupied Kalendra Wood and found advanced posts along the railway. Altogether the battalion had had only half a dozen casualties before it was relieved on November 2nd. Both Colonel Beckett and the Adjutant had now to go to hospital, 2/Lt. Harfield taking over the latter's duties.

The lack of recruits from Ireland, to which compulsory service had not been extended, was leaving Irish units much below establishment and several battalions in the Tenth Division had to be amalgamated, whereupon the three Irish Regular battalions in the Twenty-Seventh Division were transferred to the Tenth, the 10th Hampshire in exchange being posted to the 82nd Brigade under Brigadier General Brooke, now in line between the Karadajakois and Komarjan, in which they found the 2nd Gloucestershire, the 2nd D.C.L.I. and the 10th Camerons.[2]

Both General Longley and Brigadier General Vandeleur were warm in their praise of all the 10th had done in the Tenth Division and expressed their regret at losing Lt. Colonel Beckett and his fine battalion. As it turned out the transfer meant that the 10th were to see the war out in Macedonia instead of in Palestine, whither the Tenth Division moved in 1917 in time for General Allenby's penetration of the Gaza–Beersheba line and other subsequent successes, though its Service battalions were broken up or transferred to France before the final victory at Megiddo.

Meanwhile the Allied attacks West of the Vardar were continuing, the Servians making good progress towards Monastir, and though autumn rains were swelling the Struma and its tributaries, so that the valley was getting waterlogged, an active attitude had still to be maintained on the Struma to keep the enemy occupied. The 10th Hampshire thus came in for the last operations attempted that autumn by the Sixteenth Corps, an effort to secure two large farms across the Virhanli stream, which enters Lake Tahinos from the NW. These were attacked on November 16th by the D.C.L.I., the Hampshire taking post in Pheasant Wood, just short of the objective, to cover their left. The D.C.L.I. found the stream unfordable and, after failing to force the passage of a foot-bridge, had to remain out all day, pinned to the ground by the enemy's fire, before darkness allowed them to regain Pheasant Wood, where the Hampshire had spent the day under a steady fire which only caused one casualty.

The battalion was then posted at Karakaska, SW. of Tumbitza Farm, where it

---

[1] Other ranks mustered 420. The rest of the details under Captain Cowland rejoined before the end of October.

[2] A battalion formed from Lovat's Scouts.

had a long line to hold and, being none too strong, might have been hard pressed by a vigorous attack. However, though the battalion was much on the alert no attack came: after the handling they had received at the Karadajakois and Barakli Dzuma, the Bulgars were not feeling aggressive and the weakly-held defences were not tested before, on November 20th, the 10th moved back to Jeni Mahale in reserve. Here they had fairly good quarters and for a time life was a peaceful discharge of routine. Lt. Colonel Beckett and a few convalescents had before this returned from hospital, and the battalion had been re-formed as four companies (November 15th), but it was still very weak, a big draft on its way out having been held up by an outbreak of German measles.

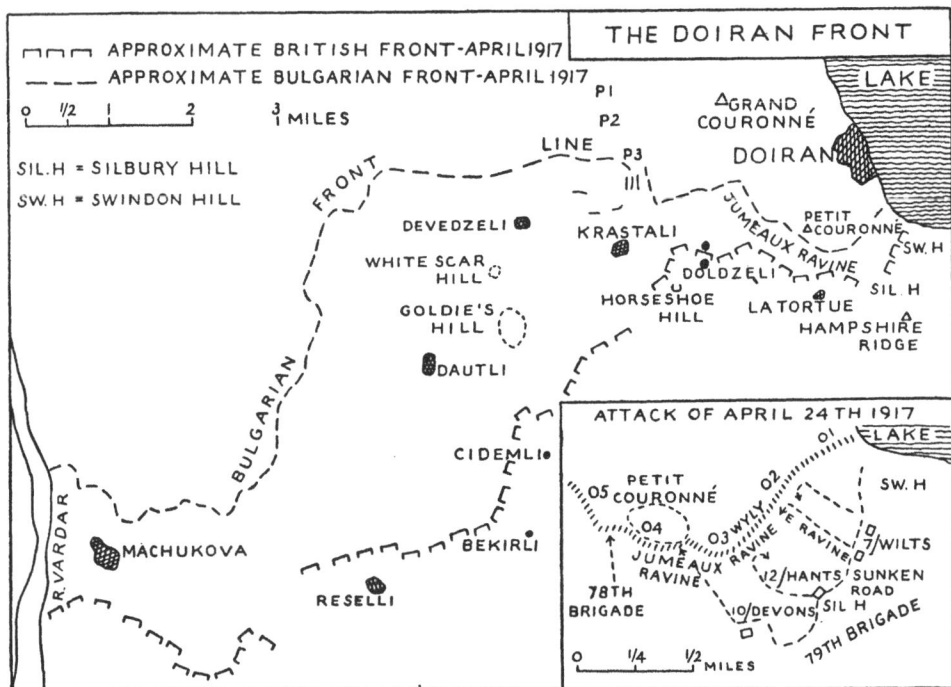

THE DOIRAN FRONT

December 4th brought another attempt upon Tumbitza and Virhanli Farms. This time the 10th Hampshire with a Greek battalion acting under Lt. Colonel Beckett's orders moved out towards Beglik Mahale, opposite Virhanli Farm, in readiness to advance against Virhanli Farm and Virhanli in co-operation with an attack from the North by two other battalions who were to cross the stream above Tumbitza Farm. The battalion remained here for two days, its patrols' efforts to reconnoitre Virhanli Farm being checked by heavy fire. It was shelled at intervals and cooking was impossible as the smoke attracted the enemy's gun-fire, but casualties were very few. Then as the main attack had had to be abandoned, the stream again proving unfordable and the passage of the bridge being checked, it went back to Beglik Mahale, where it held on until

December 10th, sending out several patrols, and then recrossed the Struma to Suhabanja to take over the watch between Gudeli Bridge and Fitoki Ford. Here it found quite comfortable quarters in well-built houses with fire-places, which were acceptable when it turned cold and snowed, and for the time could get some rest. All offensive activity had now been suspended and the main occupation was improving the defence line.

The 12th Hampshire's part of the front had seen less activity than had fallen to the 10th in the Struma valley, where the lie of the land had offered more scope for operations than on the Twenty-Sixth Division's frontage near Lake Doiran, West and SW. of which the Bulgarians were strongly entrenched on some forbidding-looking hills behind the deep and narrow Jumeaux Ravine. Of these the Petit Couronné lay South of Doiran, with the lofty Grand Couronné, due West of Doiran, NW. of it. South of the Jumeaux Ravine we were holding part of a lower ridge, running about SW. from the lake, the main features in it being Hampshire Ridge, La Tortue and Horseshoe Hill. Horseshoe Hill, South of the ruins of Dolzeli and S.E. of a rather larger village, Krastali, had been secured by the Twenty-Sixth Division in August, and thereafter a series of minor activities had gradually secured a line running SW. from Horseshoe Hill towards Reselli. A wide No Man's Land invited patrol activities and even raids, several villages in front of the main Bulgarian line being believed to be held as outposts.

The 12th Hampshire had come forward at the end of July to Mihalova, NE. of Lake Ardzan, where they spent the next three weeks in reserve, training and ' on fatigues '. The alarm of an attack then brought them up to support the forward battalions, and though this never developed they remained encamped in a ravine near Kalinova, finding large parties at night to assist the Devons and Wiltshire in entrenching. Their first turn in the front line began on September 2nd, when they relieved the Wiltshire at Cidemli. Things were not very active, except for artillery exchanges, which did little damage and only inflicted three casualties in eight days, two more being incurred by patrols, one fatal, the battalion's first loss in action. From September 10th to 17th the battalion was in support near Kalinova: ' digging and wiring as usual '. It was then back in front line for a week, during which patrols which penetrated to Goldie's Hill near Dautli found it very strongly held. Here one patrol ran into trouble; Lts. M. L. Pearce and W. C. Williams were badly hit and could not get back,[1] but Private Hinley, himself slightly wounded, brought in Corporal West, who had been more severely hit. In its next turn in front line, from October 2nd to 9th, the 12th's patrols did very useful work, Lt. Roberton and 2/Lts. Hale and Frampton bringing in excellent information. This bore fruit when, on the evening of October 11th, D Company raided Goldie's Hill with C in support and A and B as flank guards. D pushed forward behind an admirable barrage, but the enemy did not await the charge and bolted, though one prisoner was secured. On the enemy starting to shell the hill a retirement was duly

[1] They were never heard of again and must have died of wounds.

carried out with only one casualty. Another turn in front line, October 18th to 27th, led to another patrol encounter near Goldie's Hill, and then the Twenty-Second Division took over the sector to let the Twenty-Sixth relieve the French nearer the Lake. Here the 79th Brigade took over the line from the Lake Westward, the Hampshire and Wiltshire sharing the right trenches on Hampshire Ridge, the Devons and D.C.L.I. relieving each other on La Tortue on the left. Eight days ' in ' and eight ' out ' was the routine and little occurred to vary it. With the enemy's line only just across the Jumeaux Ravine, there was no scope for the patrolling which the wide No Man's Land further West had invited. The enemy usually did a little shelling each day, our guns replying, with occasional exchanges of rifle and machine-gun fire, but neither side was inclined to attack strong positions which were steadily being strengthened. Two drafts, one of 100, another of 170, arrived during November and did something to balance the wastage from sickness and other causes. Casualties were low and altogether half a dozen men were killed before the end of the year, though Lt. Reavell was killed in December when a reserve camp was shelled. Major Bazalgette had left in September to take up an appointment in England, Major Barry of the West Somerset Yeomanry replacing him. Major Bazalgette, an old officer of the 3rd Battalion, had done valuable work in helping to make the 12th.

CHAPTER XIII

MESOPOTAMIA, 1916

THE 1/4th Hampshire's head-quarters were being hurried to Kut al Amara because of the collapse of General Townshend's advance upon Baghdad. The great collection of stores and supplies at Kut was in some danger of attack by Turkish irregulars and Arabs, in whom the news of our retreat had excited hopes of plunder, and on reaching Kut on November 29th the Hampshire were promptly set to work to strengthen the defences. Apart from this immediate need, General Townshend had decided to stand at Kut, even at the cost of being invested there, and even half a battalion would be a useful addition to his much reduced British bayonets, the sheet anchor as they were to prove of the defence. Actually only one company of the 4th Hampshire was to share in that defence, for when General Nixon, who reached Kut from upstream on November 28th, tried to go on downstream, he was held up near Sheikh Saad by Arabs and Turks on the river banks and had to return to Kut. Starting off again on December 1st with as many sick and wounded as the available vessels could embark, he succeeded in forcing his way through, thanks to good work by his escort, which included D Company of the Hampshire under Captain Foster. Landing above Orah and working along the bank, keeping level with the gun-boats and the barges carrying the wounded, they thrust the enemy aside and cleared the way. The Arabs were taught to keep their distance by effective rifle fire and Sheikh Saad was safely reached. The company was then sent back upstream to escort another convoy and on its return downstream had a sharp fire-fight at Orah, without disembarking again, but merely firing from the steamer,[1] apparently with good effect as it got the convoy through. Trying again to make its way back to Kut, D found the enemy in too great force on both banks at Orah for a passage to be possible; it had therefore to retire to Ali Gharbi, 50 miles below Kut, where it entrenched a position covering Amara, ten miles further downstream.

The detachment left at Kut [2] now came under the 30th Brigade, which included a wing of the Queen's Own Royal West Kent and the 24th and 76th Punjabis,[3] with whom the 1/4th had co-operated at Nasiriya. This brigade and the 16th were detailed to hold the NW. section of the defences across the neck of the Kut peninsula, being alternatively in front line and in a ' Middle Line ' behind.

In the earlier stages of the siege the Turks pressed the garrison hard, presumably hoping to overcome its resistance before the relieving forces gathering downstream could intervene. They pressed hardest against a fort in the Eastern half of the front and against the 30th Brigade confined themselves almost entirely to fire attacks and to persistent sniping. To this the 30th

---

[1] The G.H.Q. staff joined in the shooting, for once getting a chance in action.
[2] Ten officers and 163 other ranks under Major Footner.
[3] After 1922 4/14th and 3/1st Punjab.

replied vigorously and effectively, there was no shortage of rifle ammunition, and if the Turks managed to push their trenches well forward, in places almost to within bombing range, it cost them not a little. Their efforts against the fort culminated on December 25th, when its garrison's determined resistance ultimately prevailed against particularly violent attacks, the Hampshire and Queen's Own, who worked as a provisional battalion under Major Nelson of the Queen's Own, using their rifles so effectively that on their front West of the main attack the Turkish efforts to advance were not allowed to develope.

The Turk was not the garrison's only enemy; the rising Tigris had also to be feared, and hard as the troops in reserve worked at the 'bunds' along the

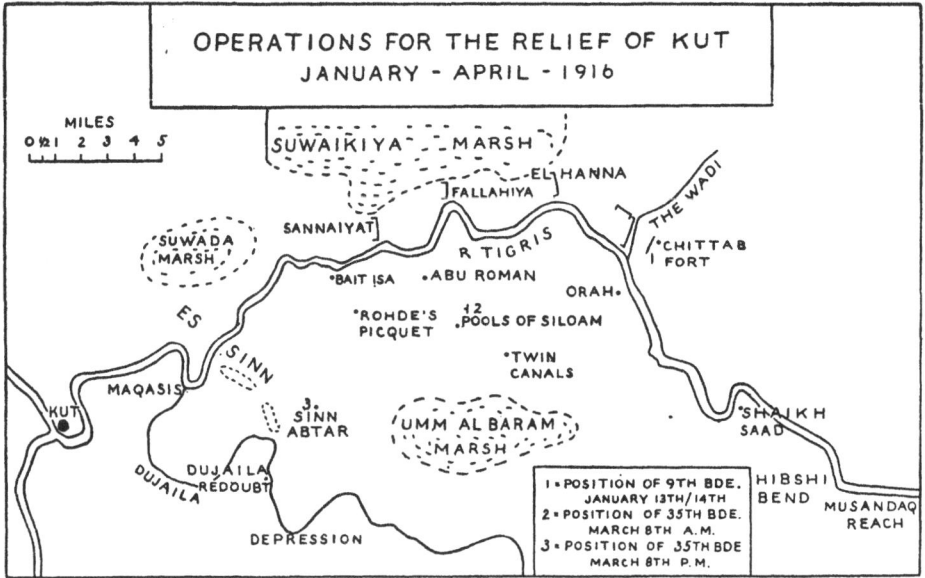

river in hopes of preventing the water breaking through, before the end of January much of our front line and immediate support trenches had been flooded, forcing the defenders to fall back to our Middle Line. As the communication trenches could not be used, they had to retire across the open under heavy fire and had several casualties, but from the Middle Line they retaliated most effectively, the Turks, themselves flooded out of their front line, having to expose themselves in the open. After this, instead of the Turks being only 50 yards away, nearly 1,000 yards separated the main lines, though the Turks occupied some sand-hills in the floods as advanced posts. The defenders did some long-range sniping, but the Turks, whose attacks had cost them very heavy losses, now abandoned any idea of capturing Kut by assault and devoted themselves to keeping the relievers at bay, leaving the garrison to be worn down by starvation.

After the New Year the all-important question was how long the food would last. At first full-scale rations were issued, partly to let the exhausted survivors of Ctesiphon recover condition. The first cut was in the tea ration, reduced by a half on January 20th, four days later half-rations of bread and meat were issued, with only half an ounce of sugar a day. The battery bullocks were the first animals sacrificed, but horse and mule meat soon made an appearance, the officers' chargers and the artillery horses being spared till after the relievers' failure in the Dujaila redoubt operations early in March, after which all ideas of the garrison's co-operating with the relievers had to be dropped. All sorts of expedients were tried to supplement the diminishing rations, fish were caught in the Tigris, weeds and grasses were used as vegetables, some proving poisonous, one officer even used a shot-gun to good effect against the flocks of starlings. Where even necessities were short, all ' comforts ' had long ago disappeared or were reserved for the hospitals.

Naturally on these scanty rations men got steadily weaker and less capable of any hard work, though guards had to be maintained and some work on the trenches could not be avoided. The sick-rate inevitably rose, dysentery affected almost everybody and deaths steadily increased, especially among the wounded. Slowly the siege dragged on, communication was maintained with the outer world by wireless, but the news of the relievers' progress was a succession of disappointments and the efforts to drop food from aeroplanes could do nothing to avert the exhaustion of the garrison and its supplies. When the end came on April 29th over 700 men had already succumbed and few of the remainder were fit for anything—let alone for the awful sufferings they were to undergo in captivity, for which Turkish incompetence and carelessness as well as sheer brutality and cruelty were responsible.

Of the 4th Hampshire in Kut all ten[1] officers survived the siege, of other ranks one return shows 154 ' believed to be prisoners of war ', nine had already died. Of these hardly 40[2] survived the trials of their two and a half years' captivity. Many perished in the terrible march to Asia Minor, which would have tried fit and fresh men severely enough but was a death sentence to men utterly enfeebled by the privations of the siege. Of those who survived to reach the prison camps of Asia Minor most succumbed to the hardships endured there, hard labour under brutal masters on a meagre diet. If the Turks may possibly be acquitted of the deliberate and calculated cruelty of the Japanese, those so unfortunate as to fall into Turkish hands fared little better than the prisoners of another generation.

When the whole situation in Mesopotamia was so radically altered for the worse by Townshend's enforced retreat to Kut, the two Indian Divisions in France were under orders for Mesopotamia, but the transfer was necessarily a lengthy affair, the leading units were not due at Basra till December, and even

[1] Major Footner, Captains Floyd, Reeks and Jones (R.A.M.C.), Lts. Forbes, Harris, Patmore, Lacy, Elton and Chitty. R.S.M. Leach, who was also among the prisoners of war, died in captivity after doing outstanding work for his fellow captives. Lt. (later Captain) Harris was awarded the M.C. for his courageous efforts to escape.

[2] 37 attended a dinner organized in their honour at Winchester n February 1919, and a few more were prevented from attending.

before Ctesiphon nearly another Division had been ordered from India to Meso-potamia, where the troops not engaged in the advance on Baghdad only came to two weak brigades.

The Turks had fortunately been too hard hit at Ctesiphon to press the retiring troops very effectively, and at first General Townshend's decision to stand at Kut seemed likely to be justified, the Turkish advance promised to be held up there till an adequate relieving force could be collected. But to collect it and even more to provide transport was not easy. The Divisions from France arrived piece-meal,[1] brigades were mixed up, several had to be changed in com-position, and when eventually an advance was begun it was very much a ' scratch ' force which went forward, with improvised formations with com-manders and troops who did not know each other, short of artillery and trans-port and shorter of medical staff and equipment.

As reinforcements reached Basra they were promptly sent on to Ali Gharbi, where the relieving force was concentrating. The bulk of the 1/4th meanwhile remained at Amara, busy with garrison duties, which fell heavily on a half battalion. Lt. Colonel Bowker returned from sick leave in India on December 11th and resumed command, and then on December 31st the two companies, 14 officers and 350 other ranks, left Amara by boat for Ali Gharbi, which they reached next day, rejoining D Company, who had been busy with outpost duties and fatigues and had been much worried by Arab snipers.

January 4th saw the Seventh (Meerut) Division start the advance, the 1/4th Hampshire following two days later. They had been allotted to an incomplete 9th Brigade, with half the 2nd Rajputs and the 107th Pioneers. The brigade was in reserve when, on January 7th, the Turks were found strongly entrenched astride the Tigris at Sheikh Saad and were only dislodged after heavy and costly fighting. The Hampshire had reached the Musandaq reach of the river late on January 6th, having covered over 28 miles in the day. Advancing again next morning to the Hibshi Bend, where a boat-bridge had been erected, they waited in reserve, with a tremendous battle raging in front; till, about 2 p.m., they were sent across the river to reinforce our right, which was being counter-attacked. They came under heavy shrapnel fire but were not actively engaged, as the attack had not developed into anything serious and they therefore escaped with only a few casualties, while after dark they were withdrawn to the bridge, to spend a miserable night in cold and wet, the ground being soaked. Besides the Turks who had counter-attacked our right, others were believed to be working Southward some way inland from the river to strike in behind us, so early next day (January 8th) the 9th Brigade was sent off down-stream to deal with the threat. It covered several miles over difficult ground cut up by ditches, but without encountering any enemy, and then returned to the bridge to take up a position on our right rear where more hostile movements were reported. Meanwhile, though held up on the left bank, we had carried the main position on the right, and this decided the Turks to clear out during the night of January 8th/9th and retire to the Wadi, six miles upstream. On find-

---

[1] One was still in France in the middle of December.

ing them gone the relievers advanced again, leaving the Hampshire to help clear up the battlefield, collect rifles and equipment, bury the dead and bring in any wounded who had been overlooked. That evening they moved forward to rejoin the main body, now preparing to attack the Wadi position.

This the Tigris Corps [1] could not attack until January 13th. With its transport so inadequate, supplies and ammunition could not be promptly replenished or satisfactory arrangements made for the numerous wounded, while the arrival of drafts and reinforcements was impeded and, in general, the difficulties of organization, already bad enough with the improvisations necessitated by what was believed to be the urgent need of reaching Kut, were hopelessly complicated. Unfortunately General Townshend, not having undertaken soon enough a careful survey of the food actually available in Kut, originally greatly underestimated the endurance of his garrison. Had it been known in January that Kut could hold out into April the hurry of the original hasty advance with all its disadvantages might have been avoided. Where improvisations and hurry were among the chief causes of failure, a systematically organized advance might well have succeeded.

The position behind the Wadi stretched about two miles inland and while the 28th Brigade, attacking frontally, sought to hold and distract the defence, three other brigades crossed the Wadi some way higher up to outflank the Turkish left. The 9th Brigade meanwhile was held in reserve near Sheikh Saad.

The attack, delivered early on Janauary 13th, started well enough; the outflanking force crossed the Wadi without meeting any opposition, though the nullah, 30 to 40 yards wide, with steep sandy banks 30 feet high, proved a more serious obstacle than was expected. However, when the three brigades wheeled round SW. and South, they soon came up against a strongly-held line thrown back almost at right angles to the Wadi and facing North, against which, despite determined efforts, little progress could be made without more artillery support. On this the 9th Brigade was ordered up to reinforce the 28th, which had driven in the Turkish outposts and advanced some way towards the Wadi before being held up. Unluckily the orders were slow to reach it, and the 9th only arrived at Chittab Fort, from which the 28th had started its attack, long after dark and was then used to throw out an outpost line behind which the 28th Brigade was withdrawn. Here the Hampshire spent another bitterly cold night, digging in under occasional bursts of heavy firing, mainly innocuous.

Moving forward before daybreak (January 14th) to renew the frontal attack, the Hampshire soon discovered that the Turkish trenches were empty: the defenders, threatened with being cut off by a renewal of the flank attack, had evacuated them and had gone back to El Hanna, at the lower end of that flankless defile between the river and the marshes [2] which formed an even more formidable position than those they had defended so tenaciously and whose capture had already cost the Tigris Corps over 6,000 casualties. These positions had been formidable enough, approached over bare and fairly level ground,

---

[1] The relieving force was known by this title.
[2] With so little land transport a move round the marshes was out of the question.

L   H.R. II.

devoid of cover, while dry water-courses had provided the defence with ready-made trenches, hard to locate even if the scanty British artillery had been assisted by the aeroplanes whose help was so conspicuously absent. But there was not even the chance of outflanking the El Hanna positions which the Wadi had offered: only a frontal attack could be made.

After clearing the Wadi battle-field and having a short rest, the 9th Brigade moved up on January 19th towards the El Hanna trenches. Persistent bad weather with much heavy rain had greatly increased the attackers' difficulties, a boat bridge had been swept away, breaking just as the Hampshire were about

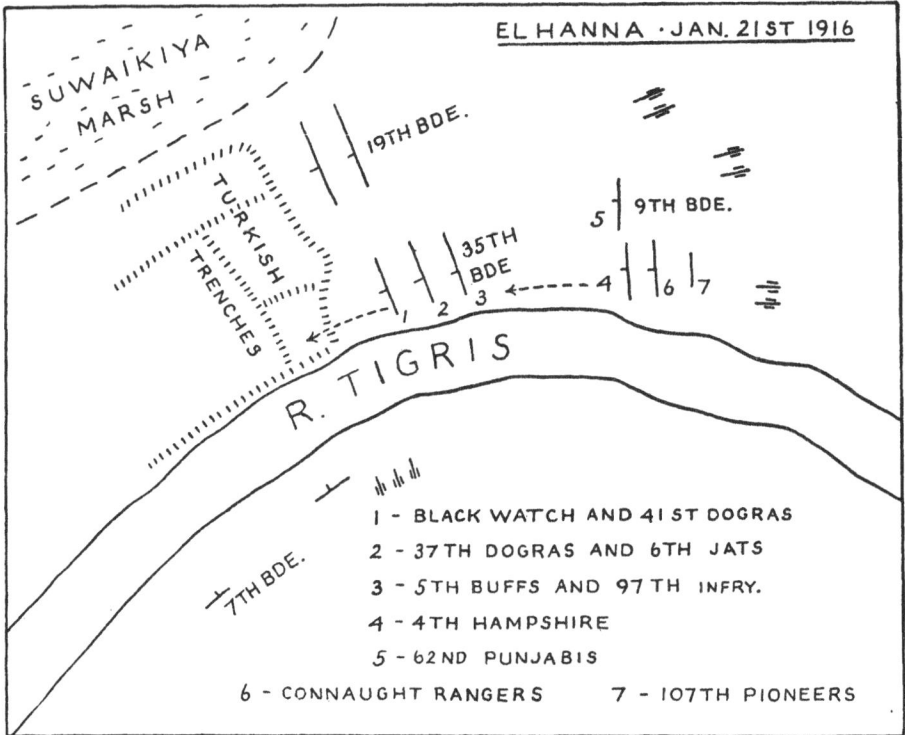

EL HANNA · JAN. 21ST 1916

1 - BLACK WATCH AND 41ST DOGRAS

2 - 37TH DOGRAS AND 6TH JATS

3 - 5TH BUFFS AND 97TH INFRY.

4 - 4TH HAMPSHIRE

5 - 62ND PUNJABIS

6 - CONNAUGHT RANGERS   7 - 107TH PIONEERS

to cross it, and communication between the banks was with difficulty maintained by ferry, all ranks had had to contend against cold and wet and the all-pervading mud, ankle-deep everywhere, and the sufferings of the sick and wounded had been much increased. However, despite the bad weather, by January 20th the British trenches were within 300 yards of the Turkish position, which had been as heavily bombarded as the limited artillery and ammunition allowed, and though Skeikh Saad and the Wadi had greatly reduced the striking power of the Tigris Corps there was no thought of suspending the attack. Townshend's need was believed to be too acute.

' Zero ' on January 21st was fixed for 6.30 a.m., but a mirage prevented the gunners from seeing their targets, so the attack had to be postponed till 7.45

a.m. by which time the Turks had fully realized what was coming. However, the 19th (right) and 35th (left) Brigades pushed gallantly forward, and ten minutes after the 35th Brigade had advanced, the 9th Brigade followed in its steps, with the 4th Hampshire on its left next the river: the Hampshire had been under fairly heavy long-range rifle fire even before ' Zero ' and had had a few men hit. The 9th Brigade pressed ahead resolutely, ' as steady and determined as if on parade ' one officer wrote, but directly the advance had begun rifles, machine-guns and field-guns had opened a heavy fire, and with the ground flat and affording no cover casualties quickly mounted up, the supports also soon being caught by the shells and suffering almost as severely from the fire as the leading brigades. Nevertheless on the 35th Brigade's left a fair number of the Black Watch effected a lodgement and besides them some Dogras also got in. Of the brigade's second and third lines some Jats entered the Turkish line and joined the Black Watch, but only a few, and those who had got in were soon hard pressed to maintain their hold.

Meanwhile the Hampshire were coming up, B Company (Lt. Needham) leading, C (Captain Page-Roberts), with which was Major Stilwell, following and D (Captain North) in support. The fire was heavy, and the battalion had a long stretch to cover even to gain our old front trench. Before reaching it Colonel Bowker, following with the third line, had been hit, but pushed on nevertheless, to be hit again and killed. The Adjutant, Captain Brandon, now joined Major Stilwell in the leading line to inform him that he was in command, but in advancing again from our old line Captain Brandon also was hit and killed and, with no support coming up and casualties heavy, the advance was held up short of the Turkish line. On the extreme left next the river, however, some men under Lts. Stilwell and Palmer managed to join the Black Watch in the Turkish trenches and lend a hand in the gallant struggle which they maintained for over an hour against heavy odds, though no more support reached them. Eventually, with their left attacked down a communication trench and their right from the uncaptured line beyond their lodgement, they were overwhelmed, only a few survivors regaining our lines. Lts. Stillwell and Palmer, wounded and disabled, were left behind. Meanwhile the rest of the battalion could merely hang on behind such cover as they could scrape together with their entrenching tools and wait till darkness allowed them to move and to try to assist the many wounded. A pelting rain and bitter cold added to the trials to be endured and stamina and endurance were severely taxed.

No better success had attended the 19th Brigade on the 35th's right and, despite a renewed bombardment, a belated advance by the 28th Brigade made no headway. Losses had been terribly heavy, and we had not even the modified success of the Sheik Saad and Wadi attacks to set against them. This time our defeat was unequivocal. Well over half the attacking infantry were casualties, even the 4th Hampshire in losing 13 officers and 230 men out of 16 and 339 in action were not actually the hardest hit battalion. Lt. Colonel Bowker, Captains North and Brandon, Lts. Needham, Bucknill, Stilwell [1] and Palmer

---

[1] Later reported as alive but a prisoner, Lt. Palmer died of his wounds in Turkish hands.

and 106 men were killed or missing, Captain Page-Roberts, Lts. Andrews, E. A. Burrell, and Jensen and 2/Lts. Pirie and Wyles and 124 men were wounded, Of the handful who were left Lt. Lester-Garland now took command, as Major Stilwell, though unhit, had collapsed from exposure and exhaustion [1] and was sent to hospital, Captain Foster having previously gone sick. Colonel Bowker's loss was much regretted: he had done much for the battalion, winning universal confidence and respect, and was greatly missed.

Nearly a month elapsed before another major attack was attempted. It was now known that the supplies in Kut would allow the garrison to hold out, if on much reduced rations, for some time longer and that the headlong attacks of January had not really been necessary, so that a more systematic and better supported attack could be prepared and reinforcements and drafts brought up.

A mere fragment like the 4th Hampshire was fit for nothing beyond camp duties and guards, and even the arrival from England on February 13th of 420 men with 13 officers [2] left it little over half its establishment. Of these men 135 came from the regiment, from the 2/6th, 3/5th and the 3/7th Battalions, 160 were from the 3/4th D.C.L.I., the rest from the Somerset L.I. and the Wiltshire. This draft had left England on December 10th, reaching Basra on January 7th, and an exhausting march up country in bad weather had reduced its original strength by over 100 through sickness.

Meanwhile the Third (Lahore) Division had been re-formed and in February the 4th Hampshire were transferred to the 35th Brigade under Brigadier General Rice, where they were combined with the 5th Buffs, also sadly reduced, as the ' Composite Territorial Battalion ', which was nick-named ' the Huffs '. It was indeed a ' composite ' unit, the Buffs' reinforcements being mostly from the Gloucestershire and Worcestershire with officers from many other regiments, while Major Thorne, who took command on February 15th, came from the 1st Royal Sussex. This battalion's [3] first active duty was finding picquets on the right bank. Here our lines had been pushed well forward upstream of the Hanna trenches, reaching the Abu Roman mounds, but though we could fire across the Tigris into the flanks and rear of the Turkish front lines, most elaborate defences had been constructed along the river bank and the Turk held on unshaken.

By the beginning of March all was in train for another attempt. This time we were to advance up the right bank to outflank the line running Southward from Es Sinn to a redoubt on the Dujaila depression.[4] To cover the concentration near the Pools of Siloam of the attacking force, the 35th Brigade, which was allotted to the Corps reserve, spent March 7th holding a line running Southward from the river towards the Umm al Baram marsh. The Turks made no attempt to interfere with the assembly of the attacking force, which apparently

---

[1] The cold and wet, added to their exertions and some shortage of rations, sent many unwounded men to hospital from all units.

[2] All subalterns and, with the exception of Lt. Beavis (2/6th) and 2/Lts. Brine, D. A. Hamley, E.A. Hamley and Weatherall (3/4th), all from other regiments.

[3] On March 7th it was returned as 33 officers and 970 other ranks.

[4] Probably an old bed of the Tigris.

they had never detected, and, early on March 8th, after the advance had started, the brigade formed up at the rendezvous and moved forward to escort the great mass of second-line transport to the point, about two miles East of Sinn Abtar, where the two attacking columns had diverged, the left crossing the Dujaila depression to attack the trenches running SW. from the redoubt towards the Shatt el Hai, the right attacking between the redoubt and Sinn Abtar. Here the brigade remained halted from midday onwards in readiness to meet the counter-attack which it was thought the Turks might attempt from their left. None developed and meanwhile, for one reason and another, the chances of a decisive success were slipping away. After a most admirably guided and conducted night march had completely surprised the enemy and brought the relief of Kut within reach, a really splendid opportunity was lamentably thrown away, and another day ended in failure and bitter disappointment.

That night the 35th Brigade spent dug in on the right flank of the force, for whose retirement orders were issued early next morning, the 35th, who were detailed as rear-guard, remaining in position till, early in the afternoon, the long train of transport and guns was all under way. When at last the brigade moved off the Turks at first seemed inclined to press the retreat and the rear-guard looked to be in for a difficult time, but the timely intervention of some British guns discouraged the pursuers most effectively, and but for shell fire, which caused a few casualties, the ' Composite Territorial Battalion ' was unmolested, regaining the starting-point shortly before midnight.

After three days in camp near the Wadi the battalion held our trenches opposite the El Hanna line from March 13th to 22nd, sapping forward to bring our front line within assaulting range of the enemy's trenches, work which cost it only trifling casualties. It was then back at the Wadi camp or at Orah across the river for a fortnight. At Orah it found outposts and had some brushes with Arabs, always on the alert to pounce on stragglers or stray animals or even to attempt to surprise a picquet.

By the first week in April the Thirteenth Division had arrived from Egypt, and on April 5th it attacked and carried the El Hanna trenches, now only lightly held, and, pushing on, also carried the Fallahiya position, three miles upstream. But the next trenches, at Sannaiyat, another three miles ahead, checked the advance, and this decided General Gorringe, now commanding the Tigris Corps, to transfer his effort to the right bank. Here again an initial success was achieved (April 17th), but violent counter-attacks coupled with the floods checked our progress and robbed us of decisive success. A final desperate effort to storm the Sannaiyat lines (April 21st) was no more fortunate, and after the gallant failure of the steamer *Julnar* to run supplies through (April 24th) the end came and Kut had to surrender.

April had given the ' Huffs ' little fighting but plenty of hard work, first in clearing the battlefield after the capture of the Hanna lines, when, among others, Lt. Bucknill's body was found and buried. Then after four days (April 8th–11th) at Falahiya, finding guards and picquets to protect the rear of the attacking force, the battalion was similarly employed across the river until April 20th, while it was in support during the last attack on Sannaiyat and then recrossed the river to take over picquet duty on the left of our front line near Rohde's Picquet, SE. of Bait Isa.

The fall of Kut after so tenacious a defence and the heavy losses incurred in the relievers' gallant efforts forms the low-water mark of our fortunes in Mesopotamia. It had been a sheer gamble to try to rush Baghdad with a force which, even had luck been with it instead of mainly against it, was unequal to its task and without any preparation for retrieving a reverse, and, as at Gallipoli, the initial error of expecting the force originally available to accomplish more than was reasonable had never been made good. Had the original advance been postponed until substantial reserves were available, the check at Ctesiphon might not have been decisive, while had the capacity of Kut to hold out been correctly estimated and unnecessary haste subsequently avoided, the 4th Hampshire might not have been cut to pieces so unavailingly.

A prolonged inactivity followed the fall of Kut. The Turks made no effort to improve their success by driving the baffled relieving force downstream and thereby allowed us to retain our advanced positions unchallenged. This may have contributed to minimize the ill-effects of our defeat. The Arabs on the whole did not stir, contenting themselves with minor activities against our outposts, communications, convoys and foraging parties. The North-West Frontier, where trouble had been feared, remained quiet, the battered Tigris Corps could gradually be brought back to strength and to full efficiency, so that before the year was out it could start the operations which were to recover Kut and carry the British flag to Baghdad.

But to the units who had to spend an unusually hot and exhausting summer far up the Tigris, at the end of an over-worked line of communications, without amenities and comforts, in an exceptionally trying climate, the time passed slowly and painfully. The daily routine was both strenuous and terribly monotonous; weakened units found themselves hardly equal to all their duties, the sick-rate was very high, rations were none too plentiful or palatable, nor did things improve until the careful and strenuous reorganization of the Basra base and of the lines of communication at last began to yield fruit upstream. Meanwhile trenches had to be held and kept in repair and picquets found, with escorts to convoys between our forward position and the camps further downstream, as the Arabs were always on the alert to descend upon any ill-guarded quarry.

During May the Hampshire were mainly at Twin Canals, occasionally holding the forward trenches, which were advanced in the middle of the month to Es Sinn, the Turks having very unexpectedly vacated that position. An outbreak of cholera cost them several lives, including those of Lt. Corser (2/6th) and of the Brigadier, but it never became an epidemic. A draft of 140 men from the 2/4th joined at the end of May, and on June 19th the Composite Territorial Battalion was broken up, the 4th Hampshire resuming their independent formation under Major Matthews of the Durham L.I., while Captain

Gribbon joined from the 6th Devons, to which he had been attached, to become Adjutant. Before this the 35th, 36th and 37th Brigades, hitherto independent, had been organized as a Fourteenth Indian Division under Major General Egerton.

July the battalion spent in the Sinn area, carrying on as before with finding escorts, guards and picquets and digging trenches. The weather was terribly hot, conditions most uncomfortable and the sick-rate naturally very high, but Colonel Matthews proved an able and inspiring commander and did much for the efficiency and welfare of the battalion. During August it was for a time at the Northern end of the Es Sinn line and found sniping picquets to look out for targets across the Tigris. The light railway from Orah had now reached Twin Canals and was creeping forward towards Es Sinn and needed guarding, block houses being established at intervals and usually held by picquets of about a a dozen men to keep the Arabs at a distance.

In September the battalion was ordered back to Sheikh Saad to be transferred to duty on the line of communications; it had marched back to railhead on September 13th, when its orders were cancelled and it was posted to the 37th Brigade under Brigadier General Walton, in which it found the 26th, 62nd and 82nd Punjabis.[1] This brigade the Hampshire joined at the Dujaila Redoubt [2] where it was employed on the usual routine, varied in October by ten days in reserve for intensive company and battalion training, after which the brigade moved up to the front and took over the line about Magasis, holding the river front. Here an advanced picquet line was being dug: No Man's Land was wide and we were gradually pushing forward our posts to bring us nearer the enemy, who had now gone well back.

November brought substantial drafts from India, seven officers and 571 men altogether from the 2/4th, 1/6th, 1/7th and 2/7th Battalions, with an officer and 28 men rejoining from hospital. The draft-finding battalions had sent good men, well trained and fit, and the opening in December of General Maude's operations for the recapture of Kut found the 4th Hampshire strong and efficient and ready for the chance to get their own back on the Turks.

Meanwhile the battalions in India had been following the usual routine of training and duties, sending ' hot weather ' detachments to ' the Hills ', and were steadily becoming both acclimatized and highly trained, the Second Line units in particular, with more lee-way to make up, improving greatly. The 2/4th, who remained at Quetta, lost Lt. Colonel Naish, invalided home in April 1916, Major J. B. L. Stilwell replacing him. They had been joined by the depot left behind by the 1/4th and had at one time 1500 men in barracks. They benefitted greatly from strenuous training in quite a good climate and had by now become quite expert in mountain warfare. The 1/5th, who had been much split up, having detachments at Benares, Cawnpore and Jhansi, were concentrated at Lucknow and moved in March to Fyzabad. Their signallers being

---

[1] Afterwards 2/15th, 1/1st and 5/1st Punjab.
[2] Evacuated by the Turks in May.

taken away for service on the Frontier a new section had to be trained, but numbers were maintained by over 200 arrivals from England, and despite large drafts to Mesopotamia and the departure of men to take commissions or for various employments the battalion ended 1916 nearly 1,000 strong, having only lost nine men by disease in two years and had 20 invalided. It lost one of its ' pre-war ' subalterns when Lt. Needham was killed at El Hanna.

The 2/5th in like manner got large drafts, over 450 in all, and could send several officers and many men to Mesopotamia. Lt. Jenner took over the Adjutancy from Captain Archdale and several officers left for Staff appointments. The men's health was good and the hot weather less extreme and less trying than in 1915.

The 1/6th, who moved from Agra to Ambala in March 1916, had two companies at Solon during the hot weather, companies exchanging stations in July: by October the battalion was concentrated again at Ambala, going into camp later for cold weather training. Drafts to Mesopotamia, where one of its officers, Lieutenant Palmer, was killed at El Hanna, were replaced from home.

The 1/7th lost Lt. Colonel Parke, invalided home in February 1916; Major Roberts-Thomson succeeding him, on which Captain Rebbeck went up to Major. The battalion moved from Meerut to Ambala in March, sent ' hot weather ' detachments to Dagshai and Kasauli and received drafts amounting to nearly 450 with several officers, itself sending drafts to the 1/4th, with whom Captain Allen was killed early in 1917 at the recapture of Kut.

The 2/7th got a change of station in March, from Secunderabad to Jubbulpore. Major Gott went home on leave in February and was replaced in command by Major Maturin, Captain Boucher becoming second in command. Captain Gribbon left in February to join the 6th Devons in Mesopotamia, Lt. W. A. de Geijer becoming Adjutant. Drafts from the 3/7th kept the battalion's numbers up, despite the drain to Mesopotamia and other wastage.

Meanwhile another Hampshire battalion had reached India, the 1/9th, who, after much work on their coastal duties, had been converted into ordinary infantry in November 1915, when they had joined a brigade of other ex-cyclist battalions. This was in turn detailed for East Africa, for Egypt and for France, but was finally sent off in February 1916 to India: the 1/9th going to Bangalore and remaining there until December 1916, when they were ordered up to the NW. Frontier. They were still under their original C.O., Lt. Colonel R. A. Johnson.

CHAPTER XIV

THE SOMME

THE OPENING PHASES [1]

THE great attack which opened on July 1st 1916 on a 25 mile front astride the Somme was undertaken at a time and in a locality dictated rather by French interests and considerations than by British. Left to himself Sir Douglas Haig would have deferred attacking till his preparations and the training of some of his troops were more complete, possibly till he could use the new weapon, the ' tank ', of which so much was expected by those in the secret of it: he would certainly have chosen a different front.[2] On the open downland of the Somme area, over and above certain tactical disadvantages and the lack of roads, railways and housing, our intentions had been impossible to conceal, the manifold administrative measures involved in the assembly of so large a force had been obvious, the construction of camps and the improvement of the communications and of the very inadequate water supply could not be hidden to the degree of which other areas might have allowed. Consequently surprise, so essential to the success of an offensive, had been lacking, except on the British right and where the French attacked, and there surprise had much to do with the success achieved: between Fricourt and Serre, where the British centre and left attacked, the Germans were expecting an attack; they were fully prepared and, effective as our bombardment had on the whole been, their counter-measures were ready; if any element of surprise came in, it was the efficacy of the deep dug-outs in which most of their trench garrisons had found safety and shelter during the bombardment.

North of the Ancre the Fourth and Twenty-Ninth Divisions were facing defences as strong or stronger than anywhere else and the task before these Divisions was difficult and formidable in the extreme. For many months the Germans had been in position here and had benefitted by the natural difficulties of the ground to construct a veritable fortress, almost warranting the epithet ' impregnable '.

The German lines here ran Northward along a ridge from which spurs projected SE. towards the Ancre, shallow valleys between them giving cover for supports and reserves. Here the key to the position was the strongly fortified Beaumont Hamel. That village confronted the Twenty-Ninth Division's left brigade, the 86th, which had to advance along a spur known as Hawthorn Ridge, while its right brigade, the 87th, faced the Southern side of a salient round the head of the deep depression known as Y Ravine, the 88th Brigade being in reserve. Beyond the Division's left was the Fourth Division, whose

---

[1] See Sketch 31 (p. 181).

[2] The late hour chosen for the attack, 7.30 a.m., was also insisted upon by the French. Sir Douglas Haig would have attacked before it was light enough for the enemy's machine gunners to see their targets clearly, a plan to be adopted with good results on July 14th.

11th Brigade, reinforced by two battalions of the Forty-Eighth Division, was attacking North of Beaumont Hamel, where two redoubts, Ridge Redoubt and the Quadrilateral, were particularly strong. It was hoped that the brigade would reach Munich Trench, 1,000 yards behind the front line, where the supporting brigades, the 10th and 12th, would go through it. On the Fourth Division's left the Thirty-First, also part of the Eighth Corps, had the village of Serre as its objective. No Man's Land, 500 yards wide South of Beaumont Hamel, was half that width further North, but it was bare of cover and the German defences were well-sited and constructed, while in places the slope of the ground had made it very difficult for our guns, and particularly the heavier pieces, to bring their fire to bear on them. Observation of our fire had not been easy and our bombardment, despite its volume, had not fulfilled expectations. It had neither silenced the enemy's batteries, subdued his machine-guns nor shattered his defences, if his wire had been well cut.[1] If hopes were high, those who had had a close view could not avoid some misgivings after the volume of machine-gun fire provoked by a discharge of smoke after the fourth day of the bombardment.

The Fourth Division had had no serious fighting since moving to the Somme and, thanks to this respite from heavy casualties and the changes consequent on them, its battalions had fully recovered from their losses and shattering experiences in ' Second Ypres '. They had had ample time to assimilate their drafts and to recover their cohesion. It has been well said [2] that the Division was as ' fighting fit as at any time in its existence ', and the 1st Hampshire had never been as near again to their August 1914 standard. It was the more unfortunate that the task set to the Division proved to be more than any infantry could have accomplished.

It had unfortunately been decided to fire a big mine under the German redoubt on Hawthorn Ridge at 7.20 a.m., ten minutes before ' Zero '. This gave away completely the one thing the Germans did not know, the exact time of our attack, and as simultaneously our heavy guns ' lifted ' off the front line, the defenders had ample time to swarm up from the safety of their undamaged deep dug-outs, to get their machine-guns into place and to man their parapets just as our heavily-laden infantry began crossing No Man's Land, while their barrage came crashing down, many batteries hitherto deliberately silent and therefore unlocated and undamaged joining in.

The 1st Hampshire,[3] following the East Lancashire on the 11th Brigade's right, went forward at 7.40 a.m., before which the East Lancashire had already been almost wiped out, less by the barrage than by the deadlier machine-guns in Ridge Redoubt, which swept both No Man's Land and the British front trenches, mowing the attackers down wholesale. Hardly any East Lancashire reached the German trenches and they were too few to achieve anything. The

---

[1] The full stength of the German defences at this point, in particular of their deep dug-outs was not revealed till the capture of Beaumont Hamel in November.

[2] *Official History*, 1916, I. 426.

[3] Even before the attack started our own ' shorts ' had buried a section of one platoon and it took nearly an hour to dig them out.

Hampshire had A, B and half C Companies in front line, the rest of C being detailed to deal with a trench on the right flank, while D was in reserve. Plunging forward into the deadly hail of fire they fared no better than their predecessors, gallantly as they advanced; Colonel Palk[1] being among the many who fell before they could get half-way across. A few bombers are reported to have got into the enemy's line, but the majority of the Hampshire were brought down at or short of the wire, only a few reaching it, and the survivors could only seek the poor shelter of the shell-holes which pitted No Man's Land. Here they had to lie for hours, mixed up with the East Lancashire, pinned to the ground, unable to move and with little chance to hit back. Captain Fawkes, though badly wounded and unable to get on, did great work in encouraging his men, while 2/Lt. Money and C.S.M. Palmer also showed conspicuous gallantry, keeping their men together and setting a fine example[2] during this long and trying ordeal.

Better fortune had attended the left of the 11th Brigade, who got rather more shelter from the ground, and despite heavy losses a fair number entered the German lines, carried the Quadrilateral and even reached the back trenches of the front system. Some of the 10th and 12th Brigades also got across and in places pushed on still further and for the moment a lodgement seemed to have been made which might be developed, heavy though losses had been. However, nothing could be done to shift those defenders who were facing the survivors of the Hampshire and both flanks of the lodgement were exposed; on the left the handfuls of the Thirty-First Division who had succeeded in entering the German lines had been speedily overwhelmed, while not only had the 11th Brigade's right been checked but hardly any of the Twenty-Ninth Division's left brigade had got in, though the mine crater at the Hawthorn Redoubt was in our hands. The Germans could therefore concentrate their attention on dislodging those of the Fourth Division who had penetrated into their position.

Of the Twenty-Ninth Division not only had both attacking brigades been engaged without avail, the 88th's leading battalions, the Essex and the Newfoundland Regiment, had also gone forward, with equally disastrous results. However, their fate had caused the Divisional commander to stop the 2nd Hampshire and the Worcestershire from advancing beyond our own lines, where they came under artillery fire but escaped serious exposure to the machine-guns. To support the Fourth Division it was now proposed to utilize these two battalions in a fresh attack upon Beaumont Hamel, while such of the 10th Brigade as was still in hand advanced on their left. Terribly congested trenches prevented this attack from being started at the time ordered, 12.30 p.m.; indeed, the orders never reached the 2nd Hampshire till long after that hour, and eventually the plan was abandoned and further fruitless sacrifice avoided. The 2nd Hampshire remained therefore in our own lines.

[1] He went forward carrying only a stick and was very soon hit : he was brought in but died in the C.C.S. that morning.
[2] All three received the M.C.

Our artillery did their best to help the Fourth Division to hang on, but the pressure on those across No Man's Land steadily increased, to reinforce them and to get ammunition and bombs across to them proved almost impossible in face of the barrage and the machine-guns, and after a stubborn resistance they were gradually forced back till at midnight we only retained the Quadrilateral. Elsewhere on the Eighth Corps' front the Germans contented themselves with having held their positions and did not attempt anything against the survivors lying out in No Man's Land. Indeed for some time our stretcher-bearers were able to go out unhindered into the open to bring in the wounded, in which work Sergeant Bone and Private Pidgeley [1] were conspicuous, carrying on even when the Germans resumed shelling in response to our renewing our bombardment.

With darkness the survivors [2] from No Man's Land could get back to our line, bringing with them many of the wounded, and what remained of the attacking battalions could be collected and to some degree reorganized. The 2nd Hampshire and the Worcestershire took over the Division's frontage, much damaged by the counter-bombardment and needing much reconstruction. During the night parties were hard at work bringing in the wounded, Privates Barton, Morgan and Parkinson displaying the greatest devotion,[3] while Pte. Mildenhall was constantly out in No Man's Land, bandaging and assisting the wounded, the Germans making little effort to interfere, even next morning, though they would not let our stretcher-bearers bring in those close to their wire.[4]

The Eighth Corps' losses had been terrible, heavier than any other Corps suffered, nearly 6000 in the Fourth Division, well over 5000 in the Twenty-Ninth and 3600 in the Thirty-First; and in the end it had nothing to show for them, as the untenable lodgement in the Quadrilateral was evacuated by order early on July 2nd. The 1st Hampshire indeed had had their worst experience of the war, comparable to the 2nd Battalion's ordeal at Cape Helles on August 6th, 1915: Second Ypres had hit them hard, July 1st 1916 had cost them eleven officers and 310 men killed and missing, 15 officers and 250 men wounded. Colonel Palk's loss was very deeply regretted. A tower of strength from Le Cateau onwards, where his coolness and calm had been an inspiration to many who were enduring their 'baptism of fire', he had taken over after Colonel Hicks had been wounded on May 8th and had been in command in the closing stages of Second Ypres and at the International Trench, where he and his men had earned the warmest praise from all above them. An officer has written of him: 'He was a great character. He used to read Gibbon to his junior officers and spoke French and German fluently. The first time I met him he said, "There are three things I will never have said to me: ' it always 'as been done, Sir '; ' never 'as been done, Sir ' and ' I thought '. It is your business to know and to act ' ". He was often a thorn in the side of the Division and the senior

[1] Of the 1st Hampshire. Both received the D.C.M.
[2] Soon after 10 p.m. it was dark enough for this, and though the Germans had put down a barrage about 9.45 p.m. this had stopped after half an hour.
[3] They received the M.M.
[4] These were mostly made prisoners.

Staff officers did not like him. He was utterly outspoken and feared nobody. He was a magnificent regimental officer, fresh and amusing, and was revered by the men '. A shrewd judge of men, kindly but firm, he was one who could ill be spared: ' the men would have followed him anywhere '. A battalion which had had two such C.O's as Colonels Hicks and Palk had been fortunate. With him had fallen Captain Bonham-Carter, the only other officer with the South African war medals, Lts. Adams and Price, 2/Lts. H. Alexander, N. H. Bell, Bramble, Cane, Goodford, Nixon,[1] F. P. Thompson and Westmore. The officers wounded were Captains K. A. Johnston, Hume, Wyld[2] and Fawkes, Lt. Shearer, 2/Lts. D. Day, Doyle, P. J. Hall, Harding, Hiddingh, Jacob, Newnham, Sims, Sweetenham and Welhams.

The 2nd Battalion had got off with trifling loss, two killed and 2/Lt. Riggs and twenty men wounded, but during the next ten days 2/Lt. Counsell and 13 men were killed and 2/Lts. Black and Tilley and 84 men wounded. These days were spent in front line at Mary Redan, repairing much damaged trenches under persistent shell fire. Large quantities of arms and equipment were recovered from No Man's Land and many dead buried, while another 60 wounded were brought in, all at night.

The battalion went out of the line on July 10th but sent 28 men under Captain Arnell up to try a raid near Y Ravine on July 14th. The raiders reached the wire and were making their way through when they came under heavy fire and bombing. They replied vigorously with rifles and bombs for 15 minutes but then had to fall back. Two wounded were brought in, but Captain Arnell and three others were missing, believed killed, while next day a party carrying a gas cylinder up to the line was caught by a H.E. shell in Auchonvillers and had 25 casualties, seven fatal, so that the month's casualties came to 150.

July 17th brought the 2nd a move back, to Acheux Wood, and after several days devoted to company training the battalion went still further back, to Beauval, to entrain on July 29th for the North. It was now to make its first acquaintance with the Ypres Salient where its Division was relieving the Sixth, the 2nd Hampshire taking over front line trenches on July 30th opposite St. Julien with one company in reserve at Potijze.

The Fourth Division had also reached the Salient and had relieved the Guards SW. of Pilkem, on the extreme British left. The 1st Hampshire had been back at Mailly Maillet and then at Bertrancourt till July 9th and had then had five days in line at Beaumont Hamel, though only six officers were available for duty. They were in line here when early on July 14th smoke was discharged all along the Divisional front and a heavy bombardment maintained for an hour to distract the enemy's attention and make him expect an attack here also, while away to the right the Fourth Army was making its highly successful dawn attack which took the Bazentins and reached Longueval and Delville and High Woods. Captain Lockhart and Lts. Smythe and Collett now rejoined and over 20

---

[1] With the Brigade Trench Mortar Battery.   [2] He lost a leg.

other officers arrived, of whom Lts. German and de Gaury had been at Gallipoli with the 10th Battalion, while over 300 men arrived, mainly from the 13th and 16th Battalions, though, unfortunately, some were of very poor physique. After a week at Mailly Maillet in support, the battalion went back, on July 23rd, to entrain for Ypres at Doullens, reaching Poperinghe on July 25th and relieving the 4th Grenadiers in front line SW. of Pilkem on the night of the 27th/28th. It was thus back near the International Trench, if not many were left to renew the acquaintance of that locality, nor were these particularly delighted to do so. Next day (July 28th) Major Armitage of the West Yorkshire arrived to assume command.

The Eighth Corps' failure on July 1st had been to some extent balanced by the success of the British right from Fricourt Eastward and of the French beyond Montauban. These gains Sir Douglas Haig did succeed in developing, and gradually and slowly the British line was pushed forward until the German defences between Thiepval and Delville Wood were mastered piecemeal in chequered and costly fighting, with the balance just in our favour; the Germans fought skilfully and stubbornly, again and again they counter-attacked in force and only by determined efforts were they held and pushed back. All through July and August the struggle raged without another Hampshire battalion being engaged: the 1st and 2nd were recuperating in the comparative ' quiet ' of the Ypres Salient, while the 11th remained at Loos, the 14th in the Neuve Chapelle area and the 15th at Ploegsteert.

Still these battalions were far from inactive. If the British attacks on the Somme gave the enemy all he could do to hold them and soon substantially relieved the pressure on Verdun, while all chance of a major counter-attack on the British front promptly disappeared, the Germans were not precluded from trying local counter-attacks to keep us occupied and to interfere with our systematic relief of exhausted Divisions by fresh troops from ' quiet ' sectors, while we with much the same end tried raids and even occasionally something more extensive.

The 1st Hampshire had two months in the Salient before returning to the Somme. They found the trenches fairly dry, but in need of repair, and at first snipers were troublesome while at night machine-guns were often active. Returning to the line on August 4th after a few days ' out ' at Elverdinghe, where a lake in the Chateau grounds provided good bathing, they came in on the evening of August 8th for the enemy's one use of gas on any substantial scale during this month, gas being released on nearly the whole front of the Eighth Corps [1] On the 1st Hampshire's front the discharge lasted ten minutes and meanwhile the trenches were heavily shelled, the S.O.S. rockets, being mostly damp, failed to go off, and some minutes elapsed before our barrage came down to co-operate effectively with our rifles in driving back Germans who attempted

---

[1] This Corps headquarters had been transferred from the Beaumont Hamel front to Ypres at the end of July.

to reach our lines, none managing to get in, though some came within bombing range. But the Hampshire had nearly 70 casualties, 14 killed or died of gas or missing, as many wounded and nearly 40 gassed, 2/Lt. Love being wounded.

From August 11th to 21st the battalion was ' out ' again, after which it relieved the Canadians South of the Menin Road, a nasty piece of line which seemed to be overlooked from all around. Here the enemy were active, and on August 26th a heavy bombardment caused 20 casualties in C Company, both Captain Smythe and 2/Lt. Prynn being buried for a time but dug out without serious injury. During the shelling about a dozen Germans started working down a trench towards A Company's bombing post, where Sergeant Clark dealt with them most effectively; well backed up by two men, he drove them off with bombs,[1] while another advance was repulsed by our fire, the Germans, big men and apparently Prussian Guardsmen, running back to the shelter of a wood.[2]

After another turn in the line East of Zillebeke early in September, the battalion was in camp at Vlamertinghe and then near Dunkirk, where it was practised in embarking. This aimed at making it appear that we intended landing on the Belgian coast, and it seems that coupled with naval activities in the Thames and elsewhere the threat did arouse German apprehensions and lead to their devoting men and materials to strengthening the coast defences. The battalion then found itself under orders to return to the Somme, and after entraining for Amiens on September 17th it spent the rest of the month training, first at Cardonette, three miles NE. of Amiens, and then at Corbie. Casualties for September only came to a dozen, but over 110 admissions to hospital considerably exceeded returns from hospital, 49, and drafts, 27. Four officers joined, including Lt. Newnham wounded on July 1st, but Lt. Sprake after a long spell as Transport Officer was detailed for a turn of home duty.

The 2nd Battalion had also been caught by the gas on August 8th but with far more disastrous results. It had gone into trenches East of Potijze on July 30th and had had ten fairly quiet days, working on defences which required much improvement, a new mine crater needing consolidation, before the gas alarm was sounded and a gas cloud was seen approaching slowly from the NE. The wind was light and the gas, moving slowly, was the more efficacious, and between it and the German barrage the battalion suffered terribly, having nearly 240 casualties, more than half fatal; Captain Hall (Buffs), 2/Lts. McCurdy, Scoggin and E. W. C. Turner[3] and no less than 125 men died, while 2/Lts. Churcher, Foster, Graham, Miller, M. T. Smith and Tollemache were incapacitated. Sergeant Graham, though gassed, stuck to his post and gave his officers valuable help in keeping the men steady while Pte. Osbourne displayed great

---

[1] He received an ' immediate ' M.M.

[2] The total casualties for August were 25 killed and missing, including deaths from gas, 38 wounded and 46 gassed. Captain Lockhart and 90 men were admitted to hospital, from which 36 men were discharged.

[3] He had only joined a week earlier.

devotion to duty in maintaining communications and repairing wires and Corporal Hopgood kept his Lewis gun in use and did much to reconstruct a damaged trench.   Here no attempt was made by the Germans to exploit what seemed to offer them a very favourable opportunity and attack: the gas, which was phosgene and particularly deadly, killing birds and rats for some distance in rear and corroding metal, had been sufficiently effective.   Luckily two large drafts, 98 men on August 12th and 125 five days later, nearly replaced the losses and for the rest of the month casualties were low, 2/Lt.Manlove and four men killed and 2/Lt. Tilley and a dozen men wounded.   With 60 admissions to hospital the battalion could produce 36 officers [1] and 773 other ranks on August 31st, ten new officers having joined.

Ten days in brigade reserve and as many in Divisional reserve had followed this gas attack, after which the battalion was in brigade reserve at Ypres for ten days, finding working parties under R.E. supervision to improve the defences behind Railway Wood.   It then had another ten in front line at Potijze, during which it came in for heavy retaliation for a raid by the 4th Worcestershire from Railway Wood on its right (September 15th).   It was again heavily bombarded on September 18th but again escaped with trifling casualties.   Chances of hitting back were few but were not neglected.   While in Divisional reserve from September 19th to 28th the battalion was inspected by General Hunter-Weston and by the Army Commander, General Plumer.   Another short spell in trenches followed, and then October 5th found it at Poperinghe in readiness to entrain for the South.   Since September 1st casualties had only just come to 20, including 2/Lt. Hayward killed, though over 80 admissions to hospital had just exceeded drafts.

Of the Service battalions the 11th and 14th reached the Somme about the same time, to be employed at the opposite ends of the fighting front, the Sixteenth Division against Guillemont and Ginchy and the Thirty-Ninth on the right bank of the Ancre, just South of the frontage of the Twenty-Ninth Division on July 1st.   The 15th came in slightly later, for the big attack of September 15th, which ushered in a new phase in the struggle.

The 11th had found the Loos salient fairly lively during July.   We were using trench-mortars against the wire and were harassing the enemy energetically to keep him from thinning his force on this front.   He retaliated fairly vigorously and parties working in back areas suffered rather severely, two officers were wounded by a shell which hit the Officers' Club at Mazingarbe, while Captain Powell was killed in the High Street at Loos on July 2nd.   The Division made several raids and a party of the 11th helped to consolidate two new craters formed by a mine explosion near Seaforth Crater on July 15th. Otherwise its work continued as usual.   At the end of July the battalion was relieved by the Pioneers of the Thirty-Ninth Division, head-quarters going back to Philosophe but moving early in August to Mazingarbe, though such changes did not mean any less work.   The Division was then (August 23rd) with-

---

[1] All battalions had now 16 Lewis guns, the heavier machine guns having been withdrawn.

drawn from the line to move Southward, the 11th Hampshire arriving at Daours on the 28th and being sent forward on September 1st to Meaulté to work under the Fifth Division. That Division had just taken over the extreme right of our line opposite Falfemont Farm and Wedge Wood, SW. of Combles: on its left was a brigade of the Sixteenth Division which had been placed under the Twentieth to assist to capture Guillemont.

After the 116th Brigade's repulse at the Boar's Head the 14th Hampshire had a brief time out of the line, but they were soon in again at Cuinchy, where mining was going on vigorously and rifle-grenades were freely used. They were then in trenches in the Ferme du Bois and Festubert sectors. At Festubert also things were active, our snipers claimed several victims and our trench mortars did some effective work, while the battalion had the satisfaction of repulsing a patrol which tried to get in between two of our posts, a wounded prisoner being brought in; it was twice heavily shelled in retaliation for raids by other battalions, having over 30 casualties in two days, and then on July 30th it tried a large raid on its own, three officers and 103 men taking part. The party detailed to get a Bangalore torpedo into place failed to do so, and thick and uncut wire held the raiders up, so they could only engage in some brisk bombing in which they threw about 200 bombs before retiring. Five men were killed, but ten wounded, including 2/Lts. Marshall and Meade,[1] were brought safely in. After another turn in front line, at Givenchy from August 6th to 11th, in which one shell, landing on their company's H.Q. dug-out, wounded three subalterns, the battalion went back by Allouagne to Magnicourt, the Division being in Army reserve. Here it had ten days training and got a useful draft of 54 men before moving South by rail on August 24th. Detraining at Le Souich, it marched to Bertrancourt, where it encamped. Here Colonel Hickie left it (August 30th) on promotion to command a brigade of the Thirty-Eighth Division, leaving Captain Skinner in command, as Majors Childe-Thomas and Finlay were both away, the former having joined the Brigade staff in July.

The 15th Hampshire were not far behind the 11th and 14th, arriving at Dernancourt on September 5th. Their Divison had been ' out ' for nearly a month, having quitted ' Plugstreet ' on August 9th and moved back to Fletre, where it entrained for Longprè on August 24th, to have a week at Villers sous Ailly, training. Its last weeks at ' Plugstreet ' had been fairly active; on July 12th rescue parties had helped to bring in wounded after an unsuccessful raid by another battalion. The work was carried out under heavy fire and 2/Lt. W. Morgan was killed, while 2/Lt. Challis and Sergeant Dugan [2] were specially commended for their gallantry and good work. In a gas attack a few days later 2/Lt. Challis was killed, and several men were gassed next day through the drifting back into our trenches of pockets of gas. Between August 3rd and 9th the battalion was active with rifle grenades, sending over nearly 100 a day without exciting much reply. Trench mortars co-operated effectively and the battalion's

[1] C.S.M. Duffin brought this officer in.   [2] Received the M.M.

M   H.R. II.

patrols were active. One under 2/Lt. Menzies-Calder ran into enemy and after a brief encounter scattered to make its way back. The subaltern, who was making his first patrol, being unable to find his way, managed to lie in hiding until next evening, apparently behind the enemy's line, and got back with useful information. Casualties during July and August had come to about 30, well below those for June.

CHAPTER XV

THE SOMME (continued)

WHEN, early in September, a Hampshire battalion was again in action on the Somme the situation there had altered considerably since the 1st and 2nd Battalions had faced Beaumont Hamel. There, indeed, the position remained unchanged, but just East of the Ancre we had advanced to the outskirts of Thiepval and, beyond that, were well past Pozieres and the Bazentins, while if we had not yet completely mastered Delville Wood and Longueval or taken Ginchy or Guillemont, our right also had gained ground, and beyond it nearer the Somme the French had made good progress. It had been ' hard pounding ' and costly, but despite the vigour, skill and determination of the German resistance the Allies had made substantial gains, while German Divisions were being used up in the struggle even faster than the Allied units [1] and were coming out reduced to a fraction of their former strength, usually with even heavier losses than their opponents. The break-through for which Sir Douglas Haig had hoped had eluded us, and the battle had developed into the attrition which Generals Joffre and Foch had all along looked upon as inevitable, reckoning, as they did, that victory must be unattainable until the hard core of German resistance had been worn down by the killing or disabling of their pre-war trained officers and men. Till the Somme German units had retained a high proportion of their trained personnel, ours had largely perished in the devoted efforts of 1914 to win time for the developement of our unready resources or in the abortive offensives of 1915; if an invaluable leaven of the ' Old Army ' still remained, in the main the British troops of 1916, if fully a match to the Germans in courage and determination, were hardly their equals in training and experience or equipment. We had to make our Armies in the field and the process was proving expensive. However, by the beginning of September the contest of endurance was turning slowly in our favour, our advance had reached a point at which our prospects were becoming more promising. If few regimental officers or men had any suspicion of the secret weapon we were about to use, they could not but realize that we were gaining ground, if but gradually, and were punishing our enemy fully as hard as he was hitting us.

The objective of our next big effort included the veritable ' fortress ' of Thiepval, and as a preliminary the Reserve Army [2] was on September 3rd to renew the attack beyond the Ancre, where it had been suspended since July 1st. In this attack the Thirty-Ninth Division, now in General Fanshawe's Fifth Corps which was holding the front from Hébuterne Southward, was to be employed, and late on September 2nd therefore the 14th Hampshire moved up through Englebelmer for their first battle. On the extreme right next the Ancre

---

[1] German regimental histories make this abundantly clear.

[2] Formed in July out of the left of the Fourth Army and commanded by General Gough. It later (October 30th) became the Fifth Army.

was a battalion of the 118th Brigade, with the 11th R. Sussex next and the 14th Hampshire beyond them, the 117th Brigade being on the left of the 116th. Across the Ancre the Forty-Ninth Division, was attacking with St. Pierre Divion and a line running down from the Schwaben Redoubt [1] on the crest of the ridge as objectives. The Thirty-Ninth Division was covering the flank of this attack which, if successful, would have established us in a good position for the big task of capturing Thiepval and the redoubts behind it.

The Thirty-Ninth Division's infantry was now much below establishment: drafts had been few and had not kept pace with casualties and other wastage, and though the Hampshire and the 11th Royal Sussex could produce about 550 rifles apiece, the supporting battalions were much weaker. The British line here,[2] NE. of Hamel, ran South of the spur stretching down from Beaumont Hamel to the Ancre and was overlooked from the German trenches, but at Zero, 5.10 a.m., the attacking battalions went forward well; a machine-gun barrage fired over their heads mowed down Germans who stood up on their parapet to fire, and the attackers were soon in possession of the front line and could press on against the next, which also was carried, 2/Lt. Leach being conspicuous for leading his men with great initiative and gallantry. Opposition then stiffened; C Company's advance towards the final objective met heavy rifle and machine-gun fire and, despite gallant efforts, it failed to penetrate the wire. Of the 11th Sussex some had even gained their final objective, but the 117th Brigade had been less successful and its failure uncovered the Hampshire's left flank. However, a determined effort was made to consolidate the ground gained, and when the 117th Brigade attempted another advance, Captain Skinner and the Adjutant, Lt. Goldsmith, collected all the men they could and went forward, almost to the wire in front of the final objective where the attack was checked, Captain Skinner being killed. Even after this failure the surviving officers, especially Lt. Goldsmith, though he was wounded, did much to hold on to the German second line and keep up a defence which was soon hard pressed, bombers assailing it on the flanks, while heavy guns bombarded the captured position steadily, inflicting heavy losses and impeding consolidation and the advance of reinforcements. The attack across the Ancre had failed and from the steeper slopes above St. Pierre Divion the enemy had good observation.

However, the 14th hung on stoutly, blocking the ends of the captured trenches, beating back several advances and using bombs, Lewis guns and rifles to good purpose. But the enemy's shell-fire prevented reinforcements and the much-needed fresh ammunition from reaching the front and made it impossible for the Pioneers to open up communications. Thus, when bombs and cartridges ran short, the Hampshire were gradually thrust back, though the second line captured was held till about 1 p.m., while after that small parties maintained themselves in the old German front line for some time. 2/Lt. Tew was conspicuous in this effort, controlling his men's fire and shooting

---

[1] North by East of Thiepval. See Sketch 37 (p. 198).
[2] It had been pushed forward since July 1st and No Man's Land was barely half as wide as on that day.

many Germans himself, Lt. Goldsmith, despite his wound, worked hard to organize the defenders and 2/Lts. Ball and Bearn also did much to maintain our

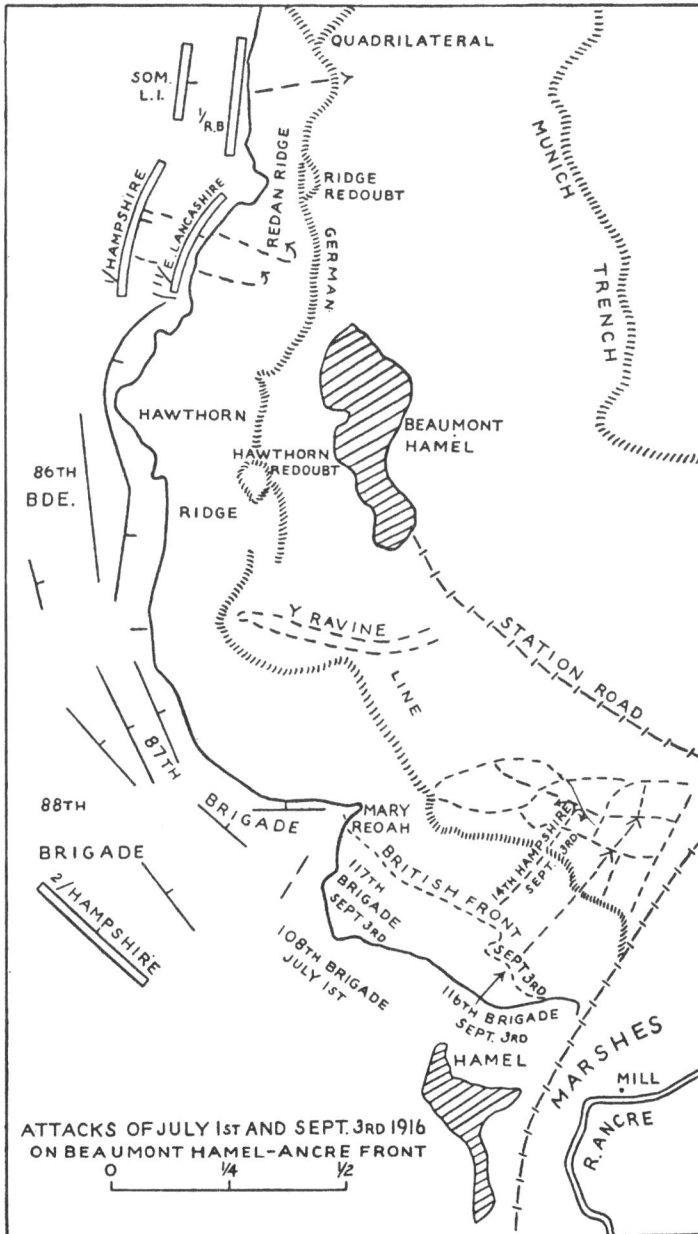

ATTACKS OF JULY 1st AND SEPT. 3RD 1916
ON BEAUMONT HAMEL-ANCRE FRONT

hold.   One party under 2/Lt. Bartlett held out till late in the afternoon before, having finished off all their ammunition, they had to get back.   In retiring 2/Lt. Bartlett was hit for a second time and fell into a shell-hole, where he remained till the night of September 4th/5th, then managing to regain our lines. After dark any men still holding out in the enemy's lines were ordered to retire, and the fragment that remained of the 14th went right back to Mailly Maillet to reorganize. Of the 570 in action, 17 officers and 440 other ranks were casualties.[1] The only consolation was that the men had fought splendidly, hanging on most stubbornly after a good attack, while the enemy's losses must have been very

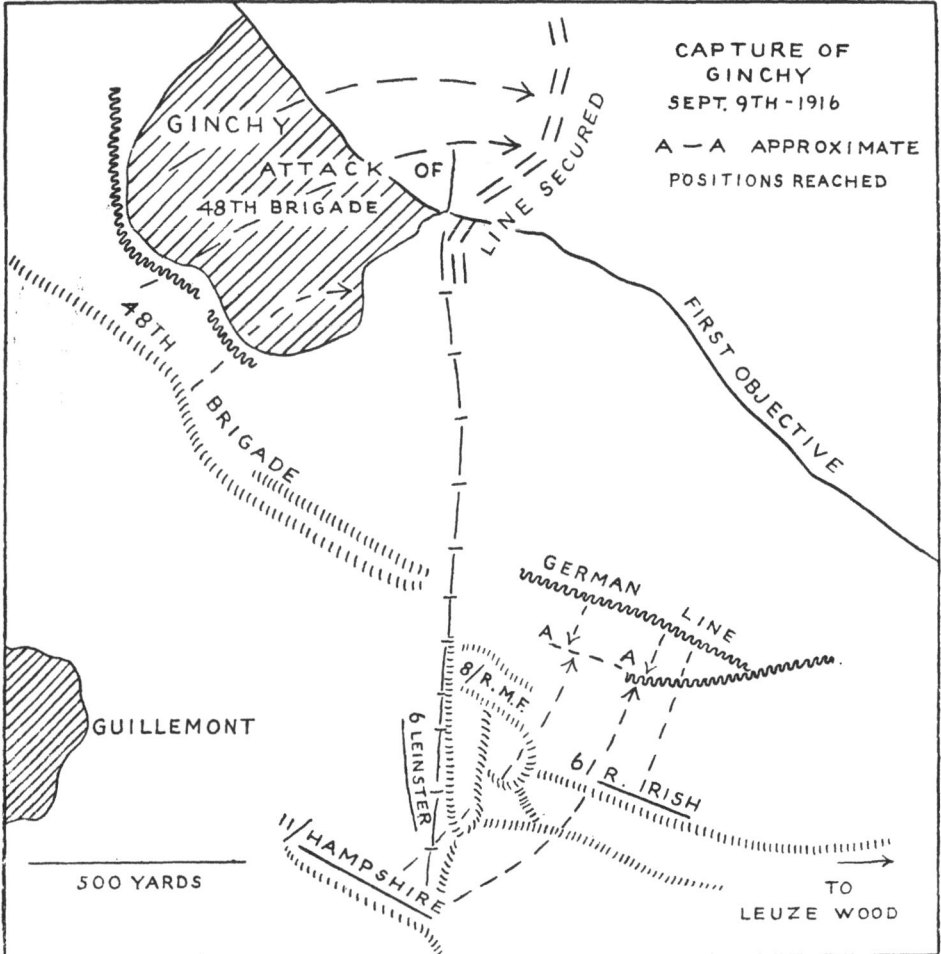

CAPTURE OF
GINCHY
SEPT. 9TH - 1916

A — A APPROXIMATE
POSITIONS REACHED

GINCHY

ATTACK OF
48TH BRIGADE

LINE SECURED

48TH BRIGADE

FIRST OBJECTIVE

GERMAN LINE

A — A

8/R.M.F.

6 LEINSTER

GUILLEMONT

6/ R. IRISH

11/HAMPSHIRE

500 YARDS

TO
LEUZE WOOD

heavy, the battered trenches captured showed how effective our bombardment had been, many dug-outs having had ' direct ' hits, while our riflemen had found

[1] Those killed included Captains Green and Rowsell and 2/Lts. Ash, Ball, Bearn, W. G. May, Peel and Rodger ; 2/Lts. Haydon and Tew were missing and subsequently reported as prisoners of war. Captain E. C. Freeman now assumed command. Lts. Goldsmith, Bartlett and Leach were awarded the M.C. The account in the battalion diary is distinctly meagre and gives little detail, not even naming the officers killed and wounded, having apparently been written up later. The Brigade's diary supplies more of the story.

and used satisfactory targets. The Germans had had to pay high for the success of their counter-attacks.

Despite this repulse, the Thirty-Ninth Division was not relieved but had on September 10th to extend its frontage, so that only it and one other were holding the whole front from the Ancre to Hébuterne. Luckily the Germans were too well occupied to think of a counter-attack, thinly as our line was held.

With the Division so hard pressed the 14th had come into line again on September 14th, in the Auchonvillers sector and almost at the point from which the 1st had attacked on July 1st. A new C.O. arrived, Major Harman of the Leinster, who relieved Captain Freeman on September 21st, when a large batch of officers also arrived, mainly of the 3rd Battalion, while drafts nearly 300 strong had appeared. These, however, came mainly from the Suffolk or the Essex, the War Office having a peculiar capacity for sending drafts to strange regiments. All three brigades were in the line, with orders to be active so as to detain as many Germans as possible while the big thrust was being made elsewhere, and accordingly trench mortars and rifle grenades were freely used, to which the enemy retaliated fairly vigorously, his minenwerfer being unpleasantly in evidence.

Meanwhile on the British right the 11th Hampshire also were having the 'liveliest' times they had yet gone through. Our line now turned sharply Southward at Delville Wood to face Ginchy and Guillemont, localities which were proving stones of stumbling. Their capture was essential to securing a good starting line for the next big attack; several Divisions had incurred heavy losses in attempts to master them, and it was to a 'sticky' point that the Sixteenth Division had found itself directed at the end of August, becoming Corps reserve to the Fourteenth Corps.

Pioneers were not allowed to be idle even in Corps reserve. Two companies of the 11th Hampshire were promptly placed under the Fifth Division to help in consolidating some hard-won gains on our extreme right. After September 4th the 11th reverted to their own Division, now about to tackle Ginchy, for Guillemont, after resisting so many attacks, had at last been captured on September 3rd. Command on this front had then passed to the Sixteenth Division and the 11th Hampshire, who now moved up to Bernafay Wood, were soon busy on the defences and in finding carrying parties for the 48th Brigade, now on the Division's left, facing North towards Ginchy, an even nastier obstacle than Guillemont. The next three days gave the 11th hard work under heavy fire, digging new trenches and helping to consolidate. On September 6th Major Hazard was badly wounded when reconnoitring along with Lt. Cade. Encountering a patrol they challenged, were answered in English and coming forward were shot, Lt. Cade being killed. Major Hazard, after lying helpless in a shell hole, was eventually found by Corporal Snelling, who went back for help and, aided by Captains Stack and Thyne, brought him safely in. September 7th brought orders to take over the defences of Guillemont from the Irish Rifles, but the 'defences' were hard to discover, the trenches being almost obliterated, while shell-holes and a few dug-outs provided only a scanty shelter, so that the battalion, which had two days of severe shelling here, was really lucky to escape with under 40 casualties.

A fresh attack on Ginchy was fixed for September 9th, and as battalions were weak, recruits from Ireland being few, A and B Companies with four extra Lewis guns under Captain Stack were attached to the 47th Brigade, the rest of the 11th going back to Bernafay Wood.

A and B had during the night to dig themselves in 300 yards behind the front line, held by the 6th Royal Irish, who were to lead the attack. It was timed for 4.45 p.m., and during a long day of waiting the two companies had to endure a good deal of shelling. Casualties fortunately were not numerous, but Captain Stack was sniped when crossing the open to report to the O.C. of the 6th Connaught Rangers, under whose orders A and B had been placed.

A heavy machine-gun fire met the Royal Irish directly their first wave went forward; it seemed that the German first line had escaped our bombardment, for many machine-guns remained in action in it; the Hampshire, following the leaders, were also mown down in numbers; Captain Bland and three subalterns were hit at once, and to avoid annihilation the men could only seek what shelter they could in shell-holes. Lt. Shaw, however, helped by Lt. Durrant, brought small parties of the second wave forward by short rushes and reached a trench just short of the German line, in which he found many Royal Irish were sheltering. Here they remained till about 7 p.m., pinned down by shell-fire, and then, as the light failed, a fresh rush carried the surviving attackers into the enemy's front line. This they held for some time till a strong counter-attack forced them back to the trench where Lt. Shaw's party had sheltered and here they checked the enemy. But if itself unsuccessful, the 47th Brigade's attack had distracted the enemy's attention from the 48th on its left, who had meanwhile mastered and held Ginchy, repulsing several counter-attacks.[1]

After dark the Guards relieved the 47th Brigade and the survivors of A and B rejoined head-quarters in Bernafay Wood, C and D meanwhile making a fruitless journey to Ginchy to construct strong points, the sites selected proving not to be in our possession. Next day (September 10th) the battalion went back to Morlancourt and thence to Corbie. Here it remained till the 18th, then going by bus to Airaines, to entrain on September 21st for Flanders and the Second Army, which was using its division to relieve some of the Canadians, now under orders for the Somme, in the line NW. of Wytschaete.[2]

With Ginchy and Guillemont taken and useful gains of ground made in Delville Wood and on our right, preparations for the big attack, now fixed for September 15th, could go forward. Several fresh Divisions were now available, among them the Forty-First, which was to attack from Delville Wood, having

[1] Lts. Durrant and Shaw received the M.C.
[2] The battalion diary does not give the casualties for the attack of September 9th or for the whole month. 2/Lts. Chubb and Jeffries were killed on that day along with Captain Bland.

on its flanks the Fourteenth Division (right) and the New Zealanders (left);
eighteen of the new secret weapons, later known as 'tanks', were to work
with it.

The 122nd Brigade was on the Division's left with the 15th Hampshire
(right) and 18th K.R.R.C. (left) in the leading line, their objective being Flers
Trench, just South of Flers, where the supporting battalions, the 11th R.W.K.
and 12th E. Surrey, would go through them and tackle Flers itself. In moving
up over-night into its assembly position the battalion had been heavily shelled,
and before Zero (6.20 a.m.) it had lost Captain Carrington of C Company and
two platoon commanders, 2/Lts. Baddeley and Parry, while ration parties had
suffered severely on the way up to the line. Advancing at Zero behind an
excellent barrage, with seven tanks to help them, the Hampshire were
quickly into the German front line, Tea Support, which was badly damaged,
though its defenders fought hard before they were overpowered. Unluckily
machine-guns on the left had done considerable damage before they were
silenced, two more company commanders, Captains Stapleton and S. Thompson,
being killed. One troublesome machine-gun was put out of action by a private
who worked along a trench until close up and then shot down the whole team,
and Lance Corporals Heath and Steer each rushed a machine-gun and disposed
of it and its crew. Some dug-outs had to be cleared, but smoke bombs were
used to good effect. Pushing on again, the Hampshire mastered the Switch Line
also, where they met more opposition, which they soon overcame, taking many
prisoners,[1] though casualties were mounting up. Here several dug-outs had to
be cleared but the advance to Flers Trench went forward according to schedule,
the 11th R.W.K. now reinforcing and going forward with the Hampshire. Flers
Trench was full of Germans, but they were readier to bolt or surrender than to
fight, being evidently terrified by the tanks, whose machine-guns had proved
very effective, though most of them were already out of action, owing mainly
to engine-trouble and other mishaps.

From Flers Trench a much disorganized advance was made into Flers, most
of the officers had already fallen,[2] and few were left to control the men or to keep
the 15th Hampshire in hand to consolidate their proper objective, and Hampshires and R.W. Kent went forward together with all formations broken up.
On the outskirts of Flers a field gun in a house at a cross-roads gave trouble, till
a tank arrived, ' spitting fire from its guns ', and disposed of it, Germans who
tried to meet the tank with bombs finding to their surprise that the bombs did
more harm to the throwers, fragments rebounding from it. Three tanks were
already out of action, but this one now headed the entry into Flers, while three
others worked along its Eastern edge. The sight of them was too much for the
Germans, Flers was quickly cleared, and parties, pressing on beyond the village,
reached the third objective, some of the 15th under 2/Lt. Menzies-Calder
collecting over 20 prisoners on their way. But, when it came to consolidating

---

[1] These were sent back under the escort of some ' walking wounded '. They were Bavarians,
two battalions of the 9th Bavarian Regiment being almost completely wiped out on this front.
[2] The last company commander, Captain Bailey, was killed in taking Flers Trench.

beyond the village, the lack of officers and senior N.C.O's [1] proved a serious trouble : with hardly anyone to take charge few men had any idea what to do, and when the Germans began to shell the captured positions some men drifted back into Flers and for a time the situation was critical, though parties of all battalions hung on North of the village and dug themselves in. Colonel Cary-Barnard and battalion head-quarters had by now come forward to Flers Trench, where a defensive position was consolidated and stragglers rallied, captured machine-guns being placed in position to strengthen the defence. Little news came back,[2] and that most confused, reports that Flers had been evacuated conflicting with others that the third objective was still occupied. 2/Lt. Hall and Corporal Murdin were indefatigable in obtaining accurate information, and eventually about 30 men under 2/Lts. Smith and Menzies-Calder [3] were dis-covered digging in beyond the village, as was also a separate party under 2/Lt. Tollemache, who had been wounded, while 2/Lt. Hall, having collected some men, took them forward to the third objective and dug in there. C.S.M. Smith also, though wounded, collected another party and consolidated a post, holding on all day until relieved at dark.[4]

Heavily as Flers and all our advanced positions were being bombarded the Germans never succeeded in regaining ground here, though they brought up large reserves and during the forenoon made several efforts to advance on Flers without success. Some of the 124th Brigade had come up into line East of Flers and secured the right flank, on the left touch was obtained with the New Zealanders,[5] while the Brigade Major of the 122nd Brigade, Major Gwyn Thomas, did much to organize the line North of the village, where Box and Cox and the Hog's Head, some trenches used for bombing practice, were occupied and consolidated, and towards evening two quite substantial counter-attacks, mainly against the 124th Brigade, were repulsed by rifle fire.

After dark the 123rd Brigade took over at Flers and the 15th Hampshire, considerably reduced in numbers, could get back to York Trench in reserve. Eight officers [6] and 97 men were killed and missing and three officers and 197 men wounded, out of the 18 officers and 557 other ranks in action, but hard as it had been hit the battalion could congratulate itself on its first battle, the capture of Flers was much to its credit, the advance here, of over 2,000 yards, being the furthest made anywhere along the front.

Elsewhere also substantial success had been achieved: we had at last cleared High Wood, Martinpuich and Courcelette had been taken and heavy punish-ment inflicted on the enemy. Unluckily our right had been checked, beyond it the French had done nothing, and this had helped to prevent further advances

[1] Three C.S.M's had been hit as well as nearly all the officers. The C.O. of the 11th R. West Kent was killed trying to organize the defence North of Flers.

[2] Three runners from C Company were killed within a space of 200 yards.

[3] 2/Lts. A. G. Smith and A. R. Hall subsequently received the M.C., C.S.M. Smith, Corporals Heath and Steer the D.C.M. and 12 men the M.M.

[4] Subsequently died of wounds.

[5] Their attack had gone very well and they were established NW. of Flers and beyond the road to Eaucourt l'Abbaye.

[6] Besides those mentioned 2/Lt. Stopford was killed.

in the centre and left and baulked us of the ' break-through ' for which the
' higher authorities ' had again hoped.[1] What the ' tanks ' had contributed

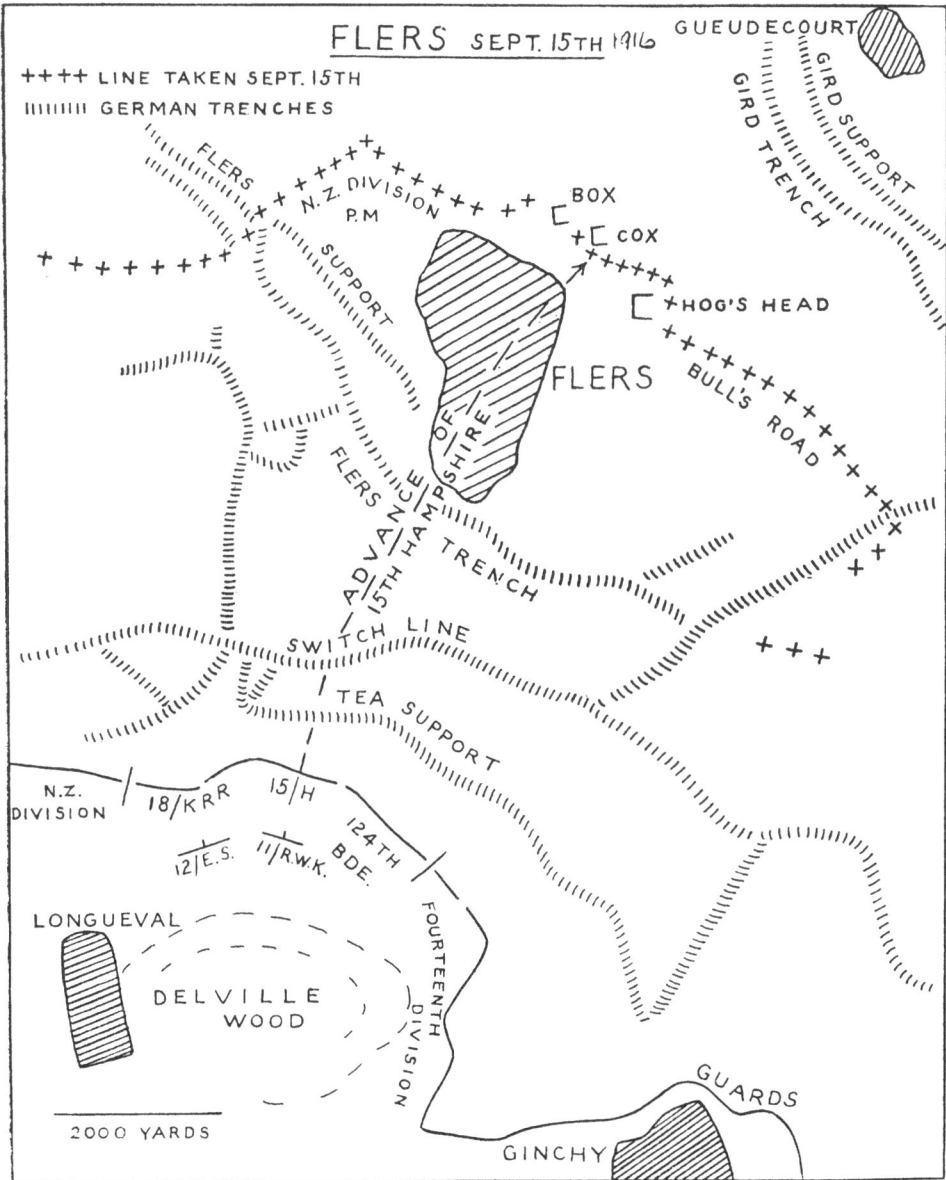

FLERS SEPT. 15TH 1916

++++ LINE TAKEN SEPT. 15TH
IIIIIIII GERMAN TRENCHES

to the day's success had largely been by their influence on German morale :
their actual performances in action had fallen far short of those prophesied, very

---

[1] The Forty-First Division's final objective had been the Gird Trenches and Gueudecourt
behind them.

few had got far, many through developing defects and putting themselves out of action. Critics who condemn their employment in September 1916 as premature would do well to examine in detail their achievements on September 15th and reflect how much worse a disappointment might have resulted from the employment at a later date of much larger numbers, if there had been no opportunity of testing them in action and there discovering their defects and the points where improvements in design were necessary; moreover if full benefit was to be reaped from their employment infantry and guns had to learn by experience how to co-operate with them. The 15th Hampshire had learnt something from what this involved but nothing to encourage extravagant ideas of what the existing model might be expected to achieve.

In the extension and consolidation of the gains made on September 15th and in the renewed attack of September 25th no Hampshires were concerned : the 15th were too much reduced to be employed again so soon and, though the Second Army had released the Fourth Division in the middle of September, it was not in action till October 7th and then the 11th Brigade was in reserve. Indeed, though they had remained a fortnight longer in Flanders, the 2nd Hampshire, were actually in action again before the 1st Battalion, as their brigade was sent on ahead of the rest of the Twenty-Ninth Division, now also returning to the Somme. With the Thirty-Ninth Division stretched out on the long inactive front from the Ancre Northward, the Hampshire had no share in the hard fighting on both flanks which filled the last days of September.

Those days which saw Lesboeufs and Morval and Gueudecourt taken on our right also saw the Fourth Army's left brought up to Le Sars, while the Reserve Army mastered the almost impregnable Thiepval, taken by the Eighteenth Division on September 26th, and broke into the lines running Eastward along the crest of the ridge towards Courcelette. Here three redoubts, the Schwaben, North of Thiepval, and Stuff and Zollern, farther East, were particularly nasty obstacles, and even after Thiepval had been taken some weeks passed before the Thirty-Ninth Division, whose 117th and 118th Brigades relieved the Eighteenth Division at the beginning of October, had really mastered them. But even then the 14th Hampshire remained North of the Ancre, holding first the Redan sector and then that opposite Y Ravine, and did not become acquainted with the Schwaben Redoubt until October 16th. They had been as active as conditions would permit and had carried out one elaborate feint attack, ' doing everything except go over the top ' one officer wrote. Casualties for September, apart from those in the attack of September 3rd, came to about 50, including Captain Gunner (Hampshire Carabiniers) wounded.

Meanwhile the 15th Battalion had had another dose of the Somme. Flers had deprived that battalion of many competent and experienced officers and N.C.O.s, but it still had its C.O. and its Adjutant, Lt. Wilkinson,[1] and the practice, now regularly followed, of leaving out of any attack a proportion of officers,

---

[1] He had recently taken over from Captain Carrington.

N.C.O.s and specialists made the rebuilding of weakened battalions much easier. ' Second Line ' Yeomanry units and Cyclist Battalions, hitherto earmarked for Home Defence, were now being utilized to provide drafts and afforded some excellent material of good physique and better trained than the raw recruits so prominent in recent drafts, and when the 15th moved up to Mametz on October 2nd, after a fortnight's rest and training at Dernancourt, if none too strong they were ready again to give a good account of themselves. They came into line just to the left of their former position, relieving the New Zealanders, who had made substantial progress West of Gueudecourt, having driven the Germans a long way back up [1] the Gird and Gird Support Trenches, which the Forty-First Division had failed to reach on September 15th. The line the Forty-First were taking over ran from the Flers-Ligny Thilloy road to the Eaucourt l'Abbaye-La Barque road, NE. of Eaucourt. Gird Support here formed our front trench, but only the Eastern portions of this trench and of Gird Trench were as yet in our hands.

The 15th had hardly taken over before, about 5 a.m. on October 4th, they were attacked in force, Germans trying to break in between C and D Companies in the left centre of the front line in Gird Support. The attack was pressed with great determination, especially on the right, where some rather higher ground was evidently their objective, but the 15th offered a stubborn resistance, using bombs and machine-guns with excellent effect and doing considerable execution. 2/Lts. Gorman and Trevett gave their men a fine lead, heading bombing attacks with great success, and 2/Lt. Gorman not only drove some intruding Germans out of our line but pushed forward along a sap and established a block 25 yards down it. New Zealand machine-gunners who had remained behind did splendid service, all but one man were hit but the survivor went on working his gun till it too was disabled, while bombers from the 18th K.R.R.C. gave useful help. The enemy pressed hardest against C Company, but they could not overcome its resistance, and after over an hour's hard fighting they withdrew, having suffered heavily, while the 15th's casualties only came to a dozen.

After their repulse the Germans did not renew the attack, contenting themselves with shelling the position vigorously, but this did not prevent our bombers pushing forward 60 yards next day ; having reached a point where the trench was blown in, they waited till a German advance to this gap gave them good targets and after holding on for an hour they withdrew, having sniped successfully and done some useful reconnoitring, while it was satisfactory to find the trenches full of German dead. That evening the battalion was reported as 'short of rations but in good spirits ' : it had again inflicted many more than its own dozen casualties. Next morning (October 6th) another but much less determined bombing attack was easily repulsed, the enemy being pushed back nearly 70 yards along Gird Support till a machine-gun checked our further progress. Then early on October 7th our bombers advanced about 60 yards along both Gird Trench and Gird Support and, though driven right back by a counter-

[1] i.e. NW.

attack, attacked again and eventually secured about half the ground previously taken. Stokes guns which enfiladed the enemy's trenches were used with good results and Sergeant Murdin handled a machine-gun most effectively.

That afternoon a fresh attack was attempted all along the Fourth Army's line. It was stubbornly opposed everywhere, machine-guns which our bombardment had failed to silence preventing much progress. The Forty-First Division's objective included the near ends of Gird Trench and Gird Support still in German hands and the Westward continuation of Bayonet Trench beyond the Flers-Ligny Thilloy road. On the 122nd Brigade's [1] right, the right of the 15th Hampshire carried the near ends of Gird Trench and Gird Support East of the High Wood-Ligny Thilloy road, but, after advancing about 200 yards, the left company was stopped by machine-guns which had been got into position because our barrage had gone ahead too soon.[2] They dug in here, beating back a rather feeble counter-attack, while our Lewis guns kept the enemy's infantry down under cover and allowed our men to dig. Here Lt. Foster and C.S.M. Smith were conspicuous for rallying men and re-organizing them, helping greatly towards maintaining and consolidating the line reached. Meanwhile German bombers working down Gird Trench were pressing our men hard, some of the ground gained was lost and the German advance threatened to cut off those of our men who had established themselves in Gird Support. A determined stand by a mixed party of Hampshire and 18th K.R.R.C., who were supporting the 15th, averted this danger, and eventually the Germans were bombed back nearly 90 yards, where a block was made and our gains secured. Meanwhile touch had been gained on the right with the 26th R. Fusiliers, who[3] also were consolidating short of Bayonet Trench but some way ahead of their starting line, and trenches were dug back to our old line. If in the main the attack had failed, some ground had been gained and the Germans had not escaped too lightly. Then on October 9th the battalion was relieved by the 123rd Brigade and went back into support, moving back again after two days to Mametz Wood and then to Meaulté. It had had nine officers [4] and 190 men hit out of the 17 officers and 319 men in action and sorely needed the drafts, nearly 400 in all and from a vast admixture of regiments, which it now received. After four days at Meaulte it entrained for the Abbeville area, whence it entrained again almost immediately, this time for the Ypres Salient.[5] Together with the rest of the Forty-First Division it had achieved not a little in its first major efforts.

At this stage in the operations the weather was beginning to take an increasingly important and unsatisfactory hand in affairs. Not only were

[1] This brigade was holding the left of the Division's frontage.

[2] The battalion on their left, who had much further to go to reach Gird Trench, also advanced some way before being forced to halt and dig in short of the objective.

[3] 124th Brigade.

[4] Captains James and Lacy and 2/Lt. Breslau were killed and 2/Lt. Philip died of wounds. Captain Amery was among the wounded, as was also 2/Lt. Gorman.

[5] Lt. Foster, 2/Lt. Gorman and C.S.M. Smith received the M.C. and Sergeant Murdin the D.C.M., while 10 M.M.s were awarded to men of the battalion.

frequent and heavy rain-storms making life in the trenches miserable and very exhausting, but reliefs were becoming increasingly slow and difficult, and the forwarding of ammunition, provisions and water to the troops in front, never easy, was now a most strenuous toil. In heavy rain the chalk of this area soon developed a glutinous stickiness over which heavily-laden men could hardly move. Communication trenches became knee-deep in sticky mud, in places they could hardly be used; movement across the open was little faster and by day was prohibitively costly. To attack in these conditions was almost to

ATTACK OF OCT. 7TH 1916

GAINED 7/10/16

TO LA BARQUE

TO LIGNY
THILLOY

GIRD

GIRD SUPPORT

GIRD TRENCH

BAYONET TRENCH

FORTY-SEVENTH
DIVISION

122ND

BRIGADE

15TH HANTS

BEAUCOURT

TAKEN BEFORE OCT. 6
124TH BRIGADE

TO HIGH WOOD

TO FLERS

invite failure ; to achieve success bordered on the miraculous, and yet, with the Germans hard put to maintain their positions even when the weather and ground were so much in their favour, the arguments for maintaining our pressure as far as possible were weighty ; moreover, if Sir Douglas Haig showed any inclination to suspend his attacks, General Joffre would not hear of it and was prompt to urge him to continue them and even pressed him to extend their scope and frontage. Urgent French needs and strong French pressure must not be overlooked, even if the difficulties against which the four Hampshire battalions contended in their attacks of October 1916 may seem to have exceeded what it was reasonable to ask troops to tackle. It is tantalizing to speculate on what might have happened had the abnormally wet autumn of 1916 only been as fine as that of 1918.

The Twelfth Division, to which the 88th Brigade was now attached, was facing a very nasty proposition when called on to tackle the German lines just beyond Gueudecourt in the mud and wet of October. The German front line

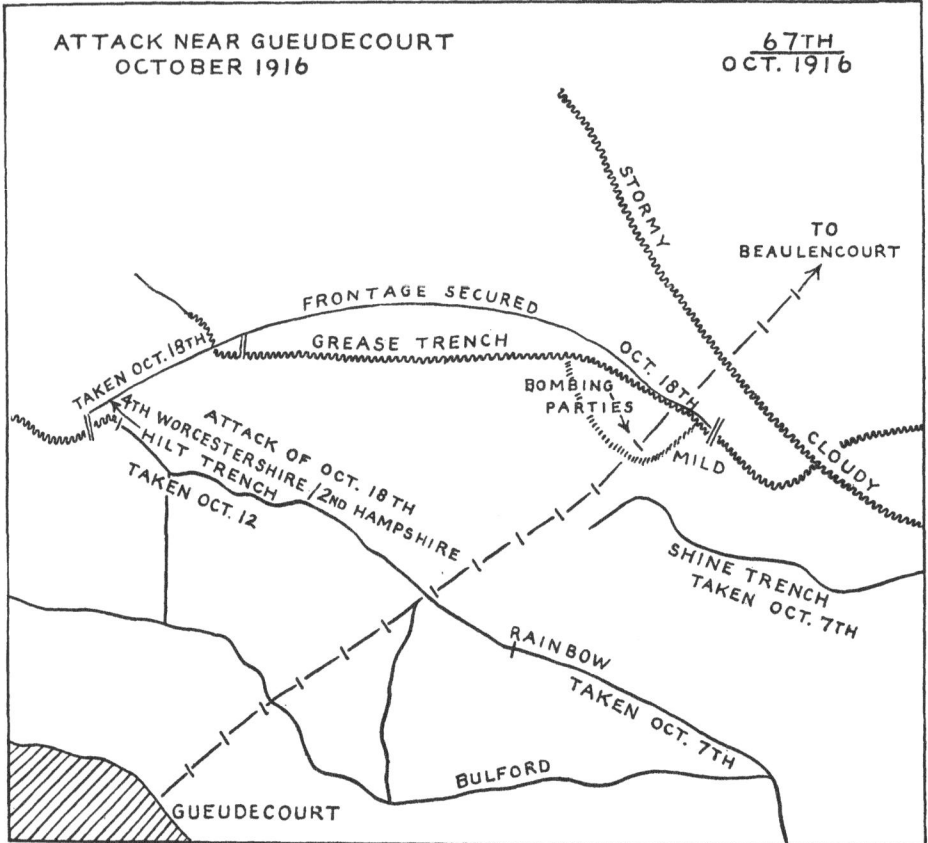

ATTACK NEAR GUEUDECOURT
OCTOBER 1916

67TH
OCT. 1916

here, Hilt Trench opposite the Division's right, the Eastern part of Bayonet Trench opposite the left, was nearly 400 yards away. Attacking on October 7th the Division had been repulsed with heavy loss, the few men who got into the enemy's lines being overwhelmed. It was therefore decided to reinforce it with the 88th Brigade, who were rushed down from Flanders, reaching Longeau on October 8th and moving up by Pommiers Redoubt to reserve trenches a mile and a half short of Gueudecourt. Before leaving Flanders the 2nd Hampshire had been inspected by General Hunter-Weston, who had an encouraging word with the few remaining Gallipoli men, Captain Lord, still Adjutant, and the Quartermaster being the only officers still present who had been at the landing.

Attacking on October 12th, the Newfoundlanders and the Essex carried Hilt Trench [1] after a hard struggle, while on the left some of the Essex reached their second objective, Grease Trench. Further to the left uncut wire in front of Bayonet Trench had checked the 35th Brigade, and the Essex, with their left uncovered, were not only driven back from Grease Trench but from Hilt Trench also. The Newfoundlanders, however, held on, and, being reinforced by Y Company (Lt. Corke), not only maintained their ground but recovered some of the lost portion of Hilt Trench.

That evening, X (Lt. Borough) joined Y in Hilt Trench, relieving the Newfoundlanders, with W (Captain Cuddon) and Z (Captain Massey) in support. Their left was ' in the air ', with Germans holding the continuation NW. of Hilt Trench, while some were actually established to the left rear, near enough to ply our open flank with rifle grenades. To this an effective reply was made and great work was done in consolidating the line, despite heavy shelling, from which the companies in support suffered almost more than those in Hilt Trench itself. Three days here cost the battalion 150 casualties, 2/Lts. Amos (Buffs) and Haly being killed with 32 men, while Colonel Middleton was wounded but continued at duty, but its hard work had made the position secure and thereby assisted the Sixth Division [2] on the right to make good the ground gained on October 7th and 12th across the Beaulencourt Road, while another dozen prisoners had been added to the 150 taken in the original attack.

After two more days in support at Gueudecourt, where more heavy shelling caused another 20 casualties, the battalion moved up into Hilt Trench on the evening of October 17th for a fresh attack on Grease Trench ; on the left the 4th Worcestershire were also attacking, while beyond them the 35th Brigade were making another attempt on Bayonet Trench. On the Hampshire's immediate right the Sixth Division was attacking with Mild Trench, and a portion of Cloudy Trench as objectives.

' Zero ' was at 3.40 a.m. October 18th, but before that the leading companies Y and Z, had formed up in No Man's Land. This drew the enemy's fire but it had little effect, and at ' Zero ' the attackers went forward well and, despite heavy fire, both Hampshire and Worcestershire, keeping close to the barrage, were quickly into Grease Trench and overpowering its defenders, of whom nearly 200 were taken by the two battalions. Grease Trench was not quite continuous and in the dark some Hampshire pushed on to Stormy Trench, 200 yards further on, but, being too far ahead, had to be brought back to Grease Trench, which was being consolidated. Unfortunately the 35th Brigade had again failed against Bayonet Trench, but the Worcestershire were constructing a block at the left end of Grease Trench, while to get touch with the Sixth Division the Hampshire began pushing along the line to the right, getting into Mild Trench and by clearing nearly 200 yards of it gave great help

---

[1] West of the Beaulencourt road, just East of which part of Rainbow Trench was also taken on Oct. 12th, most of it having been taken by the Twentieth Division on Oct. 7th.

[2] It had replaced the Twentieth.

to the battalion whose objective it was.   Captain Cornish [1] and 2/Lt. Harrod,[2] who had led the attack well, now did great work in directing the consolidation, in which C.S.M. Lund [3] was most helpful, while Lance Corporals Fiford and Gray[4] and Privates Johnson [4] and Wilkens [4] carried messages back across the open, despite very heavy shelling, and Privates Bowring [4] and Staples,[4] having salvaged a Lewis gun lying in No Man's Land, cleaned it and got it into action. Twice the enemy were seen gathering for a counter attack, but each time they were quickly and very effectively discouraged by our rapid fire.   It had been intended to construct some strong points 80 yards out to the front, but heavy fire from Stormy Trench and the steady shelling put this out of the question, though the fire did not shift the Hampshire, who held on stoutly, repulsing all attempts to dislodge them.   Captain Cornish, well backed up by 2/Lt. Harrod, was conspicuous for his cheerfulness and confidence, which greatly encouraged his men to maintain their grip on their captures despite the weather and the shelling, and, as the Brigadier [5] said, their determination and endurance were as noticeable as their dash and vigour in the attack.   Their left had been secured by the Worcestershire's success in attack and tenacity in defence, but at one moment the position on the right seemed critical.   The 71st Brigade's left in Mild Trench was very hard pressed, some ground being lost, and strong bombing attacks developed against the Hampshire's exposed right flank. These the battalion's bombers and Lewis gunners checked, Corporal Stockly,[6] Lance Corporal Whitcher [6] and Private Wood [6] all being prominent in repulsing them, while 2/Lt. Harrod followed up this repulse by taking a Lewis gun across the Beaulencourt road and thereby helped the 71st Brigade to hang on in Mild Trench, of which the Hampshire eventually consolidated 200 yards outside their own brigade's frontage.   But to hold the captured position taxed the Hampshire's endurance severely, as the Brigadier very warmly acknowledged : the shelling was very heavy, the weather atrocious, with pelting rain, and to get supplies up to those in front required real energy and determination from the carrying parties.   Useful assistance was given by our guns and by machine-guns in Gueudecourt firing overhead, and the machine-guns in the position captured were very effectively used.   The stretcher bearers were very hard worked, and among them Private Bone [6] stood out, he went from shell-hole to shell-hole getting men into the comparative safety they afforded, bandaging them and even getting some men hot tea : not a few wounded owed him their lives.

The battalion should have been relieved on the night of October 19th/20th, but with the communication trenches so deep in mud and even the open so slippery and sticky that movement was terribly slow, the relieving battalion, one from the 87th Brigade, could not complete the relief in time for the Hampshire to get away before daylight : they had therefore to remain in double-manned trenches until evening.   Since October 17th 2/Lts. Aitcheson, Cain,

[1] His orderly, Private Adams, saved his life by shooting a German who was covering him and also was most useful in the consolidation.
[2] Both officers received the M.C.   [3] Received the D.C.M.
[4] Received the M.M.   [5] Brigadier General D. E. Cayley.
[6] These four and another stretcher bearer, Private Gibbs, received the M.M.

Elton and Hailstone had been killed or were missing, with 31 men, 2/Lts. Corke, Darracott, Gilman, (E. Surrey) Graham (E. Surrey), Gravely and Rutherford were wounded with 106 men, while Captains Cuddon and Massey had to go to hospital, along with 2/Lts. Todd and Treble and 30 men.   The battalion now received many congratulations on its gallantry and tenacity : the position it and the 4th Worcestershire had captured and consolidated, despite so many difficulties and stiff opposition, was a very useful gain, and the commanders of both the Sixth and Twelfth Divisions sent them special messages of thanks for their assistance.   October 18th ranks among the 2nd Hampshire's most notable achievements.   Success at that stage in the Somme was never easily obtained and needed dash and determination to no small degree.

Before this the Fourth Division had taken over the extreme British right [1] and were experiencing the difficulties inherent in co-operating with allies whose methods were not ours.   Attacking on October 12th just East of Lesboeufs, the 10th Brigade had made a small advance, securing Antelope Trench.   The 11th Brigade had been back in reserve at Montauban that day and did not take over the front line until October 17th.   Even then the 1st Hampshire were in brigade reserve near Guillemont and merely supplied carrying and working parties on October 18th, when the Rifle Brigade and East Lancashire attacked with very scanty success.   From October 19th to 22nd, the battalion was digging assembly and communication trenches behind Lesboeufs under great handicaps from wet and mud.   It then took over the front from the Somerset L.I. who had pushed forward after dark on October 19th and secured Frosty Trench, to the left of Antelope Trench and not continuous with it.

A fresh attack was to be made on October 23rd, despite the difficulties of ground and weather, the 1st Hampshire, with the Rifle Brigade in support, seeking to capture Boritska Trench.   A (left) and C (right) companies were leading, B in support having to form a defensive flank on the right.   On the left the Dublins of the 10th Brigade were tackling Hazy Trench and beyond them the 12th Brigade was confronted by Rainy and Dewdrop Trenches.   On our right the French were attacking.

Starting at 2.30 p.m., from Antelope and Frosty Trenches, the attack had first to clear a low ridge in No Man's Land, and directly it crossed this it met a heavy fire, both from Boritska Trench and from machine-guns further back, and C Company were soon driven to shelter in shell-holes short of the objective. The French had failed completely and our right flank was therefore exposed. A Company fared better, entering and taking the Northern end of Boritska, down which they began bombing, at first with some success.   Meanwhile the Dublins had not carried Hazy Trench but had taken some gun-pits NW. of Frosty Trench and with them several machine-guns.   The Rifle Brigade, coming forward in support, were checked by machine-guns in the untaken part of Boritska Trench and only about half a company of Riflemen, working

---

[1] The 1st Hampshire came up to Meaulte on October 7th and moved forward to Montauban five days later.

forward from shell-hole to shell-hole, reinforced the hard-pressed Hampshire in Boritska Trench. Lt. Icke,[1] who had led his company admirably in the attack, recrossed No Man's Land under heavy fire to collect bombers and bring them up to reinforce the men in Boritska. These made a stout fight; 2/Lt. Gullick leading several bombing attacks, though himself wounded. As long as bombs and ammunition lasted the defence held, though the enemy were pressing them from both flanks, but after keeping the Germans at bay till well after dark the survivors, without reinforcements or supplies, had to fall back some to Frosty Trench, some to Antelope. But the fight they had made had helped the Dublins to make good the gun-pits, from which a trench was dug back to Frosty Trench, which another trench linked up with Antelope Trench, so that the attack had resulted in some improvement in our line,[2] which, with the ground in so bad a state, was no small achievement. But it had cost the 1st Hampshire over 200 casualties, Captains Cromie and Le Marchant [3] and 2/Lts. C. J. Girling and Harrison were killed, 2/Lt. Wood was missing and 2/Lts. Gullick, Hodgkins, Lapthorne, Line and Masterman wounded. Of other ranks 86 were killed and missing and 137 wounded.[4] But the Germans had not escaped lightly.

After holding on all next day and doing all they could to consolidate their position and rescue their wounded, the 1st Hampshire were relieved in the small hours of October 25th, by the 2nd R.W.F. whose Division, the Thirty-Third, was now replacing the Fourth. They now went right back, eventually finding good billets at Ramburelles, 12 miles SW. of Abbeville, where six weeks out of trenches enabled them to rest, refit and assimilate their drafts.

The 1st Battalion had thus finished with ' the Somme ', rather sooner than the 2nd, who after a week in reserve were back in front trenches North of Flers for two days at the end of October. They had returned to their own Division, which was then relieved, and before having to go back into trenches got a fortnight's rest, the 2nd Hampshire being at Mericourt. The 2nd then took over support trenches at Bernafay Wood and were there four days before taking over the front line NE. of Les boeufs on November 21st. By this time the effort to push our right further forward, over the slippery slime of the battle area, had been abandoned and the sector was ' quiet ', if nothing else could be said for it.

Beyond the Ancre, however, a last ' push ' had been made, with some success, on November 13th, Beaumont Hamel being taken, and here fighting was still raging. This final attack had completed the work on which the Fifth, the renamed Reserve, Army had been engaged since its success at Thiepval on September 26th. Gradually and only after hard fighting our lodgements in the Schwaben Redoubt had been extended and consolidated, the 117th and 118th Brigades assisting to complete its reduction during the first half of October.

---

[1] Received the M.C.   [2] Further to the left also rather bigger gains had been made.
[3] Both sons of old officers of the regiment.
[4] A few of these casualties occurred between October 17th and 23rd, 2/Lt. Currie also being wounded on October 20th.

The 116th, however, was left in its old line across the Ancre, strung out in a wide front which was but thinly held. The 14th Hampshire had four days ' out ' from October 6th to 10th after a spell of 16 days on end in the trenches, but they were back again in line facing Y Ravine for six days before being relieved by the Sixty-Third Division on October 16th and thus set free to rejoin the other brigades on the Thiepval front. If had been a trying time, if devoid of special incident, but casualties had fortunately been few.

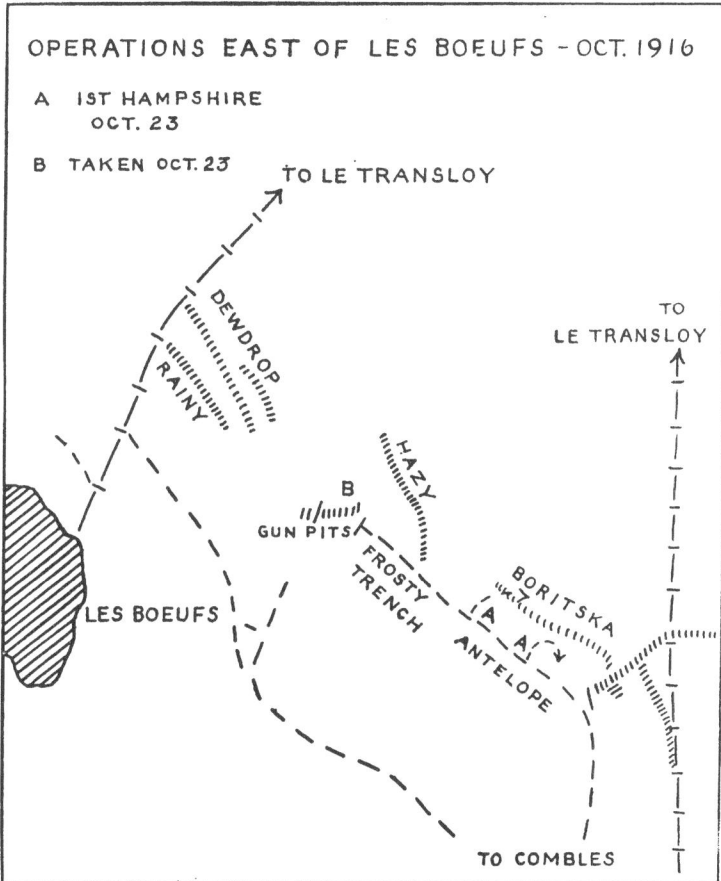

OPERATIONS EAST OF LES BOEUFS - OCT. 1916

A   1ST HAMPSHIRE
    OCT. 23

B   TAKEN OCT. 23   TO LE TRANSLOY

DEWDROP
RAINY

TO
LE TRANSLOY

HAZY

B
GUN PITS

FROSTY TRENCH

BORITSKA
ANTELOPE

LES BOEUFS

TO COMBLES

By the time the 116th Brigade were across the Ancre Stuff Redoubt also had been taken, and the next objective was formed by Stuff Trench and its Eastward continuation, Regina Trench, whose capture would complete the work already begun of driving the Germans down the reverse slope of the ridge and depriving them of the crest line and its facilities for observation.

The 14th Hampshire after a good night's rest at Engelbelmer (October 16th/ 17th) relieved the 12th R. Sussex in the Schwaben Redoubt next morning, to come in for as hard a time as they had yet known. The much battered and contested defences offered little protection against persistent heavy shelling

and even less shelter from the constant rain and bitter cold. At one point
Germans were established in a continuation of a trench which we were holding
and they more than once tried to attack along it. These attempts the 14th
quickly repulsed, but bombing and rifle-grenading continued intermittently,
while the shelling went on steadily, causing many casualties until by hard work
the defenders had done something to improve the cover. To lessen the effects
of the concussion men at times sat with their backs braced up against one
side of a trench and their feet pressing into the other. But the wet and cold
were even worse than the shelling ; men got so stuck in the mud that their
extrication took hours, at ' stand to ' some were so stiff with cold that they had
to be lifted to their feet. This rain and mud doubled the difficulties of the

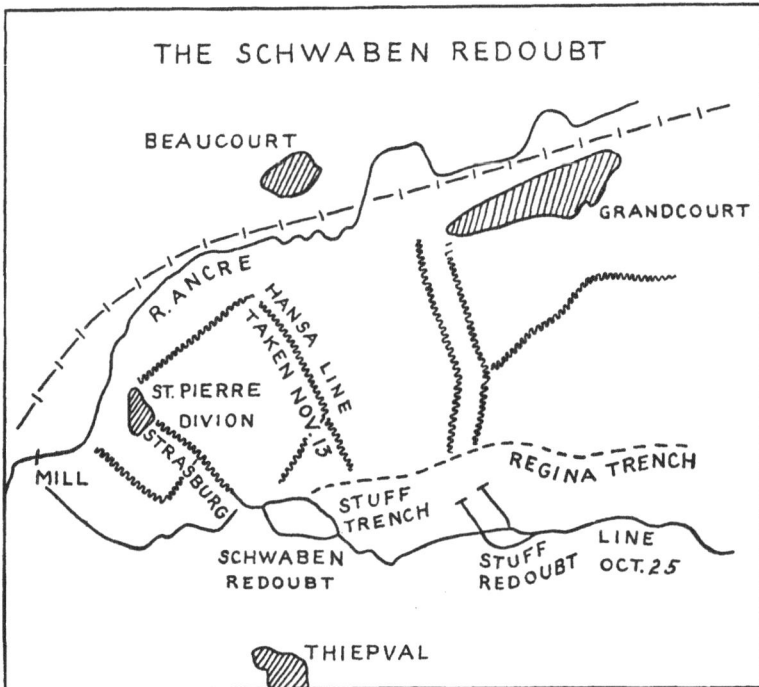

THE SCHWABEN REDOUBT

carrying parties in bringing up ammunition and rations, but fortunately the
German dead who filled the trenches, in themselves an encouraging factor, had
ample rations on them by which the Hampshire profited, as well as by the large
quantities of excellent equipment lying about. A large parcel of cigars and
tobacco, obviously lately arrived from Germany, was quickly disposed of and,
as one officer wrote, ' we wore German overcoats till they were wet through and
then put on others, we used their waterproof capes, we dug with German spades,
in fact we made full use of all Mr. Bosche's gear, and jolly good it was.'

Even with these alleviations the 14th had four very hard days, which they
endured in a manner enormously to their credit. One officer wrote in warm

admiration of his men's unflinching steadfastness ; soaked to the skin, without a chance to get dry or to get food cooked, they ' stuck it ' without a murmur, took every chance to hit back and held on until, late on October 20th, the 17th K.R.R.C. turned up to relieve them, but by then casualties had come to nearly 100, including 2/Lt. C. D. F. Pearce and 20 men killed.

As the K.R.R.C. were very weak and an attack was to be made next day, D Company under Captain Warren were left behind to reinforce them, together with some details, largely men who had not been able to get away in darkness, the difficulty of getting exhausted men out of the mud and helping them along having caused many delays. Not long after the relief had been completed a heavy barrage was put down on the redoubt, under cover of which a strong body of Germans advanced to the attack and, using flammenwerfers, established two lodgements in the the Northern face, some of the defenders being almost too cold to be able to fire. However, they rose to the occasion splendidly ; chilled and dead-beat as most of the Hampshire were, once the fight began they warmed up and ' were as fresh as paint in one minute ', as one combatant put it. Counter-attacking vigorously they and the 60th hurled themselves on the intruders, many of whom surrendered almost without a fight, while the rest were driven headlong out of the redoubt, in which they left behind many dead and more prisoners. They were apparently picked men from three regiments, but the fight they made hardly suggested it ; one account says that the Hampshire hardly knew what to do with so many prisoners, and there were officers among them.

More was to be required of D Company than merely to repulse attacks. That afternoon the 116th Brigade took part in a big attack on Stuff and Regina Trenches, three other Divisions co-operating on a frontage of 5,000 yards. D Company, who had the 11th R. Sussex on their right, were on the left of the attackers. Well led by Captain Warren, who fell at the head of his men, they attacked with great dash and were quickly successful, mastering all their objectives after sharp fighting, in which 2/Lt. Green [1] distinguished himself in the capture of a bombing post, leading his bombers with great courage and determination, and, though wounded, remaining at duty to assist in the consolidation until relieved. 2/Lt. Boustead [1] also, taking command when Captain Warren was killed, himself disposed of several Germans and directed the consolidation most effectively. Elsewhere the attack had gone well, practically the whole objective was taken, and though later on the alarm of a counter-attack caused the rest of the Hampshire to be sent up in readiness to reinforce, they were not needed and next day the whole battalion went back to a good camp at Senlis for a well-earned rest. The day's casualties had been heavy, besides Captain Warren 45 men were killed or missing, while 2/Lts. Boustead, Green and Hole and 95 men were wounded but the Germans had lost heavily and many prisoners had been taken. The 14th's achievement had been the more creditable after all they had had to endure from the shelling and the dreadful conditions : no small credit for enabling them to hold on was due to

[1] 2/Lts. Boustead and Green were awarded the M.C.

the carrying-parties, of which 2/Lt. Wallis-Wilson, the battalion's 40-year old veteran, was in charge : his unfailing energy and determination were largely responsible for the arrival of these parties with food, water and ammunition, despite all the difficulties of the approach, the mud, the lack of landmarks and the shelling ; again and again he had a nasty barrage to negotiate, but he always got his men through and ' delivered the goods '.

The weather was now making it hard to maintain the attack, but the Fifth Army had not relinquished its designs on Beaumont Hamel and of simultane-ously advancing its line on the Ancre heights, and so for the next three weeks the Thirty-Ninth Division had to be retained in the fighting line in the Thiepval sector. Conditions were too bad here for battalions to stand more than 48 hours on end in the front line, but when in reserve at Thiepval German dug-outs provided almost luxurious quarters and were full of rations and all varieties of gear and equipment. by which all ranks profited. Rats were much in evi-dence, and as one company of the 14th could produce a ' company ferret ' some excellent rat-hunting was much enjoyed. Things were fairly quiet, a German attack on Stuff Trench on October 26th fizzled out completely, nearly 50 Germans surrendering quite tamely, eight officers among them. More rain made holding the front line very unpleasant and increased the work of the carrying-parties, but casualties were few, though Lt. Harris was killed on November 6th and the M.O. badly wounded. From November 10th to 12th the battalion was in the Schwaben Redoubt, holding a bombing-block at one point with the Germans 30 yards away, just too far to throw their ' stick ' bombs effectively but within range of our Mills bombs, while a ' plum ' bomb they were using proved too small to be very effective.

By this time the weather had improved enough to allow of the Fifth Army making its projected attack on November 13th, and on being relieved on the previous afternoon the Hampshire had merely gone back to the shelter of the Thiepval dug-outs, to be called out early next morning to move up to the Schwaben. Here they were in reserve to the 118th Brigade who, with the 117th on their left nearer the Ancre, were making for St. Pierre Divion and the Hansa Line, which ran down from the Thiepval ridge to the Ancre near Beaucourt.

The Hampshire had no easy advance up to the Schwaben : when they went forward at 5.45 a.m., ' Zero' hour, it was pitch dark, a mist did not help matters, and the tape they were to follow had been shot away, but they managed to reach the redoubt without many casualties and there they waited for orders. Prisoners were soon streaming back in numbers, but patrols sent out to keep touch with the attack reported that ' 63 ', the bombing block already familiar to the 14th, had been missed by the attackers and was causing trouble by firing into the rear of the attacking waves. Captain May accordingly organized an attack upon it and was successful in overcoming its resistance, 20 prisoners, a machine-gun, two automatic rifles and some trench-mortars being captured with it. Meanwhile the attack had gone very well, having apparently taken the Germans by surprise, but here and there pockets of Germans were holding out and about 9.30 a.m. the Hampshire were ordered forward to assist in mopping up and securing the Strassburg Line, running down from the Schwaben Redoubt to St. Pierre Divion. They promptly pushed forward, Captain Bircham, who had done fine work in holding the Schwaben Redoubt in October, again distinguished himself by gallantry and good leading, reinforcing the attackers effectively and helping to secure the objective. Everywhere the advance swept forward, reaching St. Pierre Divion, collecting many prisoners and finding many German wounded, while other battalions, pushing Eastward, secured the Hansa Line half way to Grandcourt. Casualties had been negligible and the readiness of the Germans to surrender was an encouraging thing, ' the majority hardly offered any resistance ; their tails are right between their legs ' one officer wrote. Consolidation was promptly pushed on, Captain Bircham and 2/Lt. Wallis-Wilson doing valuable work, but no counter-attack developed. Elsewhere the attack had been successful, the formidable Beaumont Hamel had been taken, if all our objectives had not been reached, and the day's work was a fine ending to the Somme as far as the 14th Hampshire were concerned. Fighting continued a little longer, mainly exploiting the success of November 13th, but the 14th Hampshire had been relieved that afternoon and with the rest of their Division were soon on their way to Flanders, entraining at Doullens on November 18th and reaching Poperinghe about midnight.

If the simultaneous capture of Beaumont Hamel rather overshadowed the Thirty-Ninth Division's work on November 13th, the 14th Hampshire could congratulate themselves on a share in a notable exploit. ' The Schwaben ' had given them the chance to get their own back for September 3rd, and if their casualties had been again heavy [1] they came out encouraged by their success, by the ample evidence of the state to which quite good German units had been reduced, of which their readiness to surrender had been the outstanding proof. To the rewards gained earlier the 14th could now add the bar to the M.C. awarded to Captain May and the M.C's given to Captain Bircham and 2/Lt. Wallis-Wilson, whose good work at the Schwaben and good leading on November 15th were fittingly recognized.

[1] Not far short of 300 all told from the time of their first occupying the Schwaben Redoubt.

CHAPTER XVI

THE THIRD WINTER

WHEN ' Meredith's ' had wintered in Ghent in Marlborough's days or ' Stuart's ' in Münster in the Seven Years' War, they had enjoyed a real suspension of hostilities and repose, with only ' peace-time ' guards and duties to perform. ' Western Front ' winters between 1914 and 1918 brought no such repose and relaxation : if by 1916 the British forces were large enough to allow whole Divisions to be out of the line together, a ' resting ' Division was usually busy training reinforcements, most of whom had still much to learn. They were lucky if this training was not seriously interrupted by demands for the working parties which the preparations for another great ' push ' made increasingly insistent. Better communications, road, tramway and rail, were essential to this great effort, and better communications meant hard work for fighting units, as the various labour forces which were gradually being developed were as yet quite unequal to the requirements.

But if Divisions nominally ' resting ' were worked quite hard, holding the line during the bitter winter of 1916–1917 was arduous in the extreme. As often, the very wet autumn was followed by a hard winter, frost and snow making existence in trenches miserably uncomfortable, except so far as it banished mud and made movement easier, if the frozen ground made work on trenches almost impossible. Occasional spasms of mild weather were really almost worse than the cold, the mud was quick to re-assert itself, and the Fourth Army, above all the others, found conditions always bad, if sometimes worse. With five miles of slippery devastation, largely water-logged shell-holes, between its front and the old line of July 1st, supports and reserves, if far enough forward to be useful, were almost as exposed and unsheltered as those in front ; merely to keep the forward troops supplied threw a never-ending strain on roads, transport and men, and the trench-garrisons had to endure greater hardships than in the previous winter, when the front line had been nearer to good billets with the manifold amenities so greatly developed since the winter of 1914–1915. Moreover, while the British had had to take over from the French twenty additional miles of frontage, behind which the whole rearward organisation had to be built up from nothing, the higher command was insistent that opportunities of harassing the enemy or gaining ground should not be neglected. The Germans could not be allowed to improve and consolidate unmolested the indifferent line to which they had been pushed back, but if cogent strategical reasons supported this policy, it demanded much of those who carried it out and troops who had endured the Somme were hampered in recovering from its strain.

The 1st Hampshire were fortunate in being out of the line from November 2nd to December 7th, in good billets near Abbeville, mainly occupied with company training, route marching and other exercises, including brigade and Divisional competitions, while leave was fairly generously given. Reinforcements amounting to 168 men joined, with 30 from hospital, to which 54 were admitted, while the officers who joined included Captain K. A. Johnston and three subalterns who had also been wounded on July 1st. December 7th started a return to the front, the battalion having a week in a muddy camp near Bray before moving up on December 15th to Priez Farm near Combles, a sector just taken over from the French and hardly conforming to British standards of what a front should be. Here it spent four days in brigade reserve and then (December 19th) relieved the East Lancashire opposite St. Pierre Vaast Wood, the enemy's front line being about 500 yards away. The ' line ' here was in shell-holes,[1] not continuous trenches, and the ground was extremely muddy, but apart from some German artillery activity the time was uneventful. The battalion had three days in line, four in reserve, three in line again and then on December 29th went back to Bray. Casualties came to 15 killed and missing, with 2/Lt. R. A. B. Hall and 11 men wounded, while so bad were conditions that seven officers and 77 men were admitted to hospital, from which 20 returned, drafts amounting to 280.

The first few weeks of January were spent at Bray, encamped in a pathless sea of mud which needed any amount of work, but nevertheless much training, largely elementary, proved possible and left everyone much smartened up. The New Year's Honours List brought promotion to Captain to the Quartermaster, Lt. Tarrant, the M.S.M. to Sergeant Catley, the Orderly Room Clerk, and ' mentions ' for Captain Wyld and Lt. Flint.

January 16th brought a move to Curlu, where four peaceful days were spent in a good hutted camp, before the battalion moved up over the snow-covered ground to relieve the East Lancashire in the Bouchavesnes sector, three miles North of Peronne. The line here was continuous but too shallow to provide much cover, especially as the Germans overlooked it from higher ground. Luckily mine-shafts abounded and accommodated most of the front line garrison, and such work as the frost allowed was done at night, though a bright moon interfered with wiring, 2/Lt. Jacob being hit while directing a wiring party. Rations and ammunition had to be brought up from five miles away, which absorbed so many of the carrying parties that it left few free to carry up the materials so badly wanted in the front line. During two turns in front line two men were killed and 2/Lt. Jacob and four men wounded, but admissions to hospital came to 93, three times the discharges. A dozen officers joined, including Major Earle[2] and Lt. N. Harland, who had been at Gallipoli with the 2nd Battalion. During a fortnight in camp near Bray, fatigues greatly impeded training : 270 men under Captain Hudson[3] having to make gun emplacements near Rancourt, where another 170 under Captain German assisted a Tunnelling Company. A very unpleasant but uneventful week at Bouchavesnes followed, a thaw filled the trenches with water and they could hardly be kept passable. Then on February 22nd the Eighth Division took over and the 1st Hampshire went

---

[1] Only one company was actually in front line.
[2] Adjutant of the 5th Battalion on mobilization, he had accompanied the 1/5th to India, where he had been on the Staff for some time.   [3] He had returned from a ' course ' at Aldershot.

back West of Corbie, where they spent a week training before moving North to join the Third Army, now being reinforced for its Spring ' push '. February had cost the 1st three men killed and Lt. Harland and ten wounded, with 150 admissions to hospital, from which 35 men had rejoined. Four officers, among them Captain Prendergast, who had already been wounded twice, had joined with 11 men.

Starting on March 4th, the 1st Hampshire reached Buire au Bois, 11 miles NW. of Doullens, on the 7th, having covered 48 miles in four marches ; only 20 men had fallen out, not bad over such roads and after trying times in the trenches. They were ' out ' all March, training and being for some time at the disposal of the Army Training School for demonstration purposes. A move to Bajus near Houdain on March 21st did not interrupt the training, which included a rehearsal over ground marked out to represent the battalion's intended objective in the coming attack. Then on April 7th the battalion started for Arras, reaching Maroeuil next day. Six officers, all new-comers, and 116 men had joined in March, with another 44 from hospital, to which three officers and 85 men had been admitted, and the battalion was both strong and fit.

Like the 1st Battalion the 2nd Hampshire got through the winter without heavy casualties, having only 24 killed and 79 wounded between November 1st and March 31st, for though the Twenty-Ninth Division twice carried out minor offensives during the winter, with considerable sucess, the 88th Brigade was not employed in either, and if at times the German shell-fire was heavy, especially in retaliation for raids or bombardments, it did not do much damage. Most of the battalion's 400 admissions to hospital occurred in November and the first half of December, when they saw a good deal of the front line NE. of Lesboeufs, in trenches which heavy rain had reduced to a deplorable state, after which four weeks ' out ' in the Cavillon area followed.

The 2nd Battalion ended the year with 37 officers and 903 other ranks ; of the officers only Colonel Beckwith, who had rejoined on December 1st, and Captains Lord (Adjutant), Cuddon (O.C. ' W ' Company), and Jones (X), had been with the battalion in Gallipoli, the Quartermaster being away sick and R.S.M. Tyler acting for him.

The New Year brought Captain Lord and 2/Lt. Saunders the M.C. and Sergeant Taylor the D.C.M., Major Middleton, R.S.M. Tyler and Private Bone being ' mentioned '.

January 11th found the battalion at Hangest trying to entrain for Corbie, much hampered by snow, quantities of slush, no lights and a train which was six hours late. At Corbie it had good billets but more slush and no means of removing it. It then moved up on January 20th by Carnoy and Guillemont to take over trenches nearly two miles NE. of Morval. Ice-coated duckboards made carrying very difficult, the ground was frozen hard and the line a mere chain of isolated posts,[1] but the Germans were clearly no better off and lay quiet,

[1] Braziers were taken up to the front and did something to alleviate conditions there.

and three days in line only produced 15 admissions to hospital and two men killed. The battalion was ' in ' again from January 25th to 27th, when the 87th Brigade celebrated the Kaiser's birthday by a most successful attack, capturing 350 prisoners, which provoked a vigorous retaliation without causing the Hampshire any casualties. After two turns at Morval early in February, where casualties were heavier than usual, 11 in the first, 13 in the second, they were ' out ' at Raineville from the 10th to 20th and then had three days in trenches at Saillisel. Despite many admissions to hospital drafts kept the strength well up.

Both the Fourth and Twenty-Ninth Divisions were ' out ' when on March 17th the Fourth Army found the Germans beginning to retreat to the Hindenburg Line, the Fifth's opponents having already evacuated the nasty salient astride the Ancre in which the autumn fighting had left them. The 2nd Hampshire, having been relieved at Saillisel on March 3rd, were back at Meaulté, where they remained till March 19th, then moving to Vignacourt in the lower Somme area, where the Division was to go through the intensive training which its energetic commander organized and superintended so assiduously. The leading of junior officers during the Somme had frequently been severely criticised, they did not know how to utilise opportunities, much less develop them, and courage without knowledge or grasp of tactical principles was more likely to cause avoidable casualties than to achieve success. Special attention was therefore paid to their instruction and to musketry, in which our standard had declined disastrously through excessive concentration on the bomb. The Division was soon to show how much it had profited by the energetic and systematic instruction now provided.

Fifty men having joined with several officers, the 2nd mustered 44 officers and 883 other ranks on March 31st, companies having usually seven subalterns, though many fewer were normally present, mainly owing to ' courses '. Two marches of 12 miles each, in snow and bitter weather, took them to Mondicourt by April 2nd. A ' battle nucleus '[1] was detailed to go back to the Corps depot, and then on April 7th the battalion advanced to Humbercourt, its Division being under the Eighteenth Corps, in Army reserve to the Third Army, now about to attack in force.

All three Hampshire ' Service battalions ' in France being in the Second Army, they also saw nothing of the advance towards the Hindenburg Line with its numerous actions. On the Second Army's front the winter had seen no major activities. Its mines under the Messines Ridge were dug and ready for the offensive in Flanders which Sir Douglas Haig had so long projected, but most Divisions now under General Plumer had needed time to recuperate and re-build themselves after heavy losses on the Somme, while winter conditions in the Salient hardly encouraged attacking.

The 11th Hampshire, who had taken over De Zon Camp [2] before the end of

---

[1] This included the second in command, Major Middleton, one company commander and at least one subaltern per company with some ' specialist ' N.C.O's and men.

[2] Near Vierstraat.

September, remained there for six months, despite a change of the Divisional front in December, when the Sixteenth Division took over the Spanbroekmolen sector, but eventually moved at the end of March to a new camp, Moore Park, Divisional H.Q. having shifted to Locre. Duties and occupations during this time varied little : roads, camps and the maintenance and improvement of the line kept any Pioneers amply occupied. In the line ' strong points ' and trench-mortar emplacements had to be constructed, new trenches dug, infantry working parties supervised and assisted in draining, revetting and repairing ; in back areas more hutted camps were needed and extensive drainage schemes were being carried out, while baths, drying-rooms and wash-houses were built and roads kept in repair, with miscellaneous tasks like erecting a chaff-cutting shed and engine house, while the transport horses found peaceful employment in ploughing up ground near the camp in which to plant potatoes.

Casualties among the working parties in the line were not infrequent but in the aggregate not heavy ; Lt. Hytton, hit in November when supervising work on a ' strong point ', was the only officer killed before the Messines attack of June 6th opened the Flanders offensive of 1917, though 2/Lt. T. E. Hall was wounded in March. Changes among the officers, however, were numerous : ill-health compelled Captain Windle to relinquish his commission, Lt. Sulman taking over as Adjutant. Captain Saye went to the R.E. and Captain Bedford to the Sudan, but Major Hazard rejoined. The New Year brought Colonel Crockett and Major Bell the D.S.O. and ' mentions ', Captain Stack, Corporal Adnams and Pioneer Beck being also ' mentioned '.

Occasionally Lewis gun teams were attached to battalions in the line and came in for some activity, but incidents were few, if work was continuous and strenuous. The move to Moore Park was made in extremely bad weather, heavy snow and then a thaw, and when the Arras attack started (April 9th) activity on the Divisional front increased, several raids being made, which provoked retaliation and more work for the Pioneers, whose main activities were directed towards completing the elaborate preparations for the attack on Messines.

The Thirty-Ninth Division, after reaching Flanders late in November, enjoyed nearly three weeks welcome respite from the line. This time the 14th Hampshire spent quietly at Poperinghe, mostly in good wooden huts, training, route-marching, finding many working parties, but getting a fair amount of recreation, especially football. The Division then took over the Northern sector of the Salient, the 14th Hampshire, after four days in support on the Canal Bank, relieving the 12th Sussex at Hill Top Farm on December 16th. This quarter was very different from the Somme, the defences were mainly breastworks, to dig deeper than two feet was to reach water, both the French Territorials whom the Division relieved and their opponents seemed to have forgotten all about the war and had abstained from hostilities. This state of affairs was quickly altered and for a time the Divisional snipers enjoyed themselves, while despite some shelling only three men were wounded in four days, which were mainly devoted to repairing the trenches and reclaiming a disused line. The battalion next sampled the Boesinghe sub-sector from December 30th to January 16th, where it had the Germans within 50 yards across the Yser canal. It was now doing four days in support and four in reserve. Here again things were fairly quiet, though on January 6th the line was bombarded for forty minutes, fortunately without any casualties being inflicted. The battalion's snipers claimed several hits but bright moon-light hampered wiring parties. The weather was mainly cold with some snow and sleet and life in the line was far from pleasant. Colonel Harman being away ill, Major Finlay was commanding. A move into billets at Ypres then followed, the next sector taken over, on January 20th, being at Railway Wood East of Ypres. Here rather greater activity prevailed, guns and ' minenwerfer ' being much in evidence, and a second turn in front line from January 29th to February 1st caused the battalion nearly 40 casualties. This turn ended with a violent bombardment which seemed to show that an attack was coming. One trench-mortar bomb landed among B Company's officers, badly wounding Captain Bircham and killing 2/Lts. Colebrook and Humphrey-Davy. Despite this and heavy shelling and several casualties,[1] B and C stuck unflinchingly to their posts, and when Germans came forward in force on B's frontage a hot reception discouraged them, no Germans getting into our line. The defenders were effectively helped by the support company, which Captain Goldsmith [2] promptly brought up through a barrage. Unable to effect an entrance the enemy now fell back, whereupon Captain Goldsmith followed their retreat up with a party, capturing a prisoner and obtaining identifications. This repulse of a formidable attack was warmly commended by the Divisional commander, Major General Cuthbert, who emphasized the battalion's steadiness in defence and energy in counter-attacking.

After this the 14th were in camp West of Ypres till February 25th, training and resting, then taking over the Observatory Ridge sector, SE. of Ypres. Major Childe Thomas had rejoined and taken over from Major Finlay (February 12th).[3] In this Observatory Ridge sector the battalion continued till well into April, being usually at Zillebeke when in support or brigade reserve or back at Kruisstraat or Toronto Camp when its brigade was ' out ', being in huts and not in billets, which might have been preferable in the cold weather. Things were brisker now. Life was quite strenuous : one officer wrote in March of not having had his boots or clothes off fourteen days. Both sides' guns were more active and machine-gunners, rifle grenadiers, trench-mortar detachments and snipers were all in evidence, if casualties were few. A good deal of wiring was required and patrols were active, more so than the enemy's, one left a notice on the German wire to tell them of their retreat from Bapaume and Peronne. Colonel Harman returned on March 24th, and after being relieved at Zillebeke

---

[1] Nine men were killed and 14 wounded.   [2] He received a bar to his M.C.

[3] On February 1st of the officers with the battalion three were Regulars, four Special Reservists, three including the acting second in command, Captain Trevor Roper of the 8th Battalion, were Territorials and nine of the 14th or 15th Battalions, among them the Adjutant, Lt. Gammon.

on April 15th the battalion shifted back with its Division to the NE. side of the Salient to take over the Hill Top sector.

The Forty-First Division had been back in the Salient before the end of October, being in the front line at St. Eloi by October 29th. Here the tactical advantages lay with the Germans, to whom higher and rather drier ground gave better opportunities for observation, while a shell-pitted and mine-cratered No Man's Land, mainly water-logged, effectively discouraged any offensive or even much patrol activity. One piece of the line was significantly known as 'the Mud Patch' and much work was needed to keep the trenches in some repair. Merely to maintain the line and the approaches to it in winter weather taxed the energies and resourcefulness of the troops, and if the autumn and winter months passed without any major incidents they were not times of idleness. Luckily enough troops were available to reduce the time actually spent in trenches in 1916–1917 well below that in either previous winter,[1] even if the successive extensions of the British front South of the Somme to relieve the French involved our having to put into the trenches troops who could have done with more rest and more training.

Like other battalions the 15th Hampshire found life more strenuous the further back from the line they were : even in support or brigade reserve working and carrying parties were always being wanted, and when ' out ' working parties were even more in demand, the improvement of the communications alone requiring almost all the labour available and meanwhile training, especially of the reinforcements, had to be kept up. Drafts were largely coming now from the Training Reserve Battalions, into which the former ' K 4 ' battalions like the 13th Hampshire or ' Local Reserve ' units like the 16th had recently been converted.[2]

The change had many arguments in its favour : it had proved very difficult to refill with recruits from their own areas all battalions which had suffered heavily, already men were constantly being posted to any regiment but their own, more often probably than might have been avoided had the authorities really considered the regimental sentiments and traditions to which they so freely rendered lip-service. The change therefore rather stabilized an existing practice, but it meant that the drafts who joined a Hampshire battalion usually knew little of Hampshire or the regiment. To assimilate them and imbue them with the proper esprit de corps was therefore all the harder, while if the training staffs at home were generally allowed to retain their regimental badges and

[1] From November 1st to March 31st the 15th Hampshire had just over 40 days in front line.
[2] The 13th became the 34th Training Reserve and the 16th ranked as the 97th. Most of the senior officers and N.C.O's of both battalions remained with them for some time longer. A Garrison Battalion had come into existence in April 1916 and did duty in back areas in France, its first C.O. being Sir A. Griffith Boscawen of the 3rd Royal West Kent, and early in 1917 an 18th (Home Service) Battalion was formed under Lt. Colonel Ellicombe of the Devons. This, however, was broken up in January 1918, whereupon the Garrison Battalion was re-numbered 18th, the Provisional Territorial Battalion, for some time numbered as the 84th Provisional Battalion, being reckoned as the 17th Hampshire. It was still under Colonel Peters and was employed in Home Defence duties.

other connections, this was slender compensation for knowing that their own regiment was about the least likely of any to profit by their devotion and hard work.

One of the more notable incidents of the winter occurred when the 15th were in reserve at Dickebusch in November : a company of another battalion on its way up to the trenches was badly shelled and had heavy casualties, whom the 15th's stretcher bearers promptly and effectively succoured, assistance which was cordially acknowledged. When in front line the 15th usually found the enemy's guns troublesome, but we now had enough ammunition to respond, sometimes with compound interest. Casualties were not numerous : the battalion diary only records four in November and nine in December, including 2/Lt. Merrett killed in the Mud Patch and Captain Mee wounded, but with many officers away on 'courses' and various employments only twelve were available for duty on December 31st.

One relief in January was 'spotted' by the enemy and brought heavy fire down on the communication trenches, cutting off two platoons whose relief had to be postponed until evening, but the battalion very fortunately escaped without casualties. Incidents of importance were not numerous, but the mere maintenance of the line in a bitter winter with constant snow, sharp frosts and intervals of thaw to reduce everything to slime and mud was a fearful strain, and the cheerful endurance of hardships was really remarkable. The frequent falls of snow hampered work and training when out of the line and, if possible, increased the demands for working parties, but both January and February passed without much to vary the usual routine 'in' or 'out'. The battalion was 'in' from February 17th to 22nd in dull and misty weather without having a single casualty, and between February 27th and March 5th only seven men were wounded, despite increased artillery and mortar activity on both sides. To divert the enemy's attention from a raid on March 14th by another battalion, 2/Lt. Fowler and ten men placed two Bangalore torpedoes in his wire, as if the 15th were about to raid : one only exploded, but the whole party got back unhurt. Another turn in trenches in the last week of March brought increased activity and a dozen casualties, including three killed, but up to the Third Army's attack at Arras on April 9th no special effort had been required of the 15th Hampshire and the battalion had had ample time to assimilate some very large drafts. If the Second Army was not to start its offensive for another two months, its three Hampshire battalions were fit and ready to strike.

CHAPTER XVII

ARRAS

THE winter of 1916–1917 had brought the Hampshire few outstanding incidents. Politically and strategically, however, changes had taken place which were to affect them and the whole course of the war profoundly. Mr. Asquith's resignation and his replacement by Mr. Lloyd George brought to the head of affairs in England a man whose great energy and driving power were unfortunately largely nullified by his impatience, his ignorance of war and his utter inability to understand the practical obstacles to the superficially attractive ' short cuts to victory ' which suggested themselves to him. Impulsive and self-confident,

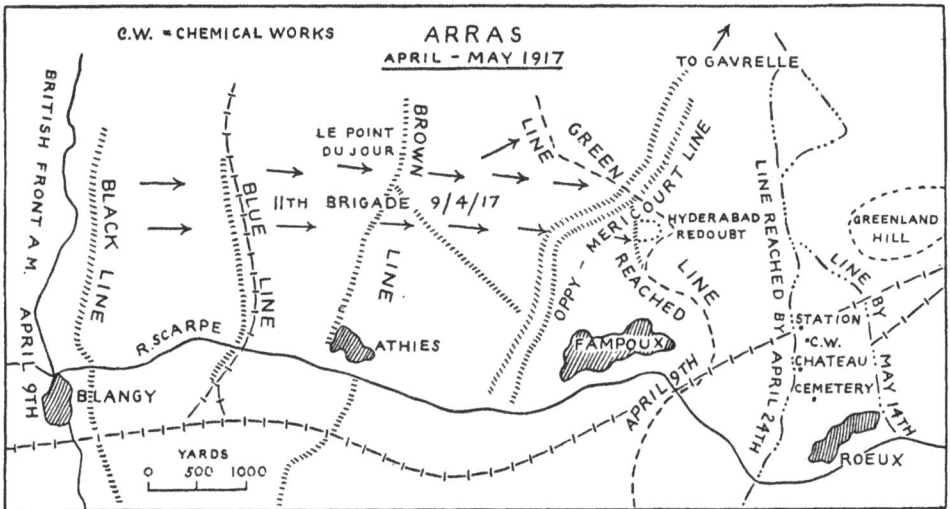

C.W. = CHEMICAL WORKS   ARRAS   APRIL – MAY 1917   TO GAVRELLE

he could not realise the extent or the consequences of his own ignorance or that his military advisers knew what they were talking about, if he did not. Moreover the supersession of General Joffre and his replacement by General Nivelle, whose ideas for the coming offensive differed so profoundly from his predecessor's, might have mattered less had not Mr. Lloyd George virtually subordinated the British Armies in France to an almost untried French Commander in Chief. The consequent changes in the British part in the projected Spring offensive, notably the wide extensions of our frontage and the consequent reduction in the force available for our attack, were of profound importance : they threw away much of the moral and practical advantages our remorseless, if expensive, wearing down of the Germans on the Somme had secured, advantages not to be measured by the relatively small gains of ground as marked on a map, especially by those who read the map without seeing below the surface. If the Germans had not been pushed back very far, they had been ousted from their really prepared defences, and the weakness of their position in March, even after some respite from serious pressure, suggests how much might have been achieved by another ' push ' had a dry October allowed Sir Douglas Haig to repeat the blows of September 15th and 25th.

The very bad winter must in any case have interfered seriously with the programme arranged at Chantilly by Sir Douglas Haig and General Joffre, while the German withdrawal to the Hindenburg Line, though an unequivocal admission that they had been worsted on the Somme, must have further thrown it out of gear. Still, both British and French might have been much better placed to impede and profit by that withdrawal had not General Nivelle's scheme been substituted for General Joffre's.

By the beginning of April the Germans were back behind the Hindenburg Line, defended as much by the belt of systematically devastated country they had left in front of it as by its own well-sited trenches and gun positions. Weeks must elapse before we could hope to attempt to breach it. On the Third Army's front, however, our preparations were virtually complete, and as the retreat had only affected the Southern extremity of the front to be attacked our plans did not need drastic re-adjustment.

This front extended Northward from across the Cojeul on our right to the Vimy Ridge, nearly 12 miles. It was being attacked by four Corps, the Hampshire being only represented in the Seventeenth, in the left centre, whose right lay on the Scarpe. The Seventeenth Corps was employing three Divisions to capture the first three of the four trench systems which confronted us, the ' Black ', ' Blue ' and ' Brown ' Lines, after which the Fourth Division, till then in reserve, would pass through the Ninth, the right Division of the Corps, and tackle a fourth system, the Oppy-Mericourt line, and then a final objective, the ' Green Line ', lying yet another 1400 yards further East, beyond Fampoux. This objective was over 6000 yards from our front line and reaching it would involve a much bigger advance than any previous attack had accomplished.

When the great attack was delivered, on April 9th, in cold and even snowy weather, the Ninth (Scottish) Division, carried out its programme most successfully and well up to time, smashing down all opposition, its prisoners alone exceeded its 2000 casualties, and thus gave a fine opening which the Fourth did not fail to exploit. April 9th had found the Fourth at Mareouil, 3½ miles NW. of Arras, whence it had advanced very early to an assembly position North of Arras, with the 12th (right) and 11th (left) Brigades in front and the 10th in support. Rain and snow wetted and chilled the waiting troops, but the ' cookers ' produced a hot meal and everyone was soon in good spirits over the good news which came back and was soon confirmed by the crowds of Germans making for the prisoners' cages. At 10 a.m. the advance to the Blue Line was begun, being made in column. One of the few German shells caused B Company of the Hampshire nearly 20 casualties, but the Blue Line was reached 30 minutes before schedule. ' Artillery formation ' was now adopted, the Hampshire, who had the Somerset L.I. on their right, having B and D Companies in front and A in support, C being detailed a carriers. On their left the East Lancashire were to form a defensive flank facing NE., and the Rifle Brigade followed, having to pass through the Hampshire and tackle the Hyderabad Redoubt, a strong position beyond the Hampshire's objective, Haggard and Hazard Trenches.

Advancing to the Brown Line almost without meeting any shelling, the Hampshire could see troops pushing ahead across the Scarpe, where the Sixth Corps was also doing magnificently. After an hour's pause on the Brown Line the 11th and 12th Brigades started their own attack at 3 p.m. behind a satisfactory barrage, some batteries having meanwhile been brought well forward. They now met some rather wild rifle fire and a few shells but were soon up to the wire of the Oppy-Mericourt Line. This was thick and practically uncut, though the Germans had failed to block their passages through it, and while some men were using wire-cutters, others, firing over their heads, prevented the enemy from manning the parapet to impede them. Before long the Hampshire were through the wire, D Company on the right capturing Heron Trench and B its Northward continuation, Hudson Trench. Pressing on, they also carried the rear line of this system, Haggard and Hazard Trenches, while A 'mopped up' behind them. All opposition was quickly overcome, 80 prisoners and three 8-inch howitzers were taken and many Germans shot down as they fled Eastward, offering excellent targets, while bombers worked their way Northward along Hudson and Hazard Trenches, extending our gains. Soon after 4 p.m. all three companies could report that their objectives had been secured.

Casualties in the assault had been trifling, only 2/Lts. Hobson, who died of wounds, Man and Soward and six men wounded. The Somerset had been equally successful and though the Rifle Brigade, who duly passed through the Hampshire, suffered considerably in getting through uncut wire, they too mastered their objective, the Hyderabad Redoubt, B Company assisting them by fire. The captured line gave good observation to the East and NE. with a fair field of fire in front, and touch having been obtained with the East Lancashire on the left, the Hampshire could settle down to consolidation, despite intermittent shelling which caused more casualties, bringing the battalion's total for the day up to nearly 60, while those of the brigade, barely 300, were exceeded by its prisoners. Meanwhile the 12th Brigade had taken Fampoux, but machine-guns behind a railway embankment had prevented its reaching the Green Line, 500 yards on, though it also was consolidating a good line.

If this fine result was due even more to the Ninth Division and the guns, which had broken the back of the resistance before the Fourth got into action, the Fourth had carried out its task admirably and had played a big part in the greatest success yet achieved on the Western Front in a single day. The other Divisions of the Seventeenth Corps, if less successful than the Fourth and Ninth, had also made big advances, and beyond them the Canadians and the Fifth Division had mastered most of Vimy Ridge. South of the Scarpe the Sixth Corps had done very well, even if it had not secured its final objective. Our right Corps, the Seventh, had also gained ground, though its right had been checked. Moreover this very substantial achievement had cost only some

12,000 casualties, whereas there was ample evidence that the enemy, who had lost 100 guns and at least 7000 prisoners, had been very hard hit.

Various hindrances impeded the exploitation of this brilliant opening blow : squalls of sleet and snow had fallen at intervals all day and continued through the succeeding days, inflicting considerable hardships on the troops and greatly increasing the difficulties, bad enough anyhow, of repairing and improving communications. Moreover, it impeded the advance of our guns, most of them now too far back to reach their distant new targets. As usual, information was so slow in getting back that orders based upon it rarely fitted the situation by

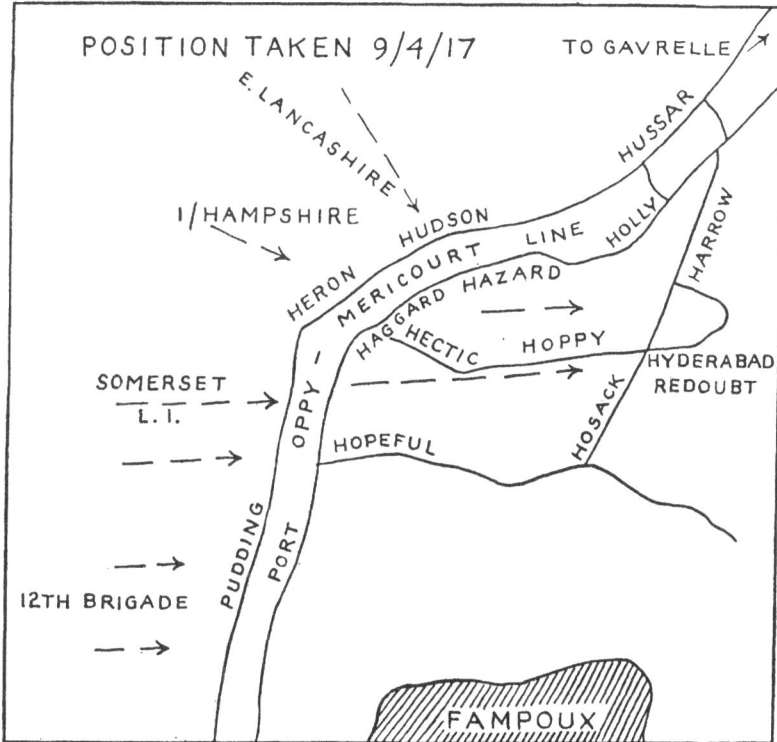

POSITION TAKEN 9/4/17   TO GAVRELLE

E. LANCASHIRE

HUSSAR

1/HAMPSHIRE   HUDSON   LINE   HOLLY   HARROW

HERON   MERICOURT   HAZARD

HAGGARD   HECTIC   HOPPY

SOMERSET   L.I.   OPPY   HOSACK   HYDERABAD REDOUBT

HOPEFUL

PUDDING   PORT

12TH BRIGADE

FAMPOUX

the time they reached the troops, and promising openings were therefore missed. Moreover, the Germans had half a dozen Divisions detailed for counter-attacking, which, if too far back to influence the first day's fighting, were near enough to the battle area to intervene on the days following it.

The 11th Brigade, while consolidating, was somewhat troubled by snipers, but in return got some fair targets for rifles and machine-guns, the Rifle Brigade indeed ran short of ammunition, but it had only one attempt at a counter-attack to repulse. About dusk Germans could be seen collecting in sufficient numbers to give good targets, and as it grew dark they came forward opposite the Hampshire, to wilt away under our rifle and machine-gun fire, while during the night the battalion's patrols were active and gathered in several more prisoners. Next day, though the enemy were clearly moving guns and transport back, opposition stiffened, the 12th Brigade's efforts to complete its task by capturing the Green Line were quickly checked and machine-guns held up patrols which the Hampshire and Somerset pushed out towards the Roeux-Gavrelle road. Eventually, late in the evening, another counter-attack developed, mainly against our left. One of our posts was severely pressed, but 2/Lt. Love, going forward under heavy fire, rallied the men and maintained the defence, while elsewhere the attackers were soon halted by our fire and lost heavily, the Hampshire having another 15 casualties during the day, mainly from artillery fire, Captain Prendergast being wounded.[1]

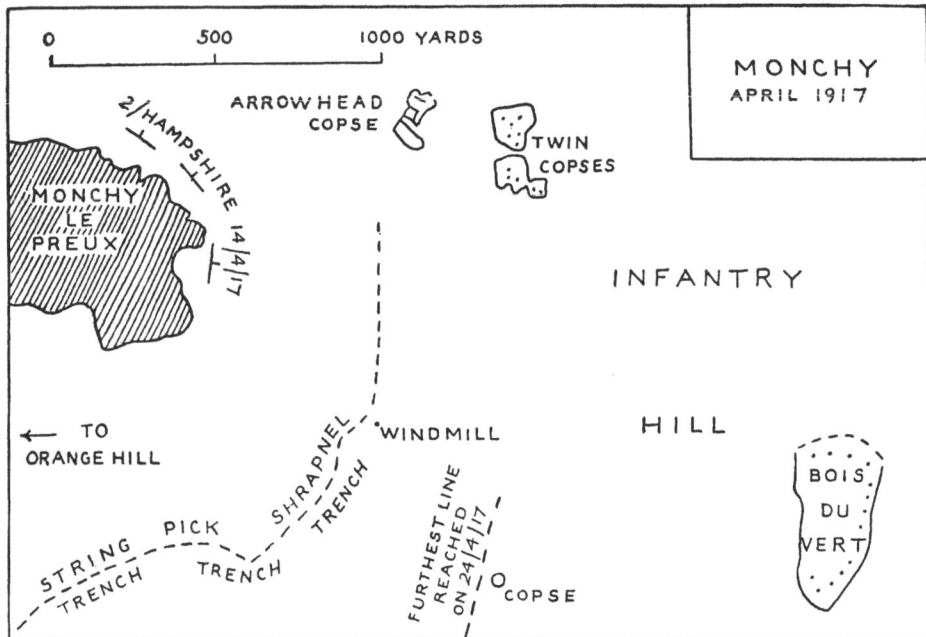

Being ahead of the flanking Divisions, before attempting a big advance the Fourth must in any case have waited till they came up level, and though on both its flanks some ground was gained, the Sixth Corps advancing nearly to Monchy le Preux, further South we were less successful and meanwhile the German reserves were arriving. The troops in front moreover, being without blankets or great-coats, were suffering greatly from more snow and sleet, the cold being bitter.

April 11th brought the Fourth Division orders to secure the road running North from Roeux to Gavrelle, 1600 yards ahead. For this the 10th (left) and 12th (right) Brigades were detailed, the 11th having to form a defensive flank on the left, but while the 12th Brigade secured part of their original objective of April 9th the 10th were held up and lost heavily. Reinforcements had now

[1] For the third time.

replaced the survivors of the original defenders, and we had not got enough guns forward to give our infantry the magnificent support which had contributed so much to our original success. The check to the other brigades left the 11th with little to do, but B Company on the Hampshire's left, bombing Northward along the Oppy-Mericourt Line, gained about 150 yards in both front and support trenches. This success they owed largely to Lt. de Gaury's fine example and skilful leading,[1] which was mainly instrumental in taking one important ' strong point ', but 2/Lt. J. P. Gilbert was killed leading his platoon gallantly and the battalion had another 30 casualties. D Company meanwhile had taken over the Hyderabad Redoubt.

Little more success attended the next day's attempt on this front, the Ninth Division, though hardly fresh, coming forward again and attacking through the Fourth, whose right and centre it subsequently relieved, leaving the 11th Brigade in line facing NE. to the left of the Hyderabad Redoubt. Meanwhile B Company's bombers had again tried to gain ground, but with little success and at the cost of nearly another 30 casualties,[2] the enemy having by now strengthened his defences.

For three more days the 1st Hampshire remained in front line. No further advance was attempted here, though our bombers made another effort on April 15th which failed, largely because our guns had almost obliterated the trenches so that our men had no cover and were exposed to machine-gun fire. The enemy's artillery fire had increased, the bad weather continued and it was a very weary battalion which was at last relieved early [3] on April 16th by the Irish Fusiliers and placed in Divisional reserve in the former German second line, where shelters in a railway cutting provided fair accommodation. The week's casualties had come to 2/Lts. Gilbert, Hobson and Seeley (died of wounds) and 48 men killed and missing, Captain Prendergast, 2/Lts. R. C. Foster, A. James, Man and Soward and 115 men wounded,[4] and all ranks badly needed the well-earned fortnight's rest they were now to get. But they could feel they had achieved a big thing and left their mark on the enemy.

Before the 1st Hampshire was relieved the 2nd had joined in the fighting. The Twenty-Ninth Division, which had moved forward from Beauval on April 1st and had spent the 9th just West of Arras in reserve, was ordered up on April 12th to take over Monchy le Preux. This village the Sixth Corps had with much difficulty succeeded in capturing and all its Divisions were now exhausted and needing relief. Monchy, as yet but little damaged, stood on a knoll at the Eastward end of a spur projecting into the plain of Douai, over which it provided fine observation, but our advance here had left us in a pronounced salient, almost inviting counter-attack.

[1] He was awarded the M.C., as was 2/Lt. Love also.

[2] 2/Lt. F.R. Seeley was wounded.

[3] D Company could not get clear of the Hyderabad Redoubt before daylight and had to remain there all day.

[4] Out of about 600 n action, so many men being employed in the manifold administratrative requirements of a big attack that few battalions ' went over the top ' much stronger.

The 2nd Hampshire had struggled forward on April 12th along the terribly congested Cambrai road to Orange Hill, a mile West of Monchy, where they bivouacked and remained in brigade reserve, going up after dark on April 13th to dig an assembly trench just East of Monchy, from which the Essex and the Newfoundlanders were next morning to attack Infantry Hill, a slight rise East of Monchy. Though heavily shelled the battalion escaped lightly, though its 20 casualties included 2/Lts. Burrage, Manton and Watson wounded, and before dawn (April 14th) it was back at Orange Hill, having left three platoons of X Company in cellars in Monchy.

For only two battalions to try to advance by half a mile an already fairly sharp salient, seemed to be asking for trouble, but Infantry Hill offered concealment to counter-attacks and its retention would have improved the position. Attacking at 5.30 a.m. the Essex and Newfoundland carried the objective, taking some prisoners. Before they could do much to consolidate they were counter-attacked in great force, in front and on both flanks. Despite an obstinate resistance both battalions had before long been overwhelmed and the Germans, a fresh Bavarian Division, seemed to have Monchy at their mercy. Apart from the head-quarters of the attacking battalions, the only troops in Monchy were the three platoons of X Company, who hastened to take up positions for its defence and helped to keep the enemy from exploiting their success, while a handful from the Newfoundland's head-quarters under Lt. Colonel Forbes Robertson, manned a bank SE. of the village and did great execution at close range, besides sending warning to the Hampshire of the critical situation.

Lt. Colonel Beckwith had already sent Y Company up to Monchy and now started forward with his remaining men. A heavy barrage was falling behind Monchy, but Colonel Beckwith noticed that this was coming down in two parallel lines with a gap between them and, utilising this skilfully, he got his men through with only 20 casualties and brought timely assistance to the hard-pressed defenders. He now disposed his men on the Northern and Eastern outskirts and several attacks were beaten off, Captain Cuddon doing outstanding work in keeping the enemy at bay and maintaining the position. Private Ferry also did well in getting an important message through at a critical moment, which led to a weak point being reinforced in time. He had to go through a heavy barrage, in which a fellow 'runner' had been hit, but he managed it. Eventually touch was gained both with the Seventeenth Division on the left and with the 4th Worcestershire, South of Monchy, who meanwhile had been holding firmly on and doing some effective shooting, and before long the Germans abandoned further efforts to advance and fell back to their original line. The battalion's good service in securing this all-important position [1] was much commended, General de Lisle declaring that it had been 'the means of saving Monchy'; it was lucky to escape with 50 casualties, including 2/Lt. Baxter and seven men killed.

[1] Colonel Beckwith, in passing on this message, added his own special congratulations to the battalion's runners and stretcher-bearers. It is unfortunate that the battalion's important share in saving Monchy should be almost ignored in the *Official History* (1917. Vol. I. 291).

Next evening the 2nd Hampshire were relieved by the 86th Brigade and went back to Arras for three days' rest, after which (April 19th) they took over trenches between Monchy and the Cambrai road. These they held for three days, being heavily shelled, gas shells being much used. The four men killed unfortunately included a mainstay of the battalion in C.S.M. Lund, while 2/Lts. Rhodes and Saunders and 14 men were wounded.

Meanwhile the whole situation had been adversely affected by the failure of General Nivelle's offensive on the Aisne to accomplish anything approaching the decisive results that he had prophesied. If much ground was gained, with 20,000 prisoners and 150 guns, the anticipated break-through was not achieved, and the heavy casualties were aggravated by the break-down of the French medical services and were largely responsible for the disastrous moral effects of this disappointment on Army and country. For the rest of 1917 the British Armies in France had to attack and continue attacking, despite many disadvantages and difficulties, so as to maintain the initiative and prevent the Germans from recovering it and exploiting the demoralisation which before long spread through the French Armies and left them quite unfit to meet a serious attack, let alone continue their offensive. Had General Nivelle's attack fulfilled anticipations or even had less been expected from it, so that its result had been less of a disappointment, Sir Douglas Haig need not have continued his attacks at Arras after the Germans had had time to prepare to meet them. In these later attacks, largely improvised, carried out by Divisions who had not been properly reinforced or rested since April 9th,[1] not supported by the full weight of artillery then available and confronted with defences that had not been adequately ' softened ', the Third Army was to incur heavy casualties and achieve no commensurate direct results, though it is easy to conjecture what might have happened had the Germans been allowed to recover the initiative.

By April 14th as much had been achieved as was needed locally to improve our positions, so but for his ally's requirements, to which he never turned a deaf ear, Sir Douglas Haig might now have turned his attention to his intended attack in Flanders. By this, his main project, he hoped to secure the Belgian coastline and deprive the Germans of the submarine bases they were using so effectively. For this the Navy, at the worst crisis of its struggle against the submarine, was extremely anxious, and he would have been glad to start operations in Flanders in May. Actually troops and guns and shells had to be expended on the Arras front, where British troops were sacrificed to shoulder their Allies' burden. If the French could point to their inadequately supported efforts of 1915, the boot was on the other foot now.

The 2nd Hampshire were immediately affected by this prolongation of the Arras battle, as in the big attack ordered for April 23rd their Division was tackling Infantry Hill and other ground East of Monchy where the German position was by now fairly strong and held in some force. The 88th Brigade

---

[1] There was hardly any relieving them by Divisions from other Armies, as on the Somme.

was attacking between Monchy and the Cambrai road, with the Worcestershire leading, the Hampshire in support and a weak composite battalion formed from the Essex and Newfoundlands in reserve. On the 88th's left the 87th Brigade was attacking Infantry Hill itself, and the 88th aimed at securing its Southern slope, including the Bois du Vert, and keeping touch to their right with the Fifteenth Division, who were attacking Guemappe beyond the Cambrai road.

The 2nd Hampshire had been relieved in front line by the Worcestershire early on April 22nd and had spent the day at Feuchy Chapel. The enemy's shelling was heavy and the Brigadier, General Cayley, was incapacitated by gas, so Lt. Colonel Beckwith took his place, Lt. Colonel McCammon [1] commanding the battalion.

' Zero ' was at 4.45 a.m., (April 23rd) and the Worcestershire, attacking with great dash, quickly forced their way up the slope ahead, advancing nearly a mile and reaching a copse on the crest about 600 yards West of the Bois du Vert. They had done splendidly but had lost heavily, and to hold their gains they needed all the support the Hampshire could give, so there could be no question of the Hampshire pushing on to the Red Line, beyond the Bois du Vert, especially as the Division on their right was not up level. Before advancing, the battalion had nearly 20 casualties from the German barrage, chiefly in Y Company on the right of the leading wave, C.S.M. Toogood being killed. In crossing a sunken road more casualties were caused by flanking machine-guns, but the men pressed on vigorously, many following the Worcestershire to the copse, while one platoon of X, the left support company, actually joined the 87th Brigade on Infantry Hill. The right support company, W, under Captain Cuddon, having captured Pick Trench, started bombing to the right flank and after two hours hard fighting cleared most of String Trench, capturing 50 prisoners. Sergeant Rowe and Private Bicknell [2] were much to the fore in this, supporting Captain Cuddon splendidly. Unluckily the Division on the right had still failed to get forward, so the Twenty-Ninth's success had accentuated the already pronounced salient. German shelling was now heavy and the Hampshire had hard work to retain their gains, let alone consolidate them effectively. Several counter-attacks were checked nevertheless, but in the afternoon the enemy came forward in great force, following a heavy bombardment by big howitzers, and despite the stubborn resistance of the Worcestershire and Hampshire they recovered the copse, most of Y and Z Companies being overwhelmed and both company commanders taken.[3] North of the copse the defence held, and in Shrapnel, Pick and String Trenches the Hampshire, mainly W Company, and some Worcestershire, reinforced by a company of the 16th Middlesex (86th Brigade), succeeded in checking the counter-attack, Captain Cuddon doing much to achieve this and maintain our hold on the

---

[1] 5th R. Irish Rifles, (attached).
[2] They received the M.M., also awarded to Private Primmer, for keeping up communications with Brigade H.Q. by repairing wires under heavy shell fire, and to Private Ferry.
[3] Captains Cornish and Robertson, the latter being badly wounded.

captured ground.¹ With the enemy checked, the Worcestershire's C.O. organized a night attack to recover the copse, in which some 40 Hampshire joined. It went forward well, but the enemy were too firmly established to be ousted and the 88th Brigade had to be content with maintaining a flank running back from Infantry Hill, where the 87th had secured and held a good position, to the Cambrai road, including String Trench and Pick Trench, over 400 yards forward from the starting line. This line they secured, their remnants, except W Company who remained behind for 24 hours, being relieved that evening by the 86th Brigade, when the battalion was taken back by bus to Simoncourt, to rest and reorganize. Losses had been severe, over half those in action ;² Lt. Colonel McCammon died of wounds, Lt. Halcrow, 2/Lt. Todd and 13 men were killed, Captains Cornish and Robertson,³ 2/Lts. Simmonds and Snyder and 67 men were missing, Lts. Fawcitt and Saunders, 2/Lts. Darracott, Hughes, G. H. James,⁴ McAvoy, Swann, Watts and Yates and 200 men wounded.

If the attack of April 23rd had nowhere reached its final objective, ground had been gained all along the front ; the Twenty-Ninth Division had advanced 800 yards on Infantry Hill, while Guemappe had eventually been secured by the Fifteenth Division's persistence, and North of the Scarpe the Fifty-First had gained ground beyond Fampoux, it it had not reached Roeux. Casualties had been heavy, but 2500 prisoners had been taken, our guns had had some fine targets in infantry advancing to counter-attack and if the enemy had dislodged it from its advanced position the 88th Brigade had taken its toll of them. Tactically the local position was therefore more than ever secure and we could have well discontinued our attacks, whose difficulties increased in proportion to their progress, especially as no fresh Divisions were available to relieve those already so severely tried and thereby give them the respite they so badly needed. The French situation, however, required the improvisation of another big attack, and for this on May 3rd the Fourth Division was brought forward again with Roeux and Plouvain as objectives, while the much depleted Twenty-Ninth, after the briefest of rests, also came up to Arras in readiness to exploit success

The Fourth Division had had ten days ' out ', the 1st Hampshire being at Izel les Hameau 12 miles West of Arras, but it had received few reinforcements and hardly a battalion was within 50% of establishment. The Hampshire, apart from nearly 200 casualties, had sent another 150 to hospital, drafts and returns from hospital had not totalled 60 and, with C Company detached to help the R.A.M.C. and A detailed as carriers, only 200 men were available for the attack.

On May 3rd the 10th Brigade was making for Roeux, with the 12th on its left, the Hampshire being in support, in trenches just North of the Fampoux-

---

¹ For this and for his good work in the defence of Monchy on April 14th he received the M.C.
² The strength on paper on April 30th was 23 officers and 565 other ranks. Colonel Beckwith being still acting as Brigadier, Captain Lord was in command.
³ Died of wounds as a prisoner of war.
⁴ Died of wounds.

Athies road. Colonel Armitage [1] being with the ' battle nucleus ', Major Earle was commanding.

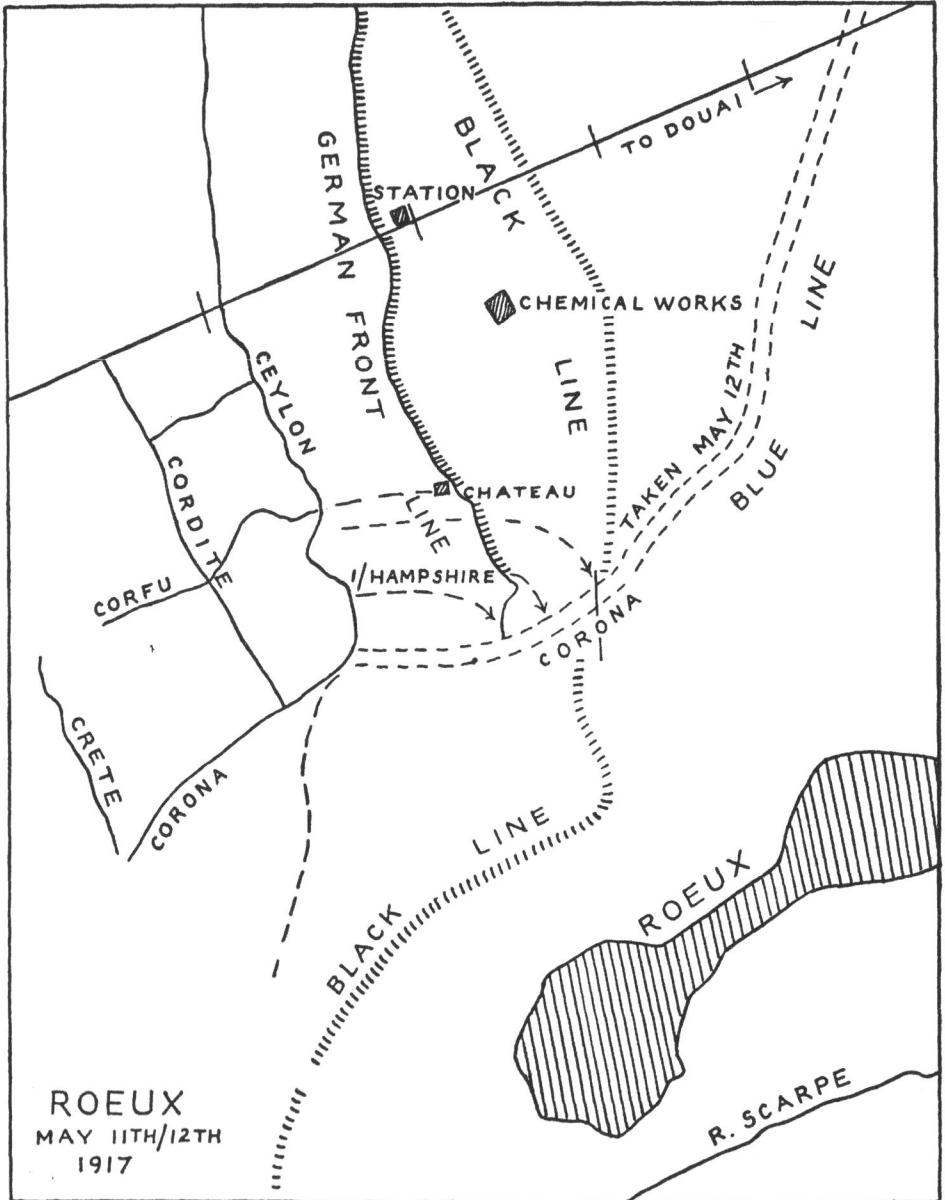

ROEUX
MAY 11TH/12TH
1917

Too early an hour, 3.45 a.m., had been fixed for ' Zero ', the darkness causing much confusion and loss of direction. A heavy barrage showed that the attack was expected and it was held up just beyond the first objective, while

[1] He was awarded the D.S.O. for his skilful leading and good work on April 9th.

even this was not finally maintained in face of vigorous counter-attacks. The Hampshire were not engaged but moved up after dark to support the Rifle Brigade, who were to make another attack on Roeux Chateau. This could not be started till 3.30 a.m. (May 4th) and made little headway, and that evening the 11th Brigade took over the front facing the Chateau and Chemical Works North of Roeux, the Hampshire having their left on the Arras-Douai railway and extending South to the junction of Corona and Ceylon Trenches. The enemy's snipers were active and both sides did some intermittent shelling, the Hampshire having a dozen casualties, including 2/Lt. Mooney died of wounds, in four days in line. The Chemical Works were steadily shelled, but patrols which reconnoitred them found them still held in force and could achieve nothing.

After two days in reserve the battalion went up into line late on May 10th for a fresh attack next day, having C (right) and D (left) Companies in front in Ceylon Trench and B in support in Cordite, A being still detached. Its task was to swing round to the right and form a defensive flank along Corona Trench, facing Roeux.

' Zero ' this time was 7.30 p.m. (May 11th), which surprised the enemy completely ; they had not detected the assembly of the attackers and these, despite their long sixteen hours' wait, went forward with much dash behind an excellent barrage, while, the counter-barrage being slow to open, our men suffered little from it. It was a lovely evening, with the ground dry enough to allow of rapid movement. The Hampshire, on the 11th Brigade's right, ably directed by Major Earle, soon mastered their objective which included Roeux Chateau, till now a real stone of stumbling, capturing 150 prisoners and seven machine-guns with trifling casualties, though 2/Lt. Hawke was killed and 2/Lts. Fall and Stringer [1] wounded. The consolidation of the line taken, ' the Black Line ', was covered by Lewis gunners in shell-holes out in front, who kept off all attempts to regain lost ground. Trouble was threatened by a big concrete emplacement near the Chateau with walls six feet in thickness and seven feet of roof cover, the first of the ' pill-boxes ' afterwards so prominent in ' Third Ypres ' which the battalion had met. However, moppers-up who were detailed to tackle it caught its occupants trying to bring a machine gun into action and disposed of them, capturing the ' pill-box ' and with it four machine-guns. Its capture aroused considerable interest as it was clear that this new form of defence was likely to give trouble. Many officers of other units came up to have a look at it.

The rest of the Division had been equally successful and next morning the 11th Brigade, attacking at 6.30 a.m. along with the Seventeenth Division on its left, advanced another 500 yards and captured Cupid Trench, North of the railway and 700 yards East of the station. [2] The enemy offered but little resist-

[1] 2/Lt. Stringer's batman, in his anxiety to get his wounded officer to safety, overlooked the fact that he was taking all the company officers' rations with him.

[2] Approximately the ' Blue Line ' on Sketch (42) : This success led to the Germans retiring between the railway and the Scarpe, the ruins of Roeux being occupied during the night of May 12th/13th.

ance and were quickly driven out, though further North the left of the Seventeenth was less successful. Captured machine-guns were used most effectively and the position was consolidated and maintained. Major Earle had again handled the attack admirably and was largely responsible for its success, and the D.S.O. awarded to him was greatly welcomed by the battalion. Once again casualties were low, 2/Lt. Bishop and three men being killed and 2/Lt. Bray and 25 men wounded.

This success was the more creditable because the Fourth Division's battalions were all far below establishment, in neither attack had the Hampshire exceeded 250 of all ranks, and to have secured all objectives and inflicted very heavy casualties on its opponents, the 4th Ersatz Division, over 500 prisoners being taken, was a satisfactory finish to the battalion's highly successful share in the Arras offensive. That night the Division's much reduced battalions were relieved by the Fifty-First Division. When it returned to the Roeux-Fampoux area in June the Arras front had become ' quiet '.

The 2nd Hampshire had also seen something of these closing stages of ' Arras '. No openings being made on May 3rd for their Division to exploit, they had remained at Arras till May 7th and then moved back to Berneville, where a welcome draft of 102 men replenished the depleted ranks, only 270 men would have been available on May 3rd. They were back at Arras by May 11th, occupying the old German front line taken on April 9th. This needed much repairing to make it habitable, while large carrying parties were called for, and then on May 17th the battalion took over reserve trenches between the Scarpe and Monchy, where its Division was now relieving the Twelfth, besides taking over Infantry Hill from the Third. Nearly 240 men from the Base had arrived at the Corps Depot and a trickle of returns from hospital had about balanced admissions.

Its first four days here the 2nd spent in digging communication trenches and shelters and in salvage work. The area had seen heavy fighting and much salvage was collected. Four days in front line (May 22nd to 25th) from Bit Lane to the Scarpe brought much hard work and heavy shelling, which caused few casualties, though 120 yards of Halberd Trench were blown in, while our guns replied vigorously. Our patrols were active and an advanced post was established in No Man's Land. The battalion was back in reserve for five days, during which it was sorry to lose its M.O., Captain Sturdy, whose gallantry and devoted work, particularly at Monchy, where he had searched houses and cellars under very heavy fire and rescued over 100 wounded, had just won him the M.C. Being in reserve meant much hard work on the trenches with large carrying-parties and much digging and was little of a relief. A dozen officers had reported, among them Major Spring, who became second in command, Lt. Colonel Beckwith having rejoined, and other ranks were up over 800 again. Lt. Askew had now taken over duty as Quartermaster, while Captain Knight, R.A.M.C., succeeded Captain Sturdy.

From May 30th to June 2nd the 2nd was in support on this front ; with plenty to do as before, repairing and improving the line, the whole battalion was thus employed on the night of May 31st/June 1st, and little rest, as the enemy's guns were active, partly in retaliation, though casualties were trifling. On the other hand the enemy had given the battalion but few chances of hitting him, rarely exposing himself. The Division made some local attacks during this spell at Monchy, but the 88th Brigade was not employed and its hard-hit units were getting a chance to assimilate their large drafts.

June 3rd saw the 2nd Hampshire at rest but under orders for the North. Like the 1st Battalion, the 2nd had had its chance at Arras and had taken it, more than once; if both had had severe losses, neither had been as hard hit as on the Somme, while both had left their mark on the enemy to some purpose.

CHAPTER XVIII

THE FLANDERS OFFENSIVE

MESSINES AND THIRD YPRES

THE prolongation of 'Arras', if unavoidable, had entailed serious disadvantages. Our heavy casualties in the later attacks had naturally diminished considerably the substantial balance in our favour of the opening stages, though the Germans had had to pay high for stopping us and their counter-attacks had often been heavily punished. The postponing of the Messines attack was another grave misfortune ; the Second Army had long been ready and could have attacked much earlier could Sir Douglas Haig have closed down 'Arras' after the first fortnight and transferred to Flanders the guns which the Third Army could not yet spare, while to crown all unusually bad weather set in just as 'Third Ypres' actually started, making conditions in the Ypres Salient a worse handicap than usual to attackers.

The Flanders offensive was eventually to give opportunities to all five Hampshire battalions in France and to win the regiment two more V.C's, but in its opening phase at Messines only the 11th and 15th Battalions were engaged, the Thirty-Ninth Division's frontage being beyond that of the attack, so that the 14th did not take part in it, while the 2nd Battalion had only just reached Flanders and the 1st was still with the Third Army.

A Pioneer battalion in Flanders had naturally seen much of the preparations, and during April and May the 11th Hampshire had been busy, the snow and sleet of April making things hard for them. Besides Major Hazard the Quartermaster, Lt. Davies, had also rejoined and the normal routine had gone on almost unchanged and with trifling casualties. On June 7th the Sixteenth Division was in the middle of the attacking line, facing Wytschaete Wood with the ruins of Wytschaete behind it. Directly the success of the attack was known,[1] C and D Companies went forward to make tracks across No Man's Land, by which guns, ammunition, rations and R.E. stores might be sent up, and so energetically did they work that by 3 p.m. one track was being used by artillery most of the way across. Work was pushed on at night, A and B taking their turn, and after a day's rest the whole battalion started on June 9th laying tramways under the supervision of the Chief Engineer of the Ninth Corps. Several bridges were constructed and, though at times impeded by shell-fire,[2] the work was so vigorously carried on that by June 18th it could be suspended and the battalion could rejoin its Division, which was enjoying a rest at Strazeele. This rest was not long extended to the Pioneers, who were dispatched on June 21st to Poperinghe to work under the Nineteenth Corps, now preparing for the next stage in the offensive. Its work now was largely

---

[1] The Division's objective was just across the Messines—St. Eloi road.
[2] The battalion diary only records half a dozen casualties from gas shelling.

road making, but wells had to be sunk, several having to be abandoned on reaching blue clay.

The 15th Battalion had had one quite sharp fight during the period of preparation and waiting. It was in front line at St. Eloi on April 20th when an attack developed in some force, aimed, it appeared, at capturing a mine-shaft in the line held by the 11th Royal West Kent on the battalion's right. After a quiet day a violent bombardment had suddenly started, knocking the trenches about badly and cutting all telephone wires. Luckily Captain Barber, who was commanding the 15th's right company, C, sent up the SOS. signals so promptly that our barrage caught the Germans just as they were leaving their trenches, while our rifles and Lewis guns also took toll of them. Sergeant Collis was quick to enfilade the attack with a Lewis gun, while Lance Corporal Windebank showed great gallantry and leadership.[1] A few Germans entered the R.W.K's front line, which the bombardment had almost obliterated, but they were either killed or driven back, the 15th's Lewis guns doing some effective shooting at the retiring raiders, catching them in flank. A second attempt was also checked, the enemy facing the 15th Hampshire hardly getting beyond his own wire, and C Company were warmly commended for their gallantry and steadiness.

If this affair cost the 15th about 30 casualties, five men being killed and Lt. Seers wounded, the enemy had been sharply punished and the damaged trenches were soon repaired. After a small patrol had had a sharp bombing encounter with a rather larger German party on April 22nd, the battalion was ' out ' from April 23rd to May 20th, two marches of over 13 miles, no small trial after a long spell in trenches, taking the 122nd Brigade back to Tournehem. Here it did some vigorous training, including open warfare and musketry, both much needed at this period in the war, but recreation was not neglected.

Returning to the St. Eloi sector the 15th were in reserve, either at Voormezesle or at Chippewa Camp, till May 31st, when they took over the front line. May had passed almost without casualties, but the 15th's total losses during its first 12 months in France came to 760, fifteen officers and 190 other ranks killed and missing, 19 officers and 536 men wounded, mainly in their two spells on the Somme.

The week before our attack was lively enough : our guns were pounding away steadily and the bombardment was clearly being effective, for our patrols, though hampered by bright moonlight, found the wire extensively cut and in places almost demolished. Gas shelling prevented attempts to penetrate the enemy's lines but useful information was obtained. The enemy retaliated vigorously, shelling our support and reserve lines almost as heavily as the front and using much gas shell, and the 15th Hampshire had had nearly 30 casualties, including 2/Lt. Collier gassed before, early on June 5th, they went back to Middle Camp for a brief rest and clean up before moving up next evening to their assembly position.

[1] Both got the M.M.

P

On June 7th the Forty-First Division was on the left of the attack, with only one other Division beyond it ; its objectives lay South and West of the Ypres-Comines Canal and included the Dammstrasse, SE. of St. Eloi, which was to be taken by the 123rd and 124th Brigades, after which the 122nd would go through them, making for a line of trenches NE. of Oosttaverne and along the back crest of the Messines ridge. This taken, the Twenty-Fourth Division would go through and make for a final objective beyond Oosttaverne.

' Zero ' was at 3.10 a. m. (June 7th), but before that the 15th Hampshire, lying out in the open to avoid the zone where the enemy's barrage usually fell, had had several casualties, including two subalterns wounded. At ' Zero ' the mines so long in readiness were exploded all along our front with devastating

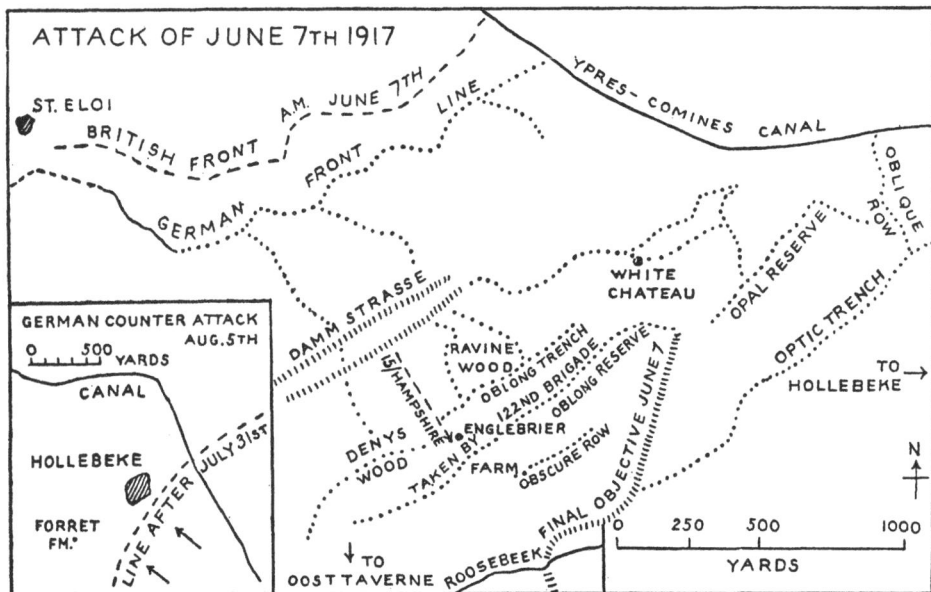

results and the Forty-First's leading brigades dashed forward, meeting only slight resistance until they reached the Dammstrasse. This, after a fierce struggle, they succeeded in mastering and, as they started consolidating, the 122nd Brigade came up in artillery formation in readiness to go through. That brigade had advanced at 5 a.m. and had only trifling casualties before deploying to attack. The 15th were in the centre, between the 11th R.W.K. and 12th East Surrey, and had Englebrier Farm as objective with Oblong Trench to be crossed on the way. They had about 500 yards of fairly flat ground to cross and their objective overlooked the valley of the little Roosebeek.

Our barrage was now rather ragged and delayed the left and centre battalions on whom it inflicted several casualties. Oblong Trench was carried nevertheless by 7 a.m. after some sharp fighting, and the attackers, pushing on, secured Englebrier Farm with Oblong Reserve behind it, overcoming some quite stubborn resistance and capturing many prisoners from dug-outs in Ravine and Denys Woods. By 9 a.m. the Division's last objective was being consolidated, and patrols were collecting prisoners from shell-holes and trenches in front ; R.S.M. Greenwood supported only by one man captured 20, while another large party who were trying to get away were intercepted and taken by 2/Lt. Whaley,[1] who pushed forward although our barrage was still falling just beyond the objective and cut off their retreat. Enemy were now seen gathering for a big counter-attack and about 10.15 a.m. a large body advanced over a ridge to reinforce those already in Obscure Row just ahead. Rifles and guns were quickly on to them and halted them, inflicting heavy casualties. Other attempts were equally successfully repulsed, though in the intervals the battalion was heavily bombarded, most of the day's casualties being due to this shelling. Then in the afternoon, just as another German advance was starting, the Twenty-Fourth Division came through the Forty-First to attack the final objective, beyond Oosttaverne, which it duly secured.

The Forty-First Division's substantial success had been fairly cheaply achieved, the 15th Hampshire, who had 2/Lts. Keep and Wright (died of wounds) and 41 men killed and missing, Captain Gorman, Lt. Newman, 2/Lts. Coope, Daniels and M. S. Moore, the M.O., Captain Hudson, and 135 men wounded, were about the battalion hardest hit, consolidating having, as so often, cost more than capturing. The battalion was back in reserve for four days, June 8th–11th, spent another four consolidating our new support line at the White Chateau, nearer the Canal,[2] and then on June 16th it took over Optic Trench, taken by the 11th R.W.K. two days earlier in an exploiting attack. This line was consistently shelled, and the 15th were lucky to escape with only 35 casualties in four days here, including five killed and 2/Lt. Powell Jones wounded. They were attacked late on June 17th, but our rifles and Lewis guns, aided by our barrage, caught the enemy as he left his trenches at dusk and drove him back. Hostile aircraft were troublesome until ours asserted themselves very effectively, while our guns replied most satisfactorily to the enemy's shell-fire.

From June 21st until July 23rd the 15th were out of trenches, though the large working parties they had to supply were usually in the shelled areas and had several casualties, 2/Lt. Warren being killed the very day after joining. Part of this time they were right back at Schakken, training hard but getting some rest and recreation. Two big drafts joined, with one of 20, and the battalion had reached a reasonable strength when, on July 23rd, its Division took over the St. Eloi–Hollebeke sector from the Forty-Seventh. The final preparations for the big attack were being completed and though the enemy plastered our lines with mustard gas, by July 31st all was ready.

The Forty-First Division, this time on the extreme right of the attack, had only to advance its line astride the Ypres-Comines canal far enough to cover the flank of the main attack. Two battalions of the 122nd Brigade sufficed to

[1] Both 2/Lt. Whaley and the R.S.M. received the M.C.
[2] To our left of the frontage attacked by the Forty-First Division on June 7th.

take Hollebeke,[1] though to accomplish this they had to fight quite hard, and the 15th Hampshire remained in support,though late that evening A and D Companies moved up to occupy Optic Trench and Oblique Row, from which the attack had started.

Thus the 14th was the only Hampshire battalion actively engaged in the day's attack ; their Division, now in the left centre Corps, the Eighteenth, was advancing from just NW. of Wieltje towards St. Julien, over 3000 yards away.

This was the ground over which ' Second Ypres ' had been fought, and its villages and farms had long ago been knocked to pieces and their ruins converted into ' strong points ', while of the woods only shattered stumps remained. It was largely open, barren or at best covered with weeds and rough grass, but bad going in rainy weather. Unfortunately the start of the Flanders offensive of 1917 coincided with some unusually bad weather, including quite torrential

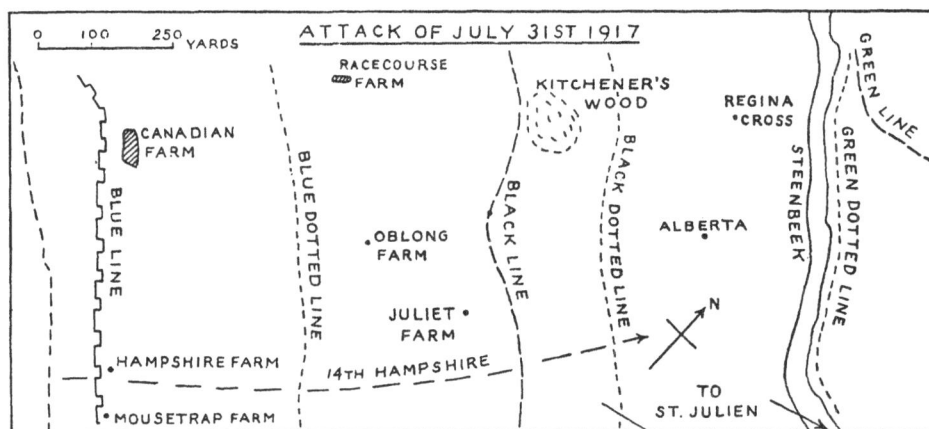

falls of rain, and throughout its course the weather was a recurrent handicap, if at times the ground dried sufficiently to be no real hindrance, while in September dust was once actually reported. But in the Salient, with the streams often so dammed up by debris as to have been converted into swamps or lakes, with the surface pitted with shell-holes which rain speedily converted into pools above a bottom of foul mire, with the natural drainage ruined by the shelling and the digging of trenches, even a little rain went a long way. The soil, if less glutinous than that of the chalk uplands of the Somme, had its own abominations ; less adhesive, it was looser and softer, and if men slipped and slithered less, those who fell into shell-holes were hard to extricate. Those few battalions who went ' over the top ' in ' Third Ypres ' without finding the going a serious impediment were fortunate.

The 14th Hampshire had had two turns in the line on Observatory Ridge in the first half of April before their Division shifted North to the Canal Bank-

[1] The 123rd Brigade was attacking between the Canal and Klein Zillebeke and secured its second but not its final objective.

Wieltje front, the 116th Brigade being on the Canal Bank when in support or in the Hill Top sector when in line.   The enemy's guns were fairly active but ours replied effectively, an SOS. from the 14th on April 24th being so promptly answered by our barrage that a threatened attack never really got going, while we cut much wire and generally damaged his trenches as much or more than he damaged ours.   From April 25th to May 16th the Division was ' out ' near Arques, [1] the 14th Hampshire getting a welcome respite from the trenches with a good spell of recreation as well as work and doing very well in Brigade Sports and competitions.   They then had ten days at Wormhoudt, continuing training, and finished May with four fairly quiet days in the Wieltje sector, having only three men hit and these in retaliation for an intense bombardment. June passed uneventfully, though in the digging of a new support trench at a very exposed spot on the nights of June 2nd/3rd and 3rd/4th Captain May and Lt. Lovelace and six men were wounded and several killed, though the line was dug all the same.   About the same time 2/Lt. Wallis-Wilson distinguished himself again when in charge of a party covering the digging of an advanced line close up to the enemy's wire.   He cleared the enemy out of a sap, which he prevented them from retaking and thus enabled the digging party to carry out its task.[2]   The Messines attack provoked some vigorous retaliation without many casualties.   Indeed, one turn in support on the Canal Bank brought double the casualties, mainly in working parties, as did the next four days in front line at Hill Top, when the 14th gained great credit by establishing safe communication by day with the Division on the left near Turco Farm.   From June 21st to July 15th the 14th was at Houlle near Watten, training, mainly rehearsing its projected attack over practice trenches.

The battalion was then back close behind the front, ' training under company arrangements ', and on July 29th it moved up to the Canal Bank to take up next evening its position for the attack.   It was in second line, behind the 11th R. Sussex, with the 13th R. Sussex on its right and the 17th Sherwood Foresters on its left.   The 116th and 117th Brigades were to capture four of the Division's five objectives, up to a ' Green Dotted Line ' 200 yards beyond the Steenbeek, the final objective, the ' Green Line ', well NE. of and including St. Julien, being left to the 118th Brigade.   From our starting-off line we had a good view to North and East for a full mile, including the ridge running NW from Kitchener's Wood on which was the second objective, the ' Black Line '. This and the ' Black Dotted Line ', 200 yards further on along the slope above the Steenbeek, the 14th had to capture as well as the ' Green Dotted Line '.

' Zero ' was at 3.50 a.m. (July 31st) when the troops, advancing behind ' the biggest barrage of the war ', were also concealed by the darkness.   The 11th R. Sussex having taken the ' Blue Line '[3] without much difficulty, the 14th Hampshire, ' leap-frogging ' them, went ahead towards the Black Line.   The

[1] On detraining at St. Omer the 14th were met by the band of the 1st Garrison Battalion of the Hampshire, later numbered as the 18th Battalion.
[2] He was awarded a bar to the M.C.
[3] This included Mouse Trap Farm.

German trenches had been only lightly held, but the 'pill boxes', dotted about quite irregularly, which had largely replaced regular trench-lines, presented the attackers with a new problem and gave much trouble. Several farms converted into 'pill-boxes' lay in the path of the 14th and their capture, mainly effected by getting round behind them and taking them in rear, caused most of the casualties, delaying and disorganizing the later stages of the advance, though the 14th, after taking both the 'Black' and 'Black Dotted Lines', pushed on down the slope to the 'Green Dotted Line' and eventually mastered this also, despite much difficulty at Alberta, a 'defended locality' NW. of St. Julien, where two tanks were very helpful, crushing uncut wire and subduing the garrison's fire. 2/Lt. Hewitt, after the capture of the 'Black Line', had reorganized his company and was waiting for the barrage to lift, when a shell burst near him, hitting him and setting fire to the signal lights in his haversack and to his clothing. He not only systematically extinguished the flames but, despite his burns and his wound, led his men resolutely forward in face of heavy machine-gun fire and played a big part in capturing the 'Black Dotted Line'; there, while superintending consolidation, he was sniped and killed. Captain West, finding the attack held up by uncut wire and a 'strong point', brought up his company from support and carried the position, pushing on over three lines of trenches, and Captain R. H. Freeman, who led his company with much skill, also did much to consolidate the captured objective. Some men went on across the Steenbeek to the 'Green Dotted Line', while the 118th Brigade took St. Julien and pressed on well across the St. Julien–Poelcapelle road, but the Thirty-Ninth was ahead of the Division on its right and, with its flank exposed, this advanced line could not be held against heavy shelling and vigorous counter-attacks and was eventually evacuated by order, the 'Black Dotted Line', which the 14th was consolidating, being adopted as the main line of resistance and successfully maintained, our artillery and machine-guns inflicting heavy casualties on the counter-attacking troops.

If the failure to retain St. Julien was disappointing, the Division had gained a substantial success and hit its enemy hard. The 14th alone claimed over 200 prisoners with three guns and 17 machine-guns, their casualties, 2/Lts. Collis, Falconer and Hewitt and 60 men killed and missing, Major Trevor-Roper,[1] Captain Gammon, Lt. Chevalier, 2/Lts. Peet and Tyler and 156 men wounded, though heavy enough, were not the crippling losses of September 3rd 1916 at Hamel, while they had the satisfaction of having carried out all they had been asked to do, and the posthumous V.C. awarded to 2/Lt. Hewitt marked the day in the battalion's record.[2]

For two days the 14th had to hold on here under heavy shelling, another 14 men being killed and 40 wounded, but posts were again established beyond the Steenbeek. Captain Collins, who had been conspicuous in the attack, took a patrol forward to occupy an advanced post where he held on while the ruins of St. Julien were reoccupied. By the morning of August 3rd the battalion was

[1] Died of wounds.
[2] Captains Collins, R. H. Freeman and West were awarded the M.C.

SECOND LIEUTENANT DENIS GEORGE WYLDBORE HEWITT, V.C.

Born on December 18th, 1897 ; elder son of the Hon. George and Mrs. Hewitt, of Field House, Hursley, Winchester. He was educated at Winchester College and gazetted to a commission in the Hampshire Regiment on 1st April, 1916. His decoration was gazetted on September 14th, 1917, when attached to the 14th Battalion, for his actions in an attack, on the Somme on July 31st, 1917. ✳ IN THE YPRES SALIEN⸱

‘ For most conspicuous bravery and devotion to duty when in command of a company in attack.

When his first objective had been captured he reorganized the company and moved forward towards his objective. While waiting for the barrage to lift he was hit by a piece of shell, which exploded the signal lights in his haversack, and set fire to his equipment and clothes. Having extinguished the flames, in spite of his wound and the severe pain he was suffering, he led forward the remains of the company under very heavy machine gun fire, captured and consolidated his objective.

He was subsequently killed by a sniper while inspecting the consolidation and encouraging his men.

This gallant officer set a magnificent example of coolness and contempt of danger to the whole battalion, and it was due to his splendid leading that the final objective of the battalion was gained.’

back on the Canal Bank and next day went further back for a week's rest, partly at Poperinghe, partly at Meteren, after which it came up to the front again, as the Division was relieving the Forty-First at Hollebeke.

The Forty-First's success on July 31st having been cheaply gained, it had been kept in the Hollebeke sector for nearly a fortnight. The 15th Hampshire were at first in support, having two companies in Oblique Row and Optic Trench, trenches taken on June 14th. Here heavy shelling caused 40 casualties, including 2/Lts. S. A. C. Pearce and Adams wounded, while constant rain filled the trenches with mud and water, making some quite untenable. Relieving the 11th R. W. Kent on August 3rd, with two companies in front line and two in close support,[1] the 15th were heavily shelled on the following evening, and early next morning (August 5th) the Germans launched a really vigorous attempt to recover Hollebeke. A mist helping them, an outpost at Forret Farm [2] was over-run and the attackers worked round behind Hollebeke, which Captain Fowler therefore evacuated, though his company checked the interceptors, cutting off and taking some of them, and prevented any further advance. Our left held firm, though one post was overwhelmed, 2/Lt. Martin and a dozen men being killed or taken. Meanwhile Major Amery had arrived from head-quarters to discover what was happening and was arranging counter-measures and the reserve companies had turned out and come forward to counter-attack. Under cover of the mist Captain Oxborrow's company now reinforced Captain Fowler's for an attempt to recover Hollebeke, some East Surrey joining in.[3] This went very well and the village was soon cleared with the bayonet, thanks largely to the good leading of Captains Fowler and Oxborrow and 2/Lt. Shields, several prisoners being taken and the surviving intruders driven out. Major Amery having been badly wounded, Major Pennell came forward to arrange to exploit the recapture of Hollebeke by recovering Forret Farm. This was accomplished by a platoon under 2/Lt. Shields, aided by more East Surreys, a dozen prisoners being added to those taken in clearing Hollebeke. Thus the position was satis-factorily re-established [4] at a cost of no more than 20 killed and missing, in-cluding 2/Lts. Martin, who was later reported to be a prisoner of war, and Sheryer (died of wounds) and Major Amery and 10 men wounded. Some picked *Sturm-Truppen* proved to have reinforced the trench garrison for this attack and its repulse was a creditable effort, seeing that our men were wet and tired and the Germans much fresher. Captains Oxborrow and Fowler and 2/Lt. Shields subsequently received the M.C. and a dozen men the M.M., among them Sergeants Warren, Cross, North and Faulkner, C.S.M. Collis getting a bar.

The Germans despite their repulse, had not relinquished hope of recovering Hollebeke. About 9 p.m. they were observed massing for an attack, but

[1] See Sketch 43 (inset). p. 226.   [2] S.W. of Hollebeke.
[3] The 12th East Surrey were on the 15th's right SW. of Forret Farm and had their outpost line rushed in the fog.
The East Surrey also recovered their outpost line and even advanced it slightly.

directly they started crawling forward our rifles and machine-guns opened up, another company having reinforced our front line, and with our barrage coming down promptly the attack never succeeded in developing. The next four days brought more heavy shelling, the enemy were apparently expecting another attack, so put down some anticipatory barrages, but early on August 10th some posts were slightly advanced beyond Hollebeke, while under cover of a barrage put down to cover an advance on our left, the 123rd Brigade sent out patrols which brought back nearly 30 prisoners. That evening the 15th were relieved, having had 2/Lts. Palmer and Spencer and 26 men wounded since August 5th and nine men killed. By August 14th the battalion was resting at Fletre, where it was inspected by its Corps Commander, Lt General Morland, and by the Divisional Commander and warmly thanked for its recent achievements.

It the 11th Battalion did not ' go over the top ' in this battle it had plenty to do. It had been busy all July, road-making, building bridges and digging wells and working on light railways. Its labours were hindered by counter-bombardments, bad weather and shortage of materials, while lorries might lose their way and fail to deliver their burden even when the required stores were available, but the daily entries in the diary record much steady progress, the result of persistent hard work of a high level of technical efficiency. Battalion head-quarters moved from Poperinghe to Brandhoek Camp on July 23rd, where for several days the 11th rested from their labours and though pestered by bomb-dropping aircraft escaped without casualties.

Shortly after ' Zero ' on July 31st A Company had started work on the roads leading to the positions taken by the Fifteenth Division [1] North of the Ypres–Roulers railway, which included Verlorenhoek and Frezenberg. It was all-important to make them fit for our heavy guns to move up and give better support to our forward troops. While thus engaged the company had the misfortune to be caught in a German barrage in which Major Bell and several men were hit, the Major's wounds unfortunately proving fatal. One of the battalion's mainstays from its earliest days, he was greatly missed. Major Hazard went forward to take his place and direct the work, which was steadily pushed on despite the shelling.

The work also much hampered by the congestion of the roads ; even where they were in good repair and had not been damaged by shell-fire, guns and lorries trying to get forward blocked them and prevented materials from reaching the front. Shell craters had to be filled or avoided by making deviations round them and all the time the shelling persisted, causing another 30 casualties, Captain Howson, who did splendid work encouraging his men and refusing to go back, despite his wounds,[2] Lt. Asfield and 2/Lts. Bennett and Pennington being wounded. But much work was done, and on August 4th the battalion handed over to the Fifteenth Division's Pioneers and moved into Ypres to be employed in screening the Menin Road forward to a spot deservedly known as Hell-fire Corner. This meant more casualties, many from gas, and

---

[1] The Sixteenth Division was in reserve.   [2] He was awarded the M.C.

the men were sorely tried. Besides more normal pioneer work, parties had at times to help in getting guns into position.

In the next major attack, that of August 16th, which brought the 2nd Hampshire into the battle, the 11th were again detailed to construct tracks across No Man's Land to the captured lines. Where their Division was attacking, in the centre towards Zonnebeke, hardly any ground was gained, but the 11th were kept hard at work nevertheless until August 17th, when all companies were brought back to camp before moving Southward, the Sixteenth Division being now under orders to join the Third Army. Since July 31st 2/Lts. Clarke and Hayman and four men had been killed, Captain Chadwick, Lt. Thorne and over 50 men being wounded or gassed.

Of the two battalions engaged in ' Arras ' the 2nd were thrown into the Flanders fighting many weeks before the 1st, who continued in their old sector North of the Scarpe till the end of June and then, after a brief rest, took over the Monchy sector across the river, which they did not finally leave till the end of August.

The 2nd had spent most of June near Candas, resting and reorganizing. Nearly 200 reinforcements joined them soon after arriving there, but many of them were really only ' C.2.,' mainly under-sized Londoners, and their musketry was little better than their physique ; other drafts and returns from hospital brought the total reinforcements up to 350, against which only 30 were sent to hospital, while the last spell at Monchy had only brought a dozen casualties ; other ranks were up to 960 by July 1st, while with Lt. Colonel Beckwith and Majors Middleton and Spring and Captain Westmorland present the battalion actually had four ' pre-war ' Regulars, of whom the C.O. was ' mentioned ' in the Honours Gazette of June 4th along with the Quartermaster, Lt. A Smith, and Sergeant Merritt,[1] while Major Middleton received the D.S.O.

Reaching Proven on June 27th the battalion went first to Dead Man's Farm near Boesinghe, where it was employed in burying cable and getting a very indifferent reserve line, the X Line, into a defensible condition. This line required almost complete reconstruction and much hard work. The 2nd then took over the Canal Bank from the 87th Brigade and after five days in support were in front line from July 10th to 13th. They found the line fairly quiet and casualties were few, if much hard work was needed. Ten days training West of Proven followed, hampered by lack of ground and of rifle ranges, while at night bomb-dropping aeroplanes were becoming unpleasantly active, on one occasion bombing an ambulance and killing 60 mules which the Hampshire had to bury. By July 24th the battalion was back East of Proven, finding large working parties. Major Middleton now left to command the 10th Northumberland Fusiliers (Twenty-Third Division), and on July 30th Colonel Beckwith received a well-earned promotion, getting the 153rd Brigade (Fifty-First Division), which left Major Spring in command. Drafts amounting to 75 with 11 men back from hospital having joined, against 39 admissions and 28 casual-

[1] Posthumous.

ties,[1] the battalion had on July 31st no fewer than 42 officers and 972 other ranks on its strength, with Captains Cuddon (W), D. Day (Y) and Westmorland (Z), and 2/Lt. Wooldridge (X) commanding companies.

The Twenty-Ninth Division was in reserve on July 31st, being on the extreme British left [2] behind the Guards, who captured Pilckem and pushed forward to the Steenbeek, securing all their objectives without heavy loss, so that the Twenty-Ninth did not have to relieve them for a week. The line it then took over ran along the Pilckem ridge, which was sticky even on top and sloped down to the marsh now formed by the swollen Steenbeek. The so-called ' line ' consisted of isolated trenches and shell-holes, though a few ' pill-boxes '

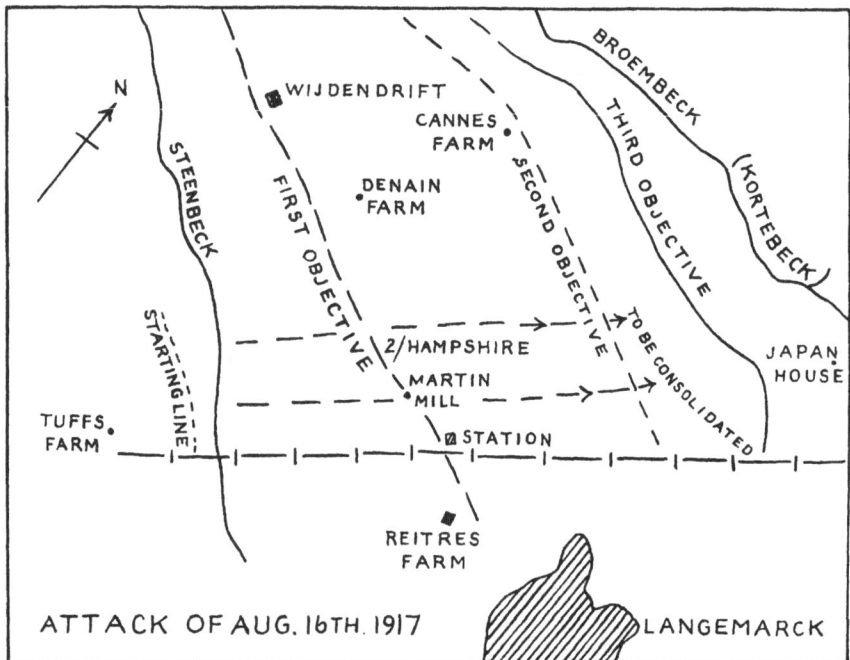

ATTACK OF AUG. 16TH. 1917   LANGEMARCK

had survived the bombardment and could be used as brigade or battalion head-quarters or as 'strong points'. The support line, which the 2nd Hampshire occupied on August 9th, existed mainly on the map and the men had to dig in as best they could. The enemy's fire was heavy and the battalion had 20 casualties, 2/Lts. Wooldridge and Powell being wounded, but the men worked well and improved the position considerably. After four days here, the battalion went forward after dark on August 15th to an assembly position NE. of Pilckem. A tape, previously laid by Captain Day, proved invaluable on a very dark night, the Essex, in support, following the battalion along it. Several men fell into shell-holes or stuck in the bog and had to be hauled out with ropes,

[1] Largely in a working party on the morning of July 10th.
[2] NW. of the frontage attacked by the Thirty-Ninth Division on July 31st.

while shell-fire caused some casualties, but the men were splendidly steady and quiet and the assembly position was reached about 1.30 a.m. (August 16th). Battalion H.Q. were at Tuff's Farm, Y (Captain Day) and W (2/Lt. Whitmarsh) Companies being across the swamps of the Steenbeek, over which the 87th Brigade had previously laid bridges, and X (2/Lt. Reid) and Z (Captain Westmorland) in 'artillery formation' on the near side behind them. On the right, beyond the Ypres–Staden railway, was the Twentieth Division facing Langemarck, the Newfoundlands being on the Hampshire's left. Beyond them was the 87th Brigade, in touch with the French.

Desultory shelling caused several casualties during the wait on the assembly position, but at 4.45 our barrage came down, 'as good as any we ever met during the war', and the men went forward well, taking full advantage of it. The leading companies' objective was a line across the Langemarck–Wijdendrift road, its right being just beyond Martin's Mill; the supports were to secure a 'Green Line', 500 yards further on and running North to Cannes Farm : on this line the Essex would come through to tackle the third objective, NNW. of Langemarck and short of the Broembeck.[1]

The advance went well, though the right companies suffered some casualties through the Twentieth Division's barrage being ragged and falling outside its proper line, while South of the railway that Division itself had soon fallen behind. In consequence enfilade fire from machine-guns in Reitres Farm and in blockhouses near it caused trouble, but those were dealt with by 2/Lt. Reid, who promptly extended two platoons along the railway and, covered by their fire, 2/Lt. Pine led a party across the railway to attack these obstructing 'strong points'. Well backed up by Corporal Whitaker, he soon captured Reitres Farm, despite stubborn opposition, and after he had been wounded the Corporal carried on, clearing the enemy out of several more posts. Meanwhile Captain Day organized an attack on other blockhouses North of the railway and Sergeant Oram brought Z Company's right platoon across to assist, while Sergeant Finch, leading an attack on another 'strong point', dashed ahead through our barrage, killed four Germans single-handed and took the blockhouses with some 20 prisoners. Thanks to their promptitude and grasp of the situation the opposition was overcome : besides Reitres Farm and the blockhouses near it dug-outs along the railway were taken, Sergeant Holdaway[2] leading a party of bombers splendidly and clearing several dug-outs, with many prisoners and several machine-guns, while with Sergeant Oram's help, Captain Day, who though wounded had continued to lead his company, soon captured his objective. Great work was done by several Lewis gunners, Privates Forrester,[2] Batten[2] and Hoath in[2] particular, who not only assisted in the capture of the battalion's objective but helped the Twentieth Division to advance and, when the enemy retired from near Langemarck Station, fired on them with great effect. Thus the first objective was duly secured and its consolidation could be started, Sergeant Oram's party rejoining their own company for the next advance.

[1] This stream is called Kortebeck in some accounts.   [2] Received the M.M.

The first objective had been captured well up to time, so the advance to the Green Line followed at 5.45. The ground was so bad that shallow columns had to be formed to cross one specially marshy bit, wave formation being resumed beyond it. Nevertheless the Green Line was reached on the heels of the barrage, 2/Lt. Reid again leading the advance admirably, while bombers of X Company cleared several more block-houses along the railway. This objective having been secured with more prisoners, bringing the battalion's captures to well over 150, its consolidation was begun, Major Spring coming forward to superintend the construction of 'strong points', while several Lewis gunners took post in front to cover the work. The men worked splendidly and soon had good cover, from which they benefitted when, about 7.30 a.m., the enemy started shelling the captured position with considerable vigour, their fire being largely directed by aeroplanes. This caused many casualties, especially among the stretcher bearers and H.Q. personnel at Tuff's Farm, where Private Gibbs, the Medical Officer's orderly, was conspicuous for good work, and made communication with Brigade H.Q. very hard to maintain. Shortly afterwards the supporting battalions, the Essex (right) and Worcestershire, came forward to attack the Red Line, just short of the Broembeek, which they duly captured, adding substantially to the many prisoners already taken. Rumours of an impending counter-attack now caused the right companies to prepare a defensive line along the railway, where the Twentieth Division, though driven back from the Red Line, was holding on to Langemarck and the Green Line. None developed, however, and the Twenty-Ninth Division was left in possession of its gains [1] and could congratulate itself on a most successful day : its losses had not been very heavy, little over 2000 all told, and the casualties inflicted on the enemy, over and above several hundreds of prisoners, had been substantial. It now retained its position despite considerable shell-fire, easily repulsing some half-hearted counter-attacks, the most threatening being promptly stopped by our artillery, and before daylight on August 17th the 86th Brigade had relieved the attacking brigades, though by some error X Company was not relieved for another 24 hours, when it rejoined head-quarters at Bluet Farm. The Hampshire's casualties, 2/Lt. Feather killed, 2/Lts. Pine and Haddy mortally wounded, 43 men killed and missing, Captain Day, 2/Lt. L. H. Brown and 148 men wounded,[2] though substantial, were not high, considering what had been achieved, and the battalion was most warmly congratulated by the Corps Commander, Lord Cavan, and by General de Lisle, who inspected it on August 19th, bringing a special message of thanks from the G.O.C. Twentieth Division for the great help the Hampshire had given his men. Captain Day and 2/Lt. Reid were given the M.C. and Sergeants Finch and Oram the D.C.M., nine men getting M.M.s.[3] Corporal Whitaker and Privates Gibbs and Wood, a ' runner '

---

[1] The 87th Brigade on the 88th's left had also captured all its objectives.

[2] The M.O., Captain Knight, 2/Lt. T.C. Pearce and 20 more men, though wounded, remained ' at duty '.

[3] Besides those mentioned, these were Sergeant Paffett, who though wounded had led his men admirably. Private Sheaf, who had taken command of a leaderless section, Privates Everiss and Ratcliffe, ' runners ', and Private Squires, who had done great work as a bomber.

who besides doing admirable work in that line, had rallied a disorganized section, seized a Lewis gun and dispersed a large party of Germans, getting bars.

The battalion was back in front line by August 20th, in the ' Red Line ' taken by the Essex and Worcestershire, where it was severely shelled and sniped and had over 50 casualties, including 2/Lt. Whitmarsh and 17 men killed. It was not inactive, the improvement of the line and of the communications provided plenty of work, while Z Company established a post beyond the Broembeek and did some useful patrolling. August 25th saw the battalion back at Proven, to begin nearly a month's respite from fighting.

The attack of August 16th, highly successful on our left, from St. Julien Northward, had been less fortunate further South, where the enemy's positions astride the narrow ridge running Eastward from Ypres had proved exceptionally strong and his resistance particularly determined. This decided Sir Douglas Haig to extend the Second Army's left Northward, giving General Plumer charge of the attack astride the Menin Road, the Fifth Army continuing the attacks further to the left. Much re-adjustment and re-arrangement was now necessary, while, to meet the pill-box and other new methods of defence, certain modifications in our tactics had to be adopted and practised and this, even more than the rain, postponed the next major attack till mid-September. In the meantime the Divisions in front line, among them the Thirty-Ninth, were kept busy enough ; many local attacks were undertaken, the line being improved at certain points, while the enemy was on the alert to hamper and hinder our preparations, shelling our lines heavily and continually, making local counter-attacks and harassing us with every available weapon, but without gaining much. Meanwhile, by keeping the Germans fully occupied, Sir Douglas Haig was fulfilling one of his major purposes, the Germans were not allowed to recover the initiative and to take advantage of it to attack the still disordered and depressed French Army.

CHAPTER XIX
THE FLANDERS OFFENSIVE, II
Third Ypres (continued)

During the month's pause which set in after the middle of August only one Hampshire battalion was in the fighting line at Ypres, the 14th, whose Division had taken over the Hollebeke sector from the Forty-First on August 12th, and remained there or at Klein Zillebeke for the next three weeks. Retaliation for the barrage fired to assist our attack of August 16th caused over 30 casualties, and at different times another 20 were suffered,[1] but the enemy was rarely aggressive and the battalion had few chances of hitting back, its main energies being devoted to improving the communications, while when it was in reserve quantities of material had to be carried up to the front line. From September 4th to 8th it was at Chippewa Camp, training, and then had three days in support in Shrewsbury Forest, ground taken on July 31st and North of the sectors it had been holding. After three days in reserve here it held the left sub-sector of this front from September 14th to 16th, when the Forty-First Division, now returning to the line, relieved it. Another attack was now very near, but artillery activity had not been pronounced on either side and the 14th escaped with six killed and a dozen wounded. On relief they went back to Curragh Camp, their brigade being in Divisional reserve during the attack of September 20th, when only the 117th Brigade was actively engaged, securing a rather limited objective SE. of Shrewsbury Forest, on the right of the Forty-First Division.

After being relieved at Hollebeke the Forty-First Division had first been at Fletre and then, on August 21st, marched back to Nieppe, whence buses took the 15th Hampshire to Acquin, where they spent three weeks. Eighty reinforcements had joined before this and another 50 with five officers, among them Major Murdoch of the 11th R.W.K., joined at Acquin, where much useful training was done, especially of signallers and other specialists. Several awards of decorations were announced and on September 9th some were presented after church parade by Brigadier General Towsey.

The return to the front started on September 14th, three marches taking the 15th back to Ridgewood, behind their old sector. Their Division was coming into line between the Twenty-Third, who were astride the Menin road, and the Thirty-Ninth, and was to attack through the Northern part of Shrewsbury Forest, with the Basseville brook to cross. As the 14th Hampshire were in Divisional reserve while the Twenty-Ninth Division was still at rest, the Fourth not yet in Flanders and the Sixteenth already with the Third Army, only the 15th Battalion represented the regiment in the big attack of September 20th.

The Forty-First Division's first and second objectives, the ' Red ' and ' Blue '

---

[1] No officer was hit.

Lines, lay West and East respectively of the Basseville brook : the 122nd Brigade was attacking on its left, with the 124th on its right, and was using the 15th Hampshire (left) and 18th K.R.R.C. (right) to capture them, after which the 11th R.W.K. and 12th E. Surreys would go through and attack a ' Green Line ', Tower Trench on the Tower Hamlets ridge beyond. The Tower Hamlets ridge, a flat-topped spur running South from the Menin road, was a position of considerable natural strength, even without the fortifications. The attackers had first to cross the open slope leading down to the Basseville brook and then to climb the sharp glacis of the spur, equally lacking in cover.

The assembly had been carried out over-night quite quietly and unevent-fully, except for more rain, and the attack duly started at 5.40 a.m. (September 20th) in a mist which soon cleared away. Soon after crossing the German front line the 15th were held up at Java Avenue by block-houses which the barrage had missed. Casualties were heavy, many officers, including all four company commanders, were hit, and the opposition was only overcome and the block-houses taken by great gallantry and good leading and with some help from the R.W.K., whose C.O., Lt. Colonel Corfe, did much to re-organize the attackers, while Captain Wigmore, now Adjutant, went forward to assist and lead the men. Before long they had carried the Red Line and, pushing on across the swampy depression formed by the brook, they mastered the Blue Line also, 2/Lts. Sergeant and Barker distinguishing themselves by good leading and initiative.

As consolidation started a counter-attack began to develop from the NE.; it was checked by our fire, and then the R.W.K. went ahead to take the ' Green Line ', where the ' Tower Hamlets ', a mass of concrete dug-outs and ' pill-boxes ', promised to give trouble, It was a formidable task, the attackers had to mount an open slope quite devoid of cover and many machine-guns were in action in the ' pill-boxes ', proof against anything short of a ' direct ' from a ' heavy '. The R.W.K. had already lost heavily and, being ahead of all other troops on their right, they came under enfilade machine-gun fire, a strongly fortified ' defended locality ' on that flank having escaped our barrage, while its fire had also checked the 124th Brigade. However, despite stubborn opposition they reached Tower Trench and gained a foothold in it, from which they were soon driven back to the Blue Line, which the 15th were consolidating, though a few men who had never received the order to retire held on stubbornly at one point. Late in the afternoon the 15th were ordered to attempt to capture the Green Line ; only about 130 men could be collected, but these pushed gallantly forward and established themselves in the Green Line, taking 40 prisoners, among them a battalion commander and his adjutant, a field gun and two machine-guns ; 2/Lt. M. S. Moore, supported only by half a dozen men, capturing nearly 30 Germans in one big dug-out. This position they consoli-dated, repulsing several counter-attacks and getting touch with the Twenty-Third Division,[1] but without ever getting touch with the handful of R.W.K. who

---

[1] That Division's *History* (p. 190) is clear on that point : ' the 15th Hampshire ' it writes ' succeeded in capturing their objective '.

had not retired and without our artillery learning that parts of the Green Line were in our hands.

This was only too evident next day, when about 10 a.m. our barrage was put down on the Green Line to assist an advance on the right by the 123rd Brigade, who established themselves across the brook but short of the Green Line, the ' defended locality ' South of the Tower Hamlets again proving a stumbling block. 2/Lt. Moore, now the senior officer left in the Green Line, showed great resourcefulness and coolness, withdrawing his men slightly so as to avoid our barrage but reoccupying his position directly it stopped, and despite another bombardment by our guns during the afternoon the position was retained all day. Meanwhile enemy had been seen preparing to counter-attack the Blue Line from the SE. but our rifles and machine-guns had dispersed them even before our barrage answered the SOS.[1]

Early next morning, (September 22nd) another dose of our barrage, which destroyed their rifles and rations, at last forced 2/Lt. Moore and the ten men who alone survived of his party back to the Blue Line, for though they had re-

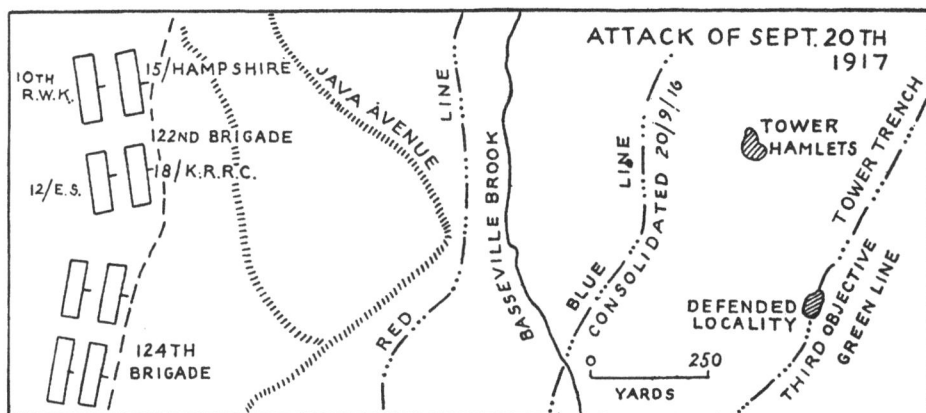

ARMED themselves with German rifles and bombs, they could not hold on any longer and had very reluctantly to leave behind an anti-tank gun and two machine-guns. They had made a gallant effort and the V.C. shortly afterwards awarded to 2/Lt. Moore was a well-earned recognition of an outstanding exploit.[2] If the Division had only secured part of its objective it had distracted the Germans' attention from the troops on its left and had contributed to their success.

After holding on throughout September 22nd under heavy shelling, though no more counter-attacks developed, the remnants of the 15th Hampshire were relieved by the 14th Battalion and another of the Thirty-Ninth Division, and went back to Ridgewood Camp. Six[3] officers and 83 men had been killed or

---

[1] The regimental histories show that the two German regiments holding the position attacked by the Forty-First Division, the 28th Bavarian Ersatz and the 395th, lost virtually all their front battalions and most of those in support.

[2] Captain Wigmore and 2/Lts. Barker and Sergeant received the M.C.

[3] Major Seers, Captain Daniels, Lts. Bender, Montagu and Stokes and 2/Lt. Savage.

SECOND LIEUTENANT MONTAGUE SHADWORTH SEYMOUR MOORE, V.C.,
Croix de Guerre

He was gazetted to a commission in The Hampshire Regiment from the R.M.C., Sandhurst, on August 16th, 1916. His decoration was gazetted on November 8th, 1917, for his actions on September 20th, 1917, at 'Tower Hamlets', East of Ypres, when attached to the 15th Battalion.

' For most conspicuous bravery in operations necessitating a fresh attack on a final objective which had not been captured. 2nd Lieutenant Moore at once volunteered for this duty, and dashed forward at the head of some seventy men. They were met with heavy machine gun fire from a flank which caused severe casualties, with the result that he arrived at his objective—some five hundred yards on—with only a sergeant and four men. Nothing daunted, he at once bombed a large dug out and took 28 prisoners, 2 machine guns, and a light field gun. Gradually more officers and men arrived, to the number of about sixty. His position was entirely isolated, as the troops on the right had not advanced, but he dug a trench and repelled bombing attacks throughout the night. The next morning he was forced to retire a short distance. When the opportunity offered he at once reoccupied his position, re-armed his men with enemy rifles and bombs, most of theirs being smashed, and beat off more than one counter-attack.

2nd Lieutenant Moore held to this post under continual shell fire for thirty-six hours, until his force was reduced to ten men, out of six officers and one hundred and thirty men who had started the operation. He eventually got away his wounded, and withdrew under cover of a thick mist.

were missing and seven officers and 251 men wounded, leaving the battalion terribly reduced ; indeed, had not 82 men joined on September 24th, the remnant would almost have been outnumbered by the influx on September 25th of twelve officers and 307 other ranks of the 1st Hampshire Carabiniers.

That regiment had continued on home duty all through 1915, though it had volunteered to serve as infantry in any theatre of war.   Early in 1916 its squadrons were attached as Divisional cavalry to Second-Line T.F. Divisions, the Fifty-Eighth, Sixtieth, and Sixty-First, all due to go overseas ; B and C Squadrons, however, went out independently in May and June , head-quarters also coming out and becoming head-quarters of the Ninth Corps Cavalry, a composite unit, of which C Squadron also formed part, B being then with the Cavalry Corps and later with the Seventeenth.   Eventually in January 1917 A Squadron also came out [1] and the regiment was re-united.   It served as Corps Cavalry to the Ninth Corps till late in July, doing useful work during the Messines attack in patrolling, locating the enemy and carrying information. By this time the difficulty of finding drafts was leading to many expedients, and among them the conversion into infantry of several Yeomanry units.   The Hampshire Carabiniers were so far allowed to retain their identity that the 15th incorporated their title and became the 15th (Hampshire Carabiniers) Battalion, the Hampshire Regiment.

This was a fine reinforcement ; if many ' originals ' of the Hampshire Carabiniers had obtained commissions or transferred to the cavalry, many remained and the 15th were glad to welcome such splendid material, men of some service and training.

The Thirty-Ninth Division, having had only limited objectives on September 20th, had only employed the 117th Brigade, so that it had two unused brigades available for the next big attack, that of September 26th, when it attacked from the line gained [2] on the 20th by the Twenty-Third and Forty-First Divisions South of the Menin road.   The 116th Brigade was on the left, its objectives being the Tower Hamlets and Tower Trench behind them, a formidable task enough.   On its right the 118th Brigade had, if possible, an even nastier nut to crack, the ' defended locality ' which had held up the attack of September 20th.

The 14th Hampshire had had two trying days in line here after relieving the remnants of the 15th Hampshire on the evening of September 22nd.   The approaches to our advanced positions were exposed to snipers and to machine-gun and artillery fire, and the battalion had been heavily shelled while consolidating a rather imperfect line, having 2/Lts. Chartney and Clarke wounded

---

[1] Its transport was nearly sunk in a collision off Havre and only beached just in time ; the men behaved admirably, several remaining on board with the horses till the vessel could be sufficiently repaired to be berthed.   Before this a Divisional squadron had ceased to form part of the Divisional organization, Corps cavalry units being formed instead.

[2] East of the Basseville brook but short of the Tower Hamlets.

with 25 men, six others being killed. After two days in reserve, it took up its position for the attack after dark on September 25th.

Directly the advance started at 5.50 a.m., it met heavy machine-gun fire and casualties soon mounted up : Major Goldsmith, who had given up his leave to be in command in this attack,[1] fell fatally wounded leading the advance, and with him Captain Nichols, Lt. Bainbridge and 2/Lt. Wallis-Wilson, a man of great bravery, who had won the M.C. and a bar, much the oldest subaltern in the battalion. However, despite the fire and the boggy ground, the 14th pressed on and reached and carried the Tower Hamlets, Captain White leading his men splendidly and keeping them close up to the barrage, while 2/Lt. Howard, after reaching his platoon's objective despite mist and smoke by keeping on a compass bearing, organized and led the clearing of several dug-outs, bombing them effectively. Captain Dawson, the next senior officer present, took charge on Major Goldsmith's fall and carried on most efficiently. Parties now pushed ahead to Tower Trench, when 2/Lt. Taberer, finding that one company detailed for this advance had lost heavily and was much disorganized, took his own company forward and by his leadership and initiative did much to ensure the success of this stage of the advance. By 7.30 a.m. about 150 men were consolidating on the left of the final objective, taking up a line just short of Tower Trench itself. Machine-guns on the left front were troublesome but touch had been obtained with the Thirty-Third Division NW. of Gheluvelt Wood, while the supporting battalion eventually reinforced the advanced party of the 14th. The 118th Brigade on the 116th's right had reached but failed to retain possession of the obstructing ' defended locality ' on the Southern end of the Tower Hamlets spur, but nevertheless the 116th's gains were retained and consolidation was energetically pushed on, despite the difficulty of getting material forward and the constant shelling and sniping. Counter-attacks developed elsewhere in considerable force and vigour, but the Tower Hamlets lay beyond their frontage, and next evening, (September 27th) on their Division being relieved the 14th Hampshire went back well behind the line. Losses had been fairly heavy, the four officers mentioned and 75 men killed or missing, 2/Lts. Barrass, Butt, Sangster and Thomas and 118 men wounded,[2] but the battalion could feel that it had achieved something substantial despite great difficulties.

The 14th and 15th Hampshire had both finished with ' Third Ypres ', for if the 14th were to return to the Salient before the offensive came to its muddy end in the swamps near Poelcapelle and Passchendaele, the Menin road sector had by then become inactive : both Regular battalions, however, were to be present for the next big attack, that of October 4th, when the Twenty-Ninth Division, on our extreme left astride the Ypres–Staden railway, had the Fourth on its right, NE. of Langemarck.

Major operations at Arras had ended before ' Messines ' started, but the Arras front did not become really ' quiet ' immediately. At several points

---

[1] He had just been through the Senior Officers' School at Aldershot.

[2] 2/Lt. Taberer was awarded the D.S.O., Captains Dawson and White and 2/Lt. Howard getting the M.C.

either Germans or British badly needed to improve their lines or were reluctant to relinquish stubbornly contested positions, and the 1st Hampshire, who remained on this front till the end of August, were active enough. They had returned to their old sector near Roeux in the middle of June. Two companies were in front line, the right, whose flank rested on the Scarpe, holding four disconnected posts, the left's line being more continuous. Patrols were active but did not find the enemy inclined to contest No Man's Land, and though the line was spasmodically shelled by night, the days were quieter and four in line

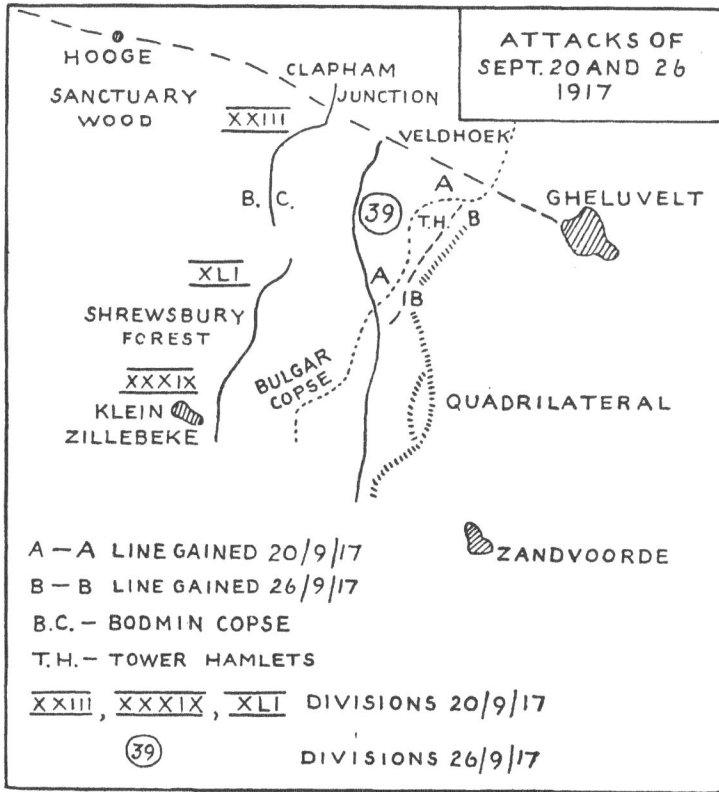

ATTACKS OF
SEPT. 20 AND 26
1917

A — A LINE GAINED 20/9/17
B — B LINE GAINED 26/9/17
B.C. — BODMIN COPSE
T.H. — TOWER HAMLETS

XXIII, XXXIX, XLI DIVISIONS 20/9/17
(39)   DIVISIONS 26/9/17

only brought eleven casualties, but in support the battalion was very hard worked, improving a poor support line. A move back to Balmoral Camp near St. Laurent Blangy, where the battalion remained from June 26th to July 13th, did not bring much rest, an intermediate line needed wiring and cable trenches had to be dug and barges got forward down the Scarpe to Fampoux. Over 120 men, with 20 discharged from hospital, joined during June, when casualties only came to 29.[1] Among the officers who now joined, Captain Smythe and Lt. Collett had been with the battalion before, but the battalion lost Major Earle

[1] 2/Lt. C. A. Huskisson, attached to the Brigade Trench Mortar Battery, was killed.

who was given command of the 1st East Lancashire, so that he remained in the 11th Brigade.

July 13th found the battalion relieving the King's Own in Himalaya Trench South of the Scarpe, and next night it took over the front line NE. of Monchy, having its support company in Bayonet Trench. Despite all the heavy fighting here, the front line was continuous and in good repair, with duck-boards nearly all its length, 1,000 yards. The enemy, who was holding his front line in some strength, as our patrols soon discovered, reserved his activities for the nights, when trench-mortars, rifle grenades and snipers were busy, but again his patrols rarely asserted themselves and ours, who were more enterprising, saw nothing of them. After four days in line and four 'out' the battalion shifted to the right into Halberd Trench, on July 22nd, with orders to raid Devil's Trench. A barrage on July 23rd on Devil's Trench, South of the point to be raided, provoked heavy retaliation, 2/Lts. Cancellor and Turner being wounded but remaining at duty. Early next morning 2/Lt. Turner was heavily fired on when reconnoitring Arrow Trench with three men. The men must have been hit, but the subaltern escaped and crawled back to report the wire insufficiently cut, so the raid was postponed for 48 hours and the wire again shelled, the gaps being kept under Lewis gun fire at night to prevent repairs. Eventually on July 26th three officers and 78 men, including seven R.E. who were to destroy any dug-outs found, under Captain Icke, carried out the raid. Crawling out 20 minutes before 'Zero', 10.45 p.m., they lined up 50 yards beyond our wire and at 'Zero' went forward behind an excellent barrage to find the wire well cut. They were quickly into the front trench, where several prisoners were taken, though most of the garrison had bolted and must have run into our protective barrage, which was being maintained on all known machine-gun emplacements on the flanks. The trench, which was in bad repair and much damaged, was carefully searched, one party advancing nearly 100 yards in a vain search for a suspected machine-gun, while bombers who attacked our left were decisively repulsed, and 25 minutes after 'Zero' the raiders were back in our lines with their prisoners, having obtained important identifications. Three men were missing and two wounded, but several enemy were left dead and wounded in the trench. Lt. Beatty, whose reconnaissances by day and night had provided most useful information for the raiders, had been conspicuous for his gallantry and leading : he was awarded the M.C., Corporal Holdaway, who had backed up his officers splendidly, getting the M.M.

The battalion spent August 2nd to 14th at Balmoral Camp, training and finding working parties, but was back NE. of Monchy by August 15th, more to the right than on previous occasions, being opposite Arrowhead and Twin Copses, but it shifted to the left again on the 18th. The enemy were quiet, but our Lewis guns and trench mortars were active and, well supported by our artillery, gave them a troubled time.

August 23rd found the battalion in brigade reserve, cleaning up and finding working parties, and then the Division was relieved and had a fortnight's training at Berles au Bois before moving to Flanders. Casualties during July and August had been low, only 12 killed and missing and 2/Lts. Cancellor and Turner and 30 men wounded. However, few drafts had arrived and with 63 admissions to hospital against 30 discharges, companies could not be completed to four platoons till 120 reinforcements joined at Berles au Bois. Lt. Harding now rejoined and half a dozen other subalterns arrived. Before entraining for Flanders on September 19th the opportunity was taken to let all survivors of July 1st 1916 visit Beaumont Hamel and see exactly what they had been facing : enough were present to fill four buses.

On reaching Flanders the battalion had some intensive training with lectures on the new methods of defence to be overcome. Major-General

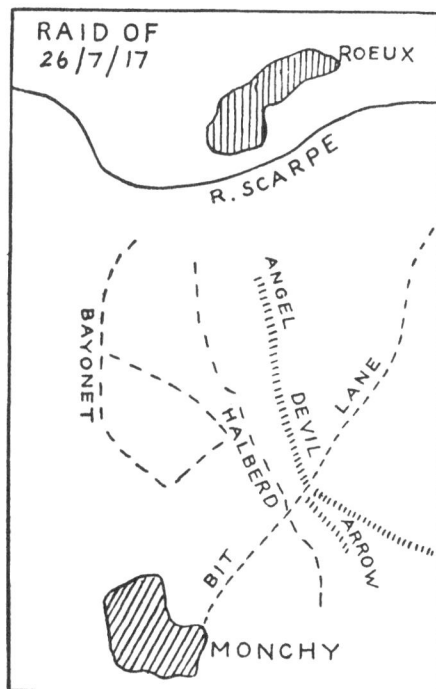

Lambton, who had been commanding the Division for the last two years, had unfortunately been disabled by an accident but his successor, Major-General Matheson, was a tried and capable commander.

A draft of 100 men joined directly the battalion reached Flanders, and with other reinforcements other ranks were up to 960 by October 4th. It illustrates the discrepancy between 'paper strength' and 'strength in trenches' that only 520 men 'went over the top' that day. Sickness and leave accounted for 60, brigade and Divisional employments for 45, 26 were detailed as carriers, 118 were with the battalion transport, 'courses' and other details accounted for 50, and the remainder formed the 'battle nucleus' left behind. Of 40 officers 22 were not in action ; Major Hudson, Captains N. Harland and Corner and eight subalterns being 'left out' and the rest away, on courses or 'employed'.

The 2nd Battalion had spent most of September either near Proven, or at Herzeele or near Elverdinghe. Several officers had joined, among them Lt. Bircham who had been with the battalion in Gallipoli and since then with the 14th at the Schwaben Redoubt, while drafts amounting in all to 175 had brought other ranks up to 900, though as with the 1st Battalion little over half were taken into action.

On returning to the line in the middle of September the Twenty-Ninth Division had relieved the Guards opposite Koekuit, where the 2nd Hampshire had four days in front line before the end of September. The enemy's guns were

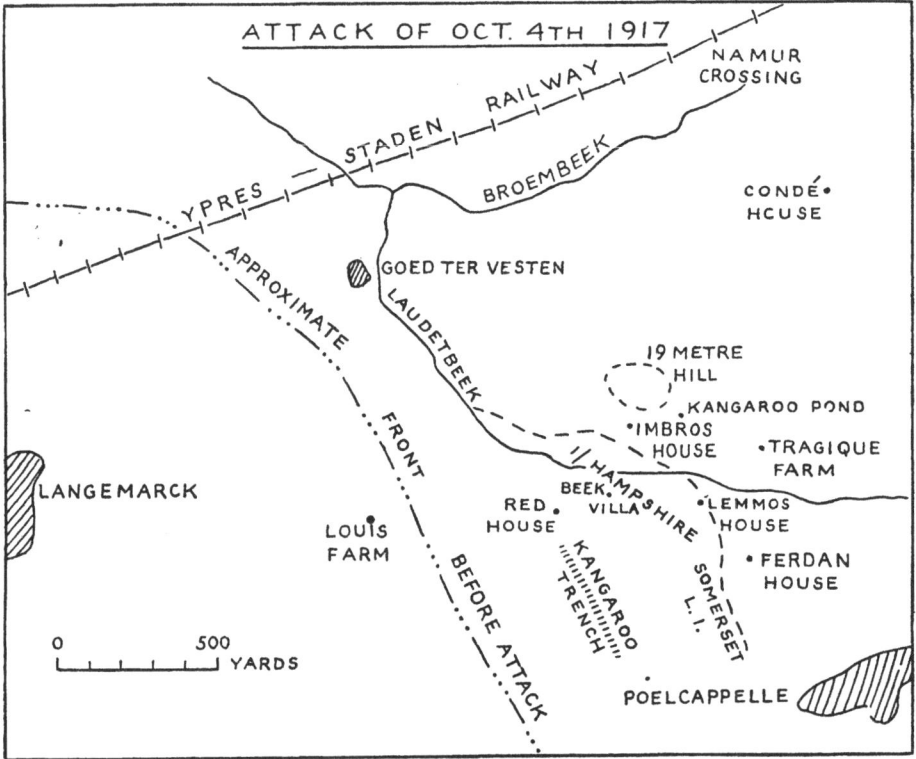

active, especially on the 26th, when a big attack was being made by our right and centre. Our patrols were active, one in particular locating an important German 'strong point'. This turn in front cost the battalion nine killed and 23 wounded, while many men were affected by gas, the area having been drenched before, as well as during, its tenure, indeed the relieved unit's head-quarters had proved almost untenable. The 88th Brigade was relieved on September 29th and was in Divisional reserve on October 4th, the next big 'push', when all that was required of the Division was to make a short advance to cover the flank of the troops on its right, a task successfully discharged by the only two battalions employed.

In that attack[1] the Fourth Division was using the 10th (left) and 11th (right) Brigades. Its starting line was East of Langemarck and its final objective lay NW. of Poelcappelle, which village the Eleventh Division on its right was attacking. The 1st Hampshire were on their brigade's left and their first objective was behind Kangaroo Trench, 350 yards away, the final objective, which included Tragique Farm, being 500 yards further on. Starting at 6.10 a.m., the battalion [2] for once found our barrage ragged and inaccurate and suffered more from it than from the enemy's fire. However, Kangaroo Trench was soon rushed, 30 prisoners and a machine-gun being taken, and by 6.50 the first objective about Beek Villa had been taken, several ' pill-boxes ' being effectively tackled. The Somerset on the right had had much trouble with ' pill-boxes ' but they also had gained their objective. After an hour's pause B Company went forward on the right through C, pushing on past Lemnos House and Imbros House, to be checked by our barrage and forced to come back and dig in short of their objectives, while the Somerset, who also had had to fall back a little way, carried on the line just short of Ferdan House. On the left A Company, after advancing some way, found itself ahead of the 10th Brigade and was checked, but touch was obtained with the troops on both flanks and consolidation was started, the battalion's front line running from Lemnos House (right) to Imbros House, with supporting posts close behind, D Company in battalion reserve being some way in rear near Red House. Some enemy who were sheltering in shell-holes in front were now dislodged by hand-grenades and shot down as they bolted.

About 1 p.m. heavy machine-gun and rifle fire developed against the left, evidently heralding a counter-attack, and the position was endangered by the 10th Brigade being driven off 19-Metre Hill to which it had advanced. The Hampshire and Somerset held on, however, though the Hampshire's left was ' in the air ' Lt. Stannard now showed conspicuous initiative and determination, going out to rally troops who were retiring and leading a counter-attack which helped to check the enemy, and before long the East Lancashire sent up a detachment which covered this exposed flank, while later they assisted the 10th Brigade to bring its line forward again. Pressure on this flank continued, and though the Rifle Brigade's intervention checked a second retirement, the left remained unsettled and the Hampshire had to establish posts behind this flank. This, however, proved sufficient, the enemy did not attempt to press any further, and as the night passed quietly some reorganization was possible and good progress made with the consolidation. Next morning also proved quiet, but the enemy's shelling became heavier in the afternoon and went on till dusk, after which the Rifle Brigade relieved the Hampshire, who spent the next two days at Louis Farm in support under shell-fire, finding parties to carry rations, water and ammunition up to the front,[3] they

---

[1] Officially known as the battle of Broodseinde.

[2] Those actually engaged in the attack came to 18 officers and 522 other ranks : Captains De Gaury (C) and German (D), and Lts. Gullick (A) and Harding (B) commanded the companies.

[3] Pack transport was now being mainly used in the battle area.

then moved back across the canal, on their brigade going into reserve.

The Hampshire's casualties came to 50% of those in action : Lt. Harding, 2/Lts. H. C. Hall, Perrett and Phippard and 64 men killed, 16 men missing, Colonel Armitage, who remained at duty,[1] Lt. Collett, 2/Lts. G. F. Ball, Chester, McCulloch, Middlemass and Scrivens and 187[2] men wounded. But the gain of ground, if less than had been hoped for, was not unsatisfactory, considering all the difficulties to be overcome.[3]

On October 9th when the Fourth Division made its second effort in ' Third Ypres ' and secured nearly all its objectives NW. of Poelcapelle, only the 12th Brigade was engaged, the 11th, who stood to all day in readiness, not being required to assist, and though three days later the Rifle Brigade was attached to the 12th to share in another attack near Poelcapelle, the 1st Hampshire were again not put in but moved back by Proven to Poperinghe to entrain on the 18th for the South, on returning to the Third Army and, as it proved, to familiar ground at Monchy. Nobody was ever very sorry to leave the Ypres Salient, but this time the 1st Hampshire had made some contribution to its expansion.

If the 1st had not shared in the attack of October 9th, that day had given the 2nd some hard fighting. The Twenty-Ninth Division was attacking North of Langemarck, now half a mile behind our front line, with its left brigade, the 88th, astride the Roulers railway. Of its objectives the 4th Worcestershire were to capture two, from Namur Crossing to Koekuit and from Tranquille Farm Westward, after which the Newfoundland Regiment would come through to take a third, from the railway, through Egypt House, to Les Cinq Chemins. It was some indication of the new German methods that both the other battalions were retained to deal with counter-attacks.

The 2nd Hampshire, who left Parroy Camp at 9.15 p.m. on October 8th, found moving up into the assembly positions more than usually difficult : the expanded Steenbeek had to be crossed, the German shelling was fairly heavy and caused both W and X Companies several casualties, while it rained hard all the time ; but if conditions could hardly have been worse,[4] somehow the positions were duly taken up, and at 7 a.m., 100 minutes after ' Zero ', the battalion started forward in ' artillery formation '. The fire was heavy, but it was some compensation for the mud that it partly smothered the shell-bursts, direction was well kept, thanks partly to having the railway line to go by, and before long the Hampshire were digging in on the Namur Crossing Line, which the Worcestershire had taken well up to time, subsequently going forward again.

Advancing again at 8.50 a.m., the Hampshire were heavily shelled but, admirably directed by Colonel Spring, established themselves just behind the

---

[1] The Chaplain, the Reverend A. E. Lawrie, was hit but remained on duty. He was an outstanding figure in the battalion, much loved and respected by all,. He set a wonderful example of courage and devotion to duty and had a remarkable hold on the battalion.

[2] Corrected figures.   [3] Lt. Stannard was awarded the M.C.

[4] Just before the advance hot tea was served out : it had been brought up in tins which were carried in packs stuffed with hay and was thus kept hot.

second objective, which also the Worcestershire had duly secured despite stubborn opposition, taking 200 prisoners. On this line they dug in, 2/Lt. Hicks, though wounded and then buried by a shell-burst near him, set a splendid example, continuing at duty and holding on to his post. Then, about 4 p.m., counter-attacks from the NE. forced the Newfoundlands back from the third objective, which they had reached, their left being pushed back across the Poelcapelle–Cinq Chemins road. They rallied, however, and Colonel Spring was prompt to reinforce them and fill up any gaps in their line, while 2/Lt. Scutt formed a defensive flank on the left with his platoon, rallied officerless men who were retiring and restored the situation. After dark the Hampshire relieved the Newfoundlands in what was now the front line, running about NW.

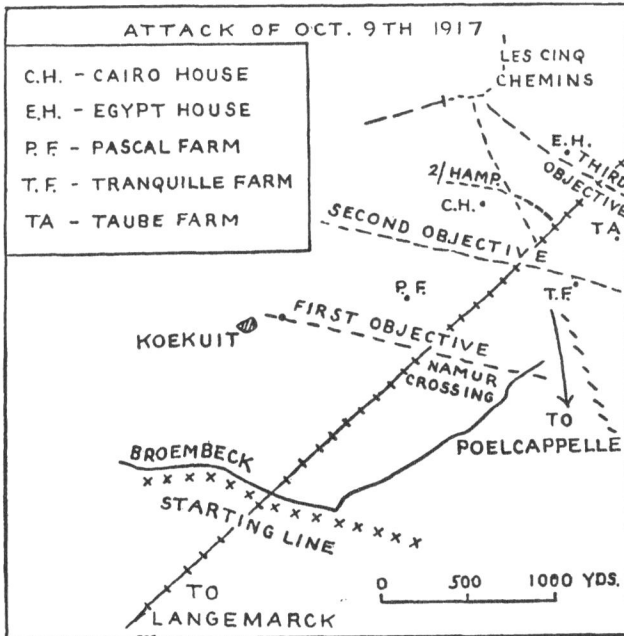

from near Tranquille Farm across the Poelcapelle–Cinq Chemins road,[1] the relief being smoothly effected. During the night, while patrols successfully located the enemy, taking several prisoners, the line was consolidated, with support and reserve lines behind it. Sergeant Sillence, acting as C.S.M., who had been conspicuous during the advance in assisting his officers and setting a fine example, was now much to the fore in directing the consolidation despite heavy shelling.

The enemy's snipers were active, especially from Taube Farm to the right front, causing several casualties, and during the night several times fighting patrols approached our lines, two of about 30 each being dispersed by Private Bray, who was out with a Lewis-gun in front of our line, while Sergeant

[1] i.e. short of the third objective.

Martin beat off another and Lance-Corporal Jerram and Private Smith did useful work in scouting and detecting the enemy's efforts to advance. Except for barraging a line the battalion was not holding, the German artillery was in-active, and though such wet ground made the work difficult, real progress was made next day with the consolidation, very good work being done by the battalion runners in keeping up communications. Early in the afternoon the Brigade Major reached battalion head-quarters, now at Pascal Farm, East of Koekuit, with orders for the capture of a troublesome 'strong point' to the left front near Cairo House. There was barely time to organize an attack before the barrage came down, but Lt. Colonel Spring went forward through a heavy barrage to W Company's head-quarters to arrange the attack, and W was just ready before our barrage began at 5.30 p.m. Advancing with two platoons in a front wave and one supporting, the company, well led and skilfully directed by Captain Cuddon, who was well backed up by Sergeants Trethewy and Parker, mastered its objective, despite stubborn opposition. Many Germans were accounted for, a Lewis gunner, Private Gosling, dispersing one party of 30 single-handed, and a good line was established 50 yards NE. of the buildings and linked up to the rest of the line.

That evening the 7th Lincolnshire (Seventeenth Division) arrived to relieve the Hampshire. A dark night made this difficult, but thanks to good arrange-ments for guides everything went off smoothly and by 8 a.m. next day (October 11th) the Hampshire were back at Elverdinghe. 2/Lt. Lloyd and 18 men had been killed and Captains C. T. Ball and Mudge, Lt. A. G. Smith, 2/Lts. Cutmore and Hicks and 74 men wounded. One noticeable feature of the action had been the increased expenditure of rifle ammunition ; in bringing up reinforcements the enemy had given better targets than of late and, with more chances of using the rifle, battalions which had been careful to maintain their standards of musketry had reaped the benefit.

Lt. Colonel Spring's skilful handling of the situation was recognised soon afterwards by a D.S.O., while Captain Cuddon was given a bar to his M.C., 2/Lts. Hicks and Scutt receiving the M.C. Sergeant Trethewy, who besides leading his platoon with great determination during the attack had done great work in consolidation, was awarded the D.C.M., while 21 M.M.s were awarded to the battalion, Lance Corporal Fielder, who had worked untiringly to succour the wounded, searching for them under heavy fire, getting a bar, while about the same time Sergeants Oram and Finch and Corporal Whitaker received the French Croix de Guerre.

The Twenty-Ninth Division and the 2nd Hampshire had thus finished their part in ' Third Ypres ' with a satisfactory success ; if the battalion had had less chance at Poelcapelle in October than at Langemarck in August it had done its bit well. Indeed the regiment could congratulate itself on having achieved some substantial success in every episode of ' Third Ypres ' in which it took part, while if its losses had been heavy it had taken a good toll of its enemies and above all won two more V.C's.

CHAPTER XX

CAMBRAI

' THIRD Ypres ' continued for some weeks after the Fourth and Twenty-Ninth Divisions had been withdrawn to ' quieter ' places. Its closing stages, in which the regiment was fortunate to escape sharing, were like those of the Somme, as much struggles against mud and swamps as against the Germans: the weather, rarely for long favourable to the attack, became worse as the autumn advanced, and what the troops in the front line had to endure rivalled even what the 1st and 2nd Hampshire had gone through in their second experience of the Somme. Attention has, however, been unduly concentrated on these closing stages and the whole offensive judged by its worst moments. That it had to be continued to keep the Germans occupied could not in 1917 be trumpeted abroad on the house tops, and unfortunately, as this essential fact could not then be divulged, it has escaped the notice of many amateur and impatient critics and is perhaps not yet properly appreciated. That the Germans were kept occupied and the French thereby given time to recover was the chief gain from its continuation : its contribution to the wearing down of the hard core of German power, the fighting strength of the German Army, was by their own admissions [1] very considerable : against our own losses and sufferings must be set what the Germans also endured, while their new counter-attacking tactics, especially when unsuccessful, were costly.[2] Very probably, once it became clear that we should not liberate the Belgian Coast, Sir Douglas Haig would have suspended the offensive sooner, if General Petain would have agreed that the state of the French Armies would allow of it, but it is hard to picture General Petain paying much attention to British interests if they clashed in the least with French or sparing the British at any expense to his own men.

Some alternative to ' Third Ypres ' might have been tried earlier had General Petain's demands allowed it. For some time the British Commander-in-Chief had been considering attacking in a quarter where the ground would be less unfavourable, where the very strength of the German defences might make surprise easier, where the tank, now greatly improved in design and manufacture and less liable to break down than those used on the Somme, might do more to justify itself than at Ypres, where the bad going was all against it. The Cambrai attack which was to give the 2nd Hampshire yet another battle in 1917, their hardest of the year, was no sudden improvisation.

The Hindenburg Line, skilfully sited and well dug, had been formidable enough in the spring when it had held up the Fourth and Fifth Armies, and such portions as had been captured during the Arras fighting had proved difficult and extremely costly to take. It had been strengthened since then, and besides the Line itself and its Support, the Germans held some strong positions in front and, as the Twenty-Ninth Division was to have reason to appreciate, they had

---

[1] *Official History* 1917. II. chapter 19.   [2]ibid. pp. 362–365.

also constructed a very formidable rearward line, the Masnieres–Beaurevoir This moreover was almost at its strongest immediately SW. of Cambrai, where it ran behind those stretches of the Scheldt and its canal which turn Westward past Crevecoeur and Masnieres to Marcoing and run thence Northward East of Noyelles.

Besides the great concentration of tanks, about whose handling and man-

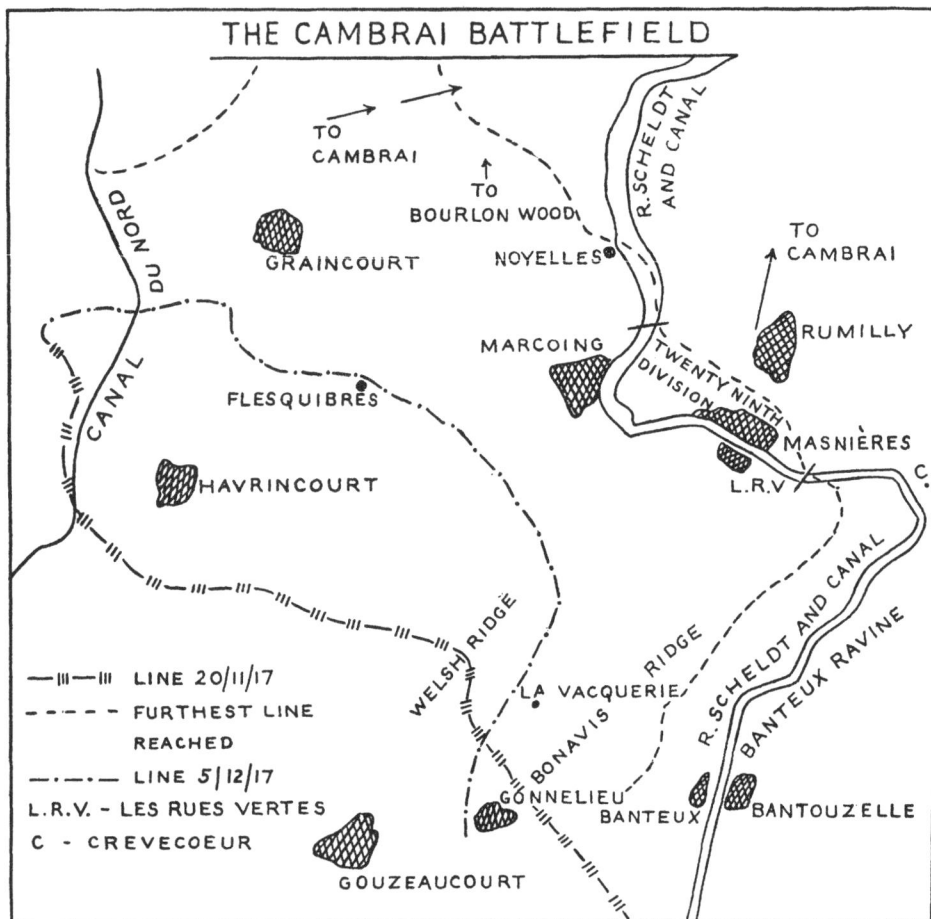

THE CAMBRAI BATTLEFIELD

TO CAMBRAI

TO BOURLON WOOD

TO CAMBRAI

GRAINCOURT

NOYELLES

RUMILLY

DU NORD

CANAL

MARCOING

TWENTY NINTH DIVISION

FLESQUIÈRES

MASNIÈRES

HAVRINCOURT

L.R.V

C.

R. SCHELDT AND CANAL

R. SCHELDT AND CANAL

—III—III LINE 20/11/17
- - - - - FURTHEST LINE
           REACHED
—·—·— LINE 5/12/17
L.R.V. - LES RUES VERTES
C - CREVECOEUR

WELSH RIDGE

RIDGE

LA VACQUERIE

BONAVIS

BANTEUX RAVINE

GONNELIEU

BANTEUX

BANTOUZELLE

GOUZEAUCOURT

oeuvring in co-operation with guns and infantry much had been learnt by experience and experiment since a solitary tank had led the 15th Hampshire into Flers, other improvements in methods had been devised. The lengthy artillery preparation, which must inevitably give warning of an impending attack, was no longer necessary, previous registration could now be much reduced without diminishing the efficiency of the bombardment, and a complete surprise was achieved when, at 6.25 a.m. on November 20th, our guns opened fire and tanks and infantry went forward: for this the Third Army's Staff deserves enormous credit.

Seven Divisions were being employed in the attack, among them the Twenty-Ninth, which, like the Fourth at Arras, was to go through the leading Divisions of its Corps, the Third, after they had taken the Hindenburg Support Line, its errand being to secure the passages over the Scheldt and its canal and, if possible, exploit that success by breaking through the German third position near Rumilly.

Since leaving Flanders the 2nd Hampshire had been at Bienvilliers for a month ; 164 men and several officers had joined before it left Flanders, and while at Bienvilliers it got reinforcements, including men rejoining from hospital, amounting to 154, together with Captain K. A. Johnston who assumed command on Colonel Spring being suddenly taken ill and having to go to hospital. The training included open-warfare exercises, much needed by nearly everyone in the battalion.

November 17th saw the Hampshire entraining at Boisleux, and after detraining near Peronne they marched to Moislains to encamp, going on next night [1] to Sorel le Grand, where instructions were received and ' battle stores ' issued.

Leaving Sorel le Grand at 2.30 a.m. (November 20th), the Hampshire duly reached the brigade's assembly area at Gouzeaucourt in good time. ' Zero ' was fixed for 6.25, just an hour before sunrise, and a thick autumn mist helped to conceal things even after it began to grow light. The German guns did not open up, even the noise made by nearly 400 tanks had actually escaped notice, and, as on July 14th, 1916, complete surprise had been achieved.

The Third Corps had three Divisions in front, of which the Twelfth and Twentieth, after taking their first two objectives, were to wheel to the right and establish a defensive flank along the slopes above the Banteux Ravine along which the Scheldt and the canal flow North to turn West at Crevecœur. This would clear the front for the Twenty-Ninth Division, whose advance from our old front line was to begin on its receiving news of the capture of the second objective. As usual information was slow to filter back, but General de Lisle was not one to wait, and at 10.30 he started the Division off, Division, brigades and battalions in ' diamond ' formation, the 88th Brigade on the right moving NE. for Masnieres, the 87th (centre) marching North on Marcoing, the 86th (left) having Noyelles and Nine Wood as objectives. In the 88th Brigade the Essex led, with the Worcestershire on their right, the Newfoundland on the left and the Hampshire behind, with Y, X, W and Z Companies in the corresponding positions in the battalion diamond.

In the Brown Line, the second objective, a formidable ' strong point ' at Good Old Man Farm was still resisting, and while the Essex with some support from the flanking battalions dealt with it, taking 150 prisoners, Y Company had a little ' show ' of its own, mopping up some ' strong points ' most successfully and taking 40 prisoners. Re-forming to continue the advance, Lt. Colonel Johnston noticed that it was going too far to the left, so he brought the companies across to the right to recover the true line. Meanwhile the Worcester-

---

[1] To ensure surprise the marches were made at night.

shire had got up level with the Essex and were approaching the canal, making for a lock half a mile SE. of Masnieres. This they secured, and two companies crossed over, while another wheeled towards Les Rues Vertes to try to secure the main bridge by which the Cambrai road crosses the canal from Les Rues Vertes to Masnieres. This the Essex should have taken, but they had diverged to the left and the Germans had had time to demolish it partially, and what they had not finished a tank now completed for them. This prevented the cavalry pushing through to secure a hold in the Masnieres–Beaurevoir Line,

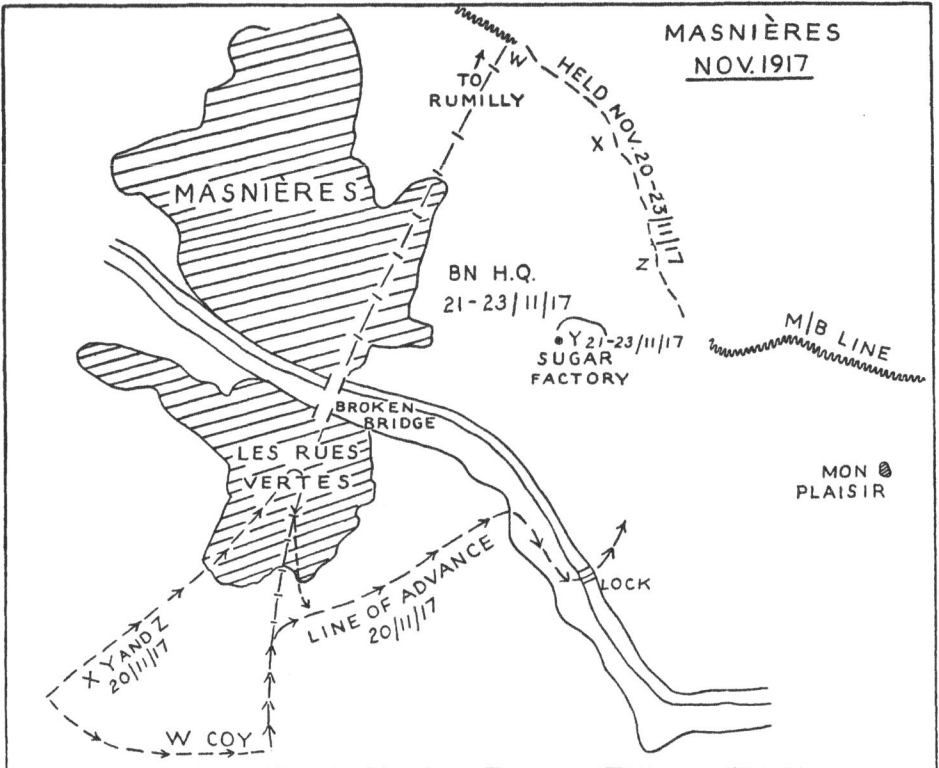

which the supporting infantry might exploit. Indeed, when the Hampshire came up the brigade seemed to be checked, though before long some of the Worcestershire had reinforced the Essex and were forcing their way in to Les Rues Vertes, and the Newfoundland were reaching the canal bank West of Masnieres. Lt. Colonel Johnston's first intention was to press the attack against the main road-bridge, and Y pushed ahead to do this, X and Z following, while W cleared some houses along the main road. However, he now learnt from a Tank officer that the bridge was impassable, so he diverted W, X and Z to the right to cross at the lock and reinforce the Worcestershire, leaving Y under Captain Bircham to help clear Les Rues Vertes and secure our end of the bridge.

Unfortunately, as the lock had to be crossed in single file under machine-gun fire and sniping, it was 3 p.m. before its passage was completed.

Lt. Colonel Linton of the Worcestershire having been killed, Lt. Colonel Johnston took command of the troops across the canal and sent X Company against Masnieres, while W and Z, attacking on the Worcestershire's left, helped them to capture Mon Plaisir Farm and make a lodgement in the Masnieres–Beaurevoir Line, between the lock and the NE. corner of Masnieres. In this stage of the fight Captain Ashling led Z very skilfully and established it in a good position, while Captain Lord took command of officerless men and led them on to the objective, whose consolidation he directed, besides organizing and leading an attack on a ' strong point ' for whose capture he was largely responsible. Thus a good position was established, Lt. Colonel Johnston making very skilful dispositions, going far to secure the right flank of the brigade, line Y, having cleared Les Rues Vertes, rejoined and was placed in reserve at the lock, and X, after clearing the outskirts of Masnieres, formed a defensive flank facing that village.

During the night orders were received that Masnieres must be cleared as a preliminary to further efforts against the Beaurevoir Line, so W and a company of the Worcestershire were detailed for this task. This took some time, the Germans resisting stubbornly, but by 4.30 next morning (November 21st) the village had been practically cleared but for a dug-out below the church which held on for some time longer, so the troops who had done the work could advance against the Masnieres–Beaurevoir trenches across the Cambrai road, which were reported not to be strongly held. Pushing forward to see whether this report was accurate, W, ably led and directed by Captain Singleton-Gates, made some headway but drew heavy fire from near Rumilly and were checked. They held on to their gains, despite having both flanks exposed, and when about 11 a.m. two German battalions came forward against Mon Plaisir our Lewis guns and the artillery helped to check them, no Germans succeeded in getting within 500 yards of the brigade's line. Eventually X came up into the gap on the right of W, where the Worcestershire had diverged to the flank, W and X eventually securing some 200 yards of the Masnieres–Beaurevoir Line, while touch was also gained with the Essex West of Masnieres.

Meanwhile, despite considerable opposition and hard fighting, the 86th and 87th Brigades had on the first day of the battle captured Noyelles and Marcoing and established a bridge-head beyond Marcoing, taking many prisoners, though the 87th's effort on November 21st to break through the Masnieres–Beaurevoir Line had been foiled. The defensive flank had been established above the Banteux Ravine, but on the other flank the Sixth Division,[1] which had taken Ribecourt, had been held up owing to an unfortunate check to the next Division on its left at Flesquieres, which also prevented the exploitation of the substantial successes gained further to the left. A deep re-entrant had thus been left in our front, whereas had it run straight NW. from Masnieres to the Bapaume–Cambrai road, a prompt attack might have been made on Bourlon Wood, the

---

[1] The left Division of the Third Corps.

dominating high ground North of that road : as things were, this Flesquieres
' bulge ' had to be flattened out first, and meanwhile German reinforcements
were arriving. Moreover, the Masnieres–Beaurevoir Line had proved unpleasantly strong : and though the 88th Brigade had established itself securely at
Masnieres and repulsed by fire an attempted counter-attack from the NE., it
could not get on. For two days the situation here remained almost unchanged.
On November 22nd W Company and the Essex tried to push forward along the
Rumilly road and to bomb along a trench, but machine-guns prevented substantial progress. More than once that day a counter-attack seemed to be
starting from the now crowded German trenches, but Lewis guns and machine-
guns quickly quashed every attempt to advance.

After two days in Divisional reserve at Marcoing the Hampshire spent three

Before daybreak on November 24th the brigade had been relieved by the
86th, whom the Sixth Division had replaced at Noyelles; it now went into
reserve at Marcoing, mainly in cellars, though the houses were as yet little
damaged. The Hampshire's casualties had so far been low : 2/Lt. Howcroft
was missing, 28 men were killed or missing, Captain Bircham and 2/Lts.
McLachlan and Niven and 56 men had been wounded, a light price for what
they had achieved. Altogether the new venture had yielded quite substantial
gains. Even if the Masnieres–Beaurevoir Line had held us up and if Bourlon
Wood had not been cleared, while the rather optimistic projects of passing the
cavalry through to exploit the success had not been fulfilled, the renowned
Hindenburg Line had been well and truly broken, the advance had surpassed
even that of April 9th at Arras, and the experience of liberating from the
Germans hundreds of civilians who had suffered three years under their heel
was both novel and exhilarating. It looked as if, were reserves available, the
opening might yet be exploited to advantage.

After two days in Divisional reserve at Marcoing the Hampshire spent three
uneventful days (November 26th–29th) in front line across the canal. They
were not attacked or even much molested, if the enemy's guns were occasionally
active and caused another 20 casualties, but the really unpleasant feature of the
situation was that the Division had now been in line since November 20th, that
before that it had had three tiring night marches in succession, with little real
rest in between, so that all ranks had earned and greatly needed a relief. No
drafts had appeared to replace the casualties, and the consolidation and improvement of the line had involved much hard and exhausting work. That the two
Divisions holding the long defensive flank on the right needed relief even more
urgently was an additional anxiety to General de Lisle, if it was not realised by
regimental officers and men, who had still less reason to know that tactically
these Divisions' position was weaker than the Twenty-Ninth's ; General de
Lisle's persistent insistence on ' digging in ' properly had driven this idea well
into his Division's heads and its line at any rate was fairly well entrenched.

That no relief was available was partly because all available reliefs and
reinforcements had been sent to the left to continue the effort to exploit our
original success and in particular to secure the key position of Bourlon Wood.
The Third Army may have persevered over long with this effort and failed to

remember that the salient created on November 20th had two flanks, not one only ; but the ruling factor was that the crisis created by the Austro-German success at Caporetto had caused French and British Divisions to be hurried to Italy to prevent collapse developing into disaster. Five British Divisions, among them the Forty-First, had had to be dispatched to Lombardy ; had they been at Sir Douglas Haig's disposal to reinforce and relieve the troops who had gained the success of November 20th, the salient opposite Cambrai might have been in very different shape on November 30th.

Meanwhile the 11th Hampshire had been employed in an operation which the Third and Sixteenth Divisions undertook mainly as a diversion to assist the Cambrai attack. This had also the local purpose of enlarging our lodgement in the Hindenburg Line near Bullecourt, effected in May after costly efforts.

On joining the Third Army the Sixteenth Division had been posted to the Sixth Corps. The 11th Hampshire's head-quarters were established at Boyelles by August 28th and companies were soon busy with different tasks, including the clearing of debris which blocked the flow of the Sensée river and threatened to cause flooding higher up. Otherwise its work differed little here from what was wanted elsewhere, improvement of the trenches, maintenance and development of communications, especially trench tramways and light railways, erecting huts in camps. Some tasks were never finished ; if any were, another was immediately forthcoming. Things were ' quiet ' here ; both sides treated this sector rather as a ' rest area ', and occasional raids and shelling did not greatly disturb the Pioneers, who only record one casualty in September and none between October 1st and November 20th. Usually during raids or bombardments working parties were not sent up to the line.

The attack of November 20th was no mere raid : any positions gained were to be incorporated into our line, which promised the Pioneers plenty to do, while some of their Lewis guns were employed under the machine-gun companies.

The attack apparently surprised the Germans, whose front line,[1] Tunnel Trench, was quickly captured on a front of 1800 yards, two important 'pill-boxes' on the right, Jove and Mars, being rushed from the rear, while many Germans sheltering in the trench were captured. At 7.30 a.m. a message came back that the Pioneers could come forward and start work on two communication trenches, across No Man's Land, Jove Lane on the right to the portion taken by the Connaught Rangers and Juno Lane to the 2nd R.D.F's lodgement in the centre. Both were soon started, though counter-attacks were developing and hampered the work, especially of Captain Howson's party who were digging Jove Lane, as the Connaught Rangers were being hard pressed by enemy who emerged from the shelter of the tunnel, and before long ' Jove ' had been lost. Lt. Hillyer and 2/Lt. Hook, who had previously reconnoitred the ground to see where the trenches were to be dug, both showed great courage and initiative, leading their men to the right places and superintending the work

[1] West of Bullecourt.

despite heavy fire.[1] By 2.20 p.m. Juno Lane had reached a depth of over four feet, despite heavy shelling, and the other party was trying to establish connection with the Rangers holding on to Mars,[2] where a stubborn defence was being offered. To reach Mars the 11th had to resort to sapping, as digging from the top was impossible, but by 9.20 p.m. this new trench was well advanced and by 1 a.m. it had been completed, Juno Lane having been reported complete before mid-night. The Rangers had meanwhile formed a defensive flank along a sap leading to Mars and there had held up the counter-attacks, and during November 21st the position was consolidated, the trenches were cleared and Mars Lane improved, while on November 23rd the 7th Leinsters [3] recaptured Jove, so that Jove Lane also would be finished.

If the Pioneers had not had much actual fighting and had only had a dozen casualties, their tasks had made big demands on discipline, endurance and skill

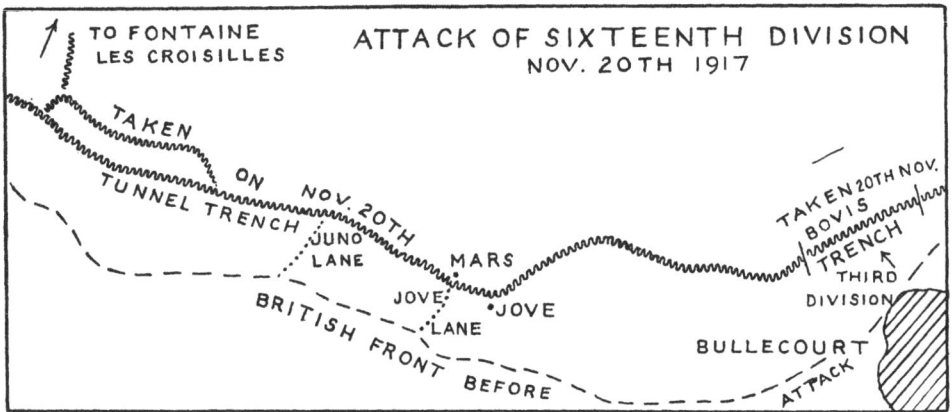

ATTACK OF SIXTEENTH DIVISION
NOV. 20TH 1917

and had contributed appreciably to the retention of the position taken, whereby our line was distinctly improved.

After their spell in front line across the canal the 2nd Hampshire returned on November 28th to Marcoing, where the 88th Brigade was concentrated in reserve. The village was heavily shelled next day, but its cellars provided excellent shelter and the troops escaped loss, while the Germans had left large quantities of stores and food of every kind behind, of which full advantage was taken. It was a lull before the storm.

During the night of November 29th/30th shelling became very much heavier and, warned by its increased violence, the Division was ‘ standing to ’ by 5 a.m. (November 30th). The 86th Brigade were holding Masnieres, the 87th being in the left sector across the canal with their reserve battalion, the K.O.S.B., in

[1] Lt. Hillyer was with the Jove Lane party, Lt. Hook with the Juno. Both received the M.C.
[2] To the left of Jove.
[3] Under Lt. Colonel Buckley, formerly a subaltern in the Hampshire and an original company commander in the 12th Battalion.

Marcoing along with the 88th Brigade. About 7 a.m. German infantry began
pressing forward in force, directing their main strength against the long flank
thinly held by the two tired and depleted Divisions who had captured it on
November 29th and had held on for ten days without reinforcements or relief.
Helped by the mist and by the dead ground in the Banteux Ravine in which
they could collect unseen, the attackers broke in at several points and were
soon thrusting Westwards against the Twenty-Ninth Division's rear, over-
running its batteries and head-quarters and threatening to roll up the whole
line in the salient. Against the 86th and 87th Brigades their frontal attacks
achieved no such success ; even when most of our supporting guns had been
taken or forced to move our rifles and Lewis guns could hold the attackers at
bay, though the 86th Brigade at Masnieres was desperately hard pressed,
Germans, who had over-run the over-matched left brigade of the next Division, penetrating into Les Rues Vertes behind it. Luckily those in charge
of the Twenty-Ninth's reserve were prompt to grasp the emergency and to act,
and their battalions responded splendidly to the call, at perhaps the most
critical situation they had yet encountered. They turned out promptly,
assembling South of the Marcoing–Masnieres road in readiness to attack Eastward and clear the 86th Brigade's rear. This was not easy ; to reach the high
ground South of Marcoing, against which the Germans [1] were advancing,
companies had to pass through a heavy barrage and some admixture of units
resulted ; thus Z Company of the 2nd Hampshire diverged on its own into
Marcoing Copse, into which the enemy had penetrated, and cleared it of them
after heavy fighting, 2/Lt. Robertson being killed. The other companies fell
into place in the general line, being on the right with the K.O.S.B. beyond them
on the Northern end of Welsh Ridge, while the Worcestershire continued
the line to the left.

Delivered with great vigour, the counter-attack first checked the leading
Germans, who were already SW. of Marcoing Copse,[2] and drove them back to
higher ground further South.[3] Against this the Hampshire advanced, along
with the rest of the brigade, and despite heavy fire they swept the Germans off
this rise, the Hampshire capturing 50 prisoners and getting good targets as the
baffled attackers retreated Eastward. The fruits of General de Lisle's training
were now reaped ; platoons combined ' fire and movement ' as instructed and
helped each other, carrying out the attack as if at practice, keeping line and
direction admirably and maintaining the advance steadily. Lt. Knott was
conspicuous in this counter-attack, leading and encouraging his men, rallying
stray men from other units and showing great initiative and resource. C.S.M.
Norris also did great work, rallying men and leading them forward to drive the
enemy back and then helping to organize a line of defence.[4] The other battalions had been equally successful, overcoming stubborn resistance, and the

---

[1] Mainly of their 30th and 9th Reserve Divisions, the 107th was attacking West of Masnieres.
[2] Approximately A—A on plan 54.   [3] Approximately B—B.
[4] He got a bar to the D.C.M. he had already earned by consistent good work in and out of the
line.

promptitude and push of the counter-attack had not only averted the threat to Marcoing and all West of it but had saved from capture many batteries still in action. These had been getting splendid targets in the masses of Germans and doing great execution. Touch was obtained with the 86th Brigade, who were holding on tenaciously at Masnieres, and on the right with the next Division, whose supports and reserves had succeeded in checking the enemy at the Hindenburg Support Line. Further to the right a line had been patched by the remnants of two other Divisions whose line had been pierced. All sorts of troops had thrown themselves into a confused fight, and while much ground and many guns had been lost and several units virtually annihilated, in the end the enemy's advance had been effectively checked. For this relief much credit must go to the splendid defence of the Twenty-Ninth Division and to its vigorous and well-handled counter-attack, for which it may well be claimed that it had averted a major disaster.

Beyond the rising ground which the 88th Brigade's counter-attack had reached, virtually the road from La Vacquerie to Les Rues Vertes, the advance was not pressed and the line was hastily re-organized so that a reserve could be formed, the Hampshire being drawn back to dig in behind the right.[1] Casualties had been fairly heavy, 2/Lt. Robertson had been killed and Captain Scott (at duty) and Lt. Knott and 2/Lt. Yates[2] wounded with 120 other ranks killed, wounded or missing. The Brigade Major having been wounded, Captain Cuddon was acting for him ; he had done good service, rallying the men at a point where the line was breaking and leading them forward again to recover their original line.[3]

This line was consolidated during the night, and though Marcoing and Masnieres were being shelled the work was little impeded, then or on the next day, the Hampshire only having nine casualties, mainly from machine-guns. But the pronounced salient now formed at Masnieres was repeatedly attacked, and the 86th Brigade was hard pressed to hold on, and though it did manage this, repulsing several vigorous efforts and inflicting heavy casualties, so exposed a position was not worth the risk or cost of its retention. Accordingly before morning (December 2nd) Masnieres and Les Rues Vertes were quietly evacuated without the Germans perceiving it. Our line now ran about half way between Marcoing and Masnieres, crossing the canal at the lock West of Masnieres. December 2nd the Hampshire spent in brigade reserve under shell-fire, varied by orders to turn out and counter-attack to re-establish the line of the Essex, falsely reported to have been broken, then to send W Company to reinforce the S.W.B. East of Marcoing and South of the lock and finally to dig in SW. and S. of Marcoing Copse,[4] where Y and Z, the latter having before this rejoined head-quarters, were in line, and X in support. This move was completed by 9.30 p.m. and the entrenching of the new line was begun.

December 3rd brought a renewal of the infantry attacks. About 11 a.m., after a heavy bombardment, infantry swarmed forward in force, pressing

---

[1] Approximately C—C on plan.
[2] Died of wounds.
[3] He received another bar to the M.C.
[4] D—D on plan.

hardest against the S.W.B. and W Company on their left near the lock.[1] These in hastily dug trenches without wire in front or dug-outs, put up a fine fight, and after the front line trenches were lost, the survivors rallied on their reserve at the S.W.B's battalion head-quarters, where a desperate resistance eventually prevailed ; indeed the Germans fell right back, abandoning the S.W.B's forward trench and allowing many wounded to be rescued. Elsewhere the German advance had been held and heavily punished, they could make no progress in face of our guns and rifles ; X Company had meanwhile been sent forward to take up a position just NE. of Marcoing Copse to prevent a further advance along the canal; this position they reached despite some casualties in going through a barrage on Marcoing Copse, and held on to it successfully. Even-

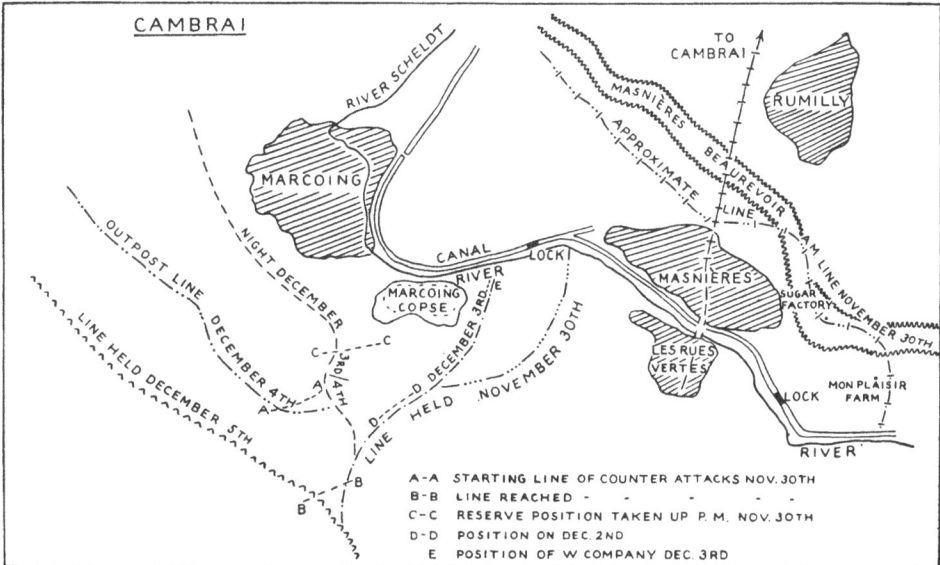

CAMBRAI

A-A STARTING LINE OF COUNTER ATTACKS NOV. 30TH
B-B LINE REACHED - - - - -
C-C RESERVE POSITION TAKEN UP P. M. NOV. 30TH
D-D POSITION ON DEC. 2ND
E POSITION OF W COMPANY DEC. 3RD

tually at 8 p.m., the rest of the battalion went up to relieve the S.W.B.,[2] now reduced to about 80.

The Hampshire[3] had hardly taken up this position before orders were received to fall back to a new line SW. of Marcoing, pivoting on the position retaken by the battalion and the K.O.S.B. on November 30th. Marcoing with the other advanced positions had now to be evacuated, as a preliminary to a further withdrawal roughly to the Hindenburg Support Line. It was clear that nothing was to be gained by hanging on to the pronounced salient which our forward line now formed, and that it was imperative to shorten and straighten out our Cambrai front.

By 1 a.m. on December 4th this first move had been carried out. Lewis gun posts had been left to cover it but by 5.30 a.m. they too had come back.

---

[1] E on plan.   [2] Some 20 survivors of W Company were with them.
[3] The day's casualties were well over 80, 2/Lt. Alexander being among those killed.

During the day the Germans frequently tried to push forward but they made little progress, being effectively discouraged by our Lewis guns which, backed by artillery and machine-guns, took advantage of some fine targets, indeed the withdrawal to the Hindenburg Support Line, ordered for that evening, was in no way molested or impeded. Before it started, outposts were posted some way in front of that line, Z Company being detailed for this duty, and soon after midnight, the outposts being in place, the rest fell back through them, to reach the Hindenburg Support Line about 3 a.m. December 5th. Here the Thirty-Sixth Division was in occupation and ready to relieve the outposts also, and when this had been done the Twenty-Ninth was at last fully relieved after a fortnight which had been strenuous even for it.

The 2nd Hampshire now went back to Ribecourt, where Z Company soon rejoined and all had breakfast, after which the battalion marched back to Elicourt and entrained. Their troubles were not over ; about 4 p.m. the train was pulled up suddenly near Farnicourt, shell-fire having torn up the track. The engine left the rails and went down the bank, taking the leading truck off the line : luckily this remained upright as did all behind and no disaster occurred. The enemy went on shelling and their aeroplanes were busy overhead, but the train was unhit and before long the battalion had detrained and shifted to another train beyond the break, so that at 8 a.m. (December 6th) it was safely at Mondicourt and could march to rest billets at Sus St. Leger.

The closing stages of ' Cambrai ' had added 2/Lt. A. H. Alexander and over 50 men to the battalion's killed and missing, mostly in W Company, and with another 50 wounded total casualties came to well over 350. But the 2nd Hampshire could congratulate themselves on their part in the battle, for which the Division was most warmly and deservedly thanked by the authorities from the Commander-in-Chief downward, the value of its tenacious defence and the orderly withdrawal after so long and arduous an effort being emphasized. Lt. Colonel Johnston received the D.S.O., Captains Cuddon and Lord and the M.O., Captain Knight, bars to the M.C., Captains Ashling and Singleton Gates and Lt. Knott the M.C., C.S.M. Milne a bar to his D.C.M., C.S.M. Norris the D.C.M. and a bar, Corporal Ridding and Private Nippard the D.C.M., L/Corporal Hoath a bar to the M.M. and 25 N.C.O's and men the M.M., while Captain Scott got a ' mention ', a list of awards which indicates the enterprise, determination and endurance which the Hampshire had shown and which places ' Cambrai ' among the greatest achievements of the Sixty-Seventh. Whatever the verdict on the battle as a whole it had given the Sixty-Seventh a fine opportunity which they had utilised to the full.

CHAPTER XXI

EGYPT AND PALESTINE, 1916–1917

GALLIPOLI had not given the 8th Hampshire and the rest of the Fifty-Fourth Division much of a chance. Thrown piece-meal into a confused struggle in which the situation was already compromised almost beyond recall, without having been able to reconnoitre the ground or know what was expected of it, the Division had had an unlucky start, and thereafter the difficult conditions with which officers and men had had to contend on the ridges running down from Chunuk Bair in an atmosphere of frustration and disappointment had offered little opportunity to recuperate. Transfer to Egypt had allowed of this, and during 1916 the Division was able to get the training it needed, to benefit by its experiences and to achieve a high standard of efficiency in all its units.

Reaching Alexandria on December 19th the 8th Hampshire were sent to Sidi Bisr Camp, where they remained for six weeks, recuperating, refitting and training. Lt. Colonel Murray of the Black Watch joined on December 22nd and took command, some of the battalion's own base details and convalescents rejoined and eight subalterns with a few men arrived from its ' Third Line ' unit. Leaving Alexandria for Cairo on February 2nd, it went to Mena Camp near the Pyramids, where the Division was collecting, its own artillery now coming out from England with other details, including transport men, whom the battalions had left behind. A draft of over 128 men arrived on March 7th, six officers, five attached from the Queen's, joined, and when on March 30th the battalion left Mena Camp for Shallufa and the Canal defences it was rested and up to a fair strength.

By this time a serious Turkish advance against the Suez Canal and Egypt was no longer considered likely. If the Turkish defence at Gallipoli had prevailed, its high cost had gone far to preclude their developing the counter-offensive that had originally been feared, before the incapacity of Turkish administration and communications to organize a large-scale invasion of Egypt had been fully appreciated. If the Canal was not to be attacked, Sir William Robertson, now installed as C.I.G.S., was not leaving troops idle in Egypt, and before long the M.E.F. was mostly on its way to France or Mesopotamia, leaving a much reduced Egyptian Expeditionary Force (' E.E.F. '), including the Fifty-Fourth Division, to secure the Canal and in due time adopt an offensive-defensive by advancing across the Sinai Desert to the gates of Palestine.

The Fifty-Fourth Division were to see 1916 out on the Canal, taking over the Southern section early in April, the 8th Hampshire's H.Q. being at Kubrit. Here ' defence works continued ' is the usual entry with which the battalion diary contents itself till it records a move to Serapeum, the central section, late in May. These defence works were being constructed in depth, with one line along the Eastern Canal bank and advanced posts pushed out about five miles into the Desert. Constructing defences in the loose and shifting sand was difficult, much revetting was required, and to keep the line in good order needed constant vigilance and hard work. The forward posts' garrisons ranged from two platoons to two companies, their rations, water and stores being brought up from the Canal by camels, whose acquaintance the 8th now had to acquire. The Yeomanry and the Australian Light Horse, entrusted with the patrolling of the front, may have occasionally sighted an Arab, but the 8th never saw an enemy and worked steadily away, with little to vary the daily routine. The Turkish advance in August, decisively repulsed at Romani by the

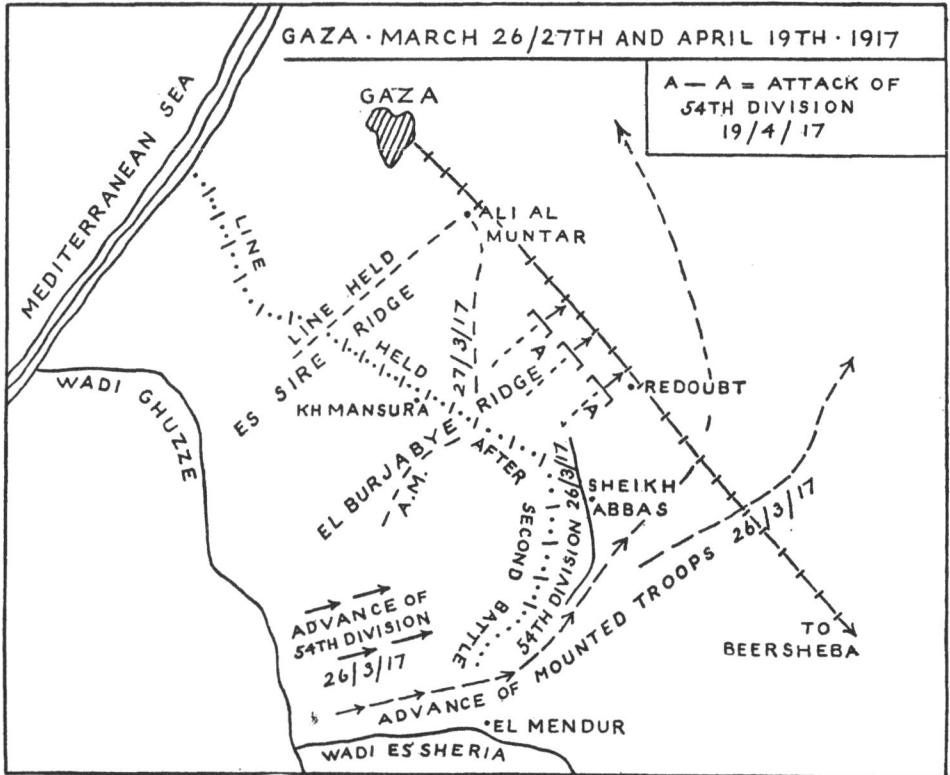

GAZA · MARCH 26/27TH AND APRIL 19TH · 1917

A — A = ATTACK OF 54TH DIVISION 19/4/17

MEDITERRANEAN SEA

GAZA

ALI AL MUNTAR

LINE HELD RIDGE

SIRE ES

LINE HELD

KH MANSURA RIDGE

WADI GHUZZE

EL BURJABYE AFTER A.M.

SECOND BATTLE

54TH DIVISION 26/3/17

27/3/17

REDOUBT

SHEIKH ABBAS

26/3/17

MOUNTED TROOPS 26/3/17

TO BEERSHEBA

ADVANCE OF 54TH DIVISION 26/3/17

ADVANCE OF

EL MENDUR

WADI ES SHERIA

Fifty-Second Division and the mounted troops, did not trouble the Serapeum front, and an extension of the 8th's line to the Southward to relieve the 4th Essex at Toussoum and Deversoir (August 25th) brought little change.

Before this Lt. Colonel Murray had left for France, Lt. Colonel Holland (Devons) replacing him. In September the battalion was withdrawn for a month's training, but it was back in front line by October 12th. Meanwhile the railway and the pipe line which supplied water were being pushed steadily Eastward across the Desert, enabling our front to be advanced, and with another Turkish attack now most improbable the battalion usually has only ' nothing of importance ' to record during these autumn months, except for departures on leave or for courses, with hospital admissions and discharges, or the occasional arrival of drafts.

1916 ended with the British occupation of El Arish, which with further successes at Magdhaba (December 23rd) and Rafa (January 7th) rendered quite unnecessary the retention in the Canal defences of any large force, so that though General Murray had to send a Division to France, he could find troops to replace it in the Eastern Force, now on the Palestine frontier, and could prepare for an attack in force on Gaza, the main bulwark of Southern Palestine. Thus the Fifty-Fourth Division at last left the Canal defences, the 8th Hampshire being relieved by dismounted Yeomanry on January 8th and moving to Moascar, where their brigade spent the rest of January, doing brigade training and route-marching, before starting its advance on February 1st. Five marches took it to Romani, where it spent a week before advancing again. Wire netting, stretched across the sand to form a roadway, made the marching easier, and on February 25th 29 officers and 881 other ranks marched into El Arish, a draft of 62 men having recently joined.

Though the notion of delivering Jerusalem from the Turk had been warmly espoused by Mr. Lloyd George, General Murray had been warned not to expect large reinforcements for an advance into Palestine. However, the force available seemed to warrant the hope of repeating on a larger scale at Gaza the useful successes achieved at Magdhaba and Rafa. The Desert Column [1] was to make the main attack, its mounted troops working round to the East to intercept the garrison's retreat, while the Fifty-Fourth Division covered their right flank and rear against any advance by relieving forces from the South-East.

The 8th Hampshire remained at or in front of El Arish until March 20th and then moved by Rafa and Khan Yunus to Im Seirat, SW. of the place where the Division would follow the Desert Column across the Wadi Ghuzze, the great watercourse covering Gaza from the SW., now dry but a considerable tactical feature.

The 162nd Brigade had reached Im Seirat late on March 26th and moved forward at 5.15 a.m. towards the Wadi. Unluckily a dense mist enveloped everything, preventing reconnaissance, delaying movement, particularly the Fifty-Third Division's, and throwing the whole time-table out of gear. Thus the 162nd Brigade did not leave its assembly position till 7.40 a.m. when it advanced in artillery formation about four miles NE. to the Sheikh Abbas ridge, where the 8th Hampshire took post, with A and C Companies on outpost. Meanwhile the Fifty-Third Division, though much delayed by the fog, was developing its attack. It met stubborn opposition but, reinforced by the 161st Brigade, eventually captured its objectives on the outskirts of Gaza, including the key position of Ali al Muntar, and obtained touch with the mounted troops who had virtually encircled the town on the East and North. Unfortunately the delay in the original advance had sacrificed precious hours of daylight and had given time for strong Turkish reinforcements to advance from NE. and East. On hearing of this the Desert Column's commander, being apparently

---

[1] The Fifty-Third Division and the mounted troops.

unaware of the Fifty-Third Division's success, warned the Fifty-Fourth to prepare to fall back to the El Burjabye ridge to get closer touch with the Fifty-Third, while he ordered the withdrawal of the mounted troops, partly because their horses were short of water. Actually the Turkish reinforcements did not really exercise any serious pressure till much later, but finding that the mounted troops' retirement was uncovering his flank, the G.O.C. Fifty-Third Division ordered a withdrawal, not knowing that the Fifty-Fourth had occupied the Sheikh Abbas Ridge and could cover his right effectively, so that it was probable that nearly all the ground captured could be retained. Too late next morning it was discovered that this withdrawal had been unnecessary, but efforts to reoccupy the positions evacuated proved unsuccessful and the Fifty-Third Division fell back to a position stretching across from the El Burjabye ridge towards the Rafa-Gaza road, almost at right angles to the Fifty-Fourth's new line, which faced East.

On the Fifty-Fourth evacuating the Sheikh Abbas ridge, the 8th Hampshire were placed in reserve near Mansura, where they remained all day, taking over the outposts after dark. The Turks had established themselves on the Sheikh Abbas ridge but had not advanced further, our guns and machine-guns keeping them at a respectful distance. It had, however, been decided to withdraw both Divisions across the Wadi Ghuzze, as no advantage seemed likely to be gained from retaining so marked a salient whose communications would be under flanking fire.[1] Accordingly during the night both were withdrawn, the 162nd Brigade acting as rear-guard, the 8th Hampshire its rear-party, leaving small covering parties to keep up a desultory fire till the rest had got away. Before midnight they were back at Im Seirat, exhausted and exasperated, if their only casualties were five missing. Next evening (March 28th) they took over an outpost line on our side of the Wadi, near El Breij, with snipers and patrols in advance who took two prisoners in some brushes with the enemy. After 24 hours here, the battalion went back again to Im Seirat ; Lt. Colonel Holland having had to go to hospital, Major Marsh was in command.

General Murray had missed success at Gaza by a narrow margin and could claim that the bad luck of the fog had been a major factor in turning the scales against him. Unfortunately his dispatches rather over-emphasized what had been achieved, greatly exaggerating the Turkish losses and leading the Home authorities to urge him to renew the attempt at once, when another effort should have been postponed until substantial reinforcements and above all much more artillery could be provided. The misfortunes which were to befall the 8th Hampshire in this second attempt must to some extent be attributed to this over-optimistic picture of the first.

Before renewing the attempt General Murray certainly pressed for more guns and more troops ; but, unfortunately, instead of insisting firmly on the urgency of reinforcements he allowed himself to be persuaded to attack without them. The authorities at Home, anxious for a big success and perhaps not

---

[1] Actually on the right the line held after the second attempt on Gaza was almost the same as the position now abandoned.

unwilling to take an optimistic view, would have done well not to urge him to an attack which the strategical situation in Egypt did not require and which had originally only been contemplated should quite substantial reinforcements be available.

Until April 16th the 8th Hampshire remained at Im Seirat, sending out patrols to cover the reconnoitring of a new outpost line beyond the Wadi and finding large parties to work on its crossings and the roads. On April 16th the battalion paraded in readiness to advance to the Sheikh Abbas ridge which its brigade was to secure as a preliminary to the new attack. The three weeks' interval between the attacks had altered the tactical situation for the worse ; whereas in March Gaza only had been prepared with defences, Turkish industry under German direction had created formidable works stretching some way SE. along the Beersheba road, so that instead of open cavalry country a fortified position would confront any turning movement in that direction. Some small additions to the attackers' artillery and even the arrival of eight rather aged tanks did nothing to off-set what the Turks had accomplished.

The attack was to be carried out in two phases, beginning with the securing of the Sheikh Abbas ridge with a line running West across the Mansura and El Sire ridges to the shore. From this in the second stage the Fifty-Fourth Division would advance against the Turkish position SE. of Gaza, the 163rd Brigade on its right making for Kh el Bir,[1] with the two Mounted Divisions covering its flank. On its left the Fifty-Second Division was tackling the defences immediately South of Gaza, with the Fifty-Third between its left and the sea.

The first stage was carried out on April 17th, when, after crossing the Wadi Ghuzze, the 163rd deployed about 4 a.m., with the 8th Hampshire (left) and 5th Suffolks leading and two tanks between them. Advancing steadily, the troops had little difficulty in clearing the Turkish outposts off the Sheikh Abbas ridge, the Hampshire having only two casualties, though one tank was disabled by a direct hit and took fire, stretcher-bearers from C Company helping to rescue wounded members of its crew. The day was spent in consolidating, a good line being established despite intermittent shell-fire. This position was retained next day, shelling causing a few more casualties, and then, early on April 19th, our bombardment opened. Two hours later, at 7.30 a.m., the two Norfolk battalions started to advance towards the Gaza-Beersheba road, with 2500 yards of undulating open ground to cross, A and B Companies of the Hampshire supporting the 5th Norfolks (right) and C and D following the 4th. The Turks, almost silent during the bombardment, started shelling directly the troops went forward, their guns having clearly been unaffected by our fire, while machine-guns soon joined in, developing a very heavy fire. The troops pushed on steadily, nevertheless, crossing a low ridge 500 yards ahead. On the right rather more favourable ground allowed of better progress, while here a tank helped the advance. Casualties, however, were heavy, the open ground providing no cover. The Hampshire were before long absorbed into the attack, which caught heavy fire from a redoubt to our right. This redoubt the tank

---

[1] Across the road to Beersheba and about North of Sheikh Abbas.

now tackled and with its aid a mixture of Hampshire and Norfolks forced their way in and took it, Sergeant Pearson being greatly to the fore and capturing 20 prisoners single-handed.[1] But the captors of the redoubt were soon hard pressed to maintain their ground, ammunition ran short, our artillery could give little help, and the 163rd Brigade's left and centre, after losing heavily, had been definitely held up 400 yards from their objective. Here the survivors hung on as best they could, pinned to the ground by the Turkish fire without any chance of getting forward. On their left some of the 162nd Brigade had been rather more successful, some men getting well across the Beersheba road, while further West the Fifty-Second Division had made a larger lodgement which it was fighting hard to maintain and extend. On the right the Mounted Divisions had failed to penetrate the defences and the whole attack was brought to a standstill; the 163rd Brigade in particular had lost very heavily, and before long its survivors were forced back, the captured redoubt being retaken and the tank destroyed. Along a slight rise an attempt at a stand was made, about 100 Hampshires with a Lewis gun being rallied by Major Marsh, and here they started to dig in. In the early afternoon the 5th Suffolk, till then in reserve, came up and extended this line to both flanks. The Fifty-Second Division was still beating off counter-attacks, but it was hard pressed and could not maintain all it had gained. The attacking Divisions had still nearly two brigades in hand and the infantry of another Division [2] were in reserve, but to have renewed the attack without far more artillery support could only have swelled the already high casualty list with little chance of achieving any more than the 8th Hampshire had accomplished.

After dark most of those lying out in the open got back to our line, while those wounded who could be reached were brought in. The 5th Suffolk had now taken over the front, and those of the Hampshire who were not collecting the wounded were consolidating part of a support line, taking in the Sheikh Abbas ridge and running thence NW. by Kh Mansura to the shore.

Casualties had been heavy, nearly 6500, well over a quarter in the 163rd Brigade, whose gallantry and determination had been so great but so unavailing. The 8th Hampshire, with 23 officers and 746 other ranks in action, had lost even more heavily than at Suvla: Captains Pittis and C. G. Seeley, Lts. Pakeman and S. G. Ratsey, 2/Lts. Atkin, Attfield, Blofield, Cox, Hills, King, Roberts and Shelton and 248 other ranks were killed and missing, of whom 2/Lts. Atkin, Cox and Roberts and 28 men were later reported as prisoners. Captains Fox, Hylton, Russell (now Adjutant) and Vincent, Lts. Butler and Harker, 2/Lts. Henville, Sutcliffe and Cronin-Wilson and 298 men had been wounded, though after the reserve not engaged in the battle had rejoined the battalion could produce twelve officers and 450 men on May 1st; a fair nucleus on which the work of reconstruction could be once again undertaken.

' First Gaza ' had been a disappointment, ' Second Gaza ' was a disastrous

---

[1] He was awarded the D.C.M.

[2] The incomplete Seventy-Fourth Division, in process of being formed from dismounted Yeomanry.

reverse. It finished all prospects of any further advance by the E.E.F., until much more artillery and substantial reinforcements could arrive. For the 8th Hampshire it meant settling down to a tedious period of trench warfare opposite Gaza, waiting for drafts. Still this long wait was far from a time of inactivity, and the battalion carried out a most successful minor operation and became most proficient in patrolling and in harassing the enemy.

After three weeks ' out ' training, reorganizing and working on second line defences, the 8th Hampshire were back in trenches by May 17th, South of Sheikh Abbas near El Mendur. Here our line faced Eastward over open country, and with the Turkish defences along the Beersheba road miles away patrolling was mainly done by mounted troops. After a week here the battalion was back across the Wadi Ghuzze in reserve till June 13th, when it relieved a battalion of the Fifty-Second Division in the trenches nearest the coast. Captains Fox and Vincent and Lt. Butler, wounded on April 19th, had rejoined before the end of May with about 80 men. Another 100 rejoined during June and with over 200 transferred from a Garrison Battalion of the Devons,[1] other ranks available for the trenches were up to 660 by July 1st. Four officers and 270 men of the 2/5th Hampshire, recently arrived from India, were attached for instruction on June 2nd.

In the coastal sector the battalion was holding a continuous trench with four posts 800 yards in advance, but communication trenches and a support line were lacking. The enemy showed little inclination to be active and rarely interfered with our patrols, which were very enterprising, one under Lt. Brannon rushing a sentry group near Sugar Loaf Hill on June 17th, taking five prisoners and returning along the beach. Much information was obtained, which proved useful in planning a big raid, carried out most successfully on July 14th by B Company with D Company of the 2/5th, in all 300 officers and men, including a large covering party and R.E. to blow up the dug-outs. The objectives included Sugar Loaf Hill and Beach Post. Everything had been carefully rehearsed, scouts having reconnoitred the ground thoroughly.

Starting off at 11 p.m. (July 14th) behind a most effective barrage which inflicted heavy casualties and drove the enemy to shelter in their dug-outs, the raiders first rushed the Sugar Loaf, Sergeant Wheeler leading them splendidly : five minutes later they were into Beach Post, Rifleman Hawes rushing a machine-gun before it could open fire, while Sergeants Early and Gray led parties which blocked the communication trenches. Some enemy showed fight but were quickly overpowered, Sergeant Palmer accounting for several, while many were caught in one dug-out and disposed of with the bayonet, on which rather than on the bomb the raiders had been trained to rely. The R.E. had soon finished their work and after 19 minutes, the raiders could begin withdrawing, bringing in 19 prisoners and a machine-gun. Casualties, three killed and missing and a dozen wounded, were very low, while it was estimated that 60 enemy had been killed, apart from those hit by the barrage during the bombardment or in seeking to escape.

----

[1] Several officers also joined.

Lt. Colonel Marsh's arrangements won much praise from the authorities, the raid being regarded as a real model. Lt. Brannon's leadership and his gallantry in bringing in a wounded man won him the M.C. and Sergeants Britten, Early, Gray, Palmer and Wheeler and Rifleman Adams were awarded the M.M.

Apart from this July was uneventful, the battalion twice co-operated by fire in raids on Umbrella Hill in the next sector, its patrols continued to be active but were almost unopposed, casualties were low and discharges from hospital considerably exceeded admissions. Septic sores caused some trouble, but malaria and enteric were infrequent and if conditions were not very comfortable the sea-bathing gave some relief and the sick-rate remained low, despite the heat.

Meanwhile a renewed offensive was in preparation. The War Cabinet hoped for great political results from a major success in Palestine and had at last agreed to provide the reinforcements and additional artillery denied to General Murray. A new, Seventy-Fifth, Division was being formed out of Indian troops already in Egypt and Territorials, including the 2/4th and 2/5 Hampshire, from India, and two Divisions with more Yeomanry were transferred from Salonica. This increase in the E.E.F. naturally involved a tremendous amount of administrative work at the base and on the lines of communication. General Allenby, now in command, was not going to strike prematurely, and as his plans included the outflanking of the Turkish line at and beyond Beersheba, water supply became a more important problem than ever.

The long pause was inevitably giving the Turks time to strengthen considerably their already formidable defences, but their troops were worse off in many ways than their opponents, their sick-rate and losses from disease were much higher, and not even German advice or assistance could introduce efficiency into Turkish administration. Moreover, the strategical deadlock did not preclude a vigorous harassing of the Turks, in which all our Divisions played their part, securing an ascendency in No Man's Land which went far to remove any legacy of discouragement from Second Gaza and its heavy casualties. If the 8th Hampshire did not repeat the Beach Post raid, their continued activity and success in patrolling maintained the feelings that exploit had inspired.

The battalion was 'out' most of August, bathing and training. Drafts brought other ranks up over 900 before the beginning of September, which month was spent in reserve to the left sector, finding large working parties every night to assist the front line battalion. Much of October was devoted to rehearsing the next attack over practice trenches and then, on October 14th, the 8th took over the coastal sector from the sea to Bunker's Hill and promptly started sending out strong patrols to secure the mastery of No Man's Land and cover working parties. After a week of this the battalion was back in the training area, completing arrangements for the attack, now very near at hand, but sending parties up to the front to carry on the patrolling. It only took up its assembly position for the attack on the evening of November 1st.[1]

[1] Its strength on October 31st was 34 officers and 887 other ranks.

Meanwhile both the 2/4th and the 2/5th Hampshire had reached Palestine, being both very different in many respects, above all in personnel, from the raw units which had left England for India in November 1915. Drafts to Mesopotamia,[1] transfers to other units or to special employments, a few deaths and invalidings and many promotions to commissions had changed them almost completely. Even so Lt. Colonel J. B. L. Stillwell, now commanding the 2/4th, had with him twelve of its original officers, including his second in command, Major C. P. Bulley, who had come out as a Captain, as had Captains J. C. Bulley, Ashmore and Goddard, while Captain Bacon, now Adjutant, had come out as a 2nd Lieutenant, but fourteen original subalterns were no longer present and Captain North had been killed with the 1/4th at El Hanna.[2]

The 2/4th had been warned for active service in April 1917, just after having found 150 men for the 2/5th, who preceded them to Palestine. They had earned a good reputation at Quetta for efficiency and for prowess in athletics, for which they owed much to the help of the Quetta Division, especially its G.O.C., General Grover, whose interest in the battalion did not cease when it left his command, but the battalion was glad to be getting a chance to prove itself in the field. It had a great send-off : all Quetta turned out to bid it farewell and wish it luck. Leaving Karachi, where it had had a great variety of guards to find, including one at Hyderabad (Sind), on April 29th, it reached Suez on May 15th [3] and was sent to Zeitoun Camp near Cairo, for a fortnight's equipping and training. New rifles were issued but heavy baggage including most of the band's instruments had to be dumped. From here the 2/4th were sent on to El Arish and thence to Rafa (June 20th), where the Seventy-Fifth Division was being assembled under Major-General Palin. The 2/4th now found themselves in the 233rd Brigade with the 5th Somerset L.I., the 4th Wiltshire and the 3/3rd Gurkhas under Brigadier-General Colston. They had now to find many guards and night outposts as well as to become acquainted with the bomb and the Lewis gun and to do a ' refresher ' musketry course with the short rifle issued to them at Zeitoun, while many officers and men went off to a variety of courses of instruction. It was very hot but the bathing, though at times dangerous, was some relaxation. In the middle of August the battalion moved up to Deir el Belah. The brigade's arrangements involved an unnecessarily exhausting march, started at 10 a.m. and carried out in the worst part of the day, which caused quite considerable suffering to the heavily-equipped men and some cases of heat-stroke. Arrived here officers and men got their initiation into trench warfare under the Fifty-Second Division, whom their Division relieved in the coastal sector on September 11th, holding the left sub-sector, the Apex. The battalion now got its first chance in action, beating off a Turkish patrol on the 20th, while its own patrols were active and several encounters occurred. On October 7th a detachment under 2/Lts. Beauchamp and Fenn

---

[1] The 2/4th in all sent 17 officers and 700 men.

[2] Three original subalterns, Durnford, Rawlings and Wilkinson, were killed in Mesopotamia or Persia

[3] It mustered 27 officers and 820 other ranks.

acted as a left flank guard in a highly successful raid by the Somerset and 3/3rd Gurkhas, though Turkish retaliation inflicted several casualties, mainly in A Company, which was in support.[1]

The battalion had some days out of the trenches in the middle of October, then taking over trenches at Queen's Hill, subsequently shifting Eastward and taking over the Mansura Redoubt. All was ready now for the big attack. Its Division, now in the Twenty-First Corps, was on its right, on the Sheikh Abbas ridge, with its right flank thrown back facing East, covering the flank of the Fifty-Second and Fifty-Fourth Divisions, who were attacking Gaza from the South-West.

The 2/5th were in Palestine before the 2/4th, having embarked at Bombay on March 19th and reached Suez on April 5th. They went first to Zeitoun, for training and re-equipping, being in the first formed brigade of the Seventy-Fifth Division, the 232nd, under Brigadier-General Huddleston, along with the 5th Devonshire, 2nd Loyal North Lancashire and 2/3rd Gurkhas.

Moving forward in May to El Arish the battalion was employed on the line of communications for a month and then moved up to the front, being attached for instruction from June 3rd to 11th to the 163rd Brigade. Colonel Day and Major Stevenson, the original C.O. and second in command, were still present. Captain Jenner had succeeded Captain Archdale as Adjutant, the latter, now Major, Captains Ellis and Kay, subalterns in 1914, and Lt. Gibbings commanding the companies. Lt. Pigden was still Quartermaster and of the subalterns six were ' originals '.

From June 26th on the battalion took over its own piece of the line, though D Company remained with the 8th Hampshire for the Beach Post raid, in which C.S.M. Graham, who led his section admirably and himself accounted for several enemy, got the D.C.M., while Corporal Wells, who led a bombing section most efficiently, and Ptes. Burgess and Goddard won the M.M.

The 2/5th had seven weeks in line from the end of June onwards, on Samson's Ridge just South of Gaza and at Hart Hill in the centre of the coastal sector. Here it greatly improved the defences, though dead ground just in front of the wire was a trouble. It maintained a steady pressure on the Turks, patrolling and harassing them with fire, to which they replied intermittently, the battalion's total casualties being under 40. Wastage from illness was larger, sand-fly fever being prevalent, and among others the C.O. was invalided. His successor, Lt. Colonel Vernon of the K.R.R.C., soon left to command a brigade, Major Stevenson carrying on until, on October 1st Lt. Colonel G.F. Perkins, who had been for some time on the Staff of the M.E.F., joined. Captain Jenner now going to the Indian Army, Captain Kay replaced him as Adjutant.

During September the battalion was in reserve, working hard on rear lines and getting much useful training, and then in October it took over front

---

[1] Major Parsons, a ' pre-war ' subaltern of the 4th Hampshire, joined in October and became second in command. Captain Bacon had been given a post on the Staff and was replaced as Adjutant by Captain Price.

trenches on the Mansura Ridge, patrolling actively and improving the line. At the end of October it was back in reserve. Drafts coming nearly to 150 had joined, mainly ' combed out ' from Garrison battalions ; these men if rather old, averaging 39, were mostly of good physique and many had had previous service. Thus the battalion was up to a fair strength and ready to give a good account of itself.

CHAPTER XXII

MESOPOTAMIA 1917

BY December 1916 General Maude's reorganization of his base and lines of communications had borne fruit and the two Corps, First and Third,[1] into which 'Force D' had now expanded, were ready for an offensive, being well up to establishment, refreshed, well equipped and trained. Ample artillery and ammunition was now available and plenty of river and road transport, with

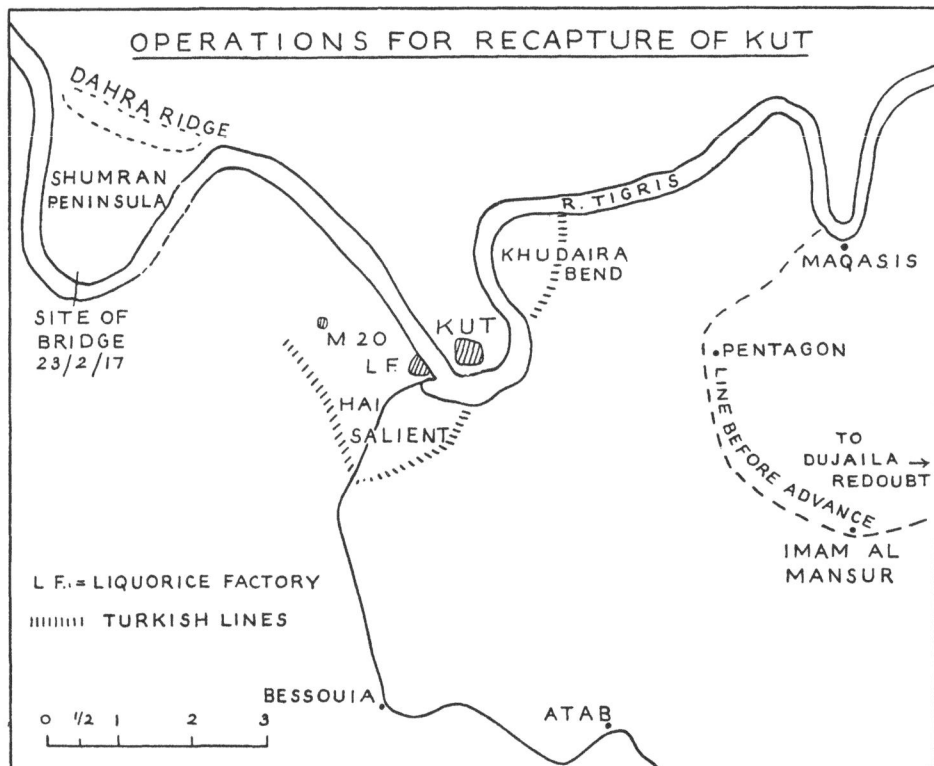

OPERATIONS FOR RECAPTURE OF KUT

DAHRA RIDGE

SHUMRAN PENINSULA

R. TIGRIS

KHUDAIRA BEND

MAQASIS

SITE OF BRIDGE 23/2/17

M 20
L.F.
KUT

PENTAGON

LINE BEFORE ADVANCE

HAI SALIENT

TO DUJAILA → REDOUBT

IMAM AL MANSUR

L.F. = LIQUORICE FACTORY

|||||||| TURKISH LINES

BESSOUIA

ATAB

0 1/2 1   2   3

adequate medical arrangements. The benefit of having maintained a forward position up the Tigris after the fall of Kut, even if at a considerable cost to the troops, was now apparent. We were well placed to start the resumption of our offensive, for which a strong strategical case could be advanced: our force was much too large to be locked up in a passive defensive, while we could hardly withdraw down the Tigris to reduce our forces without running considerable risk, both military and political. At the same time General Maude faced no easy tactical problems; the Turks were strongly posted and had had ample

[1] The Third and Seven Divisions formed the First Corps (General Cobbe), the Thirteenth and Fourteenth the Third (General Marshall).

time for improving their defences, whose strength we had already only too good reason to appreciate.

However, General Maude did not intend to start by attacking the much strengthened Sanna i yat lines. He had now the transport to enable him to operate on the right bank at some distance from the river, and by crossing the Hai well South of Kut he could threaten the Turkish line of communications by reaching the Tigris some way upstream.

Operations began on December 14th, when the Thirteenth Division and the cavalry pushed forward from Iman al Mansur to the Hai, which the cavalry crossed between Atab and Basrugiya,[1] the Thirteenth Division advancing East of the Hai towards the Turkish positions SW. of Kut. These formed a salient astride the Hai and would have to be cleared, together with some other formidable trenches across the Khudaira Bend, on the right bank just below Kut. The Fourteenth Division was supporting the Thirteenth and its tasks included protecting the Thirteenth's rear from any possible attack by Arabs. For this purpose the 36th Brigade was detailed to occupy an old line of trenches running SW. from the Dujaila Redoubt to the Hai below Atab, part of which the 4th Hampshire took over on December 15th, crossing the Hai at Atab next day to carry on the same function across the river. Here an outpost line was established, three miles in length and facing South, while the rest of the Third Corps, its rear thus safeguarded, advanced towards the Hai Salient and the Khudaira Bend.

In this line the Hampshire spent the rest of December. The Arabs were in sufficient force in this quarter to require the employment of a good many troops in keeping them off but, apart from some sniping at mounted men who hovered about in front of the battalion's position, the 4th played a merely defensive part while our troops were closing in upon the Hai Salient and the Khudaira Bend, formidable positions which were to take some clearing. An effort to cross the Tigris well above Kut and so manoeuvre the enemy out of his positions downstream had not been successful, but our lines were being pushed nearer the Turkish defences and, early in January, the First Corps started to attack the Khudaira Bend trenches in force, while the Third hammered away at the Hai Salient.

Even now the 4th Hampshire were not actively engaged. The 36th Brigade had been concentrated in reserve at Bessouia on New Year's Eve, and though it was employed on January 2nd to cover a column which went out to demolish an Arab fort and had similar work on January 14th, when the Cavalry Division raided Hai town, it had no fighting. The return march on January 2nd was carried out on one of the darkest nights imaginable : it was really impossible to see anything, and one officer addressed a mule, taking it for another officer. By January 19th the Third Division had cleared the Khudaira Bend after heavy fighting, and the weight of the attack could be transferred to the Hai Salient, the Thirteenth Division attacking astride the river on January 25th, with the 35th Brigade co-operating with fire on its left flank. The 36th Brigade was at

---

[1] SE. of Atab.

Bessouia in reserve, having spent the last few days digging assembly trenches as an alternative to the road-making on which it had mainly been employed of late.

East of the river the attack was successful and the captured line was retained ; West of it, after heavy and fluctuating fighting, the 39th Brigade was eventually thrust back to the assembly positions, the 36th being first ordered up in support and then detailed to make another assault. The lateness of the hour and the congestion of the trenches caused this to be postponed till next day, but during the night the 26th and 82nd Punjabis took over in readiness to attack with the 4th Hampshire in support.

Attacking at 10.40 a.m. (January 26th) the 82nd Punjabis carried the Turkish line [1] and started bombing along trenches leading North along the river bank and NW. To support them the 26th Punjabis went forward about 11.30 a.m., two companies joining them, though the others lost direction and made an isolated lodgement [2] well to the left. Here they held on for some time but, running short of ammunition, were forced back to the line the 82nd were consolidating,[3] their C.O., Lt. Colonel Thompson, formerly a subaltern in the Hampshire, being killed. Pressure upon the Punjabis was increasing, and about 1.30 p.m. A and B Companies of the Hampshire pushed across to assist the 82nd, while one platoon of D and some bombers joined the 26th and gave timely help in repulsing counter-attacks and maintaining the line. At 5.30 p.m. battalion headquarters and C and D went forward also, and after dark the Hampshire took over, the 26th and 82nd, both of whom had lost heavily, being withdrawn except for some bombers.

The night passed without any serious counter-attack and consolidation went on unimpeded. Next morning about 9.30 a.m. our bombers started to push up the trenches leading to the next line. They were not very seriously opposed and the objective was duly mastered, B and C occupying it about 11.30, while the bombers, assisted by those of the 62nd and 82nd, pushed on toward another line.[4] This also was taken after rather harder fighting, in which Lt. Lester-Garland was wounded, and about 2 p.m. A and D came forward to help consolidate the gains. Scouts then advanced to reconnoitre yet another line [5] to discover that it was unoccupied. Posts were established in it and during the night two companies advanced and occupied it. The Turks had evidently been hard hit, and though next day they tried to bomb back up a communication trench leading to the centre of the Hampshire's line, they were quickly repulsed and did little to impede the improvement of our line, while reconnaissance soon proved that they had fallen back to a line[6] 1200 yards in rear of that assaulted on January 26th. Equally good progress had been made East of the Hai, the Thirteenth Division having by now secured the Turkish second line.

That evening (January 28th) the 37th Brigade relieved the 36th who had meanwhile extended their front to the left, where the 35th had also advanced. The 36th Brigade had had over 600 casualties, the Hampshire having lost two

[1] P. 15—P. 12A—12B.   [2] P. 16A on map.   [3] Roughly, P. 12B to P. 15.
[4] P. 12B—15B.   [5] P. 12M—14B.   [6] Approximately from P 13M Westward.

officers [1] and eight men killed and had three officers and 80 men wounded, not a heavy price for really substantial gains in ground and the heavy casualties inflicted upon the enemy.[2]

The next few days brought minor advances and improvements of the line, the Hampshire remaining in reserve with their brigade, and then on February

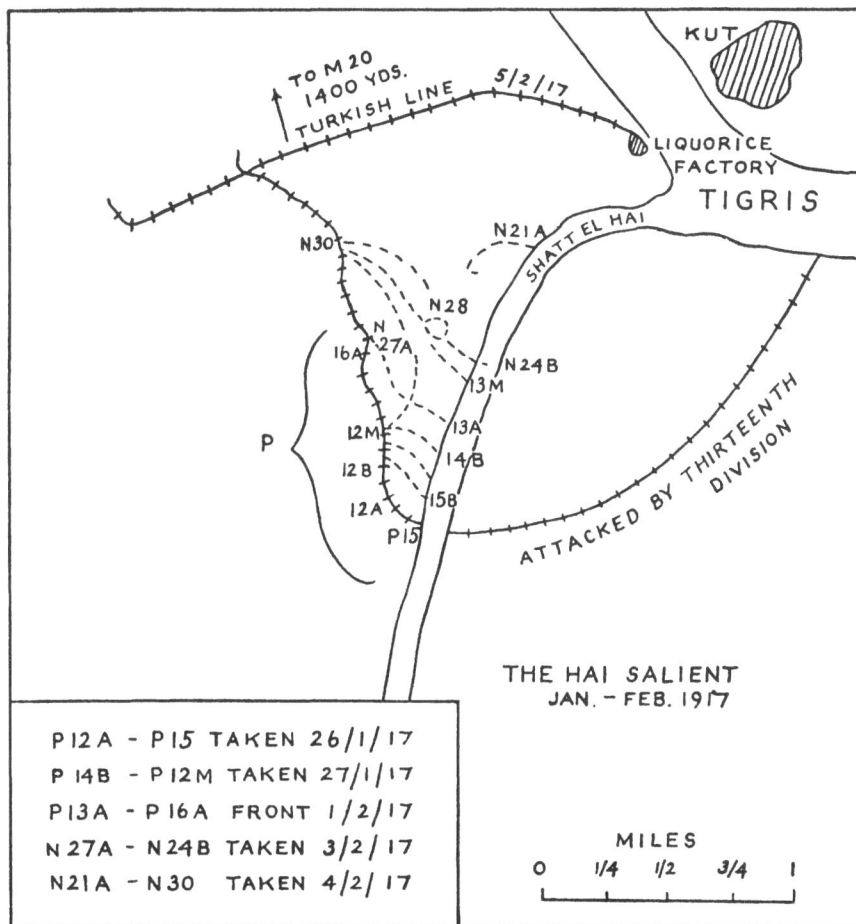

THE HAI SALIENT
JAN. - FEB. 1917

P 12A - P 15 TAKEN 26/1/17
P 14B - P 12M TAKEN 27/1/17
P 13A - P 16A FRONT 1/2/17
N 27A - N 24B TAKEN 3/2/17
N 21A - N 30 TAKEN 4/2/17

MILES
0   1/4   1/2   3/4   1

1st a fresh attack was made on both banks. On the East the Thirteenth Division took all but the last line of defence : on the West the 37th Brigade, after capturing two lines of trenches, was counter-attacked in great force and driven back to our lines, the two attacking battalions being so much reduced that they had to be withdrawn and the 4th Hampshire and the 62nd Punjabis sent up to replace them.

[1] Lt. Rawlings (6th Battalion), killed by a sniper just before the relief, and 2/Lt. H. C. Huskisson.
[2] Captain Watson, R.A.M.C., the 1/4th's M.O., received the D.S.O. ; Lt. Lamont (Middx, attached) the M.C., Corporal Langrish and Private Harris the D.C.M. and Private Sankey the M.M.

It was too late and the trenches were too congested for any fresh attack that evening, while next day mist and the need to get trench-mortars and machine guns into position caused another postponement. On February 3rd, however, the 4th Devonshire and 1/2nd Gurkhas, attacking with great dash, carried their objective [1] and, after beating off counter-attacks, started to exploit their success by bombing forward and to their left, the 62nd Punjabis reinforcing them, while the Hampshire carried bombs and ammunition across to them, C Company later on supporting the advance on the left, where a network of small trenches was hindering progress. A useful advance was nevertheless made,[2] and next morning (February 4th) the Hampshire pushed forward again. This was not too easy work ; the battalion had to negotiate a maze of trenches and direction was hard to keep, while the enemy were still fighting stubbornly and inflicted several casualties, Captain Allen [3] being mortally wounded in a patrol encounter and Lt. G. D. Andrews wounded. However, a good line was secured and consolidated, despite much sniping. Meanwhile the Turks had evacuated their last foothold beyond the Hai and by the morning of February 5th they had also fallen back West of it to a line running from the Liquorice Factory, ' Woolpress Village ' to the defenders of Kut in 1916, Westward across the Dahra Bend. The last attacks had added another 60 to the Hampshire's casualties,[4] but the many dead Turks in the positions captured showed how heavily the defenders had been hit.

Ten days passed before the Hampshire were seriously engaged again : after being relieved in front line on February 6th and working at communication trenches for three days, they were in support from February 10th to 15th at the Liquorice Factory, which the 35th Brigade had just captured. Here they were mainly occupied in digging communication trenches, while a welcome draft of 150 men from the 1/5th filled some of the gaps in the ranks. February 15th saw the 35th Brigade and the 40th [5] further to the left assault and carry a big stretch of what was virtually the last strong line [6] in the Dahra Bend, the Hampshire being in support to the 35th Brigade, whose many prisoners A Company assisted to collect and to march off to the cages. With this Turkish resistance on the right bank was virtually over, though some mopping up was needed in the Dahra Bend. The Turks were, however, still clinging on down-stream at Sanna i yat and General Maude now hoped to cut them off by crossing the Tigris above Kut.

The passage was to be attempted at the Southern end of the Shumran Bend, where converging covering fire could be given from both flanks. Where the bridge was to be laid the river was over 300 yards wide, but to secure a bridge-head three battalions were to be ferried across at points some way downstream. Heavy rain and hailstorms delayed preparation, but on February 20th the 4th Hampshire were detailed to find rowers for the pontoons in which the 37th

---

[1] P. 13M—N 27 A.   [2] The line now ran from N 24 B on the right to N 27 A.
[3] 7th Battalion.
[4] Captain Parkes (2/7th Battalion) was wounded on February 6th, when superintending consolidation.
[5] Of the Thirteenth Division.   [6] Behind and West of M 20.

Brigade was to attempt the passage, and that day and the next were spent in practising rowing on the Hai. This proved none too easy, the Hai was in flood and the pontoons were clumsy vessels and difficult to handle. Of the rowers, some 700 in all organized in three reliefs, a third were from the Hampshire, the rest from the R.E. of the Thirteenth Division and from the Fourteenth's Sappers and Miners. The operation called for no little courage and resolution, the rowers would be as unprotected as the men who had tried to land from the boats at V Beach. There would be thirteen pontoons at each crossing to carry ten passengers apiece.

At the selected crossing ramps had to be made on the bank and tracks prepared leading down to them, but all was ready in time and just before dawn on February 23rd the crossing started. The columns detailed had left their assembly positions at 6 p.m. and had been waiting since 1 a.m., after getting the pontoons down to their launching places.

The Hampshire were providing about half the rowers at the centre and right ferries, where the 2/9th and 1/2nd Gurkhas were crossing. At the centre the first trip was nearly half way across before the Turks realised what was happening, but so deadly was their fire that three pontoons never reached the shore, drifting downstream with all their crews casualties. All the rowers of another pontoon were hit, but Sergeant Combellack jumped overboard and swam ashore, towing the pontoon by taking the towing rope in his teeth ; he then, though wounded, collected rowers to take a pontoon back. Rowing back for the second trip four more crews were put out of action, and though at the second attempt five got across, none of them could return, owing to casualties among the rowers. However, enough 2/9th Gurkhas [1] had got across to establish a bridge-head and hold on, and rather later two pontoons which had got back with wounded men made another journey with ammunition and a few more men.

At the right crossing all thirteen pontoons reached the shore, the Hampshire crews rowing so strongly that, despite the current, they reached a point 400 yards above the intended landing place, but here only two pontoons got back and these, making a second attempt [2] along with two more which had floated down from the centre crossing, were again unfortunate, only one getting across, the accurate machine-gun fire being most destructive. However, here also the Gurkhas [3] maintained the foothold they had established, and as the 2nd Norfolk, crossing upstream, had been virtually unopposed and had pushed forward some way, the rest of both Gurkha battalions were diverted to this point, where they were ferried across with little loss, more rowers from the Thirteenth Division having reinforced the original crews. Thus by 2 p.m. both battalions were assisting the Norfolk to advance up the peninsula, soon gaining touch with the detachments at the lower crossings. Pressing forward despite stubborn opposition, they established themselves about half way up the peninsula, far enough forward to drive away the snipers who had till then been

[1] About a company and a half.   [2] They were now manned by Sappers and Miners.
[3] 1/2nd.

hindering work on the bridge, whose construction had been started about
8.30 a.m. and was completed before 5 p.m. when the Hampshire and the rest of
the 36th Brigade followed the 37th across.

The crossing could thus be exploited but some 200 of the rowers had been
hit, half of them from the Hampshire, whose ' steadfast gallantry ' [1] had won
general admiration and earned six ' immediate ' awards, 2/Lt. Hamilton, who
had set a fine example, greatly encouraging the men, getting the M.C., Sergeant
Combellack, Lance Corporal Gee and Pte. Craven the D.C.M. and Ptes. Jackson
and J. J. Smith the M.M.

Meanwhile on February 22nd the Seventh Division had carried the two
forward lines at Sanna i yat and during the succeeding days it was sweeping
forward across the positions which had so long defied us. The defenders of
Sanna i yat and Kut were now in full retreat and might perhaps be intercepted
by the Fourteenth Division. In this hope the 36th and 37th Brigades started on
February 24th to advance up the Shumran peninsula, across whose neck the
Turks were strongly posted on a ridge of sand-hills.

The 36th Brigade on the right had the Hampshire next the river with the
62nd Punjabis on their left. Advancing about 6.15 a.m. the troops came under
heavy fire, machine guns on the right enfilading the Hampshire, but they were in
high spirits, encouraged by their previous successes, and they pushed vigorously
forward, despite the fire and the heavy casualties it inflicted. Indeed, they
maintained ' such an unfaltering advance that observers in rear failed to notice
that anything had happened ' [2] except that the Brigade machine-gun company
had moved across to the right to answer the enfilading fire. Well supported
by the 82nd Punjabis, the Hampshire pressed resolutely on, cleared the enemy
out of a dry canal which had provided good cover and kept gaining ground
towards the ridge beyond, Lt. Durnford, though twice wounded, leading his men
skilfully and gallantly [3] and continuing in action till the objective along the
sandhills of the Dahra ridge had been secured. Their advance had covered some
3000 yards and they had taken many prisoners. The rest of the brigade kept
pace with them, and though further to the left counter-attacks delayed the
37th Brigade, it also gained ground ; by 7.30 a.m. hard fighting had given us the
ridge, though nearly 1000 yards separated our right from the river bank.[4]
Many machine-guns were in action in this gap, so that the 26th and 82nd Punjabis had to be diverted to that flank to fill it. Till it was filled, and this could
not be accomplished till about 11 a.m. and then only after really hard fighting,
the advance could not get on, indeed the Hampshire and the Norfolk further
to their left had to beat back several counter-attacks, our guns helping
considerably. Later on the 35th Brigade came up also, reinforcing the 37th,
and gained some ground in the centre, but the 36th could not get on as our
guns had failed to locate or silence the machine-guns which were still holding
us up and the troops were tired. It had been very hot and the strain had been

[1] *Official History.* Mesopotamia III, 171.   [2] Ibid. III, 176.
[3] He received the D.S.O.
[4] The peninsula widened at its base and the battalion had kept straight ahead.

great. Despite our passage of the river the Turks were still fighting hard and using their machine-guns most effectively, a strongly posted rear-guard on another ridge further back was bent on keeping us from getting across the path of the troops retiring from downstream, and though our cavalry succeeded in passing through the Fourteenth Division's line they could not outflank this

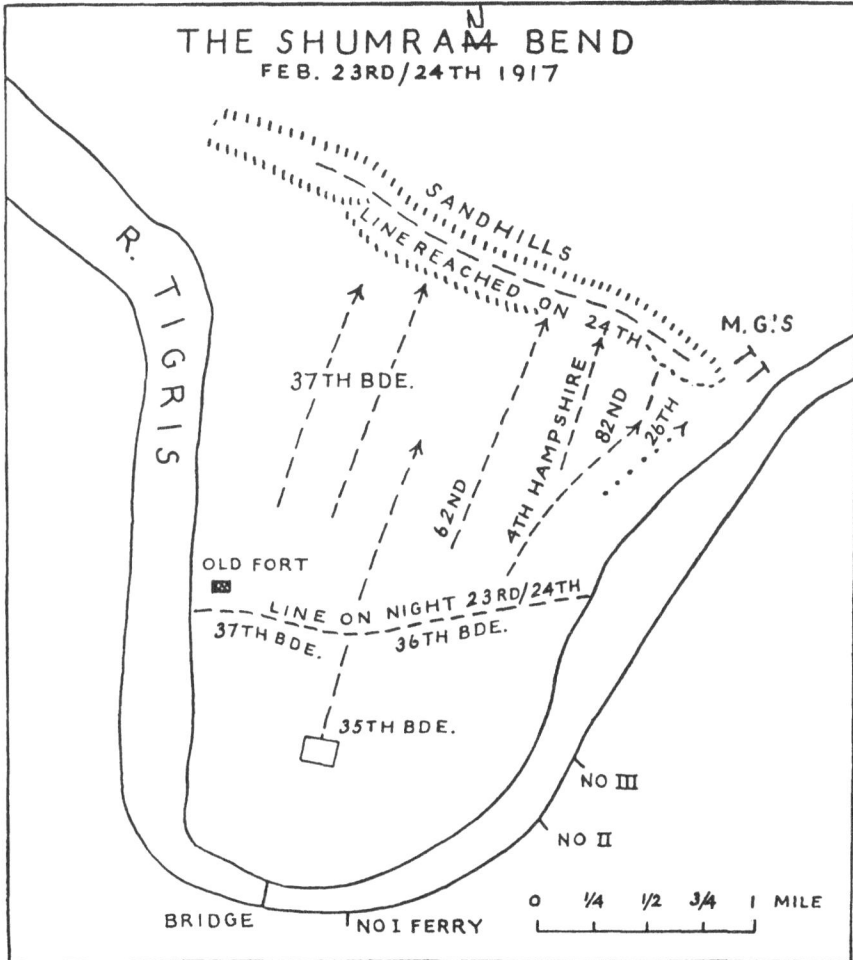

THE SHUMRAN BEND
FEB. 23RD/24TH 1917

rear-guard and clear it away, so that the endangered troops from Sanna i yat escaped interception.

The Hampshire had had a hard day's fight, with under 450 in action, apart from the rowers, their casualties, came to 180,[1] including 2/Lt. Poulter killed and Lt. Colonel Matthews [2] (slightly), Captain Rixon, Lt. Durnford and 2/Lts. Allen, Fisher, Osborne, Shaddock and Wetherall wounded, while the 82nd

[1] Rowers included, 67 men were killed, 23 missing and 180 wounded.
[2] Major Gribbon now took command, Lt. Colonel Matthews rejoining on March 3rd.

Punjabis lost even more ; still the brigade had captured over 300 prisoners and two guns and could see that it had hit the Turks hard.

If we had failed to cut off many enemy we had them on the run, and our river-craft could now push on upstream past Kut and keep our pursuing troops supplied, so we could press on after the Turks with Baghdad as our goal. Several actions were fought during the fortnight which took us to Baghdad, but the 36th Brigade missed them all. When it was advanced-guard to its Division no opposition was encountered.

If the 4th Hampshire had no fighting between the Shumran Bend and Baghdad, they had some strenuous marching with rough going and hard conditions, rations being often short so that the battalion was reduced to eat the ' atta ' usually provided for the Indian troops. However, the Quarter-master, Lt. Buckingham, rose to the occasion as usual and produced some un-expected issues of a more palatable kind. On February 26th they covered 23 miles in an effort to cut off the Turks, and if the next day's march was only eight miles, they did 18 on March 1st, when the Division reached Azizieh, 15 on March 3rd, which took them to Zor, and 15 again next day, when they reached Bastan, close to the Ctesiphon battlefield, after one of the most trying marches, through choking clouds of dust over an apology for a road.

On March 8th they came under fire again. While the 38th Brigade was trying to cross the Diala near its junction with the Tigris, a mixed column, which included the Hampshire, advanced seven miles upstream in search of a point to cross, but where they approached the river the enemy were on the alert and too well posted to warrant an attempt to force a crossing. The Hamp-shire, after deploying and advancing nearly 2000 yards, were held up by shell-fire short of the river bank and had to dig in, while patrols which pushed some way further upstream were received with machine-gun fire and could not find a passage. The column accordingly withdrew to Bawi, where the Hampshire had two days in bivouac, and before they came forward again, on March 11th, the passage of the Diala had been forced and it had been bridged. On the right bank also opposition had been overcome, the Turks were in full retreat and next day the British occupied Baghdad almost without opposition.

The 4th Hampshire entered Baghdad on March 13th and were attached to the 35th Brigade, who were in charge of the city. They now had to settle down to guard and garrison duties, finding many men as Military Police, with many guards and picquets. ' Disinfecting and cleaning up barracks ' is a suggestive entry in the battalion diary, which also records raiding houses in search of arms, arresting Arabs found in possession of weapons, collecting Turkish stores and patrolling the streets, especially at night.

The battalion now began a long spell of rather uneventful garrison duty at Baghdad, which kept it out of the sharp fighting round that city which con-tinued well into April, the Turks on the Tigris being well beaten at Mushahida (March 14th) and Istabulat (April 21st) and driven back on Tikrit, while if we did not succeed in intercepting the troops retiring Westward from the Persian border North of Baghdad, they were repeatedly defeated and thrust back into the Jebel Hamrin and reduced to inactivity there. By the end of April our position at Baghdad had been secured and we could settle down in what may be called ' summer quarters ', when the troops enjoyed a well-earned rest in readiness to resume our offensive after the hot weather, should this be expedient.

Closer acquaintance with Baghdad had hardly been pleasant : picturesque at a distance, with romantic traditions, it proved smelly and squalid, and its garrison had much unattractive work before they could make the famous city habitable, sanitary and healthy. Large quantities of Turkish stores of every kind, including ice-making machines, were found undamaged and before long the garrison's labours produced satisfactory results, while the conditions in which the hot weather had to be endured were very different from those of 1916. The comforts and amenities, then so conspicuously lacking, were now available, the transport services were working well, where there had been shortages there was plenty, and though at times the temperatures rivalled those of 1916 the sick-rate was far lower.[1] Large leave-parties could be sent off to India, the general atmosphere after the brilliant successes of the winter and spring was very different from the dejection and disappointments of 1916, and if the 4th Hampshire had little variety of duties and occupations they were not over-worked or under any strain. Baghdad even at its filthiest was better than Es Sinn or the Wadi, and after a short spell of British occupation the city was almost clean, the inhabitants had re-opened their shops and local supplies were plentiful.

The Hampshire soon moved out of Baghdad itself into a camp half a mile upstream but without any change in their duties, ' guards, picquets and police ' being the unvarying daily entry in their diary for these months. Here they remained till the middle of July: a draft from India in June of 90 men brought numbers up well over 600, and early in July the battalion was re-armed with rifles which would fire Mark VII ammunition and with long bayonets. This preceded a move along with Brigade head-quarters and the Supply and Trans-port Company and other details to Baquba on the Diala, now the Fourteenth Division's head-quarters. The march took three days ; after the first ten miles the road degenerated sadly, and the last day's march was a painful struggle over fifteen miles of exceptionally bad going, deep in dust, while the column which included 340 carts and over 1000 animals, extended to three miles. The marches were started in the early hours, so that they might be completed before the day became really hot, but even so the strain was terrible, one man died and 50 others collapsed.

At Baquba the battalion went into camp, where it continued the digging of a defensive line, with one company at a time doing company training. August brought some change of work, to railway construction, and in Sep-tember companies were employed to escort convoys going out to Beled Ruz,

---

[1] The 4th Hampshire's losses included its Quartermaster, Lt. Buckingham, who had done it excellent service and was about the last ' original ' officer left with the battalion. He died in December.

Shahraban and other places. With the return of leave parties and of convalescents and a draft of 100 men, other ranks were up to 800 by September 30th
and early in October another draft of three officers and 109 men arrived.

The suspension of active operations at the end of April had left the British
forces in the Diala valley holding a line North of Baquba and facing the Turks
in the Jebel Hamrin range. After their heavy defeats during March and April
these were no menace to us but it was always possible that the situation in
Caucasia and Persia might take an unfavourable turn. The ' Pan-Turkish '

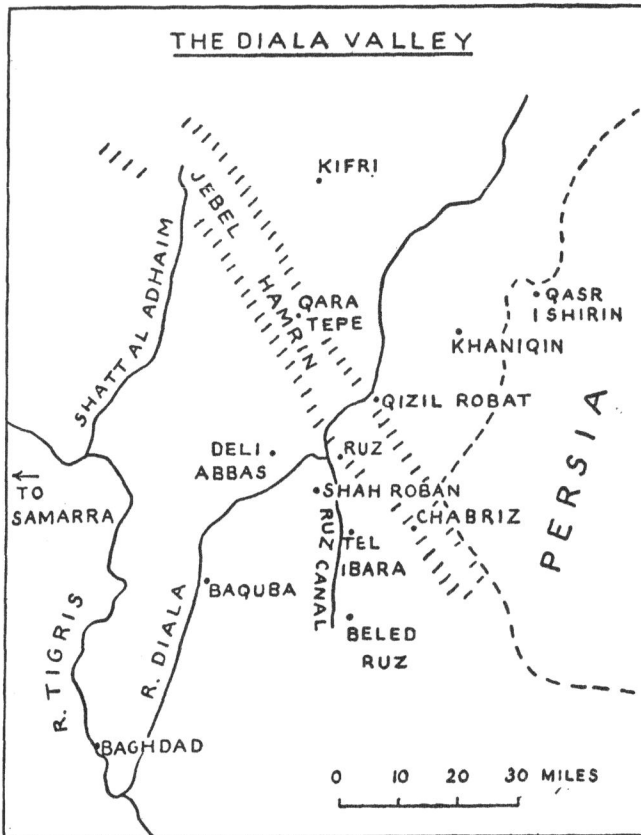

THE DIALA VALLEY

party, increasingly influential at Constantinople, had ambitions in that quarter,
which the virtual collapse of Russia during 1917 greatly encouraged. Persia
and Afghanistan and ' the Frontier ' were always sources of anxiety to the
authorities in India, and despite our capture of Baghdad possible developments
in those countries claimed more and more attention and affected our forces
in Mesopotamia.

If the prospects of any Russian co-operation against Upper Mesopotamia
were rapidly vanishing, those of a Turkish counter-offensive in force aimed at
the recovery of Baghdad seemed equally unlikely to be realised, and as cooler

weather drew near General Maude could prepare for a limited offensive, aimed rather at reducing Turkish fighting power than at extending the area we occupied, already large enough. Before the end of August a column from the Fourteenth Division had moved forward up the Diala to Shahraban, the force available for an advance having been increased by their release from garrison duties at Baghdad, units hitherto on the lines of communication but no longer needed there having replaced them.

This re-distribution of the troops on the lines of communication was setting enough units free to form a new, Seventeenth, Division, which was completed by a few fresh units from India, among them the 1/6th Hampshire, who reached Basra on September 16th, the 2/7th coming out at the same time but being allotted to the lines of communication.

General Maude's first offensive operation was directed against the Turks on the Euphrates, who were effectively smashed up at Ramadi (September 29th). His next move was made against the Jebel Hamrin, partly to push the Turks back and so make it more difficult for them to threaten our communications with Persia, should an advance into that country prove necessary, partly to prevent any interference with the water supply from the Diala, all-important for irrigation. In this advance the 36th Brigade formed part of a column which moved Eastward from Shahraban by Tel Ibara and Chabriz to attack the Turkish left.

The 4th Hampshire had reached Shahraban on October 17th, covering the 27 miles from Baquba in two marches, one of 18. Moving on next evening by Tel Ibara, they reached Chabriz about 9 a.m. on the 19th, having covered 21 miles since 6 p.m. Here the brigade remained in reserve to the 37th, before whose advance upon Qizil Robat the Turks soon cleared out, almost without offering any resistance. The 36th Brigade then moved back to Tel Ibara, where the Hampshire took over a line behind the Ruz Canal, finding several picquets. Here they remained till the end of November, twice sending a company out to Chabriz in support of cavalry reconnaissances, digging defences for a bridge-head and reconnoitring on their own into the Jebel Hamrin, while the roads were much improved and many canals and water courses bridged.

While thus engaged the battalion heard with regret of General Maude's death from cholera, November 18th. His loss was much felt ; all who had served under him knew how great had been his share in the successes at Kut and Baghdad and how much ' Force D ' owed to his skill as an organizer and administrator as well as to his leadership and inspiration. In General Marshall, who had been commanding the Third Corps, he had a competent successor, who was to bring the operation, in Mesopotamia to an almost sensationally successful conclusion by advancing as far as Mosul.

The first operation for which General Marshall was responsible was another advance early in December across the Jebel Hamrin. This involved more fighting than its predecessor of October, but the 36th Brigade was in reserve throughout the operations, the 4th Hampshire reaching the crossing place over the Kurdarrah river but then recrossing the Jebel Hamrin to Ruz Station to continue road-making. The Turks had been driven back towards Kifri, whereby their chances of advancing into Persia were reduced, but we now took up a forward position beyond the Jebel Hamrin, the head-quarters of the 4th Hampshire moving forward to Qizil Robat on Dec. 8th and next day to Khaniquin which was occupied without opposition. Here the battalion found itself within a few miles of the Persian border. The area was full of game : partridges, wild geese, duck, sand grouse and hares abounded and the rations were amply supplemented. B and C Companies, who had remained at Ruz Station, rejoined on December 31st.

Meanwhile two more Hampshire battalions had joined ' Force D ' in September, the 1/6th and 2/7th. The former had moved from Ambala to Meerut in March 1917, to be warned early in September for service in Mesopotamia, for which 28 officers and 882 other ranks under Lt. Colonel Wyatt, embarked at Bombay on September 11th.[1] Reaching Basra on September 17th, the battalion was promptly transferred to barges which took it to Qurna, where it entrained for Amara, to go by river to Kut and on by train to Baghdad, which was reached on September 24th, the battalion being located in Karrodah Camp and posted to the 52nd Brigade of the Seventeenth Division. The other units of the brigade were the 45th Sikhs, 84th Punjabis and 113th Infantry,[2] its commander being Brigadier General Andrew, Major General Gillman commanding the Division. The battalion was here all October, then moved to Iron Bridge Camp, five miles West of Baghdad, where the end of the year found it. Its duties had included guarding Turkish prisoners taken at Ramadi and elsewhere. Admissions to hospital were numerous at first, nearly 100 in October, but then declined, discharges during November and December about balancing admissions, while a draft of 107 men from India and the arrival of seven officers enabled the 1/6th to end 1917 with 28 officers and 860 other ranks for duty. By this time its Division was fully organized and complete in all respects and ready to take the field. It was likely to be needed for active work, as before the end of December the Seventh (Meerut) Division had left Mesopotamia for Palestine.

The 2/7th had left Jubbulpore, whither they had moved in March 1916 from Secunderabad, in April 1917, expecting to be sent to Egypt, but their departure was postponed and their destination changed to Mesopotamia, for which 23 officers and 859 other ranks embarked at Bombay on September 5th, Lt. Colonel Smith being in command. He had joined from England in July, replacing Lt. Colonel Maturin, originally O.C. ' A Company ', who had succeeded Lt. Colonel Gott in February 1916 but had since transferred to the R.A.M.C. Major Gribbon, the original Adjutant, had gone to Mesopotamia in February 1916 : Major Boucher had been promoted to command a Garrison Battalion in

---

[1] Colonel Playfair followed later but was invalided in October. Captain A. W. M. Addison was now Adjutant in place of Major Bowers.
[2] After 1922, 3/11th Sikhs, 10/1st Punjab and 10/4th Bombay Grenadiers.

January 1917 and Captain Palmer of B was the only original company commander remaining, Captain Davenport having gone to the ' 1/7th ' to become Adjutant. Several officers had transferred to other units or taken drafts to Mesopotamia and barely half the ' originals ' were still with the battalion.

Reaching Basra on September 11th the battalion was sent on by river to Qurna, thence by train to Amara, by river again to Kut and by train to Azizieh, where it arrived on September 16th, relieving the 1st O.B.L.I., about to join an Eighteenth Division, now being formed. Azizieh did not prove attractive, flat country covered with liquorice scrub, 18 inches high, nor was it much of a ' health resort ', 144 men being already in hospital by October 1st, though before the end of the month the number was reduced by half. Early in October the battalion lost Lt. Colonel Smith, who died of heart failure, he had done it good service both in its Volunteer and Territorial days. Major Gribbon now transferred from the 1/4th to take command and several new officers joined, including Captains Campbell and A. L. F. Smith from the 9th Hampshire, and the battalion was kept busy training and working on the river banks while companies were in turn detailed for duty with an Azizieh Mobile Column.

Of the battalions still in India, the 1/5th, 1/7th and 1/9th, the 1/5th remained at Agra throughout 1917, though two companies spent the hot weather at Chakrata and one was for a time at Delhi, where trouble was anticipated. January 1918 brought a move, but to Burma, not to an active area.

The 1/7th had also sent two companies to the hills during the hot weather, to Kasauli, head-quarters remaining at Ambala. Drafts amounting to 190 men joined, but 100 men were transferred to the 2/7th on their departure for Mesopotamia. December brought orders to mobilize for active service and on January 1st 1918, 21 officers and 717 other ranks left for Aden, where a ' little war ' had been going quietly on since early in 1915, over 250 of all ranks under Major Keene being left behind as a depot.

The 1/9th had left Bangalore in December 1916 for the Frontier, being posted to the Sixteenth Indian Division and stationed between Rawal Pindi and Peshawar. Here the battalion had strenuous training in mountain warfare in a pleasant climate, cold nights and warm days. It moved to the Simla hills in March but returned to the Plains in June, taking over quarters at Ferozepore. It had mobilized in April for employment in Waziristan but much to its disappointment it was not required. Colonel Johnson was still in command but not even he could prevail on the authorities to give the 1/9th the active service it desired.

CHAPTER XXIII

SALONICA, 1917

THE winter of 1916–1917 passed uneventfully in Macedonia, neither 10th or 12th Hampshire having anything of importance to record. The collapse of Roumania had put a stop to any immediate prospect of resuming the offensive from Salonica, and neither on the Struma or on the Doiran-Vardar front could any tactical advantage be gained by local attacks, certainly not on the Twenty-Sixth Division's front, where such information as its patrols gathered merely emphasized how forbiddingly formidable were the defences confronting us. However, General Sarrail still hankered after renewing offensive operations and when the proposal was eventually adopted it was at this very point that the British were required to attack. Strategically it may have offered greater possibilities for the exploitation of success, had the tactical situation made success attainable, let alone likely.

Despite the strategical stalemate opportunities of harassing the enemy were not altogether neglected. The Twenty-Seventh Division was holding the front between Lake Tahinos and the sea with one brigade, the others carrying on upstream of the lake as far as Orlyak Bridge, while advanced posts held Karakaska, Kispekei and Ada and were active in patrolling towards Beglik Mahale and Salmah. Occasional brushes with the enemy occurred, which have been described as ' excellent training ' and proved incidentally that Turks had replaced Bulgarians on the Lower Struma. The 10th Hampshire, after spending the first half of January at Suhabanja, then moved to Ago-mah and were responsible for Ada and Karakaska, occasionally pushing patrols out to Salmah and Beglik Mahale in hopes of ambushing scouts or patrols. Their efforts at stirring up the Turk earned the approval of their new Brigadier and Divisional Commander,[1] but though several casualties were inflicted on the enemy in minor encounters, he was chary of coming too close and gave the battalion few chances. ' He is clever at lying doggo whilst the cavalry look round and then is ready for the infantry patrols ' one account writes, and bad weather, snow and then rain, also restricted activities. A draft of 270 other ranks had joined the 10th in January, and with the mosquito inactive during the colder months the sick-rate declined, indeed returns from hospital brought the battalion nearly up to establishment, if ' employments ' and leave parties reduced other ranks actually present down below 900. From February 10th to March 16th the 10th were in reserve, in quite comfortable quarters at Suhabanja, and even after they relieved the D.C.L.I. in front line at Osman Kamilla, where head-quarters remained till the middle of June, they had little active employment : the spring offensive did not extend to the Struma front, where some minor operations were undertaken as a diversion, but the Twenty-Seventh Division was not involved, while on the failure of the offensive these operations also were aban-

[1] Brigadier General Maynard and Major General Forestier-Walker.

288

doned and the enemy did not attempt any counter-stroke. If incidents of note were few and the battalion had no chances in action, it was some compensation that only one battle casualty was recorded in the first half of the year, one missing on patrol. Sandfly fever caused some trouble but on the whole the sick-rate was low.

The 12th Hampshire had also passed the first quarter of the year with little to vary the usual routine, if there was always plenty of work to be done on the trenches and communications. They moved to and fro between front line and reserve at regular intervals. Both sides indulged in intermittent shelling, but the battalion's casualties had not reached double figures before it went back well behind the line in the second half of March for special training. One company had made a demonstration on February 9th, partly intended to draw the enemy's fire and make him disclose his dispositions before the 10th Devons raided the Petit Couronné next day; a raid which cost that battalion over 120 casualties but inflicted even heavier losses before failure of ammunition forced a withdrawal. In retreating through the Hampshire's position on Rockley and Silbury Hills, the Devons drew down a heavy barrage, but almost innocuously, the Hampshire having only two casualties. ' Work on front and main line continued : intermittent reciprocal shelling ', is a typical entry in the battalion diary for this period. Snipers were fairly active but neither side gave them many chances.

After a fortnight in the training camp the battalion was in reserve behind the front, finding working parties for the R.E. and continuing training, while its patrols examined the Jumeaux Ravine which an attack would have to cross, and then, after dark on April 23rd, the 12th moved up for the Division's attack on the formidable positions it had so long been facing.

In this attack the 79th Brigade was on the right, from the Lake to the Petit Couronné, which the Devons were again tackling, the 12th Hampshire's objective, ' O.3 ', being East of the Petit Couronné and astride a wide gully, Wylye Ravine. On their right the 7th Wiltshire were attacking ' O.1 ' and ' O.2 ' next the lake. Beyond the Devons the 78th Brigade was attacking, and on its left the Twenty-Second Division was tackling some detached works nearer Krastali.[1]

Nobody who had faced the Petit Couronné and the neighbouring defences for several months could have had any illusions about the desperate character of the venture. Our bombardment had done little damage to the formidable Bulgarian defences, their trenches having largely been blasted from the solid rock, the wire had not been very effectively cut and our guns had quite failed to master or silence those of the enemy, who had every advantage in observation and knew the ranges to a nicety. It is indeed difficult to understand how this sector should ever have been selected for an attack. Whatever the strategical arguments in favour of choosing it, without an overwhelming artillery superiority, which we did not possess, to have achieved success here against fighters as

---

[1] See sketch 26 (p. 154).

T   H.R. II.

stubborn and skilful as the Bulgarians would have bordered on the miraculous.
It was about the last place in the line where an attack promised to be successful,
but General Sarrail was insistent on it. It was not French troops whom he was
pitting against this position.

By 8.15 p.m. on April 24th the 12th Hampshire started moving forward, to
be caught by the enemy's barrage half an hour before ' Zero ', 9.45 p.m., and so
prevented from reaching their assembly position, a sunken road between Swindon and Silbury Hills, before our barrage lifted. When they did advance they
promptly came under very heavy fire. The steep and rocky sides of the narrow
Jumeaux Ravine doubled the effect of the bursting shells, creating an absolute inferno ; the Devons' rear companies, just ahead of the Hampshire, were
disordered and shattered, being unable to advance they blocked the way and
the ravine was soon congested with dead and wounded. The enemy's guns took
full advantage of their chance and poured in shell after shell. Nevertheless the
Hampshire's [1] right company somehow struggled gallantly forward, some officers
and men actually getting through the wire and gaining a foothold in O.3, only
to have the Bulgarian barrage brought down on them and to be enfiladed from
their right, where the Wiltshire had made only the slenderest lodgement near
the lake. Colonel Koebel endeavoured to bring the Hampshire's left company
across to support the right but there was no advancing through so intense
and concentrated a barrage. Casualties were heavy, Colonel Koebel himself
was among the wounded, and while the handful in the enemy's lines, unsupported and outnumbered, were killed or taken, the remnants of the battalion
were driven back by the shelling to the sunken road, where they rallied.
Captain Prior now took command and about 70 men were eventually collected
here, with a smaller party on Rocky Knoll. Meanwhile the Devons' leading
companies had established themselves on the Petit Couronné and were holding
on ; parties of the 78th Brigade had also made lodgements further West, and
while these detachments struggled hard to maintain their gains, beating back
several attacks, the D.C.L.I., the supporting battalion, tried vainly to reach
the Devons. Some Hampshires prepared to advance again with the D.C.L.I.,
but they were ordered to await reinforcements from the Divisional reserve.
Before these could intervene counter-attacks had dislodged the 78th Brigade,
the Devons, with both flanks exposed, could not possibly maintain their
precarious foothold on the Petit Couronné, and they had to be ordered back.
Still, though itself a disastrous failure, the Twenty-Sixth Division's attack had
contributed to distract the enemy's attention from the Twenty-Second, who had
captured their objectives and retained them, despite counter-attacks. But the
79th Brigade had been cut to pieces, the 12th Hampshire having 15 officers and
249 men hit, the Devons over 400 and the Wiltshire over 300. Of the Hampshire Captain Graham-Montgomery, Lt. Jarvis and 2/Lts. Bench, Gibaud
and Tidy were missing, almost certainly killed,[2] the C.O., Captain Mitchell,
Lts. Baker, Lewis and Stuart and 2/Lts. Biggar, Kellaway, Norman,

---

[1] A and B were leading with D as moppers up and C in reserve.
[2] None of them were reported as prisoners.

Vincent and Willis being wounded.[1] They had been asked to attempt the impossible.

Next day saw the much reduced battalion in camp at Piton Rocheux. Major Barry returned from leave and took command and drafts amounting to 100 men joined from an Entrenching Battalion but the brigade was unfit for any further activity. It was accordingly ordered to take over the 'Independent Brigade's' frontage on the Krusha Ridge East of Lake Doiran, a really 'quiet' sector, where its sadly shattered battalions might recover strength and efficiency.

Both Hampshire battalions in the B.S.F. were to pass the rest of 1917 uneventfully. The 10th found Osman Kamilla quiet, the enemy being inactive : they were well off for quarters, and until with the warmer weather the mosquito re-appeared and with it malaria the battalion's numbers remained high; on April 30th other ranks present numbered 874, though by June they were down to 840.

With June came orders to withdraw across the Struma to a 'summer line' along the hills West of it. This involved removing all portable trench stores, R.E. material and equipment, while the line had to be dismantled and made useless to the enemy. Not much was left behind when on June 15th head-quarters quitted Osman Kamilla for Nigoslav, the battalion's summer camp. B and C Companies under Major Davies remained behind for 24 hours, in hope of catching the inquisitive, but then withdrew unmolested across the river at Gudeli Bridge to rejoin head-quarters.

Despite this withdrawal to the hills some posts were maintained along the Struma. Some bridge-heads were held and occasionally parties crossed the river in hopes of an encounter. Thus on June 24th A and D Companies under Major Davies occupied Osman Kamilla for a night, without however having the satisfaction of a fight, and two companies were for a time forward at Demetric, holding posts along the river. Major Cowland had been transferred to the 12th Battalion early in June and in July Major Davies left to take command of a battalion in the Twenty-Second Division, Major Mackay of the Argyll and Sutherlands replacing him. Colonel Beckett, Major Davies, Captains Nicholson and Clement, Lt. Dupree, Sergeant Hodge and Privates Lane and Walker were 'mentioned' in General Milne's despatches of March 29th 1917, and Colonel Beckett was given a Brevet as Lt. Colonel, Captains Nicholson and Clement receiving the M.C.

July, August and September left the situation unchanged, almost the only incident being a satisfactory encounter on September 6th when B Company, which had occupied Osman Kamilla over-night, inflicted 20 casualties on a Bulgarian patrol, having only two men hit. Some inconvenience was caused by a water shortage, the supply in the camp being so scanty that the battalion had to go down to the Struma to bathe and wash clothes. The sick rate,

---

[1] Most of the wounded were brought in, the Bulgarians doing little to interfere with their removal.

though fairly high,[1] was much lower than in 1916, though any great exertion tended to provoke relapses in former sufferers from malaria. However, the medical authorities had learnt much about methods of combating malaria and the troops benefitted thereby. Thus with some small drafts the battalion's strength was fairly well maintained, and though on September 30th 130 other ranks on the strength were away from the battalion, with twelve officers out of 30, it had still 810 men present.

By this time the Sixteenth Corps was preparing to re-occupy a forward line, and on October 3rd battalion head-quarters evacuated Hill Camp to join the two companies already in the Gudeli Bridge sector. From this frequent patrols crossed the river to visit Osman Kamilla, Agomah and other points, bringing in useful information but without encountering any enemy. Meanwhile a ' bund ' was being built along the river from Gudeli to Komarjan Bridge, which meant some hard work.

The new ' winter line ' was not to be as far forward as in 1916-1917 but, as a preliminary to the construction of a line of redoubts, Agomah, Osman Kamilla, the Karajakois and Homondos were to be re-occupied, the 81st Brigade tackling the last two, the most formidable part of the work, while mainly to cover its operations the 82nd was to occupy Osman Kamilla on its right with the old line of works between it and Homondos. Crossing Gudeli Bridge at 10 p.m. on October 13th, by 2 a.m. the Hampshire had occupied Osman Kamilla unopposed, whereupon D Company and half A established themselves in the old line of works, B and the other half of A pushing on to the Belitsa stream, two miles ahead, to get touch with the 81st Brigade's right.

Thus secured, the 81st Brigade attacked Homondos [2] most successfully, capturing the village in fine style with 180 prisoners, besides inflicting casualties considerably exceeding its own losses, well under 50. The covering party had encountered no opposition, finding some works along the stream unoccupied. The reconstruction of the redoubt line was then taken in hand and by the evening of October 18th it had been completed, without giving the Hampshire any fighting, though the men had hard work in cold weather and had had no chance of drying their clothes, which had been drenched by heavy rain on the first night. The Hampshire, not being required to man the redoubts, were now able to re-cross the Struma.

A fortnight later they were more actively employed, when the 82nd Brigade raided Ada, Kispeki and Salmah.[3] Leaving Gudeli Bridge at 10 p.m. on October 24th, the 10th Camerons (Lovat's Scouts) and 2½ companies of the Hampshire were to pass East of Salmah and assault that village at 6 a.m. On their left the rest of the Hampshire and the Gloucesters under Colonel Beckett were attacking Ada and Kispeki from the rear. The ground was thickly wooded, with dense undergrowth in places, while heavy rain had made heavy going, many streams

---

[1] Admissions to hospital from May 1st to September 30th averaged ten a week, mainly malaria but swelled in July by an outbreak of sandfly fever.

[2] Its main column crossed the Belitsa below Homondos and wheeling round attacked the village from the NE. in rear.

[3] See Sketch 27 (p. 148).

swollen by recent rains had to be waded and the left column, moving by Osman Kamilla, found movement especially slow and difficult, while it was further delayed by having to deal with outposts near Ada. These were captured, but the encounter made the column too late to intercept the retreating defenders of Ada and Kispeki, most of whom, having taken the alarm, got away, though a Hampshire company with the right column, pushing on after Salmah had been cleared, reached Kispeki before all the garrison had withdrawn. The fighting for Salmah had been quite fierce, but before a combined frontal and flank attack the defence had collapsed. If the bulk of the enemy had got away, over 100 prisoners had been taken altogether and 70 Bulgars killed, the total British casualties being under 80, including nine Hampshires wounded, a small cost for so successful an affair.

For another fortnight the battalion remained in this sector, in good billets at Badimal but spending most of the daylight hours working on the redoubts in the forward line. Captains Clement and Gibson now left to join the Indian Army, Captains Griffiths and Mayne taking over C and D Companies, and then on November 11th the battalion started for the mouth of the Struma, where the 82nd Brigade was taking over the line the 80th had been holding for nearly two years almost without any fighting. The relief took some time as it had to be carried out in half-battalion moves by the units in reserve.

The British line here lay across the Struma and was nearer the enemy's than in the sectors higher upstream, but though our patrols were active and soon became familiar with their new piece of country, they rarely encountered the enemy, who except for occasional shelling showed little signs of activity, while our troops mainly employed themselves in improving the line, particularly by constructing galleries in which the whole trench garrison could find shelter. The end of the year found the battalion with 23 officers and 727 men actually present, another six officers and 101 men, though reckoned in the effective strength, being away.

Shortly after the 79th Brigade reached its new line another attack on the Doiran front on May 8th had uselessly involved the Twenty-Sixth Division in further crippling casualties, though the Twenty-Second had again profited by the diversion to improve its position. The sacrifices General Sarrail had demanded of the Twenty-Sixth Division were the more inexcusable because no major Allied offensive had been developed West of the Vardar, to which they might have served as diversions, the only real justification indeed for demanding the attempting of such unpromising ventures. A feeble effort had not been pressed and was soon broken off, and with that the Allied force at Salonica relapsed into over a twelvemonth of inactivity. Two British Divisions, the Tenth and Sixtieth, were now detailed as part of the reinforcements General Allenby was demanding before he would resume the offensive in Palestine, which had been so disastrously checked at Gaza (April 19th), at so high a cost to the 8th Hampshire. This reduction of the B.S.F. meant that no resumption of the offensive in Macedonia was to be expected and that meanwhile the 10th and 12th Battalions were to be left in what now became a more complete back-water than ever.

On moving East of Doiran the 12th Hampshire had gone first to Sal Grec Avancé, where they were joined by five officers and 309 men; without any time to absorb this large draft they had then had to relieve the 2nd East Yorkshire in the left centre of the frontage, from Popovo Dere on the left to a point opposite Caukli. In front stretched a wide and open plain through which the Salonica–Constantinople railway ran, with the Belashitza range behind it. Villages dotted this plain, Erdzili, Bulamac, Akindzali and others, the enemy's main position being further in rear and some distance away, with only outposts or even patrols in these villages. So wide a No Man's Land

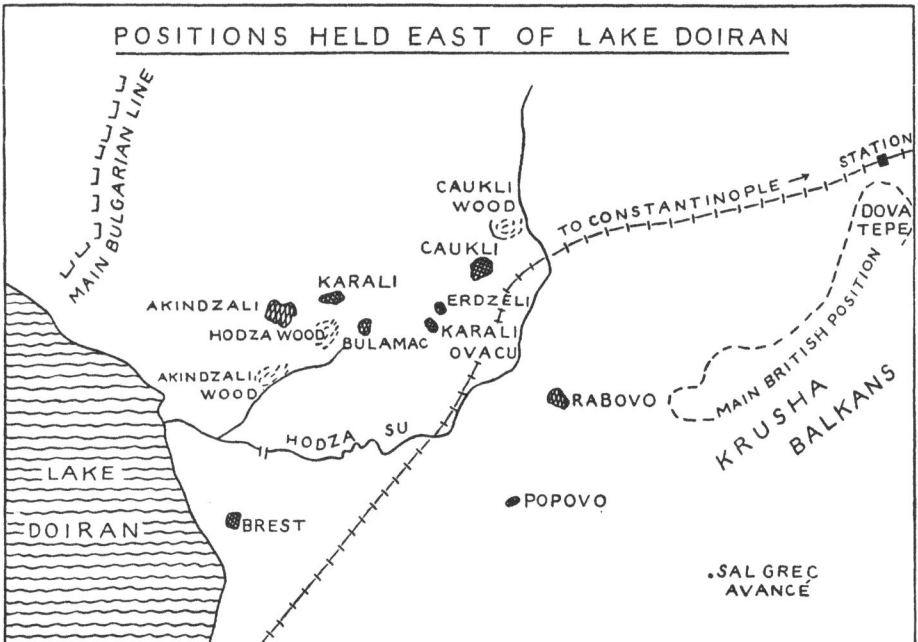

POSITIONS HELD EAST OF LAKE DOIRAN

invited patrol activities, but the enemy gave few openings and the 12th spent three uneventful weeks without any contact with the Bulgarians, during which time Lt. Colonel Lindesay, formerly of the 35th Sikhs, joined and took command, Major Barry going off soon afterwards to command a Garrison Battalion of the Irish Fusiliers.

But the 12th were not to stay long in this sector. On the Sixtieth Division's departure for Palestine the sector next the Vardar, which it had been holding, was taken over by the 79th Brigade, so that June found the 12th Hampshire with their left on that river and facing Macukovo. The enemy's line was fairly strong, but here also No Man's Land was wide and gave scope for patrol activi-ties, and while an unenterprising enemy rarely ventured far enough to meet our patrols, these acquired much information about his dispositions and defences.

Here the battalion alternated with the 10th Devons in holding the line and being in reserve, when it was in a pleasantly sited camp on a hill overlooking the Vardar. In one tour in front line at the end of June a patrol under Captain Hubback encountered the enemy at Piton l'Eglise, having three men wounded. Next day (June 27th) another party under Captain Mitchell drove the enemy's outpost off Piton l'Eglise and held that point to cover a patrol which searched Macukovo without much result. A small party remained behind in hopes of ambushing the enemy should he seek to re-occupy the Piton, but neither it nor two others which in turn remained out for 24 hours found the Bulgarian so obliging as to let himself be caught, though he was again driven from the Piton on June 28th by another patrol, while on July 1st a party under Captain Mitchell which had been searching Macukovo found the enemy again holding the Piton and cleared them off, capturing a machine-gun and many bombs but having Lt. Kininmouth wounded and a sergeant killed.

From July 3rd to 17th the battalion was in reserve. Lts. Stuart and Lewis and 2/Lts. Biggar, Vincent and Willis, all wounded on April 24th, had returned from hospital and Major Cowland had joined from the 10th Battalion as second in command, while several new subalterns had reported for duty. The battalion then had ten days in the Reselli sector, during which one company got heavily shelled though it escaped with only trifling casualties, and after a fortnight's training near Ardyan the end of August found the brigade back at the Krusha Balkans, becoming the Independent Brigade again. A draft of 100 men had joined the battalion on August 26th.

The battalion found its old position at Sal Grec Avancé quite a pleasant change of scene, forests of pine varied with some oak scrub and beech trees, with fine but distant views of the Grand Couronné across the lake and of the Belashitza mountains towering up in front. This quarter was as quiet as ever, if much work was needed on the defences. With a long frontage, the line had to be held by posts at wide intervals and to go round it was a lengthy affair, even for a mounted officer. Patrols went out constantly and collected plenty of information about No Man's Land, but encounters with the enemy were infrequent. He once tried a raid in some force but not against the line the Hampshire were holding : the experiment was not repeated. A few Bulgarian deserters gave themselves up, but little occurred to vary the normal routine of 'Quiet on our front. Work on the trenches and paths'. The weather became much colder towards the end of September and with that the mosquito became less active, having before this sent many men to hospital.

Early in October five Hampshire platoons under Captain Mitchell co-operated with eight of the Wiltshire, who were raiding Akindzali, by pushing through Bulamac into Karaki, leaving a platoon at Karaki Ovace as flank-guard. The Bulgarians were completely surprised, thanks to the steadiness and quietness of the raiders, and the raid proved most successful, the main opposition being met by the Wiltshire SW. of Akindzali and effectively overcome, the Hampshire carrying out their covering function without incurring casualties.

October saw the battalion busy over preparing a forward ' winter line ', as the mosquito's departure for his winter quarters was making the lower ground tenable again ; it was now turning quite cold, a third blanket being issued to all ranks in November, when the Belashitza range was capped in snow and severe frosts occurred, precautions were also taken against ' trench feet ', such as issuing whale oil, while the woods provided plenty of fuel. On the whole rations were good ; some canteen stores were procured, with fairly liberal supplies of a local product which could pass for beer, and in November a rum issue was authorised. Periods in reserve, largely devoted to work on the roads, allowed of musketry practice and some recreation, mainly football, while those in front line were quiet. Occasionally the enemy did a little shelling, usually when provoked by British patrol activities, which were well maintained. Occasionally again we indulged in something more extensive ; thus on December 8th, the D.C.L.I. raided Caukli Wood, six platoons under Major Cowland occupying Bulamac and Erdzili as left flank-guard. This was done without opposition, the Bulgarian outposts decamping hastily. The allotted positions were duly held for the time arranged, but without enticing the enemy to counter-attack, while the retirement was made in excellent order and with only one casualty, despite heavy shelling. A most successful smaller raid on December 18th by D Company surprised and captured an entire sentry group at Hodza Bridge, thanks largely to the good leading of 2/Lt. Willis, the Intelligence Officer, who received an ' immediate ' M.C.

The end of the year found the 79th Brigade still holding the Krusha Balkans sector, with its patrols definitely on top in No Man's Land. The 12th Hampshire had had plenty of time to recover from their shattering experiences at Doiran and in Colonel Lindesay they had an admirable commander who had done much for the battalion.

CHAPTER XXIV

PALESTINE, 1917

THIRD GAZA AND JERUSALEM

GENERAL Allenby's plan for the new offensive in Palestine did not involve an immediate assault on the Gaza defences which the three Hampshire battalions in the Twenty-First Corps were facing. Its part was rather to hold in check the strong Turkish right wing in and about Gaza, whose positions would, however, be heavily bombarded from land and sea, as if an attack on them was coming off at once. Actually any assault was to await the upshot of the move of the Desert Mounted Corps and the Twentieth Corps against Beersheba. If that succeeded, the Twenty-First Corps would strike in to assist the other two Corps to go ahead with the next stage, the rolling up of the Turkish line from its left.

The Hampshire battalions had therefore no active part in the opening stages of ' Third Gaza ', but the situation had soon developed so favourably that, to exploit the success at Beersheba and to prevent reserves being transferred to reinforce the endangered Turkish left, Gaza had to be attacked. Accordingly on November 2nd the Fifty-Fourth Division with the 156th Brigade (Fifty-Second Division) on its right attacked the defences between the Rafa road and the sea. These were strong and elaborate, and the gardens on the outskirts with their cactus hedges and enclosures added strength to the position, but it had been subjected to the heaviest bombardment yet known outside the Western Front and had been effectively battered.

The 163rd Brigade was attacking in the centre, the 5th Suffolk (right) having the El Arish Redoubt as their objective, while the 8th Hampshire were tackling Burj Trench and Redoubt, after whose capture the two Norfolk battalions would push through to secure a rear line running South from Island Wood. Before the main attack the 156th Brigade was to capture Umbrella Hill, an outpost from which the Turks could have enfiladed the attack. This was accomplished by midnight (November 1st/2nd), before which the 8th Hampshire, 21 officers and 609 men under Major Vincent,[1] were already in their assembly position.

The attack on Umbrella Hill provoked some retaliatory shelling, but the Hampshire escaped casualties and at midnight moved up to the point of deployment at Halfway House, arriving there before 2 a.m., though rifles and machine-guns had caused some casualties. At 3 a.m. the advance began : almost at once a heavy barrage came down, causing loss and some confusion in A Company on the right and in B and D in second line, with consequent loss of direction. Two platoons of A, diverging to their right, entered and captured Triangle Trench, part of the Suffolk's objective, taking a gun and 35 prisoners. The rest of A with C on their left kept the true line and reached and carried

---

[1] It was Colonel Marsh's turn to be with the ' battle nucleus ', left out of action.

Burj Trench and Burj Redoubt, while the second wave, bearing to the left, entered Zowaid Trench North of Burj Trench. Efforts to push on to the next line came under heavy enfilade fire from strong points at 'Gibraltar' and Crested Rock, and though some men reached the objective it proved to consist of mere scoops in the sand without parapets or parados, virtually untenable. Accordingly those who had advanced so far fell back to assist in consolidating the more defensible first line captured. Parties of the 5th Norfolk now passed through and established themselves at several points in the second line of defence, but the 4th Norfolk had mostly gone off to the right and joined the Suffolk in El Arish Redoubt. Eventually the brigade settled down to secure the front line from El Arish Redoubt Northward, to find consolidation in the sand far from easy, while the Turkish snipers were troublesome and their shell-fire at times heavy. On the flanks the attack had fared better, the 156th Brigade having secured its share of El Arish Redoubt, while the 161st on the left, passing over the Beach Post–Sea Post line, had swung round to take Rafa Redoubt and Rafa Trench, North of the line attacked by the 163rd Brigade. This success allowed the 162nd to go through and carry the line forward to Sheikh Hasan on the coast, 3000 yards beyond our original front at Sheikh Ajlin and so far NW. of Gaza as to threaten the garrison's retreat, and though for the moment the Turks had prevented any further advance in this direction, their counter-attacks had been heavily punished.

During the day consolidation was continued, Hampshires and Norfolks being sorted out, while the two platoons from Triangle Trench rejoined. The Turks were still shelling the captured positions and were holding their lines in some force. Our men had something to shoot at and at one time ammunition seemed to be running short, but great efforts by carrying parties made up the supply to 150 rounds a man and more bombs were brought up, as well as materials for improving the defences, rations and water. Until November 5th the battalion remained in position, consolidating, improving communications and reducing the Turks to inactivity by good sniping and the effective use of Lewis guns. Shelling swelled the casualty list slightly, but by November 5th the position was so well established that B and D Companies could be withdrawn for a wash and rest, while that evening the battalion shifted to the left, taking over Rafa Redoubt and Zowaid Trench from the 162nd Brigade, which was being concentrated to renew the attack.

This it did early on November 7th, advancing against the line Rafa-Belah to meet no opposition, whereupon Colonel Marsh, who had come forward and resumed command, pushed patrols forward, to find Island Wood and Zowaid Copse empty but for Turkish dead. Gaza had been evacuated and, though the Seventy-Fifth Division had some fighting when it also pushed forward, the town proved empty. The 8th Hampshire were now withdrawn into reserve to rest and reorganize.

Casualties had been heavy, for resistance had been stiff ; Captains Coke and Scarborough (3rd Devons), 2/Lts. Poulter (Queen's) and Wallace and 73 men were killed or died of wounds or were missing, Lt. Cross (Wiltshire),2/Lts.

Roper and Rycroft and 135 men were wounded, a third of the officers and men in action. Other units of the Fifty-Fourth Division had also lost heavily, but 500 prisoners had been taken and over 1000 Turkish dead were buried, while the attack had achieved its object and the way into Palestine now lay open.

Meanwhile the advance from Beersheba was developing fairly well, though delayed and impeded by difficulties over finding water for men and horses and by the rough and intricate country to be crossed. November 6th saw the strong defences astride the Beersheba railway at Tel es Sheria captured, whereupon the Turks evacuated the rest of their position. In hopes of intercepting the retreat of the defenders of Gaza, the troops who had turned and broken through the Gaza-Beersheba line were now directed Northward and Westward, while

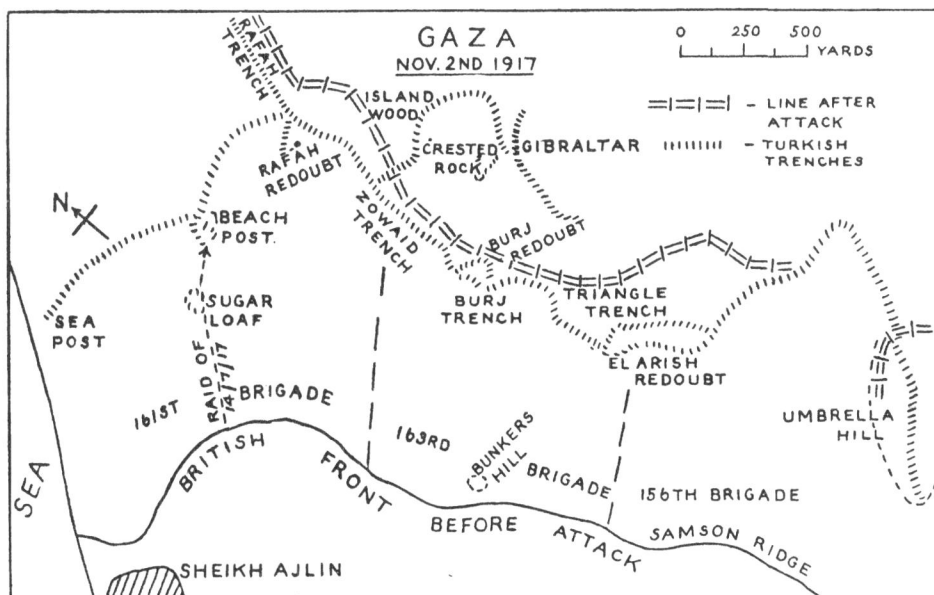

GAZA
NOV. 2ND 1917

0   250   500
|__|__|__|__| YARDS

=|=|=| — LINE AFTER ATTACK

IIIIIIII — TURKISH TRENCHES

N

ISLAND WOOD

RAFAH REDOUBT

CRESTED ROCK   GIBRALTAR

BEACH POST

NOWAID TRENCH

BURJ REDOUBT

SEA POST

SUGAR LOAF

RAID OF 14/7/17

BURJ TRENCH

TRIANGLE TRENCH

EL ARISH REDOUBT

UMBRELLA HILL

161ST BRIGADE

BRITISH

FRONT

163RD BRIGADE

BUNKERS HILL BRIGADE

156TH BRIGADE

SEA

BEFORE ATTACK

SAMSON RIDGE

SHEIKH AJLIN

the Twenty-First Corps was to advance in pursuit as soon as the return of its transport, which had been lent to the Twentieth, enabled it to move. The Fifty-Fourth Division was, however, temporarily left at Gaza, so that the 8th Hampshire saw nothing of the operations in which the 2/4th and the 2/5th now shared.

When, on November 7th, the evacuation of Gaza was discovered the Seventy-Fifth Division had just been about to attack the defences SE. and East of the town. The 233rd Brigade had promptly occupied Outpost Hill and pushed forward by Green Hill into Gaza, meeting only trifling opposition, so that the 2/4th Hampshire, in brigade reserve, had not been engaged but merely pushed on to take up an outpost line at Fryer's Hill beyond Gaza, which was harmlessly shelled, no casualties being caused. Meanwhile the 232nd Brigade, with two companies of the 2/5th Hampshire leading, had moved up to Ali al Muntar under some artillery fire to find that formidable position, which had so long seemed to dominate the surrounding area, evacuated and undefended, on which the 232nd had established itself on the 233rd's right flank and rear. These positions were consolidated during the next two days and then on November 9th the Division started its advance. Transport being short, overcoats, blankets and waterproof sheets had to be left behind.

The 232nd Brigade led the advance and, passing through Beit Hanun, reached Deir Seneid on the Wadi el Hesi before evening. The Fifty-Second

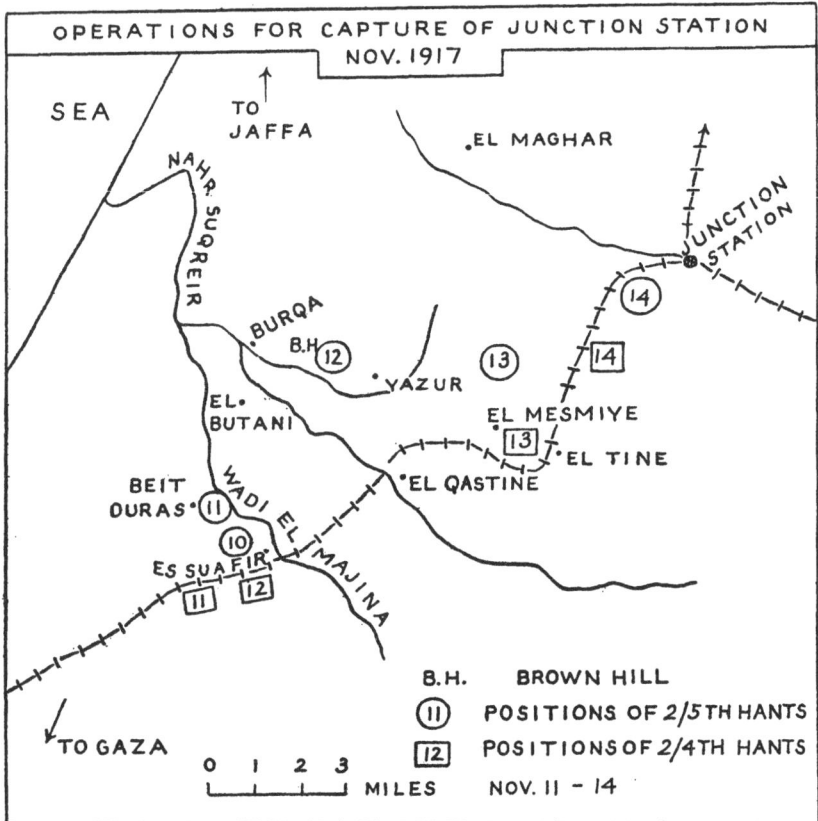

OPERATIONS FOR CAPTURE OF JUNCTION STATION
NOV. 1917

Division had already secured a passage over this obstacle and now pushed the Turks back towards the Nahr Suqreir, the next big watercourse, some way up the coast. The immediate objective was now Junction Station, where the railways from Jerusalem and Beersheba unite ; its capture would split off the Turkish Eighth Army in the coast plain from their Seventh Army, which had been pushed back into the Judæan Hills, West and SW. of Jerusalem. This Seventh Army was actually on the right flank of the British advance up the coast, but its formations had suffered severely in the battles for Beersheba and we could thrust forward up the coast plain under cover of a right flank guard without any apprehension of a counter-attack descending from the hills.

November 10th brought the 232nd Brigade to Suafir el Garbiyeh on the Wadi el Majina which flows into the Nahr Suqreir from the South. Here it was covering the Fifty-Second's Division's right flank, that Division's leading brigade, already some way ahead, being about to wheel round East towards Junction Station. At Suafir the 2/5th's outposts were in touch with enemy a mile away to the North but the Turks fell back during the night. Meanwhile the 233rd Brigade had also started forward, advancing beyond Beit Hanun.

November 11th saw the Fifty-Second and Seventy-Fifth Divisions closing up on their advanced-guards before swinging Eastwards towards Junction Station, the 2/4th Hampshire coming up nearly to Suafir, while the 2/5th moved slightly forward, halting East of Beit Duras, in touch with the Fifty-Second Division's right. That Division was now ordered to dislodge the Turks from an advanced position across the Nahr Suqreir between Burqa and Yazur. Attempting this next day (November 12th), the 156th Brigade was strongly opposed, and General Huddleston, who was forward with the artillery attached to his brigade who were supporting the attack, asked permission to assist. Accordingly about 1.30 p.m. the 2/5th were sent forward with the 2/3rd Gurkhas on their left through El Butani esh Sherkiyeh to cross the Nahr Suqreir and support the attack. A counter-attack had just dislodged our troops from Brown Hill, but while the Gurkhas reinforced them and attacked that hill directly, the 2/5th pushed forward, with A and C Companies leading, and cleared a ridge East of it, covering the Gurkhas' flank and assisting in the recovery of the hill. Outposts were now put out, and patrols pushed forward to find Yazur unoccupied. The 2/4th meanwhile had come up to Suafir and were on the 232nd Brigade's right rear with outposts on the road to El Qastine.

The attack on Junction Station could now be made, the Seventy-Fifth Division advancing from the SW., the Fifty-Second, with mounted troops covering the left, swinging round to attack more from the West. The 232nd Brigade was on the Seventy-Fifth's left with the 233rd on its right, the first objective being a line running SE. from Yazur to El Qastine. After a second line from El Mesmiye–El Tine on the railway had also been secured, the 234th Brigade was to pass through and make for Junction Station itself.

Starting off at 6 a.m. (November 13th) the 2/5th occupied Yazur unopposed and, pushing on, gained ground to the Eastward despite much machine-gun fire and distant shelling. Little artillery support was available and though progress was made it was rather slow, especially as the 232nd Brigade was ahead of the troops on its left. However, with some support from the 2/3rd Gurkhas the Turks were dislodged from their position, and though they rallied on high ground further back they evacuated this also before morning The 233rd, with the 2/4th in reserve, was delayed by flanking fire from the right, and though it took El Mesmiye nevertheless, despite some resistance,[1] it now fell behind the 232nd, which by employing its reserve battalion, had cleared a ridge North of

[1] The 2/4th remained in reserve but had half a dozen casualties from shell-fire. The casualties of the 2/5th are not given day by day but cannot have been heavy, the month's total of about 100 all told has to include those incurred in the advance on Jerusalem.

El Mesmiye, capturing several machine-guns. Flanking fire from the North checked further progress, but a substantial advance had been made without heavy casualties, though the final objective remained untaken. The Fifty-Second Division meanwhile, after overcoming determined opposition, had come up on the left, and early next morning the 234th Brigade, pushing on, secured Junction Station with a great haul of rolling stock and supplies almost without any fighting.

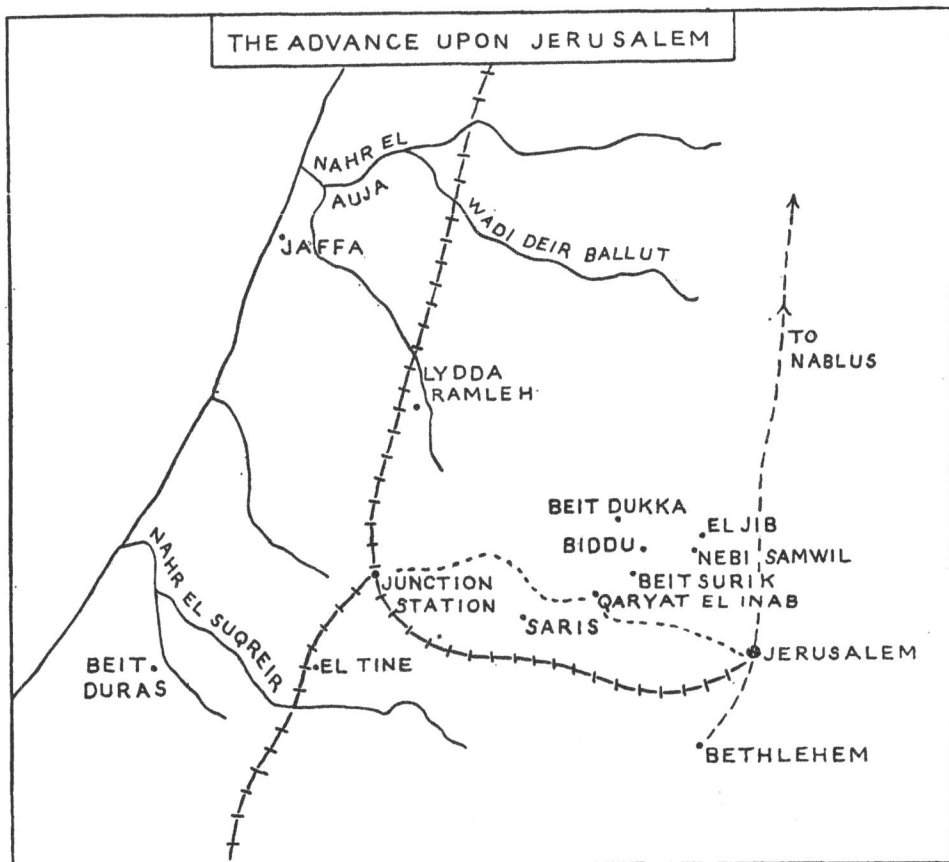

THE ADVANCE UPON JERUSALEM

With the capture of Junction Station a definite stage in the operations ended. While some further progress was made up the coast plain, Jaffa being secured and the Eighth Army pressed back behind the Nahr el Auja, the main body was now to strike Eastward through the Judaean Hills, with Jerusalem as its goal. This, in the bad weather which was now setting in, was to involve great hardships for men still wearing their summer clothing and poorly equipped for rain and cold. The advance was largely a matter of transport and communications, both presenting very considerable difficulties, as the pursuing troops already had reason to know ; if water was no longer the big trouble it had been in the breaking of the Gaza–Beersheba line, quite as formidable problems arose over keeping the attacking troops supplied and getting artillery forward through the rugged hill country ahead. Only one fairly good road leads Eastward from the coast plain to Jerusalem, that by the Valley of Ajalon from near Junction Station, the Jerusalem–Jaffa ' road ' further North being merely a rough track. Still it was urgent to press on without giving the Turks time to reorganize and recover : to take advantage of having got them on the run we could not halt for a ' breather '. The troops were not being called on for more exertions and endurance of hardship without just cause.

The Seventy-Fifth Division was selected to lead the advance by the main road, the Fifty-Second advancing on its left by the Jaffa track. The object was to get across the road to Nablus North of Jerusalem and avoid a direct attack on the city. Starting off early on November 19th, the 232nd Brigade, who led the Division, at first encountered little serious opposition, the enemy having evacuated Latron, though Turks on the hillsides above the road had to be dislodged. This was skilfully done by the 58th Rifles, a Frontier Force regiment, supported by C Company of the 2/5th, B Company also picquetting high ground North of the road. Rain made the ground slippery, and the advanced-guard did very well to get within half a mile of Saris by evening, having covered about ten miles. Resuming the advance next day (November 20th) the 2/5th worked along the hills South of the road to support the attack on Saris, which the 58th Rifles eventually carried about mid-day, D Company having been sharply engaged and having had several casualties in helping to recover ground from which one of the 58th's picquets had been dislodged. Half B had previously reinforced D, while A pushed along a ridge overlooking Saris, which the enemy evacuated about 1.30 p.m. Saris cleared, the 232nd Brigade pressed on towards Qaryat el Enab and, with some support from the 233rd, carried that village before dark, companies of the 2/4th advancing along the ridge North of the road to cover the flank of the main attack. They were now to reap the benefit of their training in mountain warfare at Quetta. Rough ground strewn with big boulders was not made easier going by heavy rain, but, though under heavy fire, the 2/4th pushed steadily on and along with the 4th Wiltshire carried a large house on our left of the objective with only trifling casualties.

Both 2/4th and 2/5th spent a miserable night, cold and wet, in bivouac in olive groves round Qaryat el Enab, and the 2/4th's bivouac was heavily shelled early next morning (November 21st), Major Bulley being wounded and nearly 30 men hit. Later they were ordered forward to assist the 234th Brigade, now advanced-guard, but had to detach D Company to occupy Beit Surik to cover the right flank of the advance, which task it duly carried out, clearing the enemy out. The 2/5th meanwhile remained at Enab where the wheeled transport had to be left, only camels going forward.[1] During the day they advanced SE. to Qustul to see if any enemy were collecting in that direction, but after dislodging a few Turks they returned before dark to Enab, another battalion

---

[1] The wounded had to be brought down in ' cacolets ', wooden cages slung in pairs on the backs of camels, and suffered considerably.

having relieved them at Qustul. They remained at Enab for three days, and though they then moved up to Biddu, they were at once sent back to Enab.

The main advance meanwhile had reached Biddu, beyond which no further move could be made unless the dominating hill of Nebi Samwil, two miles to the Eastward, were secured. This hill, where a mosque contained the traditional tomb of the prophet Samuel, was reckoned the key to Jerusalem,[1] and the vigour of the Turkish efforts to recover it after the 234th Brigade had taken it by a dashing assault was ample evidence of its importance. After dark the 2/4th came forward and took post in support, A and C Companies 150 yards in rear of the Mosque, B and H.Q.[2] a mile further back. The position was shelled during the night, though not counter-attacked, but with morning the shelling increased greatly in intensity and before long counter-attacks developed in some force. The first were quickly repulsed but the Turks came on again in greater force and succeeded in coming to close quarters, though C Company did useful work in carrying up ammunition, which was running short, while B moved up nearer to the hill in readiness to reinforce. Pressure went on increasing, the 2/4th came in for some shell-fire and had several casualties, Captain Simmons being slightly wounded, and before long the 3/3rd Gurkhas, now on the left, were specially hard beset. About 2 p.m. their left was pushed back and the position was only re-established by B Company and battalion H.Q. of the 2/4th who counter-attacked successfully, well led by Captains Ashmore and Price.[3] A and C also reinforced the defence and helped to keep the enemy at bay though under heavy fire, the mosque being a fine mark on which the Turkish guns could range, while their machine-guns were very effective ; B Company on the left was particularly harassed by flanking fire, but led and encouraged by Lt. Weekes it held on unflinchingly. Captain Simmons was hit again, this time fatally, Captain Ashmore was also wounded, but Captain Kirby carried on most effectively, while Sergeant Thompson of A did much to maintain the defence, setting a fine example and leading his platoon forward to fill a gap in the line, where, though much reduced, it kept the enemy at bay.[4]

Once Turks got within bombing range, having got into an orchard in a gap in our line, but a Lewis gunner of C Company did some effective shooting, and eventually as darkness was falling two battalions of the 156th Brigade arrived and counter-attacked most successfully. This counter-attack clinched the good work of the defence by driving the attackers right back, when the exhausted defenders were relieved. Losses had been heavy ; of the 2/4th, who were much below establishment, besides Captain Simmons [5] Lt. Beauchamp also died of wounds, 24 men were killed or missing and Captains Ashmore and Goddard and 2/Lts. Brooks, Gotelee and Phillimore wounded with 80 men. But the

---

[1] The Seventy-Fifth adopted a key as its Divisional sign.
[2] D had not rejoined from Beit Surik.　　　　　　　　　　[3] Adjutant.
[4] He got the D.C.M., which was also given to Private Thomas who had worked a Lewis gun most effectively, moving from place to place where he could do most service.
[5] Captain F. W. Simmons, one of the earliest members of the 2/4th and a fine company commander, was a great loss.

battalion had played a useful part in an operation of real importance, the retention of Nebi Samwil.

The 2/4th now went back into support, where D Company from Beit Surik rejoined next day, having been caught by shell-fire in a wadi on the way and having had 20 casualties, Lt. Fenn being wounded. A move to the left, to Beit Dukka, followed next day and then, on November 25th, the 2/4th rejoined their brigade at Enab. Their Division was now being relieved by the Sixtieth. It was much reduced in numbers and almost exhausted, but it had done great work by taking and holding Nebi Samwil, if it had been unable to capture El Jib, North of Nebi Samwil and almost as important, tactically, in the defence of Jerusalem. Hard work in bad weather had told heavily on the men, their trials being intensified by shortage of rations and by their being in their khaki drill without even waterproof sheets to cover them from the rain. All units had lost heavily and were hardly fit for much more fighting. The 2/4th's total casualties came to over 160, a large proportion out of those actually in action, and if the 2/5th had only lost just over 100 of all ranks, including an officer and 23 men killed or missing, nearly 70 men had had to go to hospital and they also needed rest and much refitting.

Meanwhile the Fifty-Fourth Division had come forward, having had a week's rest at Sheikh Hassan, just North of Gaza. Moving by Ashdud (November 17th) and El Kubeibeh (18th) the 8th Hampshire, now 25 officers and 529 other ranks, took post near Abu Shushed, SE. of Ramleh, on November 19th but soon moved up to reinforce the 162nd Brigade, now East of Lydda and in the centre of the long defensive front now held by the Desert Mounted Corps from the coast to the foothills. This front was but thinly held, but as yet the Turkish Eighth Army had shown little signs of attempting a counter-attack. Active patrolling was undertaken to get early warning of a move, the 8th Hampshire's patrols pushing out to Budrus and Kibbia and taking prisoners in a minor clash. Late in November the anticipated counter-attack did develop and pressed very hard against the troops covering the left flank of the advance against Jerusalem, who were spread in small detachments along a wide front. But the attack did not extend to most of the Fifty-Fourth Division's front and no Hampshire had a share in repulsing it, though on December 1st the 2/4th, who had been lent to the Fifty-Fourth Division and had just relieved the 5th Suffolk, had to face a vigorous local attack.

The 2/4th had just been re-equipped with warm clothing when they had to go into line again, B and C Companies taking over a ridge at Sheikh el Gharwahi, East of Lydda, with A and D further to the right. During the night (November 30th/December 1st) patrols approached near enough to D's line to be bombed and driven away, but it was against B and C that the main attack developed, just after ' stand to '. The two companies [1] had just withdrawn from the exposed forward slope of the ridge, when the Turks suddenly attacked in considerable force. The enemy came on resolutely, backed by overhead

[1] They mustered about 110 all told.

machine-gun fire, but B and C held firm, counter-attacking promptly, helped
by a company of the 3rd Gurkhas, and drove the enemy back after a sharp
fight, inflicting heavy casualties,[1] Captain Kirby leading his men with great
dash and handling the situation excellently.[2] However, the two companies had
to hold on all day under heavy fire and without food or water until relieved
after nightfall by A and D. In this position the 2/4th had to spend a week in
abominable weather. They were very weak, many men having gone sick, D
Company indeed had 42 rifles to 800 yards of front, C, the only reserve, now
consisted of under 20 rifles, while the C.O. had had to go to hospital, and when

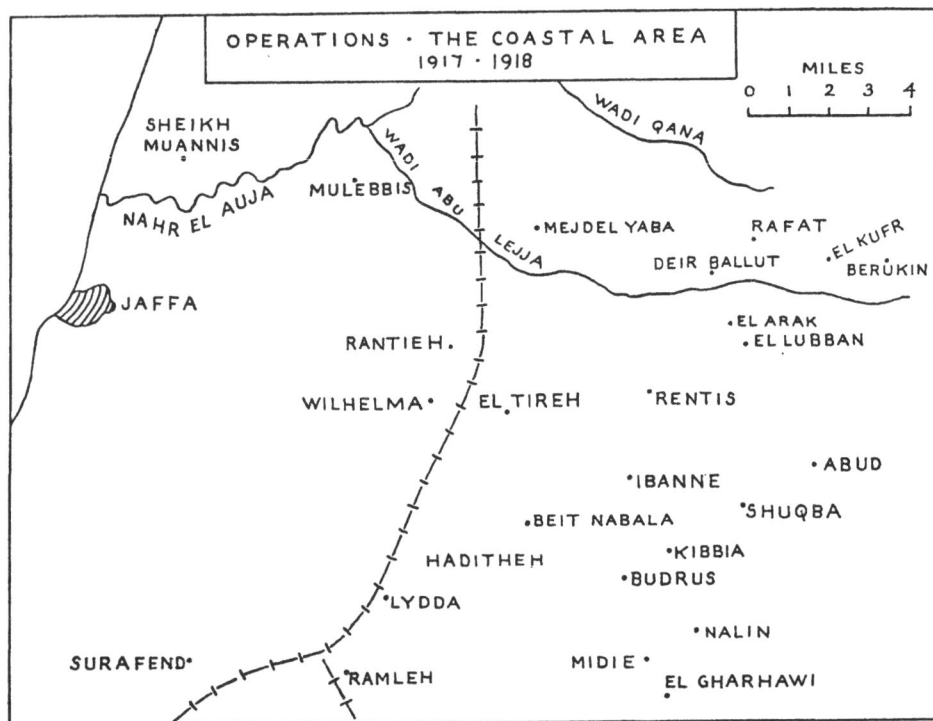

OPERATIONS · THE COASTAL AREA
1917 · 1918

relieved on December 9th by the 2/5th the battalion had only 160 men doing
duty, its fight on December 1st having cost it nine killed and 13 wounded. A
turn in Corps reserve was therefore welcome and wanted.

The 2/5th had had ten days rest before moving up to Ramleh on December
7th, in readiness to go into the line, the Seventy-Fifth Division having taken
over the right sector of the Twenty-First Corps' line, East of the railway running Northward from Lydda, the Fifty-Fourth now being on its left and astride
the line. Jerusalem having by now been taken and the Turks driven back some

[1] Nearly 50 dead Turks were left close in front of the line.
[2] Captain Kirby, who had done great work for the 2/4th, died soon after returning to England,
having undertaken active service at an age at which he should not have served.

distance to the North, no further advance was contemplated, nor could one have been attempted till the communications had been much improved and the administrative services readjusted to the new situation. Some local advances were, however, to be undertaken, notably to push the Turks back further from Jaffa, which could not be used as a port while under shell-fire, and both Fifty-Fourth and Seventy-Fifth Divisions now took part in an advance to secure the line from Kibbia ENE. of Lydda, to El Tireh on the railway, using the 163rd and 232nd Brigades.

Before this part of the 8th's line had been taken over by the 4th Wiltshire to enable the 8th to shift to Beit Nabala and relieve the 5th Bedfordshire there on December 1st. Here again they were holding a longish stretch of the outpost line with three companies in front and, as before, maintained great activity in patrolling, towards Budrus and Sheikh Obeid, both of which points the enemy seemed to be occupying regularly. On December 10th the right and centre companies were relieved by the 232nd Brigade and withdrawn into reserve, to be called upon next day to assist the 4th Norfolk, who were being heavily attacked West of Beit Nabala. This attack did not extend to the 8th's front and Colonel Marsh could spare two companies, but they arrived to find that counter-attacks had driven off the enemy. Then on December 13th the one company still in front line was relieved and the battalion concentrated, ready to attack again on December 15th.

As a preliminary the 232nd Brigade had pushed forward on December 11th, the 2/5th Hampshire occupying Midie and El Arbain virtually unopposed and later pushing patrols out towards Nalin, while the 2/3rd Gurkhas captured Budrus and beat off a counter-attack. This enabled the Divisional artillery to give effective support to a second advance on December 15th towards the Ibanne ridge, the Seventy-Fifth's objective running from Kibbia to Ibanne, whence the Fifty-Fourth carried on to El Tireh. After the 2/3rd Gurkhas had secured the right flank by occupying Kibbia, the 2/5th Hampshire, with the 58th Rifles on their left, pushed rapidly forward across some rocky ground and up a steep hillside and, after clearing the Turks off the Limepit Hill–Cantle Hill ridge, advanced again against the final objective on the ridge behind. Admirably supported by a South African field battery, the two battalions made a most dashing and successful advance, driving the Turks off the ridge and capturing several prisoners and a machine-gun, the 2/5th having only seven casualties.

On the left the 163rd Brigade had also taken its objective but at a much higher cost, the Turks' machine-guns' fire having been heavy and effective, and the 8th Hampshire were lucky in having only eight casualties, despite a sharp fight for Cistern Hill where D Company took some prisoners.

The attack had fully achieved its objects ; by thrusting the Turks back it had cleared the way for the Fifty-Second Division's attempt to cross the Nahr el Auja at its mouth and advance our line well up the coast beyond it. This the Fifty-Second did most successfully on December 21st in one of the best managed and executed minor actions of the Palestine campaigns, one result being that the Fifty-Fourth Division was able to advance its line to the Auja.

This was mainly done by the 162nd Brigade, the 8th Hampshire, who had been relieved on December 17th and had replaced the 162nd Brigade at Wilhelma, a former German settlement, co-operating by taking Round Hill (December 21st) and pushing two companies forward to seize Rantieh, where much booty was collected, at a cost of two casualties. Later the battalion moved to El Tireh.

With this a satisfactory position had been secured in the coast plain. Jaffa could be used for landing stores, which was no small help when the E.E.F's railway and road communications were being strained to the utmost to keep the troops supplied. Bad weather with torrential rains greatly aggravated the difficulties, and for administrative reasons, if for no other, the advance had had to be suspended. Whatever its political value, from the military standpoint the capture of Jerusalem had done little to improve the general situation. At Jerusalem the E.E.F. was still far from the Turkish communications with Mesopotamia, and still further from Constantinople, and though heavy punishment had been inflicted on the Turks, who had counter-attacked North of Jerusalem in great force at the end of December to be decisively repulsed and to suffer crippling losses, nothing had been done thereby to reduce the resisting power of the main enemy, the Germans on the Western Front, while the mere maintaining of its gains seemed likely to tie the E.E.F. up in a theatre of war in which no decision could be reached. The dead-lock in Palestine, which now set in, though mainly caused by administrative reasons, might well have suggested doubts whether the three Hampshire battalions in the E.E.F. were being employed to the best advantage, well as they had done in the different stages of the Beersheba–Jerusalem campaign.

CHAPTER XXV

THE FOURTH WINTER

DESPITE its brilliant start and the heavy punishment inflicted on the Germans, 'Cambrai' had inevitably provoked unpleasant reflections and forebodings. Not only had we failed to develop a promising opening, the strength and vigour of the German counter-stroke boded ill for the future : the reserves which the progress of the Russian revolution had allowed them to throw in foreshadowed the arrival of even bigger reinforcements in the spring, and though the help we might hope for from the U.S.A. might eventually compensate for Russia's defection, if the mills of American preparations were grinding thoroughly and systematically, they were grinding so exceedingly slowly that the Americans might not arrive in time.

This anxiety about the future weighed most heavily upon the Commander in Chief and the C.I.G.S., whose troubles were not decreased by any readiness on the part of the politicians to take the counter-measures the responsible military authorities deemed essential, such as finding reinforcements for France by abstaining from developing offensive activities elsewhere or ' combing out ' the ' reserved occupations ' and taking other steps to produce adequate drafts, but regimental officers and men could form their own opinions about 'Cambrai' and the prospects it suggested, nor did the events of the winter offer much encouragement, one new feature being the increased aggressiveness of the Germans, who were now making many more raids and even tried some quite substantial local attacks. No Hampshires were stationed at points where these last were attempted, but most battalions in France had raids of varying strength and seriousness to meet.

The 1st Hampshire had found their trenches at Monchy in some need of repair, which was not made easier by the attentions of the enemy's trench mortars. Gas shelling on the evening of November 3rd caused some casualties, but early next morning the battalion's left company had the satisfaction of repulsing a raid. Two strong parties advanced after a heavy bombardment, but our rifles and Lewis guns were quick to check them before they could get near and their casualties probably exceeded the ten the bombardment had inflicted. After eight days in line, in which bright moonlight cramped the activities of its patrols, the battalion had a fortnight ' out ', first at Bois les Boeufs, where a welcome reinforcement of 150 men joined, then at Arras, where many working parties were needed. It was in brigade reserve in the Pelves sector from November 24th to 28th and then took over the left sub-sector of the front line from Scabbard Trench to Bit Lane to find that our wire cutting had provoked much retaliation and damage, while a very wet line required constant pumping. A small bombing attack near Harness Lane was beaten off (November 30th), several enemy being hit and others forced to shelter in shell-holes. Four days in the line had produced nearly 20 casualties and admissions to hospital, the latter including Captain N. Harland and Lt. Beatty.

The 1st's next experience of the front line was about one mile ESE. of Monchy. While here between December 6th and 10th another heavy bombardment was followed by an advance which broke down under the battalion's rifle and Lewis guns. Our musketry was being worked up from the very low level of 1916 and during periods out of the line ' bad shots ' were being given range practice, by 1914 standards almost everybody should have been of this party.

Our patrols, usually an officer or N.C.O. with not more than ten men, were active and acquired useful information. It was thought likely that the enemy might venture on an attack, so accurate information was specially needed, while our Lewis guns were assisted to find some good targets in wiring parties. No raids were attempted by or upon the battalion, but on December 20th it had several casualties from a barrage put down to cover a raid on the battalion on its left.

January brought little change; if German activities were less marked the weather was far worse, making conditions in the line most unpleasant; a thaw followed by heavy rain made gum-boots indispensable in the trenches and severely impeded communications, though the Quartermaster managed to send up really hot soup and cocoa at night. Casualties for December and January came to six killed, 25 gassed and 18 wounded; Captain Icke, who was gassed in December, returned to duty but had to be invalided home and Lt. G. R. D. Moor went to the Army School as an Instructor. Drafts, 113 in December and 175 in January, and discharges from hospital, 73 in two months, between them much outnumbered admissions, 214, and several new subalterns appeared.

February the Fourth Division spent in Corps reserve, the battalion thus getting a welcome respite from the trenches, in camp five miles West of Arras. One unpleasant feature of the month was the reduction of brigades to three battalions, a measure which had neither administrative or tactical advantages to recommend it but which was forced on Sir Douglas Haig by sheer necessity, as the War Cabinet insisted on the retention at home of the young soldiers who might have done much more if sent out in February instead of having to try in April to lock the stable door after the steed had been stolen. The East Lancashire [1] now left the 11th Brigade after a four years' association with the Hampshire, while the large drafts who appeared, over 200 strong, came largely from ' broken ' battalions. A dozen officers joined the battalion, including a new Quartermaster, Lt. Boshell, while Captain German and Lt. Love were detailed for a turn of home duty, officers who had been long abroad without much change being now frequently given this relief.

Early in March the 1st Hampshire moved to Warlus and, after a fortnight's training there, went forward again and on March 21st, when the Germans opened their 1918 offensive, they were in brigade support North of the Arras-Fampoux road, their Division having relieved the Guards in the sector it had helped to capture nearly a year earlier.

[1] Under Lt. Colonel Earle of the Hampshire.

' Cambrai ' had left the 2nd Hampshire pretty well shattered, and with the whole Twenty-Ninth Division in the same plight nearly a month elapsed before it had to return to the trenches. The 2nd Hampshire were first at Sus St. Leger, where some 270 reinforcements joined with four subalterns, and then on December 18th they started by road for Quilen beyond Hesdin, covering 40 miles in three days, despite severe cold and snow-drifts which held up the transport. They remained at Quilen till January 3rd and then had two more days of strenuous marching to Acquin in bitter cold over roads glassy with ice ; more snow-drifts again gave the transport a very bad time, but very few men fell out in covering the 25 miles. After a fortnight here, where the training facilities were good, the battalion entrained for another spell in the Salient.

It was the apex of the Salient, the Passchendaele–Goudberg area, that the 88th Brigade, now under Brigadier General Freyberg, a Gallipoli V.C.,[1] was taking over. The ground was mainly morass, pitted with shell-holes full of stinking liquid mud and water, and only in places was digging possible, the trenches were chiefly short lengths, sometimes mere slits, not connected and hardly any of them wired. To make a defensible line was going to tax the skill, experience and energy even of a Division which General de Lisle had taught to dig. It did not make things easier that rations, water, trench stores and ammunition had to be carried up along slippery duck-boards, known to the enemy, off which a slip plunged men into an engulfing, oozy slime, and if hard frosts reduced this danger they prohibited digging. Of all the sectors any Hampshire battalion held this was perhaps the foulest, and it was greatly to the Division's credit that it made this line reasonably defensible, as the Germans were to find.

After a spell in brigade reserve at Wieltje, where they toiled away at the Division reserve defences, the 2nd Hampshire, on taking over the Goudberg sub-sector on January 26th, found much wiring needed and did not give a German effort to fraternise any encouragement. Four days here cost them 40 casualties, while on their going back into brigade reserve W Company had to be left in support to the Essex, and a party of men was carrying rations up to the front on February 1st when an attack developed. Dumping the rations, the carriers promptly reinforced the defence and helped effectively to beat off the attack. It was the last time the two battalions were to co-operate, the Essex immediately afterwards (February 7th) leaving the brigade on its reduction to three battalions. The Hampshire's drums helped to give them a great send-off.

All February the 2nd Hampshire spent at Brandhoek, Winnizeele and Poperinghe, out of trenches, the Division being ' at rest ' but training vigorously. ' Ceremonial ' and rapid-fire competitions were features of the training, and at its conclusion General de Lisle expressed great satisfaction at the standard reached. Almost immediately afterwards (March 14th) his promotion to command the Fifteenth Corps removed him from the Division he had led so

---

[1] Brigadier General Nelson had been invalided after his arduous time at Cambrai. Captain Cuddon was acting as Brigade Major.

long and so successfully and on whom he had impressed his principles : the 2nd Hampshire had learnt much from him. His successor, Major General D. E. Cayley, was no stranger, having commanded the 4th Worcestershire at ' the Landing ' and the 88th Brigade from June 1915 until September 1917.

Returning to the trenches early in March the 2nd Hampshire were holding the line North of Passchendaele when, about 6 a.m. on March 14th, the enemy put down a heavy barrage and infantry began forming up in No Man's Land. This gave the Hampshire's rifles and Lewis guns their chance, and while our barrage promptly answered the SOS. they fired away busily and effectively. After 20 minutes the German guns lifted on to our support line and two waves [1] pressed forward. Captain Scott, who had come up to the front directly the attack started, did great work in directing the fire of the machine-guns, and his coolness and disregard of danger encouraged his company to meet the attack with confidence and good effect. Only at one point did any attackers get within bombing range, elsewhere they were checked short of it and lost heavily, our guns getting well into them as they retired, while the bombers were soon driven back, 2/Lt. H. J. Morgan [2] using a revolver to such good purpose that a machine-gun the bombers were trying to silence could remain in action. As the Hampshire had only nine casualties while German stretcher bearers were busy in No Man's Land under the Red Cross flag for three hours, there could be little doubt who had had the best of it, while the capture of two prisoners provided the identification of the assailants as the 95th Reserve Infantry Regiment.

The Hampshire were less lucky next day ; during a gas bombardment, which in all inflicted 50 casualties, a shell, which had penetrated eight feet of earth, exploded at the entrance of the head-quarter ' pill-box ', wounding the sentry and drenching his clothes with liquid gas, while in crawling into the pill-box he allowed enough gas to enter with him to incapacitate the entire H.Q., Lt. Colonel Johnston, Captain Lord, the R.S.M. and the clerks all being badly gassed, along with the Signalling and Intelligence Officers. [3] Major Westmorland, who was back at Haslar Camp training a party for a raid, was sent for to take over and arrived to find that the entire H.Q. party had been removed to hospital. He had therefore to improvise a new head-quarters, Captain Harrod, the Assistant Adjutant, replacing Captain Lord and Lt. Holloway taking his duty.

After six days' rest at Poperinghe, which provided real amenities, the battalion held the Spree Farm sector from March 22nd to 26th and was able to locate some good targets by which our heavy guns profited, but when coming out on relief by the Newfoundlands it was unlucky in having a dozen casualties from the shelling of the duck-board tracks. Meanwhile the great attack further South was making unpleasantly rapid progress and all were waiting for either

[1] Prisoners said that four companies had led the attack with seven in support.
[2] Captain Scott and 2/Lt. Morgan were awarded the M.C.
[3] The M.O., Captain Knight, was also gassed.

a summons to go South and join in the effort to stem it or its extension to Flanders, while officers had been recalled from ' courses ' and leave parties cancelled or recalled. Casualties during March, especially from gas, had been quite heavy, nearly 100, including 20 killed or died of gas, and with 80 more sent to hospital, against 15 discharges, other ranks had fallen from 1003 to 927,[1] despite a draft of over 100 ; officers had also gone down, from 42 to 35.

The Cambrai counter-attack had not extended to the Bullecourt front and at the end of November the Sixteenth Division was relieved by the Fortieth. The 11th Hampshire now went back to Bapaume (December 3rd) and from there moved by Peronne to Villers–Faucon, new country for the regiment, where they were soon as busy as ever, with one company at St. Emilie and another at Ronssoy, road-making and hutting in the back areas, wiring when in the front line. Aircraft caused some trouble and casualties, and the wiring parties had some men hit, but losses were not numerous. The weather was mainly cold with frosts, when hard ground hampered work, but thaws were even more unpleasant and as serious a hindrance. January brought no change of either location or of work, with continued bad weather, but the defences were much improved, if more could have been accomplished could the infantry have found larger working parties, those who appeared being usually much below the numbers promised. A draft of 100 men from the 14th Hampshire arrived on February 2nd, and on February 18th orders were received to re-organize the battalion into three companies, though this was not carried out till March 8th, when C Company was absorbed,[2] while 100 men were sent off to the 1st Battalion. Meanwhile work went on steadily at the defences, but with the extension Southward of the British front to relieve the French nothing like enough labour was available for all that was required here, especially as French ideas and methods of defence differed radically from ours and our new front did not correspond to our standards. March brought more indications of the wrath to come, including constant amendments of the Division's defence scheme, in which the 11th Hampshire had to man the defences of Villers–Faucon.

After the attack on September 26th the Thirty-Ninth Division had had a fortnight's so-called rest, the first part spent by the 14th Hampshire in bivouac at Mount Kokereel, in wet weather and with continual calls to work on the roads and communication trenches, after which their Division relieved the Thirty-Seventh in front line at the Tower Hamlets[3] on October 15th. Since September 26th a big advance had been made North of the Menin road, Polygon Wood having been reached and cleared, but from Polderhoek and astride the Menin road little progress had achieved towards Gheluvelt ; the mud prohibited the

---

[1] Paper strength.

[2] Captains Sulman (A) and Howson (B) and Major Thyne (D) now commanded the companies with Captains Tilley, Shaw and Chadwick as seconds in command, companies having seven to nine subalterns. Lt. Colonel Crockett was still in command with Major Hazard as second in command and Captain Molyneux Adjutant.

[3] The front line was just East of Tower Hamlets and included the Northern end of Tower Trench.

917

rapid movement required in rushing pill-boxes, choked rifles and machine-guns and by smothering shell-bursts reduced the efficacy of our bombardments.

The Thirty-Ninth Division was not engaged on October 28th when a last attempt was made to advance in this quarter, and the fate of the troops who attacked just North of the Menin road cannot have made them regret they had not been employed in trying to cross the mud and slime which so effectively impeded the approach to the German line.

4 1917

During October Lt. Colonel Naden of the Cheshire had joined and taken command, and the battalion had had some intensive training. Its camp was badly bombed by aircraft early in the month, a dozen men being killed, and though 107 men joined on October 21st this still left the battalion very weak. Conditions were very bad, the ' line ' consisted mainly of shell-hole posts in a sea of mud, in which carrying parties floundered slowly and stretcher bearers could hardly get along. If this quarter was ' quiet ', to hold it even ' quietly ' was a strain. To call the sector ' pestilential ' was not libellous. While in front line again astride the Menin road early in November the 14th twice attacked a troublesome ' pill-box ' on the road ; D Company making the first attempt, on November 5th. Bad ground, soft and slippery with mud, inadequately cut wire and flanking machine-gun fire from a ' pill-box ' on our right flank, Lewis House, foiled the attackers. The officer in command of the party, Captain Finlay, about the last officer left who had come out with the battalion, was killed with five men, nine being wounded. The second attempt, early on November 8th by 2/Lt. Tower and 25 men, fared little better, despite a heavy bombardment of the objective ; ' pill-boxes ' presented small targets and, with only a ' direct ' any good, it was mainly luck if a bombardment could silence the machine-guns they sheltered.

The 14th were twice in front line again later in November :[1] fighting patrols which reconnoitred fortified dug-outs SW. of the previous objective found their wire too strong to warrant a raid. On relief the battalion moved to the Winnizeele area and was then detailed for work on roads near Wieltje. It had a week in Ypres itself, finding working parties, and spent nearly all the rest of December at Bayenghem, training and resting ; it then moved to a camp near Elverdinghe on December 30th to get another week's training before taking up a position on the Canal Bank on January 7th. ' Whole battalion on working parties day and night ' sums up its week here, but it had a dozen casualties, including 2/Lt. Crompton wounded. Three days at Hill Top Farm preceded a turn in front line in the Westroosebeke sector, where merely to reach the front was a real achievement. This quarter was fairly peaceful, and the battalion had no casualties in what was to be its last turn in the Salient, as on January 27th it entrained at Proven for the South, its Division having been transferred to the Fifth Army, now extending its line to the right to relieve the French opposite St. Quentin. With our infantry brigades being at the same time reduced to three battalions this extension seriously increased the dangers of an already sufficiently unsatisfactory situation.

[1] November 17th–20th and 24th–27th.

This front was a welcome change from the Salient in which the 14th Hampshire had suffered so much ; but they were not to see much of it for, after they had held the centre of the Division's line near Gouzeaucourt from February 1st to 3rd, an ominous sign of what was coming was given by an order to send 100 men to the 11th Battalion, the 14th being among the units to be sacrificed to the Home authorities' refusal to produce drafts. This fate did not actually befall it for three weeks, one of which it spent in support at Revelon Farm and the rest back at Henicourt. These last days were busy, 'working parties as before ', salvage, improving trenches, laying tramways and digging trenches for cables. A bombing raid by aeroplanes killed and wounded 20 transport animals at Sorel le Grand on February 16th, and after a farewell inspection by the Divisional Commander, Major General Feetham, the battalion went back to Haut Allaines, where its disbanding was completed on February 23rd, the men now being formed into two companies of a 17th Entrenching Battalion, whose members could be sure of being hard worked while they were waiting to be drafted to depleted units.[1]

The 14th had had just under two years in France : July 31st 1917, when they added a V.C. to the regiment's list, had been their greatest day, but at the Schwaben Redoubt and at the Tower Hamlets they had also been highly successful, and in many minor actions they had done well. The British Armies in France were only too soon to feel the disadvantage of the misguided policy which had deprived it of the 14th Hampshire and many other units which had done good service and played their part towards achieving the defeat of Germany.[2]

After its heavy fighting for the Tower Hamlets the 15th Battalion had moved at the end of September to the coastal area, being at Bray Dunes until October 15th and then at Coxyde Bains for a fortnight, then moving to St. Pol sur Mer. This gave its men some sea bathing and during October it received reinforcements amounting to 230 men, half from the Hampshire Carabiniers, with six officers. Lt. Colonel Cary-Bernard now received a well-deserved promotion, being appointed to command the 68th Brigade. A competent and capable commander, he had done much for the battalion, of which Major Murdoch, who had joined from the 11th R. W. Kent at the end of August, assumed command on October 8th. The 15th remained at St. Pol till November 11th, two more officers and 92 men joining, and then entrained for Italy, the Forty-First being among the five British Divisions now being dispatched thither to prevent the collapse at Caporetto developing into complete disaster.

Travelling by Paris, Lyons and Marseilles to Cannes, thence along the

---

[1] This battalion was thrown into the March battle at the very beginning in support of the Sixteenth Division, to do fine service in defending its Green Line at Tirlecourt Wood, Lt. Spencer receiving the M.C. for his gallant and skilful handling of his platoon in a rearguard action on March 23rd. He also sent back useful information and helped in the success of a local counter-attack.

[2] Without the Part II Daily Orders, which would have contained much useful information not recorded in battalion diaries, it is impossible to give lists of the honours and rewards won by members of the battalion or correct statistics for its losses.

Riviera to Genoa and on over the Apennines to Modena, it eventually detrained at Mantua on November 17th. The six days' journey had been an interesting experience, the entirely new scenes and the enthusiastic welcome received in Italy compensating for its length and cramped conditions, while everyone was glad that the battalion was not returning, as had been expected, to the Ypres Salient.[1]

From the detraining area the Division had nearly 100 miles to cover to reach the Piave, behind which river it was hoped that the Italian retreat might be stopped. The still critical situation meant that the advance had to be started without delay, and coming immediately after the long train journey it tested fitness and endurance severely, but the men, though carrying about 80 lbs apiece, responded well and, if marches were long and billets usually most uncomfortable, wine and fruit were plentiful. Actually before the British and French succour reached the Piave the Italians, encouraged by the knowledge that substantial help was close at hand, had rallied, while the Austrians' pursuit had apparently out-run the capacity of their administration to maintain its pressure and so exploit their advantage to the full.

Crossing the Adige on November 22nd and the Brenta three days later, the 15th Hampshire had two days rest before moving up to the Piave. British march-discipline and conduct made a great impression on the Italians, and the fine bearing of our troops and the good order in which they left their quarters were a revelation and an encouragement. The 40 miles between the Brenta and the Piave were covered in three marches, and on the evening of November 29th the Division began the relief of the Italians in the Montello sector, NE. of Montebelluno, where the Piave bends Southward round a steep ridge, from which splendid observation could be enjoyed over the plains to the SE. The 15th had their first turn in the front line here from December 8th to 15th. The ridge was covered largely with woods and elsewhere with vineyards and fields of maize, and with the country virtually as yet undamaged by war no greater contrast with Flanders could have been imagined. In front the Piave's shingly bed was in places a full mile in width, the river running through many channels, usually too swift, when not also too deep, to wade : these shifted and varied in depth and strength as the river rose and fell ; as crossing them was therefore both difficult and dangerous our patrol activities were severely restricted, and though in the battalion's last turn in the line, from February 17th-25th, several patrols managed to get across the river, none encountered the enemy. Contact with the enemy was therefore infrequent, if machine-guns were occasionally active and both sides did some shelling, our guns being the more aggressive, but the range was too long for snipers, and though the 15th Hampshire were in front line in Italy for 25 days altogether their casualties only just reached double figures.[2] They had found the defences very defective, the front line

---

[1] Up to its move to Italy the 15th Battalion had lost 25 officers and 360 men killed and missing, including prisoners of war, and 39 officers and 1081 other ranks had been wounded, in seventeen months in France.

[2] One killed and 11 wounded, mostly early in December.

was better dug than sited, no proper support or reserve lines existed,[1] and hard work was required to make them ready to meet a fresh attack. Actually none was attempted, the Germans had achieved their main purpose by thrusting the Italians back and distracting French and British troops to Italy and could not spare troops for another effort, while without their help the Austrians were hardly equal to effecting much, as was proved on the Asiago plateau in June, three months after the 15th Hampshire had returned to France.

Entraining on March 1st the 15th reached Warlencourt four days later. Their Division's selection for a return to France meant that, instead of remaining in Italy to be the spear-head in the final overthrow of Austria, it came in for much harder fighting and heavier losses than Italy would have brought it. Italy had been a pleasant interlude, conditions out of the line were good, billets being usually comfortable, good wine plentiful and the people friendly ; more-over, if their time in Italy had not given the 15th Hampshire any chances of adding to their laurels,[2] the Forty-First Division and the other British troops dispatched to Italy had at least done useful service in stabilizing a situation which had threatened to develop into disaster.

[1] The Italians tended to hold their front line in strength and had no idea of economizing men by a proper ' defence in depth ',

[2] In General Plumer's dispatches of April 1918 dealing with the operations in Italy he mentioned General Haking, G.O.C. Eleventh Corps, Lt. Colonel Middleton, in command of the 10th Northumberland Fusiliers, Lt. Bettinson, Sergeants Evans, Lonergan and Stone and Corporal Murden. Lt. Leybourne was subsequently awarded the M.C. for good work in Italy, C.S.M. Collis the D.C.M. and R.S.M. Greenwood and R.Q.M.S. Teague the M.S.M.

CHAPTER XXVI

1918 : I

THE MARCH OFFENSIVE [1]

WHEN, on March 21st 1918, the expected German attack developed in force along the whole front of the Fifth Army and against the Third's right and centre, the Sixteenth was the only Division with a Hampshire battalion in it to be at once engaged, its Corps, the Seventh, being the left of the four forming the Fifth Army. The Fourth Division with the 1st Hampshire was on the Third Army's left, North of the Scarpe and outside the front attacked, the Twenty-Ninth with the 2nd Hampshire was at the Northernmost point of the British front, at the apex of the Ypres Salient, while the Forty-First, in G.H.Q. Reserve behind the Third Army, was near Doullens, 25 miles from the front, so that the 15th Hampshire also were not immediately involved, if their entry into the battle was not long delayed.

The British defensive system involved three zones, a ' Forward Zone ', held usually by a third of the infantry of a Division, a ' Battle Zone ', usually about two miles back, where the main resistance was to be offered, and a ' Rear Zone ', about as much further back, to be held if the Battle Zone was penetrated, The Pioneers were in most cases among the units assigned to Division's Rear Zone, and the 11th Hampshire were back at St. Emilie, two miles West of Ronssoy, the strongly fortified village on the right of the Sixteenth Division's Battle Zone. This followed a crest, running NW. past Lempire towards Epehy. The front there ran across small spurs with valleys between them running down towards the Scheldt, and the Forward Zone had but a short field of fire. The Battle Zone was fairly strong, but so many troops [2] had to be placed in the Forward Zone that not nearly enough were left to man the rearward defences properly, the want of the fourth battalion in each brigade being very much emphasized.

The Germans had concentrated a greatly superior force ; eleven Divisions faced the three in the Seventh Corps, and the overwhelming weight of their artillery must in any case have rendered their first onslaught hard to withstand. When moreover a thick fog made it impossible to see more than a few yards, the British defence, which depended largely on the cross-fire of machine-guns in ' defended localities ', was at a crippling disadvantage. Having penetrated unseen between our posts, the enemy were attacking them from flank and rear before the defenders knew what was happening. Conditions could not have been more unfavourable for the British methods, and the contribution of the fog to the German success is hard to over-estimate.

---

[1] There is naturally so much conflict of evidence over the details of the events, owing to the heaviness of the casualties and the loss of important papers, that the story is specially difficult to piece together. Many diaries show signs of having been written up well after the event.

[2] The Sixteenth Division had five battalions in the Forward Zone.

On the Sixteenth Division's front East of Ronssoy the assault which followed the five hours of intense bombardment was rapidly successful in penetrating the Forward Zone, and by 9.30 a.m. the troops manning the Battle Zone were fighting hard, though stubborn resistance continued at several points in the Forward Zone till much later, isolated posts holding out for many hours, though surrounded, and thereby to some extent disorganizing the attack.

When the bombardment started the 11th Hampshire, who were in Divisional reserve along with the 47th Brigade, had at once stood to and manned their posts in the Villers-Faucon defences. These, though in the Rear Zone and five miles behind the front line, were very heavily shelled and the movement of the transport to a better position in the open proved difficult. At one moment the animals seemed likely to stampede, but by the coolness and good work of Lt. Robinson and Sergeant Dale this was averted and the transport was got away safely without casualties.

With the thick blanket of fog reducing the range of vision to a minimum the situation was difficult to discover and little accurate information came through. Pressure against the Battle Zone grew heavier from 10 a.m. onwards : by mid-day the enemy had forced their way into Ronssoy and, though more to the left Lempire held out longer, it proved necessary about 1 p.m. to send the 11th Hampshire up to St. Emilie to assist in manning the ' Brown Line ', the rear line of the Battle Zone. By 2 p.m. the battalion was in position here, with B Company South and D East of St. Emilie and battalion H.Q. in a railway cutting West of it. Shelling was heavy and the 11th had several casualties, Captain Sulman [1] being severely wounded. The 47th Brigade from reserve had before this also been moved forward to the ' Brown Line ', on which the surviving defenders of the forward positions had rallied, and for the time the Germans were successfully held, indeed St. Emilie, into which they had penetrated, was retaken, while on the left, where the Twenty-First Division was holding on to nearly all its Battle Zone, a brigade from Corps reserve had filled a gap. On the right patrols from B Company had, before nightfall, recovered touch with the Sixty-Sixth Division, which also had been forced back but was holding on to its Battle Zone.

Successful though the Germans had been in over-running our forward defences, the stubborn fight the Third and Fifth Armies had put up, despite the fog and other disadvantages, had been far from unsuccessful. German casualties had been heavy and their progress less than they had confidently reckoned upon. Had more adequate reserves been available the Fifth Army might have held the German advance well East of the Somme, but the heavy losses suffered, largely through fog, by the defenders of the forward lines had left several Divisions too weak to have much chance of making a successful defence of their Battle and Rear Zones, let alone to counter-attack. The Sixteenth, for instance, had only the 11th Hampshire and two battalions of the 47th Brigade intact for this purpose.

The bombardment died down sufficiently during the night for the defenders

[1] He died of his wounds.

of the Brown Line to be roughly reorganized, but it was soon renewed in force, and before dawn (March 22nd) the enemy's infantry were pressing forward again, helped once more by mist. Though the shelling was heavy the defence was stubbornly maintained, and between 7 a.m. and noon five separate efforts to advance were repulsed by the centre and left of the Sixteenth Division. Its right, however, was outflanked by Germans who had penetrated some way down the valley of the Cologne and, to escape being surrounded, the Sixteenth had to abandon its Battle Zone and to retire on Villers-Faucon. The retirement was well covered by the 11th Hampshire at St. Emilie itself, where a stubborn

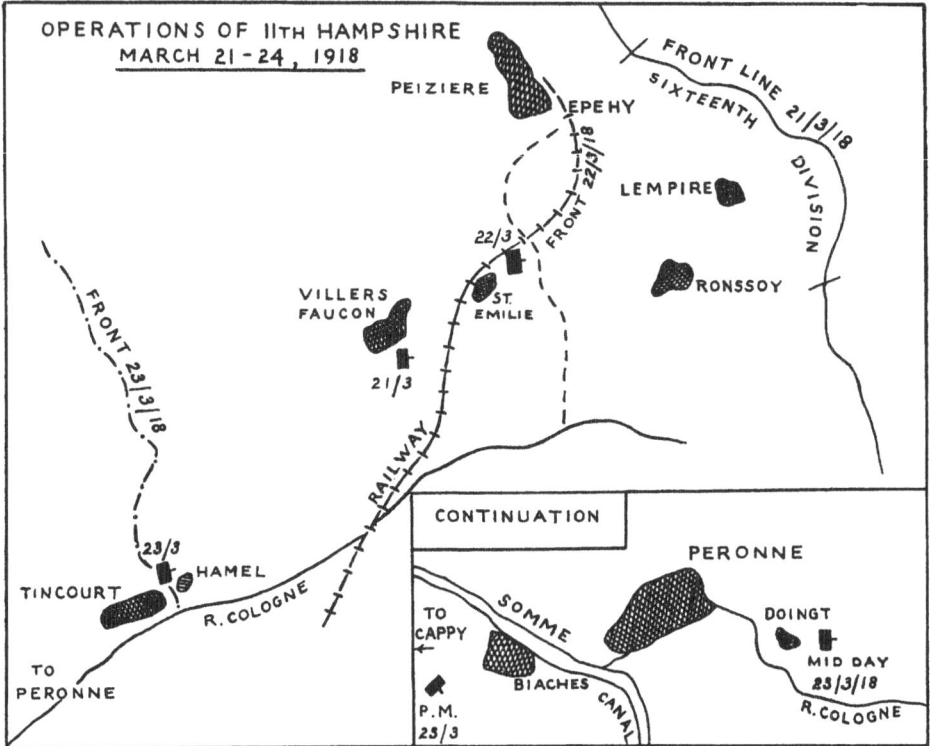

OPERATIONS OF 11TH HAMPSHIRE
MARCH 21 - 24, 1918

defence kept the Germans back for some time. D Company under Major Thyne bore the brunt of the attack in the first place, holding on tenaciously till their right was completely turned. B and A then covered D's withdrawal, whereupon B became the centre of the Germans' attentions, to be in turn forced back. Lt. Elkington had been killed just before this, while Captain Howson was captured but managed to escape.

In retiring upon Villers-Faucon the battalion suffered rather heavily but carried out the move in good order, standing first along the railway running South from Epehy, and then on high ground near Villers-Faucon. Along the ' Green Line ', marked on the map but not actually in effective existence, the remainder of the Division now took up a position running North from Tincourt and Hamel, the 11th Hampshire being on the right. The retirement had been followed up but the enemy did not attempt to come on and close with the Sixteenth, halting on high ground several hundred yards to the Eastward, from which he maintained a harassing fire, which was made more troublesome when his low-flying aeroplanes joined in. He was beginning to feel the effects of his exertions and to overstep the range of his heavier guns' ability to support him, but through an unfortunate misunderstanding a Corps further to the right retired sooner and further than General Gough [1] intended. This left a gap in the Fifth Army's centre, but for which the German advance might have been checked long enough for the line of the Somme to have been held.

The Sixteenth Division's front was held during that night (March 22nd/23rd) by the remnants of the 48th and 49th Brigade's, the Hampshire and the 47th Brigade being in support behind the Green Line. The retirement on the right making the retention of the Division's position impossible, orders were issued during the night for a retreat next day to a partially prepared line running Northward from Doingt.[2] Before this move could be begun, the enemy, about 6 a.m., renewed his attacks, but the 11th succeeded in holding them until ordered to withdraw, which was done in good order and the new position duly taken up. The trenches, dug some time ago, were in poor repair and very badly wired but they afforded a fine field of fire, being on a crest, and when, about 1 p.m., (March 23rd) infantry began coming on in great strength the 11th could take advantage of some excellent targets and inflicted heavy punishment. Meanwhile great masses of transport were making their way through Peronne and over the Somme, being effectively covered by the Hampshire with the 1st R.D.F. on their right rear. Indeed the *Official History* [3] speaks of a ' particularly fine rear-guard action fought by the 157th Field Company R.E. and the 11th Hampshire ' which allowed this move to be carried out so that the Division could eventually withdraw across the Somme and take up a line near Biaches.

When the withdrawal of the rear-guard became necessary B and D Companies went first, to halt on the downward slope of the ridge, A covering them from huts and houses on the outskirts of Doingt. Heavy casualties were inflicted on the enemy at a satisfactorily slight cost. A then withdrew through B and D, to let them repeat the operation, holding on behind on a light railway outside Peronne. This position was successfully maintained against several vigorous attacks, the steady fire of the Lewis gunners being particularly useful. Eventually B and D crossed the Somme, Major Hazard being the last man across, whereupon the bridge was duly blown up.

That evening found B and D Companies North of the Biaches–Flaucourt road, the 157th Field Company R.E. and the remnants of the 6th Connaught Rangers and 2nd Royal Irish South of it, all under Colonel Crockett's command. Despite heavy losses and the strain and hardships endured, with irregular rations and little rest or sleep, the men were in good spirits and amazingly cheerful. They had had the satisfaction of really using their rifles to good

---

[1] G.O.C. Fifth Army.   [2] 1½ miles SE. of Peronne.   [3] 1918. I. p. 359.

effect and, if driven back, they knew that they had taken a handsome toll of the enemy. For the moment they were to get the briefest of respites from exertion, as orders were received to move back to Cappy, seven miles West of Peronne. Starting at 2 a.m. (March 24th) they reached Cappy at 5 a. m. where they got a chance of a wash, though soon turned out to re-organize at the transport lines near the Bray road. That afternoon the battalion was ordered to Morlancourt across the Somme, to come into Divisional reserve : moving across country to avoid the congested traffic on the roads, it reached its destination rather before midnight to get into billets about 2 a.m. and enjoy some approach to a rest after four strenuous days.

Before this another Hampshire battalion had become involved in heavy fighting. After returning from Italy the 15th had had a fortnight at Warlencourt training with much route-marching and musketry, while its Division

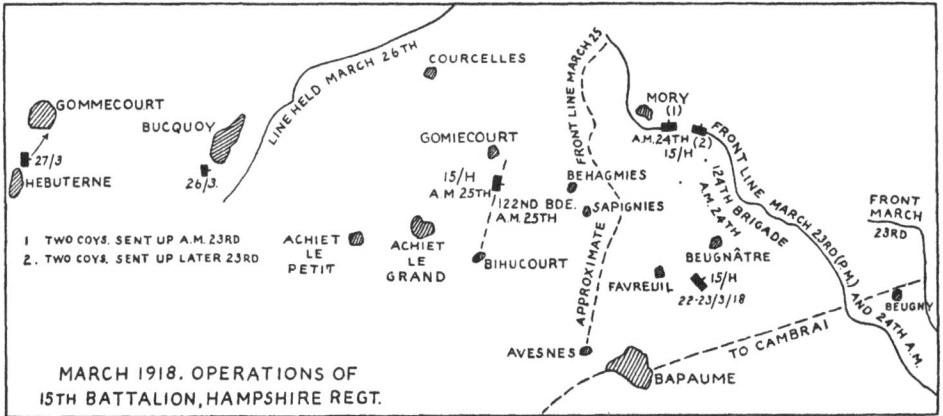

MARCH 1918. OPERATIONS OF
15TH BATTALION, HAMPSHIRE REGT.

was reduced to the new establishment, the 122nd Brigade losing the 11th R. W. Kent. When the German offensive started its Division, till then in G.H.Q. Reserve, was placed under the Third Army and sent forward, the infantry in ' tactical trains ' and the guns marching. That afternoon (March 21st) the 15th detrained at Achiet le Grand : they were short of their Lewis guns, which with the first-line transport had been sent forward by road and did not rejoin the Division for a week.

The Forty-First Division had been allotted to the Fourth Corps under Lt. General Harper, originally just West and to our left of the Flesquières salient. This Corps had been very violently attacked on March 21st and had been forced back to the rear line of its Battle Zone, after losing heavily. German pressure continued to be vigorous on March 22nd and, despite a stubborn resistance, the Corps had been pressed back before evening to a line [1] covering Beugny on the right and Beugnàtre on the left but with a gap in the centre, NW. of Beugny.

---

[1] Approximately the ' Green Line '.

Most of the Forty-First Division meanwhile had been put in almost by single battalions to patch up a rather irregular line, but the 122nd Brigade was still held back in reserve.

The 15th Hampshire had moved from about 1 p.m. (March 22nd) from Achiet to an assembly point on the Bapaume–Sapignies road. From here it moved about 6 p.m. to a position East of Favreuil [1] and SW. of Beugnatre, in front (NE.) of which last place the 124th Brigade was posted. Here the 15th dug in during the night, but soon after midnight the 12th East Surrey had to shift from the 15th's right to take post away to the left facing Mory, which meant that the 15th had to extend to the right to keep touch with the 18/60th. Then about 7 a.m. (March 23rd) two companies were ordered to move to the left and come in on the right of the 12th East Surrey opposite Mory, the other two remaining for the time in brigade reserve.

Pressure on the Fourth Corps on March 23rd bore heaviest against the right, where the advanced position covering Beugny was lost, its defenders, including some of the Forty-First Division, suffering heavily in a determined struggle : on the left the 124th Brigade dealt most successfully with a series of attacks, inflicting heavy casualties on the Germans, and the two reserve companies of the 15th Hampshire, who were called up to fill a gap in the line SE. of Mory, between the 10/11th H.L.I. (right) and 20th Middlesex (left) [2] though losing nearly 50 men, 14 of them killed, also maintained their line successfully, keeping the Germans at bay. Captain Oxborrow was conspicuous for his coolness and leadership under the heaviest shell-fire and did much to ensure the repulse of several attacks on his company, while 2/Lt. Trevett set a fine example of coolness and disregard of danger. The line here was sited on a reverse slope, and though in places the Germans got within 50 yards their corpses were piled in heaps in front of the wire and none got through. 2/Lt. Shadbolt, who, though wounded remained at duty, was another who did much to encourage his men. The day ended with the Fourth Corps holding on to the Green Line, to which the remnants of its right had been pushed back, but, beyond its left, ground had been lost and to the right a dangerous gap was developing, as some of the troops who had retired from the Flesquieres Salient were being forced NW. and others West.

March 24th brought no relaxation of pressure, all the 15th Hampshire being engaged but maintaining their positions until, early in the afternoon, the enemy's progress to the Southward forced the Fourth Corps to conform to the retirement of the Fifth, the Forty-First Division making for a line running Northward from Avesnes (North of Bapaume) to Sapignies. Until then the 15th had been quite happy, inflicting heavy loss on the enemy, who had to expose himself in advancing over the open, while their own losses were light. At one point a bayonet charge in company with some Argyll and Sutherland Highlanders helped to keep the Germans back. This withdrawal was begun on the right, the troops on the left holding on stoutly to cover the move. All three

[1] Barely two miles North of Bapaume.
[2] Battalions of the Fortieth and Forty-First Divisions were mixed up.

brigades of the Forty-First Division had been under heavy fire but had not given ground to any appreciable extent, though the enemy were round both flanks before we withdrew. They now followed up the withdrawal but did not impede it seriously, indeed some Germans were taken prisoners at this time, a counter-attack by six tanks discouraging them appreciably.

As the retirement did not really get going until dusk, there was naturally some confusion and loss of direction, but eventually a fresh line was taken up, Divisions and brigades were all mixed up, but during the night the 15th Hampshire and other portions of the 122nd Brigade were collected in reserve North of Bihucourt, where they dug in. Several battalions of the Division had been reduced to mere handfuls, but so far the 15th's losses had been very small, and they had had the satisfaction of inflicting heavy casualties on the enemy, whose attacks were beginning to flag as they passed beyond the supporting range of their heavier guns and found it increasingly difficult to get ammunition and supplies forward over the devastated battle ground, seamed with trenches and old belts of wire.

However, heavily as the Germans had lost they had still ample reserves to throw in, and though the fresh Forty-Second Division was reinforcing the Fourth Corps, fifteen Divisions were facing its five and it was hardly wonderful that March 25th saw things go badly for the defence, the Fourth Corps being pushed back some way to the NW. leaving a three-mile gap between its right and the Fifth Corps to the South.

That day's German attack had been started by patrols, who pushed forward to locate our line and feel for weak spots in it : these were followed by larger bodies and about 11 a.m. (March 25th) the front line troops of the Forty-First Division had been forced back from in front of Behagnies and Sapignies upon the Bihucourt–Gomiecourt line, where they rallied for another stand upon the 15th Hampshire and other supporting troops. Bihucourt itself was lost but the Germans could make little progress against the ridge North of it. The main trouble came on the right flank, where the Germans were exploiting and extending the gap between the Fourth and Fifth Corps. However, the Forty-Second Division was coming into action, and reinforcements from it came up to prolong and cover the 15th's line while one company of Manchesters reinforced the battalion's front. Captain Newman did much to keep the defence going and maintain the position, showing great coolness and determination under the heaviest fire, and again and again German efforts to advance were held. ' Dug in and held enemy in large numbers ' is the laconic entry in one Sergeant's diary for the day. Early in the afternoon a counter-attack by tanks, three of which advanced through the 15th's line and eight past its right, did much to relieve the situation and to discourage the enemy's efforts to advance, but although another Division was arriving to reinforce the Fourth Corps the Corps Commander decided to take up a line from Achiet le Petit to Courcelles, whereby he hoped to shorten his front and to be able to withdraw the Divisions who had borne the brunt of the fighting for a rest. Orders for this were issued about 5 p.m.

Accordingly after dark [1] the 15th Hampshire began withdrawing by companies, starting from the right. Just as A Company on the left was moving off, the enemy came on in force, covered by a machine-gun barrage. Rising to the occasion, A fought a fine rear-guard action with substantial success, extricated itself with little loss and made its way back to Bucquoy, where eventually the battalion was collected about 6 a.m. (March 26th). As before Colonel Murdoch had handled the withdrawal admirably, holding on tenaciously and inflicting heavy casualties on the enemy but not hanging on long enough to let the battalion be gripped, while Captain Wigmore made many journeys between battalion H.Q. and the front line, keeping H.Q. in close touch with the situation. When the 15th reached Bucquoy they were warmly welcomed by the Brigade Major who had never expected, he said, to see them again. Later on they went back to Gommecourt, where they arrived about 2 a.m. (March 27th). If the Division, which was now concentrating here, could not yet be withdrawn altogether from the fighting line, it was to get a brief rest and some chance to reorganize.[2]

March 26th had been notable for the conference at Doullens which marked a turn in the tide in favour of the Allies through General Foch's appointment to co-ordinate Allied operations, a step taken largely at Sir Douglas Haig's instance. This meant that French help, hitherto doled out grudgingly and therefore rather ineffectually by General Petain, was now forthcoming more freely, more vigorously and more effectively, while the Germans were finding the momentum of their advance increasingly hard to maintain and were beginning to fail to keep up the requisite pressure. Much as they had won, no break-through had been effected and the Third and Fifth Armies had made them pay high for their gains, which did not fulfil Ludendorff's hopes and requirements.

Still, if March 26th had brought better prospects for the Allies, the German advance had not yet been checked, especially South of the Somme, where Ludendorff, possibly carried away by his success in thrusting back the French who had tried to intervene, had gone rather beyond his original intentions and was exploiting local success rather than concentrating all his resources against the British further North. Despite all it had endured the Sixteenth Division could not be released from the line, so that the 11th Hampshire's hopes of a rest at Morlancourt proved elusive, and on the afternoon of March 25th they were ordered to re-cross the Somme and move to Proyart, remaining however, in Divisional reserve. They were actually in good billets here but were turned out early next day to prepare a line in front of Proyart, Chuignolles and Froissy, upon which the troops in front would fall back. The Sixteenth Division, now

---

[1] There is considerable discrepancy in the times given in the different accounts. The map in the *Official History* 1918, Vol. I, which shows the Forty-First Division as at Hebuterne on the morning of March 26th, does not allow for belated units.

[2] Colonel Murdoch was awarded the D.S.O., Captains Oxborrow and Wigmore were given bars to the M.C. and Captain Newman and 2/Lts. Shadbolt and Trevett the M.C., Sergeant Warren a bar to the D.C.M. and Sergeant Falconer the D.C.M., while 16 N.C.O.s and men received the M.M.

under the Nineteenth Corps, was on that Corps' left, with its left flank flung back to face North across the Somme, as on the other bank the Third Army's right was already some distance further West. On the right of the Nineteenth Corps the French had been pressed back SW. and three miles separated them from the British, so that Corps could not maintain its position long and about 4 p.m. the 11th Hampshire's digging was interrupted by orders to assemble in reserve behind Proyart. The selected assembly position being under heavy fire, the battalion had to move to trenches NW. of Proyart near the road leading to Mericourt. It was now under the 49th Brigade whose left, NW. of Chuignolles, A Company prolonged, while B filled a gap between the 47th and 48th Brigades, leaving only D and some Lewis guns in reserve. The German advance was now much slowed down and, weak as was the British line, partly

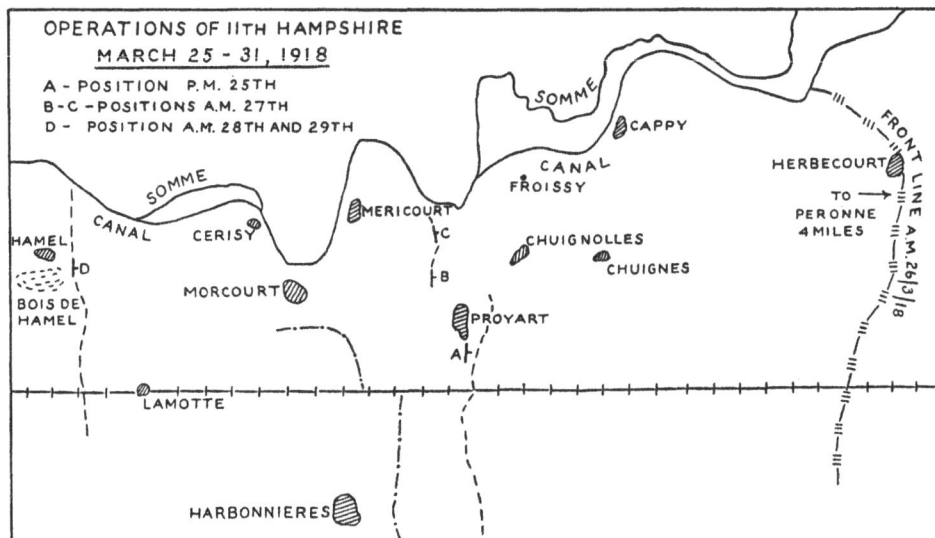

OPERATIONS OF 11TH HAMPSHIRE
MARCH 25 - 31, 1918
A - POSITION P.M. 25TH
B-C -POSITIONS A.M. 27TH
D - POSITION A.M. 28TH AND 29TH

held by improvised units, prospects of stopping the enemy were rather more hopeful. He was pressing on, however, and the next day's fighting (March 27th) was to try the 11th Hampshire hard.

Attacks started fairly early : D Company was soon thrown in, and as troops were retiring on the right the two reserve Lewis gun teams had to reinforce that flank. The pressure was too heavy to be withstood, and when the enemy reached high ground West of Proyart orders were issued to retire to the South of Morcourt. D Company, covering this withdrawal, was closely pressed and nearly all No. 16 Platoon were cut off. Captain McConnochie was killed here, while Major Thyne and 2/Lt. J. Smith were taken, with Major Hazard, who had collected some details and was last seen doing great work in checking the German advance round our right. Meanwhile other Germans crossed the Somme near Cerisy and were threatening the Division's left, which was under heavy shell and machine-gun fire. However, what remained of the battalion and a company of R.E. did splendid service by covering a retirement SW. on Lamotte. Having taken up a flank position they poured in a most effective fire, inflicting such severe casualties that the Germans recoiled towards the Somme, letting the remnants of the Sixteenth Division get back to a line running Northward from near Lamotte. This had been manned by a most miscellaneous collection known as ' Carey's Force ', largely R.E. but including a few Americans, South of whom the 11th Hampshire took post, East of the Bois de Hamel. If the outflanking of the Sixteenth Division had made the whole line of the Nineteenth Corps further South untenable, the Germans had been prevented from exploiting their success and disaster had again been averted. If the 11th had had more hard work than hard fighting before this, they were making up for it now and acquitting themselves splendidly.

The effects of the out-flanking of the Nineteenth Corps made themselves felt next day (March 28th), when the troops who had been holding their ground East of Harbonnieres and further South at Rosieres had to come back virtually into line with Carey's Force, who with the survivors of the Sixteenth Division helped to cover their move. The 11th Hampshire, however, were not called on to do more than remain in support, finding fairly good cover in sunken roads and behind banks, though they were without protection against the back-burst of shells. The day brought little loss of ground at any point and the virtual suspension of the German attacks next day was some indication that the stubbornness of the Fifth Army's defence had been effective.

While the fighting South of the Somme was now beginning to die down, North of the river the Third Army's right and centre were also holding their own with some success so that the Forty-First Division could move back to Bienvillers and get a quiet day there on March 27th. Nevertheless the Germans were far from having shot their bolt and March 28th saw their attack extended to the Third Army's left, the positions immediately East of Arras and astride the Scarpe, held by the Fifteenth and Fourth Divisions, so that a week after the opening of the great German ' push ' the 1st Hampshire were given a chance of helping to withstand it.

March 21st had found the battalion in brigade support North of the Fampoux–Arras road. Though on that day this area had been heavily shelled from 5 a.m. till 9 a.m. no attack had developed astride the Scarpe, and late that evening the 1st Hampshire moved up into the front line of the second system of the defences,[1] battalion head-quarters being established in Colt Trench. The next day (March 22nd) passed quietly, but events further South forced the Fifteenth Division to evacuate Monchy and fall back to the third system of the defences, 500 yards West of Monchy. This left the Fourth Division's right ' in the air ', and the details of the battalion had to move back from Arras to Agnez les Duisans, the transport also moving back NW. of Arras. March 23rd was misty and it was hard to discover what was going on in the Monchy area, from which heavy firing was heard. Later in the day it cleared enough to let small parties

[1] East of Fampoux.

of enemy be seen moving Westward North of Monchy, and towards evening reconnoitring patrols tried to penetrate the brigade's front line, to be driven back by the Somerset L.I. who were holding it.   About 7 p.m. A Company moved back to the reserve line of the second system, but the expected attack never developed on the Division's front and despite considerable shelling the Hampshire had no casualties.   Next day again (March 24th) no attack was attempted, but the battalion relieved the Somersets in the front line, putting three companies into the front,[1] support and ' strong point ' lines, with battalion head-quarters and the remaining company in Cadiz Trench, in the front line of the second system.

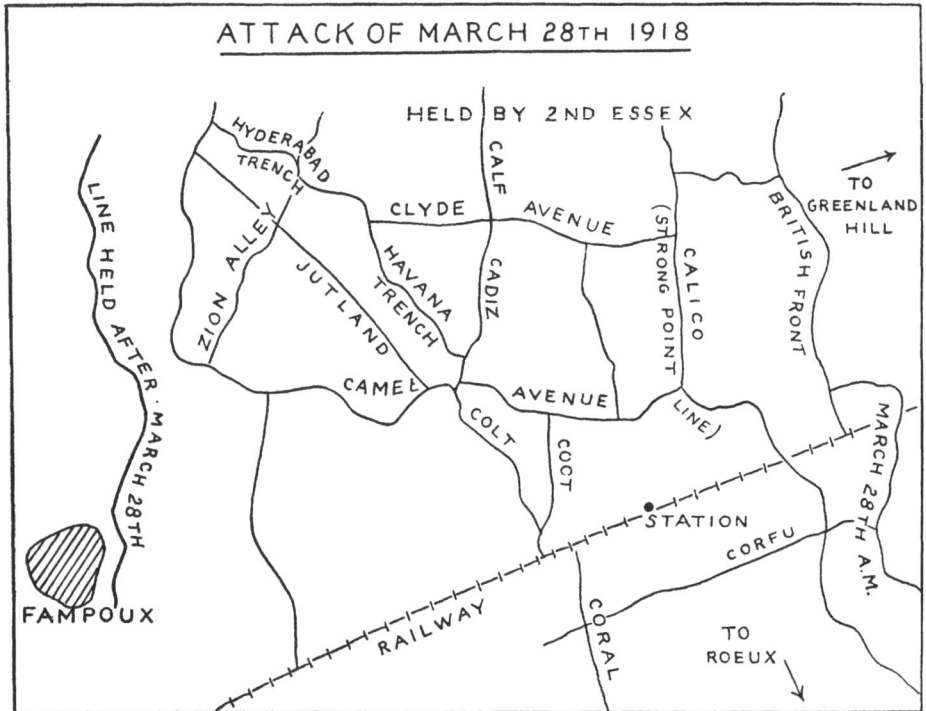

ATTACK OF MARCH 28TH 1918

Two days passed quietly enough, the Hampshire having half a dozen casualties from shell-fire and extending Southward across the railway to occupy Corfu Trench.   A heavy bombardment early on March 26th was followed by an attempted raid against our left, which D Company repulsed without difficulty or casualties, while A Company on the right assisted the Seaforths in the front line of the 10th Brigade to deal with intruders near the junction between brigades.   March 27th passed quietly, rather another lull before the storm.

March 28th brought the long anticipated attack ; an intense bombardment opened about 3 a.m. but at first fell rather uselessly behind our front system. However, before long the front and support lines were being barraged and badly

[1] The front line was about 800 yards East of the station near the Chemical Works.

damaged by trench mortars, telephone communication being completely cut, though touch was maintained by visual signalling. No infantry attack developed till about 7.15 a.m., before which the front and support lines had been evacuated in favour of the ' Strong Point ' line in Calico Trench, from which rifles, Lewis guns and machine-guns took full advantage of the splendid targets which the attackers [1] presented. Carefully sited machine-guns in particular did great damage and the attackers, delayed in the confusion of half-destroyed trenches and patches of wire, were kept under a destructive fire. For some time a most successful resistance was maintained : three times enemy who were penetrating into our line were driven back by bombing attacks headed by Lt. Edwards, who also led a counter-attack by a small party which put a machine-gun out of action.

The Essex (12th Brigade) on the left were at a disadvantage because a shallow valley on their left gave the enemy some cover, and despite a splendid resistance and a gallant counter-attack they were outflanked and nearly all killed or taken. This uncovered the Hampshire's left and by 8.30 a.m. the enemy were well beyond and round D Company's left and pressing them hard. Colonel Armitage had therefore to prepare to swing back his left, D Company eventually forming a defensive flank thrown back in Havana Trench. This move involved the evacuation of the rest of the ' strong point line ', whose defenders had now also to fall back, A Company on the right into Coral Trench, South of the railway, B in the centre along Camel Avenue, to part of which it held on. Though all the officers of A and B were by now casualties the move was successfully carried out, Sergeant Brine taking over his company and controlling its retirement most skilfully, and by about 9.30 a.m. a new line had been taken up, C Company in Cadiz Trench now coming into front line. The new line ran from Coral Trench by Coot Trench and Camel Avenue into Cadiz Trench [2] and was covered to the left flank and rear by D Company in Havana Trench, where Lt. Evans held on most successfully though his flank was exposed, repulsing repeated efforts to outflank him and inflicting heavy casualties. He had done great work in the retirement from the ' strong point ' line, getting his men away though the enemy were threatening both his flanks.

Hostile pressure continued, but for three hours the position was successfully maintained, our guns giving most effective support. Repeated efforts to advance in mass across the open, preceeded by small parties in ' worms ', were checked, whereupon the Germans had to resort to the costly method of trying to advance up the communication trenches, Clyde and Camel Avenues, in which they made but little progress. About 1 p.m., however, the pressure on the left flank forced the Hampshire to evacuate most of Cadiz Trench where C Company, with battalion head-quarters, had till then maintained their ground : they now retired into Havana Trench, but retained a hold on the

---

[1] The attack at this point was made by Bavarians of their 5th Reserve Division.
[2] The left (Northern) end of Cadiz Trench seems to have been more or less ' in the air ' except so far as it was covered by the troops holding Havana Trench behind it.

Southern end of Cadiz. The enemy pressed the withdrawal but were kept at bay by bombers and even small counter-attacks, and the new position was successfully taken up. Battalion head-quarters were in some danger of being captured, but Lt. Evans, who was stripping a Lewis gun which had had a stoppage, calmly completed the work and got the gun into action again just in time to come to their help very effectively and stopped the Germans completely. On the left beyond the Hampshire's line Germans had got into Havana Trench, but a company of the Rifle Brigade had been placed under Colonel Armitage, who used two platoons to assist in a counter-attack across the open from Jutland Trench, into which some of D Company had previously been forced back. Our bombers co-operated from the junction of Havana and Cadiz Trenches, while the Lancashire Fusiliers, who had now replaced the remnants of the Essex on the left, bombed SE. to assist in the attempt. This attack proved a complete success, the intruders being ejected, and meanwhile bombers trying to work forward along Clyde, Camel and Cadiz were successfully checked. A bombing post was established in Havana Trench and there the enemy were held at bay.

By 2 p.m. the line had been readjusted,[1] both 11th and 12th Brigades now holding the front of the Battle Zone. Casualties had been heavy, but nothing like the enemy's, as was clear from the lessened vigour of his efforts. These, though renewed at intervals during the afternoon, now lacked ' punch ' and vigour and were easily checked, our guns co-operating effectively with the infantry. On the right the Seaforth, their flank exposed by a retirement South of the Scarpe, had had to fall back on Fampoux, on which Colonel Armitage used part of the company of the Rifle Brigade to form a defensive flank along the railway, facing South, so as to secure this point. Soon after 4 p.m., however, Germans again attempted to bomb their way along Clyde and Cadiz Trenches, only to be driven back at both points, while in retiring across the open they were heavily punished, one Lewis gun at the junction of Havana and Cadiz Trenches being particularly effective and bowling over about 50 men. After this there were no more attacks and the three Divisions [2] engaged were left in possession of their Battle Zone from which the Germans, for all their numbers and all the violence of their attacks, had failed to dislodge them.

Several battalions of the Fourth Division had lost heavily, the Essex had been nearly wiped out, but the Hampshire had fared none too badly : they had had Captain Prynn and 2/Lts. House, Reid and B. A. C. Morgan and 39 men killed, while 2/Lts. Hogan and Renshaw, both wounded, were missing with 85 men, the Chaplain, the Reverend S.E. Swann, 2/Lt. Batts, and 81 men being wounded,[3] but they could reckon themselves fairly fortunate to have lost

---

[1] It ran as before from Coral Trench by Coot Trench into Camel Avenue and the Southern end of Cadiz Trench, being thrown back to the left along Havana Trench.

[2] The Fourth, Fifteenth and Fifty-Sixth.

[3] Out of 18 officers and 586 men in the line. Two officers and 96 men were with the transport, Major Hudson and four other officers and 190 men with the Divisional Depot Battalion, while sick, leave, ' courses ' and ' employed ' accounted for the remaining 14 officers and 156 men on the strength.

no more in doing so much. They could feel entitled to be well satisfied with the day's achievements.

March 28th was indeed one of the turning points in the struggle : it had incidentally vindicated the soundness, in clear weather, of the British defensive dispositions, and even if we had had to abandon our Forward Zone we had, as we calculated, held the attack at the Battle Zone. At this point it was not renewed, its reception had not been encouraging enough. The decisive check given to the Germans on this day was a factor of major importance in discouraging them and leading them soon afterwards to abandon an offensive which had failed to achieve its main purpose, much as it had gained in ground and heavy as had been the British losses in men, guns and equipment.[1]

That evening the Hampshire withdrew by order to a reserve line, covered by two platoons in Jutland Trench ; the move was not molested and the new line was duly taken up, the Division's line having been readjusted to correspond to the new front South of the Scarpe and thereby avoid forming too pronounced a salient. This new front which ran from Fampoux Lock Northward, was not attacked [2] and though the battalion was in brigade support from April 1st to 6th and then had three days in front line, with its right company actually at Fampoux, it was quite untroubled, casualties only coming to a dozen all told, and on April 8th it went back to huts four miles NW. of Arras on relief by Canadians.

If March 28th marked a very definite point in the battle North of the Somme, South of that river the offensive was not yet completely suspended, so that the 11th Hampshire had not quite finished with the struggle, while the 15th also were to see more of the last flickers of the expiring German effort.

March 29th passed fairly quietly for the scanty remnant of the Sixteenth Division, and the 11th Hampshire, though occasionally shelled, got some respite from exertions, while several men who had got detached during the fighting and had been collected at the transport line now rejoined. The respite proved, however, to be of the briefest ; next day the Germans attacked again in force, thrust back the French and thereby compelled the right of the Nineteenth Corps, South of the Luce, to conform. Extending their attacks North of the great road to Amiens they gained a foothold in our line near Hamel, just to the left of the 11th's frontage. Seeing our men retiring Captain Tilley promptly put in his counter-attack companies, A and D, who formed up on the reverse slope of a ridge and, going forward in great style, cleared the Germans out of the trenches they had taken.[3] Bolting over open ground 300 yards across, the ousted Germans gave fine targets of which the 11th's rifles and Lewis gunners took full advantage. They returned to the attack, however, and two more deter-

---

[1] Lts. Edwards and Evans were awarded the M.C. and Sergeant Brine the D.C.M., Sergeants Cox and Friend, Corporal Piper and Privates Hatcher, Miller and Penney getting the M.M.

[2] It remained unchanged till the Third Army started advancing Eastward on August 23rd.

[3] Captain Tilley was awarded the M.C. which was also given to the Adjutant, Captain Molyneux, for constant good work during this period. He had again and again rallied and reorganized men, setting a fine and encouraging example.

mined efforts had to be repulsed, in which fine work was done by an unidentified Lewis gunner who posted himself just in front of our wire so as to enfilade enemy who had reached it and were trying to make their way through, on whom he did great execution.

On the right also the enemy broke in, but D Company held firmly on and an R.E. company, counter-attacking most effectively, recovered all the lost ground, so that on the Hamel front the position remained intact. D Company had, however, lost so heavily that it had to be temporarily amalgamated with B, the battalion being reduced now to about 170 rifles with Captain Howson in temporary command. Nothing, however, was required of it next day (March 30th) and that evening it was relieved from the front line and placed in billets at Hamel, from which it went back next day to Vaire sur Corbie, to be relieved on April 3rd by the Fourteenth Division and taken right out of the fighting zone.[1]

The 15th Hampshire, like the 11th, were hardly back behind the front line before they were required again. The attacks of March 28th had extended to the Hebuterne area, which the Sixty-Second Division was holding, with the Forty-First in support. Attacking vigorously the enemy managed to penetrate into Rossignol Wood in a gap between the Sixty-Second and an Australian brigade. The Forty-First Division was therefore called up to assist in recovering this ground, and the 15th were brought forward and put into line with three companies in front and C in support. They were then ordered to put in a company to attack Rossignol Wood and then, after this had been cancelled, repeated and cancelled again, to send a fighting patrol to investigate Nameless Farm, but this last order also was cancelled, just as A Company was starting to carry it out. During a wet and stormy night the battalion's patrols were active and captured a prisoner, but no more was to be required of it, for after remaining at the front for three uneventful days, it was taken back by bus on April 3rd to Fevant, where it entrained for Poperinghe, the Division having been transferred to the Second Army. ' Back to line : bombardment day and night. Enemy completely held ' is a day's record for this time in one soldier's diary.

Of all the battalions seriously engaged in stemming the ' March push ' the 15th Hampshire must have come off with the lowest casualties. Their battalion diary [2] gives their losses for March at the incredibly low figure of 21 killed and missing, four officers and 65 men wounded.

Of the three Hampshire battalions who contributed to the checking of the great German effort short of its essential goal, the 11th stand out as having had most to do and as having done it admirably. Their worth as Pioneers

---

[1] The battalion's exact losses are not recorded. Besides those mentioned 2/Lts. Fairweather and Robinson were killed.

[2] The diary bears signs of having been written up some time after the events, as its dates do not agree with those of other units in the Division. Had not the Part II Daily Orders most unfortunately been destroyed in a ' blitz ' these figures could have been checked. The casualty returns, however, do not show any officer of the battalion as having been killed at this period. The M.O. and his orderly, however, had been killed, up in the front line attending to casualties.

they had long ago established, but their chances of showing that they would fight as well as they could dig and wire and make roads had been scanty, so that this fortnight of fighting was their ' crowded hour ' [1].

But if ' Somme 1918 ' on the King's Colour represents largely the 11th Battalion's hard work and gallant fighting, the 1st Battalion's share in its one day of desperate defence was part of a notable achievement and the 15th's part in the struggle had been by no means small.   If disaster had at moments seemed imminent, owing mainly to the refusal of the political authorities to attend to the warnings of their qualified professional advisers, and if for the same reasons more had been asked of the fighting men than was necessary, their record in the 'March Retreat' is enormously to their credit.   The Third and Fifth Armies, though by no fault of their commanders or of G.H.Q., were not given a fair chance to deal with the attack ;   that nevertheless it was stopped in time, while extremely creditable to those who fought so hard despite the odds against them, was also to no small extent the work of those who on the Somme in 1916 and at Arras in 1917 had won the vital ' elbow room ' behind our front which had so much to do with the German failure to achieve their ends.

[1] Here again without the Part II Orders to fill up the gaps in the battalion diary, neither their losses nor the rewards received by their officers and men for many valuable acts of gallantry can be accurately ascertained.

CHAPTER XXVII

1918 : II

THE APRIL OFFENSIVE

THE German failure to achieve all they had hoped for from their great attack on the British right was far from having exhausted their offensive capacities. Foiled here, Ludendorff diverted his reserves to Flanders, where the First Army's front was now held mainly by Divisions exhausted and expended in resisting his first attack, hastily replenished by drafts, consisting largely of young recruits, and far from ready to meet a fresh attack of equal violence. Normally the Lys valley would have been too wet and muddy in April to make a big attack practicable, but an unusually fine and dry spring had made it quite suitable for operations on a large scale, and the fighting astride the Somme had barely died down before, on April 9th, a new attack was delivered. Unluckily this just anticipated the relief of the Portuguese Division, then holding the Neuve Chapelle sector, whose failure to offer any effective resistance allowed the Germans to make a most dangerous advance, reaching the Lys at Estaires and outflanking the line on either flank of the breach their success had created. On the British right the fine resistance of the Fifty-Fifth Division [1] at Festubert and Givenchy prevented their exploiting their advantage effectively, on the left they were more successful, rolling up the Fortieth Division's [2] line from its exposed right, after having failed to make any impression on its front.

The First Army's only available reserves were tired Divisions just released from the Somme fighting, who badly needed a good spell out of the line to assimilate the drafts who had refilled their depleted ranks but had nevertheless to be plunged into another major battle, in which they fought at every possible disadvantage. In this extremity it was natural that the Second Army should have been called on to release its reserves to succour its hard-pressed neighbour, though of its thirteen Divisions only three had not been through the ordeal of the March offensive, the rest, among them the Forty-First, having been sent up to its supposedly ' quiet ' front to recuperate.

The three fresh Divisions included the Twenty-Ninth, who were about the first to be sent to help in stemming the German advance. The 2nd Hampshire, after holding the Spree Farm sector at the apex of the Ypres Salient from March 22nd to 26th were at Haslar Camp until April 1st, resting and working on rear defences; they then had four more days at Spree Farm, ' quiet ' but tiring, much work being required on the defences. Everyone was expecting the Division to be sent South to replace an exhausted Division in the Third or Fifth Army, but the battalion, which had been relieved on April 1st, was still at Haslar Camp on April 9th, when on the news of the new attack it was moved to Watou. Lt. Colonel Westmorland was in command, with Captains Single-

---

[1] Not engaged in the March fighting.
[2] Hastily refilled after heavy losses in March.

334

ton-Gates (W), Thompson (Y) and Ozier [1] (Z) and Lt. G. H. Brown [2] (X) commanding companies and Captain Harrod as Adjutant. Some 90 reinforcements had joined since March 31st, against half a dozen casualties and 20 admissions to hospital, and on paper the battalion had well over 30 officers and nearly 1000 other ranks.

Orders to move eventually reached the 88th Brigade before midday on April 10th, the other two brigades having already started off, to come into line near Estaires where they were very heavily engaged during the next week, when their stubborn resistance did much to check the Germans. The 88th Brigade could not follow them until the completion of its relief by the 123rd Brigade of the Forty-First Division which had just arrived from further South. Thus the 88th was some way behind the 86th and 87th Brigades, whom it would have rejoined had not the extension of the attack to the front of the Ninth Corps, North of Armentieres, diverted it to that quarter.

Leaving Watou about 12.30 p.m. by bus, the brigade reached Bailleul to find that place already under distant artillery fire, crowded with fugitive civilians and generally in a state of turmoil and confusion. Pushing on Eastward along the Armentieres road, the brigade was halted about 4 p.m., when about half-way to Nieppe, and ordered to deploy, as the enemy were reported to have taken Steenwerck and to be advancing Northward. The 4th Worcestershire were on the right and the Hampshire next, the Newfoundlands and the 2nd Monmouthshire, the Divisional Pioneers who were attached to the brigade, being beyond them. Advancing across the fields with patrols out well in front, who met and drove back some German scouts, the brigade came across a line of our guns about 1200 yards North of Steenwerck Station, firing over open sights with apparently no infantry in front. Accordingly the brigadier halted his men and started to dig in astride the railway, the Hampshire having X and Y Companies in front South of La Creche and the others in support. After dark some of the 74th Brigade fell back into line on the brigade's right and on the left touch was obtained with the Thirty-Fourth Division, now retiring from a sharp salient round Armentieres, whose withdrawal the 88th Brigade's arrival materially helped to cover, though the British line at this point still formed a pronounced salient, from which the troops had to be withdrawn during the next day's fighting.

That morning (April 11th) found X Company holding an outpost line from near Steenwerck Station towards the hamlet of Trois Arbres, while the other three companies were consolidating a line behind them, in front of La Creche. About 11 a.m. W advanced through X to investigate the position in Steenwerck, but the patrols who preceeded the advance found the place very strongly held and the move was suspended. Later in the day German patrols started working forward up the railway but were driven back, and then about 6 p.m. after our line had been heavily bombarded the enemy came on in force This attempt the Hampshire's rifles and Lewis guns promptly and successfully checked, but the day's casualties came to 40 killed and missing and 2/Lts. Sharp and Slater and

---

[1] Royal Jersey Militia, attached.   [2] Ayrshire Yeomanry, attached

50 men wounded. However, the Germans had been held and the troops, mainly Thirty-Fourth Division, holding the Nieppe Salient had been successfully withdrawn, all the guns covering them being got away. Of the operations of the Fifteenth Corps on this day the *Official History*[1] says the action of the 88th Brigade and of the 74th on its right had formed ' the pivot '. One feature of the situation was that livestock, cows, sheep, pigs and poultry, were wandering about in all directions from the deserted farms, so even if normal rations could

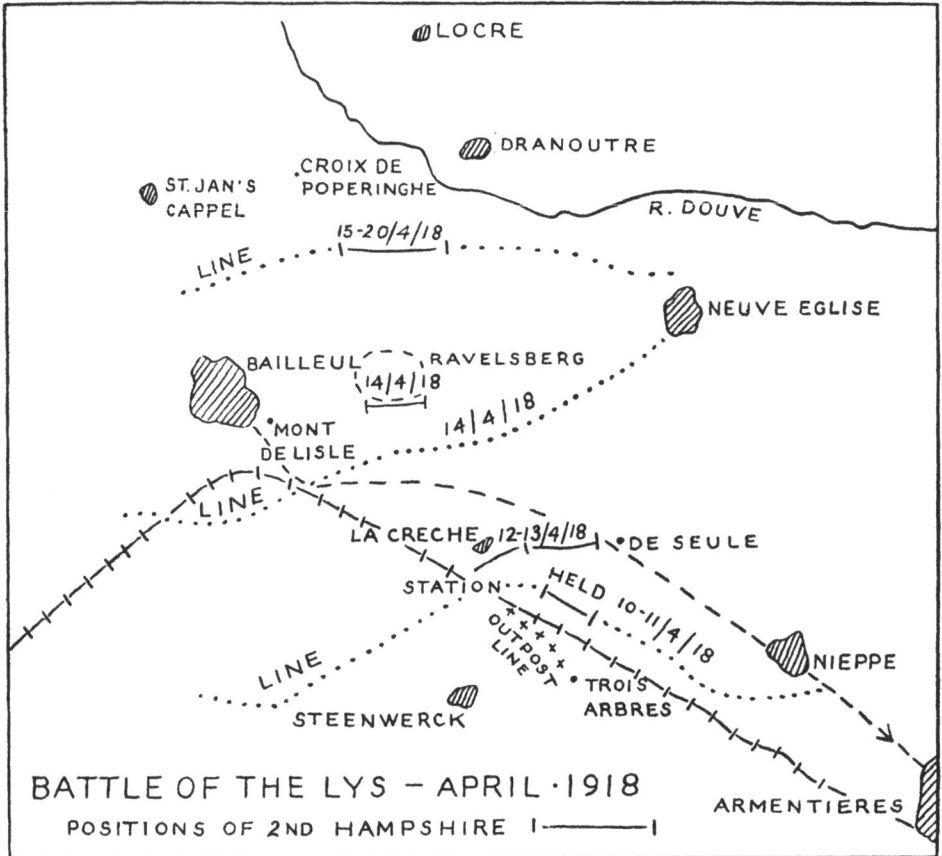

BATTLE OF THE LYS – APRIL ·1918

POSITIONS OF 2ND HAMPSHIRE I————I

not be distributed there was no lack of food. Some wire was got up and the position was considerably improved.

During the night it proved necessary to bring back the 88th Brigade's left to conform to the movements on its flank, a move which involved several casualties in X and Y Companies. In the new line Y had its left on the Bailleul–Armentieres road near De Seule with X in support behind it. Though heavily shelled at times, the battalion maintained its position throughout the day (April 12th), keeping intrusive patrols at bay, though efforts to occupy some

[1] *Official History* (1918. II. p. 234).

buildings in front as advanced posts were not successful. Heavier assaults followed, to be successfully repulsed : the highly cultivated ground with many hedges and ditches made it difficult for the Germans to get their guns forward and without substantial artillery support their infantry made little headway against our rifles and machine-guns. Casualties were again fairly heavy, over 50 in all, mainly wounded but including Captain R. E. Thompson killed, but the position had been well maintained and the enemy checked and heavily punished.

By this time the 1st Battalion also was on the fighting front, the Fourth Division, which had been relieved by the Canadians and had been in reserve NW. of Arras, having been transferred to the First Corps.   A draft of 160 men had nearly made up its March 28th losses, when on April 12th it was moved by bus to Lillers and from there marched to Gonnehem, where it was billeted ; it was now in reserve to the 11th Brigade, which was holding a frontage along the canal running from Bethune to Robecq with the Rifle Brigade and the Somerset in front, facing Pacaut Wood : the other two brigades were in reserve, the Third Division being on the right nearer Givenchy and the Sixty-First at and beyond Robecq. Though the Germans had made considerable progress in this quarter, they had been checked and had in fact reached the furthest points to which they were to penetrate.

On the Northern flank of their advance they were, however, to gain more ground yet. Bailleul, Meteren and our last foothold on the Messines ridge at Wytschaete were to be lost and the line forced back to the hills behind Kemmel, after the French reinforcements, rather belatedly sent up, had lost Mount Kemmel itself. These advances were also to compel the Second Army not only to relinquish all our gains of 1917 in the Ypres Salient but to bring back our line to the very outskirts of Ypres itself, a withdrawal which was begun on the night of April 11th/12th, the Forty-First Division being first left to hold the whole of the Eighth Corps' front and then drawn back gradually to Ypres.

For the 1st Hampshire April 13th was a quiet day ; Gonnehem was shelled in the afternoon without much result and the surplus personnel who would not be required in the local attack to be made next day were sent back to the transport lines. The 2nd Battalion, however, was actively engaged, half a dozen German Divisions being put in against the line between Bailleul (right) and Neuve Eglise, the left centre of which the 88th Brigade was holding. Fortunately the ridge behind our line here afforded the artillery good observation points, of which the gunners made good use and they, as well as the infantry, took a heavy toll of the Germans when a really strong attack developed in the early afternoon. Further to the left the Germans broke into our line near Neuve Eglise, though the Newfoundlands managed to prevent them from rolling up the 88th Brigade's line from the left. However, the line which the Hampshire and 4th Worcestershire had maintained intact had to be evacuated during the night, the brigade withdrawing to the SE. of Bailleul.[1]

[1] To a line roughly covering Mont de Lille (R) and the Ravelsberg (L).

The retirement was begun about 10 p.m. by Y Company, Z, W, and X following in that order, each leaving a Lewis gun team to cover the move. The enemy, although already round the brigade's left, made no attempt to interfere, and by 2 a.m. (April 14th) the battalion was established in its new position, which proved to be quite advantageous, being covered in front by about 1000 yards of marshy ground. Entrenching the new line was hard work for weary men, many so tired that they fell asleep while trying to dig. But they dug to some

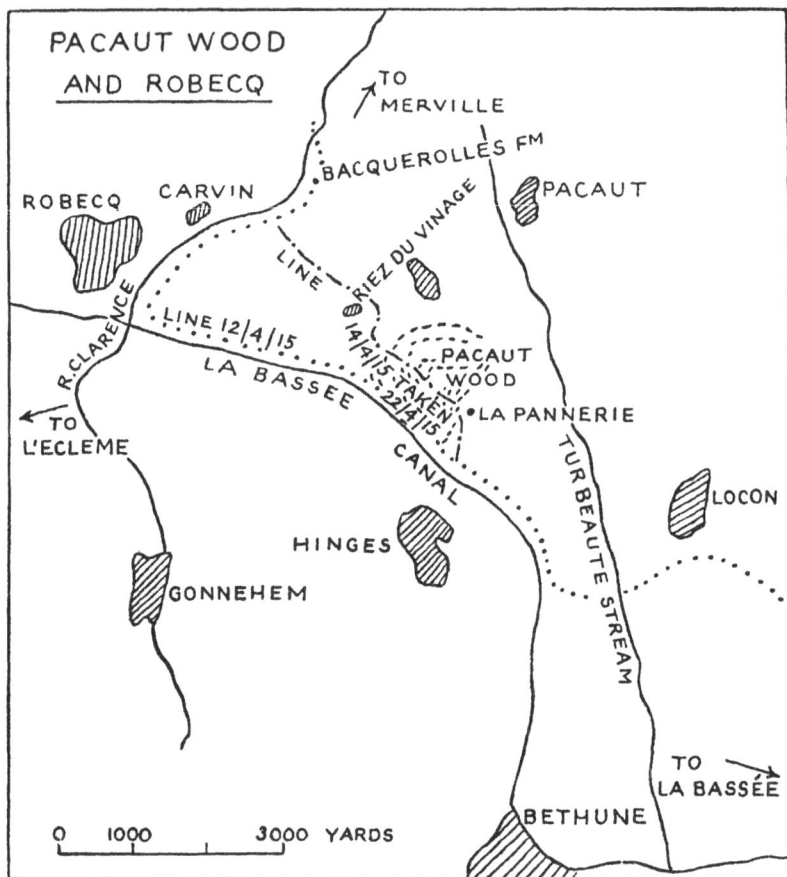

PACAUT WOOD AND ROBECQ

purpose and the German attempts to advance here were successfully held ; once the Hampshire's Lewis gunners got targets in a column of fours, and later on small parties trying to work their way forward were effectively deterred. A more solid attempt about 4.30 p.m. penetrated the line to the Hampshire's right, but the intruders were promptly ejected and the line restored, the Hampshire having meanwhile held firm. The German guns, however, had got the line fairly well ranged and discouraged much movement, if the day's casualties, six killed and 2/Lt. Heath and nine men wounded, had been even lower than the eight killed or missing, including 2/Lt. Tunks, and eleven wounded of April 13th. By now, however, all ranks were very weary, terribly short of sleep and hardly able to keep awake, and the arrival that evening of officers of the Fifty-Ninth Division to arrange for the battalion's relief was exceedingly welcome. Arrangements were not easy to make, as they depended on a fluctuating tactical situation, but about 4 a.m. the relieving unit arrived and before daylight the 2nd Hampshire had crossed the low ridge behind them and were making their way to Croix de Poperinghe, where they arrived before 7 a.m., to get a wash and a hot meal and to indulge in hopes of a well-earned rest. Casualties, two officers [1] and 65 men killed and missing, five officers [2] and 107 men wounded, had been extremely low considering the severity of the fighting ; the 2nd Hampshire's assailants had not got off so lightly.

April 14th had given the 1st Battalion a busy day. General Holland, G.O.C. First Corps, was anxious to straighten out a deep re-entrant just East of Robecq, where the frontage of his Corps joined that of General Haking's Eleventh Corps. The task was entrusted to the 11th Brigade, who after dribbling the Hampshire and the Somerset across the canal in small parties, using the half-dozen bridges still in existence,[3] formed them up to attack NE. between the canal and the Robecq-Merville road, the Hampshire on the left. For half an hour heavy guns kept the enemy's positions under a steady fire and at 6.30 p.m. the two battalions went forward behind an excellent 18-pounder barrage, moving in platoons in artillery formation.

Pushing rapidly forward some 1500 yards the Hampshire reached their objective along the road from Riez de Vinage to Carvin with only four casualties, while the Somerset, who were sufficiently seriously opposed to have 40 casualties, carried Riez du Vinage and took 130 prisoners and 20 machine-guns. Germans bolting from Riez du Vinage and neighbouring houses provided targets, which they also presented when they counter-attacked, pressing hardest against the Somerset. Altogether it was a most encouraging operation, which greatly improved our line, while the brigade had the satisfaction of recovering two 18- pounder batteries lost on April 12th. The Sixty-First Division, now on the Hampshire's left, attempting next day to push forward and secure Bacquerelles Farm, A and C Companies sent strong patrols forward to co-operate. The attackers, however, after capturing their objective were pushed back, and accordingly the advanced line, 500 yards ahead, on which the Hampshire patrols had dug in, was evacuated and the original line resumed. After maintaining its position throughout April 16th the battalion was relieved in the evening and went back to billets in L'Ecleme, where it was to have two days' rest, interrupted on April 16th by orders to turn out in readiness to counter-attack, the Fourth Division and the First, now holding the Givenchy sector, having both been violently attacked. After heavy fighting, particularly bitter

---

[1] Captain Thompson and 2/Lt. Tunks.
[2] 2/Lts. Heath, Sharp, Slater, Welsh and Whitten
[3] The Hampshire crossed in Robecq

round Givenchy, both Divisions succeeded in thwarting the attackers' efforts, though Riez du Vinage was for a time lost, without requiring the 11th Brigade to intervene ; but next day the Hampshire relieved the 10th Brigade along the canal opposite Pacaut Wood, having three companies in line and A back at Le Cauroy in support. Our patrols were active and obtained a useful identification by capturing several prisoners, while on the night of 20th/21st C Company established posts across the canal and along the Southern edge of Pacaut Wood. The German shell-fire was heavy and three days in this position cost the battalion 14 killed and 33 wounded.

Meanwhile the 2nd Battalion's hopes of rest had been disappointed. Badly mauled in the March offensive, the Fifty-Ninth Division, which had relieved it, was hardly fit for the line, certainly not to withstand an attack in force. Early in the afternoon of April 15th German pressure became increasingly severe, and the attackers, penetrating the front line NE. of Bailleul, rolled it up from the flank, so that the troops at first in support found themselves in front line again and the 88th Brigade, from being back in reserve, was once more in support, while the loss of Bailleul and other ground made it necessary to bring the flanking troops back to conform. The 2nd Hampshire had to turn to and dig in SE. of Croix de Poperinghe, while some of their officers reconnoitred the ground in front in order to know how to deliver a counter-attack if needed. This was not required of them next day (April 16th), when despite repeated attacks the new front line behind Bailleul held firm, our guns successfully breaking up several concentrations which seemed to herald an attack. Renewing the attacks early next morning, (April 17th) the Germans pressed hard against some weak battalions of the Thirty-Fourth Division, to whose support Y and Z Companies of the 2nd Hampshire were sent forward. They were heavily shelled but held on unflinchingly and about 5 p.m. restored a dangerous situation by counter-attacking most effectively. Seeing the troops in front wavering, Captain Ogier dashed forward with Z Company, arriving most opportunely just as the enemy were breaking into our line. His prompt and vigorous action was most successful, though he himself was badly wounded in the leg, the enemy were ejected and the line fully re-established.[1]

After dark the Hampshire took over the front line. It was very dark and the exact positions of the British outposts were hard to locate, nor were things made easier by the officers in the line being by this time reduced to seven, 2/Lt. Hatch also having been wounded. But the check the Germans had received all along the line on April 17th had damped their enterprise, while with plenty of guns to support our infantry we effectively discouraged attacks. Thus, though nearer Givenchy the fighting had flared up again, the 2nd Hampshire were but little troubled during the next three days and were able to put up some wire, re-site several trenches and readjust their dispositions so that two companies could be ready for an immediate counter-attack. Casualties were low, despite fairly persistent shelling, only five killed and nine wounded.

[1] Captain Ogier received the M.C.

The evening of April 20th brought a relief by French troops, now coming to the Second Army's help in substantial numbers. All ranks were dead beat but nevertheless managed to cover the ten kilometres between the front and their bivouac at Abeele in little over two hours, a fine achievement by men as tired as were the 2nd Hampshire after their ten days of hard fighting, much of it in bitter weather. From Abeele they went the next day by bus to Hondeghem near Hazebrouck where the much reduced infantry of the Twenty-Ninth Division were being concentrated for a rest. The 88th Brigade had lost heavily enough, especially the Newfoundlands, who were so much reduced that they had to become G.H.Q. troops, being replaced in the brigade by the 2nd Leinster, but the 86th and 87th had been almost cut to pieces and rest and reinforcements were badly needed.

The 2nd Hampshire, who had had two officers and 87 men killed and missing and seven officers and 161 men wounded, while another five officers and 76 men had gone to hospital, now received large drafts,[1] along with 20 officers, including the 'pre-war' Special Reservist, Captain Prendergast,[2] who took over Y Company, vacant through Captain Thompson's death, Major O'Reilly of the Middlesex, who joined as second in command, and Captain West, a 'pre-war' member of the regiment, commissioned in January 1917. The battalion was to see no more of the Flanders battle, which finished towards the end of the month with a sudden ' flare-up ' in which the French lost Kemmel, though further German progress was checked by the interposition of some of the troops they had recently relieved.

The British First and Second Armies, like the Third and Fifth in March, could claim to have prevented Ludendorff from achieving all he needed to accomplish, if we had again had to relinquish ground we were very loath to give up, especially in the Ypres Salient. We had lost very heavily in guns and men, but that we had inflicted as heavy losses on the Germans may be taken as well established.[3] In thwarting this second effort to achieve victory by a break-through the 2nd Hampshire had taken a good share and earned no little credit, and Colonel Westmorland's D.S.O. was well deserved : he had handled the situation most skilfully, organizing the withdrawals so that they were conducted in good order and that little was left behind : he had shown great disregard of danger and had frequently rallied and reorganized men and more than once had restored a situation which was becoming critical. Lt. Perry was awarded the M.C. for conspicuously good work as Transport Officer ; he had never failed to deliver the rations and without the ammunition he brought up so unflinchingly the line could hardly have been held.

At the other end of the Lys salient, the 1st Hampshire had in the last days of April had one of their most successful days. The Fourth Divison had come

---

[1] Altogether nearly 350 joined in April.

[2] He had been ' out ' several times before this, and had been wounded at ' Plugstreet ', at Second Ypres and at Arras.

[3] German methods of calculating casualties make the correct figures hard to ascertain, but their regimental histories provide ample evidence of the punishment they had received and its effect on officers and men.

into the fighting between Givenchy and Robecq fairly fresh and strong. Not many of its battalions had lost really heavily on March 28th, and it had begun counter-attacking almost from the moment it had come into line on its new front. If April 18th had seen the 10th and 12th Brigades fairly hard pressed to repulse an attack in force, directly afterwards the Division had resumed its efforts to recover some of the ground we had lost ; that lost near Riez du Vinage on April 18th was won back within two days, and on April 22nd the 1st Hampshire and the Rifle Brigade were put in with a more ambitious object, the capture of Pacaut Wood.

Pacaut Wood, just across the canal opposite Gonnehem, had considerable tactical importance, as it was still a wood and provided cover in which the enemy might mass for an attack. The attack aimed at securing a line across the wood, roughly that of a road from La Pannerie on the right to Riez du Vinage, and thereby cutting off the Southern part of the wood. The Rifle Brigade was attacking on the right, outside the wood, with La Pannerie as objective ; the Hampshire, who were attacking the actual wood, had three companies in the attack, the fourth being disposed in support along the Southern bank of the canal, to which our line had been drawn back to allow a heavy trench-mortar barrage to be put down along the wood's Southern edge. This involved re-crossing the canal by footbridges laid for the purpose, and as the German barrage answered ours within three minutes of Zero (5.15 a.m., April 22nd) many casualties were incurred in the passage, especially by the centre company, A, whose commander was killed. However, the attack went forward well, companies advancing by platoons up the various ' rides ' and along the edges of the wood and extending inwards on reaching their objectives. D Company on the right came under heavy fire from machine guns as they neared their objective, but 2/Lt. Abbott pushed forward two Lewis guns to deal with them and thanks largely to him the two right platoons were established on their objective within 25 minutes of Zero, five minutes after the left company, B, had secured its. A Company, in the centre, was delayed by its casualties, but pushed forward before long up the main ride and gained touch with B. Meanwhile D was extending to the left to close the gap, for which purpose a platoon of C was ordered up. It was sharply opposed ; Captain Causton, who was leading it, was killed in heading a rush, but despite machine-gun fire the platoon drove the enemy back, shooting many down ; following them up it over-ran a reinforcing party, while on reaching the cross-roads which formed its objective it began extending to both flanks, mainly by bombing.

By 11 a.m. the German machine-gun fire, hitherto very heavy, began to slacken, though their shell-fire increased, especially along the canal bank, and about 1.30 p.m. the battalion suffered a severe loss when Colonel Armitage was killed. Meanwhile consolidation was being pushed on, two platoons of the Rifle Brigade, having advanced behind D Company, had worked out along the road to La Pannerie, which another company had secured, and were linking up that front with the wood. Early in the afternoon the whole line had been connected, though A Company was slightly short of its objective. Meanwhile the Germans had put down a heavy barrage and opened rifle and machine-gun fire but without much effect, while after dark an attempted counter-attack was effectively repulsed, mainly by rifles and Lewis guns. By midnight the battalion was well dug in on its objective except at one point in the centre. Sharp fighting continued round this post, which had not been reduced when the Hampshire were relieved after dark by the Somerset L.I. and the Duke's and went back to billets in Lannoy.

The much regretted loss of Colonel Armitage marred what was otherwise a highly successful operation. Over 70 prisoners and several machine-guns had been taken, the Rifle Brigade taking another 60 men ; apart from the enemy's

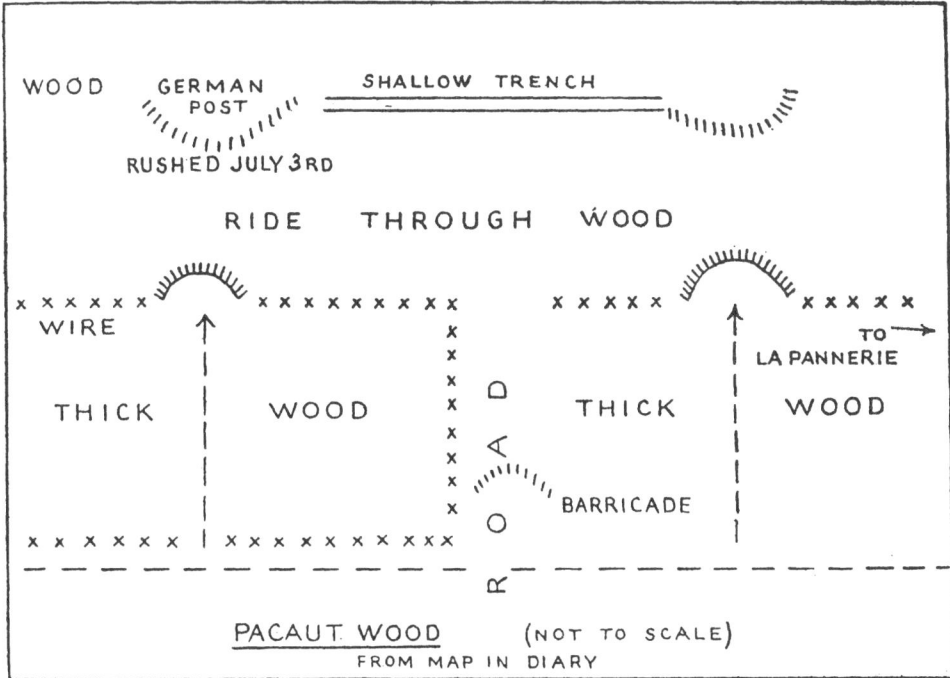

WOOD   GERMAN   SHALLOW TRENCH
POST
RUSHED JULY 3RD

RIDE   THROUGH   WOOD

x x x x x x   x x x x x x x x x x   x x x x x   x x x x x
WIRE   x   TO
x   LA PANNERIE
x
THICK   WOOD   x   THICK   WOOD
x
x
x   'BARRICADE
x x x x x x   x x x x x x x x x x

PACAUT WOOD   (NOT TO SCALE)
FROM MAP IN DIARY

casualties the ground gained in Pacaut Wood allowed of another advance at Riez du Vinage whereby the Sixty-First Division's position also was greatly strengthened. Losses had, however, been substantial, the C.O., Captain Causton, Lt. Stannard, 2/Lts. Sillence and Shirley with 43 other ranks killed or missing, Captain Newnham, 2/Lts. Clegg and Wincer and 148 men wounded out of 14 officers and 650 men in action.[1]

Colonel Armitage was much missed. Not himself of the Hampshire he had completely identified himself with the battalion from the moment of taking over the remnants of the fine unit which had been shattered against Beaumont Hamel on July 1st, 1916. He had soon shown himself a worthy successor of Colonels

[1] Those not engaged, including Major Hudson, Captains de Gaury and Edwards and 116 men forming the battle nucleus, came to 14 officers and 170 men.

Hicks and Palk, he had led the battalion in several successful attacks and had won the trust and confidence of all who served under him. He had done a great work for the battalion, which owed much to him and regretted him deeply.

The Pacaut Wood attack, whose success was recognised by the award of the M.C. to 2/Lt. Abbott and to Captain Walker, R.A.M.C., the battalion's M.O., of the D.C.M. to Corporal Alexander and of the M.M. to Sergeants Hurll and Wesley, Lance Corporals Light and Tilley and Privates Meddings and Simcock, ended the 1st Hampshire's active share in resisting the second German ' push '. On returning to the line West of Pacaut Wood on April 26th, they found things quiet. The Germans had ' shot their bolt ' in this quarter also and after April they suspended their attacks on the British front. If some British troops were to be involved in the next big German attack, that of May 25th on the Chemin des Dames—Rheims front, it fell on tired Divisions, sent to rest and recuperate in a portion of the French front which both Foch and Petain believed most unlikely to be attacked.

Of the other two Hampshire battalions in France the 11th had seen nothing of the Flanders fighting, which had affected the 15th in so far as they, having been transferred to the Second Army and put into line in the Ypres Salient, had to carry out the withdrawals which became necessary to release troops to withstand the Germans elsewhere.

The 15th Hampshire had been relieved on the Bucquoy front late on April 1st : two days later they had entrained for Flanders, reaching Poperinghe on April 4th, and after three days in camp, resting and refitting, took over trenches from the Twenty-Ninth Division at the very apex of the Salient, their relief of the 1st Lancashire Fusiliers being complete by 11.30 p.m. (April 7th). Things were fairly quiet here, dry weather had hardened the slime in which Third Ypres had come to its ' sticky ' end in November, but the ground was bare and barren and the line was held merely by shell-holes. The 15th's patrols were active but encountered no enemy, though an attempted German advance was easily beaten off on April 10th. The battalion had hardly been relieved on April 11th before it was in line again, in the ' same shell-holes ', now being held as an outpost line in preparation for the withdrawal which was becoming inevitable. Patrols were again active but the attack showed no signs of being extended to the Salient, and, early on April 16th, the first stage of the withdrawal was carried out.[1] Covering parties were left in the old front line, each company finding a Lewis gun section, but the enemy, apparently quite unaware of what we were doing, made no attempt to interfere or to follow up the move. The 15th now went right back to a camp between Ypres and Vlamertinghe, where they spent the next ten days, their brigade, though in reserve, was held in readiness to support either its own Division or those adjacent, whose own reserves had already been moved South ; it was kept busy meanwhile reclaiming an old line of trenches. Bombing by German aeroplanes, mainly at night,

---

[1] The line of resistance now ran from Pilckem by Wieltje to Zillebeke Lake, an outpost line in front having its apex at Polygon Wood.

was an unpleasant feature of the situation. Meanwhile a further withdrawal had proved necessary, the line of resistance being brought back to Ypres itself with outposts holding the Pilckem–Zillebeke position, the Forty-First Division holding the front immediately NE. of Ypres. However, the 123rd Brigade was not required for duty in the front line and May 1st found it still out of the line, working and training. The day was the second anniversary of the battalion's arrival in France : 80 ' originals ' were still present.

The 11th Battalion meanwhile had been taken right back, nearly to the coastal area, reaching Wizernes on April 11th and being put into billets at Avroult. It was then moved to the Therouanne neighbourhood, where it was quartered just East of Aire, and detailed for work on a rearward line, the Isbergues defences. This line was occasionally shelled at long range but the Hampshire escaped without casualties.

The heavy losses incurred in stemming two German attacks together with the still inadequate supply of drafts from home was now forcing Sir Douglas Haig to the distasteful expedient of reducing several Divisions, cutting them down to training cadres for the instruction of Americans, now at last beginning to reach France in some strength, the surplus officers and men being drafted to weakened units. With recruits from Southern Ireland the merest trickle the Sixteenth was an early victim of this reorganization and the 11th Hampshire, although independent of Irish recruits, did not escape. April 20th brought orders for the reduction of the battalion to a training cadre of ten officers [1] and 55 other ranks and for the remainder, eight officers and 382 men, to join a base camp at Etaples.

The reduction actually took place on May 2nd, when the training cadre moved from La Roupie to Therouanne, going on next day to Ledinghem, the surplus personnel going off to the base to be redrafted as required.[2] This was virtually the end of the Sixteenth Division of 1914 : though it was to be reconstituted later, none of its new infantry units were Irish,[3] if the reconstituted 11th Hampshire were connected with the original 11th through the officers and men of the training cadre.

---

[1] These included the C.O. and battalion staff.

[2] Owing to the loss of the Part II Orders it is impossible to trace the units to which officers and men were sent.

[3] The Regular units previously transferred to the Division were posted to other Divisions.

CHAPTER XXVIII

1918 : III

THE SUMMER MONTHS, THE 2/4TH ON THE MARNE

Two great German attacks had, with great difficulty and at a great cost, been stopped well short of their territorial objectives, and the British Armies in France, whom it had been Ludendorff's strategical object to reduce to impotence, were still far from that state, worn and exhausted as nearly every Division was after its ordeals in March and April. Thwarted and foiled, and for the moment forced to suspend his offensive so as to gather reserves for its renewal, Ludendorff, without relinquishing his original purpose of smashing the British Armies, now turned his attention to the French, mainly, it seems, in the hope of exhausting them and leaving them incapable of giving effective assistance when he should in due course renew his attack on the British. The substantial success achieved by his attack of May 27th between Rheims and Soissons may have led him to seek to exploit it beyond the limits of prudence and to renew it both in June and again in July, when he might have done better to return to his original purpose; before he was ready to strike again at the British Sir Douglas Haig had seized the initiative and on August 8th started the series of blows which were to expel the Germans from France and produce their virtual surrender on November 11th.

The three months' respite from attack which the British front was to enjoy from April to August could hardly have been anticipated by the British Commander in Chief : he could not count on being given time to build up his forces to meet another attack, still less on being able to resume the offensive ; his troops, largely recruits or units recalled from other fronts who had to find their feet in unfamiliar surroundings, wanted time for more training and for obtaining experience, new defences had to be constructed and any number of difficult administrative problems had to be grappled. The enemy still possessed large reserves, even if substantially reduced by his efforts and lavish expenditure in March and April, and while he therefore retained the initiative there was no saying how soon or where the storm might not break again or how the British would be placed for meeting it. But, as the summer wore on without another German ' push ', the British situation was gradually improving ; the drafts were being assimilated and worked up to the necessary level, substantial reinforcements, among them the 2/4th Hampshire, arrived from Macedonia, Palestine and Italy, the British defences grew stronger and the losses in guns and other material were replaced : moreover, it was becoming more and more likely that the Americans, now appearing in France in rapidly increasing numbers would after all not be too late. From the strategical standpoint these summer months gave the British one of those periods of relative ' rest ' which intervene in war between those of ' tension ' and decisive activities : to the officers and men of the British infantry the element of ' rest ' was hardly so obvious. If out of the line, they were busy training, if not needed to build defences ; in the line they had plenty to do, as in most parts of the front opportunities of harassing and worrying the enemy were not neglected. This policy was adopted largely for reasons of morale but also to benefit by the many points at which his suspended advances had landed him in unsatisfactory tactical positions, where his line showed all the disadvantages which attach to the arrested offensive, thrown back upon an unprepared defensive on a line usually ill-adapted to that purpose and often lending itself to the local counter-strokes which the British were now attempting.

In the Pacaut Wood area the German positions exhibited this weakness conspicuously and the Fourth Division, encouraged and inspired by memories of March 28th and other more recent successes, was on the alert to profit by this and do all it could to trouble and wear down the enemy. Both sides were holding improvised defences, largely disconnected posts, and few regular trench lines existed, so the tactical situation was very different from that of the almost stabilized trench warfare of 1916. This gave great chances to initiative and to activity in patrolling and allowed of occasional minor enterprises. Thus, three nights after taking over, on May 2nd, the right of their brigade's front, just East of Riez du Vinage, the Hampshire advanced their line, gaining about 100 yards. They were in line here nearly ten days and then were ' out ' from May 11th to 15th, at L'Ecleme, where Major Mordaunt of the Somerset L.I. joined and took command. On May 15th they were back in Pacaut Wood, largely thick hazel undergrowth, with rides running through it, one of which separated our front line from the German posts 30–40 yards away. Here two companies were in front line and one in reserve behind the canal. With the front lines so close rifle grenades could be used and even bombs, and the battalion did some effective shooting one day when a house in the German lines took fire and its garrison, quitting it in haste, offered good targets, while patrols found many dead Germans in a line of shelters just in front. Our snipers got some chances but were too successful to encourage the enemy to risk exposing himself and targets soon became fewer. German shelling, especially of rear areas, was quite heavy, gas being freely used, and on May 20th a ' direct ' on battalion head-quarters gassed the C.O., the Adjutant, Lt. Flint,[1] and the Intelligence and Signal Officers, though Lt. Colonel Mordaunt was back at duty four days later and the Adjutant by May 29th. On the previous day two of the battalion's advanced posts had been attacked in some force, but though all the men in them were hit the Germans failed to get in and left several dead behind when they fell back. This spell in front line lasted eight days, and the men came out in fine form, feeling they had the upper hand and could do what they liked with ' the Hun '. Four days later the battalion was back in the line, this time more to the left, in front of Riez. The line here was damp and badly drained and needed a lot of work, but things were quieter than before. Altogether May

---

[1] He had been with the battalion since early in 1915 and had taken over the Adjutancy after Captain Hume had been wounded in the attack on Beaumont Hamel.

cost the battalion 20 killed, including 2/Lts. Daines, sniped in getting an identification off a dead German, and Stevenson, with five officers [1] and nearly 70 men wounded or gassed. Ten officers joined, among them one ' pre-war ' Regular, Captain Berkeley, the original Adjutant of the 11th, with nearly 200 men, but with 110 admissions to hospital the battalion's numbers remained on balance little altered.

June was uneventful : the battalion held the Riez sector from the 1st to the 8th and Pacaut Wood from the 13th to 25th. The enemy were very unenterprising, if they gave the battalion's snipers a fair number of chances, while their guns and trench-mortars were occasionally active. After one relief the Hampshire found the enemy inclined to ' fraternize', a tendency they very quickly suppressed, getting quite a good ' bag ' in doing so, while as our posts were much better sited and constructed than his he could do little in reply. The influenza epidemic which affected all the opposing armies during the summer and autumn accounted for most of the 150 admissions to hospital. Among others Colonel Mordaunt went sick in the middle of June and in his absence Major Hudson took over, retaining command till the end of July, while of the 40 battle casualties during June 15 were fatal. Over 250 men joined, nearly half in one batch, but even so the strength in the line did not reach 600, those at the transport lines and forming the battle reserve coming to over 200. When out of the line conditions were now quite pleasant, plenty of good food could be had, especially fresh vegetables, the men could bathe in the canal and were not over-worked : indeed they amused themselves by making some 30-yard ranges to enable them to improve their shooting.

July brought increased activity. The situation had so far improved that minor operations could become more frequent and more ambitious. Despite its big initial success, the German attack of May 27th on the Chemin des Dames had been held and had landed them in an awkward salient, in which the problem of supplying the front line troops was not easy, and a subsequent attack in June had not improved their position appreciably. Moreover, the Americans, now pouring into the Atlantic ports of France in really large numbers, would before long be able to take over a ' quiet ' part of the line and even eventually to join in an attack.

The 1st Hampshire had quite a lively first half of July in front line at Riez du Vinage. Their patrols were active in taking advantage of the opportunities of surprising the small and scattered outposts which the Germans were now holding. In this 2/Lt. Powning and C.S.M. Dyer were most successful, especially in gaining information, and in an exciting duel early on July 7th a machine-gunner [2] silenced two German guns, going out into No Man's Land to get a good spot to shoot from and letting off ten drums, while on the 9th 2/Lt. Shephard and six men successfully stalked a standing patrol. Both artilleries were active but the Hampshire's casualties were under a dozen, 2/Lts. Culley and King being wounded, the former fatally. After a week in reserve, largely devoted to

---

[1] Lts. Taberer and Cheyne were gassed and 2/Lt. Shelly wounded.
[2] The battalion diary does not give his name.

musketry, the battalion took over the Pacaut Wood sector on July 20th. This time things were more ' lively ', the Duke's, whom the battalion relieved, had just made a most successful raid and the Hampshire did not relax the pressure. ' We did not give Jerry a moment's peace ' one officer wrote ; Lewis guns, rifle fire and bombs kept him well under and so quiet that on July 22nd a patrol from C Company went out to see if the enemy had actually, as it seemed, evacuated his forward posts. Covered by Lewis guns in two of our posts, Captain May, 2/Lt. Taylor, Sergeant Bax and Private Rogers made their way out to his line and worked along a shallow trench without being observed. While Captain May watched the left flank, the others made their way to the right and ran into a group of eight Germans, mostly asleep. Before the sleepers could rouse themselves the raiders had laid out the sentry and were carrying him off for identification. The other Germans bolted but several were shot by the men covering the raid with the Lewis guns, and within a few minutes of starting out the patrol was back in our lines with the prisoner.[1] Two days later patrols from A and C encountered German patrols and captured more prisoners. Another encounter on July 31st led to quite sharp fighting. Our patrol, 15 strong under 2/Lt. K. E. Potter, had searched a hedgerow and was approaching a group of houses when a large party appeared advancing down a ride in the wood. A Lewis gun promptly got on to them but did not stop them, and at the same time another party, at least 20 strong, appeared on the left. Dropping into shell-holes, our patrol gave the enemy rapid fire till they came within bombing range and then withdrew under cover of a shower of bombs and of effective fire directed by 2/Lt. Coleman from our trench behind ; several casualties were inflicted on the enemy, while of the patrol only 2/Lt. Potter was hit : he, however, had been badly wounded and had to be left in a shell-hole, but later in the day while several men crept out through the long grass and occupied some ruined buildings to cover them, 2/Lt. Coleman and a stretcher bearer made their way to the shell-hole and brought 2/Lt. Potter in.[2]

Despite much shelling the tour only produced a dozen casualties, but besides 2/Lt. Potter, Captain de Gaury and 2/Lts. Craig and Openshaw, the latter within four days of joining, were wounded. Once again admissions to hospital were well over 100, but they were exceeded by the drafts received and the return of convalescents, so that the battalion's strength was fairly well maintained and its success in so many minor enterprises had greatly encouraged and inspirited the men : C Company in particular ' had their tails a mile high ', as the Divisional and brigade commanders had held up their efforts to other units as something to be copied.[3]

---

[1] As a company commander Captain May should not have gone out and he had meant to let 2/Lt. Taylor write the report, but in getting back he encountered Major Hudson with the result that the higher authorities heard of his exploit and he was told ' not to do it again ', but a second bar to the M.C. was a better indication of the view taken of his skilful dispositions and good leading.

[2] 2/Lt. Coleman subsequently received the M.C., and Corporal Beck the M.M., as did Sergeant Bax for the July 22nd raid. 2/Lt. Potter died of his wounds in August.

[3] Their method was known as ' winkling ', but the phrase did not receive official approval.

On the Flanders front as in the Robecq area only minor operations were attempted during May, June and July. The 2nd Hampshire had been ' out ' when the German offensive on the Lys expended itself, but by May 5th they were back in line, taking over the left of the Twenty-Ninth Division's line, now SE. of Hazebrouck. Here also the line was somewhat ' fluid ', mainly held by posts. A none too quiet week here cost 25 casualties, but the line was advanced a little in places and the battalion's Lewis gunners got some good shooting at aeroplanes which came over frequently and threatened to be troublesome. After ten days' rest, partly in billets near Hazebrouck, partly

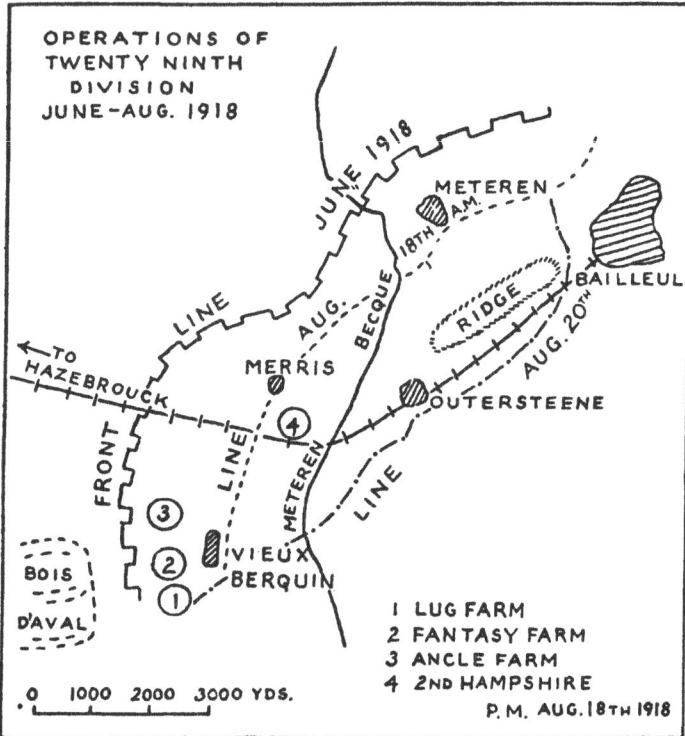

OPERATIONS OF
TWENTY NINTH
DIVISION
JUNE-AUG. 1918

METEREN
BAILLEUL
RIDGE
TO HAZEBROUCK
MERRIS
OUTERSTEENE
BOIS D'AVAL
VIEUX BERQUIN

0 1000 2000 3000 YDS.

1 LUG FARM
2 FANTASY FARM
3 ANCLE FARM
4 2ND HAMPSHIRE
P. M. AUG. 18TH 1918

at Morbecque, the battalion was in support behind Aval Wood from May 23rd to 27th and then in front till the 31st, during which time W Company raided Ferme Beaulieu without encountering any enemy, Y also trying a raid (May 30th) but without success, as the barrage fell short and did not clear the objective; 2/Lt. Quarrier and five men were missing and, with the enemy's guns rather active, the month's casualties came to 25 killed [1] and missing and 60 wounded. However, only 76 went to hospital, from which 20 rejoined and with reinforcements coming to 160, largely the young recruits now being freely pushed out, the battalion's paper strength reached 974 by May 31st, with 40 officers.

[1] Including 2/Lt. Cook.

From June 1st to 12th the 2nd Hampshire were at Morbecque Camp, resting and training. Relieving the 2nd Royal Fusiliers on June 12th in front line West of Vieux Berquin, they found that the 86th Brigade had just captured two farms, Ancle and Lug, which were being held as outposts, the Hampshire also holding some forward posts in line with and South of them. Early on June 15th the enemy attacked in some force, retook Lug Farm and Fantasy Farm North of it, and forced back the Hampshire outposts, some 40 of X Company. The rest of X were called up from support to hold the line opposite Fantasy Farm, and about 1.30 p.m. 2/Lt. Lambert and a platoon attempted without success to recover that farm. Reinforced by a platoon of W under 2/Lt. Morant, they tried again, without happier result, but about 10.30 p.m., 2/Lt. Seed and a platoon of Z having reinforced the original attackers, Fantasy Farm was retaken and the position re-established. Casualties, however, came to a dozen killed and missing, among the latter 2/Lt. Pouncey,[1] and 25 wounded.

The battalion held this position for another four days : three times it evacuated its forward line to allow of a gas discharge, which was twice cancelled but at last carried out. One patrol ran into a machine-gun post, killed four men and carried off the machine-gun, but the enemy's shell-fire was fairly effective, 2/Lt. Seed and five men being killed and Captain West, Lt. Colbert and 21 men wounded. Then, on June 20th, the Twenty-Ninth Division was taken right back for the month's rest which it had fully earned. Of this it, with all the other units of its Division, still stood in great need. Every battalion was full of drafts, mainly young, some very imperfectly trained, and wanted a chance to assimilate them and reorganize ; much re-fitting was needed and both officers and men could do with some recreation and relief from work, though the time was also largely devoted to training and some ' ceremonial ', which did much towards smartening the men. The Hampshire did well in athletics, winning the brigade cross-country run.

This rest over, the Twenty-Ninth Division returned to the front, the Hampshire arriving at Eecke (July 26th) where they were put to work on a new ' Army Line ' S.E. of Boeschepe. While the Twenty-Ninth had been resting the Ninth Division and some Australians had carried out some very successful operations, retaking Meteren (July 19th) and advancing the line towards Merris, besides inflicting considerable casualties fairly cheaply. It was a foretaste of further recoveries of ground in this quarter.

The Forty-First Division meanwhile had spent May in the Ypres defences, was ' out ' nearly all June, training and resting, and back in the line at La Clytte near Kemmel by June 30th, relieving some of the French troops who had been with the Second Army since April. It remained on this front during July.

May for the 15th Hampshire had been uneventful. They held the front or outpost line South of Potijze from May 7th to 17th and were in line again for the last week of the month, East of Goldfish Chateau. ' All water and no dug-outs ' is all one diarist has to say of the line held near Potijze. The first turn

---

[1] Later reported wounded and a prisoner.

was marked by the repulse of some small raids (May 9th, 10th and 13th) and the second by heavy gas shelling, chiefly with mustard gas, which caused 15 of the month's 40 casualties, which included four killed. Half a dozen new officers joined, with 90 men, and then from June 5th to 24th the battalion was near Watten, training, particular attention being paid to bringing the ' specialists ' up to the old level. Two long marches, each over 15 miles though no one fell out, then took the 15th back to the Watou area and on June 30th it relieved a French regiment at La Clytte. Half a dozen casualties during the relief unfortunately included C.S.M. Nunn of D Company, a D.C.M. and a highly efficient Warrant Officer.

The situation at La Clytte had hardly altered since April : the Germans had made no attempt to straighten the pronounced salient in which the holding up of their offensive had left them, and the Allies were not yet ready to strike back, except locally. The 15th were in front line from July 1st to 5th and 15th to 20th and again from July 30th to August 2nd. At other times they were either in support astride the road to Reninghelst or back in the Westoutre line. A patrol of D Company under 2/Lt. White had a sharp bombing encounter on July 17th but brought back all its wounded, and on July 23rd two platoons, one of A and one of D under 2/Lts. Lee and Kneebone, raided the enemy's line along the Klein Kemmelbeek. Machine-gun fire held up the flanking parties, but the centre one got in and inflicted several casualties, our own only coming to six, the month's total being Lt. Tollemache and 14 men killed or missing and Lt. Spencer and 54 men wounded.

What remained of the 11th Battalion had, as already mentioned, moved early in May to Ledinghem to prepare for its training duties. This involved some fairly strenuous instruction in instructing, but no Americans appeared till after the cadre had moved (May 19th) to Berneuilles, where eventually the 47th U.S. Infantry arrived on June 3rd. The first step was to instruct those Americans who were to teach the rest, after which the Hampshire instructors supervised the teaching. The Americans were a good lot of men, keen and quick, but with much to learn, while their organization was poor. After four days the 47th were replaced by the 318th, with whom a similar programme was followed, and then on June 16th came orders for the cadres of the Sixteenth Division's infantry to return to England to be reconstituted with men classified as ' B ', of good general physique but unequal to marching long distances.

Crossing from Boulogne to Folkestone on June 18th the cadre spent a night at Aldershot and then went on to Lowestoft, where a large body of ' B ' men, designated the 15th Border, was assembled to be now transferred to the Hampshire. This new 11th Hampshire remained at Lowestoft until July 3rd, various drafts arrived and several officers, four from the Reserve Battalion of the 4th Hampshire, bringing the strength up to nearly 800. It then moved back to Aldershot, where it drew mobilization equipment and transport animals, to have over 500 men rejected as medically unfit. They were quickly replaced, but except for a draft of 70 from the 3rd Hampshire the newcomers also mostly proved to be unfit and every route march was followed by more rejections. Eventually, however, a sufficient number succeeded in satisfying the medical requirements. One draft contained Maltese and Frenchmen who could scarcely speak any English, and yet the battalion staff had to organize these fluctuating reinforcements and give them elementary instruction in musketry and the Lewis gun, not to mention pioneer work. Fortunately some of the officers who reported for duty had previously served with pioneer battalions, but it speaks wonders for those responsible for it that a fairly efficient battalion entrained at Aldershot for Folkestone on August 1st. As reconstituted the Sixteenth Division was reckoned as fit to hold a sector of the line, if not for an attack.

The 11th's return to France brought the Hampshire battalions on the Western Front up again to their highest figure, five, the 2/4th's arrival at Marseilles from Palestine on June 1st having previously raised it to four. Leaving Alexandria on May 26th in the *Kaisar i Hind*, in a vessel crowded to her full capacity with two Irish battalions also on board, the 2/4th had had an unpleasantly exciting journey, submarine alarms were frequent, and one of the convoy, the *Leasowe Castle*, was torpedoed and sunk with the 2/4th looking on.[1] Five officers who had sailed for India with the 2/4th were still with the battalion, Lt. Colonel Stilwell, then second in command, Captains C. P. Bulley (D Company), Cave (B), Ledgard (C) and Bacon (now Assistant Adjutant), the last three subalterns in 1914.

The 2/4th were not a little disappointed that even after their long absence it proved impossible to grant leave to England, but the situation did not admit of it and the battalion was promptly sent up by train to Doullens, whence it marched to Amplier, a pleasant little village surrounded by green woods and fields, a welcome change after the Frontier and Palestine. Some refitting and, what was more important, training in using anti-gas respirators [2] occupied the next few days, varied by sending parties of officers and men up to the trenches near Bucquoy, held by the Sixty-Second Division to which the battalion had been posted, along with the 5th Devonshire, also from Palestine. This was a Yorkshire Territorial Division, originally ' Second Line ', but since the March reorganization containing several ' First Line ' units. The Divisional commander, Major General Braithwaite, inspected the battalion directly it reached Amplier, and it was also welcomed by Brigadier General Burnett, whose 186th Brigade it now joined.

The Bucquoy sector proved fairly ' lively ', the ruins of the village being partly in German, partly in British hands, and the parties sent up ' for instruction ' found artillery, trench mortars, machine-guns and rifles all much in evidence. The line was but thinly held by both sides, the front line [3] consisting

---

[1] Two Hampshire officers, 2/Lts. Hunt and Lainé, who were on board her, escaped.
[2] Anti-gas protectors had been carried in Palestine but not used.
[3] It ran through the middle of the ruins of Bucquoy.

of a few posts, or casualties might have been heavier. As it was, though the Hampshire took over the support line on June 15th and were in front line from June 18th to 24th, casualties were very low and all ranks gained by experience of very unfamiliar conditions. Then the Division was relieved and taken back to a camp near Souastre for rest and training. The 2/4th were here nearly three weeks, comfortably housed under canvas and having some very useful musketry practice, with other training. Colonel Stilwell now went home on

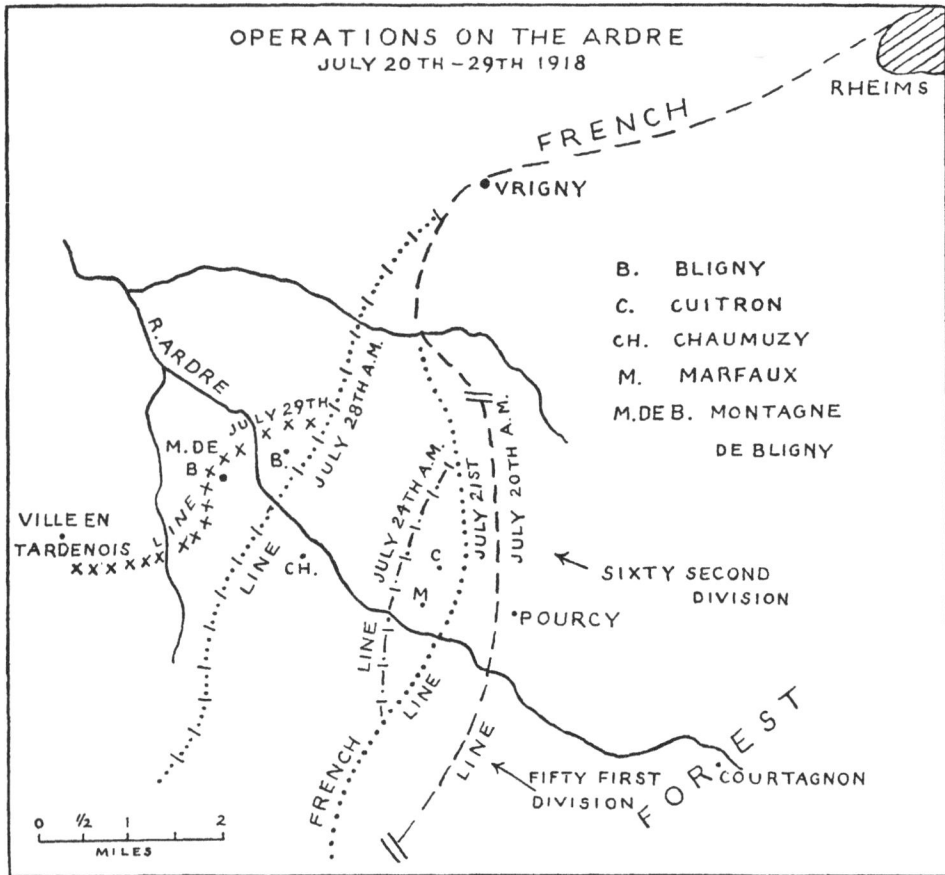

OPERATIONS ON THE ARDRE
JULY 20TH–29TH 1918

RHEIMS

FRENCH

•VRIGNY

B.   BLIGNY
C.   CUITRON
CH.   CHAUMUZY
M.   MARFAUX
M.DE B. MONTAGNE
         DE BLIGNY

R. ARDRE

JULY 29TH
JULY 28TH A.M.
JULY 24TH A.M.
JULY 21ST
JULY 20TH A.M.

M.DE
B

VILLE EN
TARDENOIS

LINE
CH.
C
M

SIXTY SECOND
DIVISION

•POURCY

LINE
FRENCH LINE
LINE

FIFTY FIRST
DIVISION

FOREST

•COURTAGNON

0   ½   1   2
MILES

medical grounds and was replaced in command by Lt. Colonel Brook of the Yorkshire L.I., who had been most helpful to the battalion when it was under instruction at Bucquoy and quickly won the confidence and respect of all ranks.

The Division was now in G.H.Q. Reserve and available for assisting the French should the attacks on them be renewed. By the first week in June the Chemin des Dames offensive had been halted, though at the cost of heavy casualties to the Allies, the five British Divisions engaged having hardly found this quarter quite the 'rest area' they had been promised. However, their gains of ground had left the Germans none too satisfactorily placed, their front here formed a deep salient, whose flanks positively invited a counter-attack, and unless they succeeded in extending it considerably, it might prove a trap. One such effort between June 9th and 14th, North and NW. of Compiegne, had failed to improve their position to any radical extent, despite another substantial gain of ground, and though the Allies were still apprehensive that the enemy might try another grand scale attack, either in the new Aisne salient or in Flanders, they were beginning to contemplate taking the offensive themselves, should the German blow be postponed much longer, or at any rate to prepare to meet a fresh attack by a counter-stroke. An attack on the Aisne salient was indeed being prepared when, on July 15th, the Germans struck again, East and West of Rheims. In anticipation of their attack the Fifty-First and Sixty-Second Divisions were already being moved to the neighbourhood of Châlons, in readiness to reinforce the French Fourth Army, on the right of the frontage attacked.

A night march in pouring rain to Mondicourt, where the 2/4th entrained in the small hours of July 15th, was followed by a tedious journey, hot and crowded, past Amiens and the suburbs of Paris to Sommesous. Detraining here late on July 16th, the battalion set out for Châlons in lorries, dangerously driven by Senegalese, some said they were Annamites, but whatever the truth they drove desperately, to be halted short of the town and ordered to Athis, a pleasant, if rather insanitary, village on a stream, of whose water full advantage was taken to wash and bathe.

Against General Gouraud's Fourth Army the Germans had made little progress. General Gouraud had held his front zone very lightly, as a covering position to his line of resistance, and the attackers, having wasted the weight and fury of their bombardment on a virtually unoccupied front zone, were effectively held at the intact line of resistance. West of Rheims, where General Gouraud's methods had not been adopted, the attack fared better, crossing the Marne above Chateau Thierry and making considerable progress between that and Rheims, astride the little river Ardre. The situation looked serious, but Marshal Foch was not deterred from carrying on with his plans for a counter-attack in force against the Western flank of the German salient, and the considerable success this counter-attack achieved was followed by its extension to the Eastern flank, where the two British Divisions [1] were put in to assist.

A long and trying march in great heat on July 19th brought the 2/4th to the Forest of Courtagnon in the Ardre valley, down which the British were to attack next day, the Sixty-Second Division being on the right, North of the Ardre. The valley, whose steep sides were thickly wooded, was open, but crops of corn concealed the German defences, especially the machine-gun posts. Villages dotted about formed centres of resistance and presented a formidable task to troops who not only did not know the ground but had had no experience of fighting over such country. But the Italians who were holding the front here had been hard hit and were shaky, so, instead of relieving them

---

[1] Two others took part in the battle on the Western flank.

and getting a chance to reconnoitre, the British were to attack through them, virtually blindfold.

The 187th (right) and 185th (left) Brigades were leading the attack, the 2/4th Hampshire [1] following in support behind the 185th. Heavy fire, largely from machine-guns which were hard to locate, met the attackers, inflicting heavy casualties, and progress was slow. The supporting battalions suffered almost as severely, at first mainly from artillery fire, but on reaching Pourcy, beyond which the leading troops were held up, the 2/4th came under machine-gun fire also. They now tried to work forward by the left to attack Marfaux, in front of which village the 185th Brigade had been checked after driving in the enemy's outposts. The thick crops made direction hard to keep, and losses were serious, 2/Lt. N. E. Smith, who was commanding D Company, being mortally wounded. Parties of A and B under 2/Lts. Scott and Holbrook, however, managed to get within 400 yards of Marfaux but had to dig in there, no easy task in the hard chalk, while after dark the position was to some extent consolidated and the numerous wounded could be succoured, great work being done by the men attached to battalion H.Q., now formed into a H.Q. Company under Captain Bacon.

The Division had captured a fair number of prisoners and machine-guns and it had advanced about half a mile, whereas the French on its right had hardly made any advance, though across the Ardre the Fifty-First Division had made rather more progress. During the next two days the 2/4th consolidated their positions. Patrols found Marfaux and Cuitron, North of it, strongly held and attempts by the 187th Brigade to push forward had little success. Attacking again on July 22nd, however, the 5th Duke's (186th Brigade) gained some ground in the woods on the right, which improved the chances of success against Cuitron and Marfaux.

These villages were the objective of the next day's attack, which was started quite early and was completely successful, largely thanks to Captain Ledgard, who had rejoined with C Company, whose arrival proved most timely, giving the attack the reinforcement needed to ensure success. Though wounded, he remained in action for some time, captured seven prisoners, it was said with an unloaded rifle, and set a splendid example, while Lt. Bennett and 2/Lt. Lord Uffington were both largely instrumental in the battalion's success, the line being carried well beyond Marfaux and 41 prisoners and eight machine-guns taken. Cuitron and a wood North of it were also secured, and with the Fifty-First Division making good progress beyond the Ardre, the day had gone well, if casualties were again heavy, those of the 2/4th including 2/Lt. G. F. Wilson killed and 2/Lt. Johnson wounded, while A and B had to be temporarily amalgamated under Captain Cottam, whose leadership and example had been conspicuous.

This position beyond Marfaux the 2/4th maintained for two days, C Company then co-operating in an advance beyond the Ardre (July 27th) by occupying Chaumuzy and then going forward again to support the Corps Cavalry, who

---

[1] C Company had been left at Mondicourt to load the trains and only rejoined on July 21st.

were trying to reach the line [1] Bligny–Montagne de Bligny. This they could not do, and the 2/4th, coming forward in the dark and rain behind the cavalry, had to halt 500 yards short of the line and dig in behind a low bank. All ranks were very tired, having had no rest for eight days, and the battalion seemed to have almost reached the end of its tether, but a stiff task had still to be tackled before it could be relieved. The pressure on the retreating Germans could not be relaxed and so, on July 28th the two British Divisions were put in again with Bligny, the Montagne and the old trench line West of them as objectives.

' Zero ' was fixed for 4.30 a.m., but the attack could not get going till half an hour later, and the barrage which the enemy promptly put down and heavy machine-gun fire on our right soon checked the advance at a sunken road East of Bligny. However, 2/Lt. Holbrook worked forward on the left with about 20 men and got well into the village, and careful reconnoitring by 2/Lts. Brierly and Lord Uffington and Corporal Williams having discovered a good line of approach by the river, more men reinforced them and enlarged the foot-hold already gained, from which a fresh advance could be made. This cleared Bligny, the battalion's objective being secured and consolidated.

That evening what was left of the 2/4th was relieved by the 5th K.O.Y.L.I., and after spending two days in reserve at Chaumuzy they went back to the wagon-lines in Courtagnon Forest. ' Minden Day ' saw them moving back to billets at Chouilly and on the way marching past the French General, Berthelot, on whom their marching made a great impression, thanks to the C.O's happy thought of giving the men a brief rest just before reaching his saluting post. Three days were spent in comfort at Chouilly, a noted wine-growing area whose products were duly appreciated, and then, reinforced by a draft of nearly 300 men, the battalion entrained on August 4th for the British area.

Bligny had been a very satisfactory ending to a week of hard fighting, if losses had been heavy, in all the 2/4th lost two officers and 172 men killed and missing on the Ardre with nine officers and 170 men wounded, but despite difficult ground and a stubborn resistance real progress had been made and the Germans well and truly beaten. Observers of great experience declared that never had they seen ground so thickly strewn with German dead as in the Ardre valley, and the two British Divisions which fought there had achieved notable results. They were the spearhead of the attack at a vital point, one of the hinges of the German line, and their success was of more than local import-ance, while they and the two other British Divisions who were engaged simul-taneously between Soissons and the Ourcq, made a tremendous impression on the French by whose sides they fought, few of them had ever worked with British troops before this. General Berthelot was most enthusiastic about them, singling out the capture of Marfaux and of Bligny as exploits specially worthy of remembrance. It had been hard going and costly, but the 2/4th could feel that in their first battle in France they had been given a really stiff task but that they had covered themselves with credit and fully established themselves in the Sixty-Second Division. The ' Second Marne ' may well be

[1] The Germans facing us had fallen back over-night to this line.

reckoned as the turn in the tide : the previous German ' drives ' had been halted short of their objectives but foiled rather than repulsed, their attack of July 15th had been an undisguisable failure, ending in an enforced retreat, while they had been unable to relieve the pressure by starting another Flanders offensive. Their failure on the Marne suggested that the initiative was passing to the Allies.

CHAPTER XXIX
1918 : IV
The Return to the Attack

WHEN the Germans had started their great attack in March only one Hampshire battalion had been on the front attacked. At the start, on August 8th, of the British ' return push ' the regiment had not even one battalion engaged : the 1st was still in the Pacaut Wood area, the 2nd and 15th were on the still ' quiet ' Flanders front, the 11th had just returned to France and was in reserve behind the First Army, while the 2/4th had just reached a rest area near Doullens and was recuperating after its strenuous and successful exertions under French command. It was, however, to be the first of the five to be actively engaged in the main advance, as the Sixty-Second Division, having been posted to the Sixth Corps (Lt. General Haldane), came into action on August 25th, by which time the fighting front had been extended Northward to the Scarpe.

August 8th, by the Germans' own admission ' the black day of the German Army ', had seen the Fourth Army with the French First Army on its right highly successful immediately South of the Somme, if rather less fortunate in the more difficult country North of the river. The exploitation of that success was not prolonged after the German reserves had been drawn to the point attacked but, on August 21st, the Third Army had taken up the attack between Albert and Arras and, while it maintained its pressure steadily, the Fourth had renewed its efforts further South. By August 26th the First Army also was joining in, and before August was out the Fourth Division, having been transferred to the Canadian Corps, was advancing with it down the Senseé, so that another Hampshire battalion was involved in the regaining of the ground lost in March. Moreover, by that time British attacks were speeding up the withdrawal from the Lys salient, which the Germans had begun early in August without being attacked.

This withdrawal had actually started in the Pacaut Wood sector on the night of August 4th/5th. The 1st Hampshire had been relieved on the previous evening and were in billets at L'Ecleme, and when they returned to the line on August 9th it had been advanced a mile East of Pacaut Wood and ran along the Turbeaute stream. The Rifle Brigade were in front, holding a line of shell-holes, which the Hampshire took over on August 14th and held for four days, the line consisting of small posts in standing wheat, while here and there German shelters could be used. The enemy's snipers and machine-gunners were active, but casualties were few and the battalion's patrols were constantly out, keeping a good watch on the enemy and locating his positions. After four days in support (August 19th to 22nd), during which the enemy made another withdrawal, beyond the Paradis–Locon road, the Hampshire went back to Lillers (August 25th), whence they moved to Chateau de la Haie, NW. of Arras.

Though nearly 150 men had gone to hospital, drafts of about the same number had arrived, with half a dozen officers, including Captain de Gaury on recovery from wounds.

The withdrawal in the Lys salient had started at its Southern end, opposite the Fifth Army,[1] but it had extended Northward, and on the first signs of it General Plumer had ordered the Second Army to take every opportunity of interfering with the movement, hoping not only to inflict casualties but to prevent any retirement ' according to plan ' to new positions of the Germans' own selection.   Thus while the Twenty-Ninth Division improved its line near Vieux Berquin, securing that village and beating off some attacks, a small advance was also made on August 9th in the Kemmel sector, the 15th Hampshire being selected to straighten out a nasty salient near La Clytte.

Attacking with great determination the battalion quickly gained its objectives on the right and centre, but had more obstinate resistance to subdue on the left.   One strongly held trench, in which were two machine-guns, was rushed by 2/Lt. Bradley, the whole garrison being accounted for : 2/Lt. G. J. Potter took command of his company when all its other officers had been hit and, though supported by seven men only, captured a strong point, killing or taking nearly 50 enemy ; another post which had been overlooked was taken by Lt. Spencer, who had pressed on so vigorously that he overshot the objective by nearly 200 yards and had to bring his unsupported party back.   Promptly attacking with only five men to help him, he rushed the post, capturing two machine-guns and disposing of its garrison of 12.   2/Lt. H. W. Green, after capturing a machine-gun in the original attack, did great service in beating off the enemy's attempts to work their way back, while Captain Leybourne was also conspicuous for gallantry and leadership : about the first to reach the objective, he did admirable work in directing its consolidation under heavy fire and sent back valuable information.   C.S.M. Williams, though wounded, remained at duty and did great work, the fine example he set in leading his men being notable.   Casualties had been fairly heavy, including Captain Gunner and Lts. Bodenham and Wedderburn (all Hampshire Carabineers) and Lt. White killed or mising with 39 men, while Lts. Spencer and Boustead and 2/Lt. Lee were wounded with 101 men, but the battalion had earned great credit by its highly successful attack.[2]   It was relieved next day by the 18th K.R.R.C., to whom it handed over a nicely consolidated line.

The 2nd Hampshire had also helped to speed up the German withdrawal. The Fifteenth Corps had now advanced up to the Outersteene Ridge East of Merris and South of Meteren, which though only 120 feet above sea level rose well above the surrounding country and gave good observation.   It was therefore attacked on August 18th, a brigade of the Ninth Division attacking from the North and securing the ridge, after which the 87th Brigade on its right

[1] Now in line between the First and Second in the La Bassée—Neuve Chapelle front.
[2] Captain Leybourne and Lt. Spencer got bars to the M.C., 2/Lts. Bradley, Green and Potter the M.C., C.S.M. Williams, Sergeant Cross and Corporal Copping the D.C.M. and 20 men the M.M.

extended the frontage of the attack, crossing the Meteren Becque and taking Outersteene village. The enemy was completely surprised and lost heavily, but when the 86th Brigade tried to work forward still more to the right, South of the Hazebrouck–Bailleul railway, it had to halt for lack of artillery support, on which the 2nd Hampshire were put in to secure the 87th Brigade's right flank by holding the railway between the Meteren Becque and our old front line. This line was consolidated, an attempt at a counter-attack being repulsed with ease, and next day the battalion covered with its fire a fresh advance which completed the capture of the previous day's objective ; a useful tactical position had been secured and substantial casualties inflicted on the enemy, while three guns and many machine-guns with 800 prisoners were taken at a cost of little over that number, the Hampshires' losses being trifling, though their position had been heavily bombarded. After this reverse the Germans fell back in front of the Fifth Army, evacuating Merville and Neuf Berquin, and also opposite the Second Army's right, thereby shortening their line so that troops could be withdrawn into reserve. Some caution had therefore to be observed in following them up ; apart from the 'booby traps' so ingeniously used in the withdrawal to the Hindenburg Line in 1917, an over-hasty advance might expose our troops to counter-attack, but all Divisions in the front line of the Second and Fifth Armies were much on the alert for signs of either a counter-attack or another withdrawal, our patrols being active and inquisitive.

After their gruelling experiences and heavy losses in the fighting astride the Ardre, the 2/4th Hampshire might have expected more than the bare fort-night's rest which they enjoyed at Authie St Leger near Doullens. Substantial reinforcements had to be assimilated and the survivors of the Ardre fighting needed a chance to recover from their exertions, while at last a fair number of officers and men could go on leave to England, from which some had been absent for nearly four years. But the enemy's withdrawal was bringing him back to the strong positions in his rear which had halted our advance in 1917 and were likely to prove much more formidable than the improvised defences from which he was retiring, so it was essential to press him hard and not let him conduct his retirement 'according to plan'. The Sixty-Second Division was therefore required to make further exertions, and August 19th found the 2/4th Hampshire moving forward to Warluzel and thence to Ayette (August 24th), their Division being now in reserve to the Sixth Corps. That Corps' front now ran N.E. from Achiet le Grand to Ervillers and faced Behagnies and Sapignies, whose defences had so far held up the Second Division and were to be attacked again on August 25th by its 5th Brigade, to whom the 186th was in support.

Attacking before dawn behind a good barrage the 5th Brigade carried successively Behagnies and Sapignies, after which the 186th went through to secure the ridge in front of Vaux Vraucourt, the 187th, on its left, making for Mory. Both brigades gained some ground, but the 5th Duke of Wellington's, who were leading the 186th Brigade, were held up on the Favreuil–Mory road and with those villages both untaken the attack was not pressed, so the 2/4th Hampshire remained in reserve. It was encouraging to see the piles of weapons and equipment left behind in the haste of the German retirement which this time was hardly 'according to plan'. Late in the afternoon the Germans counter-attacked in some force but without success, and the 187th Brigade got forward near Mory, while on the right the Thirty-Seventh Division aided by the New Zealanders cleared the enemy out of Favreuil. Fair

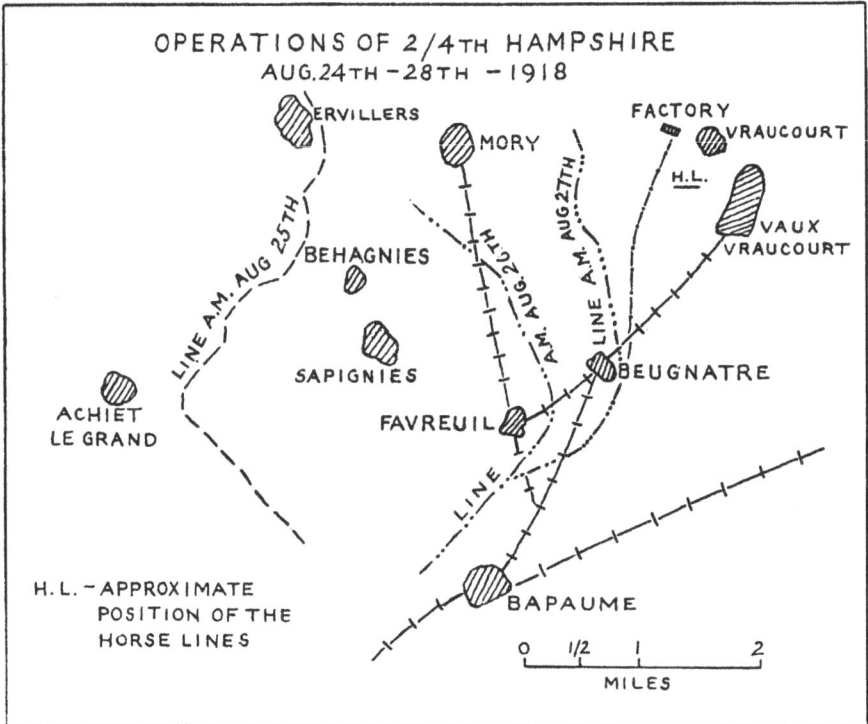

OPERATIONS OF 2/4TH HAMPSHIRE
AUG. 24TH – 28TH – 1918

progress had also been made by the right of the Third Army and by the Fourth beyond it astride the Somme. On the left the advance was closing up to the Hindenburg Line, a very much more formidable obstacle than any the 'return push' had yet encountered.

August 26th saw no major operation attempted by the Sixth Corps, but as the 187th Brigade was ahead of the 186th, the 2/4th Hampshire were ordered forward to try to get up level with it, some trenches near the Beugnatre–Vraucourt road being their objective. Heavy rain, a pitch-dark night and ground seamed with old trenches and wire impeded the move to the assembly position, but the C.O. had fought over the same ground in 1917 and, thanks largely to his guiding and knowledge, the battalion was in position just before ' Zero ' at 6 a.m., when it went forward well behind a good barrage and, despite being shelled with gas, secured a first objective without much difficulty or loss, the Germans having apparently been surprised. Advancing again later in the day with A and C in front instead of B and D, the 2/4th came under machine-gun fire from the left and from high ground behind the second objective, but Captain Cave handled A Company most skilfully, and before long, the second objective also had been gained and was being consolidated by A and C, with D forming a defensive flank facing South on the right. Pushing on again with C to secure an advanced position, Captain Bennett, who had taken over that company from Captain Ledgard, was killed, but the position was gained and a gap between it and A's line was filled by B from support. A useful advance[1] had been made at a cost of 50 casualties, including Captain Bennett and 16 men killed or missing and 2/Lt. Richmond wounded.

This line the 2/4th maintained next day, despite persistent shelling, while patrols successfully reconnoitred the ground in front, the few casualties including 2/Lt. Holbrook (Gloucestershire) wounded. By this time the Germans opposing the British Third and Fourth Armies, well-hammered and battered by a succession of blows, were going right back along the whole front. Their losses had been heavy, the reserves they had expended freely in repeated counter-attacks had not sufficed to do more than delay the British advance, and though most of their units were still fighting hard and their machine-gunners were proving difficult to overcome, their own accounts cannot conceal either the heaviness of their losses or the decline in morale which was beginning to set in. Opposite the Third Army's left the Germans were resisting more stubbornly than further South : they were holding the outposts of the Hindenburg Line and their retirement was pivoting on this point, while the right of our First Army, now coming into the battle, faced the formidable Drocourt–Queant Switch, which ran Northward from near Bullecourt. No major effort was therefore required from the Sixty-Second Division between August 26th and 30th, though every opportunity was taken of pushing fighting patrols forward to establish advanced posts. The 2/4th were active in this : early on August 28th B Company forced the enemy out of a post known as the Horse Lines, capturing a machine-gun. Sharp fire from machine-guns at a cross-roads North of the Horse Lines, however, compelled the party to withdraw, another patrol, from C Company, located several machine-guns and posts South of the Horse Lines but also had to retire after having some casualties, while later in the day heavy shelling caused more casualties in B and C, now the centre companies, the day's total being over 30. Next day (August 29th) 2/Lt. Brierly and a platoon of A again attacked the Horse Lines, the 5th Devons simultaneously attacking on the left. The Horse Lines were stubbornly defended but, a second platoon reinforcing the first, the position was carried after a sharp fight in which Private Baldwin, the battalion barber, was

---

[1] The 186th Brigade was now level with the 187th, West of Vaux Vraucourt.

conspicuous for leadership and gallantry,[1] several prisoners being taken. A line was then consolidated beyond the Vraucourt–Bapaume road, another platoon coming up to secure the left flank, where the Devons had been held up short of the 2/4th's line. About 5 p.m. lines of enemy began advancing to counter-attack from about 500 yards away, at which distance the 2/4th's rifles and Lewis guns could do some successful shooting, while our artillery co-operated effectively, though unluckily ' shorts ' caused several casualties. A timely reinforcement of the remaining platoon of A Company was brought up by Lt. Bryant and the attack was beaten off with heavy losses, and as the 2/4th's casualties, six killed and missing and a dozen wounded, were exceeded by the 21 prisoners taken, with one machine-gun, the day could be reckoned very satisfactory. That evening the 2/4th were relieved by the 2/4th Duke's

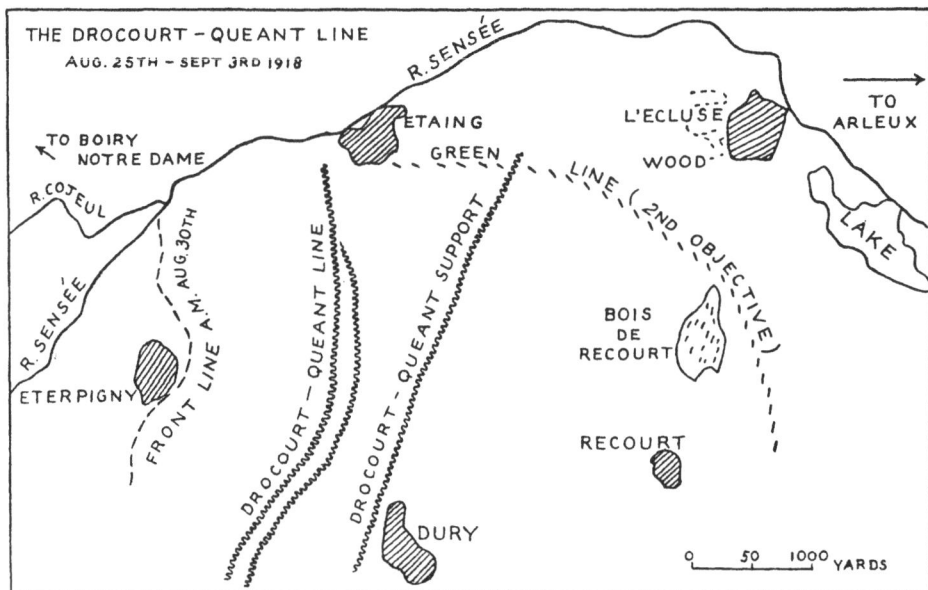

and spent the next five days in brigade support. The enemy's artillery was fairly active, they were evidently anticipating another attack, and the battalion, which was in recently dug and shallow trenches, had several more casualties. Then on September 3rd the Division, which had meanwhile taken Vraucourt and Vaux Vraucourt, was relieved and the 2/4th went back to a railway cutting near Courcelles for a week's rest. Having had nearly 150 casualties on top of their losses on the Ardre, the 2/4th welcomed the chance to incorporate the reinforcements they now received.

Before this the Northward extension of the fighting front had brought the 1st Hampshire into the battle, the Fourth Division having moved up to Boiry

[1] He received the D.C.M., also given later on to R.S.M. Hubbard, who did most useful work in organizing the supply of ammunition, leading several carrying parties forward himself.

Notre Dame on August 28th in support to the Canadians, whose advance South of the Scarpe had recovered Monchy le Preux and reached the Sensée, SE. of Guemappe. That evening the Division relieved the 4th Canadian Division NW. of Eterpigny, the Hampshire being at Boiry in support of the Somerset L.I. The battalion's posts covered the approaches to Boiry from NE. and East, two companies being in support in the village, which was heavily shelled, though luckily casualties were few. Next day (Aug. 29th) the Somerset pushed forward towards the Sensée, the Hampshire coming up on their left and advancing with them, with three companies in line and D in support. After a successful advance, in which it had had 30 casualties, the battalion was relieved by a machine-gun battalion and drawn back into reserve near Boiry, B Company being left as escort to the machine-gunners. The battalion was not long in reserve, being required that evening to relieve the Somerset and Rifle Brigade at Eterpigny, which they had just captured. The relief was difficult, the approaches to the front line being exposed to view, though small parties could be dribbled forward down a sunken road. The line was kept under shell-fire and several casualties were incurred. Eventually after dark the relief was completed, the Hampshire remaining in line here till the evening of September 1st ; patrols did what reconnoitring they could but the enemy's shell-fire caused several more casualties ; altogether during these days 17 men were killed or missing, 2/Lts. Abbott, Riggs and Woodley and over 90 men being wounded and 2/Lt. Jones gassed. On relief by the Essex on September 1st the battalion moved to a position near Boiry Lane Bridge.

The Fourth Division, now on the left of the Canadian Corps, was now confronting the formidable Drocourt–Queant line, the object of the next big attack, that of September 2nd. After capturing the portion East of Eterpigny and North of Dury, the Division was to move NE. towards the Sensée between Etaing and L'Ecluse, where that river runs through several small marshy lakes West of Arleux, which Meredith's Thirty-Seventh had known in Marlborough's days. The Division's first objective was to be taken by the 12th Brigade, after which the Rifle Brigade (right) and Hampshire (left) were to go through and reach a ' Green Line ' which curved round from Etaing to the Bois de Recourt, and if possible a ' Blue Line ' also, beyond the Sensée and the lakes.

Starting at 5.30 a.m. the Hampshire reached the rear trenches of the Drocourt–Queant line without much loss, the 12th Brigade having secured its objective. On advancing against the ' D. Q. Support Line ', however, they came under heavy machine-gun fire, especially from the left, while the Rifle Brigade were caught by artillery fire from the other flank. A gap in the wire through which the attackers had to pass was kept under specially heavy fire, but short rushes carried B Company into the ' D. Q. Support ', though Captain de Gaury was wounded, and by 8 a.m. B was established in that line with the other companies in support. Two tanks now arrived to assist in the next stage of the advance, but one was soon put out of action, and though the second helped to tackle several machine-gun nests, a ' pill-box ' at a cross-roads on the left defied all efforts, despite another determined attempt by B Company to reach the objective. Lt. Gregson [1] was wounded here and there was nothing for it but to bring the advanced men back and consolidate the position secured in the Support Line, with one platoon thrown back to cover the left flank. However, more had been achieved than had at first seemed to have been. Their failure to prevent the penetration of the ' D. Q. ' Line had evidently made a big impression on the Germans, for on September 3rd, after the 12th Brigade had attacked and taken Etaing, from which place flanking fire had held up the 11th's advance, when the 11th also began pushing forward it was to find that the enemy had gone. The Hampshire, with C and D Companies leading, now made for L'Ecluse to secure the crossings of the Sensée. C on the left was heavily shelled but got forward across the Etaing–Recourt road by short rushes and established itself on a road South of L'Ecluse. From this point patrols pushed forward into the village, which together with L'Ecluse Wood was occupied and secured, posts being established to cover and command the crossings over the Sensée. D. Company meanwhile had come up level on the right, keeping touch with the Rifle Brigade, who also had reached their objective at Recourt Wood. Despite heavy shelling and much machine-gun fire casualties had been surprisingly few, while the Division alone had taken 1000 prisoners. That night the First Division relieved the Fourth, which was to have a fortnight out of the line, the 1st Hampshire being at Caucourt. Ten officers and 150 other ranks now appeared as reinforcements, which more than replaced the 100-odd casualties incurred in breaking through the Drocourt–Queant Line, though 80 admissions to hospital reduced the numbers available for the trenches.

The piercing of the Drocourt–Queant Line was followed by a pause in the British offensive : the Germans were now mostly back behind the Hindenburg Line and the Canal du Nord North of Moeuvres, and while their retirement was being followed up systematic preparations would have to be made before these formidable defences could be attacked, among other things the Germans must be evicted from their outposts in the old British lines facing the Hindenburg position, quite a sufficiently serious task in itself. Moreover, though on the offensive, the British had no superiority in numbers : both the Third and Fourth Armies had had to use the same Divisions over and over again, both had had to overcome and rout nearly twice their number of German Divisions. The strain on the attacking troops was terrible ; both in 1916 and in 1917 much longer intervals had separated the successive attacks, and experienced officers could not but feel qualms about the ability of their units to respond to such heavy and quickly repeated demands. But the men were cheered and encouraged by the success which was attending their efforts, by their captures of ground, guns and prisoners, by the evidence of the heavy losses they were inflicting and of the weakening of the German will to resist, several quite large parties of Germans had surrendered to handfuls of attackers, and it was extraordinary how after the briefest of rests depleted units went confidently into the attack again to achieve another encouraging success.

[1] The acting Adjutant, Captain Flint being now on the staff.

Neither 1st nor 2/4th Hampshire were in action during the first half of September when the British line advanced almost to its position before March 21st, but the repercussions of the successes achieved during August had given the 2nd Battalion some active work in pressing the continued withdrawal of the enemy from the Lys salient.

The 2nd had been in line beyond the Meteren Becque from August 24th to 26th, being heavily shelled and having Lt. Currie and seven men killed and Captain Prendergast (for the fourth time) and 16 men wounded. During the last week of August large fires behind the German lines suggested preparations for a further withdrawal, and early on August 30th patrols reported that their front line had been evacuated. The 87th Brigade promptly pushed forward and advanced well beyond Bailleul, meeting hardly any enemy but ample evidence of the effective work of the British artillery in the broken-up wagons and dead animals which littered the country and in the shell-holes thickly clustered round the battery positions. The next day's advance brought the 87th Brigade to the Steenwerck–Kemmel road at La Creche, the 88th coming up next day on the left and continuing the line Northward, with the 4th Worcestershire in front and the 2nd Hampshire at an old aerodrome between Bailleul and the Ravelsberg Ridge.

September 2nd saw the advance continued, the Hampshire reaching the trenches they had dug on April 10th and so successfully defended. The Twenty-Ninth Division was now just West of Ploegsteert Wood and Hill 63, where the Germans were showing some disposition to stand, so a systematic attack had to be arranged, the 88th Brigade assailing Hill 63 and the 86th on its right going for Ploegsteert. Next day, after the Worcestershire, who had been leading the brigade, had taken the old G.H.Q. line, the 2nd Hampshire were ordered to push forward and clear Germans out of a position just East of it, to secure a good starting line for the assault. This was done mainly by W Company, now under Captain Harrod,[1] 2/Lt. Gibbons doing great work and handling his men most successfully, but when a further advance was attempted opposition stiffened, machine-guns inflicting several casualties. Z Company (Captain West), which also tried to push forward, was likewise held up and it was decided to postpone any further attempts till after dark when a fresh advance secured the objective, which lay on the Western slopes of Hill 63, but only after sharp fighting, our killed including Captain West.

The final arrangements for the next morning's attack were completed with some difficulty, as the Germans were found to be holding a large crater on our right and were only evicted by the Hampshire after sharp fighting in the dark. Eventually the 2nd Leinster having got into their assembly position on the Hampshire's left, the attack went forward at 8 a.m. (Sept. 4th) behind a good barrage. The enemy were in force and had many machine-guns, while thick belts of uncut wire had to be tackled. However, the attackers were not to be daunted ; keeping right up to the barrage, they cut the wire, swept over the hill, rushed the machine-gun posts, killing and capturing many enemy, and

---

[1] Captain Singleton-Gates was now Adjutant.

secured their objective, Gas Trench. One 'strong point' was successfully tackled by Sergeant Stone and four men who disposed of its whole garrison of 14. From here the leading companies pushed ahead and secured a trench running past Crest House, which they consolidated, while behind them a third company was 'mopping up' systematically and successfully. Consolidation was then put in hand, 2/Lt. W. M. Cooper, who had been prominent in organizing the attackers, now going out to reconnoitre and bringing back useful information after a sharp encounter with some Germans lurking in a wood, of

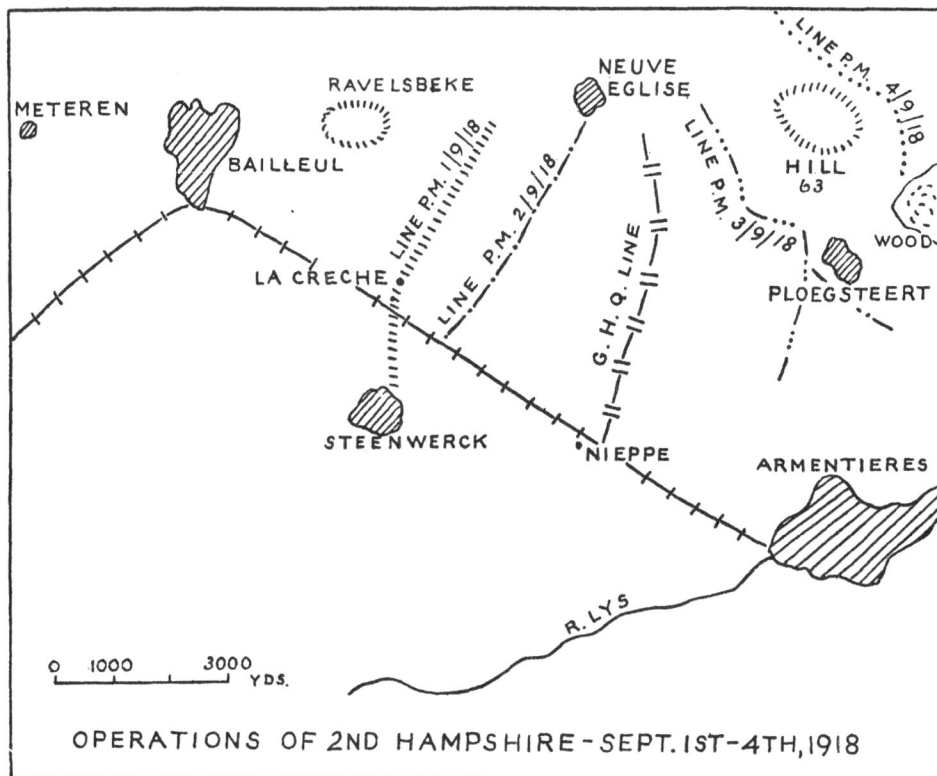

OPERATIONS OF 2ND HAMPSHIRE - SEPT. 1ST-4TH, 1918

whom his patrol disposed successfully. The Leinster also had gained their objectives and, with Hill 63 secured, the 86th Brigade's attack on Ploegsteert, which had been held up as our artillery had rather concentrated their fire on Hill 63, was now successfully renewed, another 100 prisoners being added to the 250 already taken.

The importance of the positions captured was made evident by their being persistently shelled and repeatedly counter-attacked. These efforts were successfully dealt with, the Hampshire's reserve company repulsing one advance against the right, while another attempt against the left, near Le Rossignol, was also beaten off, 2/Lt. Lambert leading a counter-attack which outflanked and drove back the attackers, taking an officer and several men and a machine-gun. A company of the Worcestershire had filled a gap which had opened between the Leinster and the Hampshire and helped to repulse the counter-attacks. The position was heavily shelled and machine-guns were pushed forward to impede our consolidation, but this went on well nevertheless, the Hampshire's hold on the hill remaining unshaken, and next day they were relieved by the Thirty-First Division and went back by La Creche to a camp near Meteren. Casualties had not been light, Captain West and 2/Lts. Irwin and Jarvis and 34 men were killed or missing with Captains Scott and Ingles and 2/Lts. Hicks and Sims and 140 men wounded. But the enemy had been hard hit, the 2nd had taken a dozen machine-guns and three large trench-mortars with at least 50 prisoners, and the capture of Hill 63 had deprived the Germans of a valuable position. 2/Lts. Cooper, Gibbons and Lambert all received the M.C., which was also awarded to Lt. Vicars-Miles, who had done devoted and invaluable work in bringing up ammunition and rations under heavy shell-fire, though once blown off a shelled road and rendered unconscious for some time.

The German withdrawal from the Lys Salient had extended considerably further North and had brought the Forty-First Division into action on the Kemmel front, rather unluckily for the 15th Hampshire, who were called upon to attack a formidable position at short notice and as a result suffered heavily.

The 15th had been in line at Westoutre from August 25th to 28th and had come back to the front on September 2nd after four days ' out ' near Lumbres, the brigade having to take over from some Americans [1] in the Vierstraat sector NE. of Kemmel.[2] Unfortunately instead of the Americans who should have been occupying the assembly positions for the proposed attack along the Vierstraat–Wytschaete road, Germans were in possession. Patrols were sent out to reconnoitre but heavy machine-gun fire soon drove them back. However, it was decided to carry on with the attack and by ' Zero ' on September 4th (4 a.m.) the attacking companies were lined up ready to attack, the 12th East Surrey being on the left. Unluckily the barrage fell behind the light railway, West of Bois Quarante, which formed the first objective, instead of in front of it, so that several machine-gun posts in front of the German line had escaped being shelled and inflicted heavy casualties. Two fine company commanders, Captains Leybourne and Newman, were killed, the C.O., Colonel Murdoch, was gassed, and the attackers were thrown into disorder. Nevertheless they pushed on and, though much weakened, managed to reach the railway line but could not make any progress towards the road beyond, which formed the second objective. Along the railway therefore they endeavoured to hold on. This, however, was more than their reduced numbers could manage in face of

[1] Some Americans had previously been attached to the battalion for instruction : the Germans were putting down some heavy barrages, under which the Americans, full of zeal to go over the top and get at the guns, became rather restive and could not understand the indifference with which the seasoned 15th treated the shelling.

[2] Kemmel had been recovered and the front advanced beyond the Kemmel—Vierstraat road.

the enemy's snipers and machine guns, and though the reserve companies of the East Surrey relieved matters for a time by coming up on the left, about 7 a.m. the Germans counter-attacked in strength and forced both battalions back. 2/Lt. G. J. Potter,[1] almost the only officer still in action, did great work in rallying and reorganizing the few men left of the 15th, and it was largely his doing that an advanced line was maintained, though short of the objective. The Brigadier[2] was warm in his praise of the courage and determination shown by both attacking battalions, but casualties had been heavy : besides the two company commanders Lt. Lowis and 2/Lts. Leedham, Pasco, Woollven, H. C. Hall[3] and Northover[3] were killed or missing with 90 other ranks, Lt. Loveridge (4th D.G.), 2/Lts. Bradley, D. A. Brown, Carley, Damp and Tibbs[3] were wounded or gassed with another 220 men.[4] This left the battalion terribly

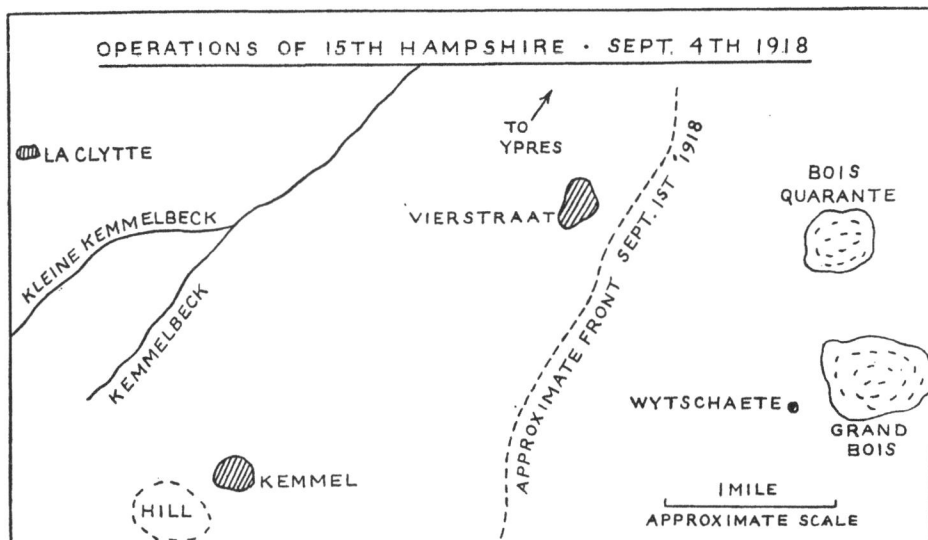

OPERATIONS OF 15TH HAMPSHIRE · SEPT. 4TH 1918

depleted, but Major Puttick was available to assume command and sufficient reinforcements were before long forthcoming to enable it to take part effectively in the next attack.

One quarter only of the British line had remained unchanged since the beginning of 1918, the portion of the First Army's front between the La Bassée Canal and Lens, and even here September brought a move. The Sixteenth Division had been sent to this front on being reconstituted, taking over the line South of the La Bassée Canal after the middle of August. This had brought the 11th Hampshire, who had been training their men in the pioneer work of which many were quite ignorant, up to Sailly–Labourse, where they took over on August 22nd and were soon busy on their usual duties, mainly keeping the

[1] He received a bar to the M.C.   [2] B. General Weston, who had taken over in June.
[3] Wiltshire.   [4] The East Surrey lost nearly 250 all told.

light railways, tracks and communication trenches in order. German shelling and occasional visits by aircraft caused some casualties, C Company having 15 men hit on September 5th, when Vermelles was heavily bombarded, and after the Sixteenth Division had on September 13th advanced its line by taking Auchy the shell-fire increased slightly : the 11th's work, however, remained little changed, though more attention was being paid to the forward area, tracks having to be made across what had been No Man's Land and was now behind our front. Colonel Crockett had meanwhile received command of an Army Musketry School and Major Stewart, R.E., had taken over from him.

During the middle weeks of September no major operation was attempted anywhere, but in dislodging the enemy from their outpost positions covering the Hindenburg Line several Divisions had quite as heavy fighting as any experienced earlier in our advance, among them the Sixty-Second, which was brought forward to assist to clear the Havrincourt area. The Division came into line on September 12th as the left Division of the Sixth Corps, having the Second Division beyond it on that flank and the Thirty-Seventh on its right. The British line here ran about SSE., from the bend in the Canal du Nord near Hermies to the NE. projection of Havrincourt Wood, and the Sixty-Second Division was to advance NE. with the 186th Brigade on its right, its leading battalions having to capture part of the Hindenburg Line front system [1] after which the 2/4th Hampshire would attack Havrincourt village. It was a formidable enough task : the enemy were on the alert, the defences were strong and the attackers had to carry out an awkward change of direction, advancing North at first till level with the village, and then swinging round to their right. A Company (Captain Cave) was on the right, C (Captain Brierley) in the centre and D (Captain Bulley) on the left, with B (2/Lt. Weekes) in support. Starting off at 1 a.m. (Sept. 12th) the battalion made its way through what had once been Havrincourt Wood to its assembly point in the open beyond. There was some shell-fire and hostile aeroplanes dropped a few bombs, but the assembly position was reached with little loss, and at 5.45 a.m., 20 minutes after ' Zero ', the 2/4th went forward. No less than eight brigades of field-guns were supporting the Division and the leading battalions made good progress, so that the 2/4th reached their wheeling point without much loss, and at 7.15 a.m., on the barrage lifting, they pushed forward into Havrincourt. On the right A Company, well led by Captain Cave, quickly captured Havrincourt Chateau, to have much trouble from machine-guns nearby, of which also it managed to dispose, thanks to Captain Cave, who went forward himself with a few men to tackle one very troublesome gun, shot the gunner, took the gun and four prisoners and enabled the advance to carry on, 2/Lt. Wheeler, about the first man into the village, headed a rush which captured two machine-guns, after which he established his men on the far side of the village and took a large part in repulsing a counter-attack, shooting several men himself, while a little

---

[1] The Division had attacked at this point on November 20th, 1917, the opening day of ' Cambrai '.

later on, when two more machine-guns were holding up the efforts of the
2/4th Duke's to advance Eastward along the Hindenburg trenches, Captain
Cave took a platoon of A forward and rushed them, nearly 20 prisoners
including six officers being taken. C Company, meanwhile, met stubborn
opposition round the Church, while D had the misfortune to catch several
heavy shells and was for a time disorganized, but Captain Bulley rallied his
men and led them forward to help the 5th K.O.Y.L.I. to dispose of some
troublesome machine-guns on the Graincourt Road which were holding that
battalion up. The supporting platoons were by now 'mopping up' to some

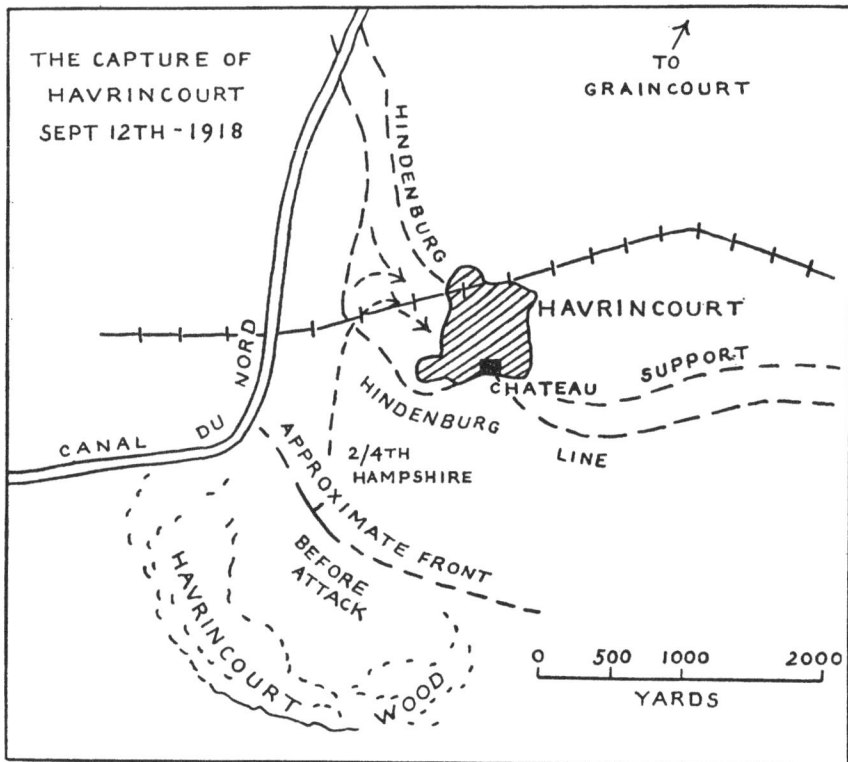

THE CAPTURE OF
HAVRINCOURT
SEPT 12TH - 1918

purpose, searching and clearing cellars and dug-outs and roping in many
prisoners.

B Company should now have gone forward to a final objective East of the
village, but it had suffered fairly heavily, being caught in the German barrage
and having all its officers hit, and it was unable to keep up with our barrage.
However, 2/Lt. Lainé came over from C to take command, crossing open
ground in face of heavy shelling. Reorganized and inspired by him, B pushed
on again, taking several prisoners and, though unable to reach the final objective, it eventually joined the other companies along the railway NE of Havrincourt.

The Germans testified to the importance of our gains by the vigour of their efforts to recover them. They brought up a fresh Division [1] which came forward just about dusk, supported by low-flying aeroplanes and covered by a violent bombardment. The frontage it attacked was that held by the 2/4th Hampshire and 5th K.O.Y.L.I., whose rifles and machine-guns received it with so steady and effective a fire that it was completely checked, our guns assisting to break it up. Night therefore found the Hampshire in possession of their gains, though depleted by over 200 casualties and ready for relief, which soon arrived. R.S.M. Hubbard, as at Vaux, had been indefatigable in keeping up the ammunition supply and in helping to get the wounded away. A very dark night with torrents of rain did not make the relief easier and when, about 3 a.m., the battalion was collected at its assembly position, it was found that several posts had not been relieved. Accordingly Captain Cave went back to take charge of them, to find that meanwhile the enemy had broken through beyond the Hampshire's left and had taken several posts in rear ; in one five of the 2/4th were subsequently found, all killed, having evidently defended their post to the last. Other Hampshires had thrown back a flank on the left and played a useful part in beating the enemy back.

September 13th and 14th the 2/4th spent in reserve in the assembly position, heavy shelling causing several casualties, Captain Bulley being badly hit in the leg, which was subsequently amputated. He and Captains Bacon and Cave were the only remaining officers who had sailed with the 2/4th for India ; he had been one of the battalion's mainstays and his loss was much felt. These two days brought the total casualties up to nearly 300, including 2/Lt. Bryant and 75 men killed and missing, among them C.S.M. Churcher of A Company, an admirable Warrant Officer. Besides Captain Bulley 2/Lts. Gadsby, Isaacs, Pratt, Lord Uffington, Weekes and W. T. Wilson had been wounded with 207 N.C.O.s and men.[2] Against that the 2/4th claimed over 100 prisoners with seven machine-guns, and the congratulations of the Corps and Divisional commanders left no doubt as to the value attached to the capture of Havrincourt,[3] one of the preliminaries essential to the great attack on the Hindenburg Line and Canal du Nord which was about to be delivered.[4]

In the next of these, the Fourth Army's attack of September 18th, which secured a good position for the main blow against the Hindenburg Line from Vendhuille Southward, no Hampshires were engaged, though the 1st Battalion had returned to the line on September 18th, having had much less than its promised month's rest after the piercing of the Drocourt–Queant line. The Fourth Division was now between the Scarpe and the Canal du Nord and was astride the Sensée, holding a long front. Here the 1st Hampshire spent six days in line, on a ridge overlooking the Trinquios stream which the Germans

---

[1] The 20th, it had been in reserve for ten days.

[2] The battalion's casualties since arriving in France now came to 800 and companies were down to platoons in strength.

[3] Captain Cave got the D.S.O. and Captain Bulley and 2/Lts. Lainé and Wheeler the M.C.

[4] The battalion now went back again to Achiet.

had dammed so as to flood both its banks. During retaliation for operations by the Division on the left (September 21st) all D Company's officers and 30 men were gassed and on the night of September 23rd/24th one of B Company's posts was rushed and three men taken. The Germans were apparently trying to rush and set fire to a big dump they had left behind. A previous effort a little earlier had been stopped by C Company, who had put the fire out in time, and now one of C Company's posts, though attacked in rear, drove the enemy off, inflicting several casualties and taking a prisoner, whereby a useful identification was obtained. Two other posts were also attacked but beat off the enemy successfully. When the battalion was relieved (September 24th) 50 of B under Lt. Aldworth and 2/Lt. Kelly were left behind to carry out a raid across the Trinquios. By careful reconnaisance Lt. Aldworth had previously discovered a suitable point for crossing the stream, and his party not only remained on the far side for several hours, making thorough examination of the ground, but attacked a German post, inflicting several casualties.[1] But the battalion was out of the line when on September 27th the British Armies started the second and as it was to prove the final stage of the ' Advance to Victory '. Undeterred by the marked lack of support, let alone encouragement, he was receiving from the War Cabinet, Sir Douglas Haig had resolved to make the attempt to reach a decision in 1918 and his troops were to justify his daring and resolution to the full.

[1] Lt. Aldworth was awarded the M.C. The C.S.M. of C Company and two Lance Corporals who had been in command of the party which had repulsed the enemy's attempt to raid them got the M.M. The battalion diary does not give their names.

CHAPTER XXX

1918 : V

THE FINAL ADVANCE

IN the operations between September 27th and November 11th, the second and decisive stage of the Allied counter-attack, the 1st and the 2/4th Hampshire were engaged in the main British thrust Eastward, through the Hindenburg positions and past Cambrai towards the Sambre, the 2nd and 15th Battalions took part in the Second Army's separate but simultaneous offensive in Flanders and the 11th came forward with the Fifth Army, whose work was the linking up of the inner wings of the big attacks. No Hampshires were included in the Fourth Army who actually achieved the feat of penetrating the Hindenburg Line between Vendhuille and St. Quentin, but the 2/4th in the Third Army and the 1st in the First, who had to face the Scheldt Canal SW. of Cambrai and the Canal du Nord further North, had quite sufficiently formidable obstacles to pierce and stubborn enough resistance to overcome.

The main attack was started on September 27th by the First and Third Armies, the latter including the Sixty-Second Division, whose leading brigades, the 185th and 187th, came through the Third Division on the right of the Sixth Corps and assisted to secure Ribecourt and the Hindenburg Support Line between that village and Flesquieres, though they failed to reach the day's final objectives, Marcoing and the Scheldt Canal. The 186th Brigade, which was in support, moved up from a bivouac near Beaumetz to a position SW. of Havrincourt but was not put into the fighting that day. The 2/4th Hampshire, who had been joined by a dozen new officers, had also received substantial drafts which a longer rest would have given them more chance to assimilate, but Sir Douglas Haig had no reserves to spare and, with the whole front in movement or about to move, ' rests ' had to be cut short and Divisions to be put in again after the briefest of intervals. It was wonderful how the men responded ; the successes already gained were a great encouragement, and each new advance produced ample evidence that the enemy was wilting under the heavy punishment he was receiving.

September 28th saw the attack renewed, the Sixty-Second Division having to capture the rest of the previous day's objectives, including Marcoing. This was to be attacked by the 5th Duke's with the Hampshire in support,[1] but Colonel Brook was warned that the Duke's might not reach the assembly position by ' Zero ' (6.30 a.m.) and that the Hampshire might have to attack in their place. The Duke's did not arrive and therefore the 2/4th had to go forward, with the disadvantage of being a mile behind the barrage. However, the battalion set off at a brisk pace, A (Captain Cave) and C (2/Lt. Young) leading on a two-platoon front, and by great exertions overtook the barrage just short of the first trench to be taken, Dago Trench, just West of Marcoing.

---

[1] The battalion was to form up on the Flesquieres—Ribecourt road.

This was quickly rushed, and A had the satisfaction of shooting down teams which had just come up to get three guns away. Besides these guns several machine-guns and trench-mortars were taken with several prisoners. Pushing on again, A had some sharp fighting at a house near the road to Marcoing, where more prisoners and machine-guns were taken, before reaching the outskirts of Marcoing, where B (Captain Cottam) and D (Captain Gotelee) were to pass through. C meanwhile, after clearing Premy Support fairly easily, had met stubborn opposition further on, but 2/Lt. Young negotiated a barrage very skilfully and C reached and mastered its objective, capturing a field gun and several machine-guns on the way.

B and D now passed through and got into Marcoing, to be fiercely opposed there, but made good progress, B's leading platoons reaching the canal despite much machine-gun fire, which the Lewis guns of No. 5 Platoon did much to

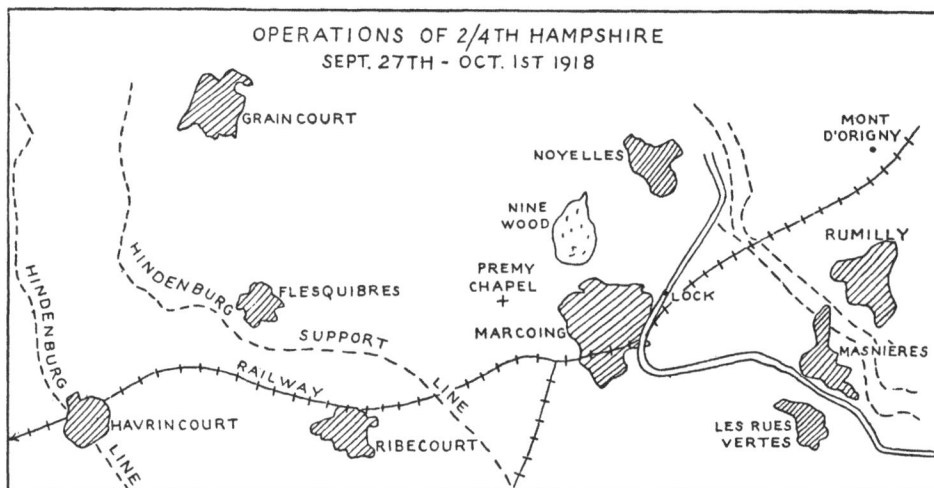

OPERATIONS OF 2/4TH HAMPSHIRE
SEPT. 27TH - OCT. 1ST 1918

subdue, while No. 7 worked round another machine-gun post, dislodged the defenders and took the guns. The passage of the canal proved difficult; machine-guns and rifles behind the embankment beyond had to be silenced, but eventually Captain Cottam led some of B across, and on B's left, near the Marcoing Lock, D also established a footing beyond the canal, Captain Gotelee, himself the first man across a plank bridge, leading a successful rush which dislodged some enemy and secured a position. This assisted the 5th Duke's to get over also and go ahead, but they were unable to get much further, their most advanced parties being driven back to the line the Hampshire were consolidating.

Satisfactory progress had been made by the whole Third Army, while the First on its left had extended the previous day's substantial gains, but next day (September 29th) efforts to exploit this success did not achieve all that was hoped for, the Sixty-Second Division failing to take Rumilly in the Masnieres–

Beaurevoir Line.[1] Elsewhere, however, the bridge-heads over the canal were extended and large stretches of the Marcoing Line taken, while the Fourth Army achieved its great feat of penetrating the Hindenburg Line on a wide front between Vendhuille and St. Quentin, a success which it was quick to exploit.

All that was required of the 2/4th on September 29th was to advance in the late afternoon in support of the 2/4th Duke's, who had made a lodgement in the Rumilly trenches but could not extend it and were being counter-attacked. Part of the battalion had to cross the canal in single file under heavy shell-fire, and consequently it lost the barrage, while on its coming up level with the Duke's such heavy machine-gun fire developed from Mont d'Origny on the left front that no advance beyond Rumilly Trench was possible.

Next morning showed that some Germans were hanging on to Rumilly Support North of the 2/4th's position, so a defensive flank was formed here, while arrangements were being made to deal with this party, on whose position two attacks were subsequently made, the first by some of C Company under 2/Lt. Turner, a second by 20 men under 2/Lt. Shorland and Sergeant Hamilton, the latter a veteran of the South African War. Both were gallantly pressed, but the Germans were strongly posted and could not be dislodged, and the surviving attackers had to regain their previous positions, 2/Lt. Shorland being the last of his party to quit the lodgement that had been made. Apart from this, that afternoon brought the 2/4th a much-felt loss, when Captain Cottam was killed ; ' our best company commander ' he has been called by another officer of the battalion, for which he had done outstanding work. Casualties, mainly from artillery fire, were rather heavy, but our snipers and rifle-grenade men retaliated effectively.

Next day (October 1st) the Sixth Corps detailed the Third Division to renew the attack on Rumilly, the Second simultaneously attacking on the left, from which much of the obstructing fire had come. In this attack, which started at 6 a.m., some of the 76th Brigade ' leap frogged ' the 2/4th, passing over Rumilly Trench, and pushed on into Rumilly where they established themselves. Suspecting that Germans might be lurking in the deep dug-outs in Rumilly Trench, Colonel Brook detailed C Company to follow the 76th Brigade and mop up carefully. The precaution was more than justified ; the right platoon, led by 2/Lt. Shorland, discovered and disposed of 70 Germans with five machine-guns in one dug-out, the left platoon dealt drastically with others who emerged from another dug-out hoping to fire into the backs of the 76th Brigade, while altogether over 30 machine-guns were captured. 2/Lt. Shorland was again conspicuous for skilful leadership and was well supported by 2/Lt. Turner, who carried on though wounded until disabled by another wound.[2]

The Marcoing fight, one of the 2/4th's most successful efforts, had cost

---

[1] The point at which the Twenty-Ninth Division had been held up during the Cambrai battle of 1917.

[2] 2/Lt. Shorland was awarded the D.S.O. and 2/Lt. Turner the M.C.

them nearly 100 casualties, including besides Captain Cottam 20 men killed or missing and 2/Lts. Matthews and Turner wounded, but they had hit the Germans hard, taking four field guns, two trench-mortars and 46 machine-guns with prisoners who considerably exceeded our casualties. After this the 2/4th were to have nearly three weeks' well-earned respite, not coming into action again till October 20th, when they found our front well forward beyond Cambrai towards the Selle.

The 1st Battalion meanwhile had been on the edge of the battle. During the big attack of September 27th the Fourth Division had made vigorous demonstrations as if about to attack, and during the following week its artillery was active, while patrols tried to keep touch with the enemy and get early information of any withdrawal. This, however, was difficult, because the Germans had flooded so much of the area. Then, on October 6th, the battalion was relieved and went back beyond Arras to Berneville for a little rest and training, which latter included instruction in riding for as many officers as could be mounted, a rather painful experience for several. From Berneville the battalion moved up on October 11th to Fontaine Notre Dame near Cambrai. This was a much-battered village, all rubble and rubbish, which provided little shelter, but the battalion's next move, which took it beyond Cambrai to Escaudoeuvres, brought it into country which had so far escaped the ravages of war, if the houses bore ample evidence of the unpleasant habits of German ' kultur ': even so it was in great contrast to the devastated areas over which the fighting had swayed to and fro between Arras and Cambrai, and the German retreat had been too hurried for them to do more than befoul and contaminate. Then on October 17th the battalion moved up into front line, its Division having relieved the Forty-Ninth between Villers en Couchies and Avesnes le Sec,[1] to the left of the point at which the Sixty-Second Division was about to come into line again. Lt. Colonel Mordaunt having gone to England for a rest, Major Hudson was commanding.

If neither 1st nor 2/4th Hampshire were very heavily engaged during the first half of October, the extension of the Allied attacks to Flanders had brought the 2nd and 15th Battalions into the fighting, as the Twenty-Ninth Division, now in the Second Corps, was attacking from Ypres itself astride the Menin road ridge, while the Forty-First, at first in reserve to the Nineteenth Corps on the right, soon came up into front line.

Attacking early on September 28th the Second Corps was promptly and completely successful, the Twenty-Ninth Division, which began by clearing Hooge and then pushed on by Polderhoek towards Gheluvelt, and the Ninth on its left, which advanced through Polygon Wood on Broodseinde, carrying all their objectives and driving the enemy headlong. The 88th Brigade, at first in reserve, came up with the leaders about 9.40 a.m., the advance having then reached Tower Hamlets. Here the 88th went through and, with the 4th

---

[1] Country which the Thirty-Seventh had known in 1794.

Worcestershire leading, were into Gheluvelt within half an hour, capturing a battery of heavy howitzers and many prisoners. The 2nd Hampshire now took on the lead, making for the high ground round Oude Kruiseecke, which was duly reached and occupied. Opposition now stiffened, a fresh German Division had been thrown in, and the terrible state of the ground, a maze of old trench lines littered with debris and punctuated with craters, mostly full of water, was delaying the advance of our guns and reserves. A defensive position was therefore taken up with X Company on outpost, W and Z in

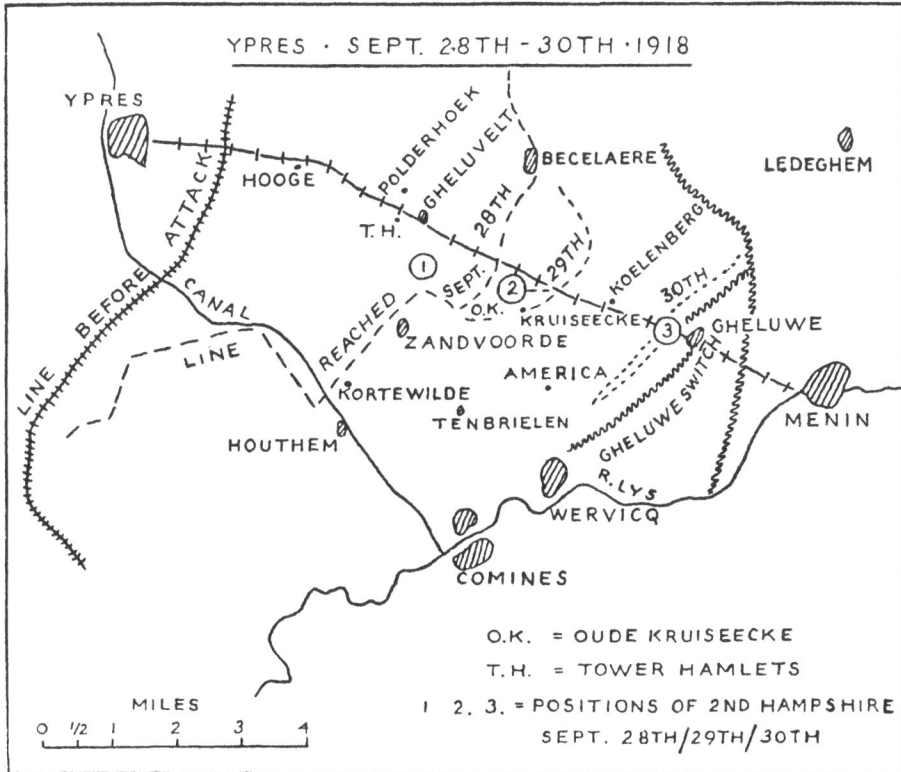

YPRES · SEPT. 28TH - 30TH ·1918

O.K. = OUDE KRUISEECKE
T.H. = TOWER HAMLETS
1. 2. 3. = POSITIONS OF 2ND HAMPSHIRE SEPT. 28TH/29TH/30TH

support and Y in reserve. This was subjected to much machine-gun fire, but no real counter-attack developed, though the Hampshire had the satisfaction of shooting down two low-flying aeroplanes. Casualties had been light, the Hampshire's were under 40 all told, and as over 1,000 prisoners had been taken, with many guns and machine-guns, a substantial success had been achieved: never before had five miles been gained in one day at Ypres.

The 15th Battalion had not been actively engaged; the Forty-First Division, following the attacking Divisions of the Nineteenth Corps, whose success had almost equalled that of the Second, had merely pushed its leading brigade, the 124th, forward to a line running from the canal at Kortewilde towards Zandvoorde, meeting but little serious opposition ; the 122nd Brigade being further back, in reserve, had not had any fighting. Further South the right of the Second Army had also advanced, without encountering much opposition, and the Germans were evidently preparing to quit the Messines-Wytschaete ridge.

The success achieved on September 28th was more successfully exploited next day on the flanks than in the centre of the attack, as fresh troops were flung in to face the Twenty-Ninth Division, whose guns were struggling pain-fully forward over the devastated ground, and when, about 7 a.m., the 88th Brigade resumed the advance with the Hampshire in reserve, adequate artillery support was lacking. After advancing over half a mile towards Koelenberg, the leading battalions were held up by machine-guns in ' pill-boxes ' and, as no touch could be obtained with any troops to the South, the Hampshire formed a defensive flank, on the right of the 4th Worcestershire and facing South towards Kruiseecke. German snipers and machine-guns continued to be active and another 40 casualties were added to the previous day's total, 2/Lt. Phelps being killed. The Forty-First Division meanwhile had gained ground North and East of the Ypres–Comines Canal, but again the 15th Hampshire were not actively engaged, being in support to their brigade, which had ad-vanced past Kortewilde towards Tenbrielen, the 123rd Brigade also advancing on its right. Beyond the canal the advance had almost reached the Lys : here the Germans were yielding ground more readily than between Ypres and Menin, where a strong Gheluwe Switch had to be pierced.

This was discovered next day (September 30th) when the 124th Brigade, again leading the Forty-First Division, got forward to the Lys between Wervicq and Comines, but the 88th on approaching Gheluwe met stubborn opposition, the Worcestershire after initial success being held up. Before this 2nd Hamp-shire patrols had cleared Kruiseecke and ' America ',[1] taking some prisoners, but the battalion was in reserve and only came up into front line after dark, relieving the 4th Worcestershire in front of Gheluwe and about 500 yards from the outskirts. The right flank was somewhat exposed, no troops having come up level. Next morning, however, some of the Forty-First Division came up here, the 122nd Brigade having been brought across from near Tenbrielen and linking up with the 88th Brigade, but the latter made no attempt to attack the Gheluwe Switch, though both sides were active with guns, trench-mortars and machine-guns, the 2nd Hampshire having nearly 40 casualties, nearly all wounded. The Forty-First Division also was confronted by the Gheluwe Switch.

The strength of the positions covering Gheluwe became fully apparent when the attack was renewed on October 2nd, the 2nd Hampshire leading its brigade's advance. Though Gheluwe had been heavily bombarded for half an hour before ' Zero ' (7 a.m.), machine-guns were still in evidence when the attackers tried to force their way in. This they did with some success ; on the right two

---

[1] A cabaret on the road to Wervicq.

platoons of X under Lt. G. H. Brown worked their way down the Reutelbeck and occupied a cemetery East of the village. Here machine-guns on their right proved troublesome, but a 'pill-box' was rushed by Private Bone and taken with two machine-guns and nearly 30 prisoners. Meanwhile W, the other attacking company, had been delayed by a check to the brigade on its left and was unable to clear the Northern part of Gheluwe to which the enemy were clinging, being well supplied with machine-guns. Eventually after Z, which was in support, had pushed into the village, reaching the church, most of W got forward and joined X near the Wervicq road, South of Gheluwe. One platoon under 2/Lt. Guy, though reduced to a handful, worked its way through

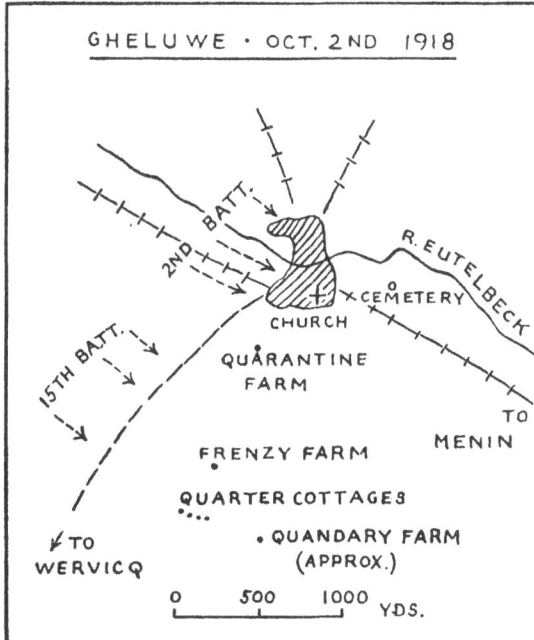

GHELUWE · OCT. 2ND 1918

the village to its SE. corner, disposing of many enemy, and helped a platoon on its left to get forward. Before this counter-attacks had led to the evacuation of the advanced position at the cemetery, Lt. Brown and Private Bone remaining to the last to give covering fire and giving great help to the most advanced platoon, which was in danger of being cut off, while Colonel Westmorland, whose energy and ability were again conspicuous, also helped to extricate this party.[1] Meanwhile, thanks largely to the inspiring leading and example of 2/Lt. Mitchell, who himself disposed of half a dozen Germans, most of Y had established themselves NW. of the village, facing NE. so as to deal with any counter-attack from the North, and despite heavy shell-fire the battalion retained its hold on its gains, though no further advance could be attempted. Several more machine-guns were put out of action, the crew of one who took refuge in

[1] He received a bar to the D.S.O.

an aid-post and came out adorned with Red Cross brassards being summarily dealt with. About 5 p.m. the enemy's fire developed much greater intensity and strong parties of infantry began working forward; the Hampshire, however, though unsupported on the right, held on and drove back the attackers with rifles and Lewis guns, 2/Lt. Ewens doing much to help in the repulse of the attack, and when about 10 p.m. the K.O.S.B. turned up to relieve them, the Hampshire were able to hand over most of Gheluwe to them. Casualties had not been excessive, 27 men killed and missing, Lt. G. H. Brown (at duty), 2/Lts. Guy, Hill, Parkham and Perry and 46 men wounded, bringing the total since September 28th to one officer and 50 men killed and missing and ten officers and 140 men wounded.[1]

The 15th's attack had also met stubborn opposition. The battalion had moved forward to ' America ' on the previous afternoon, (October 1st) coming under sharp fire from the direction of Wervicq and having Lt. Colonel Puttick and the Adjutant, Captain Wigmore, wounded, whereupon Captain Good took command. Orders had been too late in reaching it to allow the battalion to attack the Gheluwe Switch that evening as intended, and it had to dig in quite half a mile short of the German line. Attacking under a good barrage at 5.30 next morning (October 2nd), it made good progress at first, carrying the trenches and getting well forward across the Gheluwe–Wervicq road, while on the right one company managed to penetrate to Quandary Farm, where 2/Lt. Seal (Hampshire Carabineers) and a party maintained themselves tenaciously for some time, although isolated and unsupported, while elsewhere Lt. Graham, after capturing a concrete dug-out, also held on under heavy machine-gun fire. Sergeant Barton was much to the fore, leading the advance and then, though wounded, helping in the consolidation of the position reached, and C.S.M. Burch, after succouring his wounded company commander under heavy fire, rallied men to lead an attack on a ' pill-box '.

After Lt. Seal's party had been forced to evacuate Quandary Farm, ,an effort was made to maintain a line from Quarter Cottages through Frenzy Farm to Quarantine Farm, but violent counter-attacks forced back the next battalion on the right and the 15th had to give ground, though they retained a lodgement in the Gheluwe Switch SW. of the village and to the right of the 2nd Hampshire's position. That evening they were relieved by the Thirty-Fourth Division, to get a fortnight's respite from fighting. Casualties had been heavy, Captain Reynolds [2] and 33 men killed or missing, eight officers and 120 men wounded, but the 15th had taken a heavy toll of the enemy, capturing a dozen machine-guns and many prisoners.[3]

The Flanders attack was now suspended, partly for administrative reasons, partly because the French and Belgians had not kept level with the Second

[1] Lt. Brown and 2/Lts. Ewens, Guy and Mitchell received the M.C. and Private Bone the D.C.M.
[2] D.G. attached. Capt. Whaley and Lts. Graham and G. J. Potter were among the wounded.
[3] Lt. Graham and 2/Lt. Seal received the M.C., C.S.M. Burch and Sergeant Barton getting the D.C.M.

Army, whose left was therefore rather exposed, while reserves had reinforced the defenders of the ' Flanders Positions '. Thus for the next ten days, four Hampshire battalions out of five were back ' resting ', while, if the 11th remained in the line, its work was hardly affected by the advance which carried the Fifth Army up to the Haute Deule canal and over the Aubers Ridge, the Sixteenth Division being nearly four miles East of Auchy by October 5th. This meant the usual hard work for the Pioneers on roads, light railways and communications generally : they might change their position after an advance but their work remained the same, varied occasionally by assisting the R.E. in bridging.

The 2nd and 15th Battalions were in action again before either the 1st or 2/4th. October 14th saw the Flanders advance resumed, the Second Army seeking to reach the Lys as far downstream as Courtrai and thereby to cover the thrust of the Belgians and French Eastward towards Ghent. The Twenty-Ninth Division had now shifted to the left, facing the Flanders II Position from Ledeghem Northward, the Forty-First being the next but two to the South and confronting the still untaken portions of the Gheluwe Switch and the Terhand Line North of Gheluwe.[1]

Attacking a full hour before sunrise the leading troops of both Divisions made speedy progress. The Germans had apparently realised that an attack was coming and had put down a heavy barrage a full hour before ' Zero ', but on lines which had been noted and our troops were well placed to avoid it, though the front wave of the 15th Hampshire, A and B Companies, had a few casualties. Machine-guns in defended farms were the chief obstacle, but a thick mist reduced their efficiency, if it caused some loss of direction and mixture of units.

The 122nd Brigade was leading the Division's attack with all three battalions in line. ' Pill-boxes ' caused much trouble, but the 15th Hampshire attacked with great dash and determination : the men by now knew how ' pill-boxes ' should be tackled and did not let themselves be held up, and the first objective was taken according to programme. Despite the mist direction had been extraordinarily well maintained. C and D Companies now went through the leaders and carried on to the battalion's final objective[2] with equal success. Resistance was weakening : many Germans were not fighting with their old toughness. Here the 124th Brigade came through to carry on the attack while the 15th Hampshire set to work to consolidate the ground gained. Casualties had been light, about 80, including a dozen killed and missing and five officers wounded, 2/Lt. Sumption mortally, but the prisoners were nearly four times as many [3] and several machine-guns and an anti-tank rifle were also taken.

The Forty-First Division had secured its entire final objective, making an advance of over three miles and reaching Wynberg ; the Twenty-Ninth, which

---

[1] Its starting line was more to the West than that of the Twenty-Ninth.
[2] Approximately North of Menin and across the line of the road to Roulers.
[3] One account claims as many as 840.

used the 86th and 88th Brigades to lead its attack, did almost as well. The 2nd
Hampshire, whose recent losses had been to some extent made good by the
arrival of a dozen officers and about 120 men, had come forward to Becelaere
on October 11th and moved up into position West of the Menin–Roulers road
on the evening of October 13th. They were in reserve to the 88th Brigade,
which had the Leinster in front and the Worcestershire in second line.

Moving forward through the mist, thickened somewhat unnecessarily by
our smoke shell, the Hampshire found direction hard to keep. Y and Z Companies were leading and made as rapid progress as the mist allowed, any Germans who had escaped the leading battalions proving more anxious to be
accepted as prisoners than to fight. East of the Ledeghem road, a halt was
made for reorganizing, units having got mixed in the mist and smoke. Another

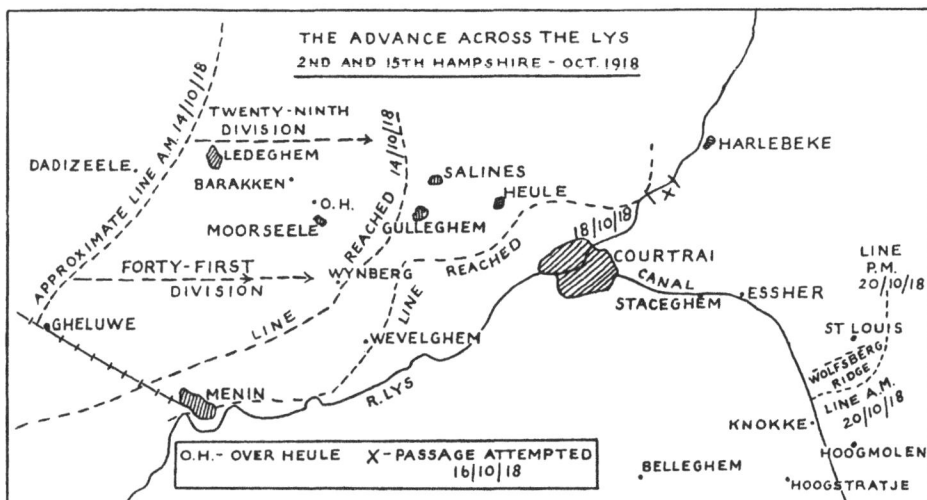

advance having reached Barakken, Y and Z pushed forward through Sovereign
Wood and came up with the Worcestershire, now in front line,[1] through whom
Y and Z advanced again, cleared a ridge in front and reached the Driemasten–
Gulleghem road, Z taking several prisoners, while two platoons of Y pressed
on some way SE. to secure a large house. Opposition was now stiffening,
mainly from machine-guns and trench-mortars, and no further advance could
be made, though W Company came up on the right to form a defensive flank
facing Gulleghem, in front of which the Thirty-Sixth Division had been checked.
Losses had not been heavy, 15 men killed and missing and Lt. Parry and 2/Lts.
Ewens and Holloway wounded with 76 men, while the Division had captured
some 50 guns and over 1,000 prisoners, besides advancing nearly three miles.
Major O'Reilly, who had been in command, had led the advance very skilfully
and received the M.C. for his good work.

Nothing more was required of the 2nd Hampshire next day than to retain

---

[1] Approximately on the line Overheule—East of Barakken.

their position, while the 87th Brigade went through and carried on most success-fully, advancing another three miles, capturing two large villages with many prisoners and guns and getting nearly to the Lys, on whose banks it established itself on the following day (October 16th) between Harlebeke and Courtrai, the K.O.S.B. and the Ninth Division on their left actually getting parties across the river. That evening the 88th Brigade relieved the 87th, the Hamp-shire taking over from the K.O.S.B. and putting two platoons of X across the Lys to assist the Ninth Division.

The foothold across the Lys was, however, precarious : the bridges connect-ing the advanced detachments with the left bank were under shell-fire and were so repeatedly hit that, far from more being constructed, those already laid were rendered useless. Meanwhile the advanced parties were being hard pressed, one attack, about 5 a.m. (October 4th) being gallantly repulsed by the party of X Company, under 2/Lt. Cotten, who charged and drove the enemy back, restoring the situation. But with the bridges virtually demolished it was clear that the advanced detachments could not be supported,[1] and after Brigadier-General Freyberg had himself come across to investigate orders were given to withdraw them. To cover the operation a selected party of Hampshire Lewis gunners was ferried across in pontoons, so quickly and silently that, though the night was bright, the enemy never detected the move. This party having taken up its covering positions, the Ninth Division's men were safely withdrawn, all their wounded being brought away, after which the Hampshire covering party was also ferried back, General Freyberg and Colonel Westmorland only leaving with the rear-party under 2/Lt. Milne.[2]

The passage of the Lys was merely being postponed until more systematic preparations could be made. The success achieved by the left of the Second Army had had considerable effect elsewhere, enabling its two right-hand Corps to cross upstream of Menin. These now advanced on a broad front down the right bank, in touch on their right with the Fifth Army, before which also the Germans were retiring, abandoning Lille and other places of importance. Their advance threatened the flanks of the troops opposing the Second Army's left on the Lys, and on the evening of October 19th the 2nd Hampshire had the satisfaction of leading their Division across that river. The 11th Queen's of the Forty-First Division had already got across at Courtrai earlier in the day, so X and Z Companies were ferried across behind them and extended their line towards Harlebeke, securing a bridge-head. An infantry bridge having been completed, the rest of the battalion came over about 11 p.m. and lined up along the Harlebeke road in readiness to attack next day.

Having meanwhile shifted to its left, the Forty-First Division was now on the Twenty-Ninth's immediate right. The 15th Hampshire had moved to Heule on the outskirts of Courtrai on October 16th, being so unlucky as to have nearly 30 casualties from one shell on the Gulleghem–Heule road, and had

---

[1] The Ninth Division's *History* says that food and ammunition had to be dropped by aero-planes.
[2] 2/Lts. Cotten and Milne received the M.C.

remained in reserve, following the rest of the Division across the Lys. They were not, however, engaged on October 20th, when the Second Army started the thrust that was to carry it from the Lys to the Scheldt, as their Division was retained in reserve, only coming into the battle on its second day.

This advance was to give both 2nd and 15th Hampshire their last battle. Both, however, had some sharp fighting to end their war, the 2nd leading the Twenty-Ninth Division's attack on October 20th. ' Zero ' was at 6 a.m. and, with the Leinster in immediate support, the battalion was soon across the Courtrai–Harlebeke railway and forging ahead over rather difficult country, seamed with small streams and dotted with farms and cottages surrounded by hedges and gardens, while recent rain made the going heavy. As the leading waves neared Staceghem the enemy could be seen retiring in disorder and showing no disposition to stand and fight, except at one point North of Staceghem where 30 men were killed or taken. Field guns firing over open sights gave some trouble but were successfully tackled, the battalion took four in all, and soon after 9 a.m. Esscher on the Courtrai-Bossuyt Canal had been reached and the line running thence NE. was being consolidated. The Leinster were up now, gaps having developed in the front line, and while some platoons of the Worcestershire were mopping up in rear, others were coming forward to join in the attack.

Pushing on again, the 88th Brigade's left reached St. Louis about 1 p.m., the Hampshire halting here till other troops came up on the right and secured a line running SW. to the canal. The Germans had rallied on the Wolfsberg ridge sufficiently to prevent the 88th Brigade advancing any further without more adequate artillery support, but a counter-attack soon faded away under the fire of the 88th's rifles and machine-guns, and in the afternoon the 86th Brigade came through and gained a little more ground. That allowed the Hampshire to be sent back into billets at Staceghem in reserve. Losses had again been light and, tired as the men were, they had attacked with great dash and determination. One feature of the day had been the enthusiasm and readiness to help of the inhabitants whom the advance was liberating.

At Staceghem the 2nd Hampshire had four days' rest, while first the 86th and then the 87th Brigade carried on the attack. The country was difficult, it was hard to get enough guns forward to give the artillery support required, and with the British ahead of the French on their left, progress was none too rapid. Moreover, most battalions in the Second Army were much below establishment, so that heavy casualties could not be risked. The Twenty-Ninth Division, however, could now be rested : by October 25th it had been relieved and the 88th Brigade moved South to billets near Tourcoing, where they were made very welcome by the recently liberated inhabitants.

The 15th Battalion's active share in this advance towards the Scheldt had begun on October 21st, when their Division was ordered to pass through the Thirty-Fifth on the Kreupel and Hoogstraatje ridges SE. of Courtrai and continue the advance. The 122nd Brigade was on the left, with all three battalions in line and the Bossuyt–Avelghem road, just short of the Scheldt, as objective. The Courtrai–Bossuyt canal, which ran diagonally across its line of advance, proved a trouble, all the bridges having been blown up. However, the 18th K.R.R.C. managed to get across to the Eastern side in the Twenty-Ninth Division's area and pushed forward towards the Hoogmolen ridge, and the Hampshire, having negotiated the ruined bridge at Knokke in single file, came up on their right and advanced nearly 600 yards before machine-guns stopped them. Little more progress had been made by the right brigade, and before the advance could be resumed next day (October 22nd) the Germans were counter-attacking with some vigour. One attempt during the night was re-pulsed by the 15th, but a disturbed night left them weary and, though about 7 a.m. another attack was beaten off, further to the right the Germans re-gained some ground and thus prevented the next battalion from reaching its assembly position by 9 a.m., when it should have cooperated with the 15th in a renewed attack. The Hampshire had therefore to extend their line and take over the whole frontage, and try as they would could make little progress having great difficulty in mastering a machine-gun nest at the Southern entrance to the tunnel by which the canal pierces the main ridge between the Scheldt and the Lys. After a time they were reinforced by the 10th Queen's (124th Brigade), who crossed the canal and came up on their right, and a renewed effort in the afternoon, supported by a good barrage, gained some ground, the Queen's eventually taking the obstructing end of the tunnel. After dark the 123rd Brigade took over, allowing the Hampshire to withdraw to billets near Knokke. They had had another 100 casualties, including 2/Lts. Colyer and Sabine killed and 2/Lts. Darking, Ferris, Langdon and Seal wounded.

The next three days saw the Division gain more ground, clearing the Hoog-molen ridge and reaching a line from Herstert to the outskirts of Ooteghem, to which the 122nd Brigade came up late on October 25th with orders to pass through the 123rd next day and continue the advance, with the Scheldt at Avelghem as objective. Patrols soon discovered that the enemy was retiring on this front, which involved some changes of plan and redrafting of orders, but about mid-day an advance could be started. It encountered considerable opposition, but machine-guns gave most useful covering fire and on the 15th's left C Company soon reached the objective. D on the right were held up by machine-guns on the flank, but a well-executed flanking move by A, who were in support, cleared several machine-gun nests and allowed D to get forward. A heavy barrage was now put down by the enemy, but the leading companies pushed rapidly forward so that the barrage came down behind them, though B, in support to C, were caught by it and became disorganized but were rallied and brought up to support the left. Meanwhile the other companies, attacking with great dash and determination, had reached a line just short of the Scheldt [1] and were consolidating, taking advantage of a deep ditch which provided a ready-made trench, only needing a fire-step. Outposts were pushed out to cover the consolidation, but no counter-attack was attempted and soon after

[1] They could not secure the bridge at Avelghem.

midnight the 15th were relieved and went back to billets for four days' rest. For the moment the Second Army's advance was suspended : it was close up to the Scheldt but could not force a passage until the French and Belgians came up level on its left.

The 15th Hampshire had fared surprisingly well in this last and most successful attack, having had the amazingly low number of 20 casualties, only one being fatal. If some German units were fighting with much less than their old skill and determination, the country had given their machine-gunners

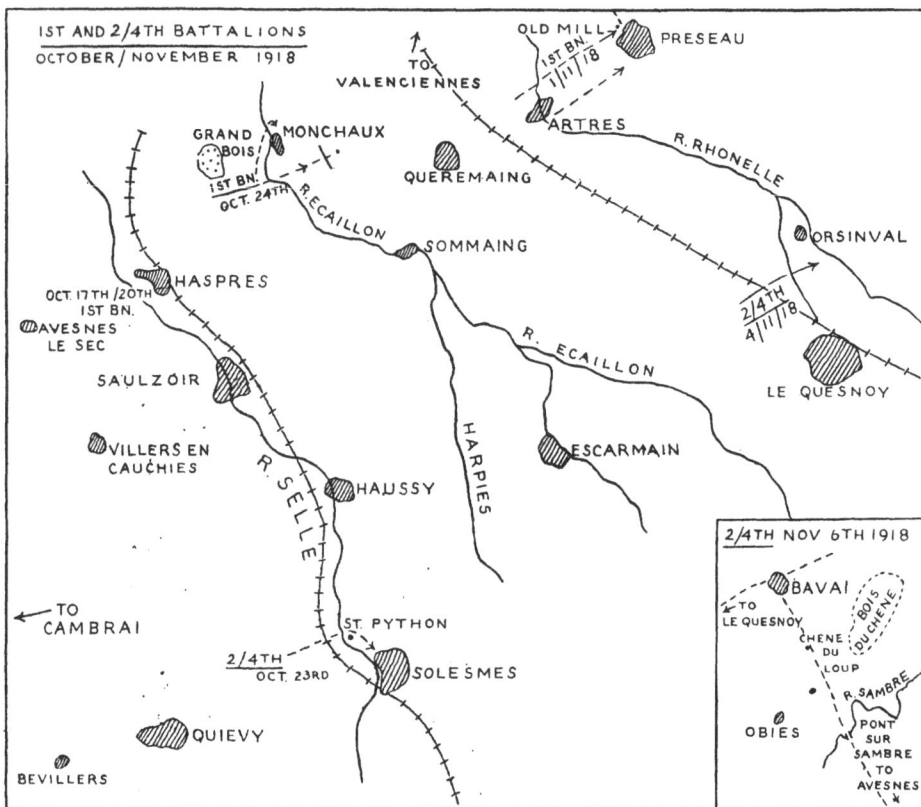

many good positions and the opposition had been far from negligible, especially as all our battalions were weak and, as before, owing to the heavy going which delayed the replenishment of empty limbers, adequate artillery support to the infantry attacks had been lacking. The Second Army had had to fight for its gains.

October 20th, when the 1st and 2/4th Hampshire again came in action, marked a second stage in the fighting along the Selle, behind which river the Germans, after being driven out of the Hindenburg Line and other positions covering Cambrai, were trying to stand. Their line here formed part of the so-called ' Hermann Position ', which existed mainly on paper and was in no way comparable to the formidable defences the British Armies had already penetrated. No elaborate trench systems remained to be pierced, no net-work of old trenches and belts of wire had to be tackled, the fighting now took place in open country, hardly scarred by war, villages really existed and were not mere heaps of rubble and ruins, marked on the map but not too easy to identify on the ground, and when captured or by-passed they actually afforded real shelter, all the more welcome as autumn was already well advanced and nights were getting quite cold, though the weather was far finer than in the corresponding months of 1916 or 1917. This ' open warfare ' was a new experience for officers and men ; in August and September they had been fighting over the area of devastation between the old British front of July 1916 and the Hindenburg Line, where nearly all buildings and woods had long been razed to the ground ; where countless old trench-lines hampered movement and afforded ready-made defensive positions. The bomb had still been in constant use, but in the new conditions battalions who had maintained some standard of musketry were to find themselves well repaid.

The Fourth Division, now in the Twenty-Second Corps on the right of the First Army, had relieved the Forty-Ninth Division opposite Saulzoir and Haspres on October 17th.[1] The 1st Hampshire had taken over after dark on October 17th from the 4th K.O.Y.L.I. opposite Haspres, holding the whole brigade front on the near side of the Selle with battalion head-quarters at Avesnes le Sec, a locality which attracted an unpleasant amount of attention from the enemy's guns. The line here was one of rifle-pits in the open, not much more than a chain of outposts, and to keep touch with the enemy and find out his intentions active patrolling was necessary. On the 18th Lt. Colonel Earle, who had for some time been commanding the 1st East Lancashire,[2] arrived to take command, and on the same day C Company repulsed a raid on one of its posts, capturing a prisoner, to the great satisfaction of the Intelligence, who badly wanted an identification at this moment.

All was in train here for the attack of October 20th, to be begun by the Hampshire (right) and the Rifle Brigade (left) on the 11th Brigade's front, with the passage of the Selle and the capture of the railway line beyond as objectives. However, during the night of the 19th/20th the enemy fell back here, and after the 10th Brigade on the right had pushed forward to the Division's first objective, just short of the Ecaillon stream, the 11th Brigade advanced unopposed through Haspres and continued the line NW. to Grand Bois, facing the village of Monchaux across the Ecaillon, the Hampshire now being on the

---

[1] Major General Lipsett, the new Divisional Commander, who had succeeded General Matheson, transferred to the Guards in September, had been killed in reconnoitring the position on October 14th : he was succeeded by Major General Lucas, a Brigade Major in the Twenty-Ninth Division at the Cape Helles landing.

[2] That regiment's *History* speaks with great enthusiasm of Colonel Earle's work for its 1st Battalion, which greatly regretted losing a commander who had won its confidence and had led it most successfully at Ypres in October 1917 and in hard trials in March and April 1918.

left, in touch with the Fifty-First Division. The first patrols to penetrate into Haspres received a wonderful welcome from the inhabitants, wild with joy at being delivered from German hands. Hostile shelling had caused a few casualties, including some of the civilians who were making their way out to avoid being caught in a counter-attack, but the enemy's evacuation of a fairly strong position was some indication of his weakening will and capacity to hold out very much longer.

The 2/4th Battalion, unlike the 1st, had really hard fighting on October 20th. Since their fight for Marcoing they had not been in action again, having been back near Havrincourt for a week ; they had then come forward past Cambrai to Quievy, enjoying the unusual experience of finding billets in virtually undamaged villages, a pleasant contrast to trenches and dug-outs. The Sixth Corps was using the Guards (left) and the Sixty-Second Division (right) in the new attack and the latter's objective included Solesmes, near to the point where the 1st Hampshire had had their first touch with the enemy in August 1914. To take Solesmes the Selle had to be crossed, which promised some trouble, as in places it was six feet deep and 20 across, with a high bank beyond, while above Solesmes dams had expanded it into a lake. However, one battalion got across in the next Division's sector upstream, and, while it attacked Solesmes from the South, the 5th Duke's managed to wade across further downstream at St. Python and to cover the erection by the R.E. of footbridges.

The 2/4th Hampshire, who were to follow the 5th Duke's across, had some difficulty in reaching their assembly positions in the dark and in pouring rain ; that they accomplished it successfully was due to the Intelligence Officer, Lt. Greenhalgh,[1] who, though gassed while reconnoitring the ground, guided the companies to their places nevertheless and then directed their advance.

Moving forward at 2 a.m. the 2/4th were soon across the Selle and making, as ordered, for Solesmes to assist the attack from the South. A Company (2/Lt. Wheeler) had to clear some houses at St. Python and for a time were held up, but a skilful move disposed of the opposition ; that done, they pushed on and established a footing in Solesmes, despite stubborn resistance on its outskirts, taking two machine-guns and 30 prisoners. D (Captain Gotelee) followed, meeting considerable opposition at a loopholed wall, which was overcome by an outflanking movement, skilfully led by 2/Lt. Neil, who had located the obstructing machine-guns. B (Captain Lainé), who supported D, also had trouble with machine-guns and a trench-mortar, but 2/Lt. Barker and a party rushed a machine-gun post, taking the gun and disposing of all its crew, and the advance went on. C (Captain Brierley) had been detailed to mop up Solesmes, in which work the reserve platoons of the other companies assisted, and by 7.15 a.m. the battalion was established on its objective, having taken 250 prisoners with a dozen machine-guns and two trench-mortars at a surprisingly low cost, only eight killed and 2/Lt. Matthew and 20 men wounded. The

---

[1] Lancashire Fusiliers (attached).

enemy had been surprised by the speed of the attack, but much was due to the skilful planning of the acting C.O., Major Cockburn of the Inniskilling Fusiliers, Colonel Brook being on leave.

Meanwhile the 185th Brigade had gone ahead and secured the Division's final objective, on the ridge overlooking the Harpies stream, a tributary of the Ecaillon, which the 1st Hampshire were facing some miles to the left ; the 1st would have to cross this obstacle before they had finished with the attack begun on October 20th, but the 2/4th, after holding on at Solesmes till relieved by the Third Division on the evening of October 22nd, went back to Bevillers to enjoy ten days' respite before returning for their last battle.

The 1st Hampshire had an active share in finishing off the ' battle of the Selle '. They had spent three nasty days (October 21st–23rd), dug in just East of Haspres, under steady shelling, largely gas, and in heavy rain, while the Fourth Division was closing up to the Ecaillon, in readiness to force its passage on the 24th, when the First Army was to attack again, the Third and Fourth having done so successfully on the previous day. The Ecaillon, like the Selle, was a troublesome obstacle, four feet and more deep in places, with a muddy bottom, 20 feet and more wide, with steep banks and running quite fast. The country was closely cultivated, with many orchards, and the Germans had been able to put up enough wire on both banks to be an appreciable obstruction, while they held the river with machine-gun posts on the far (right) bank.

The Division's first objective on October 24th, the ' Blue Line ', was formed by the sunken road from Monchaux to Sommaing, about 200 yards beyond the enemy's bank of the river. The Hampshire were on the left of their Division, in touch with the Fifty-First and facing Monchaux : they were also to secure a ' Yellow Line ', 1000 yards beyond the ' Blue Line' , and would consolidate there.

B (left) and D (right) Companies led the attack, supported by A and C and advancing behind an excellent barrage. Unfortunately the bridges which had been provided proved too short to span the stream and the attack seemed bound to be checked. Luckily the thick mist hampered the enemy's machine-gunners, whose fire was to some extent kept down by bombing across the stream and by rifle-fire. On the right, 2/Lt. Cancellor of C promptly swam the river, armpit deep and icy cold, and rushed a machine-gun post single-handed,[1] Captain May and 2/Lt. Holmes and some men, having hauled themselves over along a wire across the river, tackled the other machine-gun posts so successfully that before long C and D could report themselves as across. Once the attackers reached their bank the German resistance had crumpled up and the majority were quick to surrender, over 100 being taken at the first objective. With the enemy putting up so poor a fight, Captain May pushed on with C and D, though their left flank was open, as A and B had found even deeper water, impossible to wade. His enterprise was rewarded by getting an ideal target in Germans who were quitting the village in haste. A and B were now diverted

[1] He was awarded the M.C.

to follow C and D, who by 6.15 a.m. were reported to have taken the Yellow Line as well as the Blue and to be consolidating, of which success the arrival soon afterwards at battalion head-quarters of a large batch of prisoners, including an officer, gave tangible evidence. A and B were held up for a time in front of Monchaux, but a small party under 2/Lts. Rayner and Kelly, who had scrambled across the Ecaillon lower down, in the Fifty-First Division's area, now made their way into Monchaux from the North, establishing themselves in a barn and taking several prisoners. These included an officer, of whom 2/Lt. Rayner, finding that he could speak English, now made use, telling him that our troops were all round the village and that further resistance would be futile. The officer having explained this to his men, over 100 surrendered, and this allowed A and B to push on through Monchaux to their positions in the Yellow Line, where they gained touch with C and D, beyond whose right the Somerset also had gained their objective and were consolidating. Both Hampshire and Somerset, however, were ahead of the 10th Brigade, which was held up short of the Yellow Line but captured its share of it in the late afternoon, thereby making the 11th Brigade's position secure.

Meanwhile the Hampshire had carried on with their consolidation. Casualties had been unexpectedly low, seeing how naturally strong the position was and in what force it was held. The battalion, whose strength had been considerably reduced by sickness,[1] so that on October 27th it could not muster 400 all told for an attack, had got off lightly with only 20 killed and missing and 90 wounded with four officers :[2] against this it could set 250 prisoners and 40 machine-guns.

The battalion retained its position for two days, soaked to the skin, with its food almost too wet to be eaten and under heavy shell-fire, while the 12th Brigade was exploiting the success of October 24th by advancing to the Rhonelle and establishing itself on the right bank after taking Artres (October 26th) ; on this the Hampshire were drawn back to get a brief rest at Monchaux before they took over the left of the new front with head-quarters at Querenaing (October 28th). A fresh attack was in preparation and active patrolling [3] was carried on to keep touch with the enemy, now back behind the Rhonelle. Like the Selle and Ecaillon this stream was quite an appreciable obstacle.

The next large-scale attack by the First, Third and Fourth Armies was to be combined with another thrust in Flanders, where the Second Army had yet to achieve the passage of the Scheldt, towards which the Fifth also had been advancing on a wide front for the last fortnight. But before this attack was made the First Army had to push forward SE. of Valenciennes so as to out-flank that town and thereby force the Germans to evacuate it, which would avoid a direct

---

[1] The influenza epidemic had caused many admissions to hospital and, not a few deaths were reported, the regiment's most notable loss being that of Lt. G. R. D. Moor, A.D.C. to Major General W. de L. Williams, commanding the Thirtieth Division. He had again distinguished himself, adding to his V.C. the M.C. and a bar.

[2] 2/Lts. Holmes, Kelly (R. Sussex) R.V. Taylor and Wynn.

[3] The battalion had several casualties in this period, Captain May being wounded for a third time.

attack on the town, known to be crowded with civilians. The Twenty-Second Corps, which now had the Forty-Ninth (left) and Fourth Divisions in line, was to carry out this operation by attacking across the Rhonelle on November 1st, Canadians co-operating on its left and the Third Army's left Division on its right.

The attack of November 1st started at 5.35 a.m. in the dark : it went very well nevertheless, the men kept close up to an excellent barrage and made short work of crossing the Rhonelle. The Hampshire had nearly two miles to cover to reach their objective North and East of Préseau, which village the Rifle Brigade on their right were attacking, but though Germans entrenched in scattered posts offered some opposition, many surrendered promptly, nearly 20 being taken in one house by Corporal Dennett, who pushed his way in ahead of his platoon [1] and the objective, just beyond Préseau, was taken well up to time and many prisoners with it. Consolidation was now started but the brigade had not half enough men for the length of its frontage, and before long counter-attacks were developing, pressing hardest against the Rifle Brigade in Préseau and pushing them back West of the village. This exposed the Hampshire's right and made it necessary to bring the line back to a sunken road running North from an old mill on the outskirts of Préseau. This position was successfully defended, the enemy being checked, thanks largely to our guns. About 3.30 p.m. an urgent appeal for ammunition came back from B Company, as the enemy were pressing forward strongly and assembling in a sunken road to counter-attack, so four boxes were now hurried up. B Company, however, were not content to meet the advance with fire alone but, as the enemy advanced, charged most effectively, a company of the Somerset co-operating on the right, and the Germans were sent bolting back. After this the Hampshire were not troubled again, and during the small hours they were relieved by the King's Own, and went back across the Rhonelle to Haspres, having covered themselves with credit in the last but not the least satisfactory of their actions during the war. A very promising young officer, 2/Lt. Cancellor, had been killed and 2/Lt. Burns was missing, while eleven men were killed or missing, Lt. Reid and 2/Lts. Powning and Walmsley and 30 men being wounded, but over 250 prisoners had been taken, with several machine-guns, and the battalion's stubborn resistance had prevented the counter-attack from achieving any substantial success and paved the way for a most successful continuation of the attack by the 10th Brigade. A hard fortnight had ended well for Colonel Earle and his battalion.

With the Fourth Division out of the line, only the 2/4th Hampshire were left to be ' in at the death ' of the great ' advance to victory '. They had had ten days good rest at Bevillers, during which Colonel Brook rejoined, and then moved up by Solesmes to Escarmain, SW. of Le Quesnoy, in readiness for the attack to be delivered on November 4th all along the line. In this the Sixty-Second Division's objective lay NW. of Le Quesnoy, which the New Zealand

[1] He was awarded the D.C.M.

Division was attacking. The forming-up line, from which the 2/4th Hampshire was to lead its brigade's advance, ran roughly NW. and SE., along the Le Quesnoy–Valenciennes railway, whose low embankment here gave a little cover to the leading companies, A and B. The first objective was a wooded ravine, where stubborn opposition was to be expected and was indeed encountered, while the advance caught the enemy's barrage before reaching the ravine. However, A Company (2/Lt. Wheeler) forced its way down the steep slope, fighting hard and refusing to be checked. Many Germans were killed here and over 50 taken with three machine-guns. On A's left B (Captain Lainé) had difficulty over a copse from which machine-guns swept the ravine, and only after really hard fighting was it taken with 80 prisoners. C (Captain Brierley) and D (Captain Gotelee) now went through, up the slope beyond the ravine and forced their way to the Le Quesnoy–Orsinval road despite heavy fire from machine-guns, the battalion's final objective being reached within three hours of ' Zero '. Several more machine-guns, four trench mortars and 160 prisoners were taken in this stage of the advance, in which Captain Brierley was wounded after having gone unhit through every other action in France, while the prisoners now taken swelled the total to over 300. Casualties came to nearly 100, but only 20 were killed.

The 186th and 187th Brigades having secured their objectives, the 185th should have continued the attack, but partly owing to the congestion of the roads this move had to be postponed till next morning (November 5th), when the 2/4th followed it towards Bavai, to take over the lead next day. The advance was now becoming more of a pursuit : the Germans had been well and truly beaten on November 4th, especially by the Fourth Army, which had forced its way across the Sambre, and on starting their attack on November 6th, the 2/4th, who had the Bavai–Avesnes road as objective, met few enemy at first though they were heavily shelled ; machine-guns enfilading the left then delayed them for a time, but after some orchards had been cleared and two machine-guns and some prisoners taken, the advance went ahead again. At Quene au Loup D Company was checked but soon broke through, driving the enemy back to Bois du Chêne. This brought it ahead of the rest of the battalion, but it maintained its ground and helped to cover the advance of the other companies across the Bavai–Avesnes road, though B was held up till 2/Lt. Wheeler rushed an obstructing machine-gun and enabled the company to get on.

The 2/4th having secured their objective, the 185th Brigade and the 5th Duke's went through, leaving the 2/4th, who had spent the night of November 6/7th in pouring rain without any shelter, to have two days' welcome rest in farms near Obres where the countryfolk could not do too much for their liberators. The Germans were going back fast, and though on November 9th the 2/4th moved up again to the suburbs of Maubeuge, expecting to have to force the passage of a canal, the enemy had withdrawn and did not oppose the advance. Next day the 2/4th crossed the Sambre and relieved the 2/4th K.O.Y.L.I. in the outpost line East of Maubeuge, where the news of the armistice reached them (November 11th).[1]   After all that the battalion had gone through the news came as something of an anti-climax; there was no excitement, no enthusiasm, most men were perhaps too tired and too strained quite to realise that they had finished with fighting.

The 2nd Battalion also had ended up in front line.   After a week's enjoyment of the rare experience of being billeted in undamaged houses, the Division had returned to the line by November 8th, the 86th Brigade being along the Scheldt about Bossuyt, with the 2nd Hampshire at Achterhock in support.

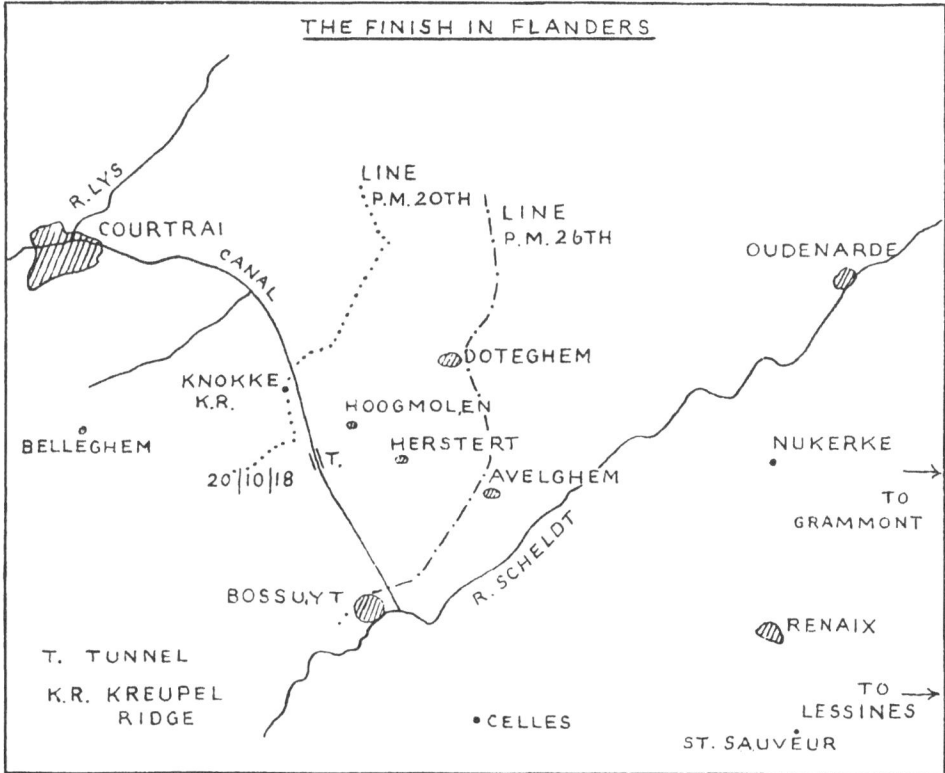

THE FINISH IN FLANDERS

The river here was 60 yards wide and forcing a contested passage threatened to prove difficult and costly, as the enemy's bank commanded the left.   However, early on November 9th reports came in that the Germans had withdrawn, whereupon the 2nd Hampshire followed the leading battalion of the brigade across the Scheldt and pushed forward to Celles.   Here X and Y took over the outposts in preparation for taking on as advanced-guard next day, when the battalion pushed steadily forward behind a screen of cyclists without encountering any enemy, the only signs of his existence being the extensive damage done to the roads, which slowed down the advance considerably.   Vehicles, even

[1] Casualties since November 1st were just under 100, including 21 men killed and missing and two officers wounded.

guns, found it hard to get forward and rations had to be brought up by pack animals. That evening the Hampshire reached St. Sauveur, some miles from the Dender at Lessines. A squadron of the 7th D.G. had now reached the front to assist in the advanced-guard duties, and next morning (November 11th) it pushed ahead with the Brigadier, who was determined to secure the bridges at Lessines before 11 a.m., at which hour the armistice would come into force. Pressing on hard with the cavalry, General Freyberg just achieved his purpose, but the 2nd Hampshire did not have to fight again, halting short of the river. They had come a long way from Cape Helles.

The end of hostilities found the 15th Battalion also moving forward, its Division advancing towards the Dender below Grammont. The 122nd Brigade was, however, in reserve and the 15th had not regained touch with the rapidly retreating enemy before the armistice. They then halted at Nukerke, which they had reached over-night, and promptly turned on to road-repairs, an urgent and essential task even if, after all the fighting, men might have hoped for a little relief from effort.

The Fifth Army meanwhile had continued to advance steadily. Spread out on a wide front, including much difficult and water-logged country, it contained several Divisions which, like the Sixteenth, had been reconstituted with men originally classified as fit for 'garrison' duties, from whom much more had since then been required. These 'B' men had responded splendidly and had more than once overcome really stiff and determined opposition, but the Army's main work was the rather restricted function of keeping connection between the First and Second Armies, and, though several battalions of the Sixteenth Division were fairly sharply engaged in the final advance, the Division had no reason to call on its Pioneers to down tools and to show again, as they had in March, that they could fight as well as work. Each successive advance merely meant the same work farther forward, assisting the R.E. in bridging and occasionally ferrying infantry across rivers being the only variation on road repairs. The successive changes in battalion head-quarters [1] provide almost the only variable feature in the battalion's diary for October and November. The work was hard and continuous, the weather was breaking and increasing its difficulties, but there could be no relaxing. Working parties and billets were occasionally shelled but casualties were few. In the later stages of the advance it was a new experience for the 11th to find themselves surrounded by a liberated population, mainly old men and women or mere children but quite capable of giving the battalion a very warm welcome. On November 10th, the day before the armistice, the battalion's band played in the square at Antoing, rousing the population to great enthusiasm when, after four years under the German heel, they again heard the strains of the Brabançonne.

[1] October 3rd Cambrin, October 8th Douvrin, October 9th Haisnes, a move caused by Douvrin being heavily shelled, October 16th Dynamite Factory (near Carvin), October 18th Pont a Marcq, October 22nd Rumes, November 9th Taintignies, November 10th Antoing.

CHAPTER XXXI

MESOPOTAMIA AND PERSIA, 1918

THE Fourteenth Division's advance across the Jebel Hamrin, which had left the 1/4th Hampshire at Khaniqin, had far-reaching consequences for that battalion, bringing it some remarkable experiences and taking it to places never previously visited by British troops. As already mentioned, Turco-German aims in Trans-Caucasia and the Caspian region had been stimulated by Russia's collapse. That the Bolsheviks, now supreme in Russia, would offer any resistance to Turkish penetration into this region was very doubtful, nor could the attitude of the local population, the Armenians and Georgians in particular, be predicted, while the Persian government's probable action was equally speculative. The British authorities were naturally reluctant to extend the sphere of military operations into Persia, where a small force would be impotent and substantial forces could not be maintained without devoting to their service nearly all ' Force D's ' land transport, but some intervention was becoming unavoidable.

It was at first hoped to confine intervention to the dispatch of a military mission to organize and train such local forces as would be likely to resist a Turkish advance. This mission eventually took shape as that ' Dunsterforce ',[1] with whose fortunes the 1/4th Hampshire's were to be so closely connected, but the first task which actually took the Hampshire over the Persian border was to assist to extricate a survey party and an Australian wireless detachment formerly with the Russians under Colonel Bicharakoff, whom that officer's unexpected withdrawal to Kermanshah had left in some peril. Orders to attempt the rescue of this party reached Colonel Matthews on January 1st, and next day he started for Qasr i Shirin with a mixed column in which the Hampshire were included. The road was bad but, despite this and heavy rain, the 20 miles between Khaniqin and Qasr i Shirin were covered between 8 a.m. and 4.30 p.m., the ' cookers ', for which two horses were quite inadequate, only getting in some hours later. The next day's march, to Sar i Pol, struck a better road and rather better weather, and by leaving two ' cookers ' behind and using their horses to pull the others, they also completed the 17 miles' march successfully. Another march of 12 miles took the column to Pai Tak (January 4th), the road being fair but the weather bad. From Pai Tak two companies advanced on January 6th to meet Colonel Kennion, the British Consul at Kermanshah, with the survey party and the wireless section, who were duly brought back to Pai Tak, the whole column then returning to Qasr i Shirin in three marches. Great difficulties were encountered in getting the transport along, the weather was bitterly cold with rain and sleet, and the men finished the march on half-rations, a barren and impoverished countryside producing no supplies. On regaining Qasr i Shirin the battalion was ordered

[1] General Dunsterville's *Adventures of Dunsterforce* helps to explain the operations in which the 1/4th Hampshire took part in Persia.

to remain there, and on January 18th it was joined by a column which was to co-operate with Colonel Bicharakoff and any Russian forces he might manage to keep in the field against the Turks. This column, which included the 14th Hussars and two R.H.A. guns, did not at first advance beyond Qasr i Shirin, largely because of the badness of the road, which the Hampshire were turned on to improve,

Thanks to the battalion's labours the road was soon made quite practicable for an advance by Sar i Pol (January 20th) and Pai Tak (January

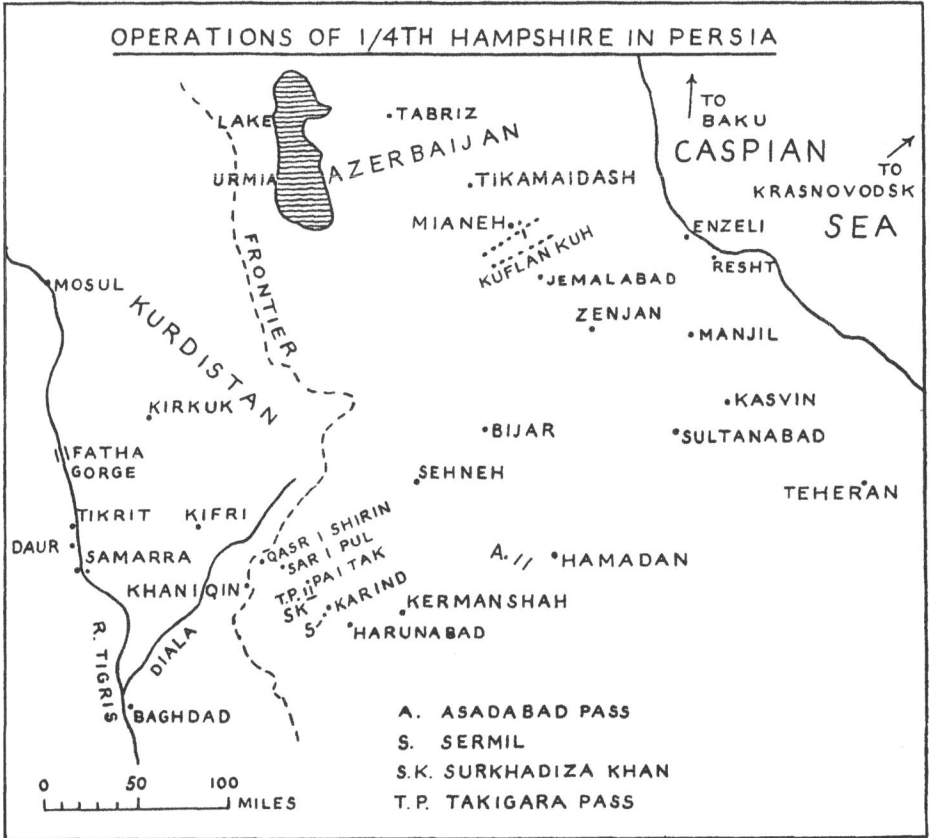

OPERATIONS OF 1/4TH HAMPSHIRE IN PERSIA

A. ASADABAD PASS
S. SERMIL
S.K. SURKHADIZA KHAN
T.P. TAKIGARA PASS

0   50   100
└┴┴┴┴┴┘_____┘ MILES

21st) to Surkhadiza Khan, 4,200 feet above sea-level, where battalion headquarters were established by January 23rd, having dropped D Company at Sar i Pol and C at Pai Tak on the way. At these places the battalion remained almost all February, employed on guard and picquet duties, escorting convoys and, so far as the weather allowed and heavy snow rarely permitted it, on road work. Late in February D Company moved up to Sayed Hussain and a platoon of B escorted a motor repairing party to Karind and brought it back again. Meanwhile General Dunsterville and his mission had passed through early in February, eventually reaching Enzeli on the Caspian by February 17th, but to avoid capture by the Bolsheviks he had to return to Hamadan.

Prospects of Russian assistance in checking a Turkish advance grew steadily fainter, and little progress could be made towards organizing any effective local assistance. Our intervention was none too popular in Persia, the country SW. of the Caspian was largely in the hands of the Jangalis, the followers of Mirza Kuchik Khan, a local chieftain, whose men were little better than brigands and very hostile to the British,[1] and the whole situation was most difficult and obscure. Meanwhile another Division from Mesopotamia, where no further offensive was intended, was reinforcing General Allenby in Palestine, and though this was to be replaced, mainly from India, it meant more obstacles to embarking on substantial operations in Persia

However, General Dunsterville was working hard to extend our influence, and it was agreed in March to push forward some detachments to secure the road as far as Hamadan, now ' Dunsterforce's ' head-quarters. Accordingly on March 15th A Company advanced to Sermil, one platoon under Lt. Hamilton going on to Karind, so that the battalion was now spread out over 40 miles, and on March 20th 50 rifles of B Company under 2/Lt Weatherall started for Kermanshah, which they reached, despite much snow and bad weather, four days later. However, General Dunsterville wanted them at Hamadan, so they pushed on, their arrival there on March 28th, by General Dunsterville's own account, doing much to secure his position. Small as the party was its value was far greater than its numbers.

The battalion was now more widely scattered than ever, with head-quarters and parts of B and D Companies at Surkhadiza Khan, detachments of B at Kermanshah and Hamadan, A (less one platoon at Karind) at Sermil, C at Pai Tak, one platoon of D at Sar i Pol. Luckily the battalion was well up to establishment, having 27 officers and 987 other ranks present on March 31st, so the detachments were fairly strong.

April brought no major changes. Guarding the road and keeping it clear for convoys brought occasional brushes with marauding Kurds and would-be rifle thieves, several of whom were shot, but nothing more. Sniping by the hostile Sinjabis caused the reinforcement of Karind by a platoon of B from Surkhadiza Khan, while the platoon at Sar i Pol was joined by one of C from Pai Tak. Later in the month two platoons of A escorted a convoy to Khosinabad [2] and remained there till the end of the month to cover the establishment of telegraphic communications, while C and D were concentrated at Surkhadiza, Pai Tak having been evacuated, but they moved on April 28th to the top of the Takigara Pass,[3] a fresh camping ground covered with young grass and surrounded by oak trees being much appreciated. Work on the road went steadily on and a leave party of 80 went off to India.

Meanwhile the Fifteenth Division had disposed of the Turks on the Euph-

---

[1] Mirza Kuchik was in touch with the Germans, who were supplying his men with arms and instructors.

[2] S.W. of Kermanshah.   [3] Between Pai Tak and Surkhadiza.

rates at Khan Baghdadi (March 26th/27th) and the Third Corps had greatly improved our positions in Southern Kurdistan (April), successes which indirectly improved our position in Persia, where a squadron of the 14th Hussars had gone forward to Hamadan and some local levies were being organized. However, the situation remained chaotically obscure and unsatisfactory, though luckily the other powers concerned in this quarter were at cross-purposes and did not co-operate cordially, even against the British : Germans, Turks and Bolsheviks all had their own aims and ideas.

A further increase of our force in Persia was sanctioned during May, most of the 36th Brigade coming forward beyond Khaniquin and the Third Corps taking over the road up to Kermanshah, to which place most of A and B Companies advanced during the month, Captain Walkinshaw taking three platoons of A on to Hamadan. An outbreak of typhus at Kermanshah affected many men but caused only a few deaths, and at the end of May H.Q. and C and D Companies were posted to a mobile column under Lt. Colonel Matthews, to be carried in Ford vans, 500 of which were available, which was to bring us to the Caspian by securing the Hamadan and Enzeli road. This column, which also included half the 1/2nd Gurkhas and two mountain guns, eventually moved forward from Takigara on June 7th and reached Kermanshah next day, despite the badness of the stony road, having covered 60 miles in two days. Another two days took it to Hamadan, 105 miles on, the Ford cars being severely tested by having to climb the Asadabad pass, 6500 feet up. From here Colonel Matthews and D went on to Kasvin, leaving C to follow as soon as enough cars to carry it had been sufficiently repaired. The Mobile Column had found four platoons already at Kermanshah, one of A and three of B, the other platoon of B being at Hamadan. The rest of A had already reached Kasvin but, on D Company's arrival there, moved back to Sultanabad. By June 16th the Mobile Column was collected at Kasvin, where want of petrol halted it for some days. Two platoons of D, however, moved to Manjil and meanwhile Bicharakoff's Russians defeated the Jangalis and occupied Resht and Enzeli.

To Resht the bulk of the Mobile Column followed on June 20th, to meet serious opposition at a bridge beyond Manjil. The country was thickly wooded and the Jangalis were well concealed, and in the first effort to clear the way the 1/4th lost a good officer when Captain Durnford was killed. However, the C.O. handled the situation admirably and the men were quickly in occupation of good firing positions with the result that the Jangalis' fire was soon mastered. Pushing on again, we encountered fresh opposition ; ' the trees seemed alive with Jangalis ' writes one account, and for a time they resisted stoutly, but after Lewis guns had subdued the enemy's fire a party rushed the Jangali position and they bolted into the woods. Besides Captain Durnford two men were killed and 2/Lt. Wallace and four men wounded, but the Jangalis had left at least 20 dead behind them. Resht, quite a large place with many quite Europeanized houses, was reached on June 21st without further opposition, and parties were pushed on to Enzeli. Thus by the end of June General

Dunsterville had secured the road to Enzeli,[1] and such opportunities as the Hampshire and Gurkhas had had of teaching the Jangalis a lesson had been fully utilized, both 'had acquitted themselves well'[2] and 'inspired in the Jangalis a wholesome respect'.

June ended with eight officers and 368 other ranks with the Mobile Column at Resht and Enzeli, five officers and 179 other ranks at Kermanshah, three officers and 206 men at Sultanabad and Hamadan. As before, guarding the road and escorting convoys provided the main occupation, punctuated by occasional brushes with the Jangalis, who were known to be gathering in some strength in the neighbourhood of Resht. A party out reconnoitring on June 18th ran into some 100 Jangalis two miles from Resht and had a sharp encounter, driving off the enemy and burning several houses, besides beating off efforts to prevent its return to Resht.[3]

The Mobile Column[4] was not actually in Resht but in billets on the outskirts, though the Bank and the telegraph office and the British Consulate were defended by guards. The place was largely surrounded by jungle, which made it easy for the Jangalis to approach our positions undetected, and early on July 20th, in foggy weather, both the billets and the posts in Resht itself were attacked in some force. The Hampshire, however, were not caught napping, and the Jangalis, though greatly superior in numbers,[5] could make little impression on an efficient defence. For a time, however, the situation was obscure, but Lt. Stokes[6] did most useful work in finding out what was happening despite the heavy fire and brought back valuable information, while L./Corporal Morgan, though badly wounded, kept on using his Lewis gun most effectively, setting a fine example. Before long the defenders could pass to the counterattack, Lt. Wilkinson and a party from battalion head-quarters crossing the river and driving the enemy back most successfully. Pressing gallantly on in pursuit with a few men, Lt. Wilkinson was killed and with him Sergeant Coles, the Pioneer Sergeant, but C.Q.M.S. Kemp took charge and effected a masterly withdrawal.

In this quarter the enemy had been too hard hit to renew the attack; several had been taken while their losses had been heavy. Meanwhile C Company from the other side of the town, after repulsing its attackers, was fighting its way through the bazaar North of our billets; assisted by 50 Gurkhas and an armoured car, it drove off assailants who had been pressing the Bank and telegraph guards hard. To achieve the relief of the British Consulate which a party under Sergeant Mills, though heavily and persistently attacked, had defended stubbornly, a strongly-held hotel in the main square had to be cleared with the bayonet and kukri, but this done the Consulate was reached just in time to prevent its being set on fire. Meanwhile Lt. Fisher and the platoon from Enzeli, having removed under fire several barricades across the

---

[1] This allowed of the subsequent move of the 39th Brigade to Baku.
[2] *Official History, Mesopotamia*, IV. 184.   [3] It had one man killed.
[4] Besides the Hampshire two companies of Gurkhas had reached Resht.
[5] They were put at 2,500.
[6] He was awarded the M.C. for ' conspicuous gallantry and devotion to duty '. L/Corporal Morgan got the M.M.

road, had forced their way through after sharp fighting, having half a dozen casualties. If the British force was too small to occupy the whole town, it retained possession of all the important points and must have inflicted on the Jangalis[1] many times its own 30 casualties,[2] while this decisive repulse certainly gave the Jangali leader reason to reconsider his attitude.

Apart from a little sniping, opposition now died down and a convoy came in unopposed from Kasvin with 50,000 rounds of rifle ammunition, though escorted by only 20 men, while on July 24th 100 Hampshires and 200 Gurkhas with an armoured car penetrated into Resht, completely cleared the town of Jangalis, burnt two houses from which they had sniped us and occupied a hotel and the Customs House. After that frequent patrols met little opposition, though the Jangalis were believed to be lurking in some force in the jungle West of the town : convoys went to and fro unchallenged and early in August the chief Jangali leader asked for terms of peace. Meanwhile the parties at Kermanshah under Captain McKenzie and at Hamadan and Sultanabad under Captain Walkinshaw,[3] were carrying on as before, having occasional brushes with hostile parties, and towards the end of July [4] a detachment from Kermanshah moved to Sehneh,[5] where it anticipated an occupation by the Turks.

A leading motive for obtaining control over the Caspian was that of securing the oil wells at Baku, or at any rate denying them to our enemies, and General Dunsterville was anxious to send some force there to encourage the local authorities, largely Armenians, to resist both the Turks and the Bolsheviks. Reinforcements, including the 39th Brigade of the Thirteenth Division, were on their way to Persia, the persistent labours of the troops along the road having helped considerably to make the maintenance of additional forces possible. Before this reinforcement could arrive an anti-Bolshevik coup d'etat put Baku in the hands of those elements of the population which were most friendly to us, and on August 4th Colonel Stokes, acting as General Dunsterville's representative, arrived there to arrange for our co-operation with them. As escort he had Lt. Fisher's platoon of D Company, 44 all told, who were thus the first British troops to reach Baku. Though the small size of the party was a disappointment to our friends, it was an earnest of more help to come, and eventually about half the 39th Brigade reached Baku and were the mainstay of such defence as was offered there. Lt Fisher's platoon had, however, embarked in a steamer as escort to General Dunsterville before the Turkish attack developed and, though back by September 15th to assist in the evacuation, they took no active part in the defence. Before this H.Q. and other Hampshires at Resht had moved during August to Kasvin, while C Company embarked on August 26th for Krasnovodsk across the Caspian to assist the

---

[1] Over 50 were taken, including several Austrians.

[2] The Hampshire had two O.R. killed and 16 wounded. C.Q.M.S. Kemp and Sergeant Mills received the D.C.M.

[3] A and B Companies.

[4] On July 31st there were nine officers and 350 O.R. with headquarters, four officers and 175 O.R. at Kermanshah and three officers and 180 O.R. at Hamadan and Sultanabad.

[5] N.W. of Hamadan.

Trans-Caspian government against a threatened Bolshevik attack from Astra-khan in co-operation with other Bolsheviks from further North. A few Indian troops had already been sent to their help but reinforcements were needed.

The remaining troops at Kermanshah had meanwhile moved to Hamadan, while Captain Walkinshaw's two platoons of A from Sultanabad had taken the field on August 22nd, moving by motor towards Persian Azerbaijan and crossing the Kuflan Kuh (Panther's Hill) ridge had reached Mianeh. From here half the party under Lt. Gow pushed on another 60 miles on the Tabriz road to Tik-maidasht [1] where some Dunsterforce officers had hopefully taken post with Persian levies. A squadron of the 14th Hussars, 150 Gurkhas and half a dozen guns were in the same area. These troops on September 3rd reconnoitred the Turkish position and drove in its outposts, to find they had caught a Tartar, as two days later the Turks attacked in force and the prompt flight of our untrustworthy Persian levies compelled the little British detachment to fall back past Mianeh to the Kuflan Kuh, where a stand was made. Colonel Matthews now arrived to take command, his force consisting of 75 Hampshire, 200 Gurkhas, 60 Hussars and about 200 very shaky levies with six guns, later reinforced by about 70 Worcestershire. He took up a position on the North of the pass across the hills with the Hampshire in the centre astride the road. The position was too extensive for the numbers available, and when on September 12th the enemy's attack developed, the speedy flight of the levies made it quite untenable. The enemy were in greatly superior strength, at least 500 sabres and 1500 rifles and good Turkish troops at that, and when they occu-pied the heights evacuated by the levies and brought heavy fire to bear on the guns, Colonel Matthews had to order a retirement on Jemalabad. The Hamp-shire had for some time held at bay about six times their numbers, who were advancing along the road, and thanks largely to their stubborn resistance and to the timely support of the Worcestershire,[2] who held a bridge over the Kijil Urnan river, the guns could be got away and the whole force reached Jemalabad without much loss. From there it had to retire again towards Zenjan, where reinforcements, including about 150 Hampshire, joined it and entrenched a strong defensive position at Yangijah, 40 miles NW. of Zenjan. This was not tested : the Turks were content to have pushed us off the Kuflan Kuh and did not follow us up, or attempt to press on against our lines of communications at Kasvin. Here therefore the Hampshires with Colonel Matthews remained until October 23rd when they moved back to Zenjan, other ranks were now up to 250, various details having rejoined head-quarters. The other outlying parties, except for C Company in Trans-Caspia, were now under orders to concentrate at Zenjan, but distances were considerable and reliefs slow to arrive and by the end of October few had rejoined.

Before this the Turks had already drawn back in the Bijar and Sehneh areas, we had collected something of an armed flotilla on the Caspian and

---

[1] About 50 miles short of Tabriz.
[2] The Worcestershire's *History* speaks warmly of the gallant fight put up by the Hampshire and Gurkhas to save the guns.

were exercising control there, and General Marshall's successful advance up the Tigris had taken him almost to Mosul before the conclusion on October 30th of the armistice with Turkey, news of which reached Mesopotamia two days later. In Persia and the adjacent countries the political situation continued confused, the Turks were reluctant to relinquish their designs and the Bolsheviks in Trans-Caspia were another source of trouble, so that the 4th Hampshire and the other British troops in Persia were to remain there for many months after the close of hostilities in Europe.

General Marshall's final advance up the Tigris had given the 6th Hampshire a share in a major operation. The battalion had previously taken the field in January, when its brigade was employed on an expedition to Najaf on the Euphrates, to punish the inhabitants for the murder of certain Indians. Leaving Baghdad on January 19th, the battalion reached Hillah on the 22nd and Kefl next day. From here a detachment under Captain Miller was sent out to support cavalry employed in punitive operations, but though a hostile village was duly burnt the 6th had no fighting and rejoined head-quarters in camp at Kufa on January 26th. Here the 6th remained till February 3rd when, the object of the expedition having been achieved, the column started its return to Baghdad, reaching Iron Bridge Camp on February 9th.

The operations had cost the battalion over 100 admissions to hospital, leaving other ranks available below 700, but before the end of February, discharges had brought them back nearly to the 850 of January 1st. By this time the battalion had moved up the Tigris to Balad, whence it went on again to Samarra, as its Division was relieving the Third (Lahore) Division, now under orders for Palestine. To assist in General Brooking's operations on the Euphrates, which resulted in the crushing defeat of the Turks at Khan Baghdadi (March 26th) the Division carried out a demonstration toward Tikrit, after which the 6th Hampshire went back to Alajik, just above Samarra. Here they remained till April 7th, then moved up to Daur and took over duty there, in support to the cavalry and armoured cars who patrolled the valley for some way upstream, occasionally getting in touch with the Turks, from whom a fairly constant trickle of deserters came over. Discharges from hospital and several small drafts had brought rank and file well up over 800, and the battalion ended April with 900 of all ranks.[1] It was then back at Tel Mahaijir, working on the defences and roads, moved with its brigade on May 8th to Tikrit and back on May 17th to Alajik where it remained till June 28th. Two-thirds of the battalion were then detailed for railway construction, which occupied them all through July and well into August, when, the railway having reached Tikrit,[2] the battalion was turned over to road-making again. This kept it busy till the end of September, shortly after which it moved forward

[1] Of 25 officers half, including Lt. Colonel Wyatt (commanding), Major Radwell, Captains Miller, Webb, Curtis, Roper and Riddock (Adjutant), belonged to the 6th Battalion and six to other battalions of the regiment.

[2] The First Corps had occupied Tikrit earlier on to cover the advance of the railway.

again and was on outpost at Abu Rajash, fifteen miles above Tikrit, from October 8th onward.

By this time developments in the Balkans and in Palestine had warranted a resumption of the offensive in Mesopotamia also to drive the Turks back up the Tigris. With much of his transport devoted to maintaining the long line of communications of the troops in Persia, General Marshall found this none too easy, but on October 20th the First Corps started our last advance. The Turkish positions at the Fatha Gorge, where the Tigris cuts a passage between the Jebel Hamrin on the East and the Jebel Makhul, were about 30 miles up-stream of Tikrit. They were strong, but the force holding them was weak and our superiority in numbers was substantial, although a battalion had been withdrawn from every Indian infantry brigade in Mesopotamia to reinforce the B.S.F., while effectives had been much reduced by an epidemic of influenza, from which Force D, like our troops in other theatres of war, had been suffering.

The Seventeenth Division was making the main attack East of the Tigris, the Eighteenth co-operating on the right bank. Leaving Abu Rajash on October 20th the 52nd Brigade, the Division's advanced-guard, reached the lower end of the Fatha Gorge next evening and early on October 22nd it moved forward, the 6th Hampshire [1] being on the right near the river, with the 113th Infantry on their left. A and B led the 6th in four lines at 200 yards distance, C and D following in small columns widely extended. A first objective was soon secured, but after that the enemy's guns opened up. General Marshall was not ready to press the attack home as yet, so the infantry halted and re-mained lying out under some shell-fire from 9 a.m. till after dark, while the guns came up and got into position. After dark another advance was made and a picquet line taken up, about a mile short of the Turkish trenches. This position was maintained next day, while the guns registered and engaged occasional targets, and in the evening the 52nd Brigade pushed forward again about 800 yards, the 51st having come up on its right between the 6th Hamp-shire and the Tigris. From the position now occupied the Turkish lines would have been attacked early next day (October 24th), but by 6 a.m. our patrols reported that the Turks had evacuated the position and gone right back upstream.

The badness of the road and our shortage of transport impeded the pursuit ; the 52nd Brigade had to hand over most of its mules to the 34th and 51st and so had little further part in the operations, though the 34th and 51st had quite stiff fighting on October 26th and again two days later. The 6th Hampshire got forward as far as Qalah Jibbah on the Jebel Makhul on October 27th, after a difficult march over rough ground, where movement was in places only possible in single file, but they were kept in reserve and then sent back to clear up the previous day's battlefield, after which they moved back to Fatha and were there when on November 1st the conclusion of the armistice was announced.

---

[1] They mustered 18 officers and 718 other ranks, having sent nearly 100 men to hospital since October 1st.

The 1/6th Hampshire [1] had just 'smelt powder', the 2/7th did not get even that amount of fighting.   The battalion had moved down the Tigris to Amara in January and remained there until nearly the end of September, detaching a company each to Masharah and Qalet Saleh.   Few incidents occurred, training and work on the defences being the battalion's occupations.   The move in September took it by steamer to Kut and by rail from there to Table Mountain in the Jebel Hamrin, where it was attached to the 38th Brigade and had a complete change of scene, if its only change in occupation was that a company at a time was usually employed on road repairing.   It had had no chance in action before hostilities ended.

[1] They had had six men wounded.   Just before the advance the battalion had lost Captain Riddock, the Adjutant, who died on Oct. 17th.

THE pause in active operations in Palestine which followed the repulse of the great Turkish attempt to recover Jerusalem lasted until March, except that in February we pushed down into the Jordan valley and secured Jericho. This move was so far defensive in purpose as it diminished any chance of an attack on our right from across the Jordan, though the idea of a thrust Eastward to cut the Hedjaz railway and distract the enemy's attention to that quarter was already being entertained. The three Hampshire battalions, however remained in the coast plain and spent January and February in much the same way, finding themselves really busier when in reserve than when in the line, road-making alone requiring frequent 'fatigues' and providing unending occupation.

The 2/4th had spent most of December in Corps reserve at Surafend, mostly working on the roads. Several officers and 160 men joined and then on December 27th the battalion went back into line near El Beida,[1] where it spent an uneventful January. Colonel Stilwell rejoined from hospital with several other officers and nearly 100 men, and the opening up of railway communications with Egypt meant that rations improved and that comforts and ordnance stores were more readily obtained. On February 6th the battalion went back to Haditheh,[2] going into Divisional reserve, and remained there till March 11th. Another 100 men and more officers rejoined from hospital, many of them recovered wounded. On March 11th the battalion moved up to Rentis but remained in reserve, road-making, till March 18th, when it went into line again well South of the Wadi Deir Ballut, one of the main water-courses draining down from the Judaean Hills, relieving the 2/5th.

That battalion had held on to the positions taken on December 15th for ten days without being troubled by the enemy : it had then gone back to Surafend, where it found ample occupation in road-making. It moved to Lydda on January 8th and was in brigade reserve at Budrus from January 19th to February 12th, when it relieved the 5th Devons at Kh Ibanne but did not go into front line till March 2nd. It then took over the front line near Shuqba. Returns from hospital had greatly exceeded admissions, if few drafts had arrived.

The 8th meanwhile had spent the first half of January in reserve, followed by a fortnight in line without incident or casualties, it then had all February in reserve, after which, early in March, it took over the left of its Division's line NE. of Mulebbis and across the Wadi Abu Lejja, an important affluent of the

---

[1] NE. of Lydda.   [2] East of Lydda.

Nahr el Auja. Several officers had joined, and by February 28th drafts and returns from hospital had raised the 640 other ranks of January 1st to 770.

The Twenty-First Corps was now about to undertake a local operation aimed at bringing its right level with the line held by the Twentieth, which before this had advanced some five miles astride the Nablus road. This would secure a better line from which to launch the big offensive now in contemplation. The Seventy-Fifth Division had therefore to push forward to the Wadi Deir Ballut. This meant an advance of four miles on the right, the Fifty-Fourth Division nearer the coast having a much shorter advance to make.

Meanwhile the 2/5th Hampshire had moved up on March 10th from Shuqba to Abud and were starting work on a track leading forward from Abud when heavy fire was opened from a hill in front and news came back that a survey party of the Sappers and Miners on reconnaissance had been attacked and was in difficulties. A party was promptly dispatched to its help, the Turks were cleared off the hill and the endangered surveyors rescued.

On March 12th the attacking brigades were the 232nd (right) and 234th of the Seventy-Fifth Division and the 162nd of the Fifty-Fourth. The main Turkish line of defence followed the bed of the Wadi Deir Ballut, but they had many outposts in front, usually held by machine-guns in sangars. Several of these, Tinans Point, Halfway Hill and others, the 2/5th's advanced-guard had to clear before tackling the main objective on the El Arak ridge, SE. of Deir Ballut. The battalion came under flanking fire from its right but after clearing Stopbutt Hill, NE. of El Lubban, B and C Companies, effectively supported by the artillery, advanced and captured the El Arak ridge also, the battalion's casualties coming to 30 all told. Elsewhere the objectives were also captured, though the 234th Brigade had sharp fighting at Deir Ballut, and the Turks taken, apart from those killed, about equalled the Seventy-Fifth Division's 100 casualties, so the operation, which had secured a much better forward line,[1] could be reckoned very successful.

After six days in line consolidating their gains, the 2/5th were relieved by the 2/4th and spent the rest of March at El Lubban, getting baths, having their clothes disinfected and training when not working on the roads. By April 8th they were back in the line in readiness for another advance.

The 2/4th meanwhile had bad luck while holding the position taken by the 2/5th, a ' direct ' hit on C Company's H.Q. on March 20th causing a dozen casualties, including 2/Lts. Dixon and Donner wounded. Patrols were active, and on March 24th the first German the battalion had met was brought in as a wounded prisoner. On March 27th, after two strong patrols had established themselves on the Deir Sinan ridge, three companies moved forward and occupied it. This roused the Turks to shell the ridge fairly steadily, 2/Lt. Holbrook being wounded, while there was much sniping and bombing round

---

[1] The Fifty-Fourth Division also came forward, securing the line Mejdel Yaba—Ras el Ain, but the 8th Hampshire were not engaged.

our advanced posts down the far slope. But the Turks were kept at bay and when, on March 31st, they made a small attack, A Company repulsed it without much difficulty. Lt. Colonel Stillwell having gone to hospital, Captain Bulley took command on April 5th, Major Parsons being in Egypt on a Senior Officers' course.

The first effort to advance into the Trans-Jordan hills and cut the Hedjaz railway at Amman (March 21st to 31st) achieved a certain success, Amman was reached but not taken and some but no lasting damage was done to the railway, while heavy casualties were inflicted on the Turks, but our enforced retirement was our first real check since the start of the attack on the Beersheba line.

Meanwhile the development of the German offensive in France had already caused the Fifty-Second and Seventy-Fourth Divisions to be ordered to France, while it was decided to set free many other British battalions by ' Indianizing ' three other Divisions,[1] Indian battalions replacing all but one British in each brigade and thereby assimilating their composition to that of the two Indian Divisions now arriving from Mesopotamia.

Despite this General Allenby did not abandon a plan he had formed for another advance on his left. As originally planned the operations might have developed into something quite substantial, as after the Seventy-Fifth and Fifty-Fourth Divisions had advanced East of the railway, the Fifty-Fourth was to wheel round and sweep West, rolling up the strongest part of the Turkish lines between the railway and the coast from the flank, while a Mounted Division pushed ahead to cut off the retreat of the defenders of this section. The first stage was to be an advance North of the Wadi Deir Ballut by the Seventy-Fifth Division, its objectives including Berukin on the right, Rafat in the centre and Three Bushes Hill NW. of Rafat ; in a second stage the Seventy-Fifth, pivoting on its right, would wheel round NE. and cross the big Wadi Qana, five miles further on, thrusting the Turks back and thereby covering the right flank and rear of the Fifty-Fourth, who would also advance some way North before swinging round to face Westward, in readiness to cross the railway.

The Seventy-Fifth started the attack on April 9th, with the 232nd Brigade on the right, as far as Berukin, the 233rd in the centre, facing Rafat, and the 234th on the left making for Three Bushes Hill. The advance started at 5.10 a.m., the 2/5th Hampshire supporting the 2/3rd Gurkhas, who took El Kufr [2] without difficulty, whereupon A and D Companies of the 2/5th pushed on to attack objectives East of El Kufr. A were soon checked, the company commander being wounded, and though C supported them little progress could be made in face of artillery and rifle fire. On A's right D fared better, establishing themselves on Necklace Hill East of El Kufr and getting touch on their right with the 2/4th Somerset L.I., who had been much impeded by flanking fire

---

[1] This process was not extended to the Fifty-Fourth, as it was earmarked for transfer to France should another Division be required.

[2] SW. of Berukin.

but eventually took Tin Hat Hill, SE. of Berukin, by 10 a.m. Here for a time D also were held up. Then about 1.30 p.m. the 5th Devons were put in to take Berukin, which they eventually succeeded in capturing, while later on, about 5 p.m., under cover of a fresh bombardment, B Company of the 2/5th relieved the pressure on A and C by advancing Northward from Necklace Hill against the next ridge, later called Toogood Hill. This was captured without much difficulty, so A and C could now come forward also and secure the Sh Nufukh [1] ridge, A's original objective. The other brigades meanwhile had taken their first objectives but they could not advance till Berukin had been cleared, and there and on Three Bushes Hill savage fighting was going on, the Turks counter-attacking vigorously. The 2/4th meanwhile had not been engaged.

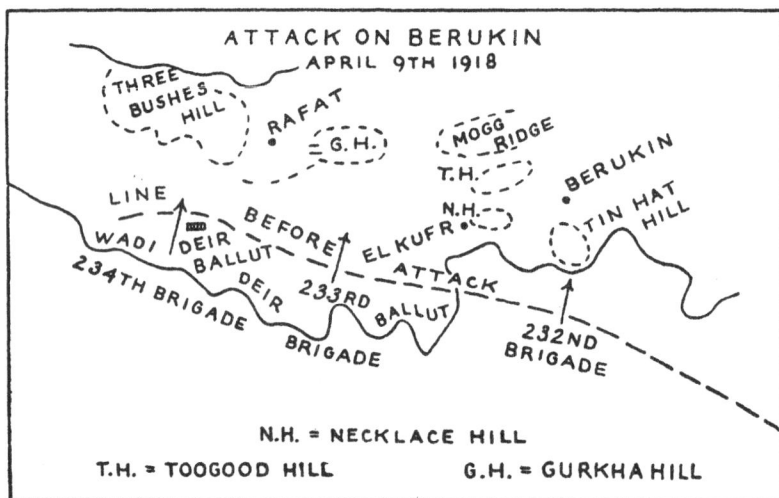

During the night the fight for Berukin went on, the Devons being repeatedly attacked but holding stoutly on and retaining their ground, while B Company on Toogood Hill repulsed one small attack. The Devons having been absorbed into the struggle for Berukin, the 2/5th had next morning (April 10th) to support the 2/3rd Gurkhas who were tackling Mogg Ridge NW. of Berukin. B Company pushed forward about 8 a.m. and despite considerable casualties reinforced the Gurkhas on its lower slopes. Even with this support the Gurkhas could not carry the hill, and an attempted advance in the centre was also checked ; here the 3/3rd Gurkhas, who had carried the Eastern end of the ridge, later known as Gurkha Hill, were held up by ' the Pimple ', a redoubt at the Western end, so the 2/4th Hampshire were ordered to assist them. Advancing over a crest A and D Companies of the 2/4th met heavy fire from machine-guns and were checked, 2/Lts. Aitchison, Brierley and Hallam were hit, the last named being brought back into safety by Captain Ashmore and 2/Lt. Greenhalgh despite heavy machine-gun fire. Luckily boulders and rocks

[1] Between Berukin and Mogg Ridge.

gave good cover and reduced casualties,[1] but the fire was too heavy to allow of any further advance and the troops could merely hang on and retain the ground already gained. Early in the afternoon C and D Companies of the 2/5th made a fresh effort to carry Mogg Ridge, and with the help of the 58th Rifles its crest was reached and for a time we seemed to have secured it. A counter-attack in great force, in which Germans of the Asia Corps were put in, backed by a devastating bombardment by trench mortars, dislodged the attackers and forced the 2/5th back to Toogood Hill, where they rallied and held their ground. Their losses had been severe, four officers, Captain Sprigg, Lts. G.S.W. Spencer-Smith, Pite and Beddy, and nearly 50 men killed and missing, nine officers, including Captains Kenny and Toogood, and 90 men wounded, and that evening the battalion was relieved and went back behind the Wadi Ballut. On the left gallant efforts by the 234th Brigade had failed to secure the whole of Three Bushes Hill, and with the enemy evidently in considerable strength and holding strongly prepared defences, while our casualties had been heavy, no further advance was attempted, though Berukin, Toogood Hill and Rafat were retained despite several counter-attacks.

The critical situation on the Western Front was mainly responsible for the decision to break off the attack. The Seventy-Fourth Division was following the Fifty-Second to France, the 'Indianization' of the other Divisions was being pushed on, and while the 2/5th Hampshire were among the battalions whose fate it was to be broken up to provide drafts for the E.E.F., the more fortunate 2/4th was one of those to be sent to France to replace battalions shattered in resisting the great German offensive. The Fifty-Fourth Division went as far as being placed under orders for France in June and actually began its withdrawal towards the embarkation area. These orders were, however, cancelled but, as it still remained 'ear-marked' for transfer to France should need arise, the Division continued 'all-British' to the end of hostilities.

After the Berukin fighting had died down the 2/4th remained at the front for another fortnight, being frequently shelled and having a few more casualties. Major Parsons returned from Egypt and took command, and on April 29th the battalion left the brigade and moved back to Lydda, where it entrained for Egypt, to have three weeks training at Kantara before embarking at Alexandria on May 22nd. Lt. Colonel Stilwell had rejoined with details who had not been with the battalion in the line. The 2/4th had done well in Palestine and acquired no small reputation : what lay ahead of them was to be an even sterner test.[2]

The 2/5th, though marked down for reduction, were not broken up until August. After a short rest they had taken over the front again at Necklace Hill and Toogood Hill on April 17th, where they remained for a fortnight,

---

[1] These only came to three killed, three officers and 34 men wounded.

[2] For its work in Palestine the battalion gained one M.C., Lt. Brooke, a Croix de Guerre, 2/Lt. Weekes, two D.C.M's, Sergeant Thompson and Pte. Thomas, three M.M's, Privates Goddard, Papadopoulos and Wyatt, and two 'mentions', Captains Goddard and Kirby. Its casualties had come to nearly 240.

strengthening and improving the line and effectively repulsing two attacks on the night of April 30th/May 1st, one of which, trying to get in between the battalion and the 5th Devons on its right, actually reached our wire before it was halted : thanks to its good work on the defences, the battalion escaped with only four men wounded, despite the heavy bombardment before the attack. It held part of the Division's left sector most of May and until June 19th, but it was little troubled by the enemy and did much to strengthen the defences. It was ' out ' for ten days, then back in support and finished its active career near Berukin, where its patrols were very active and established a mastery over No Man's Land which the enemy failed to challenge. Colonel Perkins had gone back to England at the end of April and Major Ffrench-Blake of the 10th Buffs commanded the battalion in its last three months. No drafts joined, though returns from hospital considerably outnumbered admissions and maintained the battalion at a fair strength. On disbandment [1] over half the 540 other ranks joined the 4th Wiltshire, in whose ranks they played a big part in General Allenby's final victory in September, when their casualties were appreciable, including 2/Lt. S. D. Stevenson died of wounds, and Lt. Kimm and 2/Lt. Bessant wounded.

The 2/5th had had a good record in their year of active service, Lt. Colonel Perkins and Major Crosson received the D.S.O., Captains Burnett and Collins and Lt. Kimm the M.C., R.S.M. Cousens, C.S.M. Graham, Sergeant Harris and Privates Braby and Cole the D.C.M., Corporal Wells, Lance Corporal Gray and Privates Burgess, Goddard and Turner the M.M., while Colonel Perkins, Major Crosson, Captains Archdale, Burnett, Ellis and Toogood, Lt. Kimm and Serjeant Kemp were ' mentioned ', R.S.M. Cousens also getting the Croix de Guerre. More fortunate in seeing active service than their ' First Line ', the 2/5th had certainly ' done their bit ' well and were unlucky to lose their identity before the end of hostilities.

The 8th were thus the only Hampshire battalion to see the Palestine campaigns out to their triumphant finish. Their Division was not engaged in the Berukin operations, the 8th being in line at Ras el Ain part of April, then out, mainly digging second-line defences, till the middle of May, when they came back to the trenches in front of Mejdal Tomba. Patrolling was actively carried on here and on June 18th D Company covered a successful raid by the 4th Norfolk. Some drafts joined, mainly men ' combed ' out from ' departmental ' corps, who needed much training. Then at the end of June the Third (Lahore) Division from Mesopotamia began relieving the Fifty-Fourth, now under orders for France. The 8th Hampshire actually marched to Lydda on June 27th to entrain, only to have their orders cancelled and to return to Surafend, where and at Mezeireh, they spent most of July, training and working on the roads. A move to Sheikh Muannis [2] brought no change in occupation and the battalion remained out of line until the middle of September. All this time the prepara-

---

[1] Without the Part II Orders the destination of the remainder cannot be given.
[2] In the coastal sector, just across the Auja.

tions for the coming big attack were being pushed on : these involved the concentration in the coastal area of the bulk of the E.E.F., the line East and North of Jerusalem being more lightly held, the intention being that the infantry should break through in strength on our left, thrusting the Turks back NE. into the foothills and so opening the way for the mounted troops, now including the Indian cavalry formerly in France, to sweep forward right round the enemy's flank into the Plain of Esdraelon and then plant themselves across his rear. The Fifty-Fourth Division, whose right had reached the foothills, would be the pivot of the move.

If the long summer halt had been necessary for the reorganization of the E.E.F. and to give the new Indian units, now so large an element in its infantry, the training and the experience they lacked, it had contributed appreciably to make success more likely because of the strain imposed on the Turkish troops, ill-fed, ill-equipped, badly administered and increasingly weary of the war. If in the spring the German successes had inspired hopes of victory, the disappointing German failure to clinch the original successes could not be disguised. Sickness thinned the Turkish ranks, the constant raids, often very successful, by which the British educated the new Indian units, accentuated Turkish war-weariness and dejection, desertion grew serious, some surrendering to the British, many more slinking off homeward. The actual rifle strength of the Turkish Divisions sank far below their establishment, and it was on a weakened and demoralized enemy, very unlike the Turks who had held Gaza and struggled so hard for Nebi Samwil and Jerusalem that General Allenby's hammer-stroke was to fall.

The Fifty-Fourth Division's frontage, which extended Westward from the Rafat salient to the railway near Ras el Ain, was nearly six miles long, much wider than those of the Divisions beyond the railway, who were massed in depth on much narrower fronts. On its right was the French detachment, a strong brigade, on its left the Third Indian Division.

The 163rd Brigade, with the 8th Hampshire (left) and 5th Suffolk in front line, had its right just West of Three Bushes Hill, the hamlet of Kh ed Duweir and a spur beyond it and across the Wadi el Ayun being the Hampshire's objective. Patrols sent out on the evening of September 16th and again on the 18th, just before the attack, had reconnoitred the approach to Merj Kesfa, where the battalion would deploy. Those sent out on the 18th took up positions to cover the battalion's advance down the Wadi Orwell to the Wadi Ikba, and under their protection the deployment was duly carried out by 3.15 a.m., though the enemy was decidedly ' jumpy ', sending up many flares and firing away freely. This rifle-fire, however, passed harmlessly over the Hampshire's heads, and though shortly before Zero his guns opened up, their fire missed the deployed battalion, falling harmlessly behind it in the Wadi Ikba. At ' Zero ' (4.15 a.m.) A Company (Captain Villar) and D (Lt. Carr) went forward on left and right respectively, with C (Captain Freeman) and B (Captain Brannon) supporting them. Advancing with great dash, A was at Kh ed Duweir under ten minutes, capturing several prisoners. Captain Villar was killed here but 2/Lt. Brown led the company forward into the Wadi el Ayun, machine-guns on

Merj Kesfa giving splendid covering fire. After a halt to let the barrage lift the attackers went on, D keeping level with A, and Hill 502 beyond the Wadi was soon captured, with more prisoners and a machine-gun. B then pushed forward and secured the next ridge to the North, being effectively covered by Lewis guns and the captured machine-gun, which kept down snipers.

Meanwhile on the left, the 161st Brigade, trying to advance beyond Kefr Qasin, was checked by heavy shell-fire, and therefore for a time most of the 8th had to seek shelter on the reverse slope of the hill they had taken, Lewis guns on the crest engaging any targets which appeared. Eventually some of the 162nd Brigade came through the Essex to deal with the works North of Kefr Qasin, after which they pushed on East to clear Kh Nejjara and Kh

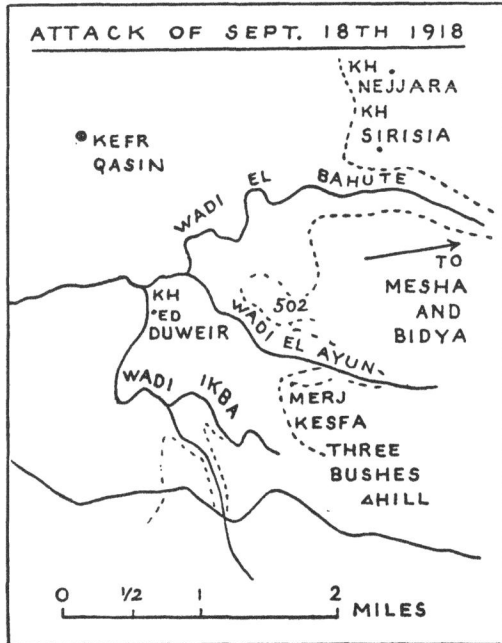

ATTACK OF SEPT. 18TH 1918

Sirisia, D Company being ordered forward across the Wadi el Bahute, coming in on the 162nd's right. This movement was successful and the two Norfolk battalions then went ahead Eastwards toward Mesha and Bidya, the 162nd Brigade on their left also making good progress. The 8th meanwhile were concentrating in reserve South of Kefr Qasin with one platoon escorting an advanced battery. They did not have to be put in again. The volume and accuracy of the bombardment and the very effective support of the machine-guns had kept casualties very low. Only three men were killed and 20 wounded, though besides Captain Villar, 2/Lt. Bartlett,[1] working under the Division's A.P.M., was killed, 2/Lts. Butt and A. W. Evans being wounded ; 40 prisoners had been taken.

[1] Dorsets attached.

The Fifty-Fourth Division was not required to share in the great pursuit. The complete success of the infantry's attack had made the gap the cavalry wanted; they were now forging ahead fast and soon left the Fifty-Fourth behind, after its leading units had, early on September 20th, reached a line running North and South through Bidya. Everywhere Turkish resistance was collapsing, and though the Divisions on the Fifty-Fourth's left were pushing on towards Nablus, the exploitation of the victory was mainly left to the cavalry and the 8th Hampshire saw nothing of it. They had spent a week in salvage work on the battle-field before their Division was ordered forward to Haifa, which the cavalry had occupied on September 23rd. Starting on September 28th the 8th reached Haifa in six marches, arriving on October 3rd.[1] Here they found guards and did some training and then started on October 24th up the coast for Beirut, doing the distance in nine marches and hearing on the way on October 31st of the armistice with Turkey. They were in camp near Beirut when on November 11th the armistice with Germany brought an end to hostilities in Europe also.

[1] The strength on reaching Haifa was 28 officers and 768 other ranks.

CHAPTER XXXIII

SALONICA, 1918

THE dead-lock which had prevailed at Salonica after the abandonment in May 1917 of the Allied offensive was to remain unbroken for most of 1918. General Sarrail's recall in December 1917 had transferred the command to General Guillaumat, a man of very different character, much readier to listen to other people's points of view, who soon became no less trusted and respected by his allies than by the French contingent. If he was soon to be recalled to France for more urgent work, he had done much to make the Allied 'Army of the East' a happier and a more harmonious force and had laid the foundations for the eventual success the Allies were to achieve in the Balkans. Any plans he had had in preparation for active operations early in the year were, however, perforce abandoned when the German March offensive developed in France, and neither 10th nor 12th Hampshire had any chances of gaining distinction while under his command.

The New Year had found the 10th still on the extreme British right, between the mouth of the Struma and Lake Tahinos. January passed uneventfully, a carefully planned ambush for a hostile patrol (January 23rd) failed to entrap any enemy, and the Bulgarians made no attempt to interfere with our establishing a new outpost on Sniper's Knoll and thereby advancing our line slightly. Neither side used their guns more than occasionally, though the defences required constant attention and a party was detailed for work on the railway at Stavros. February brought the 10th and the regiment a much regretted loss, Colonel Beckett being killed in a bomb accident. He was returning from visiting his day posts and passed a party being instructed in throwing bombs. Stopping to see what was being done, he had got down into the bombing pit when a premature explosion wounded the man who was about to throw, injured the bombing officer slightly and hit Colonel Beckett in the head. He died almost at once, to the great sorrow of the 10th, of whom he had made a very fine fighting battalion and by whom he was much respected and greatly liked. He had won the D.S.O. and a Brevet Lt. Colonelcy, and his fine record both with the 1st Battalion in France and with the 10th marked him out as one of the regiment's best and most promising officers, whom it could ill afford to lose. Major Taylor of the Royal Irish, who had recently joined as second in command, succeeded him, being promoted to Lt. Colonel on February 26th.

From the middle of February until April 30th, the 10th were back at Bluff Camp, getting a good opportunity for training, with some work on roads, railways and rear defences. Officers and men who had developed into 'chronic malarias' and were generally back in hospital soon after being discharged were now being sent back to England, but few drafts were available to replace them, though the 'departmental corps' were being 'combed' to find fit men for transfer to the infantry; but if the battalion's nominal strength fell from 850 of all ranks on January 1st to 770 on June 30th there was no corresponding decline in those really effective.

By June 30th the 10th Hampshire were preparing to move Westwards, the 82nd Brigade being in process of being relieved on the Lower Struma. The political changes which had placed the Venizelists in power and had brought Greece into the war on the Allied side had made it possible to hand over most of the Struma front to the Greeks, setting the Twenty-Seventh Division free for transfer to the Doiran–Vardar front. Here it was to relieve French troops on the five miles of frontage immediately West of the Vardar. The Allied dispositions were being re-adjusted in preparation for the offensive now in contemplation, which General Guillaumat had so strongly advocated, while even after his return to France[1] to become Military Governor of Paris he did much to secure the approval of the Allied War Council for it. Greeks and Servians were both anxious for it, and it was even advocated as a counter-stroke to the German offensive in France, as an Allied advance in the Balkans might distract thither German or Austrian troops or, more probably, prevent troops from Macedonia reinforcing those in France.

Most of May and June the 10th Hampshire had spent in front line across the Struma. Their patrols were active and on May 16th 40 men under Lt. Hetherington successfully raided a post at the Picquet Bank. The advance was detected when the raiders were 100 yards from the post, whose garrison opened a heavy fire but bolted directly the raiders charged forward, though according to a Bulgarian deserter who came in next day they had outnumbered the attackers by two to one.[2] The post was carefully searched and the raiders withdrew in their own time, having had only one man wounded.

June was marked by the departure for France of Lovat's Scouts, all brigades of the B.S.F. being reduced to three battalions to provide reinforcements for France, the 79th Brigade likewise losing the 7th Wiltshire.

The 12th Hampshire had spent the opening months of 1918 in the Dova Tepe sector, the 79th Brigade remaining as ' the Independent Brigade ' until early in April, when Greek troops took over part of our Struma frontage and readjustments followed. Like the 10th, the 12th had neither heavy fighting nor casualties to record, but they too had a new C.O., losing Colonel Lindesay, who transferred to the 8th R.S.F. in January and was replaced by Major McNaught of the Cheshire. The small number of casualties was not due to any lack of activity on the battalion's part : its patrols were active and enterprising but got few chances, as the Bulgarians were rarely to be met in No Man's Land, here wide and little damaged by war. A big raid on January 1st, aimed at searching Akindzali Wood, in which seven platoons took part under Major Cowland, was greatly hampered by swampy ground which impeded and so much delayed movement that the operations had to be curtailed. This cost

---

[1] He was succeeded by General Franchet d'Esperey, who had commanded the Fifth French Army at the Marne in 1914.

[2] Lt. Hetherington subsequently received the M.C.

eight casualties, three fatal, almost the only battle casualties recorded at Dova Tepe, A Company, who co-operated with the 3rd Middlesex and 7th Wiltshire in a successful raid on April 6th, doing so without suffering any loss.

The first quarter had brought much cold and snow and rain, which had increased the difficulty of maintaining the defences and interfered with the training programme when the battalion was out of the line, but the 12th had mainly bright and clear weather for their four days' march in April to Kirac, East of Lake Ardzan, where their brigade was placed in Corps reserve. It remained here until the middle of June, training and working on the roads and on a defence line. Several new officers joined, but with the claims of France on draft-producing units paramount, few reinforcements appeared. From June 14th to 30th the battalion was in brigade reserve at the Crag, working hard at gun positions and on second-line defences, it then took over the front line at Reselli from the D.C.L.I. Hostile guns were fairly active, but our patrols could wander freely about No Man's Land without provoking a ' scrap ', unless, as they often did, they pushed up to the enemy's wire, when they usually drew fire and even occasionally had some bombing. Only seven casualties were recorded during July, throughout which month the battalion remained in front line, though it lost 30 mules early in the month when a shell landed in the transport line.

From August 1st to 16th the 12th were back at the Crag and then took over front line trenches near Bekirli Ford, the right portion of the 79th Brigade's line. The Bulgarian guns were now more active and at times shelled our lines quite vigorously but without inflicting many casualties, and as before their patrols were rarely in evidence, energetically as ours sought them out.

Before this the 10th Hampshire were in line on their new front across the Vardar. Their relief by Greek troops had been completed by June 24th, and they had left Stavros by rail on July 6th for Gumendje, where the railway up the Vardar valley crosses the river. Detraining here on July 7th, they next day took post in two ravines, des Cascades and Pactol, behind the villages of Mayadag and Kara Sinantsi, being in Divisional reserve. Rocky ridges separated by ravines were a change from the Struma front with its water-courses and trees and presented the 10th with new problems, Several small drafts arrived, mainly men discharged from hospital, strength on July 31st being 31 officers and 729 other ranks, of whom 145 men and no less than 19 officers were away from the battalion, sick or on leave, at courses or employed.

Preparations for the coming offensive were now being pushed on vigorously, General Milne rather anticipating the final approval of the Home authorities in order to be ready to co-operate. The main attack was to be made West of the Vardar by the Servians with French support, the British having been again assigned the thankless task of attacking the formidable positions just West of Lake Doiran to distract the enemy's attention. A subsidiary attack was also to be made East of the Lake by the Greeks, supported by the Twenty-Eighth Division.

This time the Twenty-Second Division, with a Greek Division on its right next the Lake, was to tackle the defences of which the Twenty-Sixth had such bitter memories ; they were no less uncompromisingly formidable than in 1917 and the 12th saw no reason to regret that they were not to try again. The Twenty-Sixth Division was merely to try to distract the enemy, while across the Vardar the Twenty-Seventh also was not taking part in the first attack but would join in directly the main thrust by the Servians succeeded. Before the main attack, however, the 82nd Brigade was to carry out a minor operation of some importance. This was the capture of the strongly-held and entrenched Roche Noire Salient, which projected from the main Bulgarian line, North of the village of Alcah Maghale. It would have to be taken before the main line in this sector could be attacked, and it was hoped that the enemy would inter-pret our enterprise as indicating our intention to make the attack here, whereas the main blow was to come in some way further West.

The 10th Hampshire and the 2nd Gloucestershire, who were to attack here, were given ten days' intensive rehearsing over a full-sized reproduction of the position. Patrols were sent out frequently to reconnoitre the line of advance and make themselves familiar with the ground, which was dotted with trees thickly enough to give quite good cover, and all ranks were thoroughly drilled in every detail of what they had to do.

The Hampshire, who faced the Western half of the position, had about 300 yards to cross to reach their first objective, La Table. From here they were to push on to a second row of works, La Roche Noire and Les Deux Roches, two more works, the Dos du Mulet (East) and La Tranchée des Roches (West), forming the final objective. On their right the Gloucestershire were tackling a strong closed work, the Mamelon des Buissons. Of the Hampshire, A Company (2/Lt. Collins) on the right had Les Deux Roches and the Dos du Mulet as objectives, C (Captain Green) in the centre was tackling La Roche Noire and La Tranchée des Roches, D (Captain Grellier) on the left had to mop up La Table and secure the left flank, B (Captain Lowy) was in reserve.

The Bulgarian front line was continuous, with a strong belt of wire in front and many machine-gun emplacements, but it had been steadily bombarded for several days before the attack, which was timed for September 1st, and the enemy's efforts to repair the gaps in the wire had been effectively hampered. ' Zero ' was to be at 5.30 p.m., as the enemy's trenches seemed usually much more strongly held at night than by day. This involved a long wait for the attacking troops, who had had to take up their positions before it became light and to lie low all day and keep quiet in the hopes of avoiding observation. It was a strain, but the attackers' discipline proved equal to it ; their presence was not discovered and the attack surprised the enemy, whose barrage only came down after all the Hampshire but the reserve company were across No Man's Land and through the wire and were getting into the front line, having had trifling casualties. B Company, however, being late in starting, caught the barrage and suffered quite severely, Lt. Sparrow being among those killed, and for the time it was disorganized. This mattered less because the leading companies had carried out their programmes without a hitch or check, thanks largely to the careful preliminary training. The Divisional commander, Major General Forestier-Walker, wrote that he had never seen so steady or so

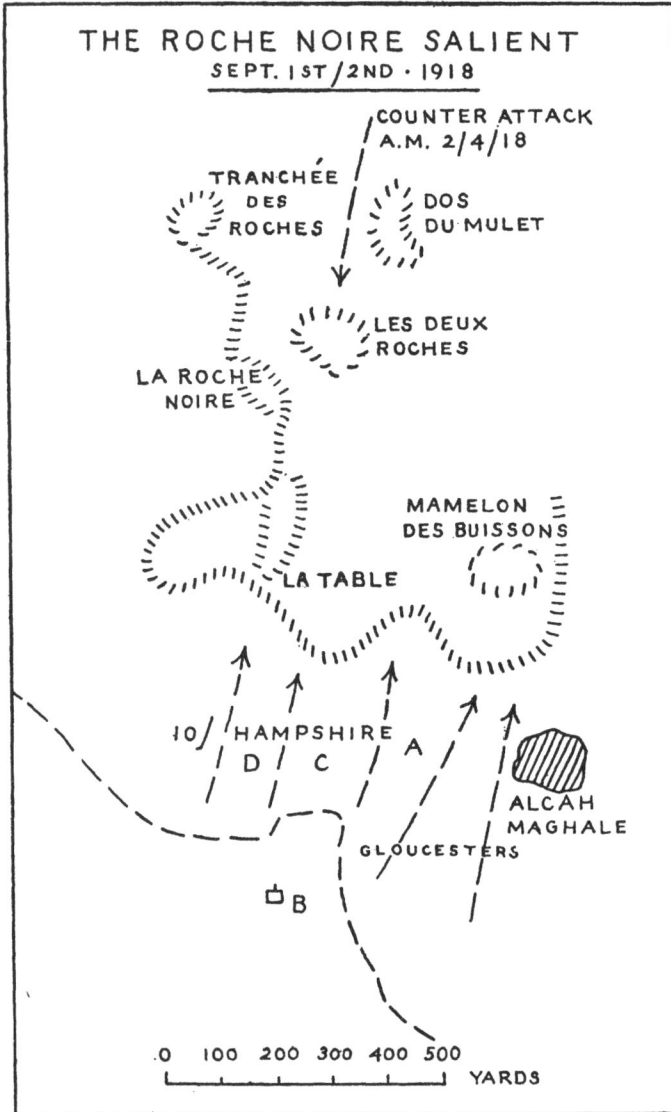

THE ROCHE NOIRE SALIENT
SEPT. 1ST/2ND · 1918

gallant an advance, everything being done as if on parade, while the men showed a remarkable dash. Opposition in the front line was soon overcome, the enemy had been caught at a disadvantage, and by 6 p.m. A Company, pushing ahead, had over-run Les Deux Roches, capturing 28 prisoners : pressing on they soon secured the Dos du Mulet, 2/Lt. Collins, though wounded, leading his men on till all objectives had been taken and a defensive position secured. C took a machine-gun and 12 prisoners at La Roche Noire and went on to capture the second objective at La Tranchée des Roches well up to time. D had rather more trouble and was for a time held up by machine-guns and bombers ; one platoon suffered severely, but Captain Grellier, though wounded, reorganised it and captured the strong point which had been causing the trouble, so that before long D also was in possession of all its objectives.

With the Gloucestershire equally successful on the right flank, consolidation could now be started, carrying parties from the 4th R.B. giving valuable help. It was much impeded by the concentration of fire the enemy now brought to bear ; casualties, light at first, soon mounted up, nearly all wires were cut and communication was mainly maintained by runner, though the R.A. liaison officer did wonders in keeping touch with our guns. However, the men stuck splendidly to their work, their resolution and tenacity being, described by the G.O.C., ' as notable as their dash and determination in the attack,' while Captain Grellier and 2/Lt. Collins, despite their wounds, directed the consolidation most effectively. B Company had before this come up to assist, and eventually two platoons of B with all A were detailed to hold the position, C and D withdrawing into reserve. Meanwhile the other platoons of B, pushing forward to reconnoitre, discovered enemy advancing up a ravine towards Les Deux Roches, and almost simultaneously the enemy's barrage came down in renewed strength. D Company had already gone back, and C were following but promptly turned back and manned La Roche Noire in readiness to counter-attack, and when, just before 5 a.m. (September 2nd), an attack developed in strength and enemy began gaining a foothold on Les Deux Roches, Captain Green took two platoons forward to thrust the attackers back by a vigorous and timely charge, clearing them off the slope. C.S.M. King had just before this collected a party to bring up some much-needed ammunition, having to pass through the enemy's barrage to reach the firing line. By 6 a.m. the position was so well established that battalion H.Q. could withdraw C to the assembly position, B Company and some details under Captain Lowy holding the captured position.

Until September 7th the Hampshire remained in occupation of their gains, completing the consolidation and patrolling up to the enemy's main line. They were left unmolested except for some shelling, but the few additional casualties it caused included Captain Lowy, one of the few ' originals ' left with the 10th,[1] who was mortally wounded on September 2nd. These casualties brought the total loss up to three officers, Captain Lowy, Lt. Sparrow and 2/Lt. Fishlock, and 47 men killed and missing, with Captain Grellier, 2/Lt. Collins and 132 men wounded, about half those engaged in the attack, the Gloucesters' casualties being just under 100. The attack had fully achieved its objectives, tactical and strategical,[2] and both battalions were warmly congratulated by the

---

[1] Major Scott and Captains Dupree and Grellier were also ' original ' officers.
[2] Its success forced the Bulgarians to evacuate their advanced position between Alcah Maguale and the Vardar, which the 81st Brigade occupied.

authorities on their fine achievement. An 'immediate' D.S.O. was awarded to Lt Colonel Taylor, with M.C.s to Captains Green and Grellier and 2/Lt. Collins ; C.S.M. King, Sergeants Oborne (died of wounds), Buckingham and Seabrook, Corporal Johnson, Lance Corporal Sims and Private Manders and Richards received the M.M..

After two days out of the front line the battalion on the night of September 10th/11th relieved the D.C.L.I. in the Dromedaire sector of the front to the left of the Roche Noire salient. It had been here ten days, patrolling vigorously, when the success of the main offensive was admitted by the Bulgarians evacuating the trenches facing the 82nd Brigade. On September 20th they started blowing up ammunition dumps and setting fire to stores they could not remove, a sure sign of their intention to withdraw. By September 21st the Twenty-Seventh Division was free to advance in pursuit, although in no very fit state for this : the influenza epidemic, the 'Spanish Flu', which had already run rampant through our Armies in France in the early summer, had fastened its grip on the B.S.F., many of whose men, debilitated by their long endurance of the Macedonian climate and the other drawbacks of that 'front', fell ready victims to it. The 10th's ranks had been terribly depleted by its ravages, Captain Dupree and 2/Lt. Collins, who had returned to duty, being among those admitted to hospital, and the whole battalion could hardly produce one company up to establishment.

The 12th's share in the offensive, whose success was so soon to bring the Macedonian campaigns to an end, had consisted of carrying out along with the 8th D.C.L.I. the minor operation which the Twenty-Sixth Division was to undertake to assist the Twenty-Second and the Greeks in their attack just West of Doiran.

The 12th had been in line at Bekirli since the middle of August. Our guns were blazing away freely as if the attack was coming on this front, thereby drawing considerable but fairly harmless retaliation, while our patrols were active and brought back useful information. On September 8th, the 12th had extended their line to the right to include Glengarry Hill, from which, early on September 18th, B Company under Major Jones went forward to expel a Bulgarian outpost from White Scar Hill, SW. of Krastali, the D.C.L.I. attacking another outpost on Flatiron Hill just to the Eastward. Advancing by the Dautli track, the 12th were in their assembly position by 4.30 a.m., 20 minutes before 'Zero'. Covered by a good barrage B Company rushed the hill, killing several Bulgarians, and though promptly counter-attacked beat off the enemy most successfully. However, the hill was soon under heavy shell-fire and causalties began to mount up. One platoon of D Company, 25 strong under 2/Lt. Marshall, which was providing a left-flank guard, was vigorously attacked by a much larger detachment, which reached one of our posts and was only driven off after hand to hand fighting, the other posts having kept the enemy at bay by fire. A right-flank guard of C Company in Ham Ravine was not troubled by any attack but was heavily shelled, and the repulse of the Twenty-

Second Division allowed many more guns to be turned on to White Scar and Flatiron Hills, until, in the words of one officer, ' every gun in Macedonia ' seemed to be shelling them. About 10 a.m., a runner having got through from Brigade H.Q. with orders to withdraw, we fell back without the enemy trying to interfere. Major Jones, who had handled the situation with great coolness and done much to encourage his men to hold on despite the shelling, now conducted the withdrawal skilfully and got away all the wounded but a few too bad to be moved. Casualties had been heavy, 2/Lt. Medcraft and 19 men killed or missing,[1] Lt. Frampton and 2/Lts. Marshall and Pringle and 39 men wounded. The enemy's loss could not be ascertained, but his counter-attack had certainly been costly, and the company's dash in attack and tenacity in defence were much praised.[2]

Shortly after midnight the Bulgarians began bombarding the 12th's positions with great vigour and about 1 a.m. (September 19th) they attacked Glengarry Hill in force. A Company had had several casualties from the bombardment, but its men were quite unshaken and never let the enemy reach our trenches, though several were shot down in trying to cut our wire. Two quiet days followed on this front, no diversion being attempted to assist the Twenty-Second Division's renewed attack on the Doiran position (September 19th), as costly and unsuccessful as its predecessor, and then, early on September 21st, explosions and fires in the enemy's lines seemed to indicate that the success of the main Allied attack further West was causing the Bulgarians at last to relinquish the positions they had so tenaciously and successfully defended.

Both 10th and 12th Hampshire, despite their weakness, now started in pursuit, though as the Twenty-Seventh Division had to recross the Vardar to rejoin the rest of the B.S.F., the 10th never got into touch with the enemy. Their brigade being the rear-most of the Division, which was delayed by having to bridge the Vardar, the 10th Hampshire did not cross till September 26th, reaching Bogdanci that evening and Dedeli next day, where they remained till the 30th. Much reduced by casualties and sickness, the battalion had been reorganised in two companies under Lt. Englefield and Captain Grellier and, as the other battalions were scarcely stronger, an 82nd Composite Battalion was now formed under the Gloucestershire's C.O. with Colonel Taylor as second in command, the 10th, who had under 200 men available, supplying one company with 12 Lewis guns, under Major Scott. This unit would have moved on to Kosturino on September 30th, had not news came in that Bulgaria had asked for an armistice.

The 12th Battalion had had rather more to do. Directly it became evident that the Bulgarians were quitting the Twenty-Sixth Division had pushed patrols forward to investigate, and on September 22nd the 12th Hampshire had had the satisfaction of entering Servian territory and finding themselves well

---

[1] Several were found later in Bulgarian hospitals, wounded and taken prisoners. The D.C.L.I. lost even more heavily in proportion to the numbers in action.
[2] Major Jones got the D.S.O.

in rear of the old Bulgarian lines. Much war material had been abandoned, but no live enemy were encountered, though the R.F.C. was taking toll of the retreating Bulgarians. Pushing through Stojakovo,[1] the 12th reached Bogdanci next evening, while the following day's advance took them to Rabrovo, where it found several of its wounded taken on White Scar Hill. The enemy had offered a little resistance, mainly rather innocuous shelling, while during the night (24th/25th) our outposts were sniped and there was some bombing.

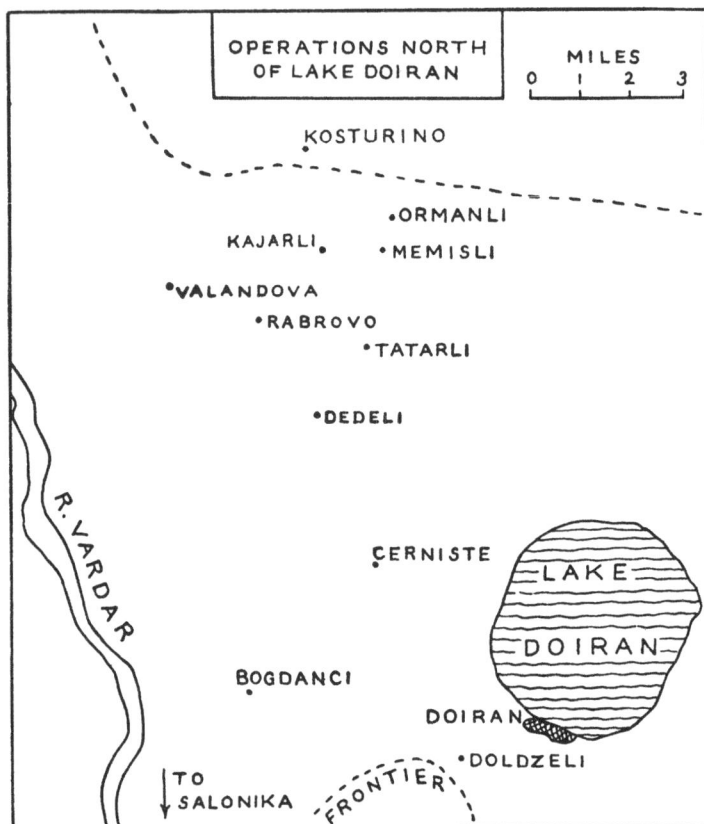

OPERATIONS NORTH OF LAKE DOIRAN

MILES
0 1 2 3

Starting off for Kosturino before dawn on September 25th, the 12th saw more evidence of the effective work of the R.F.C. : long-range shell-fire caused a few casualties, but the opposition was trifling, though the 78th Brigade on the left met rather more, and by 9 a.m. Kosturino had been occupied by the 79th Brigade's advanced-guard and the Division entered Bulgarian territory, though the 12th only crossed the frontier next day, when after a most strenuous march over part of the Belashitza range, they reached Strumica. Arduous as the march had been few men fell out, but the advance was out-pacing the A.S.C's

[1] The Division was now leading the left wing of the B.S.F's advance.

capacity to keep it supplied, though fortunately plenty of captured supplies were available, including a local plum brandy which proved a most invigorating refreshment to the exhausted. Consequently the Twenty-Sixth Division had to remain halted round Strumica till the afternoon of September 28th, when the 79th Brigade, advancing again, occupied villages on the road to Berovo. Next day it found the enemy inclined to stand at the pass leading to Berovo, both mountain artillery and machine-guns being in action and holding up the brigade's advanced-guard. This position the 12th Hampshire were about to attack next day (September 30th), but before their outflanking movement could be started the news of the armistice, which would come into force at midday, suspended hostilities.

Neither 10th or 12th Hampshire or indeed any part of the British force at Salonica had played any prominent part in the final operations against the Bulgarians, the first of Germany's vassals to be eliminated from the war, but whatever the Macedonian campaigns may have contributed to the Allied victory, what the B.S.F. had endured in its three weary and apparently futile years in Macedonia must not be underestimated. It had had little to encourage it ; if in many minor actions it had shown itself superior to its enemies when given a reasonable chance, its attacks on the Doiran front had never had the least prospect of success. The B.S.F. had had a vile climate to endure, its conditions of service had been trying, little leave, few amenities or opportunities of relaxation, much hard and monotonous work and duty, with little to show for it, and some sense of frustration and of doubt about the part the force was playing in the war. Its final effort had been demanded of units more than usually weakened by illness, with many of their men hardly fit for duty, let alone for great exertions, and no fair estimate of its achievements will overlook these factors. General Franchet d'Esperey, on taking command in Macedonia, had been greatly impressed by the bearing and spirit of the British troops, and that in the final attack he gave them the nastiest piece of the work was no light compliment. Neither 10th nor 12th Hampshire had found Macedonia exactly a 'station for honour,' both had acquitted themselves well enough to show that given better chances they should have done much more : both, despite many disadvantages, had achieved a high reputation for discipline, spirit and efficiency and had done credit to the regiment.

Bulgaria's defection left the B.S.F. with Turkey to face, but if a month elapsed before the Turk followed the Bulgar's example, neither 10th nor 12th got into action against him. The advance against Turkey was not the only problem before the Allies ; the victory over Bulgaria had to be exploited by the liberation of Servia, by the occupation of Bulgaria and by an advance to the Danube to deal with the Germans and Austrians holding down Roumania. The allotment of the Allied troops to these different tasks gave rise to some discussion and several changes of plan ; eventually General Milne with a mainly British force was given the advance against Turkey, in which our Navy could effectively co-operate. For political reasons, however, a British Division was to advance to the Danube, the Twenty-Seventh being selected, while the Twenty-Sixth, who had started to march North by the Struma valley, was diverted Eastward towards the Maritza, behind which such troops as Turkey might muster for the defence of Constantinople were likely to be found. Before the Twenty-Sixth could cross the Maritza Turkey had capitulated (October 30th), while the Twenty-Seventh, whose advance to the Danube was held up by heavy falls of snow, was eventually sent back to Salonica, the Twenty-Sixth being sent to the Danube in its place.

The armistice with Bulgaria had found those actually present in the field with the 10th Hampshire down below 200 all told, another 280 nominally ' effective ' being detached, including some in the field ambulance. About 30 convalescents had rejoined before the 82nd Composite Battalion was split up again on October 8th, but even then the 10th could only produce two skeleton companies of about 50 apiece, battalion H.Q. absorbing 50 all told and the transport 60. The battalion moved camp to Rabrovo on October 7th and started its advance into Bulgaria on the 17th, halting for five days at Petric (October 21st–26th). Resuming the march North, the 10th crossed the Struma on October 26th, making for Sofia, but was halted at Dupnica [1] on November 2nd, the Division being now ordered back to Salonica. The battalion then spent nearly a whole day waiting for a train to take it South; when this did at last arrive its engine promptly collapsed and Marianopolje was not reached till late on November 8th. Taking to the road again here, the battalion marched through the Rupel Pass and found itself back in the familiar country of the Struma valley. It recrossed that river at Orlyak and, pushing on by the Seres road through heavy snow, reached Guvesne on November 14th, a train taking it on to Janesh three days later. Here it settled down to await orders and to hear about demobilization prospects, having plenty to do meanwhile in improving the poor accommodation which the camp provided.

News of Bulgaria's surrender had deprived the 12th Hampshire of their last chance of distinction. They waited near Hamzali five days, resting and doing a little training, before advancing Eastward with their brigade by Jenikoi (October 6th) to Radomir, which was reached on October 20th, partly by light railway, partly by road. The marches were never long, the population was anything but hostile, and at one halting place hot sulphur springs gave everyone a most refreshing bath. From Radomir the whole 79th Brigade went by a broad gauge railway to the Turkish position near Mustafa Pasha (October 22nd), where it took post in readiness for an advance which Turkey's surrender anticipated. Apart from a few hostile aeroplanes no enemy had been seen and the chief feature of the time had been a welcome issue of much-needed socks and shirts with an extra blanket per man.

Bulgaria and Turkey were out of the war, but with Austria and Germany still fighting it looked as if the Division's selection to move to the Danube

[1] Thirty miles South of Sofia.

might give the 12th more fighting yet.   However, November 4th brought news of the armistice with Austria, and when on November 11th they reached Rust-chuk on the Danube, having travelled by train through Philipopolis and the Shipka Pass, news met them that Germany also had capitulated.   They were the first British troops to reach the Danube but French troops were already across.   If a long spell of duty as part of an Army of Occupation was ahead of the 12th, their warfare was accomplished.

CHAPTER XXXIV
AFTER THE ARMISTICE—DEMOBILIZATION
NORTH RUSSIA

NOVEMBER 11th might have brought the end of hostilities, much had to be done before peace could be concluded and the Army brought back to a peace establishment and more normal conditions. The terms of the armistice had included the occupation by the Allies of Germany West of the Rhine, other defeated countries had also to be occupied, and however desirable it was to beat swords into plough-shares and restore men to their civilian occupations, this could not be done quickly. The problems of demobilization were intricate : industry wanted 'key' men and skilled men, but these included many long retained in industry and only lately 'combed out', so by length of service they had little claim to an early release. It was hard to make the surviving volunteers of 1914 and 1915 appreciate the reasons for letting men only recently 'fetched' have precedence in being demobilized, especially as many of those who had left good positions to serve could not calculate on getting back to these or finding an equivalent : they were naturally anxious to return to civil life before all the best posts had gone. Men like the original Hampshire Territorials who had gone out to India in 1914, many of whom were still there or in other Eastern countries and had not been home since they left, had very strong claims to 'priority' in demobilization, and it was hard to reconcile the claims of the individuals with the exigencies of the service.

With the fighting over it was not too easy to find satisfactory employment for the large numbers who had still to be retained in reserve for possible developements. Germany had been beaten and had surrendered : the German Army had yet to be disarmed and demobilized, and until that was completed the British troops could not relax their standards of training ; they might be needed to fight again. Some 'ceremonial' was now practised, with brigade and Divisional competitions to give extra reason for it, and everything was done to provide adequate recreation for the men, for whose energies and interests Association Football provided an outlet which was a safety valve of really great value, while boxing and cross-country runs and other forms of athletics were also a great help. Inter-platoon and inter-company ties, going on to brigade and Divisional competitions and eventually to Army of the Rhine championships, in every branch of games and athletics played a big part in the activities of 1919, while much was done to give men training for civil life ; an Education Officer now became an important member of a battalion's headquarters, and lectures, partly recreational, partly educational, became frequent. Occupation was also found for troops in France and Belgium in efforts to repair the damages of war ; 'salvage' in all its forms was necessary, miles of trenches needed filling in, great stretches of wire had to be cleared away, and if the ruined towns and villages could not as yet be rebuilt, the repair of roads and railways, the reconstruction of bridges and some effort to restore the natural drainage of the countryside could be started.

The problems of this period were complicated for the 2nd, 2/4th and 15th Hampshire by their forming part of the force to occupy Western Germany : and while a Service battalion like the 11th was naturally marked down for disbanding, a Regular unit like the 1st Hampshire had to be reconstituted for its peace duties as soon as possible. This meant the discharge or transfer to other battalions of men not serving on a Regular attestation or not liable to retention in the service for some little time and their replacement by 'serving' soldiers, not many were left, or men ready to re-enlist for a limited period.

The Fourth Division was not selected for the advance to the Rhine and the 1st Hampshire did not set foot on German soil. They remained near Valenciennes till the first week in January, first at Curgies, moving to Saultain on November 20th and passing close to one of the Thirty-Seventh's old battlefields at Famars. They moved again to Preseau (November 22nd) and thence to Sebourg on December 16th, going on into Belgium on January 4th and being quartered at La Louvière, a mining town ten miles East of Mons. Barely 20 men were demobilized in December, but after the New Year demobilization started in earnest, nearly 150 men leaving, another 460 following in February. Discharges from hospital, the return of 'details' from 'employments' and the much appreciated arrival of the Band from Winchester on January 13th did something to keep up numbers, but in February the battalion was re-formed, one company being composed of men liable for 'retention' and the rest 'serving' Regulars or men due for demobilization, while ten officers and 200 men went off to the 2nd Battalion. Further reductions followed as more men were demobilized or, if re-enlisted,[1] went home on leave, usually joining the 3rd Battalion, now at Catterick, out of which the Regular battalions were to be constructed. By June the battalion had been reduced to a cadre, the remaining 'retainables' having been posted to the 2/6th R. Warwickshire, while Lt. Colonel Earle took command of the 51st (Young Soldiers) Battalion on the Rhine. This cadre, under Major Corner, left Binche, to which it had previously moved, got held up at Antwerp for several days and eventually crossed from Boulogne to Dover on June 20th, reaching Winchester late that evening. Of its 64 men over half belonged to the Band, the others included four who had gone to France from Colchester in August 1914, R.S.M. Palmer, who had won the M.C. and the D.C.M., Sergeants Goode, a drummer in 1914, and Pearce and Lance Corporal Hills. A formal civic reception was given to the cadre next day by the Mayor and Corporation, a Colour party from the Depot being also on parade with the Colours.

The 2nd Battalion's cadre had come home nearly three months before the 1st's, the 2nd having been reduced to cadre first, as it was nominally on a

[1] Up to February 6th the 1st Battalion had re-enlisted 150 men.

foreign service tour, which it was to resume as soon as possible, as the war was to be ignored in calculating reliefs.

The 2nd Hampshire had moved to Lessines two days after the armistice and then advanced across Belgium to the Meuse, which they reached at Huy on November 29th, having on the way crossed the field of Waterloo. A party of 100 2nd Hampshires had been among the detachments of the Ninth and Twenty-Ninth Divisions to represent the British Army at the formal re-entry of the King of the Belgians into Brussels (November 22nd), a memorable occasion to which the fine turnout of the 2nd Hampshire did full credit.

Pushing on Eastward the 2nd plunged into the Ardennes, largely pine-clad hills with the roads winding along the bottoms of deep and rocky valleys, country in which it was just as well to be unopposed. On December 5th they crossed the German frontier near Malmedy, to be naturally received in sullen silence, though as they advanced it was evident that the good behaviour of the leading British troops had clearly reassured the Germans and shown them to their relief and surprise that they would not be done by as they had done. December 10th found the 2nd Hampshire at Frechen, just short of Cologne. Nearly 250 miles had been covered, largely in bad weather, but the battalion had marched splendidly, hardly having any stragglers and with no more men going to hospital than might have done if in billets.

Two days' halt gave a chance to clean up before the ceremonial entry into Cologne on December 13th, when the Ninth, Twenty-Ninth and 1st Canadian Divisions marched in and crossed the Rhine, the Twenty-Ninth in the centre using the great Hohenzollern Bridge, at the end of which General Jacob, the Corps Commander, took the salute. The troops marched with fixed bayonets, and their turn-out and carriage were worthy of this historical occasion, the Hampshire being specially commended for their smartness and bearing. Once across the Rhine the battalion took up billets at Mulheim, ' a dirty place full of factories ', but soon moved to Berg-Gladbach where it made itself quite comfortable in a paper-mill, but it had to turn out again and move to Wermels-kirchen, 20 miles NE. of Cologne, where it was to remain till the middle of January. It was now on the forward edge of the ' occupied zone ' and had to put out outposts on the frontier. The Colour party, which had been sent to Winchester to fetch the Colours, was received with due honour on December 25th, and the battalion settled down to a routine in which education and recreation played a big part, though training was not neglected. An Army of Occupation in a country which largely assessed things in terms of military efficiency could not afford to relax, and rapid-fire, snap-shooting and other competitions kept up the standards of musketry.

Demobilization started in the last days of 1918, though on a small scale, only 34 leaving, but 140 went in January. February 1st found the battalion again on outpost duty, at Dhunn, having to find examination posts on the line of demarcation marking the ' occupied ' zone. The weather was cold with much snow, which gave chances of tobogganing but was not allowed to interfere unduly with other activities. The 2nd Hampshire, being now detailed for reduction to cadre before being reconstituted, were relieved on February 23rd by the 2/4th and went back to Mulheim and thence to Bamberg, leaving their football XI behind to get through to the semi-finals of the Divisional Cup, to be then beaten by the K.O.S.B. Reduction to cadre was virtually completed by March 12th, before which all those ' retainable ' had been transferred to the 2/4th, and on March 31st the cadre under Captain Singleton-Gates, who had been acting as Adjutant since August, reached Aldershot, where the Foreign Service Details, under Major Baxter, recently released from internment in Holland, were already established in Salamanca Barracks. Late as was the hour of its arrival, nearly midnight, the cadre was given the warmest of welcomes, the Aldershot Volunteers turning out in force to help with the baggage.

The 2nd Battalion, however, was not to be given much chance to re-form and resume its normal peace routine, a new call was to be made upon it which postponed that for several months. The 2nd Hampshire, or rather a provisional unit to which the authorities had attached that name, was to take part in a rather unsatisfactory enterprise. British intervention in North Russia early in 1918 had been largely due to fears that the Germans might secure a grip on Murmansk and Archangel and, besides getting hold of the munitions the Allies had landed there, use these ports as submarine bases. Operations had been continued to assist those ' White ' Russians who were friendly to the Allies, but the troops originally sent out were mostly units of ' low category ' men, including many due for demobilization, and early in 1919 it was decided to relieve them with Regulars. No Regular battalions were as yet sufficiently advanced in reconstruction to provide much more than a company, and the troops sent out were really provisional battalions, that described as the ' 2nd Hampshire,' who provided a battalion head-quarters and one company, being completed by companies from the Somerset L.I., the Dorset and the Wiltshire.[1] The C.O., Lt. Colonel Sherwood-Kelly, who came from the Norfolk, was one of the Twenty-Ninth Division's most reputed fighting men, who had won a V.C. at Cambrai when commanding the Inniskillings. Major Baxter was second in command and the Hampshire officers with the battalion included Captains Berkeley, Edwards, Flint (Adjutant), May, McIvor, Smythe and Spencer-Smith and Lts. Cotten, Gorman and M.S. Moore.

The battalion was collected at Crowborough, which it left on May 15th, sailing from Tilbury that evening. Rounding the North Cape on May 19th at midnight, its ship called at Murmansk next day and from there slowly followed an ice-breaker through the ice to Archangel, which it reached on May 21st., the battalion landing next day. Its arrival[2] had a considerable effect on the local population, whose rather fluctuating adherence to the Allied interests was for a time consolidated, while the importance of the occasion was emphasized by several ceremonial parades. But the troops were needed up the Dwina, and

[1] To complete these companies details were drafted in from many other regiments, nearly 30 in all being represented.

[2] It formed part of the 238th Special Brigade, whose Brigadier, General Grogan of the Worcestershire, was another V.C.

on June 2nd the battalion started for Bereznik in large barges towed by steamers. Progress against the current did not exceed 50 miles a day, and not till June 6th was the front reached at Kurgoman, just above Bereznik.   Here the battalion landed, H.Q. with the Dorset (Y) and Wiltshire (Z) Companies on the right bank, the Hampshire (W) and Somerset (X) under Major Baxter being across the river, here over 1200 yards wide, at Tolgas.   The country, flat and sandy, was covered with thick forest and inclined to be swampy, while mosquitoes were troublesome.   The line held consisted of a chain of block-houses on the outskirts of a group of villages.   The Bolshevik outposts were just

upstream, actually within artillery range, but they were not sufficiently active to give our patrols many chances, though on June 12th Captain Smythe and a party from No. III Platoon had a successful brush on the left bank, killing four enemy, and on the right bank the C.O., who took out a patrol himself, ran into another party and disposed of one man in a personal encounter.

It had been decided to attack the main Bolshevik positions at Topsa and Troitsa, 15 miles above Kurgoman, the 2nd Hampshire [1] having to work round through the woods to a position East of Troitsa, threatening the retreat of the enemy holding Topsa, some miles downstream, which White Russians were

[1] Battalion headquarters with W and Y Companies were to be employed with trench mortars and a section of machine-gunners.

attacking. The column, which started its move about 4 a.m. on June 19th, had nearly 18 miles to cover through swampy forest in great heat,[1] and much delay was caused by the ammunition mules getting bogged, as after about six miles the track faded out and the column had to struggle through swamps. However, by midnight the intended position was duly reached and about 3 a.m. (June 20th) the advance began. Y Company led the way and emerging from the forest into a clearing East of Troitsa opened fire to cover W's advance upon the village. This was quite stubbornly opposed, the Bolsheviks were apparently nervous of being intercepted and were in considerable force here, and little progress could be made against machine-gun fire ; indeed the enemy seemed to be getting round our flanks. Colonel Kelly, therefore, called off the attack and drew off, successfully evading the effort to surround his column. If the attack had to be abandoned, by drawing off the enemy it had appreciably assisted the White Russians to capture Topsa with 500 prisoners. He now took his men to Topsa, which was reached after an exhausting march, just after the repulse of a counter-attack. Next day a move was tried on the left bank, Captain Berkeley with 150 rifles, half of them Hampshires, trying to work round the enemy's inland flank in conjunction with a naval attack. He reached the intended position to find the enemy in force, strongly posted and awaiting attack, while nearly 300 yards of bog extended in front of the Bolsheviks' line ; seeing this, after a sharp exchange of rifle-fire, Captain Berkeley decided not to press the attack. The total casualties in the battalion, about a dozen, included Lt. Gorman of the Hampshire, who died of wounds, and Sergeant Batten, a very capable N.C.O. of 17 years service, who was killed. One Hampshire private was wounded.

Patrols now discovered that the enemy had retired some way upstream, but before an advance could be made against their new position a mutiny in a ' White Russian ' battalion at Ust Pinega, 50 miles above Archangel, caused the '2nd Hampshire' to be taken back to Bereznik and from there to Ust Pinega, from which W Company was sent on up the Pinega (i.e. NE.) to Nishin Palenga, then on to Leunovo. It was now extremely hot ; with almost perpetual sunshine the air never cooled at night, and as fresh fruit and vegetables were lacking, many men's digestions were upset. Plenty of fish could be obtained, largely by exploding trench-mortar shells in the river and collecting the proceeds. Another mutiny on the Onega front soon followed, battalion headquarters and two companies, Y and Z, being hurried back to Archangel and from there by the railway to Obozerskaya (July 23rd) leaving the other two on the Pinega. From here they advanced 25 miles further South, along the railway, but were soon brought back to Obozerskaya, leaving one company in the forward positions near Yemtsa. A raid should have been made on August 17th but had to be cancelled as the wind was insufficient for the discharge of smoke. Colonel Sherwood-Kelly now left for England, Lt. Colonel MacLeod of the 4th South African Infantry replacing him. Conditions on the railway front were slightly less uncomfortable than on the Dwina, more supplies were available and other

---

[1] In the Arctic Circle there was no night.

rations besides ' bully ' and biscuits. Meanwhile W Company had moved again to Pinega, from which it sent out frequent patrols which were able to worry the enemy by threatening his communications.

Later in August a patrol of Z Company (Wiltshires) had a brush with Bolsheviks South of Obozerskaya, killing several, and rather before that C.S.M. Norris and Corporal Tilly got the chance to earn the M.M. in a successful raid by a party from the detachment at Pinega, in which several enemy were killed and others taken, while useful information was obtained, while on September 1st the Wiltshire company repulsed a strong attack on the advanced positions, inflicting heavy casualties.

September 18th saw the head-quarters wing back on the coast at Isakagora, where the companies from the Pinega front rejoined a few days later, and by September 27th the battalion was on its way back to England, as the British troops were being withdrawn from North Russia.

Whatever the reasons for the intervention in that country and whatever the degree of success it may have achieved, it had hardly been a very enjoyable experience for the troops. Conditions of service had been unpleasant, neither climate nor country had anything to recommend it, and the troops had had few opportunities of a blow at the Bolsheviks, though in such encounters as had occurred they had fully had the measure of them and were confident in their ability to deal with them. Losses had been small : the whole ' 2nd Hampshire '[1] had only seven killed and missing [2] and 17 wounded. Sickness had on the whole been lower than might have been expected considering the climate and conditions.

Reaching Tilbury on October 6th, the battalion landed and went into camp at Purfleet, moving on to Crowborough, where it arrived on October 8th and started its real reconstruction, non-Regulars being demobilized, men of other regiments sent off to their units and Hampshiremen given leave. Then on November 3rd 530 of all ranks under Majors Frisby and im Thurn arrived from Catterick, having been separated there from the 1st Battalion, while Colonel French, who had had several important Staff posts during the war, arrived to take command. A week later another 300 men arrived from the 1st Battalion at Gosport, and on the same day an advanced party left for Ireland, to which troubled country the Sixty-Seventh was now to pay its last visit instead of returning to India.

The 2nd Hampshire's departure had left the regiment still represented in Germany by three battalions, forming a brigade in the Southern Division of the Army of Occupation. These were the 2/4th, the 15th and the 51st, one of the 'Young Soldiers' Battalions which had recently replaced the former Training Reserve Battalions, though the authorities, going back on their

---

[1] On disembarkation 154 of the battalion's 866 other ranks were actual Hampshires, 184 were Wiltshires, 118 Somersets, 70 Dorsets, 37 Guardsmen, 40 Scots and 100 Irishmen. Twenty-seven regiments altogether had been represented in the battalion.

[2] Lieutenant Gorman and Sergeant Batten were the only members of the regiment killed.

previous plan, had allotted these units to regiments, the Hampshire having also a 52nd and a 53rd ' Graduated ' battalions,[1] whose task it was to train recruits and pass them on to the ' Young Soldiers ' units.

The 2/4th had started for Germany within a week of the last shot being fired. Entering Belgium on November 19th near Console (SE. of Maubeuge), they crossed the Meuse between Namur and Dinant and reached Barcenal on November 27th. Here they halted for ten days in pleasant country well outside the war area, where some of the officers went shooting in the forests, using .303 rifles against the local roe-deer. They were glad to be in billets now that the weather had broken and turned cold. Resuming their advance on December 9th, six more marches through Belgian Luxembourg took them to the German frontier, which they crossed at Poteau on December 16th,[2] ending their pilgrimage at Mechernich ten days later. They had covered over 170 miles, some of them over quite deep snow.

Mechernich was a mining town, unbeautiful but with pleasant country round it, while it provided quite good billets, while the inhabitants, finding themselves decently treated, responded by making the men as comfortable as they could. There was not much for the men to do, but demobilization started on a small scale. Here the 2/4th spent two months, then moving forward to cross the Rhine and replace the 2nd Battalion at Wermelskirchen. That battalion now handed over all its ' retainables ', while 150 men whom the 2/4th had just previously sent to the 15th were re-posted. The move had involved leaving the Sixty-Second Division, but their new Brigadier, General Cayley, was no stranger to other Hampshiremen and a friendly rivalry soon developed in athletics and other competitions with the two other Hampshire battalions in the brigade, though cricket pitches were almost impossible to find and football grounds none too easy.

Rhine Army units were kept fairly busy, especially those on outpost, who had to be on the look-out for smugglers, who were active. Ramschied, the big town just beyond the outposts, was a great centre of the separatist, ' Spartacist ', movement and intercourse between the Allied Zone and the country beyond was very strictly supervised, the sentries being warned to be very vigilant. In June the presentation of the peace treaty to the Germans for signature caused some excitement : it was rumoured that they would refuse, and all was in readiness for this : they thought better of it and signed (June 29th), and after that the main question which occupied most peoples' minds was what units would be required for the British contingent in the Army of Occupation for the left bank of the Rhine and who would be demobilized.

Colonel Westmorland now took command of the 2/4th but reverted to Major and second in command in June, on Colonel Sidney of the Northumberland Hussars being posted to the battalion. Officers came and went rapidly, but despite constant changes in its composition the battalion managed to run

[1] These two battalions had joined the Sixty-Seventh (2nd Line Home Counties) Division by December 1917.
[2] One officer who had sailed for India with the battalion was still present, Captain Bacon.

quite a good cricket XI and to make a very satisfactory showing when inspected ; both Sir William Robertson, G.O.C. Rhine Army, in May and Sir Claud Jacob, the Corps Commander, in August being very complimentary.

July had brought another turn of outpost duty, which prevented the battalion from taking part in a great Victory Parade at Brussels, for which it had been selected. This was followed by a return to Wermelskirchen. Demobilization began in earnest in September, over 200 officers and men being ' released ', and then on October 31st the battalion was broken up, 13 officers and 160 men going to the 15th Hampshire and 18 officers and 266 men to the 51st Battalion ; fourteen N.C.O.s and men were still present who had left England with it in November 1914 and had remained with it throughout.[1]

The 2/4th had seen almost more fighting than any other Hampshire T.F. battalion, if their active part in the war had been briefer than that of the 4th and the 8th, who had started fighting in 1915, and their contribution to the regiment's record in the war was notable. They had been fortunate in that their original members had included a good sprinkling of officers and men who supplied a connection with Colonel Cave's old 1st V.B. to start them on the right way.

The Forty-First Division, though selected for the Army of Occupation, did not enter Germany during 1918. On November 11th it had just reached the Dender near Grammont, but it remained halted between Lessines and Grammont until the middle of December [2] and halted again on the Meuse from December 21st to January 6th, when it began entraining for Germany, where it took over part of the Cologne bridgehead. The 15th Hampshire, of whom Lt. Colonel Puttick had resumed command before the end of November, had had a good rest before moving up to the Meuse, where they found billets at Vieux et Robert, below Namur. At Cologne, where they were billeted at Overath, one company was wanted each day for guards, the others training and doing a fair amount of shooting. Competitions, athletic and others, also kept them busy and they took their share of the rather tiresome and exacting outpost duties. By March 7th demobilization had brought other ranks down below 600, but large drafts from the 1st and 5th Dorsets and from the Somerset L.I. raised them to over 1100 by May 3rd. The reorganization of the Rhine Army in March caused the 15th Hampshire's transfer to the Southern Division and meant a move to Wermelskirchen to be brigaded with the 2/4th and the 51st Battalions. In May Lt. Colonel Brand (R.B.) took over command, which he retained until the battalion was eventually disbanded. As with the other Hampshire battalions as much recreation and education was given as the training programme and general maintenance of efficiency allowed, and though the battalion was becoming rather a collection of men from many units, its stan-

[1] They included R.Q.M.S. Emberton, C.S.M. Samways, O.R.S. Cousins, Sergeant Drummer James and Sergeants Dixon and Meaden. Captain Bacon, the last of the original officers to leave the battalion, had been demobilized a few weeks earlier.
[2] It was said that the men's boots were too worn out for a long march.

dards were not allowed to relax, nor did its numbers fall below the 1000 till well into September, while the big draft from the 2/4th in October, shortly before the battalion was disbanded, increased the proportion of real Hampshiremen.

The last formed of the five Hampshire Service Battalions who saw active service, the 15th had seen more fighting than any of the others and have left a fine record, starting with a big share in the capture of Flers in September 1916 and including a V.C. at the Tower Hamlets a year later. The incorporation of the Hampshire Carabineers had brought the battalion some fine material, while this helped it to escape disbanding in 1918 [1] and thereby to survive to take its part in the final successes.

The Sixteenth Division had not been required for the Army of Occupation and the 11th Hampshire saw nothing of Germany. The Division, which had just been squeezed out of the fighting line on November 9th, had halted on the Scheldt with head-quarters at Seclin, South of Lille, and in that area its units were to remain.

The end of hostilities meant less to Pioneers than to others, their work on roads, railways and bridges remained as essential as ever, and the 11th Hampshire's daily routine, as recorded in their diary, would hardly indicate that anything special had happened on November 11th, were it not for occasional references after that date to recreation, to educational training and to demobilization. The 11th moved back to Le Neuville en Phalempin on November 16th and there it remained until at the end of March it was transferred to Frétin. Some 30 coal miners were the first men demobilized, agricultural workers being about the next for ' priority ', and during February nearly 250 of all ranks left the battalion. The chief event of that month was the presentation of a ' King's Colour ' by the G.O.C. First Corps, Lt. General Holland, but March saw demobilization carried a good way further, equipment, vehicles and transport animals being handed over to the appropriate authorities, while ' retainables ' went off to other units, about 120 men going to the 2/8th Worcestershire on March 31st. By May 1st the 11th were down below cadre establishment, and the last day of May brought orders for its return home, when the cadre was to ' proceed ' to Scotland for disbanding, not a very obvious place for a nominally Southern English battalion.

Pioneer battalions had had more hard work than fighting : they were often under heavy fire without much chance of retaliating, and if the 11th Hampshire had in the aggregate had quite substantial casualties, only March 1918 had given them a real chance to show their fighting capacities. They had done so to some purpose then and had shown that they could hit as effectively as they could dig.

Of the battalions on other fronts, the 1/4th in Persia were not likely to be very immediately influenced by the end of hostilities in Europe : the 5th, still

---

[1] Service battalions which had incorporated Yeomanry units were not among those disbanded.

in India, could not be spared till re-formed Regular battalions could replace the Territorial and Garrison units doing duty in that country, threatened as it was with trouble on the Frontier and from Afghanistan ; the 6th and 2/7th in Mesopotamia and the 8th in Palestine might be needed for occupation duties for some time yet ; the 1st/7th, which had got to Aden, were taking part in the local ' little war ' which had been smouldering on ever since 1915, and the 9th, after some remarkable adventures, were deep in Siberia. None of them were likely to be able to ' stand down ' just yet, any more than could the services of the units still at home be dispensed with immediately.

Of these last, the armistice had found the 3rd Battalion still at Gosport, carrying on with the dual duties of manning defences and finding drafts which it had done so efficiently since August 1914 ; the 4th Reserve Battalion, which had absorbed the other draft-finding Territorial units, had moved to Belfast, while the 17th (Home Service) Battalion,[1] was now at Southwold. While serving as a training battalion, it was also responsible for an extensive stretch of coast defences, duty which involved having to train men as gunners, the detachment of R.A. under the command of the 17th's C.O. being too weak to man all the guns it had on charge. Another battalion, the 2/9th, formerly Cyclists, had just ceased to exist ; it had given up its bicycles at the same time as the 1/9th and had since then been largely employed in draft-finding, having first completed the 1/9th for service in India by providing over 400 men, while after July 1st, 1916 it had sent out 300 men to the 1st Battalion. In April 1918 it had discontinued its coastal patrols, all outlying detachments rejoining head-quarters at Sandown, after which the battalion was transferred to Herringfleet in Suffolk and posted to a ' Mixed Brigade ' attached to the Sixty-Eighth [2] Division. It had moved to Lowestoft before being disbanded.[3]

Most unfortunately hardly any record of the 3rd Battalion's activities during the war seems to have survived : the MS Book entitled ' Digest of Service, 3rd Battalion, Hampshire Regiment ' merely contains a page for the years 1915–1919, recording very briefly Colonel Powney's retirement in January 1916 and Major Daniell's promotion to succeed him, the battalion's move from Gosport to Catterick in February 1919, the fact that altogether the battalion sent 500 officers and 22,000 men overseas as reinforcements and the battalion's disembodiment on July 3rd 1919, when its officers and men became the 1st Battalion and the ' Head-quarters and Permanent Regular establishment ' of the 3rd, consisting actually of Major Hackett with the R.S.M., the Orderly Room Sergeant and the Sergeant Drummer, returned to Winchester. Gummed into the volume is a letter of February 22nd 1919 from Lt. General Sir H.

---

[1] The final form taken by the provisional battalion formed in February 1915 from the home service men left behind by the Territorial battalions.

[2] Second Line Welsh T.F.

[3] The 1st Garrison Battalion appears in the Army List from June 1918 as the 18th (Garrison) Battalion : it was disbanded early in 1920. Just before it was given its number the 18th (Home Service) Battalion, formed in December 1916, had been broken up. It had served in the Seventy-First (Home Service) Division until December 1917, doing coast defence duty on the East Coast.

Sclater, G.O.C. Southern Command, expressing his high appreciation of the splendid work done by the battalion during the war, especially by the instructors responsible for the training, and of its excellent conduct and unfailing readiness to respond to any call made upon it, with his regret at the departure from his command of so admirable a battalion.

Catterick, the new Aldershot in the making for the Northern Command was not an improvement on Gosport, far from it. It lacked any kind of amenities, and with many men impatient to be demobilized and little to occupy them, it was anything but an attractive or popular station. The reconstitution of the 1st Battalion was a not unwelcome step as promising an early move.

Command of the reconstituted 1st Battalion was now taken over by Colonel Beckwith, with Sergeant Jeffery,[1] repatriated after being taken at Le Cateau, as R.S.M. in place of R.S.M. Withers, who now went to pension after 25 years' service : a first-rate R.S.M., the battalion owed him much. The Colours, carried by Lt. Beatty and 2/Lt. Newby, were sent to Paris for the Victory March of July 7th and to London for another Victory March, in which Lt. Black, C.S.M. Ralfs and R.S.M. Smith of the 3rd Battalion and 12 others acted as escort.

On their return to Catterick the Colours were ' trooped ', it was the reconstituted battalion's first ' ceremonial ' parade and was admirably carried out, the Brigadier, who was present, being much impressed with the battalion's steadiness. Shortly after this Lt. Colonel Barlow, another released prisoner of war, joined and took over command, after which a railway strike gave the battalion some tiresome duty. This fortunately did not last long, and by October 16th an advanced party had left for Gosport where the battalion was to be quartered. Before this, as the battalion was several hundreds over establishment, the surplus, over 500 all told, were formed into a separate 2nd Battalion under Major Frisby, so that for the moment the Thirty-Seventh and Sixty-Seventh were again quartered side by side as at Secunderabad in 1887 and at Minorca 120 years before.[2]

The surrender of Turkey had found the head-quarters of the 1/4th Hampshire with some 300 rifles at Zenjan,[3] to which Colonel Matthews and his force had fallen back ten days earlier. C Company was in Trans-Caspia and details of the other companies were under orders to rejoin head-quarters. The main occupation was now the construction of new barracks, but in November head-quarters with A and B Companies were ordered back to Kasvin, leaving D at

[1] He had distinguished himself greatly by splendid work in captivity ; finding himself in a camp of over 4,000 prisoners without officers, he had set to work to organize the life of the camp, setting a fine example of courage and patience and refusing to knuckle under to the Germans. He was awarded the M.S.M.
[2] On the Sunday before the 1st Battalion left Catterick there had been a combined church parade, both battalions being present in full strength.
[3] 70 miles SE. of Enzeli.

Zenjan. The march took several days, 106 miles being covered, with 18 miles as the longest day's march. No change in the distribution of the battalion occurred until the middle of February, when C Company, now only 80 all told, rejoined from Merv : the little British force in Trans-Caspia, engaged in a ' side-show ' of the Persian ' side-show ' of the Mesopotamian ' side-show ', had achieved no little success in thwarting Bolshevik attempts to ferment trouble in Central Asia and C Company's efforts had not been wasted.[1] This company, under Captain Fardell had joined the troops engaged against the Bolsheviks the day (Aug. 29th) after they had repulsed an attack on their position near Meshe. Two rather half-hearted attacks by the Bolsheviks were repulsed during September, and in October an advance was made to Merv, which was occupied after more sharp fighting, the brunt of which fell on the 19th Punjabis. The Hampshire detachment remained in occupation of Merv, where it suffered severely from influenza, until recalled to head-quarters early in 1919, before more fighting occurred. D Company from Zenjan soon followed, and by February 25th the battalion was re-united after nearly a year. It now mustered twelve officers and 627 other ranks, the first men demobilized ' on compassionate grounds ' having gone off a few days earlier. Demobilization went on rapidly during March, the homeward journey being usually made by Enzeli, the Caspian, the Caucasus and the Black Sea, British troops, mainly the ' B.S.F. ' from Salonica, having occupied those areas. By March 20th, the available rifles having been reduced to 250, demobilization was suspended[2] but was resumed on a small scale in April. Drafts, mainly ' retainable men ' from other units, brought other ranks up again above 400 in July, but by October 1st they had fallen well below that figure.[3]

October brought orders for the battalion's return to England and on October 28th, the head-quarters party of 140 all told under Major Bowers, who had taken over from Colonel Matthews in June, started in lorries for Basra, another 120 following the next day. All those ineligible for demobilization had been transferred to other units or duties. Journeying by lorry though Hamadan and Karind to Quariba, and thence by train to Kut, the battalion took ship there (November 6th) and arrived at Basra on November 9th. Here it was reduced to a cadre, which left Basra for Bombay on November 28th. For a unit raised originally for Home Defence it had had some really remarkable wanderings and experiences.

Meanwhile the 5th Battalion had at last had a taste of active service. It had returned to India from Burma in October 1918 and had been sent up to Ambala, where it relieved the 9th Hampshire, under orders for Vladivostock. It was still at Ambala in the spring of 1919 when serious riots broke out in the

---

[1] No account of its doings is included in the battalion diary, but the operations in Trans-Caspia are briefly described by in the *Journal* of the Royal United Service Institution for 1919.

[2] Strength on March 31st was 11 officers and 317 other ranks.

[3] By this time R.Q.M.S. Shore and Sergeants Hart and Smith were the only, ' originals ' still with the 1/4th.

Punjab, involving a great increase in ' internal security ' duties, not only at Ambala itself but in the country round, while 200 men had to be sent up to Simla and escorts to be found for train-loads of European women and children who were being sent to the Hills. Things had hardly settled down when the threatened trouble with Afghanistan led to hostilities, whereupon the 5th Hampshire were ordered to Kohat to join a 46th Mobile Brigade. *- arrived 31 May 1919*

At Kohat the battalion found itself in an insanitary camp in very hot weather, with a poor supply of bad water and fresh rations almost unobtainable. To move out to Mohammed Zai Fort to man some partly constructed lines was a relief and gave the 5th its chance, the lines being twice attacked by Afghans or local tribesmen, who were easily beaten off, the second time largely by the artillery, without any loss to the 5th. Here the battalion remained all through June, in great discomfort from the heat, the lack of water and the generally bad conditions. Cholera broke out in Kohat and spread to the 5th Hampshire, who lost six men, while others succumbed to a ' heat wave ', so that a return to Ambala in June was welcome, as the Ameer had soon repented of having begun hostilities and all chance of more active service was over. *left Kohat 22 June*

Back at Ambala the battalion was soon sent up to the Hills, head-quarters and B and C Companies to Solon, A and D to Dagshai, but in September it moved down to Bombay to embark. Leaving Bombay on October 15th, by November 8th the battalion was back at Southampton. The thirty men whom it had lost in action had mostly fallen in the ranks of the 1/4th in Mesopotamia, where 16 of the 1/5th had had the misfortune to be taken by the Turk ; that in five years it should have only lost 30 men by disease was a great tribute to good ' interior economy ', its men's temperate habits and the carefulness of the medical authorities. *＊ 3rd Afghan War*

The 1/6th were home well before the 1/4th or 5th. Immediately after the armistice with Turkey escorting prisoners downstream kept them busy, but they were soon at work again on the railway, near Jift, and then on November 24th returned to the Jibin Wadi near Tikrit. A draft of 60 men was sent off to Salonica, but the battalion was still over 800 strong.[1] January brought a move downstream to Alajik, where dismantling the Samara defences and taking up a pipe line and other salvage work provided ample occupation. Demobilization started in earnest in February, 320 men leaving on the 7th, and when reduced to cadre on March 13th the battalion barely mustered 400 other ranks. Five officers and 160 men were then detailed to join the 1/4th Hampshire, the remaining officers and men being sent to the base for demobilization. The cadre, with Lt. Colonel Wyatt still in command, left Baghdad on March 17th, embarking at Basra for England on March 31st.

The other Hampshire battalion in Mesopotamia, the 2/7th, had also been demobilized long before the 1/4th. It had spent November 1918 and most of December up the Diala at Mansuriyeh, mainly employed on the roads, had sent

---

[1] Including roughly 150 ' on command '.

a draft of 160 men off to Salonica at the end of November and had moved back to the Tigris line of communications just before the New Year, to be mainly employed in supervising Turkish prisoners of war at work on ' bunds ' along the river bank. A return showing the men's civil occupation and consequent claims to early demobilization gave 90 each as employed in agriculture and building, with 30 carters and carmen but only four fishermen and one miner. This indicated the approach of demobilization, which started in earnest in February and was soon completed.[1]

Like the 1/5th, the 1/7th had in the end ' smelt powder '. Hostilities on a small scale had been going on at Aden ever since Turkey's entry into the war. An ' unfortunate incident ' in the summer of 1915, mainly caused by the employment of unacclimatised troops in great heat, had created a nasty situation, but after the arrival of reinforcements the Turks had been pushed back and the water supply secured. Since then an Aden Field Force, a weak brigade, had sallied out several times for a minor offensive ; mainly to keep the Turks from renewing their attacks and thereby to ensure the security of Aden, though neither the troops nor the transport required for the expulsion of the Turks from the Aden Protectorate could be spared. Meanwhile the garrison was quite hard worked ; it was none too large for its duties and, as the 1st Hampshire had found in 1903, the climate was trying, the British infantry unit in the garrison usually being relieved after a year of the amenities of Aden. When therefore the 1/7th Hampshire moved to Aden in January 1918 to relieve the 6th East Surrey, they were not coming to a bed of roses.

The 1/7th had been warned for service at Aden before the end of 1917 and they actually left Ambala for Karachi on January 1st 1918, taking out 20 officers [2] and some 700 men and leaving another 250 under Major Keene as a depot at Ambala. Lt. Colonel Roberts-Thomson, who was in command, had under him six officers who had sailed with the 1/7th to India. A return showed that, besides the original 800, 680 men had joined since the battalion reached India, but meanwhile over 200 had gone as drafts to Mesopotamia, another 130 had transferred to the Machine-gun Corps, the Supply and Transport and the Signal Service and 40 to a Garrison Battalion, while 30 had obtained commissions. Discharges, invalidings and a few deaths accounted for nearly another 100.

Reaching Aden on January 9th the battalion at once took over the outpost position at Sheikh Othman, ten miles out and covering the main water supply. Here it remained till the end of March, when it was relieved, half the battalion now taking over the duties at Steamer Point and head-quarters going to the Crater. Earlier in the month the 1/7th had twice taken part in demonstrations, intended to draw the Turks, make them disclose their dispositions and inflict casualties on them. Neither action resulted in any serious fighting, though in the first the Lewis guns had to cover our retirement and the second gave B

[1] The last monthly diary is for February 1919.
[2] Two more rejoined at Aden.

Company and the scouts a little shooting. Still in the thick scrub, in which connection and direction were not easy to keep, the work was difficult, especially the withdrawals, the Turks were fairly quick to follow them up and were skilful skirmishers, quite prompt at taking advantage of any blunder or accident. However, all went quite well and the authorities expressed themselves as fully satisfied with the way the work had been carried out.

Little happened during the summer months, beyond occasional alarms of a Turkish attack, when reinforcements were railed up to Sheikh Othman, while a draft of 90 men from India more than filled up any gaps made by the climate. In September the battalion took over the outpost line again and was in reserve on October 1st, during a demonstration near Robat ; it was again ' out ' on October 21st for another reconnaissance toward Darb, when the Lewis guns and scouts got some targets.

After hostilities with Turkey were over, the 1/7th lost several men from influenza, the epidemic having reached Aden. Guarding prisoners of war and escorting them to Suez were now among the duties, but early in 1919 the troops were withdrawn from the outposts and concentrated in Aden. Two regimental badges cut on Inscription Hill by the 1st Battalion in 1903 were now discovered and cleaned up. So many men went home to be demobilized that by July the battalion, now down to 500 all told, had only just enough men available for the station and regimental duties : about 120 of these were 1914 men who had gone out with the 1/7th and, though eligible for demobilization, wanted to see things out and return with their battalion. Of the 1914 officers four were still present, Lt. Colonel Jenkins, Captain of A Company in 1914, being in command, as Colonel Roberts-Thomson had gone home in April.

The 1/8th, at Beirut on November 11th, were not left there long, their Division having been selected for duty in Egypt. Embarking on December 2nd, they disembarked at Kantara two days later and, after spending some weeks near Cairo, were transferred to Khartoum in March, travelling by Suez and Port Soudan. Shortly before this seven officers and 350 men of the 2nd Dorset had been turned over to them, only about 250 of the 8th being available for the Soudan and all those eligible for demobilization being left at Cairo. Colonel Marsh now assumed duty as O.C. British troops at Khartoum, where the battalion remained throughout the year. Detachments were found for duty at different out-stations, the Atbara, Assouan, Luxor and Wadi Halfa, while several drafts, mostly from units being demobilized, brought the battalion's numbers up to 750 by the end of August. Life at Khartoum was fairly peaceful ; that the temperature usually averaged well over 100°, it touched 116° in May and the minimum in the summer months was 80°, did not prevent the men from playing football vigorously. In October substantial drafts joined from the 12th Hampshire and the Royal Berkshire, which allowed of the demobilization of all who had enlisted before July 1st 1916, mainly ' Derby ' men, and on December 14th a company of the 2nd King's arrived [1] to relieve the 8th Hampshire. By

[1] A Regular battalion, returning from India.

the New Year handing over was virtually complete and the battalion was preparing to quit Khartoum, though some time yet was to elapse before its final reduction to a cadre, which eventually reached England in March.

The 9th Battalion's final adventures were among the most remarkable episodes of the war. The battalion, which had actually begun to mobilize for service on the Frontier, only to be disappointed and have its orders cancelled, was at Ambala in October 1918, with two companies at Kasauli, when it was again ordered to mobilize, this time for service with a force, largely Canadian, which was being sent to assist the anti-Bolshevik elements in Siberia. Unluckily the battalion had just been attacked by the influenza epidemic, and, though on October 29th 33 officers and 990 men embarked at Bombay for Vladivostock, the ravages of the epidemic made the journey a very trying experience, as the numerous sufferers completely swamped the very limited hospital accommodation. Several men died, others had to be left in hospital at Colombo, Singapore and Hong Kong, which last place was reached on November 16th. Here Colonel Johnson tried to have the battalion landed to give the sick a chance to recover and to get the men fit by some marching and physical drill, but his representations were over-ruled and the battalion was sent on at once to Vladivostock, already in the grip of winter.

Reaching Vladivostock on November 25th, the 1/9th landed next day and were quartered in a cavalry barracks, where they were issued with Arctic clothing supplied by the Canadian authorities, including knee boots, mocassins and wool-lined overcoats, before starting on December 18th on the 4,000 miles train journey across Siberia, which was to bring the battalion to Omsk, the headquarters of Admiral Koltchak, the anti-Bolshevik leader. It travelled in trucks which contained about 20 men each and were imperfectly warmed by stoves, two men having to remain on duty all night to keep the fire alight. The lighting, by candles, was also miserable, but luckily the rations were ample, which, with the temperature down to 20° below zero,[1] was fortunate. Omsk was eventually reached on January 7th, much to the relief of Colonel Ward, the C.O. of the 25th Middlesex, already there, who welcomed this reinforcement warmly.[2] Here the 9th were to remain until May, when they were sent on again to Ekaterinburg at the foot of the Urals. What purpose their presence here was serving it was hard to say : they made a great impression on the Russians by their fitness, it was extraordinary how little sickness there was despite the intense cold of the winter months, by their good conduct and cheerful bearing, but a tiny handful of troops could do nothing to influence the always obscure and rapidly changing political situation. The anti-Bolshevik elements soon proved incapable of putting up any serious resistance, and in August the 9th had to quit Ekaterinburg and gradually to retrace their steps across Siberia to Vladivostock, which they left for Vancouver on November 1st. From there, after completing their circuit of the world, they got back to Southampton on

[1] Later it went down to 70°.
[2] Cf *With the Die-hards in Siberia*.

December 5th, to be most warmly received. Major Robson, a Captain on mobilization, brought the battalion home.[1]

The 10th and 12th Battalions had seen more than enough of Macedonia before hostilities ended, but for neither of these was an early departure possible. An Army of Occupation had to be found for Constantinople and for the Caucasus, and as Regular units were first for home, to be reformed for peace duties, Service battalions were naturally retained in the Eastern theatres till reconstituted Regulars could relieve them.

The 10th had returned to Salonica as a mere skeleton, and though discharges from hospital did a little to replenish their ranks, they were still very weak, only 250 other ranks present and 100 ' on command ', when they left for Constantinople in March. On arriving there, on March 19th, they joined the 85th Brigade of the Twenty-Eighth Division, now in occupation of Constantinople and the Dardanelles. Little worth recording had happened in their last four months at Salonica, routine duties, a little education, a little training and some recreation, while several officers and men got leave to England and a few were demobilized, Colonel Taylor leaving in February and being replaced by Major Eley (Suffolk).

' Duties ' at Constantinople were fairly heavy, especially as most battalions were weak, the 10th Hampshire only having 230 men present on April 1st. With the terms of the peace treaties still unsettled, disturbances were always possible,[2] and much patrolling was necessary, while large inlying picquets had to be always in readiness. Detachments were occasionally sent out into the country round to maintain order, discourage brigandage, search for concealed fire-arms and military stores and show the inhabitants that the Allies were going to keep order. Demobilization went on steadily, the battalion's numbers being to some extent kept up by the absorption of the remnants of the 10th Devons (September) and the 8th D.C.L.I. (October). Colonel Eley left to rejoin his own regiment in September, Lt. Colonel Plowden of the K.S.L.I. replacing him in command of what was now ' Hampshire ' mainly in name and retaining command until the formal disbanding on December 31st.

The 12th Hampshire had been disbanded some months sooner. November 11th had found them at Rustchuk, the first of their Division to reach the Danube. On the 15th three officers and 100 other ranks represented the British forces at the formal entry into Roumania of General Berthelot, who was commanding the Allied Army of the Danube, and the battalion was to have taken part in the official re-occupation of Bucharest but was sent instead to Cerna Voda in the Dobrudja to take over ' occupation ' duties there and in the surrounding country. After three weeks there the 12th moved again to Silistria (December 15th), to carry on with the same duties and help in the establishment of the Roumanian authorities in the liberated territory. Here

---

[1] Lt. Colonel Johnson and several other officers were ' mentioned ' for good services in Siberia.
[2] More serious troubles did occur later, but not in 1919.

they remained till early in April, fairly busy with a variety of duties but without special incidents. Good quarters assisted the battalion to endure some bitter cold with much snow tolerably well, but demobilization and the departure of leave parties had brought other ranks down to 150, when the 12th were detailed in March 1919 to move to Egypt. Leaving Silistria on April 7th they reached Varna three days later, Major Jones being in command as Colonel McNaught was on leave. After ten days in camp there, they went on to Alexandria, arriving on April 26th and being accommodated in a camp five miles outside the town. Here they spent some uneventful months, drafts, including 23 from the 3rd Hampshire, gradually increased the strength, till orders arrived for the demobilization of all men over 37 together with all those who had enlisted in 1914, after which numbers fell rapidly and by September 19th the battalion had ceased to exist.

The 10th and even more the 12th Hampshire may be reckoned unlucky in having spent most of their war on the Salonica ' back-water ', where chances of distinction were limited, while the unhealthiness of the climate, the distance from England and the lack of any facilities for recreation made service unpleasant and monotonous. The why and wherefore of the Allied operations in Macedonia did not perhaps trouble regimental officers and men much : they were there and what there was to be done they did, but opportunities were few and far between, and as a theatre of war Macedonia had nothing to to recommend it. The 10th had had hard fighting and taken hard knocks at Gallipoli, but there the object of the operations was clear and understandable : to be thrown in against an almost impregnable position, as the 12th were in their one real ' battle ', was a cruel fate. It says much for both the 10th and 12th that in the adverse conditions of Salonica they should have borne themselves so well and earned such favourable reports.

Between 1914 and 1918 the various battalions of the Hampshire Regiment added ninety battle honours to those already on the regiment's Colours. Of these fifty-six were earned on the Western front, ten in Egypt and Palestine, eight at Gallipoli, eight in Mesopotamia and Persia, four at Salonica, with ' Aden ', ' Archangel ', ' Italy ' and ' Siberia ' to complete the tale. Many of those for France and Flanders like ' Somme, 1916 ' or ' Ypres, 1917 ' were won by several battalions, if ' Retreat from Mons ' and ' Ypres, 1915 ' are to be identified with the 1st Battalion, ' Landing at Helles ', ' Krithia ' and ' Cambrai ', with the 2nd, ' Flers-Courcelette ' with the 15th and ' Kut el Amara ' with the 1/4th.

To show so many honours on the Colours was clearly out of the question, and the solution arrived at, of obtaining the King's approval for putting ten specially selected honours on the King's Colour, was perhaps the least unsatisfactory method of meeting the difficulty. The choice was not easy : some honours which meant much to individual battalions represented achievements of less general importance than others more widely shared. The ten finally adopted by the Hampshire Regiment include one at least which recalls every battalion which saw heavy fighting, the two Regular battalions, all the five Service battalions which went overseas and the 1/4th, 2/4th, 2/5th and 1/8th Territorial battalions. ' Retreat from Mons ', ' Ypres 1915, 1917, 1918 ', ' Somme 1916, 1918 ', ' Arras 1917, 1918 ' and ' Cambrai 1917, 1918 ' between them cover all the main fighting on the Western Front, if it may be regretted that ' Armentieres ' could not have been included to cover the 1st Battalion's stubborn defence at ' Plugstreet ' or ' Ourcq-Tardenois ' for the 2/4th's fine debut in France. ' Landing at Helles ' could not have been omitted and ' Suvla ', ' Doiran 1917–1918 ', ' Gaza ' and ' Kut el Amara 1916–1917 ' make the list fully representative of a magnificent record of achievements which, however inadequately recorded in these pages, enhance appreciably an already high reputation.

HONOURS AND AWARDS

V.C.

2/Lt. D. G. W. Hewett	Ypres	31. 7. 1917
2/Lt. G. R. D. Moor	Gallipoli	4. 6. 1915
2/Lt. M. S. S. Moore	Ypres	26. 9. 1917

K.C.B.

General Sir R. C. B. Haking

K.C.M.G.

Lt. General R. C. B. Haking

C.B.

B. General A. T. Beckwith   B. General G. H. Nicholson

(civil)

Captain H. L. Wheeler

C.M.G.

B. General A. T. Beckwith	B. General G. H. Nicholson
Lt. Colonel C. N. French	Lt. Colonel H. W. Tompson
Colonel S. C. F. Jackson	Major General W. de L. Williams

C.B.E.

Colonel Sir T. S. Cave   Lt. Colonel R. A. Johnson

Lt. Colonel L. C. Morley

O.B.E.

Captain I. P. F. Campbell	Captain L. N. Montefiore
Captain W. G. L. Cheriton	Major J. O'Brien
Lt. Colonel J. E. Dixon-Spain	Captain Sir W. L. Parker
Major C. L. Ellery	Colonel C. C. P. Powney
Major P. Hackett	Captain W. D. Price
Major C. J. Hazard	Lt. Colonel A. C. Richards
Captain H. M. Howgreave-Graham	Major J. C. F. Richards
Captain P. G. McMaster	Major A. Robson

Captain C. M. H. Venour

M.B.E.

Major C. N. L. Blackmore	Captain W. Englefield
Lt. J. Bradford	Lt. H. H. M. Fawcitt
Lt. H. Browning	Captain E. C. Reeves
Captain H. A. B. Bruno	Major F. Smith

Captain S. D. M. Wilson

---

¹ This list has been mainly compiled from the *Regimental Journal* and checked by the War Diaries and *London Gazette*. The rank given is that at the time of the award, whether substantive or temporary. Attached officers are not included.

D.S.O.

Lt. Colonel R. S. Allen
Captain J. D. M. Beckett
Lt. Colonel A. T. Beckwith
Lt. Colonel B. E. Bell
Major G. M. Bell
Lt. Colonel W. D. Bewsher
Captain W. S. Cave
Major W. S. Cowland
Lt. Colonel B. E. Crockett
Major W. F. Crosson
Lt. Colonel H. C. Dolphin
Captain R. S. Durnford
Lt. Colonel F. W. Earle
Captain A. Foster
Lt. Colonel W. C. Garsia
Lt. Colonel H. H. Gribbon
Major B. B. von B. im Thurn.
Lt. Colonel K. A. Johnston

Major R. H. Jones
Lt. Colonel J. D. Mackay
Lt. Colonel J. F. H. Marsh
Lt. Colonel W. H. Middleton
Lt. Colonel G. Molyneux
Lt. Colonel C. Murdoch
Lt. Colonel the Hon. L. Palk
Major B. E. T. Parsons
Lt. Colonel G. F. Perkins
Captain T. E. Rodocanachi
Major O. A. Scott
Lt. J. W. Shorland
Lt. Colonel T. C. Spring
Major W. B. Stillwell
2/Lt. T. C. M. Taberer
Lt. Colonel H. C. Westmorland (and bar)
Captain A. M. Wilkinson (and bar)
Major H. J. de C. Wymer

M.C.

2/Lt. C. B. M. Abbott
Captain L. G. J Adams
Lt. G. H. J. Aldworth
Captain E. M. Allen
Captain G. D. Amery
2/Lt. G. D. Andrews
Captain L. Ashling
and Qr. Mr. S. H. Askew
Lt. H. E. Avins
Captain C. R. Barber
2/Lt. A. H. Barker
Lt. G. H. Barker
2/Lt. E. F. P. Bartlett
Lt. H. J. Beatty
Lt. B. P. G. Beanlands
Lt. J. H. Bell
Captain F. G. J. Berkeley
2/Lt. C. L. P. Biggar
Captain B. O. Bircham
2/Lt. P. M. N. Boustead
2/Lt. A. A. Bradley
Captain H. M. E. Bradshaw
Lt. C. W. Brannon
2/Lt. A. E. Brown
2/Lt. E. J. S. L. Brooke
2/Lt. H. Bryant
2/Lt. J. G. Bucknill
Captain C. P. Bulley
Captain F. H. Burnett
Captain G. P. Burrell
2/Lt. D. B. Cancellor
Captain R. L. Chidlaw-Roberts
Captain J. Clement

2/Lt. S. C. Coleman
2/Lt. H. J. Collins
Captain S. H. Collins
2/Lt. W. H. Collins
2/Lt. W. M. Cooper
Captain P. A. Cornish
Captain H. C. B. Cottam
2/Lt. L. J. Cotten
Captain P. B. Cuddon (and two bars)
2/Lt. F. H. J. Damp
Captain A. M. Dawson
Captain D. Day
2/Lt. R. R. Dear
Lt. G. S. V. de Gaury
2/Lt. V. H. Donnithorne
2/Lt. G. W. Dore
Lt. H. Durant
Lt. G. E. Edwards
Lt. B. Evans
2/Lt. A. Ewens
2/Lt. P. G. Fall
Lt. C. D. Fawkes
Lt. R. P. Fenn
2/Lt. L. E. P. Fisher
Captain H. Flint
2/Lt. A. G. Forbes
Lt. A. D. Foster
Captain C. H. Fowle (and bar)
Captain J. P. Fowler-Esson
Lt. G. W. Fox
Captain R. H. Freeman
Lt. A. O. Gammon
Captain W. C. Garsia

Lt. I. H. German
2/Lt. W. M. Gibbons
2/Lt. E. A. Girling
Captain F. B. Goldsmith (and bar)
2/Lt. C. J. H. Goodford
Lt. D. T. Gorman
Lt. R. H. Gotelee
Lt. K. Graham
2/Lt. H. W. Green
Captain J. R. Green
2/Lt. R. A. Green
R.S.M. F. Greenwood
Captain C. Grellier
2/Lt. J. L. Griffin
Lt. W. M. Gullick
2/Lt. F. J. Guy
2/Lt. A. R. Hall
Lt. J. A. de C. Hamilton
Captain J. H. Harris
2/Lt. H. G. Harding
Lt. F. H. Harrod
Captain C. J. Hazard
Lt. T. H. Hetherington
Lt. E. J. Hicks
Lt. A. C. Hillyer
2/Lt. C. H. Hirst
Lt. D. G. Hook
2/Lt. A. C. Howard
Captain G. A. Howson
Major P. H. Hudson
2/Lt. H. G. Hullum
Captain H. N. Hume
Lt. H. J. G. Icke
Captain B. B. von B. Im Thurn
Lt. R. M. Jerram
Captain R. H. Jones
Lt. A. E. Kimm
Lt. D. C. Knott
2/Lt. L. H. Lainé
Lt. L. W. Lamb (and bar)
2/Lt. H. F. Lambert
Lt. C. La Trobe
Lt. T. S. Leach
Captain W. H. Ledgard
Captain P. A. Ledward
Lt. J. L. Leith (and bar)
Captain V. G. Lewis
Captain P. E. Leybourne (and bar)
2/Lt. H. R. Lockyer
Captain R. P. Lord (and bar)
Lt. J. Love
Lt. E. R. Maddox
2/Lt. F. R. Mann
Major H. Marshall

Captain H. W. M. May (and two bars)
Lt. M. McConnochie
Lt. J. W. Milne
2/Lt. W. A. Mitchell
Captain H. T. Molyneux
Lt. G. C. D. Money
Captain G. R. D. Moor V.C. (and bar) { M.C. }
2/Lt. H. J. Morgan
2/Lt. E. M. Neil
Captain F. Newcomb
Captain C. C. Newman
Captain H. C. C. Newnham
Captain G. Nicholson
Captain C. C. Oxborrow (and bar)
2/Lt. J. F. Pain
R.S.M. J. Palmer
Lt. J. H. Perry
Captain C. S. Pittis
Lt. G. J. Potter (and bar)
Lt. H. G. Powers
2/Lt. E. C. Rayner
2/Lt. T. E. B. Reid
2/Lt. T. E. Rodocanachi
2/Lt. H. C. Saunders
Lt. and Qr.Mr. W. J. Saunders
Captain R. J. Scott
2/Lt. J. A. H. Scutt
Lt. S. R. Sebastian
2/Lt. G. O. H. Sergeannt
2/Lt. F. R. Shadbolt
2/Lt. R. D. Shaw
2/Lt. P. E. Shields
2/Lt. G. R. Singleton-Gates
2/Lt. W. S. Singleton-Gates
2/Lt. A. G. Smith
C.S.M. J. E. Smith
2/Lt. M. T. Smith
Captain C. C. Smythe
Lt. J. L. Spencer (and bar)
2/Lt. J. A. Stannard
Lt. H. F. S. Stokes
Lt. A. W. Street
Captain W. V. Strugnell (and bar)
Captain P. L. Sulman
Captain F. Sutcliffe
Captain T. P. Thyne
Captain J. E. Tilley
Lt. E. M. Trevett
2/Lt. T. Turner
Lt. R. E. R. Upton
Lt. A. L. W. Vicars-Miles (and bar)
Captain E. W. N. Wade
Lt. B. A. Wallis-Wilson (and bar)
2/Lt. W. J. West

2/Lt. F. J. Whaley
Lt. G. P. Wheeler (and bar)
2/Lt. H. F. Wheeler
Captain A. H. White
Captain S. H. Wigmore (and bar)
2/Lt. H. B. Willis

2/Lt. H. L. Willsher
2/Lt. L. S. Winn
Lt. & Qr.Mr. W. Wood
Lt. W. R. Wood (and bar)
Captain J. W. F. Wyld
Lt. W. G. Young

D.C.M.[1]

240590 Aldridge, Corporal W.
7762 Alexander, L/Corporal A. V.
8777 Alexander, L/Corporal C. ʜ ʜ ᴀɴᴅ ʙᴀʀ
9008 Atkey, Sergeant W.
10161 Ayling, Private F.

27722 Baddams, Private E.
19676 Bailhache, Private J. H.
202740 Baldwin, Corporal F.
6950 Baldwin, C.S.M. H. T.
19057 Barton, Sergeant E. G.
18163 Bastable, Private G.
12928 Benny, Sergeant G. A.
14740 Biddlecombe, Private F.
2462 Blake, Corporal A. H.
5121 Blake, C.S.M. J. A.
14201 Bone, L/Corporal E.
7909 Bone, Corporal F. W.
10205 Bowers, Sergeant S.
202649 Braby, Private F. E.
5802 Brine, Sergeant R.
3/4579 Brown, C.S.M. E.
2772 Buddams, Private E.
5360 Budden, Sergeant W. M.
26991 Burch, C.S.M. E.

15708 Chambers, L/Corporal W.
330009 Clark, Sergeant B.
241021 Cole, Private H.
18024 Collis, C.S.M. F.C.
202053 Combellach, Sergeant R.J.
20908 Copping, L/Corporal B. A.
29528 Cotton, Private J. W.
201687 Courtney, Private R. F.
240009 Cousens C.S.M. W. H.
202992 Craven, Private W.
27891 Crook, Private J.
11775 Cross, Sergeant E.

28104 Dalton, Corporal R. S.
14304 Dennett, Corporal R.
201105 Dennett C.S.M. H.
9603 Dollery, Sergeant B. E.
16457 Duggins, Private A.

7633 Eldridge, Drummer H. A.
2825 Elkins, Private H. W.
8013 Empringham, Sergeant H. C.

26960 Falconer, Sergeant G.
2139 Feary, Corporal H. D.
8244, 8644 Finch, Sergeant W. ᴅᴄᴍ. ᴍᴍ
3892 Fisher, Sergeant F.
28490 Fooks, C.S.M. F.
380505 Fremantle, Sergeant J. E. ?

6228 Gannon, Sergeant H. G.
203403 Gee, Corporal F. C.
9896 Gilkes, Corporal F. W.
240129 Graham, C.S.M. M.
42304 Greedy, C.S.M. H.

1888 Halsey, Sergeant W.
200031 Hamilton, Sergeant T. H.
241459 Hammond, Private I.
8650 Hampton, Private G.
9890 Hanna, Sergeant H.
7335 Harden, Private J.
6804 Harris, Private A.
5924 Hayden, Sergeant W. J. H.
18722 Heath, L/Corporal P.
200798 Hester, Private A.
2665 Hill, Private J.
4096 Holdway, R.S.M. T.
20893 Hubbert, R.S.M. A. R.

12411 Ivens, Private C. J.

12856 Jarvis, Sergeant C. E.

200248 Kemp, C.Q.M.S. P.

26741 Lane, Sergeant T.
202370 Langrish, L/Corporal W.
8605 Leamon, Sergeant J. W.
5955 Lewis, Private E.J.
8017 Ley, Sergeant E. G.
7222 Lund, C.S.M. G. W.

[1] In several cases the regimental number and initials have not been recorded in the battalion's diary or in the Journal, which seems to have copied the lists in the *London Gazette*.

208051 Macgregor, Private J. A.
330380 Matthews, Sergeant M.
201870 Mells, Sergeant F.
11484 Mersh, R.Q.M.S. F. J.
5576 Milne, C.S.M. J. W. (and bar)
230619 Mowbray, Private W. G.
36448 Munday, Sergeant W.
330232 Newnham, Private A.
9478 Nippard, Private A. F.
5200 Norris, C.S.M. J. (and bar)
12646 Norton, Sergeant G. H.
8481 Nunn, C.S.M. J.
10890 Odell, Sergeant F.
8949 Oram, Sergeant F.
5395 Palmer R.S.M. J. E.
201316 Parfitt, Private G. C.
330031 Parrack, Sergeant W. H.
503838 Pearson, Sergeant J. W.
17492 Pidgley, Private N.
40473 Pillar, L/Corporal C. A.
2942 Player, Private N. W.
11017 Price, Sergeant J. E.
305223 Puttock, Sergeant E. T.
40224 Pyne, C.S.M. W.

5756 Ralfs, C.S.M. E. S.
334 Read, Sergeant V.
241193 Rees, Sergeant C. F.
42449 Richardson, Sergeant C. H.
14564 Riding, Corporal A.
314319 Ross, Sergeant W.
8000 Rycroft, Sergeant E.

201254 Samways, Sergeant C.
200305 Shadwell, Sergeant W. C.
8316 Sharpe, Sergeant W. J.
6228 Shearing, Col. Sergeant M.
11107 Shepperd, Sergeant G.
2219 Sinsbury, Sergeant E.
Smith, L/Corporal F. J.
17389 Smith, C.S.M. T. E.
15628 Snelling, Corporal R.
1472 Snow, L/Corporal R.
18801 Steers, Corporal W.
7806 Stone, Sergeant F. L.
38473 Stone, Private F. T.
4505 Sturges, C.S.M. T.
17215 Taylor, Corporal G.
231766 Thomas, Private R. J.
9613 Thomas, Sergeant W.
8903 Thompson, Sergeant H,
7826 Thorne, Private W.
200343 Tilson, C.S.M. J. H.
200037 Tompson Sergeant W.
3/4029 Treagus, C.S.M. B.
202036 Trethewy, Sergeant W. J.
5086 Trump, C.S.M. F.

2887 Verrall, Private E. G.

8048 Warren, Sergeant G. (and bar)
9419 Weaver, Corporal W. H.
8504 Wheeler, C.Q.M.S. W. L.
3/ Wilkins, Private J. S.
202607 Williams, Sergeant A.
6651 Williams, C.S.M. F. C.
2030 Woolridge, Private H. G.

M.M.[1]

8343 Abbott, C.S.M. W. J.
20023 Adams, L/Corporal A.
204693 Adams, B. A.
38865 Adams, F.
27524 Adams, Sergeant F. C.
7926 Adams, J.
8895 Adams, R. C.
12251 Adaway, A.
242811 Adlam, H.
120340 Adnams, L/Sergeant W.
28259 Aldridge, M.
8777 Alexander, L/Corporal C. J. (and bar)
330766 Allen, Sergeant C.
201562 Allen, L/Corporal F. J.
30039 Amor, C.

22425 Anderson, L/Corporal G.
8816 Andrews, D.
26989 Angell, J. W.
205037 Anger, Corporal C. A.
33550 Anstey, S.
9081 Argyle, L/Corporal F. (and bar)
Arnold, E. V.
20236 Ash, Sergeant G. W. (and bar)
9008 Atkey, C.S.M. W.
205041 Austin, J.
12718 Avis, W.

11192 Baker, F. A.
19937 Baldry, Sergeant A. W. (and bar)
Bampton, D. G.
201652 Banning, C. J.

[1] Where no rank is given the recipient was a private.

202524	Barfoot S. A.	356847	Broadley, Corporal W.
19133	Barker, Sergeant R. E.	40896	Brogden, Corporal E. G.
243245	Barker	12171	Brookling S.
10823	Barnes, A.	21245	Brown, L/Corporal E.
26767	Barnes, L/Corporal A.	11780	Brown J. H.
31493	Barnes, C. W. J. (and bar)	31663	Brown P.
31403	Barnes	11589	Browning, L/Corporal F.
201152	Barney, C.Q.M.S. A. E.	49925	Browning W. F.
9047	Barrow F. J.	205440	Buckett W.
21667	Bartin, G.	19819	Buckingham, Sergeant G.
16866	Barton J. T.	18261	Bucknall L/Corporal E.
19057	Barton Sergeant R. C. (and bar)	202836	Budden F. C.
18163	Bastable, Corporal G.	33361	Buist A.
8311	Bath W.		Bull C.
29957	Battam H.		Bullen, Sergeant
14873	Batten A. H.	204703	Bunker S. G.
6549	Batten, Sergeant J.	204970	Burden H. G.
19407	Beale, L/Sergeant E. R.	45581	Burden
23395	Bealing, L. F.	202096	Burgess C.
28245	Beattie A.	27518	Burridge, L/Corporal H. S. P.
14858	Beck, Corporal E.		Burrow, Corporal F.
21126	Beech, C.	16517	Burton, Sergeant G.
8539	Belbin, Sergeant H.	11593	Bush S. H.
29537	Bellows, Corporal S.	18261	Bushnell, L/Corporal E.
26969	Bennett, Corporal G.		
201752	Bennett V.	14732	Cake H. F.
31551	Bessant, T.	38593	Campbell F.
8790	Bettridge, Sergeant G.	202475	Carter, G. H.
17922	Bicknell E.	202475	Cawte G. H. (and bar)
8566	Bigwood, Sergeant W. C.	202746	Chapman D.
17880	Binstead L/Corporal	24998	Chandler B. F. T.
24829	Birt, L/Corporal A. W.	5042	Charlton T. (and bar)
19074	Bishop, Sergeant F.	4176	Cheek E. C.
12189	Bithell, Sergeant J.	7096	Cherrett, Sergeant H. C.
17779	Bloxham A.	14614	Cherrett J. D.
31737	Blunn J.	28558	Chetland, L/Corporal H.
16063	Board, L/Corporal F.	26956	Chignell, L/Corporal H.
144	Bogie, C.Q.M.S. A. W.	12334	Childs, L/Corporal F. R.
27557	Bolton, Sergeant W. J.	201159	Churcher, C.S.M. H. T.
8895	Bone A.	16960	Clark G.
200613	Bone, Sergeant W.	12348	Clark, Sergeant H. G.
	Bonner T.		Clarke C.
22733	Bowers G.	202461	Clarke F. W.
8173	Bowman, Sergeant S.	16968	Clarke G.
29671	Bowring H.	15198	Cleeve W. G.
17301	Boyes A. J.	28282	Coates J. T.
27928	Box J.		Cole F.
15877	Box, Sergeant W.	241021	Cole H. A.
201329	Brandon S. V.	26472	Coleman P. W.
29542	Bray E.	389176	Coles A.
22505	Brazier H.	26535	Collins H. E.
32138	Bree, C.S.M. M. W.	42936	Collins, J. C.
3822	Brine, Sergeant R.	27496	Collins, L/Corporal J. N.
311564	Britten, Sergeant H. G.	26465	Collins T.

28454 Collins T. W.
23238 Collinson W. H.
18024 Collis, Sergeant F. (and bar)
3/4120 Cook, L/Corporal J. H. (and bar)
204591 Cooke D.
10836 Coombes L/Corporal P. G.
16399 Coombs W.
Cooper C. E.
11200 Cooper E. H.
12114 Cooper, Corporal T.
Coote, Sergeant A. E.
14430 Copper, Sergeant H. V.
11044 Cotton A. B.
10554 Cox, Sergeant A. C.
11601 Craker G.
9089 Crompton P.
15733 Crosdee H.
11775 Cross, Sergeant E. (and bar)
Crosthwaite D.
205017 Croucher E.
4560 Curran S. A.
16319 Curtis, Corporal W. B.

12128 Dale, Sergeant R. W.
28104 Dalton, Corporal E.
44119 Davie J.
26885, Davies, G.
18448 Davis, E. A.
21190 Day T.
26501 Deane, L/Corporal E. D.
29968 de Gruchy, W. P.
26607 Denny, L/Corporal W. W.
31795 Dew B.
201090 Diggance M.
200534 Digweed, Corporal J. R.
Dixon, Sergeant N.
9603 Dollery, Corporal B. E.
28285 Donson A.
44199 Dowie J.
✓ 25554 Dowland H.
12036 Down, A. E.
331275 Drake, W. G.
29970 Druin, Corporal F. T. (and bar)
20394 Dugan, C.
19102 Dugan, Sergeant G. M. P.
11053 Dumper, Sergeant H.
14613 Dunaway, Sergeant W.
7862 Duvan, Corporal F.

06836 Eady, C
19924 Eady, C. B.
356223 Earley, L/Corporal F. C.
202427 Earley, J. A.
330254 Early, Sergeant W. J.

31875 Eastwood, H. F.
Eaves, G. A.
11487 Edwards, Sergeant A.
204937 Edwards, Sergeant H.
23158 Edwards, Sergeant H. H.
27872 Edwards, W.
6209 Eeles R.
25102 Elliot, A.
200757 Ellis, J.
40900 Ellis, R.
Erith, Corporal H. H.
12175 Essex, Sergeant H. A.
7805 Everiss F.
38603 Everitt, J.

11617 Falder, L/Corporal C. E. (and bar)
27517 Farr, Corporal A. W.
28061 Farr, Corporal G. H. K.
26971 Faulkner, Corporal F. S. (and bar)
26451 Fay, E.
6301 Fever, Sergeant A. U.
27315 Felkit, Corporal C.
15351 Ferry, P. W. H.
29772 Fielder, L/Corporal J. E. (and bar)
17773 Fiford, L/Corporal C.
18669 Fisher, T.
16255 Flack, W. R.
242499 Flook, H.
11260 Foot, C. G.
45617 Ford, L/Corporal R. W.
4228 Ford, L/Corporal V. R.
14809 Forrester, F.
16015 Foster, E. W.
21934 Fowler, L/Corporal T.
14031 Fox, L/Corporal A.
27700 Frampton, E.
22651 Friend, Sergeant, R.
Frost, M. S.
380993 Frost, Sergeant R. J.
26452 Fry, E.
42293 Fugett, R. G.
11617 Fuller, L/Corporal S. E. (and bar)
307291 Fuller, W. G.
8244 Finch W. JCM. MM (1st MM
9857 Gardner, Sergeant A. E.
14081 Gibbon, Sergeant A. J.
22398 Gibbons, E.
15328 Gibbs, W. F. (and bar)
14915 Gibson, R. E.
203150 Gillingham, Corporal H. G.

204855 Gladwell, J. E.
58074 Glenister, F.
Goble, H. H.
205555 Goddard, A. J.
201373 Goddard, C.
65304 Goddard, L/Corporal F.
241607 Goddard, G.
54972 Godwin, H. C.
14343 Goff, H.
4587 Golding, Corporal C.
204767 Goodchild, W. G.
15662 Goodman, W. E.
10629 Gosling, A.
32634 Gosling, J.
19235 Gosney, F.
200212 Goss, J. P.
17053 Graham, L/Sergeant T.
23298 Grandly, L/Corporal E.
15133 Grant, L/Corporal J. G.
24134 Gray, L/Corporal A. F.
330461 Gray, Sergeant B. B.
16899 Gray, L/Corporal W.
26913 Green, Corporal H. A.
9055 Gregory, Corporal A. W.
280056 Gregory, Sergeant J.
33391 Gregory, W.
12920 Grey, Sergeant A. E.
26088 Groves, Sergeant W. F.
Grubb, Corporal W.
201328 Gundry, Sergeant A.
22690 Guy, Corporal E.

17667 Hack, F.
Hall, F. C.
39030 Hall, S.
12154 Hammerton, F.
28886 Hampton, Corporal R. O.
28107 Hampton, Corporal W.
202769 Hampton, W. J.
6338 Harding, F.
25755 Hardy, G
27018 Harris, C.S.M. W. D.
19706, Harrison, Sergeant H. G.
204772 Harvey, Sergeant A.
11462 Hastings, J.
31512 Hatcher, R. S.
332144 Hawes, H.
33369 Hawke, Corporal F. H.
204785 Hay, L/Corporal
5924 Hayden, C.S.M. W. J. H.
Hayley, Corporal F. A. H.
13334 Hazlewood, Sergeant.
10768 Heard, Sergeant A.
12474 Heath, L/Corporal G.

Heath, Corporal S. G.
9557 Heath, W. C.
19368 Hedger, T. J.
6957 Henbest, Corporal J.
204775 Hendry, W.
8233 Herrington, L/Sergeant A.
20488 Herriott, H. G.
27630 Hewitt, H.
11466 Higho, Corporal T. W.
Hill, Corporal E.
202848 Hillier, J.
32403 Hillman, A. J.
220336 Hixon, Corporal H.
21233 Hoath, L/Corporal A. W. (and bar)
11476 Hobart, P. J.
26463 Hobbs, L/Corporal C. W.
204787 Hodges, L/Corporal F.
205069 Hogg, J.
10866 Holdaway, Sergeant E.
19538 Holdaway, Corporal L.
55034 Holland, A.
37635 Hollis, Sergeant W. (and bar)
27359 Honeychurch, L/Corporal B.
15607 Hooper, A.
202341 Hopkinson, Corporal J. J.
17549 Hopwood, Corporal J. T.
205032 Horner, Corporal C. W.
7770 Hould, F.
242239 Hudson, E. A.
45661 Hughes, A. E.
7719 Hughes, C.S.M. C. E.
12371 Hughes, Sergeant W. J.
26782 Humphries, L/Corporal J.
33276 Hunnybell, L/Corporal L.
204161 Hunnybell, W.
21392 Hurford, Sergeant F.
4711 Hurll, Sergeant W. G.
45642 Hussey, A. E.
356107 Hyde, L/Corporal F. G.

7770 Ifould, J.

204146 Jackson, H.
27113 Jackson, J. C.
209799 Jacques, L/Corporal J. S.
Jago, L/Corporal J. C. G.
205037 James, F. C.
35662 Jameson, L/Corporal
1285 Jarvis, Sergeant C. (and bar)
11267 Jefferies, Sergeant S. S.
33373 Jerram, L/Corporal H. H.
27263 Johnson, J.
8512 Johnson, R. E.

8492	Johnson, L/Corporal W. J.	204813	Matcham, Corporal H. (and bar)
7885	Jones, A.	19111	Matthews, C.Q.M.S. W. E.
260082	Jupp, E. S.	200296	May, H.
			May, H.C.
11480	Kempton, Sergeant G.	2163	Maybourn, L/Corporal M.
24289	Kenning, Sergeant A.	204683	McClemments, L/Corporal L.
39011	Kenny, A.	28436	McIlwaine, W. J.
202440	Kent, L/Corporal R. A.		McKerrell
21832	Kenton, L/Corporal G.	200100	Meaden, Sergeant G.
202427	Kervill, A. E.	4367	Meddings, J. G.
25199	Kibby, A. E.	15303	Meggs, Corporal W. J.
28527	Kiddle, R.	356839	Merson, F. C.
	Kidman, Corporal C. W.		Middleton, L/Corporal C.
8755	Kimber, A.	14262	Mildenhall, S. J.
297182	King, H. J. ✓ 26073 . No.6Aug18	205525	Miles, J. C.
7326	King, C.S.M. W. H.	27787	Millard, Corporal J.
8747	Kneller, P.	32522	Miller, W. G.
8679	Knight, A. F.	202785	Millett, L/Corporal W.
17347	Knight, Corporal W.	10676	Mills, Corporal A. J.
171	Knott, J. T.	33230	Milne, Sergeant G. F.
		7380	Mintram, Corporal A.
20615	Lake, W. J.	356410	Mitchell, A.
15896	Lane, A.	202711	Mitchell, J.
13714	Langston, Corporal G.	✓27273	Molesworth W.
15931	Lark, Corporal H. W.	14263	Monger, W. J.
235017	Lea, W. H.	17087	Moore, L/Corporal H. W.
33126	Lewington, E.T.	313482	Moore, L/Corporal W. J.
28799	Lewy, E. P.	6755	Morey, L/Corporal W.
	Lewis, Sergeant J.	203271	Morgan, J.
68476	Light, L/Corporal A. J.	37240	Morgan, Corporal J.
54909	Linnington	06621	Morgan, L/Corporal T.
	Little, Sergeant W. H.	10178	Morris, A. W.
235016	Livesey, J.	11317	Morris, Sergeant L. G.
24943	Loader, H.	11865	Morrow, H. L.
41707	Lockett, Sergeant S.	205050	Moscrop, L/Corporal T.
20403	Lonergan, C.S.M. J. T.	11342	Moy, H. C.
797	Lovegrove, Corporal J.		Muckett, L/Corporal F. H.
34348	Lowman, A.	26761	Mumford, C.
27169	Luscombe, W.	18700	Munden, L/Corporal F.
18303	Lush, L/Corporal A.	17976	Murden, B. H.
		20089	Murrell, Corporal J. H.
16419	Macdonald, T.	19798	Myers, Corporal J.
15301	Maggs, Corporal W. C.		
17859	Mallard, Sergeant A. J.	11351	Nash, Sergeant F. J.
202875	Mannock, F.	7397	Neal, L/Corporal F. C.
16574	Manders, G. W.		Neale, H.
✓ 35660	Manson	28757	Neate, L/Corporal A.
7728	Marshall, Corporal W. C.	7971	Neile, Sergeant E.
18357	Martin, Sergeant A. T.	202792	Newington, H. G.
28215	Martin, H.	21269	Nickalls, J.
15260	Martin, Corporal H. F. (and bar)	17186	Nolan, P.
7619	Martin, Sergeant J. T.	26973	North. Sergeant C.
356089	Mason, J.	23342	Nunan, L/Corporal A.
204807	Mason, W. G.	8481	Nunn, C.S.M. J.

297 N . . Sgt A E

5765 Noon . C WO2

8325	Oakley, G.
33429	Oakley, R.
	Oborne, Sergeant G.
19142	O'Brien, Sergeant J.
11319	O'Hea, M. O.
8265	Oliver, Sergeant A. J.
27119	Oram, L/Corporal W. M.
7960	Osbourne, T.
	Over, W. T. E.
18730	Paffet, L/Corporal A. E,
7938	Paffett, Sergeant W. H.
11216	Page, Sergeant C.
	Page, J. T.
8130	Paice, Sergeant, J. J.
	Paige, S. J.
11686	Painting, Corporal A.
32692	Palmer, A. J.
331437	Palmer, L/Sergeant T.
202642	Papadopoulos, N. E.
201600	Parker, A.
7701	Parker, Sergeant A. A.
15935	Parkinson, H.
11340	Parkinson, W. H.
21700	Parris, C.
330237	Parsons, E. W.
202235	Parsons, G.
19256	Parsons, R. H.
27123	Patten, Corporal S.
3804	Patterson, A. H. (and bar)
16819	Pearce, L/Corporal J. E.
20986	Pegg, L/Corporal A,F.
	Penney, E. C.
8435	Penny, C.S.M. W. H.
15767	Penny, F. G.
32972	Perry, L/Corporal J.
26524	Perry, Sergeant P. A.
45677	Pickard, H.
9404	Pickard, N. T.
	Pink, E.
	Pillard, Sergeant L.
✓ 33597	Pinchbeck, L/Corporal E.
27913	Piper J.
20350	Piper, Corporal, W.
264560	Pitts, L/Sergeant F. J.
26863	Plant, S. C.
240251	Plumley, L/Corporal H.
	Poffett, E.
10856	Polino, Corporal J.
	Pope, Sergeant F.
	Portlock, P.
255002	Pragnell, L.
11170	Pragnell, Corporal
11017	Price, Sergeant J.

29017	Pries, E. C.
5312	Primmer, F.
29114	Pudney, A. L.
8470	Purdue, Corporal W. (and bar)
9162	Purdy, Sergeant A. H.
8630	Purkiss, F. W.
29313	Purkiss, Sergeant H. (and bar)
11963	Pym, C.S.M. R.
14335	Quelch, C. T.
∕ 18452	Quick, Corporal S.
19495	Raggett, Sergeant A. W.
08009	Rand
32674	Ratcliffe, J.
8547	Ratley, Sergeant G. A.
17079	Raybould, T.
201136	Raymont, Sergeant D. W.
29720	Reed, L/Sergeant A. C.
306830	Redman, Sergeant G.
8911	Redman, Sergeant R.
18865	Reed, L/Corporal S.
14673	Richards, H.
3/4319	Richards, R. J.
241452	Richardson, A.
42449	Richardson, Sergeant C. H.
33412	Richardson, Corporal J. G.
	Richardson, R.
356427	Rickman, G. H.
29481	Rigg, T.
304985	Rippon, L/Corporal L.
201140	Rivers, H.
22029	Rivers, P.
6600	Roberts, Sergeant J.
12536	Robinson, E.
45692	Robinson, W. H.
28254	Robson, Sergeant W.
4100	Rogers, B.
9315	Rogers, Sergeant H.
33363	Rogers, L/Corporal W.
200923	Rolfe, Sergeant H.
11102	Rowe, Sergeant C. W.
33270	Rowe, L/Corporal F. W.
8904	Rowe, Sergeant H.
9351	Rowland, L/Corporal L. C.
235019	Ruckley T. A.
27503	Russell, E.
	Sampsomme, P. J.
26695	Sallis, T. F.
330587	Salmon, A. V.
280373	Sandy, Sergeant V.
200211	Sankey, A.
27979	Savage, F. L.

7961 Scammell, Sergeant, J. H.
25158 Scott, Corporal C.
330885 Scouse, A.
17795 Scuffle A.
19829 Seabrook, Sergeant A.
202586 Seevior, S.
45697 Sellars, A.
54888 Seymour, S.
28183, Shaxton, E. H.
34237 Sheaf, T.
202409 Sheath, A.
11327 Shergold, C.S.M. H. V.
20800 Shipp, Sergeant
7612 Sillence, Sergeant J.
25968 Silver, J.
201139 Silvester, Sergeant E.
257312 Silvester, J.
16480 Simcock, J.
18537 Simmonds, F.
3/4416 Sims, L/Corporal A.
204988 Sims, L/Corporal E. T.
11221 Skinner, A.
31507 Skinner, Sergeant G.
203767 Smith, F.
28956 Smith, Corporal F. G.
22075 Smith, G.
203077 Smith, J. J.
10729 Smith, R. H.
6774 Smith, S.
Smithurst H. V.
27504 Sole, W.
241206 Sparkes, Sergeant E.
18203 Spencer, A.
34163 Squires, L/Corporal H. R.
21480 Squires, J. F.
26981 Stansbridge, L/Corporal
29725 Staples, W. J.
27021 Starr, L/Corporal G.
8800 Stead, Corporal B.
18801 Steere, Sergeant W.
Stevens, Sergeant A.
21215 Stevenson, W. N.
201232 Stewart, Corporal G. H.
7806 Stone, Sergeant F. L.
7399 Stone, C.S.M. H.
11112 Stone, J.
02425 Street, A. G.
Suddick, J.
27857 Suddick, L/Corporal R. V.
44940 Sullivan, F.
26566 Surridge, W. R.
22738 Sutton, L/Corporal T. H.

17982 Taplin, L/Corporal G. H.

202815 Tappenden, F.
331100 Tarry, W.
8608 Tarvis, Sergeant T. W.
204475 Taylor, Corporal J.
204984 Taylor, S.
27915 Terry, L. F.
18750 Thomas, J. R.
Thompson, C.
203833 Thresher, F. J.
10566 Tilley, L/Corporal C.
200343 Tilson, C.S.M. J. H.
55152 Tilzey, C. V.
331348 Titt, Corporal S. C.
Todd, A. W.
28430 Tomkinson, L/Corporal J.
33267 Tonge, L/Corporal S. (and bar)
33560 Tonkin, F. A. L. (and bar)
15325 Topp, F. H.
35736 Townsend, Corporal E. J.
45763 Townsend, H. C. (and bar)
9555 Travers, J.
27130 Tremlett, L/Corporal
202577 Trent, F.
Trickett, S. F.
12358 Trinder, Sergeant G.
20995 Trowbridge, E.
23500 Tubbs, L/Corporal A. E.
202820 Tucker, Sergeant N. J.
280896 Turner, Sergeant A.
202429 Turner, D. G.
15587 Turner, F. C.
13670 Turner, Corporal G.
8608 Turner, Sergeant G. W.
Turner, Corporal

242403 Underwood, F.

11332 Veal, F. F.
55162 Vidler, F. A.
28714 Vincent, Sergeant A. C.
8118 Vine, Corporal F. A. (and bar)
40836 Virgo, G. R.

200069 Walsh, C.S.M. W. F.
45716 Ward, W. J.
26769 Ware, Sergeant A. S.
18351 Ware, W.
8048 Warren, Sergeant G.
12847 Waters, E. P.
Webb, Sergeant T. L.
204571 Webber, J. (and bar)
242248 Wells, Corporal P.
8148 Wesley, Sergeant A. H.
201825 West, P.

11186 Westbrook, F.
15537 Whatley, J.
330307 Wheeler, Sergeant A. B.
17543 Wheeler, J. R.
17783 Whitaker, Sergeant S.
209562 Whitaker, L/Corporal W. (and bar)
8417 Whitehead, Corporal W.
331227 Whittington, O. F.
26232 Wickens L.
14319 Williams, C.
8951 Williams, P. I.
202609 Williams, Corporal W.
17184 Willis, W. T.
7500 Wilson, Sergeant B.
13938 Wiltshire, Corporal W.
19025 Windebank, L/Corporal G.

20737 Wingate, C. A.
204630 Winn, J.
17785 Witcher, Sergeant S. W.
17031 Wood, A. E. (and bar)
42430 Wood, F.
Woodham, Sergeant W. F.
330888 Woodmore, W.
Woods, Sergeant C.
56601 Woods, L/Corporal G.
6119 Woods, Corporal W.
27566 Wright, L/Corporal E.
3/5150 Wright, L/Corporal H.
202822 Wyatt, W. J.

Yardy, C.
12434 Young, Sergeant A. V.
14465 Young, Sergeant G. E.

M.S.M.

200866 Adams, Sergeant E.
240900 Annett, Private E. E.
305731 Arnold, R.Q.M.S. G. W.
200745 Avery, Private P.
11692 Ayres, C.Q.M.S. W. C.

11633 Barker, C.S.M. E. T.
10923 Bartlett, C.Q.M.S. F.
305004 Bishop, R.Q.M.S. H. H.
202213 Brown, Private J.
331339 Bulfitt, Q.M.S. L. G.
20294 Burrows, Sergeant S.

9179 Catley, Sergeant R.
7005 Charter, Private L.
28631 Chase, C.S.M. J. W.
6974 Coates, Corporal E. G.
305223 Collins, R.Q.M.S. A. E.
330699 Connolly, Sergeant A. H.
3/4895 Cross, C.S.M. H.
305861 Cull, Sergeant E. A.

28001 Dobson, R.S.M. G. H.
200204 Dorman, Private H. J.
0841 Dyer, Private E. C.

200934 Elderfield, Sergeant P. L.
202044 Enstile, Corporal E. J.
229203 Evans, Sergeant J.

200715 Farmer, Private E.
200878 Fosbury, Sergeant L. F.
6888 Foster, Corporal J.
974 Fowkes, C.Q.M.S. C.
200777 Foyle, Sergeant R. B.

14718 Frankum, Private W. J.
200758 Friend, Private A. J.
22651 Friend, Sergeant R. E.

200430 Garrett, Sergeant, A. G.
205460 Gatrell, Corporal G.
380532 Geary, C.S.M. G. F. J.
4589 Glasspool, S.M. H.
8322 Glover, Sergeant F.
200500 Goodman, O.R.S. G. W. H.
20209 Greenwood, R.S.M. F.
3/1613 Gritt, Sergeant F.

23840 Hall, Sergeant J. T.
7219 Hansell, Sergeant C.
7219 Hansell, Private W.
380395 Harris, Sergeant C.
Herbert, Corporal W.
5372 Houghton, R.S.M. W.

17276 Irving, Private D.

19436 James, Corporal C. W.
7504 Jeffery, Sergeant H. J.
11475 Jenn, C.Q.M.S. J.

15473 Kempley, C.Q.M.S. E. L.
380802 King, S/M. E. C.
King, Private F.
240001 Knox, R.Q.M.S. J. C.

3808 Lawley, Corporal W.
201327 Laurence, C.Q.M.S. T. G.
3/4640 Lewis, R.Q.M.S. F. C. H.

30032 Low, Sergeant P. W.
281021 Lunt, R.S.M. A.

202061 Male, L/Corporal H. H.
355407 Martell, S/M. H. V.
865 [200363] Mathieson, Private R. A. J.
19111 Matthews, C.S.M. W. E.
3/4409 Mills, C.Q.M.S. A. W.
35324 Morss, Private W.

3/4525 Newman, Sergeant F.
320921 Nicholls, C.S.M. W.

29876 Parish, L/Corporal W.
41937 Patten, Private W. R.
200736 Pearce, Sergeant E.
200017 Porter, Q.M.S. S.
200060 Potter, R.Q.M.S. T. F.
240400 Prentice, Private T.

12808 Radford, R.Q.M.S. N.
240870 Reed, Private C. E. R.
201324 Richardson, Sergeant J. T.

200462 Saunders, Sergeant A.
8702 Saunders, Private W. E. G.
8316 Sharpe, C.Q.M.S. W. J.
3/4410 Smith, R.S.M. J.
24476 Stephenson, C.S.M. J. M.

24137 Taylor, C.Q.M.S. F.
5196 Teague, S/M, A.
17399 Treagus, R.Q.M.S. H. D.
11674 Tubb, C.S.M. J.

22557 Walden, Sergeant D. E.
280040 Waller, Sergeant A.
306170 Walton, Private I. C.
5324 Watts, C.Q.M.S. W.
0850 Wareham, Private H.
355038 West, C.Q.M.S. F. E.
17970 West, C.S.M. H. W.
3/4299 Whitbread, R.Q.M.S. W.
18434 Wilkinson, Corporal H.
4573 Withers, S/M. T.
6119 Woods, Sergeant W.
8392 Wootten, C.Q.M.S. H. J.
205623 Wray, Corporal C. A.
~1606 WRIGHT L/Cpl J

MENTIONED IN DISPATCHES [1]

200856 Adams, Sergeant E.
12340 Adnams, Corporal W.
Allen, Lt. Colonel R. S. (3)
Andrews, Major A. E.
4941 Andrews, Private E. A.
Andrews, Major & Qr. Mr. G.D.
(2)
204090 Annett, Sergeant E. E.
Archdale, Captain I. G. H. C.
Ashmore, 2/Lieutenant G. M.
Attwood, Lieutenant, W.
16683 Austen, L/Corporal G.
200475 Avory, Sergeant P. A.

Babington, Lieutenant
11040 Back, Private A. R.
241375 Bailey, L/Sergeant W.
27090 Ball, Private C. M.
Ball, Lieutenant C. T.
15623 Barber, L/Corporal F. W.
10811 Barnes, Sergeant, A.
4961 Barnes, Sergeant G. A.

Barnes, Captain K. R.
10490 Barrett, Private J.
Barrett, Captain W. F.
330493 Bartrum, Corporal F.
Bassett, Lt. Colonel J. C.
Baxter, Major N. E.
10281 Bayley, Sergeant C.
Beckett, Lt. Colonel J. D. M. (4)
Beckwith, Brigadier General A. T
(4)
Bell, Major G. M.
Bennett, Captain J. F.
Bessant, 2/Lieutenant S. J.
Bettinson, 2/Lieutenant G.
Bewsher, Lt. Colonel W. D.
14740 Biddlecombe, Private F.
Biggar, 2/Lieutenant G. L. P.
9013 Bird, Corporal R.
Blackmore, Major C. H. L.
8589 Bone, Private A.
Boshell, Lieutenant & Qr.Mr.
H. S.

r P. BiṣṢue, Cav. 2i/SH

[1] This list also includes those ' brought to notice ' by the Commander in Chief, Home Forces and the Secretary of State for War for good services. Where more than one ' mention ' was earned the rank shown is the highest reached, otherwise it is that held at the time of the ' mention.' The number in brackets gives the total mentions.

241992 Bowers, Private E.
       Bowers, Major H. M.
10205 Bowers, Private S.
       Bowker, Lt. Colonel F. J.
       Bradford, Captain J.
21273 Brewer, Private H. F.
280355 Bridle, Private E. H.
       Brown, Lieutenant, S. R. S.
       Browning, Lieutenant H.
       Bruno, Captain H. A. B.
       Bryan, Lieutenant G. W. S.
7928 Bryant, R.S.M. G. E.
       Buckingham, Lieutenant & Qr.
       Mr. H.
       Bullen, Major R.
4073 Burgon, C.S.M. A.H. P.
       Burnett, Captain F. H.
202916 Burrows, Sergeant S.
       Butler R.S.M.

       Campbell, Captain I. P. F.
       Carnegy, Major General P. M.
16211 Carpenter, Private E.
       Carruthers, Lieutenant H. B.
       Cave, Captain W. S.
       Chadwick, Captain L. W.
13265 Challis, Corporal F.
       Chastney, 2/Lieutenant F. W.
       Cheriton, Lietenant W. G. L. (2)
       Chevallier, Lieutenant C.
7843 Chidley, Sergeant G. J.
330009 Clark, R.S.M. B.
       Clement, Captain J.
13221 Cleves, Sergeant A.
10932 Coates, C.S.M. J.
20098 Cole, Sergeant S.
2315 Coleman, Sergeant J. I.
33326 Collins, C.Q.M.S. L. H.
335811 Collis, Sergeant M. H.
       Colson, Major R. J. (2)
       Connellan, Major P. M. (2)
       Cooke, Lt. Colonel C. E. A.
       Cooney, R.S.M. P. A.
21301 Cooper, Private H. J.
8250 Cordery, L/Corporal E.
200924 Cousins, Sergeant W. H.
4130 Courtney, Private R.
       Cowland, Major W. S.
       Cox, Lieutenant R. K.
       Crichton, Lt. Colonel Sir H. G. L.
       Crockett, Lt. Colonel B. E. (4)
11775 Cross, Private E.
4895 Cross, S/M. M.
       Crosson, Major W. F.

42085 Croxson, Sergeant F. S.
280057 Cunningham, C.Q.M.S. J.
       Cuddon, Lieutenant P. B.

       Dale, 2/Lieutenant F. J.
       Daniell, Lt. Colonel R. H. A.
       Dare, Captain F. C.
19375 Daridge, Sergeant H. F.
51412 Davies, L/Corporal R.
203312 Davis, Sergeant A. E.
3624 Davis, Sergeant I.
14668 Dawson, C.S.M. E.
11432 Day, Sergeant E.
10297 Dean, Sergeant F. V.
25631 Dennis, Private T. E.
       Dennison, Major C. D.
240735 Dewey, Sergeant A. W.
       De Winton, Brigadier General
       L. C.
18182 Dickens, S/M. A.
TR8/8102 Dickenson, R.Q.M.S. E.
       Dobson, Lt. Colonel A. T. A.
17501 Dorrell, L/Corporal H.
       Dove, Lieutenant G. R. A.
6920 Downer, C.S.M. A.
357868 Doyle, Sergeant E. C.
4300 Dradge, C.Q.M.S. T. F.
201737 Drage, C.Q.M.S. H. T.
7460 Drinkwater, L/Corporal F.
9697 Driscoll, Private W.
       Drower, Major E. M.
       Duffield, Major E. W. (3)
       Duffy, Lt. & Qr.Mr. J. A. H.
305379 Dugdale, Private H. T.
43797 Duncan, Private F.
       Dupree, Lieutenant E.
       Durant, Lieutenant H. T.
       Durham, 2/Lieutenant D. I.
       Durnford, Lieutenant R. C.
14930 Dyer, Private F.

       Earle, Lt. Colonel F. W. (4)
       Earle, Major G. H.
305565 Eaton, Sergeant T.
210920 Edwards, W. T.
200730 Elderfield, Sergeant P. L. (2)
8167 Eldridge, Sergeant E.
       Ellery, Captain C. L.
       Ellis, Captain C. M. J.
       Englefield, Lieutenant W. (2)
       Ennis, Captain A. B.
202044 Eustice, J. T.
22923 Evans, Sergeant J.

Fidler, Captain F.
8242　Finch, Private W.
7857　Finnemore, S. J.
3392　Fisher, C.Q.M.S. J.
Fisher, 2/Lieutenant L. E. P.
19934　Flaxman L/Corporal E. L.
Flint, Captain H. (2)
20569　Foot, Private G. J.
Foster, Captain B. S.
Foster, Major M. R. W.
200973　Foyle, Sergeant R. B.
Franklin, Lieutenant E. T.
French, Lt. Colonel C. N.

Gammon. Lieutenant A. O.
200430　Garratt, Sergeant A. G.
Garsia, Lt. Colonel W. C. (2)
201202　Cantrell, L/Corporal A. C.
Giddens, Lieutenant & Qr.Mr.
　G. (2)
6932　Gibbs, Private A.
Gill, Captain A. R.
Goddard, Captain B. R.
8635　Goodall, Sergeant F. H.
8980　Goode, Sergeant H. W.
Goodford, 2/Lieutenant C. J. H.
Gott, Major J.
20082　Grace, Sergeant A. J. G.
26872　Grant, Sergeant A. G.
20209　Greenwood, R.S.M. F.
Gribbon, Lt. Colonel H. H. (2)
Griffith, Captain C. C.
26847　Grout, Sergeant A. G.
20351　Groves, L/Corporal A.
4291　Groves, C.S.M. T.

Hackett, Capt. & Qr.Mr. P.
330186　Hagger, Private O. D.
4605　Haine, R.S.M.
21155　Hains, Private E.
Hake, Captain G. D.
Haking, General Sir R. C. B. (6)
1888　Halsey, Sergeant W.
37350　Hambley, Private W. H.
Hamilton, Lieutenant D. J. W.
Hamley, Captain C. E. O.
8652　Hampton, Private G.
Hampton, Major & Qr.Mr. E.
Hancock, Lieutenant R.
Hanson, Captain J. C.
21131　Hard, Sergeant H. C.
Harding, 2/Lieutenant H. G.
Harpfield, Major D. H. B.
Harris, Captain J. H.

7991　Harris, L/Corporal K.
TR8/619　Harrison, C.S.M. W. J.
Harrod, Captain F. H.
2875　Haster, Private A.
Hazard, Major C. J.
8508　Hear, L/Corporal C. J.
200225　Heard, Sergeant W.
Hellyer, Lieutenant F. E.
Henderson, Captain A. D.
24828　Herbert, C.Q.M.S. E.
2871　Hester, Private A.
Hicks, Captain F. M.
Hill, Captain & Qr.Mr. J. W.
Hirst, Captain C. H.
Hobart, Lt. Colonel G. V. C.
5360　Hobbs, R.Q.M.S. G. W.
20107　Hodge, Sergeant F. J.
68805　Holloway, Private J.
Holdway, Lieutenant T.
5772　Houghton, R.S.M. W.
Howgrave Graham, Captain H. M.
Howson, Captain G. A.
Hubbard, Captain G. F.
Hubbuck, Captain G. M. (2)
Hudson, Captain P. H.
Hume, Captain H. N. (2)
29331　Huxtable, Sergeant C.

Im Thurn, Major B. B. von B. (5)
22412　Ingram, Sergeant G. A.
Irwin, Captain. L. C.
291015　Izod, Sergeant, H. M.

Jackson, Colonel S. C. F.
Jacob, Captain E. F.
24309　James, L/Corporal W.
12054　January, Private E.
Jay, Captain D. S.
Jeffries, Sergeant W. A.
7504　Jeffery, Sergeant H. J.
Jensen, Captain C. L. R.
Johnson, Lt. Colonel R. A.
Johnston, Lt. Colonel K. A.
Jones, Major R. H.
24994　Judd, Sergeant C.

5766　Keeping, C.S.M. G.
31173　Keeping, Private T.
204840　Kellett, R.Q.M.S. A. H.
230075　Kemp, Sergeant R. J.
13473　Kempley, C.Q.M.S. E.
Kendall, Major W. P.
Kennedy-Shaw Lt. Colonel F. S.
　(2)

Keylock, L/Sergeant F.
Kimm, Lieutenant A. E.
7326 King, C.S.M. W. H. (2)
Kingswell, Captain, L. W.
Kirby, Captain W. R.
Kneebone, 2/Lieutenant C.

25100 Lane, Private C. G.
La Trobe, Captain C.
205425 Laurence, L/Corporal H.
13808 Lawley, Private W.
205028 Leach, R.Q.M.S. W. F.
Ledgard, Captain F. W.
3/4335 Lee, Sergeant J.
3/4021 Lewis, Corporal R. L.
20403 Lonergan, Sergeant J. J.
Lordan, Captain W. L.
200417 Lovelock, Private A.
Lucas. Lieutenant, T. H.

8439 Macgregor, Private J. P.
30603 Mallott, C.Q.M.S. B. C.
Mann, 2/Lieutenant F. R.
355407 Martell, S/M. A. V.
Marsh, Lt. Colonel J. F. H. (3)
Marshall, Major H.
7616 Martin, Sergeant J.
330330 Matthews, Sergeant M.
May, 2/Lieutenant H. W. M. (2)
McConnochie, Lieutenant H.
6439 McGregor, Private J. A.
McLachlan, 2/Lieutenant G. W.
Mead, Lieutenant R.
7136 Mears, C.S.M. F. W.
Mee, Captain F. G.
Mellor, Captain J. E. P.
Merritt, Sergeant A. E.
11784 Mersh, R.Q.M.S. F. J.
330202 Mew, Sergeant J.
Middleton, Colonel W. H. (5)
Miles, Lt. Colonel A. E. (2)
Miller, Major M. R.
330371 Mobray, Private W. G.
Money, Captain G. D. C.
Montefiore, Captain L. N.
10034 Moody, Private J.
Morley, Lt. Colonel L. C. (2)
203048 Morris, Sergeant H. L. (2)
Moulton, Lieutenant W. R.
9817 Moxham, Private J. C. R.
18700 Munden, L/Corporal F.
Munro, Colonel L.
200634 Murphy, C.Q.M.S. D. E.
201895 Muspratt, L/Corporal R. A. L.

Naish, Lt. Colonel W.
Newbery, Captain
8174 Newby, Sergeant E. J.
Nicholson, Captain G. (3)
Nicholson, Brigadier General
G. H. (2)
25793 Nobes, Corporal C. W. E.
305234 Noble, R.S.M. L.
Norman, L/Sergeant E.

7280 Oakford, L/Corporal H. (2)
Oakley, Captain J. G. (2)
O'Brien, Major J.
281295 Oliver, L/Corporal C.
5639 Oner, C.S.M. A. E. (2)
5139 Owen, C.S.M. A. E. (2)
Oxborrow, Captain C. C.

10442 Page, O.R.S. H. J.
Page-Roberts, Captain F. W.
8130 Paice, Sergeant T.
Palk, Lt. Colonel Hon. L. C. W.
(3)
Palmer, Major E. W. G.
607 Parfit, Private F. G.
Parish, Captain W. E.
Parker, Major G. H.
19812 Parker, Private W.
Parker, Captain Sir W. L.
Parkes, Captain R. G. (2)
5499 Parr, L/Sergeant T.
330371 Parrack, Sergeant W. H.
5972 Parrant, Sergeant H.
Parsons, Major B. E. T.
201957 Patten, Private W. H.
20044 Payne, C.S.M. C.
Paynter, Lieutenant A. T.
330184 Peachey, R.Q.M.S. H. G.
200836 Pearce, Sergeant E. P. (2)
201982 Pearce, C.S.M. W. T.
Pelly, Brigadier General R. T. (2)
Perkins, Lt. Colonel A. B.
Perkins Lt. Colonel E. K.
Perkins, Lt. Colonel G. F. (5)
Picton, Lieutenant W. R.
Pinnock, Lieutenant, B. C.
Pittis, Captain C. S. (2)
Playfair, Lt. Colonel F. H. G.
Playford, Lieutenant C. R. B.
8591 Poole, R.S.M. A.
380897 Pope, Private W.
1339 Potter, R.Q.M.S. T. F.
Powney, Lt. Colonel C. du P. P.
5689 Pragnell, C.Q.M.S. J.

	Pragnell, Captain & Qr.Mr. J.	2219	Sinsbury, Sergeant F.
	Prile, Captain W. D.	82107	Smallwood, L/Corporal D.
	Pugh, Sergeant H. W.		Smith, Lieutenant & Qr.Mr. A.
	Puttick, Lt. Colonel A. W.	8595	Smith, Sergeant E. C.
8470	Purdue, Private W.	13513	Smith, Sergeant E. V.
19875	Purey, Corporal E. C.		Smith, Major F.
40224	Pyne, R.S.M. W. (2)	29497	Smith, L/Sergeant H.
			Smith, Captain H. A. H.
305486	Radford, R.S.M. H.	4400	Smith, R.S.M. J.
	Ralston, Captain T. H.		Smith, 2/Lieutenant M. T.
43801	Reed, Private W. G.	280855	Smith, Sergeant N. C.
19975	Reed, Sergeant H.	5274	Smith, C.S.M. W. J.
	Reeves, Lieutenant E. C.	114605	Smithers, C.S.M. D.
240632	Reeves, Sergeant T. C.	201325	Soper, Private V. T.
	Richards, Major J. C. F. (2)	6586	Southam, Private A.
9917	Rickman, Sergeant H.		Spencer, Lieutenant J. L.
355273	Ridge, Sergeant C. J.		Spencer-Smith, Major R. O.
8232	Robins, Sergeant J. G.		Spring, Lt. Colonel T. C. (2)
	Robertson, Captain W. P.	14032	Squibb, Sergeant W. L.
	Rodoconachi, Lieutenant T. C. (2)		Stack, Captain J. W. (2)
		16818	Steele, Corporal S. A.
200927	Rolfe, Sergeant A. (2)		Stevens, 2/Lieutenant A. E.
211265	Rose L/Corporal A. P.		Stewart, Corporal J. W.
	Rosser, Major G. A.		Stratton, Captain G. F. S. (2)
	Robson, Major A.		Street, Lieutenant A. W.
200181	Rothery, C.Q.M.S. H.	7399	Stone, Sergeant H.
307126	Russell, Private E. W.	30218	Stone, Corporal W. J.
	Rutherford, 2/Lieutenant D. C.	3/4565	Stubbington, Corporal C.
	Rutherford, Major J. A.	4545	Sturges, L/Sergeant T.
280053	Rye, Private J.		Sulman, Lieutenant G. H.
		6657	Sumner, R.Q.M.S. E. J.
20369	Saffery, Sergeant W. F.		Sutcliffe, Lieutenant F.
8964	Sampson, Col. Sergeant G.		Symes, Lt. Colonel G. S. (2)
11219	Saunders, Col. Sergeant A.		
	Saunders, Captain & Qr.Mr. W. J.		Taberer, 2/Lieutenant T. C. M.
7245	Sawyer, C.S.M. W.	5499	Tarn, Private R. H.
	Scott, Major O. A.		Taylor, 2/Lieutenant F. M.
	Scott, Captain R. J. (3)	4362	Taylor, C.Q.M.S. W.
	Sebastian, Captain S. R. (2)	11575	Thomas, Sergeant R. L.
	Seeley, Captain C. G.	3/4603	Thorne, L/Corporal L.
	Sears, Captain W.	6588	Tille, Sergeant G. W.
28459	Sellars, Private R.		Tilley, Captain J. E. (2)
10754	Senior, Sergeant I.	200889	Titley, Private C.
200795	Sharpe, Private A.		Tims, Lieutenant & Qr.Mr. E. G.
14296	Shave, Private E. P.		Tollemache, 2/Lieutenant H. M.
	Sheffield, Lieutenant S.	16742	Toman, Private G. W.
	Sheppard, 2/Lieutenant C. H.		Tompson, Colonel H. W.
11327	Shergold, C.S.M. H. V.		Toogood, Captain S. L.
	Shorland, Lieutenant J. W.	16742	Towner, Private C. W.
315203	Sillence, C.S.M. J.		Trevitt, 2/Lieutenant E. M.
6726	Simmonds, Sergeant R.	17120	Troy, L/Corporal T.
8842	Simpson, C.S.M. D.		Turner, Lieutenant E. C.
395603	Simpson, Sergeant H. T.		Turner, 2/Lieutenant P. S.
3/4416	Sims, L/Corporal A.	5128	Tyler, R.S.M. A.T. J. (2)

Unwin, Captain L. U.

306183 Vaughan, Sergeant A. L.
Veasey, Major A. C. T.
Victor, 2/Lieutenant H. B.
Vincent, Major C. W.

Wade, Captain E. W. N.
Wadham, Lieutenant V. N.
10240 Walker, Private C.
202003 Walkey, Sergeant W. B.
Walkinshaw, Captain C. C.
280040 Waller, Sergeant A.
355429 Wallis, Sergeant C.
Wallis, Lieutenant E. C.
Ward, 2/Lieutenant E.
200162 Warner, Sergeant P.
6954 Warr, C.S.M. W. L.
5324 Watts, C.S.M. W.
6101 Weal, C.S.M. J. L.
200902 Webb, Sergeant A. R.
6651 Webley, C.Q.M.S. F. J.
20216 Welch, Private P. L.
Wells, Major C. A. (2)
10396 Werner, Corporal J. W.

21327 West, L/Sergeant G. P.
330042 Westmore, R.Q.M.S. T. R.
Westmorland, Lt. Colonel H. C. (3)
Westmorland, Lt. Colonel H. G.
7042 Whatmore, Q.M.S. A.
8504 Wheeler, C.Q.M.S. H. L.
Wigmore, Captain, S. H.
Wildish, Lieutenant H. B.
Wilkinson, Captain A. M.
330274 Williams, Corporal D. R.
Williams, Major General W. de L. (4)
Wise, Corporal E.
4513 Withers, S/M T.
33081 Woodmore, Private J. H.
15548 Wool, R.S.M. W.
8223 Woolston, C.S.M. R.
Wyld, Captain J. W. F. (3)
Wymer, Major H. J. de C.
Wyatt, Lt. Colonel A. T. D. (2)

27962 Yates, R.Q.M.S. J. T. P.
Young, Major E. C.
Young, Private W.
306276 Young, Sergeant J.

SPECIAL PROMOTIONS

to be Lt. General—Major General Sir R. C. B. Haking
to be Major General—Colonel R. C. B. Haking, Colonel W. de L. Williams
to be Colonel—Lt. Colonel R. H. A. Daniell, Lt. Colonel C. N. French, Lt. Colonel
    W. de L. Williams
to be Lt. Colonel—Majors R. S. Allen, J. D. M. Beckett, A. T. Beckwith, F. W. Earle,
    C. N. French, H. H. Gribbon, W. H. Middleton, R. T. Pelly,
    G. F. Perkins, W. F. Pothecary, G. S. Symes
to be Major—Captains F. Foster, B. B. von B. im Thurn, F. S. Kennedy-Shaw,
    G. Nicholson, R. T. Pelly, G. F. Perkins, E. W. N. Wade.
to be Hon. Captain—Lts. & Qr.Mr.'s A. Smith, E. N. Tarrant
to higher rates of pay—Lts. & Qr.Mr's C. Giddens, A. Smith.

FOREIGN ORDERS AND DECORATIONS

BELGIAN

Ordre de la Couronne   Commandeur Major General W. de L. Williams
    Officier Colonel C. N. French

Ordre de Leopold   Chevalier Captain P. B. Cuddon

Croix de Guerre   2/Lieutenant T. H. Bennett
    31138 Bree, C.S.M. W.

H.R. II.

Croix de Guerre

14284 Brown, Corporal J.
20808 Brown, Private J.
31663 Bunn, Private F.
Captain P. B. Cuddon.
26935 Chambers, Sergeant A. E.
26872 Grant, Sergeant A. C.
19706 Harrison, Corporal H. G.
2/Lieutenant L. A. Le Brun
33230 Milnes, L/Sergeant G. G.
5619 Oner, C.S.M. H. E.
12808 Radford, Q.M.S. H.
27521 Read, C.S.M. V.
Captain R. J. Scott
24683 Vibert, Private A. G.
Major General W. de L. Williams

EGYPTIAN

Order of the Nile

Lt. Colonel W. C. Garsia (3rd Class)
Lt. Colonel J. F. H. Marsh (4th Class)
Major D. Mills (1st Class)

FRENCH

Croix de Guerre

2/Lieutenant T. H. Bennett
8589 Bone, L/Corporal A.
Lieutenant H. Browning
42264 Caddy, Private L. J.
24009 Cousens, C.S.M. W. H.
Major W. S. Cowland
11775 Cross, C.S.M. E.
31875 Eastwood, Private H. F.
7633 Eldridge, Drummer H. A.
22963 Evans, Sergeant J.
8244 8644 Finch, Sergeant W. *DCM, MM*
Lt. General Sir R. C. B. Haking
27015 Harris, C.S.M. E. C.
Captain F. H. Harrod
9071 Hunter, Corporal W.
Captain C. J. M. Kenrick
7326 King, C.S.M. W. H.
19414 Little, Sergeant W.
24933 Loader, Private E. H.
350689 Mason, Private J.
200296 May, L/Corporal H.
Merritt, Private G. H.
Lieutenant M. S. S. Moore
Captain R. J. Mounsey
8949 Oram, Sergeant, F.
Major J. C. F. Richards
3/4416 Sims, L/Corporal A.
8316 Sharpe, Sergeant W. J.
Major E. W. N. Wade
2/Lieutenant H. J. Weeks

Croix de Guerre
                                     Lt. Colonel H. C. Westmorland
29562 Whitaker, Corporal W.
Major General W de L. Williams
58136 Wykes, Sergeant F. H.

Legion of Honour
  Croix de Commandeur   Lt. General Sir R. C. B. Haking
  Croix d'Officier   Colonel C. N. French
Lt. Colonel L. C. W. Palk

  Medaille d'Honneur   9905 Bailey, Private A. A.
201625 Martin, Private Y.
314563 Stubbington, Sergeant G.
Lieutenant H. B. Willis

  Medaille Militaire   9081 Argyle, L/Corporal F.
13992 Bicknell, Private E.
8589 Bone, L/Corporal A.
39003 Duffy, Sergeant G.
8904 Rowe, Sergeant H.
11220 Titcombe, Sergeant A. F. C.
17379 Treagus, C.Q.M.S. H. A.
23500 Tubbs. L/Corporal A. E.

GREEK

Military Cross
                                       Captain C. C. Griffith
32403 Hillman, Private W.
8942 Johnson, Corpoal W. K.
6119 Wood, Sergeant W.
Order of King George   Lieutenant W. P. Kendall

ITALIAN

Order of the Crown of Italy,
  Grand Officer   Lt. General Sir R. C. B. Haking
Order of St. Maurice and St. Lazarus   Colonel C. N. French
Silver Medal for Military Valour   Lt. Colonel W. H. Middleton
Lieutenant G. W. S. Bryan
Bronze Medal for Military Valour   Sergeant Bone, J.
C.S.M. Dacombe, A.

PORTUGUESE

Order of Avis, 1st Class   Lt. General Sir R. C. B. Haking
Order of Avis, Chevalier   Lieutenant M. P. Levy

RUSSIAN

Order of St. Stanislaus   Lt.Colonel C. N. French
Order of St. Vladimir   Lt. General Sir R. C. B. Haking

SERVIAN

Order of the White Eagle   Lt. Colonel J. D. M. Beckett
Captain C. Grellier
Order of Karageorge, Gold Medal   3256 Dicker, Private H.
8577 Dutch, Private F. J.
2922 Fosbury, Private F. C.
8538 Lamport, Private H.
2083 Mowbray, Private W. C.

Silver Medal

3795 Elderfield, L/Corporal P. L.
19934 Flaxman, Private E. L.
04888 Hedger, Sergeant C. O.
16982 Michades, Private F.
19012 Parker, Private W.
1861 Rudd, Corporal E.
6009 Warren, L/Corporal F. A.

ROLL OF OFFICERS

(I) REGULAR BATTALIONS

AUGUST 1914–DECEMBER 1918 (INCLUSIVE)[1]

Charles Benjamin Knowles — (Major-General 11. 10. 1890) COLONEL 7. 2. 1908 →

Sydney Charles Fishburne Jackson — Lt. Colonel 24. 3. 1911. Colonel [7. 9. 1910] 14. 12. 1914 →

Herbert Carrington-Smith — Lt. Colonel 25. 1. 1913 *K.I.A.* 25. 4. 1915.

Edward Leigh — Major 22. 7. 1905. *K.I.A.* 1. 5. 1915.

Frederick Richard Hicks — Major 8. 8. 1908. Lt. Colonel 29. 11. 1914. *Died of wounds* 12. 6. 1915.

Weir de Lancey Williams — Major 3. 1. 1909. Lt. Colonel 28. 4. 1915. Colonel [3. 6. 1915] →

Nelson William Barlow — Major 17. 7. 1909. Lt. Colonel 13. 6. 1915 →

George Hastings Parker — Major 14. 2. 1910. *K.I.A.* 19. 12. 1914.

John Henry Deane — Major 8. 10. 1910. *K.I.A.* 30. 4. 1915.

James Donald Mackay — Major 19. 4. 1911. Lt. Colonel 13. 6. 1915 →

Arthur Thackeray Beckwith — Major 29. 12. 1912. Lt. Colonel 1. 10. 1915 →

Laurence Charles Walter Palk (Hon.) — Captain 11. 11. 1900. Major 20. 11. 1914. *K.I.A.* 1. 7. 1916.

Charles Newenham French — Captain 14. 2. 1903. Major 29. 11. 1914. Brevet Lt. Colonel 3. 6. 1916. Brevet Colonel 1. 1. 1918 →

Albion Ernest Andrews — Captain 21. 9. 1904. Major 20. 12. 1914 →

Lyddon Charteris Morley — Captain 21. 9. 1904. Major 28. 4. 1915. Brevet Lt. Colonel 1. 1. 1919 →

Alfred Charles Addison — Captain 21. 9. 1904. *K.I.A.* 25. 4. 1915.

Noel Edward Baxter — Captain 21. 9. 1904. Adjutant 9. 8. 1911–9. 8. 1914 →

Reginald Seymour Allen — Captain 18. 1. 1908. Major 1. 5. 1915. Brevet Lt. Colonel 1. 1. 1918 →

Francis Cecil Moore — Captain 20. 6. 1906. Major 4. 5. 1915 →

William Henry Middleton — Captain 21. 7. 1906. Major 13. 6. 1915 →

John Charles Field Richards — Captain 21. 7. 1906. Major 1. 9. 1915 →

Frederick St John Barton — Captain 22. 1. 1907. *K.I.A.* 24. 7. 1915 →

Herbert Julian de Crespigny Wymer — Captain 16. 3. 1907. Major 1. 9. 1915 →

George Stewart Symes — Captain 9. 5. 1907. Major 1. 9. 1915. →

Peter Martin Connellan — Captain 9. 5. 1907. *K.I.A.* 20. 10. 1914.

John Douglas Mortimer Beckett — Captain 9. 5. 1907. Major 8. 1. 1916. Brevet Lt. Colonel 3. 6. 1917. Killed accidentally 9. 2. 1918.

Francis William Earle — Captain 21. 3. 1909. Major 8. 1. 1916 →

Willoughby Clive Garsia — Captain 12. 6. 1909. Major 8. 1. 1916 →

Basil Stewart Parker — Captain 12. 6. 1909. *K.I.A.* 6. 8. 1915.

George Whiteley Reid — Captain 17. 7. 1909. Adjutant 21. 3. 1912. *K.I.A.* 4. 5. 1915.

Trevor Coleridge Spring — Captain 24. 3. 1911. Major 8. 1. 1916 →

Claude Cronster Black-Hawkins — Captain 1. 8. 1911. *K.I.A.* 10. 8. 1915.

[1] Only officers Gazetted to permanent commissions are included and acting and temporary ranks are not shown.

Henry Guy Fellowes Frisby	Captain 1. 8. 1911. Major 22. 10. 1917 →
Duncan Mills	Captain 9. 8. 1911. Major 28. 1. 1918 →
George Forder Perkins	Captain 9. 8. 1911. Adjutant 9. 8. 1914–June 1915. Major [18. 2. 1915] 22. 4. 1918 →
Lancelot Francis Urquhart Unwin	Captain 9. 8. 1911. *K.I.A.* 27. 4. 1915.
Reginald Wickham Harland	Captain 9. 8. 1911. *K.I.A.* 30. 10. 1914.
Robert Douglas Johnston	Captain 1. 1. 1912. Major 22. 4. 1918 →
Herbert Mounsel Bowers	Captain 13. 12. 1912 →
John Leonard Lockhart	Captain 13. 1. 1913 →
Henry Hugh Gribbon	Captain 1. 2. 1913 →
William Penn-Gaskell	Captain 3. 12. 1913 →
Edgar Alan Corner	Captain 22. 1. 1914 →
Francis Alexander Aitchison	Lt. 22. 1907. Captain 21. 10. 1914 →
George Stevenson Pletts	Lt. 4. 5. 1907. Captain 21. 10. 1914 →
Claude Malcolm Hamilton Venour	Lt. 9. 5. 1907. Captain 23. 10. 1914 →
Archibald Courtenay Hayes Foster	Lt. 19. 10. 1907. *K.I.A.* September 1914.
Eric John Weston Dolphin	Lt. 9. 3. 1909. Captain 29. 10. 1914. *K.I.A.* 7. 11. 1914.
Edwin William Noel Wade	Lt. 13. 3. 1909. Captain 31. 10 1914 →
Bernard Basil von Brumsye im Thurn	Lt. 12. 6. 1909. Captain 1. 11. 1914 →
John le Hunte	Lt. 12. 2. 1910. Captain 10. 11. 1914 →
Charles Heathcote Fowle	Lt. 24. 3. 1911. Captain 29. 11. 1914 →
Francis George Joseph Berkeley	Lt. 24. 3. 1911. Captain 29. 11. 1914 →
Caryl Lermitte Boxall	Lt. 1. 4. 1911. Captain 29. 11. 1914. *Died of wounds* 4. 5. 1915.
Edward Montague Swayne Kent	Lt. 1. 4. 1911. *K.I.A.* 26 8. 1914.
Owen Heathcote Lacy Day	Lt. 15. 7. 1911. Captain 11. 12. 1914. *K.I.A.* 6. 8. 1915.
Richard Osbaldestone Spencer-Smith	Lt. 1. 8. 1911. Captain 17. 12. 1914 →
Arthur Paget Knocker	Lt. 8. 8. 1911. *K.I.A.* 7. 2. 1915.
George Archibald Rosser	Lt. 1. 11. 1911. Captain 13. 4. 1915 →
Edmund George Wheeler	Lt. 20. 3. 1912. Captain 28. 4. 1915 →
Clement Reuben Smith	Lt. 13. 12. 1912. Captain 28. 4. 1915. H.P. 13. 12. 1916.
Sydney Vincent Halls	Lt. 11. 12. 1912. Captain 28. 4. 1915 →
Patrick Garnet Walsh McMaster	Lt. 13. 1. 1913. Captain 28. 4. 1915 →
Thomas Mewburn Chetwode Lloyd	Lt. 1. 2. 1913. Captain 28. 4. 1915. Died 25. 4. 1916.
George Lynton Edsell	Lt. 10. 9. 1913. Captain 1. 5. 1915 →
Victor Alexander Cecil	Lt. 8. 10. 1913. Captain 4. 5. 1915 →
Henry Roundell Greene	Lt. 22. 1. 1913. Captain 27. 5. 1915. Died 27. 6. 1918.
Edward Capel	Lt. 11. 2. 1914. Captain 27. 5. 1915 →
William Douglas Maclean Trimmer	Lt. 18. 3. 1914. *K.I.A.* 30. 10. 1914.
Kenneth Alfred Johnston	Lt. 5. 8. 1914. Captain 1. 10. 1915 →
Gerald Vernon Tisdell Webb	2/Lt. 11. 10. 1911. Lt. 1. 10. 1914. *K.I.A.* 6. 8. 1915.

Frederick Albert Silk	2/Lt. 20. 12.. 1911. Lt. 10. 10. 1914. Captain 1. 10. 1915 →
Douglas Henderson Cowan	2/Lt. 22. 5. 1912. *K.I.A.* 26. 8. 1914.
Leonard Herbert Sweet	2/Lt. 5. 2. 1913. Lt. 21. 10. 1914. *K.I.A.* 22. 6. 1916.
John White	2/Lt. 24. 5. 1913. Lt. 23. 10. 1914. *K.I.A.* 4. 6. 1915.
Herbert Campbell Westmorland	2/Lt. 3. 9. 1913. Lt. 31. 10. 1914. Capt. 3. 3. 1916 →
Geoffery Nicholson	2/Lt. 17. 9. 1913. Lt. 31. 10. 1914. Captain 17. 3. 1916 →
Charles John Wingfield Packenham	2/Lt. 10. 12. 1913. Lt. 1. 11. 1914. *K.I.A.* 30 4. 1915.
Ralph Ponsonby Watts	2/Lt. 23. 1. 1914. Lt. 10. 10. 1914. Captain 23. 7. 1916 →
Philip Herbert Hudson	2/Lt. 25. 2. 1914. Lt. 10. 11. 14. Captain 25. 8. 1916 →
Cecil Cooper Waddington	2/Lt. 10. 6. 1914. Lt. 15. 12. 1914. Captain 10. 12. 1916 →
Vivian Hugh Nicholas Wadham	2/Lt. 10. 6. 1914. Lt. 17. 12. 1914. T./Captain 25. 5. 1915. Died 17. 1. 1916.
Patrick Hackett	Quartermaster and Hon. Captain 25. 4. 1910. Major 25. 4. 1915 →
Edwin Victor Tarrant	Quartermaster and Hon. Lt. 7. 9. 1907. Hon. Captain 1. 1. 1917 →
Alfred Smith	Quartermaster and Hon. Lt. 15. 6. 1912. Captain 1. 7. 1917 →
Cyril Dalton Fawkes	2/Lt. 14. 8. 1914. Lt. 8. 2. 1914. Captain 1. 1. 1917. Adjt. 8. 4. 1918. Depot →
Eric William Thomas Rowe	2/Lt. 14. 8. 1914, from Spec. Res. Lt. 13. 4. 1917. Captain 1. 1. 1917 →
John William Fortescue Wyld	2/Lt. 15. 8. 1914. Lt. 28. 4. 1915. Captain 1. 1. 1917→
Christopher Castlehaw Smythe	2/Lt. 15. 8. 1914. Lt. 28. 4. 1915. Captain 1. 1. 1917 →
Albert Richard Gill	2/Lt. 15. 8. 1914. Lt. 1. 5. 1915. Captain 23. 2. 1917 →
William John Saunders	Quartermaster and Hon. Lt. 25. 8. 1914. Hon. Captain 25. 8. 1917 →
Hume Nutcombe Hume	2/Lt. 15. 9. 1914. Lt. 1. 5. 1915. Adjt. 1. 12. 1915–16. 4. 1917. Captain 27. 4. 1917 →
Frederick Fidler	2/Lt. 1. 10. 1914. *K.I.A.* 25. 4. 1915.
Ernest Henry Coulter	2/Lt. 1. 10. 1914. Lt. 4. 5. 1915. H.P. 25. 5. 1916.
Samuel Sprake	2/Lt. 1. 10. 1914. Lt. 17. 5. 1915. Captain 27. 4. 1917 →
Francis Henry Lambert	2/Lt. 1. 10. 1914. *Died of wounds* 14. 6. 1915.
Edward Herbert Charlie Drouet Le Marchant	2/Lt. 2. 10. 1914 (from S.R.) Lt. 5. 6. 1915. *Died of wounds* 29. 10. 1916.
Edward Charles Reeves	2/Lt. 7. 10. 1914. Lt. 15. 6. 1915. Captain 27. 4. 1917 →
Percy Humphries Heathcock	2/Lt. 17. 10. 1914. To S. Staff R. 10, 2. 1915.
John O'Brien	2/Lt. 7. 11. 1914. Lt. 1. 10. 1915. Captain 27. 4. 1917 →
H Parker	2/Lt. 7. 11. 1914. Died of wounds 28. 4. 1915.
Arthur Howard	2/Lt. 7. 11. 1914. *K.I.A.* 30. 4. 1915.
Adam Hillis	2/Lt. 7. 11. 1914. Lt. 1. 10. 1915. Captain 27. 4. 1917. H.P. 7. 5. 1918.

Reginald Percy Lord	2/Lt. 7. 11. 1914. Lt. 17. 10. 1915. Captain 27. 4. 1917 →
William Henry Day	2/Lt. 18. 11. 1914. Lt. 1. 12. 1915 →
Ernest Ward	2/Lt. 10. 12. 1914. Lt. 1. 12. 1915 →
Thomas Brian Gravely	2/Lt. 11. 12. 1914. 11. 12. 1916 from 13 Bn. Lt. 11. 6. 1918 →
Horace Claude Charles Newnham	2/Lt. 16. 12. 1914. Lt. 7. 1. 1916 →
Haslitt Seymour Beatty	2/Lt. 16, 12. 1914. Lt. 11. 1. 1916 →
Clement Morley Bromley	2/Lt. 17. 12. 1914. Lt. 1. 3. 1916. To Tank Corps 4. 8. 1918.
William Englefield	2/Lt. 20. 12. 1914. Lt. 1. 3. 1916 →
Bernard Paul Gascoyne Beanlands	2/Lt. 23. 12. 1914. Lt. 3. 3. 1916. Died 8. 5. 1919.
Charles James Henry Goodford	2/Lt. 23. 12. 1914. *K.I.A.* 1. 7. 1916.
Oliver Robson Walford	2/Lt. 13. 1. 1915. *K.I.A.* 26. 4. 1915.
Arthur Taylor Penny	Major [24. 3. 1911] 2. 2. 1915 from H. P. Died 28. 9. 1915.
Christopher Moor	2/Lt. 15. 2. 1915 (from S.R.). *K.I.A.* 6. 8. 1915.
Henry Simms	2/Lt. 6. 3. 1915. Lt. 1. 1. 1917. To H.P. 7. 5. 1918.
Thomas Gawn	2/Lt. 9. 4. 1915. *K.I.A.* 6. 8. 1915.
Arthur Leonard William Vicars-Miles	2/Lt. 17. 4. 1915. Lt. 15. 5. 1916 →
George Drover	2/Lt. 26. 4. 1915. Lt. 25. 5. 1916 →
Thomas Holdway	2/Lt. 4. 5. 1915. Lt. 25. 5. 1916 →
Frank Richards	2/Lt. 4. 5. 1915. *K.I.A.* 14. 5. 1915.
Hugh Flint	2/Lt. 9. 5. 1915. Lt. 31. 5. 1916. Adjt. 17. 4. 1917→
Harold Lancelot Hodgkins	T./2/Lt. 12. 5. 1915. 2/Lt. 12. 2. 1916. Lt. 12. 8. 1917
George Simmonds	2/Lt. 13. 5 1915. Lt. 31. 5. 1916. Ret. 14. 3. 1919.
William Athelston Hiddingh	2/Lt. 16. 6.. 1915. Lt. 15. 6. 1916 →
Cecil Roach Bullen Playford	2/Lt. 25. 5. 1915. Lt. 15. 6. 1916 →
Dudley William Baring	2/Lt. 20. 5. 1915. Lt. 15. 6. 1916→
Reginald Charles Keller	2/Lt. 2. 6. 1915. Lt. 15. 6. 1916 →
Robert Leslie Chidlaw-Roberts	2/Lt. 16. 6. 1915. Lt. 3. 7. 1916 →
Norman Prynn	2/Lt. 16. 6. 1915. Lt. 3. 7. 1916. *K.I.A.* 28. 3. 1918.
William Victor Strugnell	2/Lt. 27. 6. 1915. Lt. 25. 8. 1916 →
Harold Gwynne Wiggins	Lt. 28. 6. 1915 (from S.R.). To Coldstream Guards 2. 3. 1916.
Charles Aloysius Kenny	2/Lt. 1. 7. 1915. Lt. 25. 8. 1916 →
George Evelyn Edwards	2/Lt. 14. 7. 1915. Lt. 25. 8. 1916 →
Eric William Manning Price	2/Lt. 14. 7. 1915. *Died of wounds* 1. 7. 1916.
Henry John Diamond	2/Lt. 1. 8. 1915 (from North. Fus.). Lt. 15. 6. 1915. To D.C.L.I. 1. 1. 1917.
Henry George Harding	2/Lt. 1. 6. 1915 (from North Fus.). Lt. 25. 8. 1917. *K.I.A.* 4. 10. 1917.
Charles Chafin Newman	2/Lt. 29. 7. 1915 (from Hamp. Yeo.). Lt. 1. 1. 1917 → *K.I.A.* 3. 9. 1918.
Frank Reginald Seely	2/Lt. 11. 8. 1915. *Died of wounds* 13. 4. 1917.
Norman Henderson Bell	2/Lt. 11. 8. 1915. *K.I.A.* 1. 7. 1916.
George Raymond Dallas Moor, V.C.	2/Lt. 15. 8. 1915 (from S.R.). Lt. 30. 10. 1916. Died 3. 11. 1918.
Cecil Archibald Burrage	2/Lt. 4. 9. 1915. Lt. 1. 1. 1917 →
John Wilton Watts	2/Lt. 20. 10. 1915. Lt. 1. 1. 1917 →
Lionel Henry Churcher	2/Lt. 20. 10. 1915. Lt. 27. 4. 1917 →

Roland James Mounsey	2/Lt. 20. 10. 1915. Lt. 27. 4. 1917 →
Frank Milner Black	2/Lt. 20. 10. 1915. Lt. 27. 4. 1917 →
Lionel Percy Walsh	Captain 2. 10. 1915 (from R. Dublin Fus.). To R. Dublin Fus., March 1916.
John Edward Dixon-Spain	Captain 2. 10. 1915 from R.A. (Spec. R.) →
Walter Manning Gullick	2/Lt. 23. 11. 1915 (from Spec. Res.). Lt. 27. 4. 1917 →
Francis Lavington Porter	2/Lt. 24. 11. 1915. Lt. 27. 4. 1917 →
Ernest Fraser Jacob	2/Lt. 24. 11. 1915. Lt. 27. 4. 1917 →
Hugh Alexander Doull Mackay	2/Lt. 24. 11. 1915. Lt. 27. 4. 1917 →
James Leith Leith	2/Lt. 20. 12. 1915. Lt. 1. 7. 1917 →
George Parker	2/Lt. 24. 12. 1915. Lt. 1. 7. 1917 →
Guy Douglas Clifford Money	2/Lt. 27. 12. 1915. Lt. 1. 7. 1917 →
William McAvoy	2/Lt. 20. 1. 1916. Lt. 20. 7. 1917 →
R. Sweetenham	2/Lt. 30. 1. 1916. Lt. 30. 7. 1917 →
Harold Lancelot Hodgkins	2/Lt. 12. 3. 1916. Lt. 12. 8. 1917 →
John Binsted Breacher	2/Lt. 30. 3. 1916. Lt. 4. 9. 1917 →
Robert Henry Armstrong	2/Lt. 7. 4. 1916. Lt. 7. 10. 1917 →
Denis George Wyldborn Hewitt, V.C.	2/Lt. 7. 4. 1916. K.I.A. 31. 7. 1917
Frederick Charles Borough	2/Lt. 30. 4. 1916. Lt. 30. 10. 1917. Ret. 27. 6. 1918.
Arthur Palmer Halcrow	2/Lt. 11. 5. 1916 (from 23 Lond. R., T.A.). Lt. 1. 6. 1916. K.I.A. 23. 4. 1917.
Vivian Cuthbert Edwin Smith	2/Lt. 4. 6. 1916. Lt. 4. 12. 1917 →
Phillip Cuddon	2/Lt. 4. 6. 1916 (from Queen's). Lt. 14. 9. 1917 →
John McCurdy	2/Lt. 13. 6. 1916. Died of wounds 9. 8. 1916.
Henry Clementts	2/Lt. 12. 6. 1916. Lt. 12. 12. 1917 →
Alfred Tilley	2/Lt. 13. 6. 1916. Lt. 13. 12. 1917 →
Geoffery Oswald Hamilton Sergeant	2/Lt. 19. 7. 1916. Lt. 19. 1. 1918 →
Evelyn Victor Allen Bell	2/Lt. 19. 7. 1916. Lt. 19. 1. 1918 →
Arthur Francis Barker	2/Lt. 19. 7. 1916. Lt. 19. 1. 1918 →
Claud Catton Oxborrow	2/Lt. 19. 7. 1916. Lt. 19. 1. 1918 →
Gilbert Stanley Ash	2/Lt. 4. 8. 1916. K.I.A. 3. 9. 1916.
Hercules Montague Edwin Bradshaw	2/Lt. 8. 8. 1916 (from S.R.). Lt. 8. 2. 1918 →
James Lewis Spencer	2/Lt. 16. 8. 1916. Lt. 16. 2. 1918 →
John Passmore Fowler	2/Lt. 16. 8. 1916. Lt. 16. 2. 1918 →
Montague Shadworth Seymour Moore, V.C.	2/Lt. 16. 8. 1916. Lt. 16. 2. 1918 →
Frederick Newcombe	2/Lt. 16. 8. 1916. Lt. 16. 2. 1918 →
Francis John Whaley	2/Lt. 16. 8. 1916. Lt. 16. 2. 1918 →
Victor Oliver Reynolds	2/Lt. 19. 8. 1916. Lt. 19. 2. 1918 →
Hugh Alan Bruno Bruno	2/Lt. 4. 9. 1916 (from S.R.). Lt. 4. 3. 1918 →
Denys Frederick Hook	2/Lt. 27. 10. 1916. Lt. 27. 4. 1918 →
Donald Thomas Gorman	2/Lt. (20. 10. 1916) 20. 2. 1918. Lt. 20. 4. 1918. K.I.A. 18. 6. 1919.
Basil Algernon Cecil Morgan	2/Lt. 27. 10. 1916. K.I.A. 28. 3. 1918.
George Rolland Atkinson Dove	2/Lt. 27. 10. 1916. Lt. 27. 4. 1918 →
Montague Shearing	2/Lt. 10. 11. 1916. Lt. 10. 5. 1918 →
William Ernest Aitcheson	2/Lt. 13. 11. 1916. Lt. 13. 5. 1918 →
Thomas Brian Gravely	2/Lt. 11. 12. 1916. Lt. 11. 6. 1918 →
William James West	2/Lt. 2. 1. 1917. K.I.A. 3. 9. 1918.
George Hubert Ellis	2/Lt. 8. 1. 1917. Ret. Pay. 11. 6. 1918.
John Collinson	2/Lt. 13. 1. 1917. Lt. 13. 7. 1918 →

James George Bench	2/Lt. 4. 3. 1917. *K.I.A.* 24. 4. 1917.
John Anderson	2/Lt. 11. 3. 1917 →
Henry William Mends May	Captain 2. 4. 1917 (from Spec. Res.) →
Ernest George Baker	2/Lt. 4. 4. 1917 →
W H Look	2/Lt. 14. 4. 1917 →
William Henry Collins	2/Lt. 16. 4. 1917 →
Leonard John Lionel Cotten	2/Lt. 1. 5. 1917. Lt. 1. 11. 1918 →
Sam. Whetton	2/Lt. 1. 5. 1917 →
Leslie William Tattersall Pine	2/Lt. 1. 5. 1917. *Died of wounds* 18. 8. 1917.
John Brookman	2/Lt. 1. 5. 1917 →
William Gilbert Craven Hackman	2/Lt. 1. 5. 1917 →
Richard	2/Lt. 27. 7. 1917. *K.I.A.* 9. 4. 1918.
Sydney Gleeson	2/Lt. 2. 7. 1917 →
Ernest Reynolds Maddox	2/Lt. 5. 7. 1917 →
Jack Graham Hogan	2/Lt. 5. 7. 1917. *K.I.A.* 28. 3. 1918
Eric Archibald Reid	2/Lt. 5. 7. 1917. *K.I.A.* 29. 3. 1918.
Norman Robert de la Lee Gill	2/Lt. 4. 8. 1917 (from S.R.) →
Richard John Stevenson	2/Lt. 28. 8. 1917. *Died of wounds* 10. 5. 1918.
Alfred Robert William Smithwick Koe	2/Lt. 12. 9. 1917 →
John Ambrose Clegg	2/Lt. 12. 9. 1917 →
Thomas Martin Bell	2/Lt. 12. 9. 1917 →
Richard Flack	2/Lt. 26. 9. 1917 →
Richard Vivian Taylor	2/Lt. 26. 9. 1917 →
John George Frederick Shirley	2/Lt. 31. 10. 1917. *K.I.A.* 22. 4. 1918.
Arthur George Downer	2/Lt. 31. 10. 1917 →
William John Jones	2/Lt. 9. 11. 1917 →
William Percival Foot	2/Lt. 9. 11. 1917 →
Henry James Thomas Riggs	2/Lt. 28. 11. 1917 →
Gifford Miles Miles-Bailey	2/Lt. 4. 12. 1917 →
Reginald George Whicher	2/Lt. 8. 12. 1917.
William Arthur Mitchell	2/Lt. 11. 12. 1917 →
Reginald John Payne	2/Lt. 15. 12. 1917 →
Henry Francis Lambert	2/Lt. 21. 12. 1917 →
Ernest Stephen Boshell	Quartermaster and Hon. Lt. 17. 1. 1918 →
James Sillence	2/Lt. 8. 2. 1918. *Died of wounds* 24. 4. 1918
Albert Edward Bradley	2/Lt. 12. 4. 1918 →
John Crawford Claud Pascoe	2/Lt. 24. 4. 1918. *K.I.A.* 4. 9. 1918.
John Wynn	2/Lt. 24. 4. 1918 →
William Henry Penney	2/Lt. 31. 5. 1918 →
Joseph K W Milne	2/Lt. 3. 6. 1918 →
Edgar John Newby	2/Lt. 19. 6. 1918 →
Thomas Budd	2/Lt. 26. 6. 1918 →
Frank Stanley Guy	2/Lt. 26. 6. 1918 →
Horace William Halls	2/Lt. 26. 6. 1918 →
Frederick George Highman	2/Lt. 5. 7. 1918 →
Arthur Keen	2/Lt. 14. 8. 1918 →
Ernest Gaston	2/Lt. 14. 8. 1918 →
Owen John Price	2/Lt. 21. 8. 1918 →
William Allan Dore	2/Lt. 21. 8. 1918 →
d'Eyncourt Goddard Chamberlain	2/Lt. 21. 8. 1918 →
Allan Christopher Walter	2/Lt. 21. 8. 1918 →

William Vivian John Naish	Lt. (31. 5. 1916) 3. 9. 1918 from Terr. Force →
Herbert Leonard Wheeler	2/Lt. 25. 9. 1918 →
James Campbell Kelly	2/Lt. 9. 10. 1918 →
Percy Alexander Terrey	2/Lt. 9. 10. 1918 →
Percy Hanks	2/Lt. 9. 10. 1918 →
Thomas Maughan	2/Lt. 9. 10. 1918 →
James Wright	2/Lt. 9. 10. 1918 →

(II) SPECIAL RESERVE

AUGUST 1914–DECEMBER 1918

William Waldegrave Selborne Earl of	COLONEL 23. 7. 1904. 21. 6. 1908 →
Cecil de Pre Penton Powney	Lt. Colonel 27. 9. 1913. Res. 4. 1. 1916.
Henry Milburn Humphery	Captain 9. 6. 1902. Major 26. 2. 1915 →
Roger Henry Averill Daniell	Captain 30. 4. 1904. Major 3. 9. 1914. Lt. Colonel 4. 1. 1916 →
John Theodore Ford	Captain 29. 4. 1907 →
Densil Cope	Captain 29 4. 1907. Rel. Com. 22. 1. 1918.
George Hughes Earle	Captain 22. 1. 1914. 22. 1. 1914. Major 19. 9. 1914 →
George Guy Heywood	Captain 8. 1. 1911 (Depot. 21. 9. 1914). Rel. Com. 25. 2. 1916.
George Amelius Crawshay Sandeman	Lt. 6. 9. 1905. Captain 13. 4. 1915. *K.I.A.* 26. 4. 1915.
Cecil Francis Harvey Twining	Lt. 17. 11. 1908. Captain 19. 9. 1914. *K.I.A.* 3. 5. 1915.
Roundell Cecil Palmer (Viscount) Wolmer	Lt. 5. 4. 1909. Captain 19. 9. 1914 →
Edward Faringdon Lane	Lt. 1. 4. 1911. Captain 2. 2. 1915 →
Cecil Edward Morgan	Lt. 6. 9. 1911. Drowned 3. 7. 1915.
Guy Townsend Rose	Lt. 16. 9. 1911. Captain 26. 2. 1915 →
Henry John Collins	Lt. 16. 9. 1911. Captain 26. 2. 1915 →
Robert Eric Wilson	Lt. 30. 6. 1913. Captain 26. 2. 1915 →
Charles Lionel Wells.	Lt. 30. 6. 1913. Captain 26. 2. 1915 →
Hubert Audsey Bierenaki Harrington	Lt. 17. 1. 1914. *Died of wounds* 9. 12. 1914.
Gerald Griffith	Lt. 12. 8. 1914 →
Arthur Frederick Claude Vereker Prendergast	2/Lt. 25. 6. 1912. Lt. 19. 9. 1914. Captain 6. 4. 1916 →
Ridley Merill Colebrook	2/Lt. 9. 10. 1919. Lt. 19. 9. 1914. Captain 6. 4. 1916 →
Edward Herbert Charles Drouet Le Marchant	2/Lt. 1. 4. 1914. To Regulars 2. 10. 1914.
Percy Edward Standen	2/Lt. 16. 5. 1914. Lt. 4. 12. 1914. Captain 6. 4. 1916 Died 21. 10. 1918.
Gerald Burke Collet	2/Ltl 3. 6. 1914. Lt. 2. 2. 1915 →
Arthur Cecil Willison	2/Lt. 3. 6. 1914. Lt. 2. 2. 1915 (to Sherwood Foresters) 2. 7. 1915.

John Edward Malmesbury, Earl of	Captain 5. 9. 1914. →
Michael Holroyd	2/Lt. 15. 8. 1914. Lt. 2. 2. 1915. Captain 6. 4. 1916 →
Geoffrey Frederick John Reeves	2/Lt. 15. 8. 1914. *K.I.A.* 6. 6. 1915.
Hercules Montague Edwin Bradshaw	2/Lt. 15. 8. 1914. To Regulars 8. 8. 1916.
Harold Gwynne Wiggins	2/Lt. 15. 8. 1914. To Regulars 28. 6. 1915.
Kenneth Wiggins	2/Lt. 15. 8. 1914. Lt. 2. 10. 1915 →
Lionel Booth-Wilbraham	2/Lt. 15. 8. 1914. Rel. Com. 15. 4. 1915.
Neville Harland	2/Lt. 15. 8. 1914. Lt. 29. 10. 1915. Capt. 27. 4. 1917 →
Charles Cecil Harland	2/Lt. 15. 8. 1914. Lt. 2. 10. 1915. To S. Staff R. 24. 2. 1916.
Christopher Moor	2/Lt. 15. 8. 1914. To Regulars 15. 2. 1915.
Herbert John Gough Icke	2/Lt. 13. 8. 1914. Lt. 15. 2. 1915. Captain 27. 4. 1917 →
Henry Julien Cromie	2/Lt. 15. 8. 1914. Lt. 3. 5. 1915. *K.I.A.* 23. 10. 1916
Maurice Francis Cromie	2/Lt. 15. 8. 1914. Lt. 3. 5. 1915. *K.I.A.* 4. 6. 1915
Reginald Bousfield Gillett	2/Lt. 15. 8. 1914. Lt. 29. 10. 1915 to Oxf. and Bucks. 10 1. 1917.
Arthur Samuel Radcliffe	2/Lt. 14. 8. 1914. Lt. 2. 2. 1915. To A.S.C. Spec. R. 11. 8. 1915.
Hamilton Augustus Haigh Smith	Lt. 15. 8. 1914. Captain 3. 5. 1915 →
George C Weston	2/Lt. 25. 8. 1914. Lt. 2. 2. 1915 to S. Lanc. R. 11. 1. 1916.
William Dudley Keith Thellusson	2/Lt. 17. 8. 1914. Lt. 29. 10. 1915. Rel. Com 17. 2. 1916.
Charles Richard Etches	Captain 31. 10. 1914 (Hon. Maj. Ret., Spec. Res., E. Surr. R., Major. 6. 4. 1916). →
George William Bradley, Visct. Uffington	2/Lt. 21. 11. 1914 →
Murray Thorold Smith	2/Lt. 9. 1. 1915. Lt. 6. 4. 1916. To 21 Lancers 5. 7. 1917.
Richard Iles Vick	2/Lt. 18. 1. 1915. Lt. 4. 6. 1916 →
Robert Avalon Montagu Chambers	2/Lt. 20. 1. 1915. *Died of wounds* 15. 10. 1915.
Owen Geoffrey Powell	2/Lt. 27. 1. 1915. Lt. 26. 2. 1917 →
George Francis Mason	2/Lt. 3. 2. 1915. Lt. 6. 4. 1916. Killed 1. 9. 1917.
William Gerald Nixon	2/Lt. 3. 2. 1915. *R.I.A.* 1. 7. 1916.
Reginald Bertram Lambourne	2/Lt. 10. 2. 1915. *Died of wounds* 5. 1. 1916.
Theodore Emmanuel Rodocanachi	2/Lt. 27. 2. 1915. Lt. 6. 4. 1916 (to R.F.C.) →
Hugh Alan Bruno Bruno	2/Lt. 6. 3. 1915. Lt. 6. 4. 1916 (to Regulars) →
Skinner Raymond Sebastain	2/Lt. 6. 3. 1915. Lt. 26. 2. 1917. *Died of wounds* 27. 3. 1918.
Henry William Mends May	2/Lt. 6. 3. 1915. Lt. 26. 2. 1917. To Regulars 2. 4. 1917.
Walter Burnaby Sparrow	2/Lt. 13. 3. 1915. Lt. 26. 2. 1917. *K.I.A.* 1. 9. 1918.
Robert Baldwin	2/Lt. 13. 3. 1915. Lt. 26. 2. 1917 →
Robert Burnaby Sparrow	2/Lt. 13. 3. 1915. Lt. 26. 2. 1917 →
Herbert James Burnell Quicke	2/Lt. 13. 3. 1915. Lt. 1. 7. 1917 →

Godfrey Roydon Hughes	2/Lt. 13. 3. 1915. Lt. 1. 7. 1917 →
James Hamilton Currie	2/Lt. 13. 3. 1915. Lt. 1. 7. 1917. *K.I.A.* 25. 8. 1918.
William Herbert Gunning	2/Lt. 17. 3. 1915. *Died of wounds* 31. 10. 1916.
Albert Victor Cain	2/Lt. 20. 3. 1915. *K.I.A.* 19. 10. 1916.
Leslie Arthur Allen	2/Lt. 25. 3. 1915. Lt. 1. 7. 1917 →
George Henry Joseph Bramble	2/Lt. 26. 3. 1915. *K.I.A.* 1. 7. 1916
Alexander Keith Faulkner	2/Lt. 27. 3. 1915. Lt. 1. 7. 1917 →
Cecil Aubyn Masterman	2/Lt. 31. 3. 1915. Lt. 1. 7. 1917 →
George Raymond Dallas Moor, V.C.	2/Lt. (29. 10. 1914) 2. 4. 1915. Lt. 30. 10. 1916. Died November 1918.
Richard G Mills	2/Lt. 4. 4. 1915. Lt. 1. 7. 1917 →
Norman Robert de la Lee Gill	2/Lt. 8. 4. 1915 To Regulars 4. 8. 1917.
Kenneth George de Jongh	2/Lt. 10. 4. 1915. Lt. 4. 3. 1918 →
Graham Sandeman	Captain 13. 4. 1915.
Bertram Okeden Bircham	2/Lt. 20. 4. 1915. Lt. 1. 7. 1917 →
Frederick Cecil Man	2/Lt. 21. 4. 1915. Lt. 1. 7. 1917 →
Christopher Herbert Counsell	2/Lt. 26. 4. 1915. *Died of wounds* 6. 7. 1916.
John Ernest Tilley	2/Lt. 3. 5. 1915. Lt. 1. 7. 1917 →
Leonard Cecil Tong Manlove	2/Lt. 4. 5. 1915. *K.I.A.* 3. 8. 1916.
Neville Eden Cobbold	2/Lt. 25. 5. 1915. Lt. 1. 7. 1917 →
Fendall Powney Thompson	2/Lt. 26. 5. 1915. *K.I.A.* 1. 7. 1916
Sidney Francis Clayton	2/Lt. 2. 6. 1915. Lt. 1. 7. 1917 →
Richard Eustace Stockdale Gregson	2/Lt. 10. 6. 1915. Lt. 1. 7. 1917 →
John Henry Bell	2/Lt. 11. 6. 1915. Lt. 1. 7. 1917 →
Joseph Bardell Line	2/Lt. 11. 6. 1915. Lt. 1. 7. 1917 →
Thomas Herbert White	2/Lt. 11 6. 1915. Lt. 1. 7. 1917 →
Murray Carteret Tollemache	2/Lt. 14. 7. 1915. Lt. 1. 7. 1917 →
William Henry Attfield	2/Lt. 24. 7. 1915. Lt. 1. 7. 1917 →
Reginald Kennedy Cox	2/Lt. 24. 7. 1915. Lt. 1. 7. 1917 →
Charles Douglas Woolridge	2/Lt. 24. 7. 1915. Lt. 1. 7. 1917 →
John Barrow Simmonds	2/Lt. 24. 7. 1915. Lt. 1. 7. 1917 →
Reginald Aubery Hone	2/Lt. 31. 7. 1915. Lt. 1. 7. 1917 →
Gerald Huntley Philip	2/Lt. 4. 8. 1915. *Died of wounds* 11. 11. 1916.
John Percival Love	2/Lt. 26. 8. 1915. Lt. 1. 7. 1917 →
Edward Jago	2/Lt. 26. 8. 1915. Lt. 1. 7. 1917 →
Edwin Charles Turner	2/Lt. 26. 8. 1915. Lt. 1. 7. 1917 →
Douglas Carstairs Arnell	Lt. 14. 9. 1915. Captain 20. 1. 1916. *K.I.A.* 13. 7. 1916.
Richard Michael Rycroft	2/Lt. 9. 9. 1915. Lt. 1. 7. 1917 →
Colin Nevill Peel	2/Lt. 25. 9. 1915. *K.I.A.* 3. 9. 1916.
Robert Campion	Captain 6. 10. 1915. From Roberts' Horse →
James William Massey	Captain 16. 10. 1915 →
Arthur George Stock	2/Lt. 4. 11. 1915. Lt. 1. 7. 1917 →
Eric Walter Carpenter-Turner	2/Lt. 22. 11. 1915. *Died of wounds* 9. 8. 1916.
William Heli Haly	2/Lt. 27. 11. 1915. *K.I.A.* 14. 10. 1916.
Gifford Miles Miles-Bailey	2/Lt. 28. 12. 1915. Lt. 1. 7. 1917 (to Regulars). 2/Lt. 4. 12. 1917 →
Charles John Girling	2/Lt. 13. 1. 1916. *K.I.A.* 23. 10. 1916.
Eric Horace Wood	2/Lt. 22. 1. 1916. *K.I.A.* 23. 10. 1916.
Arthur Palmer Halcrow	2/Lt. (30. 9. 1914) (11. 5. 1916). Lt. 26. 2. 1916. *K.I.A.* 23. 4. 1917.

Walter Manning Gullick	2/Lt. (23. 2. 1915) 23. 5. 1916 (from S. Lanc. R.) to Regulars 27. 4. 1917.
Thomas Stephen Leach	2/Lt. 7. 7. 1916. Lt. 7. 1. 1918 →
Robert Anthony Green	2/Lt. 7. 7. 1916. Lt. 7. 1. 1918 →
Frederick Le Gros Clark	2/Lt. 5. 8. 1916. Lt. 5. 2. 1918 →
Walter Percival Osmond	2/Lt. 5. 8. 1916 →
Travers Charles Melville Taberer	2/Lt. 5. 8. 1916. Lt. 5. 2. 1918 →
Dudley Irwin Durham	2/Lt. 26. 9. 1916. Lt. 26. 3. 1918 →
Douglas Glasspool Baker	2/Lt. 26. 9. 1916. Lt. 26. 3. 1918 →
Allan Tabor Austin Dobson	2/Lt. 25. 10. 1916. Lt. 25. 4. 1918 →
George Henry James	2/Lt. 25. 10. 1916. *Died of wounds* 8. 5. 1917.
Thomas Edward Boyd Reid	2/Lt. 22. 11. 1916. Lt. 22. 5. 1918 →
Kenneth Wiggins	2/Lt. 2. 12. 1916 →
John William McCarthy	2/Lt. 19. 12. 1916 →
Richard Martin	2/Lt. 19. 12. 1916. Lt. 19. 6. 1918 →
Alfred Cycil Howard	2/Lt. 25. 1. 1917 →
Alec Phillip Watson	2/Lt. 25. 1. 1917. *Died of wounds* 14. 4. 1917
George Edis Niner	2/Lt. 25. 1. 1917 →
Robert Harry Powell	2/Lt. 1. 3. 1917. Rel. Com. 25. 5. 1918.
Lyndsey Lloyd	2/Lt. 1. 3. 1917. *K.I.A.* 9. 10. 1917.
Francis Charles Augustus McCullock	2/Lt. 1. 3. 1917. Lt. 1. 9. 1918 →
George Douglas Machin	2/Lt. 1. 3. 1917. Lt. 1. 9. 1918 →
Gilbert Recklaw Singleton-Gates	2/Lt. 28. 3. 1917. Lt. 28. 9. 1918 →
William Heaps	2/Lt. 28. 3. 1917 →
Conway Hastings	2/Lt. 28. 3. 1917 →
Christopher Hume Middlemass	2/Lt. 26. 4. 1917 →
Wilfred Ambrose Slater	2/Lt. 27. 6. 1917 →
Robert Hamilton Robertson	2/Lt. 1. 8. 1917. *K.I.A.* 30. 11. 1917.
Thomas Samuel Greves	2/Lt. 1. 8. 1917→
Horace Victor Walter Pite	2/Lt. 1. 8. 1917. *K.I.A.* 10. 4. 1918.
Harry Edwin Avins	2/Lt. 29. 8. 1917 →
Frank William Henry Jones	2/Lt. 29. 8. 1917 →
William Edgar David John Boghurst	2/Lt. 29. 8. 1917 →
Robert Courtney Gardam Shaw	2/Lt. 26. 9. 1917 →
Wilfrid Gordon Wakefield	2[Lt. 26. 9. 1917 →
Maurice Andrew	2/Lt. 31. 10. 1917 →
Cecil Rudolph Boehr	2/Lt. 31. 10. 1917 →
Hugh James Moren	2/Lt. 31. 10. 1917 →
Harry Newman	2/Lt. 31. 10. 1917 →
John Petty	2/Lt. 31. 10. 1917 →
Ivan Gordon Hewlett	2/Lt. 31. 10. 1917 →
Edwin Frank Whittington	2/Lt. 28. 11. 1917 →
Chamberlain Jesse Gilbert	2/Lt. 28. 11. 1917 →
Richard Haslen McMullen	2/Lt. 28. 11. 1917 →
Albert John Barson	2/Lt. 18. 12. 1917 →
Herbert Thomas Fulford	2/Lt. 18. 12. 1917. Rel. Com. 2. 5. 1918.
Edward John Quarrier	2/Lt. 18. 12. 1917. *K.I.A.* 31. 5. 1918.
Robert Vernon Woodley	2/Lt. 30. 1. 1918 →

Alfred Churchill Matthew	2/Lt. 30. 1. 1918 →
Joseph Duncan Shilling	2/Lt. 30. 1. 1918 →
Philemon Henry James Street	2/Lt. 30. 1. 1918 →
Arthur Henry David Bennett	2/Lt. 30. 1. 1918 →
William Harry Harold Hayward	2/Lt. 30. 1. 1918 →
William Francis Cuthbush	2/Lt. 27. 2. 1918 →
Geoffrey Holmes	2/Lt. 27. 3. 1918 →
John Humphrey Woollven	2/Lt. 27. 3. 1918 *K.I.A.* 4. 9. 1918.
Alfred Goslin	2/Lt. 1. 5. 1918 →
Sidney Robert Hepworth	2/Lt. 1. 5. 1918 →
Leslie Bernard Oscar Hellbrun	2/Lt. 1. 5. 1918 →
Cyril Curtis	2/Lt. 28. 5. 1918 →
Arthur Ewens	2/Lt. 28. 5. 1918 →
Charles Lambert-Manuel	2/Lt. 29. 5. 1918 →
Harry Lyons Barber	2/Lt. 26. 6. 1918 →
Arthur James Webb	2/Lt. 26. 6. 1918 →
Reginald Charles Gadsden	2/Lt. 26. 6. 1918 →
William Oliver Leal	2/Lt. 28. 8. 1918 →
Cecil Charles Alexander	2/Lt. 25. 9. 1918 →
Harold Goodwin	2/Lt. 25. 9. 1918 →
Harry Crees	2/Lt. 13. 11. 1918 →
William John Symons	2/Lt. 13. 11. 1918 →

INDEX OF PERSONS AND PLACES[1]

Abbeville, 190, 197, 202
Abbott, 2/Lt., 342, 344, 365, 449
Abdelrahman Bair, 100, 105
Abeele, 341
Abud, 408
Abu Rajash, 405
Abu Roman, 164
Abu Shushed, 305
Acheux Wood, 173
Achi Baba, 71, 76, 78, 79, 91, 93
Achiet le Grand, 322, 323, 361, 373
Achiet le Petit, 324
Achterhock, 395
Acquin, 238, 311
Ada, 288, 292, 293
Adams, F. J .,2/Lt., 231
Adams, H. I., Lt., 173
Adams, Pte., 194, 452
Adams, Rifleman, 270, 452
Aden, 287, 438, 442, 443, 446
Addison, A. C., Capt., 42, 69, 74, 75, 469
Addison, A. W. N., Capt., 286
Adige, the, 316
Adnams, Corpl., 206, 452
Adriatic, the, 141
Afghanistan, 284, 438, 441
Afriat, 2/Lt., 140
Africa, East, 133, 168
Africa, South, 26, 43, 50, 133, 136, 173, 377
Africa, S.W., 136
Agnez les Duisans, 327
Agomah, 151, 288, 292
Agra, 168, 287
Aghyl Dere, the, 97
Ahwaz, 119, 120
Airaines, 184
Aire, 27, 345
Aire Kavak, 104
Aisne, the, 15, 20, 22, 23, 24, 25, 26, 28, 29,
    217, 355
Aitcheson, T. C., 2/Lt., 194
Aitchison, F. A., Capt., 26, 31, 34, 130, 470
Aitchison, W. E., 2/Lt., 410, 474
Aivatli, 147, 150
Ajalon, Vale of, 303
Akaika Channel, the, 121, 122, 123, 125
Akindzali, 294, 295, 417
Alajik, 404, 441
Albania, 141
Albany Barracks (Parkhurst), 44
Albert, King of the Belgians, 430

Albert, 359
Alberta, 230
Albuera, 91
Alcah Maghale, 419, 420
Aldershot, 3, 52, 53, 132, 138, 139, 242, 352,
    353, 431, 439
Aldworth, Lt., 374, 449
Alexander, A. H., 2/Lt., 261, 262
Alexander, A., 2/Lt., 173
Alexander, A., L/Cpl., 81, 451
Alexander, C., L/Cpl., 344, 451, 452
Alexandria, 54, 70, 92, 114, 132, 136, 263,
    353, 411, 446
Al Huwain, 121
Ali al Muntar, 265, 300
Ali Gharbi, 157, 160
Ali Ibn Husain, 120
Allahabad, 47, 117
Allen, E.M., Lt., 139, 449
Allen, L. J. S., Capt., 168, 280
Allen, R. S., Capt., 82 ; Lt. Col., 449, 460
Allen, W., 2/Lt., 281
Allenby, General, 153, 270, 293, 297, 409,
    412, 413
Allouagne, 177
Amara, 119, 121, 126, 157, 160, 286, 287,
    406
Ambala, 168, 286, 287, 440, 441, 442
Ameer, the, 443
' America ' (cabaret), 380, 382
America, South, 101
America, U.S., 309
Americans (troops), 327, 345, 346, 352, 369
Amery, Capt., 140, 190 ; Major, 231, 449
Amiens, 26, 128, 131, 175, 331, 355
Amman, 409
Amos, 2/Lt. (Buffs), 193
Amplier, 353
Anafarta Hills, 101
Anafarta Ova, 102
Anafarta Sagir, 108
Ancle Farm, 351
Ancre, the, 128, 129, 133, 137, 169, 176, 179,
    180, 182, 188, 197, 200, 205
Andrew, B.Genl., 286
Andrews, A. A., Capt., 132
Andrews, G. D., 2/Lt., 119, 126, ; Lt., 164,
    280, 449
Annamites, 355
Annequin, 138
Antelope Trench, 195, 196

[1] Roman figures apply to a chapter, Arabic to pages.
Names which occur in Honours and Awards or in the Rolls of Officers are not indexed unless
they also appear in the text.
Where an officer or man did not belong to the Hampshire, the regiment is given.

Antoing, 396
Antwerp, 26, 28, 429
' Anzac ', 92, 93, 106, 111, 112, 114, 116
Anzac Cove, 100
Anzac Sap, the, 100
Apennines, the, 316
Apex, the (Gaza), 271
Arabistan, 119, 120
Arabs, X, 157, 160, 165, 166, 167, 274, 275, 282
Archangel, 431, 433, 434
Archdale, Capt., 168 ; Major, 272, 412, 460
Arctic Circle, the, 433, 444
Ardennes, the, 18, 430
Ardjan, Lake, 150, 155, 295, 418
Ardre, the, 355, 356, 357, 361, 364
Argentine, the, 50
Arleux, 365
Armenians, 397, 406
Armentières, 28, 29, 335, 336, 447
Armitage, Lt. Col. (W. Yorks), 174, 220, 248, 329, 330, 342, 343, 344
Armitage, Lt. (E. Surreys), 90, 96
Arnell, Lt., 136 ; Capt., 136, 138, 172, 478
Arras, 27, 36, 133, 204, 206, 209, XVII, 224, 233, 243, 251, 253, 256, 309, 310, 315, 331, 333, 341, 359, 378, 447
Arrowhead Copse, 244
Arrow Trench, 244
Arques, 229
Artres, 392
Asadabad Pass, 400
Asami Bend, 123
Asfield, 2/Lt., 232
Ash, 2/Lt., 182
Ashdud, 305
Ashling, Capt., 255, 262, 449
Ashmore, A. C., Capt., 271, 304, 410
Ashmore, G. M., Lt., 139, 460
Ash Ranges, 52
Asiago plateau, 317
Asia Minor, 159
Asiatic shore (Dardanelles), 70
Askew, Lt. and Qr.Mr., 222, 449
Asquith, Mr., 210
Assouan, 443
Astrakhan, 407
Atab, 274
Atabiya, 123
Atbara, the, 443
Athies, 220
Ati's House, 122, 123
Atkin, 2/Lt., 268
Atlantic Ports, the (France), 348
Attfield, 2/Lt., 268
Aubers Ridge, 27, 29, 138, 353
Auchonvillers, 173, 182
Auchy, 371, 383
Auja (Nahr el), 307, 308, 408
Australia, 41

Australians, see under Units and Formations, 80, 81, 93, 97 105, 332
Austria, 3, 426, 427
Austrian troops, 55, 141, 257, 316, 317, 402, 417, 425
Auteuil, 134
Authie St. Leger, 361
Aval Wood, 350
Avesnes (near Bapaume), 323
Avesnes (near Maubeuge), 394
Avesnes le Sec, 323, 378, 379
Avonmouth, 345
Avroult, 345
Ayette, 361
Azerbaijan, 403
Azizieh, 282, 287
Azmak Dere, 104

Bacon, Capt., 117, 271, 272, 353, 356, 373, 435, 436
Bacquerolles Farm, 339
Baddeley, 2/Lt., 185
Badimal, 293
Baghdad, 119, 126, 157, 160, 166, 282, 283–286, 404, 441
Bailley, Capt., 188
Bailleul, 27, 40, 57, 335–337, 340, 361, 367
Bainbridge, Lt., 242
Bait Isa, 166
Bajus, 204
Baker, Lt., 290, 474
Baker, Lt. Col. (R. Fus.), 149
Baku, 401, 402
Balad, 404
Baldwin, B. Genl., 97
Baldwin, Pte, 363, 451
Balkans, the (see Salonica), 405, 416
Ball, B. H., 2/Lt., 181, 182
Ball, C. T., Capt., 250, 460
Ball, G. F., 2/Lt., 248
Balmoral Camp, 243, 244
Bamberg, 431
Bangalore, 168, 287
Banteux Ravine, the, 253, 255, 259
Bapaume, 207, 255, 313, 323, 364
Baquba, 283–285
Barakken, 384
Barakli Dzuma, 153, 154
Barcenal, 435
Barber, Capt., 225, 449
Barber, Sergt., 98
Barker, A. H., 2/Lt., 390, 449
Barker, G. H., Lt., 239, 240, 449
Barlow, Major, 4, 14, 15, 17 ; Lt. Col., 439, 469
Barnes, R.Q.M.S., 49
Baron, 16
Barrass, 2/Lt., 243
Barratt, Lt. (R. Warwickshire), 87, 96
Barratt, O.R.S., 49

Barrosa, 116
Barry, Major (W. Somerset Yeo.), 156, 252, 294
Bartlett, E. F., 2/Lt., 181, 182, 449
Bartlett, W. B., 2/Lt., 101, 112
Bartlett, 2/Lt. (Dorsets), 414
Barton, Capt., 46, 119, 129, 469
Barton, C.Q.M.S., 49
Barton, Sergt., 382, 451
Barton, Pte., 172, 453
Basingstoke, 50, 52, 53
Basra, 119, 120, 121, 159, 160, 164, 285, 286, 287, 440, 441
Basrugiya, 274
Basseville brook, the, 238–241
Bath, 53
Bathwick, 53
Batt, 2/Lt., 414
Batten, Sergt., 433, 434, 453
Batten, Pte., 235, 453
Batts, 2/Lt., 330
Bavai, 394
Bawi, 282
Bax, Sergt., 349
Baxter, C. W., 2/Lt., 216
Baxter, N. E., Capt., 4, 8, 9, 13 ; Major, 431, 432, 460, 469
Bayenghem, 314
Bayonet Trench (Monchy), 279
Bayonet Trench (Somme), 190, 192, 193
Bazalgette, Major, 50, 131, 156
Bazentins, the, 173, 179
Beach Post, 269, 270, 272, 298
Bearn, 2/Lt., 181, 182
Beatty, 2/Lt., 66 ; Lt., 244, 310, 431, 449 472
Beauchamp, 2/Lt., 271, 304
Beaucourt, 132, 200
Beaudicourt, 133
Beaulencourt, 193, 194
Beaumetz, 375
Beaumont Hamel, 134, 137, 169, 170, 171, 173, 174, 179, 180, 197, 200, 201, 245, 343, 347
Beaurevoir, 13, 252, 254, 255, 256, 377
Beausant, 134
Beauval, 133, 134, 173, 215
Beauvois, 6
Beavis, 2/Lt., 164
Becelaera, 349
Beck, Pioneer, 206, 453
Beckett, Capt., 26, 31, 36, 37, 58, 59, 60 ; Major, 143 ; Lt. Col., 143, 144, 146, 151, 153, 154, 291, 292, 416, 449
Beckwith, Major, 69, 73–77, 87 ; Lt. Col., 94, 204, 216, 218, 219, 222, 233, 439, 448, 449, 460, 465, 469
Beddy, 2/Lt., 411
Bedford, Capt., 206
Beek Villas, 247

Beersheba, 153, 267, 269, 297, 299, 300, 303, 308
Beggar's Bush Barracks (Dublin) ,49
Beglik Mahal, 154, 288
Behagnies, 324, 361
Beirut, 405, 443
Beit Duras, 301
Beit Dukka, 303
Beit Hanun, 300, 301
Beit Nabala, 307
Beit Surik, 303–305
Bekirli Ford, 418
Belah, 298
Belashitza Mountains, 294–296, 424
Beled Ruz, 283
Belfast, 438
Belgian troops, 26, 382, 388
Belgium, 3, 5, 16, 26, 52, 65, 175, 217, 251, 428, 429, 430, 435
Belitsa, the, 29
Bell, G. M., Capt., 132 ; Major, 206, 232, 449, 460
Bell, N. H., 2 Lt., 173, 473
Bell, P. L., Lt., 99
Bellevue Farm, 5
Benares, 117, 167
Bench, 2/Lt., 290, 474
Bender, 2/Lt., 240
Bengal, 3
Bennett, J. F., Lt., 356 ; Capt., 363, 460
Bennett, 2/Lt., 232
Bereznik, 432, 433
Berg-Gladbach, 430
Berkeley, Lt., 49, 50 ; Capt., 134, 348, 431, 433, 449, 470
Berkshire, 52
Berles au Bois, 244, 245
Berlin Wood, 57, 59, 60, 62
Bernafay Wood, 183, 184, 197
Berneuilles, 352
Berneville, 322, 378
Berovo, 425
Berthelot, Genl. (French), 357, 445
Bertrancourt, 134, 173, 177
Bertry, 5
Berukin, 409, 410, 411, 412
Beshik Lake, 146, 147
Bessant, 2/Lt., 412, 460
Bessouia, 275
Bethune, 27, 327
Bettinson, Lt., 317, 460
Beugnâtre, 322, 323, 362
Beugny, 322, 323
Bevillers, 393
Bewsher, Lt. Col., 39, 49, 97–100, 112, 449, 460
Biaches, 321
Bicharakoff, Colonel (Russian), 397, 400
Bicknell, Pte., 218, 453
Biddlecombe, Pte., 106, 451, 460

Biddu, 304
Bidya, 414, 415
Bienvillers, 253, 327
Biggar, 2/Lt., 290, 295, 449, 460
Bihucourt, 324
Bijar, 403
Billy sur Ourcq, 26
Binche, 429
Bircham, 2/Lt., 108, 115 ; Capt., 201, 207, 246, 254, 256, 449, 477
Bird, Captain (R. Warwickshire), 87
Bird, C.S.M., 137
'Birdcage', the, 34, 36
Birdwood, Genl., 93, 104, 108, 114
Birr, 53
Bishop, 2/Lt., 222
Bit Lane, 222, 309
Black, 2/Lt., 173 ; Lt., 439, 473
Black-Hawkins, Capt., 49, 98, 99, 469
Black Sea, the, 440
Bland, Captain, 132, 184
Blaringhen, 138
Bligny, 357
Blofield, 2/Lt., 268
Bluet Farm, 236
Bluff Camp, 416
Blyth, 47
Boar's Head, the, 139, 177
Bodenham, Lt. (Hants Carb.), 360
Boeschepe, 207, 233, 351
Boesinghe, 207, 233
Bogdanci, 423, 424
Boiry Lane Bridge, 365
Boiry Notre Dame, 364, 365
Bois de Hamel, 327
Bois de Recourt, 365
Bois du Chêne, 394
Bois les Bœufs, 309
Boisleux, 253
Bois Quarante, 369
Bolsheviks, the, 402, 403, 404, 432, 433, 434, 440
Bomb Alley, 90
Bombay, 41, 42, 47, 272, 286, 440, 441
Bone, W., Sergt., 172, 453
Bone, F. W., L/Cpl., 62, 451
Bone, A., Pte., 199, 204, 453, 460, 466
Bone, F., Pte., 381, 382, 451
Bonham-Carter, Capt., 133, 173
Boomerang, the, 88
Boritska Trench, 195, 196
Borough, Lt., 2/193, 473
Boshell, Lt. and Qr.Mr., 310, 461, 474
Bossuyt, 386, 387, 393 (see Courtrai-Bossuyt Canal)
Bouchavesnes, 203
Boucher, Capt., 164 ; Major, 286
Boulogne, 352, 429
Bourlon Wood, 255, 256
Bournemouth, 46

Bousfield, Capt., 87
Boustead, 2/Lt., 199 ; Lt., 360, 449
Bovington, 52
Bowers, Capt., 46 ; Major, 286, 440, 461, 470
Bowers, Sergt., 106, 451
Bowker, Major, 43 ; Lt. Col., 47, 119, 124, 160, 164, 461
Bowring, Pte., 194, 453
Boxall, Capt., 69, 72, 470
'Box and Cox' (trenches), 187
Boyd, Capt. (Leinster), 14, 15
Boyelles, 257
Braby, Pte., 412, 451
Bradley, 2/Lt., 360, 370, 449
Bradshaw, 2/Lt., 63, 449, 473, 476
Braika, 120
Braithwaite, M., Genl., 353, 373
Bramble, 2/Lt., 173, 477
Brand, Lt. Col. (R.B.), 431
Brandhoek Camp, 232, 311
Brandon, Capt., 119, 126, 163
Brannon, 2/Lt., 101 ; Lt., 114, 269, 270, ; Capt., 413, 449
Bray, 2/Lt., 222
Bray, 203, 322
Bray Dunes, 315
Brenta, the, 316
Breslau, 2/Lt., 188
Brewer, Pte., 62
Briastre, 6
Brie Comte Robert, 17
Brierley, 2/Lt., 357, 363, 410 ; Capt., 371, 390, 394
Briggs, Lt. Genl., 152
Brine, 2/Lt., 164
Brine, Sergt., 329, 331, 451, 453
Britten, Sergt., 270, 453
Broodseinde, 247, 378
Broembeck, 235–237
Brook, Lt. Col. (K.O.Y.L.I.), 354, 362, 375, 377
Brooke, B. Genl., 153
Brooke, Lt., 411, 449
Brooking, M. Genl., 404
Brooks, 2/Lt., 306
Brown, A. O., 2/Lt., 413
Brown, D. A., 2/Lt., 370
Brown, G. H., Lt. (Ayrshire Yeo.), 335, 381, 382
Brown, R. H., 2/Lt., 236
Brown, Sergt., 63, 451
Brown Hill, 301
Brunker, B. Genl., 92
Brussels, 430
Bryant, 2/Lt., 364, 373, 449
Bryant, R.S.M., 102, 461
Bucharest, 445
Buckingham, Lt. and Qr.Mr., 119, 282, 287, 461
Buckingham, Sergt., 422, 453

Buckley, A. D. B., Col., 44
Buckley, G. A. M., Capt., 50, 53 ; Lt. Col., 258
Bucknill, Lt., 119, 124, 126, 163, 165, 449
Bucquoy, 325, 344, 353, 354
Bucy le Long, 22, 24, 26
Budden, Sergt., 132, 451
Budrus, 305, 307, 407
Buire au Bois, 204
Bulamac, 294–296
Bulfin, M. Genl., 57
Bulford, 45, 46
Bulgaria (see Salonica)
Bulgarians (see Salonica)
Bullecourt, 257, 258, 263
Buller, Sergt., 63
Bulley, C. P., Major, 271, 303 ; Capt., 353, 371–373, 449
Bulley, J. C., Capt., 271
Bülow, Genl. von (German), 15, 19
Bunker's Hill (Gaza), 270
Bunch, C.S.M., 382, 451
Burford Hancock, Lt. Col., 46
Burge, 2/Lt., 65
Burgess, C.S.M., 272
Burgess, Pte., 272, 412, 453
Burj Redoubt, 297, 298
Burj Trench, 297, 298
Burka, 301
Burma, 287, 440
Burnett, B. Genl., 353
Burnett, Capt., 412, 449, 461
Burns, 2/Lt., 393
Burrage, 2/Lt., 216, 473
Burrell, E. A., Lt., 119, 126, 164
Burrell, G. P., Capt., 119, 124, 449
Burrell, H. A., Lt., 119
Bury St. Edmunds, 101
Busigny, 5
Bustan, 282
Butkova Lake, 150
Butler, Lt., 126
Butler, Lt. (Wiltshire), 268, 269
Butt, 2/Lt., 243, 414
Byrne, Sergt., 139

Cachy, 131
Cade, Lt., 183
Cadiz Trench, 328, 329, 330
Cain, 2/Lt., 194, 477
Cairo, 263, 270, 443
Cairo House, 250
Calderwood, 2/Lt., 93 ; Lt., 105, 106
Calico Trench, 329
Calshot Castle, 51
Cambrai, 8, 216, 218, 219, XX, 309, 311, 313, 371, 375, 377, 378, 388, 390, 431, 446, 447
Cambrin, 396
Camel Avenue and Trench, 328–330

Campbell, Captain, 287, 448, 461
Canada, 129
Canadian Farm, 63
Canadian troops, 39, 56, 57, 58, 65, 337, 393
Canal :
    Bossuyt-Courtrai, 386, 387
    du Nord, 336, 371, 373, 375
    La Bassee, 27, 39, 128, 337, 339, 340, 342, 347, 348, 370
    Ruz, 285
    Scheldt, 252, 253, 258, 375–377
    Suez, 149, 263, 265
    Ypres-Comines, 226–228, 380
    Ypres-Yser, 57, 60, 62–67, 206, 207, 228–230, 233, 314
Cancellor, 2/Lt., 244, 293, 391, 393, 449
Candas, 233
Cane, 2/Lt., 173
Cannes, 315
Cannes Farm, 235
Cantle Hill, 307
Cape Helles, 51, V–IX, 173, 193, 389, 396, 446
Capel, Lt., 38, 49, 60, 470
Capes, 2/Lt., 119
Caporetto, 257, 315
Cappy, 322
Cardonette, 132, 175
Cardy, Capt., 136
Carley, 2/Lt., 370
Carnoy, 204
Carr, Lt., 413
Carrington, Capt., 185, 188
Carrington-Smith, Lt. Col., 69, 72, 73, 79, 469
Carvin, 339, 396
Cary–Bernard, Lt. Col. (Wiltshire), 140, 187, 188, 215
Caspian Sea, 397, 402, 403, 439, 440
Catley, Sergt., 203, 459
Cattenières, 7, 10
Catterick, 429, 431, 438, 439
Caucasia (the Caucasus), 284, 391, 440, 445
Caucourt, 366
Caudry, 6, 10, 11
Caukli, 294, (Wood) 296
Caullery, 11
Causli, 143
Causton, Capt., 342, 343
Cavan, Lord, Genl., 236
Cave, Sir T. S., Colonel, 436
Cave, W. S., Capt., 353, 363, 371–373, 375, 449
Cavillon, 204
Cawnpore, 117, 167
Cayley, B. Genl., 194, 219 ; M. Genl., 312, 435
Cecil, Lt., 4, 12, 38, 470
Celles, 398
Cerisy, 326

Cerna Voda, 445
Ceylon Trench, 221
Chabriz, 285
Chadwick, Capt., 233, 313
Chailak Dere, 97
Chakrata, 287
Chalk Pit Wood, 175
Challis, 2/Lt., 177
Châlons, 355
Champagne, 55
Channel Ports, the, 25, 31
Chantilly, 210
Chapman, Capt. (E. Surrey), 58
Chartney, 2/Lt., 241
Chasseur Island, 151
Château de la Haie, 359
Château Thierry, 20, 355
Chaumuzy, 356, 357
Cheeseman, Lt., 98, 99
Chemical Works, the (Roeux), 221, 328
Chemin des Dames, the, 20, 24, 344, 348
Cheshire Ridge, 99, 100
Chester, 2/Lt., 248
Chevallier, 2/Lt., 230, 461
Chevry, 18
Cheyne, Lt., 347
Chichester, 48
Childe-Thomas, Major, 177, 207
Chipilly, 132
Chippewa Camp, 445
Chilton, Lt. (A. & S.H.), 86
Chittab Fort, 161
Chitty, 2/Lt., 119, 159
Chocolate Hill, 104, 107
Chocques, 132
Chouilly, 357
Christchurch, 43
Chubb, 2/Lt., 184
Chuignolles, 325, 326
Chunuk Bair, 96–98, 100, 263
Church, Capt., 50, 51
Churcher, 2/Lt., 175, 473
Churcher, C.S.M., 373, 453
Cidemli, 155
Cinq Chemins, 249
Cistern Hill, 307
Clark, Sergt., 175, 451
Clarke, A. B., 2/Lt., 241
Clarke, S. F., 2/Lt., 233
Clegg, 2/Lt., 343
Clement, Lt., 100, 111 ; Capt., 151, 153, 291, 293, 449
Clery, 11, 13
Cloudy Trench, 193
Clyde Trench, 329, 330
Cobbe, Lt. Genl. Sir A., 274
Cockburn, Major (Inniskillings), 391
Coddington, Major, 44
Codford, 50
Cojeul, 211

Coke, Capt., 298
Colaba, 42, 47
Colbert, Lt., 351
Colchester, 3, 4, 429
Cole, Pte., 412, 451
Colebrook, L. C., 2/Lt., 207
Colebrook, R. M., Lt., 44, 476
Coleman, 2/Lt., 349, 451
Coles, Sergt., 401
Collett, Lt., 104, 173, 243, 248, 476
Collier, 2/Lt., 225
Collins, H. J., Capt., 412, 449
Collins, S. H., Capt., 230, 449
Collins, W. H., 2/Lt., 419, 420, 421, 422, 449
Collins, L/Cpl., 61, 453
Collis, 2/Lt., 230
Collis, Sergt., 225 ; C.S.M., 231, 454
Cologne, 430, 436
Cologne, river, 320
Colombo, 444
Colquhoun, Major (Leinster), 111, 142
Colston, B. Genl., 271
Colt Trench, 327
Colyer, 2/Lt., 387
Combellach, Sergt., 279, 280, 451
Combles, 177, 205
Comines, 226, 227, 380 (see Ypres-Comines Canal)
Compeigne, 15, 355
Condé, 22–24
Connellan, Capt., 4, 5, 9, 11, 16 ; Major, 14, 24, 29, 461, 469
Console, 435
Constantinople, 52, 92, 153, 284, 294, 309, 426, 445
Cook, 2/Lt., 350
Coope, 2/Lt., 227
Cooper, B. Genl., 52, 99
Cooper, H. F., Lt., 119
Cooper, W. M., 2/Lt., 368, 369, 449
Cooper, 2/Lt. (Dorsets), 87
Coot Trench, 329, 330
Cope, Capt., 26, 31, 44, 475
Copping, Corporal, 360, 451
Coral Trench, 329, 330
Corbie, 175, 184, 209
Cordite Trench, 221
Corfe, Lt. Col. (R.W.K.), 239
Corfe Castle, 48
Corfu Trench, 328
Corke, 2/Lt., 193, 194
Corner, Capt., 69, 75, 245 ; Major, 439, 470
Cornish, Lt., 126 ; Capt., 197, 218, 219, 449
Cornwallis, Lord, 45
Corona Trench, 221
Corser, Lt., 166
Costeker, Capt. (R. Warwickshire), 72
Cottam, Capt., 356, 376–378, 449
Cotten, Lt., 85, 431, 449

Coulomniers, 18
Coulter, 2/Lt., 25, 35, 471
Counsell, 2/Lt., 173, 477
Couperey, 17
Courcelles, 324, 364
Courcelette, 183, 188, 446
Courtagnon, 355, 357
Courtrai, 383, 385–387 (see Courtrai-Bossuyt Canal)
Cousens, R.S.M., 412, 451, 466
Cousins, O.R.S., 436
Cox, 2/Lt., 268
Cox, Sergt., 331, 454
Cowan, D. A., Lt., 119
Cowan, D. H., 2/Lt., 4, 10, 13, 471
Cowan, Lt. (R. Scots), 136
Cowland, Capt., 87, 89, 148, 153 ; Major, 291, 295, 296, 417, 449, 461
Coxyde Bains, 315
Crag, the, 418
Craig, 2/Lt., 349
Crater, the (Aden), 440
Craven, Pte., 280, 451
Crawford, Pte., 62
Crease, Sergt., 137
Crepy en Valois, 16
Crested Rock, the (Gaza), 273
Crest House, 368
Crete Rivet, 144, 145
Crete Simonet, 143–145
Crevecœur, 252, 253
Crockett, Lt. Col., 52, 132, 206, 313, 321, 371, 449, 461
Crofts, Lt. Col., 51
Croix de Poperinghe, 339, 340
Cromer, 3
Cromie, H. J., Capt., 196, 476
Cromie, M. F., Lt., 83, 85, 86, 476
Crompton, 2/Lt., 314
Cronin-Wilson, 2/Lt., 268
Cross, Lt. (Wiltshire), 298
Cross, Sergt., 231, 361, 451, 454
Crosson, Major, 412, 419, 461
Crowborough, 431, 434
Ctesiphon, 128, 159, 160, 166, 283
Cuddon, Lt., 111, 115 ; Capt., 136, 138, 193, 195, 204, 216, 218, 234, 250, 260, 262, 311, 449, 461, 465
Cuffs, Pte., 62
Cuinchy, 39, 138, 139, 177
Cuitron, 356
Culley, 2/Lt., 347
Cupid Trench, 221
Curragh, the, 52, (camp) 238
Curgies, 429
Curlu, 68, 213
Currie, 2/Lt., 197 ; Lt., 367, 477
Curtis, G. M., Capt., 404
Curtis, R. H., Lt., 101
Cuthbert, M. Genl., 207

Cutmore, 2/Lt., 250

Dago Trench, 375
Dagshai, 168, 441
Dahra Ben, the, 278 ; ridge, 280
Daines, 2/Lt., 348
Dale, 2/Lt., 130, 132, 461
Dale, Sergt., 319, 454
Dalton, Sergt., 42
Damakjelik Bair, 98–100, 104, 106, 108
Dammartin, 17
Dammstrasse, the, 226
Damp, 2/Lt., 370, 449
Daniell, Major, 438, 461, 465
Daniels, 2/Lt., 227 ; Capt., 240
Danube, the, 425–427, 445
Daours, 177
Darb, 443
D'Arcy, 2/Lt., 67
Dardanelles, the, 51, 54, 68, VI–IX, 128, 141, 445
Darling (see Kingsley-Darling)
Darracott, 2/Lt., 195, 219
Daur, 404
Dautli, 155, 422
Davenport, Capt., 287
Davies, M. Genl., 95
Davies, Lt. and Qr.Mr., 132, 136, 224
Davies, Major (R. Warwickshire), 148, 151, 291
Dawson, Capt., 242, 243, 449
Day, C. R. L., Major, 46 ; Lt. Col., 272
Day, D., 2/Lt., 173 ; Capt., 234–236, 449
Day, O. H. L., Capt., 69, 80, 81, 90, 94, 95, 470
Dead Man's Farm, 233
Deane, Major, 69, 77, 79, 469
Dedeli Pass, 145, 146, 423
De Gaury, 2/Lt., 100 ; Lt., 174, 215 ; Capt., 247, 343, 349, 360, 365, 449
De Geijer, Lt., 168
Deir Ballut, 408
Deir el Belah, 271
Deir Seneid, 300
Deir Sinan, 408
Delhi, 287
DeLisle, M. Genl., 96, 103, 216, 236, 253, 256, 259, 311
Delville Wood, 173, 174, 179, 182, 184
Demetric, 291
Dender, the, 396, 436
Dennett, Corpl., 396, 451
Denys Wood, 227
Dernancourt, 177, 189
Derry, 2/Lt., 96
Desert, the (see Sinai)
De Seule, 336
De Tott's Battery, 76
Deversoir, 264
Devil's Trench, 244

Devonport, 53
Dewdrop Trench, 196
De Winter, B. Genl., 92, 103, 130, 461
De Zon Camp, 165
Dhunn, 420
Diala, the, 282–285, 441
Diamond, 2/Lt., 68, 472
Dickchurch, 285
Dinapore, 47, 117
Dinant, 435
Dixon, 2/Lt., 409
Dixon, Sergt., 436, 454
Dobrudja, 445
Doingt, 321
Doiran, Lake, 141, 143, 145, 146, 149, 150,
    153, 155, 156, 288, 289, 290, 291, 293,
    294, 296, 417, 418, 422, 423, 425, 441 ;
    Station, 146
Doljeli, 130, 133
Dollery, L/Corpl., 130
Dolphin, E. J. W., Lt., 11, 16, 29 ; Capt.,
    33, 34, 470
Dolphin, H. C., Lt. Col., 11, 44, 449
Donner, 2/Lt., 409
Donnithorne, 2/Lt., 134, 135, 449
Doran, B. Genl., 83
Dorsale des Trois Arbres, 144, 335
Dos du Mulet, 419, 420
Douai, 215
Double Crassier, the, 134, 136
Doughty-Wylie, Colonel, 74
Doullens, 128, 175, 204, 318, 325, 353, 359,
    361
Douve, the, 30–32
Dova Tepe, 417, 418
Dover, 429
Doyle, 2/Lt., 173
Drake, Sir F., 91
Dremiglava, 148, 150–152
Driemasten, 384
Drocourt-Queant Line, the, 363, 365, 366,
    373
Dromedaire Sector, the, 422
Dublin, 49
Dublin Castle, 104
Duffin, C.S.M., 177
Dugan, Sergt., 177, 454
Dujaila depression and redoubt, 159, 162,
    164, 167, 174
Dum Dum, 117
Dundas, General, 45
Dunkirk, 175
' Dunsterforce ', XXXI
Dunsterville, M. Genl., 397–399, 401, 402
Dupnica, 426
Dupree, 2/Lt., 100 ; Lt., 111, 147, 291 ;
    Capt., 421, 422, 461
Durant, 2/Lt., 184, 449
Durnford, Lt., 271, 280, 283 ; Capt., 400,
    449, 461

Dury, 363
Dwina, the, 431, 433
Dyer, C. S. M., 348
Dyer, Pte., 106, 461
Dynamite Factory, the, 396

Earle, F. W., Capt., 46 ; Major, 203, 220,
    221, 243 ; Lt. Col., 310, 389, 393, 429,
    449, 461, 465, 469
Earle, G. H., Major, 132, 134, 461, 475
Early, Sergt., 269, 270, 454
East Africa, 133
East Coast, the, 438
Eaucourt l'Abbaye, 187, 189
Ecaillon, the, 389–391
Edinburgh, 42
Edsell, Lt., 4, 34, 35 ; Capt., 130, 470 ;
Edwards, Lt., 329, 331 ; Capt., 342, 419,
    447, 472
Eecke, 351
Egerton, M. Genl., 167
Egypt, 69, 79, 104, 133, 134, 136, 142, 148,
    149, 165, 168, XXI, 286, 407, 409, 411,
    443, 446
Egypt House, 248
Ekaterinburg, 444
El Arak, 405
El Arbain, 307
El Arish, 265, 271, 272 ; (redoubt) 297, 298
El Beida, 407
El Breij, 266
El Burjabye, 266
El Butani, 301
El Hanna, 161, 163, 164, 168, 271
El Jib, 305, 309
El Kubeibeh, 305
El Kufr, 409
El Lubban, 408
El Mendur, 269
El Mesmiye, 300–302
El Qastine, 300
El Sinn, 164, 165, 166, 283
El Sire, 267
El Tine, 301
El Tireh, 307, 308
Eldridge, Drummer, 64, 132, 451, 466
Eley, Major (Suffolk), 445
Elicourt, 266
Elizabeth, Queen, 69, 91
Elkington, Lt., 320
Elkins, Pte., 123, 451
Ellery, Capt., 101, 113, 448, 461
Ellicombe, Lt. Col. (Devons), 208
Ellis, C. M., Capt., 272, 412, 461
Ellis, G. L., 2/Lt., 139
Ellis, Y. P., 2/Lt., 139
Elton, G., Lt., 126, 159
Elton, G. K., 2/Lt., 195
Elverdinghe, 62, 174, 246, 250, 314
Emberton, R.Q.M.S., 436

Enab (Qaryat el), 303–305
England, 15, 42, 47, 49, 50, 52, 53, 137, 142, 143, 156, 164, 168, 263, 271, 306, 352, 353, 361, 378, 412, 416, 433, 434, 436, 440, 441, 445
Engelbelmer, 128, 179, 197
Englebrier Farm, 266
Englefield, Lt., 425, 461
Ennis, Capt., 44, 461
Enzeli, 399–401, 439, 440
Epehy, 318, 320
Erdzeli, 294, 296
Erle, Capt., 49
Erquinghem, 28
Ervillers, 361
Escarmain, 391
Escaudœuvres, 378
Esdraelon, plain of, 413
Eski Line, the, 77, 115
Esmery-Hallon, 15
Esscher, 386
Essex, 4
Essex Ravine, 110
Estaires, 334, 335
Estreé St. Denis, 26
Etaing, 365, 366
Etaples, 345
Eterpigny, 365
Euphrates, the, 119, 121, 123, 124, 285, 399, 402
Evans, A. W., 2/Lt., 414
Evans, B., Lt., 329, 330, 331, 449
Evans, Capt. (R. Warwickshire), 84–86
Evans, Sergt., 317, 461
Everiss, Pte., 232, 454
Ewens, 2/Lt., 382, 384, 449, 479

Fairlie Cunninghame, 2/Lt., 139
Fairweather, 2/Lt., 332
Faith, Capt., 49, 100, 148, 151
Falcon, Lt. (E. Surrey), 90, 96
Falconer, 2/Lt., 230
Falconer, Sergt., 325, 451
Falfemont Farm, 177
Fall, 2/Lt., 221, 449
Fallahiya, 165
Famars, 429
Fampoux, 211, 212, 219, 228, 243, 310, 327, 330, 331
Fanshawe, Lt. Genl., 179
Fantasy Farm, 351
Fardell, Capt., 101, 440
Farm, the (Gallipoli), 97–99
Farnicourt, 262
Fatha Gorge, the, 405
Faulkner, Sergt., 331, 454
Favreuil, 323, 362
Fawcitt, Lt., 219
Fawkes, Capt., 171, 173, 449, 470
Feather, 2/Lt., 236

Feetham, M. Genl., 314
Felixstowe, 3
Ferdan House, 247
Ferme Beaulieu, 350
Ferme du Bois, 179
Ferme 14, 66
Fenn, 2/Lt., 271, 305, 449
Ferozepore, 287
Ferris, 2/Lt., 387
Ferry, Pte., 216, 218, 454
Festubert, 138, 177, 334
Feuchy Chapel, 218
Fevant, 382
Ffrench-Blake, Major (Buffs), 412
Fidler, 2/Lt., 25, 31, 37 ; Capt., 59, 462, 471
Field, Capt., 136
Field, Corporal, 58
Fielden, L/Corpl., 250, 454
Fiford, Corpl., 194, 454
Finch, Sergt., 235, 236, 250, 451, 466
Fine, 2/Lt., 126
Finlay, Capt., 51, 125 ; Major, 177, 207, 314
Fir Tree Spur, 79, 80, 83, 84
Fir Tree Wood, 77, 79–83
Fisher, Lt., 281, 401, 402, 449, 462
Fisher, C.Q.M.S., 96
Fisher, Sergt., 85, 451
Fisherman's Hut, the 97, 100
Fishlock, 2/Lt., 421
Fitoki Ford, 155
Flanders, 13, 26, 27, 51, 184, 188, 192, 201, 205, 206, 217, XVIII, XIX, 253, 315, XXVI, 357–359, 375, 378, 380, 383
Flanders II Position, the, 383
Flatiron Hill, 424, 425
Flaucourt, 321
Flaxman, Pte., 194, 462
Flers, 185–187, 189, 190, 197, 242, 437, 446
Flers Trench, 185, 187
Flesquieres, 255, 256, 322, 323, 378
Fletre, 177, 232, 235
Flint, Lt., 203, 347 ; Capt., 366, 429, 449, 462, 472
Floyd, Capt. (Norfolk), 126, 159
Foch, Marshal, 179, 325, 344, 353
Folkestone, 352, 353
Fontaine au Pire, 6–8
Fontaine Notre Dame, 378
Fonquevillers, 134
Footner, Major, 119, 126, 157, 159
Forbes, Lt., 119, 120, 124, 159, 449
Forbes-Robertson, Lt. Col. (Newfoundland), 216
Ford, Capt., 83, 87, 475
Forestier-Walker, M. Genl., 238, 420, 421
Forrester, Pte., 225
Forret Farm, 231
Fortescue, Sir J. W., 91
Fort Gillicker, 51

Fort Gomer, 51
Fort Monckton, 51
Fort St. George, 127
Fortin, 17, 66
Fortuin, 57, 59
Foster, A. D., Lt., 190, 449
Foster, H. M., Capt., 119, 126, 152, 164
Foster, R. C., 2/Lt., 175, 215
Fowler, 2/Lt., 209 ; Capt., 231, 449, 473
Fox, 2/Lt., 101, 113 ; Capt., 268, 269, 449
Frampton, 2/Lt., 155 ; Lt., 423
France, I–III, V, XI, XIV–XX, XXV–
    XXX, 41, 42, 52, 53, 69, 82, 95, 141,
    148, 149, 153, 409, 411, 416, 417, 422,
    426, 427, 447
Franchet d'Esperey, Genl. (French), 18,
    417, 425
Frechen, 430
Freeman, E. C., Capt., 413
Freeman, E. P., Capt., 182
Freeman, R. H., Capt., 230, 449
French, C. N., Colonel, 438, 462, 465, 467,
    469
French, Field Marshal Sir J., 5, 6, 16, 29,
    68, 132
French troops (see France) 70, 76, 77, 78,
    80, 84, 88, 90, 111, 142, 143, 145, 146,
    149, 150, 290, 416, 418, 427
Freniches, 15
Frenzy Farm, 352
Fretin, 413
Freyberg, B. Genl., 311, 385, 396
Frezenberg, 61, 63, 233
Fricourt, 169, 174
Friend, Sergt., 331
Frisby, Major, 434, 439, 470
Froissy, 325
Frontier, the N.W. (India), 117, 166, 168,
    284, 287, 353, 438
Frosty Trench, 195, 196
Fryer's Hill (Gaza), 299
Furley, Major, 138
Fusilier Bluff, 88, 89, 103
Fyzabad, 167

Gadsby, 2/Lt., 373
Gallipoli, 42, 51, 52, 54, VI–IX, 136, 137,
    141, 142, 143, 148, 150, 166, 192, 203,
    204, 246, 263, 311, 446
Gammon, Lt., 207 ; Capt., 230, 449
Garsia, Capt., 35, 66, 132 ; Major, 150, 151,
    152, 449, 462, 469
Gas Trench, 368
Gates (see Singleton-Gates)
Gavrelle, 214
Gawn, Sergt., 42 ; C.Q.M.S., 56 ; 2/Lt., 93,
    95, 472
Gaza, 153, XXI, 293, 297, 298, 299, 303,
    305, 413, 447
Gee, L/Corpl., 280, 451

Genoa, 315
Gentelles, 131
George V, H.M. King, 41, 43, 52, 140, 441
Georgians, 397
German, 2/Lt., 100 ; Lt., 174 ; Capt., 203,
    347, 380, 450
Germany, 1, 415, 425, 427, 428, 430, 434–
    437
German troops, passim
Ghell, Sergt., 137
Gheluvelt, 313, 378, 379, (Wood) 243
Gheluwe, 380–383
Ghent, 202, 387
Gibaud, 2/Lt., 290
Gibbings, Lt., 272
Gibbons, 2/Lt., 367, 369, 450
Gibbons, Sergt., 139
Gibbs, Pte., 194, 236, 454
Gibraltar, 92
' Gibraltar ' (Gaza), 295
Gibson, Capt., 293
Giddens, Lt. and Qr.Mr., 101, 462
Gilbert, F. C. H., 2/Lt., 133
Gilbert, J. F., 2/Lt., 215
Giles, C.Q.M.S., 96
Gill, A. R., 2/Lt., 25, 35, 60, 462, 471
Gill, N. R., 2/Lt., 108, 477
Gillett, 2/Lt., 69, 76 476
Gillman, M. Genl., 296
Gilman, 2/Lt. (E. Surrey), 195
Ginchy, 176, 179, 181, 183, 184
Ginn, Corpl., 44
Girling, 2/Lt., 196, 478
Gird Trench and Support, 187, 189, 190
Givenchy, 39, 138, 139, 177, 337, 339, 342
Glasspool, C.S.M., 50
Glasspool, Pte., 38
Gledhill, Sergt., 67
Glengarry Hill, 422, 423
Goddard, Capt., 271, 306, 411, 462
Goddard, Pte. (2/4th Bn.), 272, 411, 455
Goddard, Pte. (2/5th Bn.), 412, 455
Goldfish Château, 351
Goldie's Hill, 155, 156
Goldsmith, Lt., 180–182 ;　Capt., 207 ;
    Major, 242, 450
Gomiecourt, 324
Gommecourt, 325
Gonnehem, 337
Good, Capt. (Hants Carb.), 380
Goodall, C.Q.M.S., 41
Goode, Sergt., 429, 462
Goodford, 2/Lt., 130, 132, 173, 450, 462, 472
Good Old Man Farm, 253
Gorman, 2/Lt., 189, 190 ; Capt., 229, 431,
    433, 434, 450
Gorringe, M. Genl., 121, 163
Gosling, Pte., 250, 455
Gosport, 51, 434, 438, 439
Gotelee, 2/Lt., 304 ; Capt., 376, 390, 394, 450

Gott, Major, 127, 163 ; Lt. Col., 287, 462
Goudberg, 311
Gough, General Sir H., 179, 321
Gouraud, General (French), 355
Gouzeaucourt, 253, 315
Gow, Lt., 403
Graincourt, 372
Graham, K., Lt., 382, 450
Graham, K. G., 2/Lt., 175
Graham, 2/Lt. (E. Surrey), 195
Graham, C.S.M. (2/5th Bn.), 272, 452
Graham, C.S.M. (14th Bn.), 139
Graham, Sergt., 175, 455
Graham-Montgomery, Capt., 290
Grammont, 395, 436
Grand Bois, 369
Grandcourt, 201
Grand Couronne, the, 155, 295
Grand Morin, the, 19
Gravely, 2/Lt., 195, 472
Gravenstafel, 56, 57
Gray, Sergt., 269, 270, 455
Gray, L/Corpl., 194, 455
Grease Trench, 193
Greece, 141 (*see* Salonica)
Green, E. M., Capt., 182
Green, H. W., 2/Lt., 360, 450
Green, J. K., Capt., 419, 421, 422, 450
Green, R. A., 2/Lt., 199, 450, 472
Green, Sergt., 140
Greenhalgh, 2/Lt. (L.F.), 390, 410
Green Hill (Anzac), 99
Green Hill (Gaza), 299
Greenwood, R.S.M., 227, 317, 450, 459, 560
Gregson, Lt., 366, 477
Grellier, 2/Lt., 48, 100, 143, 144 ; Capt.,
   152, 153, 419, 421, 450, 467
Gretz, 18
Gribbon, Capt., 46, 167 ; Major, 280, 286,
   287, 449, 462, 470
Gridiron, the, 90
Griffith, C. C., Lt., 100 ; Capt., 293, 462, 467
Griffith, 2/Lt., 4, 13
Griffith Boscawen, Lt. Col. Sir A. (R.W.K.),
   208
Grigg, Capt., 45
Grimsby, 48
Grogan, B. Genl., 431
Grover, M. Genl., 126, 271
Groves, C.S.M., 49, 112, 462
Gudeli Bridge, 155, 291, 292
Gueudecourt, 188, 189, 192–194
Guemappe, 218, 219, 365
Guillaumat, General (French), 416, 423
Guillemont, 176, 177, 179, 180, 183, 184,
   191, 204
Guise, 15, 16
Gulleghem, 384, 385
Gullick, 2/Lt., 196, 197, 243, 450
Gully Beach, 83, 87, 96

Gully Ravine, 76, 79, 80, 85, 86, 88, 90, 94,
   103, 119
Gully Spur, 80, 83, 84, 90
Gumendje, 418
Gunner, Capt. (Hants Carb.), 188, 360
Gurkha Bluff, 83
Guvesne, 426
Guy, 2/Lt., 381, 382, 450
Gwynne, Capt. (R.A.M.C.), 15, 62, 67
Gwyn-Thomas, Major, 187

Haanebeek, the, 59, 60
Hackett, Lt. and Qr.Mr., 4 ; Capt., 17, 33,
   51 ; Major, 438, 448, 462, 471
Haddy, 2/Lt., 236
Haditheh, 407
Hafles, C.Q.M.S., 50
Haggard Trench, 212
Hai river, *see* Shatt al Hai
Hai Salient, the, 274, 276
Hai (town), 275
Haifa, 415
Haig, F.M. Sir D., 5, 169, 174, 179, 199,
   205, 210, 217, 224, 237, 251, 257, 309,
   310, 325, 345, 346, 374, 375
Hailstone, 2/Lt., 195
Haisnes, 396
Haking, Sir R. C. B., B. Genl., 3 ;
   Lt. Genl., 132, 317, 339, 448, 462,
   465–467
Halberd Trench, 222, 244
Halcrow, 2/Lt., 219, 473
Haldane, Lt. Genl., 359, 373
Hale, 2/Lt., 155
Halfway Hill, 408
Halfway House (Gaza), 297
Hall, A. R., 2/Lt., 187, 450
Hall, H. C., 2/Lt., 248
Hall, R. A. B., 2/Lt., 203
Hall, T. E., 2/Lt., 206
Hall, Capt. (Buffs), 175
Hall, 2/Lt. (Wiltshire), 370
Hallam, 2/Lt., 410
Halls, Lt., 4, 6, 9, 13, 470
Halsey, Sergt., 114, 451
Haly, 2/Lt., 193, 478
Ham, 14
Hamadan, 399, 400, 401, 402, 403, 438
Hamel (sur Ancre), 128, 129, 133, 186, 230
Hamel (near Peronne), 321, 322
Hamel (Somme), 331
Hamilton, General Sir I., 70, 72, 92, 96, 101,
   102, 106, 112, 114
Hamilton, J. C., 2/Lt., 286 ; Lt., 299, 450
Hamilton, Sergt., 377, 452
Hamley, D. A., 2/Lt., 164
Hamley, E. A., 2/Lt., 164
Hammar Lake, the, 121, 122, 125
Hampshire, 48
Hampshire Cut, 95 ; Farm, 62 ; Ridge, 158

Hampton, Pte., 95, 451
Ham Ravine, 422
Hamzali, 426
Hangest, 204
Hanna, Sergt., 86, 451
Hanna (see El Hanna)
Hansa Line, 200, 201
Harbonnieres, 327
Harden, Pte., 132, 451
Harding, 2/Lt., 68, 132, 133 ; Lt., 245, 247, 248, 450, 462, 472
Harding, Lt. (E. Surrey), 90, 96
Hardy, Sergt., 63
Hare, B. Genl., 73
Hare, Corpl., 58
Harfield, 2/Lt., 153, 462
Harker, 2/Lt., 268
Harland, C. C., 2/Lt., 69, 76, 82, 85, 86, 103, 104, 476
Harland, N., 2/Lt., 83, 86 ; Lt., 203, 204 ; Capt., 245, 310, 476
Harland, R. W., Capt., 3, 4, 9, 16, 20, 31, 33, 470
Harlebeke, 386
Harman, Lt. Col. (Leinster), 182, 207
Harness Lane, 309
Harper, Lt. Genl., 322, 324
Harpies, 391
Harrington, Lt., 26, 33, 44, 476
Harris, H. J. L., Lt., 200
Harris, J. H., Lt., 119, 159, 450, 462
Harris, Sergt., 412
Harris, Pte., 277, 451
Harrison, 2/Lt., 197
Harrison's Crater, 136
Harrod, 2/Lt., 199 ; Capt., 312, 335, 367, 451, 462, 466
Harrow, 4
Hart, Sergt., 440
Hart's Crater, 136
Hart Hill, 272
Harvey, Lt. Col. (O.B.L.I.), 140
Haslar Camp, 312, 362
Hasler, B. Genl., 57, 60
Haspres, 389, 390, 391, 393
Hatch, 2/Lt., 340
Hatcher, Pte., 330
' Hatfield Park ', 114
Haucourt, 5, 7, 10
Haut Allaines, 315
Haute Deule Canal, 383
Havana Trench, 329, 330
Havre, 4, 5, 131, 132, 138, 140, 141
Havrincourt, 371, 372, 375
Hawes, Rifleman, 269
Hawke, 2/Lt., 221
Hawthrone Redoubt, 169, 171 ; Ridge, 169, 170
Haydon, 2/Lt., 182
Haydon, Sergt., 37

Hayes, Capt., 99
Hayman, 2/Lt., 233
Hayward, 2/Lt., 176
Hazard, Capt., 132, 135 ; Major, 187, 206, 224, 232, 313, 329, 346, 450, 462
Hazard Trench, 212
Hazebrouck, 32, 140, 341, 350, 361
Hazy Trench, 195
Hearden, Lt. (R.W.K.), 90, 96
Heath, 2/Lt., 338, 339
Heath, L/Corpl., 187, 189, 451
Hebuterne, 68, 139, 182, 325, 332
Hedjaz railway, the, 409
Helles (Cape Helles), VI–VII, 72–96, 103, 110, 114–16, 137, 192, 446, 447
' Hellfire Corner ', 232
Hellyer, Lt., 98, 99, 100 ; Capt., 105, 106
Henicourt, 315
Henville, 2/Lt., 265
Herlies, 29
Hermann position, the, 359
Hermies, 371
Herm Trench, 212
Herringfleet, 438
Herstert, 387
Herzeele, 246
Hesdin, 313
Hetherington, Lt., 417, 450
Hetman Chair, 104
Heule, 385
Hewitt, 2/Lt., V.C., 230, 448, 473
Hibshi Bent, the, 160
Hickie, Lt. Col. (R. Fus.), 138, 177
Hicks, E. J., 2/Lt., 249, 250, 369, 450
Hicks, F. M., Capt., 98, 99, 100, 112, 148, 462
Hicks, F. R., Major, 4, 6, 7, 11, 13, 14, 17 ; Lt. Col., 35, 37, 38, 57, 58, 59, 63, 172, 173, 344, 469
Hiddingh, 2/Lt., 173, 472
High Wood, 177, 187
Hill, 2/Lt., 382
Hill, Pte., 124, 451
Hill Q (Anzac), 97
Hill 10 (Suvla), 110, 111
Hill 28 (Suvla), 101, 102
Hill 60 (Suvla), 104, 105, 106, 111, 112, 113
Hill 63 (Ploegsteert), 367, 368, 369
Hill 100 (Suvla), 112
Hill 112 (Suvla), 104
Hill 114 (Helles), 73, 76
Hill 138 (Helles), 73, 76
Hill 141 (Helles), 74
Hillah, 404
Hill Camp, 292
Hillis, 2/Lt., 42 ; Lt., 130, 471
Hills, 2/Lt., 268
Hills, L/Corpl., 429
Hill Top Farm, 206, 208, 229, 314
Hillyer, Lt., 257, 258, 450
Hilt Trench, 194, 195

Himalaya Trench, 244
Hindenburg Line, the, 205–10, XX, 361, 363, 366, 371, 372, 375, 377, 379
Hinley, Pte., 155
Hoath, Pte., 235 ; L/Corpl., 262, 455
Hobson, 2/Lt., 212, 215
Hodge, Sergt., 291, 462
Hodgkins, 2/Lt., 197, 473
Hodson, Capt. (R. of O.), 80, 81
Hodza Bridge, 296
Hogan, 2/Lt., 330, 474
Hog's Head, the, 187
Hohenzollern Bridge, the, 430
Holbrook, 2/Lt. (Gloucestershire), 357, 361, 408
Holdaway, Sergt., 235, 455
Holdaway, Corpl., 244, 455
Holdway, R.S.M., 42, 69, 77 ; 2/Lt., 82, 83, 462, 472
Hole, 2/Lt., 199
Holland, Lt. Genl., 339, 433
Holland, Lt. Col. (Devons), 264, 266
Holland, 431
Hollebeke, 227, 231, 232, 238
Holloway, Lt., 312, 389
Holmes, 2/Lt., 391, 392
Holmes-Gore, Capt., 101, 103
Holman, Sergt. Cook, 137
Holman, Sergt. Drummer, 137
Holroyd, 2/Lt., 60, 64, 476
Homondos, 292
Hondeghem, 27, 341
Hong Kong, 444
Hooge, 61, 66, 375
Hoogmolen, 387
Hoogstraatje, 386
Hook, 2/Lt., 357, 358, 450, 474
Hopgood, Corpl., 176
Hopkins, C.S.M., 50
Hornby, B. Genl., 138
Horsea Island, 51
' Horse Lines ', the, 363
Horseshoe Hill, 155
Houdain, 204
Houlle, 229
Hounslow, 44
Houplines, 28
House, 2/Lt., 320
Howard, A., 2/Lt., 42, 69, 77, 471
Howard, A. C., 2/Lt., 242, 243, 450
Howcroft, 2/Lt., 256
Howson, Capt., 232, 269, 313, 320, 332, 458, 462
H Trenches (Gallipoli), VII, 92–6, 103, 115
Hubback, Capt., 295, 462
Hubbard, R.S.M., 364, 383, 452
Huddleston, B. Genl., 272, 301
Hudson, 2/Lt., 4, 49 ; Capt., 93, 105, 106, 203 ; Major, 245, 330, 343, 349, 358, 375, 450, 462, 471

Hudson, Capt. (R.A.M.C.), 229
Hudson Trench, 212
Hughes, 2/Lt., 219
Hulluch, 135
Humbert, Lt. (R. Berkshire), 86
Humbercourt, 205
Hume, 2/Lt., 61 ; Lt., 68 ; Capt., 132, 173, 387, 450, 462, 471
Humphery, Major, 40, 44, 66, 475
Humphrey-Davy, 2/Lt., 207
Hunt, 2/Lt., 353
Hunter-Weston, B. Genl., 3, 8, 10, 11, 12, 14, 22, 29, 32, 33, 59 ; M. Genl., 72, 95 ; Lt. Genl., 137, 176, 192
Hurll, Sergt., 344, 455
Huskisson, C. A., 2/Lt., 243
Huskisson, H. G., 2/Lt., 377
Huy, 430
Hyderabad, 271
Hyderabad Redoubt, the, 212, 213
Hylton, Capt., 268
Hylton, 2/Lt., 206

Ibanne, 307
Icke, 2/Lt., 196 ; Capt., 244, 310, 450, 476
Illah, 120
Iman al Mansur, 274
Imbros, 82, 104, 108, 110, 114, 116
Imbros House, 247
Im Seirat, 265, 266
Im Thurn, Lt., 4, 22, 32 ; Capt., 34, 35, 37, 38 ; Major, 434, 449, 450, 462, 465, 470
India, 4, 31, 39, 41, 42, 46, 47, 49, 117, 126, 127, 160, 167, 168, 269, 279, 271, 283, 285, 286, 287, 353, 399, 434, 438, 442, 443
Infantry Hill, 216, 217, 218, 219, 222
Ingles, 2/Lt., 369
Inkerman, 65
Inscription Hill (Aden), 443
International Trench, the (Ypres), 66, 67, 68, 172, 174
Ireland, 3, 49, 52, 53, 153, 184, 345, 434
Irish, L/Corp., 35
Iron Bridge Camp, 286, 404
Irwin, 2/Lt., 369
Isaacs, 2/Lt., 373
Isakagova, 434
Isbergues, 345
Island Wood (Gaza), 297, 298
Isle of Wight, 3, 43, 47, 54
Istabulat, 282
Italy, 257, 315, 316, 317, 346
Izel les Hameau, 219

Jackson, Colonel, 4, 11, 14, 448, 462, 469
Jackson, Sergt. (2nd Battn.), 76
Jackson, Sergt. (1st Battn.), 130
Jackson, Pte., 280, 455
Jacob, Lt. Genl. Sir C., 430, 436

Jacob, E. F., 2/Lt., 173 ; Lt., 203, 462, 473
Jaffa, 302, 303, 307
James, A., 2/Lt., 215
James, G. H., 2/Lt., 219, 478
James, J. W., Lt., 140 ; Capt., 190
James, Sergt. Drummer, 436
Janesh, 426
Jangalis, the, 399, 400, 401, 402
Japanese, the, 159
Jarvis, E. G., 2/Lt., 369
Jarvis, P. W., 2/Lt., 290
Java Avenue, 239
Jebel Hamrin range, 282, 283, 288, 392, 405, 441
Jebel Makhul range, 405
Jeffery, Sergt., 439, 459, 462
Jeffries, 2/Lt., 184
Jenikoi, 426
Jemalabad, 403
Jeni Mahale, 151
Jenkins, Lt. Col., 443
Jenner, Lt., 168 ; Capt., 472
Jensen, Lt., 126, 164
Jericho, 407
Jerram, L/Corpl., 250, 455
Jerusalem, 265, 300, 301, 302, 303, 304, 305, 306, 308, 407, 413
Jhansi, 167
Jhelum, 119
Jibin Wadi, 441
Jift, 441
Joffre, General (French), 17, 18, 179, 181, 210
Johnson, R. A., Lt. Col., 48, 168, 287, 404, 445, 448, 462
Johnson, R., 2/Lt., 356
Johnson, Corpl., 422, 455
Johnson, Pte., 194, 455
Johnston, K. A., Lt., 4, 38, 49, 60 ; Capt., 130, 203, 253 ; Lt. Col., 253, 254, 255, 262, 312, 449, 462, 471
Johnston, R. D., Capt., 4, 18, 22, 33, 65, 120, 470
Jones, A. le P., Capt., 115, 116, 136, 138, 204
Jones, I. F., 2/Lt., 365
Jones, R. H., Major, 431, 433, 446, 449, 460, 462
Jones, Capt. (R.A.M.C.), 119, 126, 159
Jordan, the, 407
Jourdain, Lt. Col. (Connaught Rangers), 143
' Jove ' (Jove Lane), 257, 258
Jubbulpore, 168, 286
Judaean Hills, 300, 302, 407
Jumeaux Ravine, 155, 156, 289
Junction Station, 300, 301, 302, 303
Juno Lane, 257, 258
Jutland Trench, 330, 331

Kabak Kuyu, 106
Kaiajik Dere, 104, 112
Kaiser, the, 205
Kajarli, 143
Kalendra, 153
Kalinova, 155
Kangaroo Trench, 247
Kantara, 411, 443
Kara Bail, 146
Karachi, 47, 49, 271, 442
Karadzakoi Bala, 152, 153, 252
Karadzakoi Zir, 152, 153, 292
Karakaska, 153, 288
Karaki, 295
Kara Sinantsi, 418
Karind, 395, 399, 400
Karrodah river, 286
Karun river, 120
Kasauli, 168, 287, 442
Kasvin, 400, 402, 403, 439
Kay, Capt., 272
Keene, Major, 287, 442
Keep, 2/Lt., 227
Kefl, 404
Kefr Qasin, 414
Keir, Lt. Genl., 65
Kellaway, 2/Lt., 290
Kelly, Lt. Col. (see Sherwood-Kelly)
Kelly, 2/Lt. (R. Sussex), 374, 392
Kemmel, 337, 341, 351, 360, 367, 369
Kemmis, Lt. Col., 50, 52
Kemp, C.Q.M.S., 401, 402, 451
Kemp, Sergt., 412, 465
Kennedy-Shaw, Capt., 44, 462, 465
Kennion, Colonel, 397
Kenny, Capt., 411
Kent, 2/Lt., 4, 10, 13, 471
Kent, C.Q.M.S., 401, 402
Kermanshah, 397, 399, 400, 402, 403
Khafajiyah, 120
Khan Baghdadi, 400, 404
Khaniquin, 286, 287, 400
Kharkla river, 120
Khartoum, 445, 446
Khan Yunus, 265
Kh el Bir, 267
Kh ed Duweir, 413
Kh Ibanne, 407
Kh Mansura, 268
Kh Nejjara, 414
Khosinabad, 399
Kh Sirisia, 414
Khudaira Bend, the, 270, 271
Kibbia, 305, 307
Kidney Hill, 103
Kifri, 286
Kijil Urnan, 403
Kilindir, 146, 156
Kilworth, 53, 132

Kimm, Lt., 412, 450, 463
King. A. J., 2/Lt., 328
King, R. D., 2/Lt., 268
King. R.S.M., 68
King, C.S.M. (10th Bn.), 49
King, C.S.M. (II) (10th Bn.), 421, 422, 456, 463
King, Corpl., 139
Kingdom, 2/Lt., 101
Kingsley-Darling, Capt. (R. Scots), 10, 115, 136
Kininmouth, Lt., 291
Kirac, 418
Kirby, Capt., 304, 306, 411, 463
Kiretch Tepe Sirt, 101, 103, 104, 107, 112
Kirte Dere (see Krithia Nullah)
Kispeki, 288, 292, 293
Kitchener, Lord, 4, 41, 52, 123
Kitchener's Wood, 229
Klein Kemmelbeek, 352
Klein Zillebeke, 228, 235
Kluck, General von (German), 3, 13, 15, 16, 17, 19, 20, 25
Kneebone, 2/Lt., 352, 463
Knight, Capt. (R.A.M.C.), 222, 236, 262, 312
Knocker, Lt., 4, 14, 22, 28; Capt., 37, 38, 470
Knokke, 387
Knott, 2/Lt., 259, 260, 261, 451
Koebel, Lt. Col. (N. Staffordshire), 140, 290
Koekuit, 246, 248, 250
Kortewilde, 379
Kohat, 441
Koltchak, Admiral (Russian), 444
Komarjan, 151, 157, 292
Kortebeck, the, 235
Kortewilde, 380
Kosturino, 141, 151, 423, 424
Krasnovodsk, 402
Krastali, 155, 289, 422
Kreupel, 386
Krithia, 76, 77, 78, 79, 83, 85, 91, 446
Krithia Dere (Nullah or Kirte Dere), 78, 79, 84, 85, 95, 115
Krithia Spur, 85
Krusha Balkans, the, 291, 295, 296
Kruiseecke, 380
Kruisstraat, 207
Kubrit, 263
Kuchik Khan, 399
Kufa, 404
Kuflan Kuh, 403
Kum Kale, 75
Kurdistan, 400
Kurds, the, 399
Kurdarrah river, 285
Kurgoman, 432
Kut al Amara, 119, 126, 136, 148, XIII, 274, 275, 276, 278, 280, 282, 285, 287, 406, 440, 446, 447

La Barque, 189
La Bassée, 27, 29, 39, 360; (canal) 27, 39, 238, 337, 339, 340, 342, 347, 348
La Brique, 65
Lacey, 2/Lt., 119, 126; Lt., 151
La Clytte, 351, 352, 361
La Creche, 335, 367, 369
Lacy, Capt., 190
La Ferté sous Jouarre, 19, 21
Lake Ardjan, 152, 418
Lake Beshik, 146, 147
Lake Butkova, 150
Lake Doiran, 143, 145, 149, 150, 155, 156, 289, 291, 418
Lake Langaza, 146, 147
Lake Tahinos, 150, 153, 288, 416
Läiné, 2/Lt., 353, 372; Capt., 390, 399, 450
Lala Baba, 112
La Louvière, 429
Lambert, F. H., 2/Lt., 38, 83, 85, 86, 471
Lambert, H. F., 2/Lt., 351, 368, 369, 450
Lambert, C.S.M., 50
Lambourne, Lt., 115, 477
Lambton, M. Genl., 245
La Montagne Farm, 22, 24
Lamont, Lt. (Middx.), 277
Lamotte, 367
Lancashire, 45
Lane, Lt., 44; Capt., 104, 108, 475
Lane, Pte., 291, 456
Le Neuville en Phalempin, 437
Langaza, 148 (see Lake)
Langdon, A. C., 2/Lt., 387
Langdon, L., 2/Lt., 138
Langemarck, 235, 236, 243, 247, 248, 250
Langrish, Corpl., 277, 451
Lannoy, 343
Lanrezac, General (French), 5, 6, 15, 16, 17
La Pannerie, 342
Lapthorne, 2/Lt., 197
Lark, Corpl., 137, 456
La Roche Noire, 419, 421
La Roupie, 345
La Table, 419
Latham, Lt., 101, 112
La Tortue, 155, 156
La Tranchée des Roches, 419, 421
Latron, 305
La Vacquerie, 260
Laventie, 138
Lawford, M. Genl., 139, 140
Lawrie, Rev. A. E., 248
Leach, 2/Lt., 180, 182, 450, 478
Leach, R.S.M., 159
Learey, Sergt., 140
Le Cateau, 3, 5, 6, 8, 13, 14, 15, 17, 172
Le Cauroy, 340
L'Ecleme, 339, 343, 359
L'Ecluse, 365

Ledgard, Capt., 352, 356, 450, 463
Ledeghem, 383, 384
Ledinghem, 345, 352
Lee, 2/Lt., 352, 360
Lee, Sergt., 139
Leedham, 2/Lt., 370
Le Gheer, 29, 31, 32, 34, 35
Le Hunte, Lt., 4, 13, 470
Leigh, Major, 42, 69, 71, 73, 76, 77, 78, 469
Le Marchant, Lt., 58, 59 ; Capt., 196, 471, 476
Lembet, 149
Lemnos, 70, 71, 90, 91, 92, 93, 94, 101
Lemnos House, 246
Lempire, 318
Lens, 27, 370
Le Quesnoy, 393, 394
Le Rossignol, 368
Lerouf, M., 13
Le Sars, 188
Lesbœufs, 188, 195, 196, 204
Les Cinq Chemins, 248, 249
Les Cloyes, 15
Les Corbières, 19
Les Deux Roches, 419, 420, 421
Le Souich, 177
Les Rues Vertes, 254, 258, 259, 260
Lessines, 396, 430, 436
Lester-Garland, Lt., 119, 123, 164, 276
Le Touquet, 29
Leunovo, 433
Le Verguier, 14
Levi, Capt. (R.A.M.C.), 94, 96
Levy, Pte., 130
Lewes, Major, 101, 105
Lewis, R. J., Lt., 290, 295
Lewis, Sergt., 100
Lewis House, 314
Ley, Sergt., 55, 63, 132, 451
Leybourne, Lt., 317 ; Capt., 360, 369, 450
Light, L/Corpl., 344, 456
Ligny, 7, 8, 9, 10, 11, 13
Ligny sur Marne, 17
Ligny Thilloy, 189, 190
Lille, 27, 385, 437
Lillers, 337, 359
Limepit Hill, 307
Lincolnshire, 48
Lindesay, Lt. Col. (I.A.), 294, 296, 417
Line, 2/Lt., 197
Linton, Lt. Col. (Worcestershire), 255
Lipsett, M. Genl., 389
Liquorice Factory, the, 278
Liverpool, 92, 101
Lloyd, 2/Lt., 252, 278
Lloyd George, Mr., 210, 265
Lloyd Payne, M. Genl., 42
Loader, Capt., 101, 103
Lockhart, Capt., 173, 175, 470
Locon, 359

Locre, 206
Lombardy, 257
Lonergan, Sergt., 317, 456, 463
London, 48, 439
Lone Pine, 93
Longeau, 131, 132, 192
Longley, M. Genl., 151, 153
Longpré, 177
Longueval, 173, 179
Longuevilliers, 134
Loos, 3, 128, 130, 134, 135, 136, 174, 176
Lord, 2/Lt., 42, 69, 77, 88 ; Lt., 94, 96, 104 ; Capt., 115, 136, 137, 192, 204, 219, 255, 262, 312, 450, 472
Lorraine, 9, 17, 18
Louis Farm, 247
Louvencourt, 134, 137, 138
Louth, 45
Love, 2/Lt., 175, 214, 215 ; Lt., 310, 450, 477
Lovelace, 2/Lt., 229
Loveridge, Lt. (4th D.G.), 370
Lowestoft, 352
Lowis, Lt. (Hants Carb.), 370
Lowy, Lt., 92, 142, 146 ; Capt., 419, 421
Lucas, M. Genl., 389
Luce, the, 331
Lucheux, 133
Lucknow, 167
Ludendorff, Genl. von (German), 325, 334, 342, 346
Luffmann, Lt., 87
Lug Farm, 351
Lumbres, 369
Lund, C.S.M., 194, 217, 451
Luxembourg, 438
Luxor, 443
Lydda, 305, 306, 307, 407
Lyndhurst, 46
Lyons, 315
Lys, the, 3, 27, 28, 29, 30, 339, 341, 350, 359, 360, 367, 389, 380, 383, 385, 386, 387
Lyster, Capt. (Leinster), 142, 143

McAvoy, 2/Lt., 219
McCammon, Lt. Col. (R. Irish Rifles), 218, 219
McConnochie, Capt., 326, 450, 463
McCormick, Capt., 49
McCulloch, 2/Lt., 248
McCurdy, 2/Lt., 175
Macedonia (see Salonica), 141, 146, 153, 288, 293, 346, 440
McIvor, Capt., 431
Mackay, J. D., Major, 4, 449, 469
Mackay, Major (A. & S.H.), 291
Mackay, Capt. (A. & S.H.), 87
McKenzie, Capt., 402

MacLachlan, 2/Lt., 256, 463
Macleod, Lt. Col. (S. Africa), 433
McNair, Lt. (R. Warwickshire), 86
McNaught, Lt. Col. (Cheshire), 417, 446
Macrae, 2/Lt., 119, 121, 122, 123
Macukovo, 294, 295
Madras, 126
Magasis, 167
Magdhaba, 265
Magnicourt, 177
Mailly, 134
Mailly-Maillet, 137, 138, 173, 174, 182
Maiyadiya creek, the, 123
Majendie, Lt. Col. (60th), 131, 148
Majinina creek, the, 123, 124
Makina Masus, 119
Malet, Lt. (R. Warwickshire), 86
Malmedy, 430
Malmesbury, Earl of, Capt., 43, 476
Malone, Lt. Col., 139
Malta, 42, 70, 92
Mamelon des Buissons, 419
Mametz, 189, (wood) 190
Man, 2/Lt., 212, 215, 477
Manders, Lt. (R. Berkshire), 89, 96
Manders, Pte., 423, 456
Manjil, 400
Manlove, 2/Lt., 176, 477
Mann, 2/Lt., 94, 96, 450, 463
Mansura, 266, 267, 272, 273
Manton, 2/Lt., 216
Mantua, 316
Marcoing, 252, 253, 255, 256, 258, 259, 260,
    375, 376, 377, 390 ; copse, 259, 260 ;
    Lock, 376
Marfaux, 356, 357
Marianopolje, 426
Marlborough, Duke of (1st), 202, 365
Marne, the, 16, 17, 18, 19, 20, 24, 25, 355,
    357, 358, 417
Mareouil, 204, 211
' Mars ' (Mars Lane), 257, 258
Marseilles, 132, 136, 315, 351
Marsh, Capt., 101, 114 ; Major, 266 ; Lt.
    Col., 270, 297, 307, 449, 463
Marshall, Lt. Genl. Sir W., 274, 285, 404,
    405
Marshall, C. T., 2/Lt., 177
Marshall, H. R., 2/Lt., 423
Martin, 2/Lt., 231
Martin, Sergt., 250, 456
Martinpuich, 185
Martin's Mill, 235
Mary Redan, 137, 138, 173
Masharah, 406
Masnières, 252, 253, 254, 255, 256, 258, 259,
    262, 376
Massey, Capt., 138, 193, 195, 478
Masterman, 2/Lt., 196, 477
Matheson, M. Genl., 245, 389

Matthew, 2/Lt., 390
Matthews, Lt. Col. (D.L.I.), 166, 167, 281,
    397, 400, 403, 437, 438
Maturin, Major, 168 ; Lt. Col., 286
Maubeuge, 394, 435
Maude, Genl. Sir F. S., 167, 234, 278,
    285
Maudhuy, Genl. (French), 27
Maunoury, Genl. (French), 17, 19, 20
Mauritius, 3, 40
May, H. W. M., 2/Lt., 129, 130, 132, 133 ;
    Capt., 200, 201, 229, 349, 391, 392, 431,
    450, 463, 474, 477
May, W. G., 2/Lt., 182
Mayadag, 418
Mayne, Capt., 293
Maynard, B. Benl., 288
Mazingarbe, 135, 176
Meade, 2/Lt., 177
Meaden, Sergt., 436, 456
Meaulté, 177, 190, 195, 205
Meaux, 17
Mechernich, 435
Medcraft, 2/Lt., 423
Meddings, Pte., 344, 456
Mediterranean, the, 26, 129, 140
Mee, Capt., 209
Meerut, 168, 286
Megiddo, 153
Mejdal Tomba, 412
Mejdel Yaba, 408
Melliss, M. Genl., 120, 123, 124
Mena Camp, 263
Menin, 383, 384, 386
Menin road, the, 178, 232, 237, 238, 239,
    241, 243, 313, 314, 378, 380
Menzies-Calder, 2/Lt., 178, 185, 187
Mercer, Lt., 94, 96
Meredith, Lt. Genl., 204, 365
Mericourt, 197, 211, 212, 215, 326
Merj Kesfa, 413, 414
Merrett, 2/Lt., 209
Merris, 351, 360
Merritt, Sergt., 233, 463
Merv, 438
Merville, 339, 361
Mesha, 414
Meshed, 438
Mesopotamia, 41, 42, X, 136, 148, XIII,
    263, 271, 308, XXXI, 409, 412, 434,
    438, 439, 440, 446
Messines, 32, 205–7, XVIII, 241, 327, 380
Meteren, 27, 140, 231, 327, 356, 360, 369
Meteren Becque, the, 361, 367
Meuse, the, 430, 435, 436
Mezeireh, 412
Mhow, 41, 42
Mianeh, 403
Middle Camp, 225
Middlemass, 2/Lt., 248

Middleton, Capt., 43 ; Major, 130, 133 ;
  Lt. Col., 134, 137, 193, 204, 205, 233,
  317, 449, 463, 465, 467, 469
Midie, 307
Midlam, Corpl., 239
Mihalova, 155
Mildenhall, Pte., 172, 456
Mild Trench, 193, 194
Mill, the (Ancre), 129, 130, 133
Miller, M. R., Capt., 404, 463
Miller, G. A., 2/Lt., 136, 175
Miller, Pte., 331, 456
Mills, Capt., 130, 466, 470
Mills, C.Q.M.S., 49
Mills, Sergt., 401, 456
Milne, Genl., 150, 291, 418, 425
Milne, Sergt., 86 ; C.S.M., 263 ; 2/Lt., 385
Minorca, 437
Mirza Kuchik, 399
Mitchell, G., Capt., 290, 295
Mitchell, W. A., 2/Lt., 381, 382, 449
Moascar, 265
Modena, 316
Mœuvres, 366
Mohammed Zai, 441
Mogg Ridge, 410, 411
Moislains, 251
Molyneux, Capt., 313, 331, 450
Monastir, 153
Monchaux, 389, 391, 392
Monchy le Preux, 214, 215, 216, 217, 219,
  222, 223, 233, 244, 248, 309, 310, 327,
  328, 365
Mondicourt, 205, 206, 262, 355, 356
Money, 2/Lt., 171, 450, 463, 473
Mon Plaisir, 255
Monro, Genl. Sir C., 114
Mons, 3, 5, 6, 8, 18, 55, 80, 429, 446, 447
Montagne de Bligny, 357
Montagu of Beaulieu, Lord, Lt. Col., 48, 126
Montagu, Lt., 240
Montaubon, 185
Mont de Lille, 337
Montdenis, 19
Montdidier, 26
Mont d'Origny, 337
Montebelluno, 316
Montello, the, 316
Montmirail, 18
Mooney, 2/Lt., 221
Moor, C., 2/Lt., 83, 87, 93, 95, 472, 476
Moor, G. R. D., V.C., 69, 77, 83, 87, 91, 96,
  108 ; Lt., 310 ; Capt., 392, 448, 450,
  473, 477
Moore, Genl. Sir J., 7
Moore, F. C., Capt., 4, 11, 14, 19, 26 ; Major,
  130, 469
Moore, M. S. S., V,C., 2/Lt., 227, 239, 240 ;
  Lt., 431, 448, 466, 473
Moore Park Camp (Belgium), 206

Moore Park Camp (Ireland), 54
Moores, Sergt., 42
Morant, 2/Lt., 351
Morbecque, 350, 351
Morcourt, 326
Mordaunt, Lt. Col. (Somerset L.I.), 342,
  348, 378
Morgan, B. A. C., 2/Lt., 330, 473
Morgan, C. E., Lt., 26, 44, 475
Morgan, H. J., 2/Lt., 312, 450
Morgan, W., 2/Lt., 177
Morgan, L/Corpl., 401, 456
Morgan, Pte., 172, 456
Morlancourt, 184, 322, 325
Morland, Lt. Genl., 232
Morley, Capt., 4, 49 ; Major, 93, 100, 105,
  106, 463, 469
Mormal, Forest of, 5
Morris, Lt., 87, 95
Morris, L/Corpl., 130
Morse, 2/Lt., 99
Morto Bay, 70, 75, 76, 78, 79
Morval, 188, 204, 205
Mory, 323, 362
Mosselmarkt, 59
Mosul, 404
Mouse Trap Farm, 61, 62, 64
Mount Kemmel, 337
Mount Kokereel, 313
Moxham, Pte., 101, 463
Moxley, Lt., 139
Mudge, Capt., 250
Mud Patch, the, 208, 209
Mudros, 92, 93, 102, 112, 114, 115, 142
Mulebbis, 407
Mulheim, 430, 431
Mullingar, 49, 52, 53
Munden, Corpl., 140, 456
Munich Trench, 139
Munro, Colonel, 44, 462
Munster, 202
Murdin, Corpl., 187 ; Sergt., 190, 317
Murdoch, Major (R.W.K.), 238 ; Lt. Col.,
  315, 325, 359
Murdoch, C.S.M., 50
Murmansk, 431
Murphy, Lt., 101
Murray, Genl. Sir A., 265, 266, 270
Murray, Lt. Col. (Black Watch), 263, 264,
  266, 270
Musandaq Reach, the, 160
Mushahida, 282
Mustafa Pasha, 426

Nablus, 303, 408, 415
Naden, Lt. Col. (Cheshire), 314
Nahr el Auja, 307, 408
Nahr Suqreir, 300, 301
Naish, W., Lt. Col., 46, 169, 463
Naish, W. V. J., Lt., 119, 475

Najaf, 404
Nalder, 2/Lt., 93, 96
Nalin, 307
Nameless Farm, 332
Namur, 435, 436
Namur Crossing, 248
Napier, B. Genl., 42, 72, 79
Narrows, the (see Dardanelles)
Nasiriya, 121, 124, 125, 157
Nauroy, 13
Nebi Samwil, 304, 305, 412
Necklace Hill, 409, 411
Needham, Lt., 126, 163, 168
Neil, 2/Lt., 290, 451
Nelson, B. Genl., 310
Nelson, Major (R.W.K.), 158
Nery, 16
Neuf Berquin, 361
Neuve Chapelle, 3, 38, 174, 334, 360
Neuve Eglise, 337
Nevoljen, 152
New, Sergt., 130
Newby, Lt., 437, 463, 475
Newman, Lt., 227 ; Capt., 324, 325, 369, 450, 473
Newnham, 2/Lt., 173, 175 ; Capt., 343, 450, 472
New Zealand troops, 70, 80, 81, 82, 93, 97, 98
Nichols, Capt., 242
Nicholson, G., 2/Lt., 4, 14, 16, 26 ; Capt., 151, 153, 291, 450, 463, 465, 471
Nicholson, G. H., B. Genl., 39, 45, 132, 448
Nieppe, 27, 28, 29, 238, 335, 336
Nigoslav, 291
Nineteen Metre Hill, 247
Nine Wood, 253
Nippard, Pte., 262, 452
Nishin Palenga, 431
Nivelle, Genl. (French), 210, 217
Niven, 2/Lt., 256
Nixon, Lt. Genl., 120, 126, 157
Nixon, 2/Lt., 173, 477
Nœux les Mines, 132
Noote Boom, 40
Norman, 2/Lt., 290
Norris, Sergt., 137 ; C.S.M., 259, 262, 431, 452
North, Capt., 126, 163, 271
North, Sergt., 231, 456
North Cape, the, 431
North Russia, 431-4
Northover, Lt. (Wiltshire), 370
Noyelles, 253
Noyon, 15
Nukerke, 396
Nunn, Corpl., 108 ; C.S.M., 352, 452

Oblique Row, 225
Oblong Reserve, 226 ; Trench, 226

Oborne, Sergt., 422, 457
Obozerskaya, 433, 434
Obres, 394
O'Brien, 2/Lt., 42, 463, 471
Obscure Row, 227
Observatory Ridge, 207, 228
O'Farrell, Lt. Col., 51, 54, 139
Ogier, Capt. (R. Jersey Militia), 335, 340
Oise, the, 26
Oiselle, 26
Omsk, 442
Onega, the, 433
One Tree Gulley, 104
Ooteghem, 387
Oosttaverne, 226, 227
Openshaw, 2/Lt., 349
Oppy, 211, 212, 215
Optic Trench, 227
Orah, 157, 165, 167
Oram, Sergt., 235, 236, 250, 452, 466
Orange Hill, 216
O'Reilly, Major (Middlx.), 341, 384
Orfano, 146
Orlyak Bridge, 151, 288, 426
Ormanli, 144
Ormond, Sergt., 63
Orsinval, 394
Ortiach (Hortiach), 144, 150
Osborne, D. G., 2/Lt., 281
Osborne, H. J., Lt., 119, 121, 124
Osman Kamilla, 288, 291
Oude Kruiseecke, 380
Ourcq, the, 17, 19, 357
Outersteene Ridge, the, 360, 361
Outpost Hill, 299
Overath, 436
Overheule, 384
Oxborrow, Capt., 231, 323, 325, 450, 463, 473

Pacaut Wood, 337, 340, 342, 343, 344, 347, 348, 349, 359
Pactol Ravine, 418
Padmore, Lt., 126, 159
Paffet, Sergt., 236, 457
Page Roberts, Capt., 119, 163, 164, 463
Pai Tak, 397, 398, 399
Pakeman, Lt., 238
Pakenham, Lt., 69, 77, 471
Palestine, 153, XXI, 293, 294, XXIV, 346, 353, 398, 399, 404, 405, XXXII, 438
Palin, M. Genl., 271
Palk, Hon. L. C., Capt., 4, 9, 11, 19, 35, 36 ; Major, 37, 38, 60, 62, 63 ; Lt. Col., 133, 134, 171, 172, 173, 340, 449, 463, 469
Palmer, C. W., Capt., 287
Palmer, D. C., Major, 132
Palmer, G. C., 2/Lt., 232
Palmer, Hon. R. S., Lt., 126, 163, 168
Palmer, C.S.M., 171 ; R.S.M., 429, 450, 452

Palmer, Sergt., 269, 270, 457
Papadopoulos, Pte., 411, 457
Paradis, 359
Paris, 17, 315, 355, 437
Parke, Lt. Col., 46, 168
Parker, B. S., Capt., 42, 69, 80, 91, 94, 98, 470
Parker, G. H., Major, 25, 37, 43 ; Lt. Col., 49, 463, 469
Parker, H., 2/Lt., 42, 69, 77, 471
Parker, Sergt., 250, 457
Parkes, Capt., 278, 463
Parkham, 2/Lt., 382
Parkhurst, 43, 44
Parkinson, C.S.M., 49
Parkinson, Pte., 172, 457
Parris, Pte., 140, 457
Parry, F. M., Lt., 185
Parry, F. W., 2/Lt., 100 ; Lt., 384
Parson.s Capt., 119, 124 ; Major, 272, 408, 411, 463
Pascal Farm, 250
Pascoe, 2/Lt., 370, 475
Passchendaele, 56, 243, 311, 312
Pavey, 2/Lt., 113
Payne, Pte., 144
Pearce, C. D. F., 2/Lt., 199
Pearce, H. F., 2/Lt., 136
Pearce, T. C. E., 2/Lt., 236
Pearce, 2/Lt. (E. Surrey), 90, 96
Pearse, H. L., 2/Lt., 155
Pearse, S. A. C., 2/Lt., 140, 231
Pearse, Sergt., 429, 463
Pearson, Sergt., 268, 452
Peckham, Corpl., 42
Peel, 2/Lt., 180, 478
Peet, 2/Lt., 251
Pelves, 309
Pennell, Major, 239
Penney, C.Q.M.S., 137
Penney, Pte., 327, 453
Penn-Gaskell, Capt., 69, 74, 75, 80, 470
Pennington, 2/Lt., 232
Perkins, A. B., Major, 48 ; Lt. Col., 463
Perkins, G. F., Capt., 4, 5, 32, 34, 35, 38, 39 ; Major, 68, 130 ; Lt. Col., 272, 412, 449, 463, 465, 470
Peronne, 203, 207, 253, 313, 321, 322
Perrett, 2/Lt., 248
Perry, Lt., 341, 382, 450
Persia, 118, 271, 282, 284, 285, 286, XXXI, 440, 446
Persse, Lt., 50
Peshawar, 287
Petain, Genl. (French), 251, 325, 344
Peters, Lt. Col., 46, 47, 208
Petersfield, 46
Petit Couronné, 284, 290
Petit Morin, 19
Petric, 426

Pezelhoek, 64
Pheasant Wood, 153
Phelps, 2/Lt., 380
Philip, 2/Lt., 190, 477
Phillimore, 2/Lt., 304
Phillips-Jones, Lt. (R. Berkshire), 86
Philipopolis, 427
Philosophe, 176
Phippard, 2/Lt., 248
Piave, the, 316
Pick Trench (Monchy), 218, 219
Picquet Bank, the, 417
Pidgley, Pte., 172, 452
Pierrefonds, 15
Pigden, Lt. and Qr.Mr., 272
Piggott, C. B., Capt., 87, 89, 94
Piggott, L. B., Lt., 93, 96
Pilckem, 173, 175, 234, 344, 345
Pilleau, Major, 49, 97, 98, 99
Pindi (see Rawal Pindi)
Pine, 2/Lt., 235, 236, 474
Pinega, the, 433, 434
Pink Farm, 83
Piper, Corpl., 327, 457
Pirbright, 132
Pirie, 2/Lt., 164
Pitcairn-Campbell, Lt.-Genl., 53
Pite, 2/Lt., 411, 478
Piton l'Eglise, 295
Piton Rocheux, 295
Pittis, Lt., 101, 102 ; Capt., 268, 451, 463
Player, Pte., 124, 452
Playfair, Major, 43 ; Lt. Col., 46, 286, 463
Ploegstreert (' Plugstreet Wood '), 28, 29, 30, 31, 32, 33, 37, 39, 63, 128, 130, 140, 174, 197, 341, 367, 368
Plouvain, 219
Plowden, Lt. Col. (K.S.L.I.), 445
Plumer, Genl. Sir H., 66, 68, 176, 205, 317, 360
Plymouth, 42, 48
Poelcappelle, 56, 230, 243, 247, 248, 249, 250
Poland, 146
Polderhoek, 313, 378
Polygon Wood, 313, 344, 378
Pommiers Redoubt, 192
Pont a Marcq, 396
Pont de Nieppe, 28
Poole, Lt. (A. & S.H.), 87, 88, 94, 96, 104
Poona, 47, 117
Poperinghe, 57, 64, 176, 201, 206, 220, 231, 232, 248, 312, 332, 344
Popham, Capt., 93, 96
Popovo, 294
Portsmouth, 45, 46, 48, 51, 139 (see 14th and 15th Battns.)
Port Soudan, 493
Poteau, 435
Potijze, 65, 173, 175, 176, 351

Potter, G. J., 2/Lt., 360, 370, 452
Potter, K.E., 2/Lt., 349
Poulter, J. C., 2/Lt., 381
Poulter, 2/Lt. (Queen's), 298
Pouncey, 2/Lt., 351
Pourcy, 356
Powell, J. S., Capt., 132, 176
Powell, R. H., 2/Lt., 234
Powell-Jones, 2/Lt., 227
Powney, Col., 43, 438, 448, 463, 475
Powning, 2/Lt., 348, 393
Pozieres, 179
Pratt, 2/Lt., 373
Premy Support, 376
Prendergast, Lt., 26, 30, 37, 40, 44, 64 ; Capt., 204, 215, 341, 367, 476
Préseau, 393, 429
Price, E. W. M., Lt., 173, 472
Price, H., Capt., 272, 300
Price, Sergt., 132
Priez Farm, 303
Primmer, Pte., 218, 457
Pringle, 2/Lt., 423
Prior, Capt., 290
Proven, 235, 237, 246, 248, 311
Prowse, B. Genl., 62, 68, 129
Proyart, 325, 326
Prynn, 2/Lt., 175 ; Capt., 330, 472
Pulteney, Lt. Genl., 16
Punjab, the, 441
Purfleet, 3, 439
Purnell, C.Q.M.S., 50
Puttick, Major (R.W.K.), 370 ; Lt. Col., 382, 436, 464
Pyramids, the, 263

Qalah Jibbah, 405
Qalet Saleh, 406
Qaryat el Enab, 303
Qasr i Shirin, 397, 398
Qizal Robat, 285, 286
Quadrilateral, the, 170, 171, 172
Quandary Farm, 382
Quarantine Farm, 382
Querenaing, 392
Quariba, 440
Quarrier, 2/Lt., 350
Quarter Cottages, 382
Queant, 363, 365, 366, 373
Queen's Hill (Gaza), 272
Quene au Loup, 394
Quetta, 47, 117, 126, 167, 271, 303
Quievy, 390
Quilen, 311
Qurna, 119, 120, 121, 125, 286
Qustul, 303, 304

Rabrovo, 424, 425
Radomir, 426
Radwell, Major, 404

Rafa, 265, 266, 271, 297 ; Redoubt, 298 ; Trench, 298
Rafat, 409, 411, 413
Rake, Major, 50, 53
Railway Alley (Loos), 188
Railway Wood (Ypres), 176, 207
Rainbow Trench, 193
Raineville, 205
Rainy Trench, 195
Raleigh, Sir W., 69
Ralfs, C.S.M., 439, 452
Ramadi, 285, 286
Ramburelles, 197
Ramleh, 305
Ramsbotham-Isherwood, Col., 51, 138
Ramshied, 438
Rancourt, 203
Rantieh, 308
Ras el Ain, 408, 412
Ratcliffe, Pte., 236, 457
Ratsey, C., Capt., 101, 103
Ratsey, D. W., Capt., 101, 103
Ratsey, S. G., Lt., 101 ; Capt., 268
Ravelsberg, the, 339, 367
Ravine des Cascades, 418
Ravine Wood, 227
Rawal Pindi, 117, 119, 126
Rawlings, 2/Lt., 271, 277
Raymond, F. C., 2/Lt., 101, 103
Raymond G., Capt. (R.A.M.C.), 101, 102
Raynbird, Sergt., 119, 121
Rayner, 2/Lt., 392, 450
Read, Lt., 101
Reavell, 2/Lt., 156
Rebbeck, Capt., 168
Recourt Wood, 365, 366
Redan Redoubt, 188
Red House, the, 247
Reeks, Capt., 119, 126, 159
Reeve, 2/Lt., 113
Reeves, E. C., 2/Lt., 37, 464, 471
Reeves, G. F. J., 2/Lt., 83, 87, 476
Regina Trench, 197, 198
Reid, E. B., 2/Lt., 380
Reid, G. W., Capt., 42, 69, 78, 469
Reid, T. E. B., 2/Lt., 235, 236 ; Lt., 363, 450, 478
Reitres Farm, 235
Rendell, C.Q.M.S., 50
Reninghelst, 352
Renshaw, 2/Lt., 330
Rentis, 427
Reselli, 155, 295, 414
Resht, 400, 401, 402
Reutelbeek, the, 301
Reynolds, Capt. (D.G.), 382
Rheims, 344, 346, 358
Rhine, the, 428, 429, 430, 435, 436
Rhodes, J. E., Lt. Col., 80, 101, 113
Rhodes, S. T., 2/Lt., 217

Rhododendron Spur, 97, 98, 99, 108
Rhonelle, the, 392, 393
Ribecourt, 255, 262, 375
Rice, B. Genl., 164, 166
Richards, A. C., Major, 44
Richards, F., 2/Lt., 81, 472
Richards, J. C. F., Capt., 4, 11, 18, 25;
    Major, 464, 466, 469
Richebourg St. Vaast, 139
Richmond, 2/Lt., 363
Riding, Corpl., 262, 452
Riddock, Capt., 404, 406
Ridge Redoubt, 171
Ridgewood, 238, 240
Riez du Vinage, 138, 339, 340, 341, 343, 348
Riggs, H. J., 2/Lt., 365, 474
Riggs, W. C., 2/Lt., 173
Riviera, the, 316
Rixon, Capt., 281
Robat, 443
Robecq, 337, 339, 342, 350
Roberton, 2/Lt., 155
Roberts, 2/Lt., 268
Robertson, Genl. Sir W., 203, 209, 431
Robertson, J. F., Major, 50, 53
Robertson, N. C., Capt., 218, 219
Robertson, R. H., 2/Lt., 259, 260, 478
Roberts-Thomson, Major, 168 ; Lt. Col.,
    442, 443
Robinson, 2/Lt., 319, 332
Robson, Major, 445, 464
Roche Noire, the, 419, 421
Rockley Hill, 289
Rocky Knoll, 290
Rocky Peak, 144
Rodger, 2/Lt., 180
Rodocanachi, 2/Lt., 133, 449, 463, 477
Rœux, 214, 219, 221, 222, 243
Rogers, Pte., 349, 457
Rohde's Picquet, 166
Romani, 264, 265
Romsey, 42
Ronssoy, 313, 318, 319
Roosebeek, the, 226
Roper, F., 2/Lt., 299
Roper, G. R., Capt., 404
Rose, Lt., 4, 13, 475
Rosieres, 16, 17, 327
Rosser, Lt., 69, 70, 79 ; Capt., 80, 81, 85,
    464, 470
Rossignol Wood, 332
Roulers, 64, 232, 248, 383, 384
Roumania, 150, 425, 445
Round Hill, 308
Rowe, Sergt., 218, 457
Rowsell, Capt., 182
Royal Barracks (Dublin), 49
Rozoy, 17
Rumes, 397
Rumilly, 253, 377

Rupel Pass, the, 426
Russell, B. Genl. (N.Z.), 104
Russell, Capt., 268
Russell's Top, 97
Russia (Russian troops), 55, 69, 141, 284,
    309, XXXI, 431-3, 444
Rustchuk, 427, 445
Rutherford, D. C., 2/Lt., 195, 464
Rutherford, J. S., 2/Lt., 119
Ruz Canal, the, 285
Ruz Station, 285, 286
Rycroft, 2/Lt., 299, 478

Saba, 120
Sabine, 2/Lt., 387
Saillisel, 205
Sailly Labourse, 370
St. Eloi, 208, 224, 225, 226, 227
St. Emilie, 313, 318, 319, 321
St. Jean, 57
St. Julien, 56, 57, 60, 173, 229, 230, 237
St. Laurent Blangy, 243
St. Louis, 386
St. Omer, 27, 229
St. Pierre Divion, 180, 200, 201
St. Pierre Vaast, 203
St. Pol, 315
St. Python, 390
St. Quentin, 314, 375, 377, (Canal) 14
St. Sauveur, 15
St. Yves, 30, 31, 32
Salamanca Barracks (Aldershot), 431
Sal Grec Avancé, 294, 295
' Salient ', the (see Ypres)
Salisbury, 45
Salmah, 289, 292, 293
Salmon, C.S.M., 137
Salonica, 107, 125, XII, 271, XXIII,
    XXXIII, 440, 441, 445, 446
Salt Lake, the (Suvla), 104
Samarra, 404, 441
Sambre, the, 375, 394
Samson's Ridge, 272
Samways, C.S.M., 436
Sanctuary Wood, 61
Sandeman, Capt., 22, 44, 58, 475
Sandhurst (R.M.C.), 35, 43
Sandown, 47, 438
Sangster, 2/Lt., 139, 243
Sankey, Pte., 277, 457
Sanna i yat, 165, 274, 278, 280, 281
Sapignies, 322, 324, 361
Sari Bair, 51, 92, 93, 96, 101, 143
Sar i Pol, 398, 399
Saris, 302
Sarrail, Genl. (French), 149, 152, 288, 290,
    293, 416
Saultain, 439
Saulzoir, 389
Saunders, H. C., 2/Lt., 137, 204, 217, 450

Saunders, W. J., Lt. and Qr.Mr., 49, 99, 100, 106, 111, 450, 464, 471
Savage, H., 2/Lt., 240
Savage, H. W., Capt., 49, 99
Sayed Hussain, 399
Saye, Capt., 206
S. Beach (Gallipoli), 70, 76
Scabbard Trench, 309
Scarborough, Capt. (Devons), 298
Scarpe, the, 212, 217, 221, 222, 233, 243, 244, 318, 327, 331, 359, 373
Schakken, 227
Scheldt, the, 252, 253, 318, 375, 386, 387, 388, 392, 437 ; (canal) 252, 253, 375, 376, 377
Schwaben Redoubt, the, 180, 188, 197, 201, 209, 246, 315
Scimitar Hill, 104
Sclater, Genl. Sir H., 439
Scoggin, 2/Lt., 175
Scotland, 47, 437
Scott, A., 2/Lt., 356
Scott, O. A., Lt., 92, 143 ; Major, 421, 423, 451, 464
Scott, R. J., Capt., 260, 262, 312, 369, 452, 464, 466
Scott, Sir W., 9
Scrivens, 2/Lt., 248
Scully, Major (R. Irish), 143, 144, 148
Scutt, 2/Lt., 249, 250, 452
Seabrook, Sergt., 422, 458
Seaforth Crater, 176
Seal, 2/Lt. (Hants Carb.), 380, 387
Sebourg, 429
Seclin, 437
Secunderabad, 47, 117, 286, 287
Sedd el Bahr, 71, 73, 74, 75, 76, 87
Seed, 2/Lt., 351
Seeley, C. C., Capt., 101, 268
Seeley, F. R., 2/Lt., 215, 473
Sears, Lt., 221 ; Major, 246, 464
Sehneh, 402, 407
Selle, the, 388, 389, 390, 391, 392
Selvigny, 12
Senlis, 199
Sensée, the, 257, 359, 365, 373
Septmonts, 22
Serain, 11
Serapeum, 263, 269
Seres, 150, 426
Sergeant, 2/Lt., 239, 240, 450, 473
Sermaize, 15
Sermil, 399
Serre, 169, 178
Servia, 3, 111, XII (see Salonica)
Shadbolt, 2/Lt., 323, 325, 450
Shaddock, 2/Lt., 281
Shahraban, 285
Shaiba, 120
Shallufa, 263

Sharp, 2/Lt., 335, 339
Shatra Channel, the, 122, 123
Shatt al Hai, 119, 165, 274-9
Shaw, 2/Lt., 184 ; Capt., 317, 450
Shaw, Pte., 106
Sheaf, Pte., 236, 458
Shearer, 2/Lt., 173
Shearing, Col. Sergt., 132, 452
Sheffield, Lt., 87, 94, 96
Sheik Abbas, 265, 266, 267, 268, 269, 272
Sheik Ajlin, 298
Sheik el Gharwahi, 305
Sheikh Hassan, 298, 305
Sheikh Muannis, 412
Sheikh Nufukh, 410
Sheikh Obeid, 307
Sheikh Othman, 442, 443
Sheikh Saad, 157, 160, 162, 163, 169
Shelly, 2/Lt., 347
Shelton, 2/Lt., 100, 268
Shephard, 2/Lt., 348
Sherwood-Kelly, Lt. Col. (Norfolk), 431, 433
Sheryer, 2/Lt., 231
Shields, 2/Lt., 231
Shillingston Hill, 30
Shipka Pass, 427
Shirley, 2/Lt., 343, 474
Shone, Capt., 99, 100
Shore, R.Q.M.S., 440
Shorland, 2/Lt., 377, 449, 464
Shrapnel Gully (Gallipoli), 93, 99 ; Trench (Monchy), 218, 219
Shrewsbury Forest, 238
Shumran Bend, the, 278, 279, 280, 282
Shuqba, 407, 408
Siberia, 418, 444, 445, 446
Sidi Bishr, 114, 263
Sidney, Lt. Col. (Northbld. Hussars), 435
Silbury Hills, 289, 290
Silk, 2/Lt., 41 ; Lt., 69, 79, 87, 103, 104, 471
Sillence, C.S.M., 249 ; 2/Lt., 343, 458, 464, 475
Siloam, Pools of, 164
Silistria, 443, 446
Simcock, Pte., 130, 344, 458
Simmonds, 2/Lt., 219
Simmonds, R.S.M., 50
Simmons, F. W., Capt., 304, 306
Simmons, P. E. H., Capt., 119, 124
Simms, O.R.S., 50
Simms, L/Corpl., 62
Simoncourt, 217
Sims, 2/Lt., 134, 173, 369
Sims, L/Corpl., 422, 458, 464
Sinai, Desert of, 263, 264, 271
Singapore, 444
Singleton-Gates, G. R., Capt., 255, 262, 334, 437, 450, 478

Singleton-Gates, W. S., Lt., 340, 450
Sinjabis, the, 399
Sinn (see El Sinn)
Sinsbury, Sergt., 95, 452, 464
Sixteen Palms, 123
Skegness, 48
Skinner, Capt., 177, 182 ?
Slater, 2/Lt., 335, 339
Smith, A.Lt. and Qr.Mr., 69, 80, 81, 87, 96,
    115, 204, 233, 464, 465, 471
Smith, A. G., 2/Lt., 185 ; Lt., 250, 450
Smith, A. L. F., Capt., 287
Smith, C. R., Lt., 42, 69, 79, 470
Smith, J., 2/Lt., 326
Smith, M. T., 2/Lt., 132, 174, 450, 476
Smith, N. E., 2/Lt., 356
Smith, S. A., 2/Lt., 99
Smith, S. G., Lt. Col., 286, 287
Smith, V. C. E., Lt., 134, 474
Smith, J., R.S.M. (3rd Bn.), 438, 439, 460
Smith, J., R.S.M., 49, 112, 464
Smith, E., R.Q.M.S., 96
Smith, R. E., C.S.M., 187, 190, 452
Smith, Sergt., 440
Smith, R. H., Pte., 250, 458
Smith, T., Pte., 62
Smith-Dorrien, Genl. Sir H., 5, 6, 7, 13,
    15
Smythe, C. C., 2/Lt., 35 ; Capt., 130, 173,
    175, 243, 431, 432, 450, 471
Snelling, Corpl., 181, 452
Snow, M. Genl., 3, 7, 22
Snow, Corpl., 124, 452
Sniper's Knoll, the, 416
Snyder, 2/Lt., 219
Sofia, 426
Soissons, 20, 346, 357
Solesmes, 5, 6, 390, 391, 392
Solon, 441
Somaliland, 95
Sommaing, 391
Somme, the, 26, 131, 133, 136, 139, XIV,
    XV, 202, 205, 210, 217, 223, 225, 228,
    251, 319, 321, 322, 325, 327, 331, 333,
    334, 359, 362, 446, 447
Sommesous, 355
Sorel le Grand, 253, 315
Souastre, 354
Soudan, the, 206, 443
South Africa, 26, 43, 133, 173
South America, 101
Southampton, 4, 46, 54, 441, 444
Southwold, 438
Sovereign Wood, 384
Soward, 2/Lt., 212, 215
Spaabrockmolen, 206
Sparrow, 2/Lt., 419, 421, 477
Spencer, 2/Lt., 232 ; Lt., 315, 352, 360, 450,
    464, 473
Spencer-Smith, G. S. W., Lt., 411

Spencer-Smith, R. O., Capt., 69, 72, 73, 74,
    75, 77 ; Major, 104, 115, 132, 137, 464,
    470
Spinney, Capt., 119
Sprake, 2/Lt., 25, 37, 38 ; Lt., 68, 175,
    471
Spree Farm, 312, 334
Sprigg, Capt., 411
Spring, Major, 222, 233, 236 ; Lt. Col., 248,
    249, 250, 253, 449, 464, 469
Squibb, Sergt., 130, 464
Squires, Pte., 276, 458
Staceghem, 386
Stack, Capt., 132, 181, 184, 206, 464
Staden, 235, 243
Standen, Lt., 26, 32, 33, 44, 476
Stannard, 2/Lt., 247, 248 ; Lt., 343, 450
Staples, Pte., 194, 458
Stapleton, Capt., 185
Stavros, 146, 147, 416, 418
Steamer Point (Aden), 442
Steenbeek, the, 229, 230, 284, 285
Steenwerck, 335, 367
Steers, Corpl., 185, 187, 452
Stevens, A. E., 2/Lt., 59, 62, 66, 132, 464
Stevens, B. F., Capt., 50, 52
Stevenson, A. L., Major, 272
Stevenson, R. J., 2/Lt., 348, 474
Stevenson, S. D., 2/Lt., 412
Stewart, Major (R.E.), 371
Stilwell, J. B. L., Major, 167 ; Lt. Col., 271,
    353, 354, 407, 409, 411
Stilwell, J. G., Lt., 119, 163
Stillwell, W. B., Major, 119, 124, 126, 163,
    164, 449
Stockley, Capt., 194
Stojakovo, 424
Stokes, Lt. Col., 402
Stokes, C. C., 2/Lt., 240
Stokes, H. F., Lt., 401, 450
Stone, Capt. (Norfolk), 48
Stone, F. C., Sergt., 368, 452, 458
Stone, H., Sergt., 317, 458
Stone, Corpl., 77
Stopbutt Hill, 408
Stopford, Lt., 187
Stormy Trench, 193
Strassburg Line, the, 201
Stratford on Avon, 42
Strazeele, 224
String Trench, 218, 219
Stringer, 2/Lt., 221
Stuart, Genl., 202
Stuart, Lt., 290, 295
Struma, the, 148, 149, 150–5, 288, 291, 292,
    293, 416, 417, 418, 426
Strumica, 424, 425
Sturges, C.S.M., 106, 452
Stuff Redoubt and Trench, 188, 197
Sturdy, Capt. (R.A.M.C.), 222

Suafir el Garbiyeh, 301
Suez, 271, 272, 443
Suez Canal, the, 136, 263, 264, 265
Suffolk, 438
Sugar Loaf Hill, 265
Suhabanja, 155, 289
Sukash Shuyukh, 121
Sulajik, 101
Sulman, Lt., 206 ; Capt., 313, 319, 450, 469
Sultanabad, 400, 401, 403
Summerhill Camp, 149
Sumner, R.Q.M.S., 136, 464
Sumption, 2/Lt. (Hants Carb.), 383
Surafend, 407, 412
Surkhadiza Khan, 398, 399
Surrey, 52, 138, 139
Susak Kuyu, 106
Sus St. Leger, 262, 311
Sussex, 48
Sutcliffe, 2/Lt., 268, 450, 464
Sutton, 2/Lt., 101, 103
Sutton Veney, 53, 131
Suvla, VIII, IX, 268, 447
Swann, Rev. S. E., 330
Swayne, Lt., 104
S.W.B. Gully, 106
Sweet, 2/Lt., 4, 26, 471
Swettenham, 2/Lt., 134, 173
Swindon Hill, 290
Switch Line (Flers), 185
Symes, Capt., 130, 464, 465, 469

Table Mountain, 406
Taberer, 2/Lt., 242, 243 ; Lt., 347, 449, 464, 478
Tabriz, 403
Tahinos Lake, 150, 153, 288, 416
Taintignies, 396
Takigara Pass, the, 399, 400
Taku Forts, the, 42, 87
Talbot-Ponsonby, Lt., 48
Tanner, 2/Lt., 100 ; Lt., 151
Tarrant, Lt. and Qr.Mr., 51, 68 ; Capt., 203, 465, 471
Tatarli, 143, 145
Taube Farm, 249
Taylor, Lt. Col. (R. Irish), 416, 422, 423, 445
Taylor, 2/Lt., 249, 392
Taylor, Sergt., 204, 452
Teague, R.Q.M.S., 317, 460
Tea Support Trench, 185
Tekke Burnu, 71
Tekke Tepe, 102
Tel es Sheria, 299
Tel Ibara, 285
Tel Mahaijir, 404
Tenbrielen, 380
Tenedos, 71
Terhand Line, the, 383

Tertry, 14
Tew, 2/Lt., 180, 182
Thames, the, 175
Therouanne, 345
Thiepval, 128, 179, 180, 188, 197, 200
Thomas, Capt. (E. Surrey), 90, 96
Thomas, 2/Lt., 243
Thomas, Pte., 304, 413, 452
Thompson, F. P., 2/Lt., 173, 477
Thompson, I. F. R., Lt. Col. (I.A.), 276
Thompson, R. E., Capt., 335, 337, 339, 341
Thompson, S., Capt., 185
Thompson, Sergt., 204, 411, 452
Thompson, O.R.S., 137
Thorn, Corpl., 42
Thorne, Major (R. Sussex), 164
Thorne, Lt., 233
Thornton, Major, 51
Three Bushes Hill, 409, 410, 411, 417
Thyne, Capt., 132, 181 ; Major, 313, 321, 326, 450
Tibbs, 2/Lt., (Wiltshire) 370
Tidy, 2/Lt., 290
Tigris, the, 119, 126, XIII, XXII, 404, 405, 406
Tikmaidasht, 403
Tikrit, 202, 404, 405, 441
Tilbury, 431, 434
Tilley, A., 2/Lt., 176
Tilley, J. E., 2/Lt., 173 ; Capt., 313, 331, 450, 464, 477
Tilly, L/Corpl., 344, 458
Tinans Point, 408
Tincourt, 320
Tinhat Hill, 410
Tirlecourt Wood, 315
Todd, 2/Lt., 195, 219
Tolgas, 432
Tollemache, C. H., 2/Lt., 135
Tollemache, H. M., 2/Lt., 352, 464
Tollemache, M. C., 2/Lt., 175
Tompson, Major, 44, 448
Toogood, Capt., 411, 412, 464
Toogood, C.S.M., 218
Toogood Hill, 410, 411
Topsa, 432, 433
Toronto Camp, 207
Tourcoing, 386
Tournan, 18
Tournehem, 225
Toussoum, 265
Tower, 2/Lt., 314
Tower Hamlets, the, 239, 240, 241, 242, 243, 313, 315, 378, 427
Tower Trench, 241, 242, 243, 313
Townshend, M. Genl., 121, 126, 157, 159, 161, 162
Towsey, B. Genl., 238
Tragique Farm 247

Tranchée des Roches, 419, 421
Tranquille Farm, 248, 249
Trans-Caspia, 403, 404, 439, 440
Trans-Caucasia, 397
Trans-Jordan, 409
Treble, 2/Lt., 195
Trethewy, Sergt., 250, 452
Trevett, 2/Lt., 189, 323, 325, 450
Trevor-Roper, Capt., 207 ; Major, 230
Triangle Trench, 297, 298
Trimmer, Lt., 4, 31, 32, 33, 470
Trinquois, the, 373, 374
Trois Arbes, 335
Troitsa, 432, 433
Tuff's Farm, 235, 236
Tumba, 147, 150
Tumbitza Farm, 157
Tunks, 2/Lt., 339
Tunnel Trench, 257
Turbeaute Stream, the, 359
Turco Farm, 229
Turkey, 118, 425, 426, 439, 441, 442, 443
Turks, the, VI–IX, X, XXI, XXII, 288,
    XXIV, 396, 402, 403, 405, 406, XXXII,
    441
Turner, E. W. C., 2/Lt., 175, 478
Turner, J. W., 2/Lt., 244, 245
Turner, T., 2/Lt., 377, 378, 450
Turner, Corpl., 62, 458
Turner, Pte., 412, 458
Tweedie, Major (Gloucestershire), 149
Twelve Tree Copse, 83, 85, 87, 88
Twin Canals, 166, 167
Twin Copses, 244
Twining, Lt., 25, 27 ; Capt., 40, 44, 62, 475
Tyler, 2/Lt., 230
Tyler, R.Q.M.S., 69 ; R.S.M., 204, 464

Uffington, Lord, 2/Lt., 356, 359, 476
Umbrella Hill, 297
Umm al Baram, 164
Umm as Sabiyan, 123
United States, the, 309
Unwin, Capt., 3, 26, 27, 29, 32, 33, 34, 39,
    60, 465, 470
Unwin, Commander (R.N.), 70
Upson, Pte., 130
Urals, the, 444
Ust Pinega, 433

Vaire sur Corbie, 332
Valenciennes, 393, 394, 429
Vancouver, 444
Vandeleur, B. Genl., 153
Vardar, the, 141, 149, 150, 153, 288, 293,
    294, 417, 418, 419, 440
Varna, 446
Vaucelles, 16
Vauchelles les Quesnoy, 137
Vaux Vraucourt, 361, 362, 363

V Beach (Gallipoli), 71, 72, 73, 74, 76, 91,
    100, 279
Veasey, Capt., 48 ; Major, 101, 102, 465
Vendhuille, 375, 377
Venizel, 22
Venizelists, the, 417
Venour, Lt., 34, 470
Ventnor, 48
Verberie, 15, 16
Verdun, 55, 133, 136, 148, 174
Verlorenhoek, 57, 232
Vermand, 14
Vermelles, 371
Vernon, Lt. Col. (60th), 272
Vernon, 2/Lt., 126
Verrall, Pte., 124, 452
Vesle, the, 22
Vicars-Miles, Lt., 369, 450, 472
Vierstraat, 205, 369
Viesly, 6
Vieux Berquin, 351
Vieux et Robert, 436
View Farm, 64
Vignacourt, 205
Villar, Capt., 413, 414
Ville Montoire, 26
Villeneuve le Comte, 19
Villers Cotterets, 16
Villers en Couchies, 378
Villers Faucon, 313, 315, 320
Villiers sur Ailly, 117
Villiers sur Morin, 19
Vimy Ridge, 211, 212
Vincent, C. W., Capt., 268, 269 ; Major,
    297, 465
Vincent, 2/Lt., 291, 295
Vineyard, the, 85
Virhanli, 154 ; farm, 154 ; stream, 153
Vladivostock, 444
Vlamertinghe, 57, 175, 344
Voormezeele, 225
Voyennes, 15
Vraucourt, 362

Waddington, 2/Lt., 4, 49 ; Capt. 100, 471
Wade, Lt., 25, 31, 33 ; Capt., 34, 450, 465 ;
    Major, 466, 470
Wadi, the, 160, 161, 162, 163, 165, 283
Wadi Abu Lejja, 407
Wadi Deir Ballut, 407, 408, 409, 411
Wadi el Ayun, 413, 414
Wadi el Bahute, 414
Wadi el Hesi, 300
Wadi el Majina, 301
Wadi Ghuzze, 265, 266, 267, 269
Wadi Halfa, 443
Wadi Ikba, 413
Wadi Orwell, 413
Wadi Qana, 409
Walford, Capt. (R.A.), 74

Walford, O. R., 2/Lt., 59, 472
Walker, Colonel, 50, 131
Walker, Capt. (R.A.M.C.), 344
Walker, Pte., 291, 465
Walkinshaw, Capt., 400, 403, 465
Wallace, Colonel, 48
Wallace, T. V. W., 2/Lt., 298
Wallace, 2/Lt. (Yorkshire), 400
Wallis-Wilson, 2/Lt., 200, 201, 229, 242, 450
Walmsley, Lt., 393
Walton, B. Genl., 167
Wambaix, 6
Ward, Lt. Col. (Middlx.), 444
Ward, 2/Lt., 132, 465, 472
Warlencourt, 317, 328
Warlus, 310
Warluzel, 361
Warminster, 8
Warnelle, the, 6, 7, 8, 11
Warren, F. R. F., Capt., 199
Warren, H., 2/Lt., 227
Warren, Sergt., 230, 235, 452, 458
Warwick, 42, 69
Warwickshire, 42
Waterloo, 430
Watford, 101
Watou, 334, 335, 352
Watson, A. R., 2/Lt., 216, 475
Watson, L. C., 2/Lt., 101, 103
Watson, Capt. (R.A.M.C.), 277
Watten, 229, 252
Watts, J. W., 2/Lt., 219, 473
Watts, R. P., Lt., 59, 471
Waziristan, 287
W. Beach (Gallipoli), 71, 73, 114, 116
Weale, C.Q.M.S., 50
Weatherall, 2/Lt., 164, 281 ; Lt., 399
Webb, G. V. T., Lt., 69, 79, 83, 87, 88, 92, 95, 470
Webb, H. J., Capt., 404
Wedderburn, Lt. (Hants Carb.), 360
Wedge Wood, 177
Weeding, 2/Lt., 101
Weeks, 2/Lt., 307, 371, 372, 411, 466
Welhams, 2/Lt., 173
Wells, Sergt., 42
Wells, Corpl., 272, 412, 458
Wellstead, Capt., 136
Welsh, 2/Lt., 339
Welsh Ridge, 259
Wermelskirchen, 430, 435, 438
Wervicq, 380, 381, 382
Wesley. Sergt., 344, 458
West, Capt., 230, 341, 351, 367, 369, 450, 474
West, Corpl., 155
Watmore, 2/Lt., 173
Westmorland, H. C., 2/Lt., 4 ; Lt., 25, 130; Capt., 134, 232, 234, 235 ; Major, 312 ; Lt. Col., 334, 341, 380, 385, 435, 449, 465, 471

Westmoorland, H. G., Major, 44, 465
Wessex Bridge, 151
Weston, 2/Lt., 34, 44, 60, 476
Weston, B. Genl., 370
Westoutre, 352
Westroosebeke, 314
Whaley, F. J., 2/Lt., 217 ; Capt., 381, 451
Whaley, O. S., 2/Lt., 99
Wheeler, G. P., 2/Lt., 371, 373, 390, 394, 451
Wheeler, C.Q.M.S., 182, 465
Wheeler, Sergt., 269, 270, 459
W. Hills (Suvla), 104
Whitaker, Capt., 44
Whitaker, C.S.M., 49
Whitaker, Corpl., 235, 236, 250, 459
White, A. H., Capt., 242, 243, 451
White, A. R., 2/Lt., 146
White, A. W., Lt., 352, 360
White, J., Lt., 69, 76, 79, 80, 82, 85, 471
White Chateau, the, 227
White Scar Hill, 422, 423, 424
Whitmarsh, 2/Lt., 235, 237
Whitten, 2/Lt., 339
Whittome, 2/Lt., 100
Wieltje, 57, 61, 63, 229, 311, 318, 344
Wieltje Farm, 64
Wight, Isle of, 3, 43, 47, 48
Wigmore, Capt., 239, 240, 325, 332, 451, 465
Wilde, 2/Lt., 133
Wilhelma, 308
Wijdendrift, 235
Wilkens, Pte., 194, 452
Wilkinson, J. C., Lt., 271, 401
Wilkinson, P. S. M., Lt., 188
Williams, P. C., Lt., 98, 100
Williams, W. C., Lt., 155
Williams, W. deL., Major, 4 ; Lt. Col., 73, 74, 75, 78, 83, 85, 87 ; B. Genl., 115 ; M. Genl., 492, 448, 465, 466, 467, 469
Williams, Capt. (R.A.M.C.), 4, 13, 18
Williams, C.S.M., 360, 452
Williams, Corpl., 357, 459
Williamson, Sergt., 33
Willis, 2/Lt., 290, 295, 296, 451
Wilson, C. F., 2/Lt., 356
Wilson, W. T., 2/Lt., 373
Wilson, B. Genl., 22 ; M. Genl., 66 ; Lt. Genl., 131
Wiltshire, 50
Wincer, 2/Lt., 351
Winchester, 43, 46, 50, 51, 132, 138, 429, 438
Windebank, L/Corpl., 285, 459
Windle, Capt., 206
Winnizeele, 311, 314
Winter, Pte., 58
Withers, R.S.M., 439, 460, 465
Witley, 138, 139
Wizernes, 26, 345

Wolfsberg, the, 386
Wombwell, Major, 50
Wood, 2/Lt., 197
Wood, Pte. A., 194, 459
Wood, Pte. F., 236, 459
Woodford, C.Q.M.S., 137
Woodley, 2/Lt., 365, 479
Wool, 54
Woollven, 2/Lt., 390, 479
Woolpress Village, 278
Wooldridge, 2/Lt., 234
Wootten, Sergt., 63, 460
Wormhoudt, 229
Wright, 2/Lt., 227
Wyatt, Lt. Col., 286, 404
Wyatt, Pte., 411, 459
Wyld, 2/Lt., 35, 38 ; Lt., 59 ; Capt., 130, 132, 173, 203, 451, 465, 471
Wyles, 2/Lt., 126, 164
Wylye Ravine, the, 289
Wymer, Capt., 69, 72, 79, 80, 81, 85, 449, 465, 470
Wynberg, 383
Wynn, 2/Lt., 392
Wytschaete, 224, 237, 380, (Wood) 224

X Beach (Gallipoli), 71, 73, 74, 76

Yangijah, 403

Yates, 2/Lt., 260
Yazur, 301
Y Beach (Gallipoli), 71, 77, 83, 87, 89
Yemtsa, 152
Yenikoi, 152
York, 4
York Trench, 181
Young, 2/Lt., 375, 376
Young-James, Lt., 101, 103
Ypres, 3, 28, 31, 36, 40, 51, V, 128, 170, 173, 174, 176, 190, 206, 207, XVIII, XIX, 311, 312, 314, 316, 334, 337, 341, 344, 345, 351, 378, 379, 380, 389, 446, 447
Ypres-Comines canal, 226, 227, 228, 380
Ypres-Yser canal, 57, 60, 62, 63, 64, 65, 66, 67, 206, 207, 228, 229, 231, 236, 314
Yvrencheux, 134

Zandvoorde, 380
Zeitoun, 271, 272
Zenjan, 403, 439, 440
Zillebeke, 178, 207, 344, 345
Zollern Redoubt, the, 188
Zonnebeke, 234
Zor, 282
Zouave Ford and Wood, 150, 151
Zowaid Copse, 298
Zowaid Trench, 298

INDEX OF FORMATIONS AND UNITS

ARMIES
  B.E.F., the, 5, 6, 13, 15, 16, 17, 18, 19, 20, 22, 24, 26, 40, 65, 80, 125
  First Army, 138, 334, 341, 359, 360, 363, 370, 375, 389, 391, 392, 396
  Second Army, 66, 68, 116, 184, 188, 205, 209, 224, 257, 332, 334, 337, 341, 344, 351, 360, 361, 375, 380, 383, 385, 386, 392, 396
  Third Army, 68, 128, 131, 133, 137, 205, 209, 210, 217, 224, 233, 238, 248, 252, 256, 257, 318, 319, 322, 325, 327, 331, 333, 334, 341, 359, 362, 363, 366, 375, 376, 391, 392, 393
  Fourth Army, 173, 179, 188, 202, 205, 251, 324, 359, 362, 363, 366, 373, 375, 377, 391, 392, 394
  Fifth Army (formerly Reserve), 179, 197, 205, 237, 251, 314, 318, 319, 321, 325, 327, 333, 341, 360, 361, 375, 382, 385, 391, 392
  B.S.F., the, XI, XXIII, XXXIII
  E.E.F., the, XXI, XXIV, XXXII
  Force D, 42, X, XIII, XXII, XXXI
  M.E.F., the, 52, VI–IX, 130, 283
  New Armies :
    First (K 1), 48, 49, 50, 52, 112, 128, 131
    Second (K 2), 48, 49, 50, 128, 131
    Third (K 3), 49, 50, 128, 131
    Fourth (K 4), 51, 53, 54, 84, 90, 205
    Fifth (K 5), 53, 54
  Desert Column (Egypt and Palestine), XXI
  Eastern Force (Egypt and Palestine), XXI
  Army of the Rhine, 429, 430, 434, 435, 436, 437
FRENCH
  First, 359
  Fourth (Gouraud's), 355
  Fifth (Lanrezac's, Franchet d'Es- perey's), 5, 6, 15, 16, 17, 18, 417
  Sixth (Maunoury's), 17, 19, 20
  Tenth (Maudhuy's), 27
GERMAN
  First (Kluck's), 5, 13, 15, 16, 19, 24, 25
  Second (Bülow's), 15, 19, 24
TURKISH
  Seventh, 300
  Eighth, 300, 303, 305
BRIGADES
  5th, 3, 361
  10th, 4, 5, 6, 19, 57, 61, 63, 70, 171, 195, 211, 214, 219, 247, 328, 337, 340, 342, 389, 392, 393
  11th (see 1st Hampshire)

12th, 4, 5, 6, 8–19, 20, 22, 27, 28, 29, 61, 63, 170, 171, 195, 211, 212, 214, 219, 248, 329, 330, 337, 342, 365, 366
19th, 16
23rd, 138
29th (see 10th Hampshire, to p. 153)
30th, 143, 144, 146, 152
31st, 144, 145
34th, 104
35th, 193
38th, 97, 99, 100, 282, 406
39th, 275, 401, 402
40th, 278
47th, 183, 317, 321, 326
48th, 183, 184, 321, 326
49th, 321, 326
68th, 315
71st, 194
74th, 335
76th, 377
78th, 289, 290, 424
79th (see 12th Hampshire)
80th, 293, 421
81st, 152, 292
82nd (see 10th Hampshire, from p. 153)
85th, 57, 445
86th, 71, 73, 77, 78, 80, 88, 90, 96, 103, 109, 165, 169, 217, 218, 236, 253, 255, 258, 259, 260, 335, 341, 351, 361, 367, 368, 386, 395
87th, 77, 79, 80, 85, 88, 102, 104, 110, 115, 169, 194, 205, 218, 233, 235, 236, 253, 255, 258, 259, 325, 341, 361, 367, 385, 386
88th (see 2nd Hampshire)
116th (see 14th Hampshire)
117th, 180, 188, 197, 200, 229, 238, 241
118th, 180, 188, 197, 200, 229, 230, 241, 242
122nd (see 15th Hampshire)
123rd, 187, 190, 227, 228, 230, 240, 335, 380, 387
124th, 187, 227, 239, 323, 380, 383, 387
127th, 79, 80
128th (Hampshire Territorial), 45, 46
153rd, 233
156th, 87, 88, 297, 298, 301, 304
157th, 90
161st, 112, 113, 265, 298, 414
162nd, 92, 103, 268, 298, 305, 414
163rd (see 1/8th Hampshire)
185th, 356, 375, 391, 399
186th (see 2/4th Hampshire from p. 353)
187th, 357, 361, 362, 375, 399
232nd (see 2/5th Hampshire)
233rd (see 2/4th Hampshire to p. 353)

234th, 301, 302, 303, 304, 408, 409, 411
238th (Special), 431
7th Mounted, 148
INDIAN
9th, 160, 161, 162, 163
19th, 163
28th, 161, 165
29th, 79, 83, 88, 93, 106
30th, 120, 121, 123, 124, 157
33rd, 119
34th, 405
35th, 163 (see 1/4th Hampshire, pp. 164–167), 275, 276, 278, 280, 282
36th (see 1/4th Hampshire from p. 167)
37th 167, 276, 277, 279, 280, 285
46th (Mobile), 441
51st, 405
52nd (see 1/6th Hampshire from p. 286)
N.Z. at Gallipoli, 80, 81, 97, 98
CORPS
Cavalry, 241
First, 5, 15, 19, 20, 22, 24, 28, 31, 34, 337, 339, 437
Second, 5, 6, 7, 8, 12, 15, 19, 20, 22, 26, 27, 29, 31, 33, 34, 35, 378, 430
Third, 16, 17, 19, 20, 22, 26, 27, 29, 32, 34, 65, 252, 255
Fourth, 322, 323, 324
Fifth, 39, 57, 179, 323, 324
Sixth, 65, 212, 214, 215, 267, 359, 361, 362, 371, 375, 377, 390
Seventh, 212, 318
Eighth, 93, 95, 103, 114, 137, 170, 172, 174, 337
Ninth, 95, 101, 102, 103, 108, 224, 241, 325
Eleventh, 317, 319
Twelfth, 131, 133, 150
Thirteenth, 360
Fourteenth, 182, 236
Fifteenth, 311, 336, 360
Sixteenth, 150, 151, 153, 292
Seventeenth, 211, 212, 241
Eighteenth, 205, 228
Nineteenth, 294, 326, 327, 331, 378, 379
Twentieth, 297, 299, 408
Twenty-first, 272, 297, 299, 306, 408
Twenty-Second, 389, 393
Anzac, 70, 82, 93, 97, 104, 105
Canadian, 212, 359, 360
Desert Mounted, 297, 305
Indian (France), 26, 33, 128
First Indian (Mesopotamia), 274, 405
Third Indian (Mesopotamia), 274, 275, 285, 400
Tigris, 161, 162, 165, 166
GERMAN
Guard, 34
Asia, 259
II, 16, 17, 18, 19

IV, 17, 18, 19
IV (Reserve), 10
XIX (Saxon), 37
XXVII (Reserve), 62
DIVISIONS
Guards, 173, 184, 235, 310, 390
First, 236, 339, 366
Second, 3, 361, 371
Third, 6, 10, 14, 24, 224, 257, 377, 391
Fourth (see 1st Hampshire)
Fifth, 13, 23, 26, 55, 65, 132, 177, 182, 212
Sixth, 27, 28, 29, 65, 173, 193, 195, 255
Seventh, 26, 28, 31, 128, 139
Eighth, 128
Ninth, 140, 211, 212, 215, 351, 360, 384, 430
Tenth (see 10th Hampshire to p. 153), 293
Eleventh, 52, 93, 101, 104, 247
Twelfth, 192, 195, 224, 253
Thirteenth, 52, 90, 93, 97, 108, 114, 165, 274, 275, 277, 278, 279, 402
Fourteenth, 185, 332
Fifteenth, 135, 218, 219, 232, 327, 330
Sixteenth (see 11th Hampshire)
Seventeenth, 221, 223, 250
Eighteenth, 188
Twentieth, 177, 193, 235, 236, 253
Twenty-First, 319
Twenty-Second, 146, 149, 156, 289, 290, 291, 293, 419, 422, 423
Twenty-Third, 233, 238, 239, 241
Twenty-Fourth, 226, 227
Twenty-Sixth (see 12th Hampshire)
Twenty-Seventh, 53, 56, 64, 65, 128, 131, 152 (see 10th Hampshire after p. 153)
Twenty-Eighth, 55, 56, 57, 59, 63, 64, 65, 128, 153, 418, 445
Twenty-Ninth (see 2nd Hampshire)
Thirtieth (of 1914–1915), 54
(of 1915–1918), 54, 115, 392
Thirty-First, 170, 171, 172, 369
Thirty-Second (of 1914–1915), 49
Thirty-Third, 197
Thirty-Fourth, 335, 340, 352
Thirty-Fifth, 54, 386
Thirty-Sixth (Ulster), 130, 262, 386
Thirty-Seventh (of 1914–1915), 54
(of 1915–1918) 128, 313, 362, 371
Thirty-Eighth (Welsh), 177
Thirty-Ninth (see 14th Hampshire)
Fortieth (of 1914–1915), 54
Fortieth, 313, 323, 334
Forty-First (see 15th Hampshire)
Forty-Second (E. Lancashire), 79, 82, 83, 84, 85, 86, 98, 324
Forty-Third (1st Wessex), 39, 45, 46, 47
Forty-Fifth (2nd Wessex), 39, 46, 47
Forty-Seventh (London), 134, 135, 227
Forty-Eighth (S. Midland), 39, 170
Forty-Ninth (W. Riding), 180, 378, 389

Fifty-First (Highland), 219, 233, 355, 356, 390

Fifty-Second (Lowland), 88, 90, 115, 267, 268, 269, 271, 272, 297, 301, 302, 303, 307, 409, 411

Fifty-Third (Welsh), 93, 101, 102, 265, 266, 267

Fifty-Fourth (E. Anglian), *see* 8th Hampshire

Fifty-Fifth (W. Lancs), 334

Fifty-Sixth (London), 330

Fifty-Eighth (London), 241

Fifty-Ninth (2nd N. Midland), 339, 340

Sixtieth (London), 241, 293, 294, 305

Sixty-First (2nd S. Midland), 241, 339

Sixty-Second (2nd W. Riding), 332 (*see* 2/4th Hampshire after p. 353)

Sixty-Third (R.N.D.), 84, 85, 90, 197

Sixty-Sixth (2nd E. Lancashire), 319

Sixty-Seventh (2nd Home Counties), 435

Sixty-Eighth (Welsh), 438

Seventy-First (Home Service), 438

Seventy-Fourth (Yeomanry), 268, 409, 411

Seventy-Fifth (*see* 2/4th Hampshire *and* 2/5th Hampshire)

Southern (Rhine Army), 434, 436

INDIAN

Cavalry, 275, 279, 281,

First (Quetta), 126, 271

Second (Rawalpindi), 119

Third (Lahore), 31, 159, 164, 274, 275, 404, 412, 413

Fifth (Mhow), 41, 42

Sixth (Poona), 118, 126

Seventh (Meerut), 159, 160, 274, 280, 286

Twelfth, 123

Fourteenth (*see* 1/4th Hampshire)

Fifteenth, 399

Sixteenth, 287

Seventeenth, 285 (*see* 1/6th Hampshire)

Eighteenth, 405

CANADIAN, 39, 56, 57, 58, 128, 175, 212, 451

NEW ZEALAND, 185, 187, 189, 362, 393

GERMAN

2nd Cavalry, 16

4th Ersatz, 224

5th Bavarian Reserve, 319

9th Reserve, 259

20th, 373 ; 30th, 259 ; 107th, 259

UNITS [1]

7th Dragoon Guards, 396

11th Hussars, 29

14th Hussars, 398, 403

North Irish Horse, 17

Hampshire Carabiniers, 241, 437

37th Battery R.F.A., 129

68th Battery R.F.A., 31

88th Battery R.F.A., 31

157th Field Coy. R.E., 321

Grenadier Guards, 4th Battalion, 174

Royal Scots, 5th Battalion, 42, 77, 78, 88, 109 ; 11th Battalion, 140

Queen's, 10th Battalion, 387 ; 11th Battalion, 385

Buffs, 2nd Battalion, 62 ; 5th Battalion, 164, 166, *see* ' Huffs '

King's Own, 1st Battalion, 29, 63

R. Warwickshire, 2/6th Battalion, 429

R. Fusiliers, 2nd Battalion, 73, 78, 80, 84, 85, 87, 351 ; 3rd Battalion, 58, 59 ; 4th Battalion, 47 ; 26th Battalion, 190

King's, 2nd Battalion, 443

Norfolk, 2nd Battalion, 279, 280 ; 4th Battalion, 92, 102, 267, 297, 298, 307, 414 ; 5th Battalion, 92, 102, 103, 267, 297, 298, 414

Lincolnshire, 7th Battalion, 250

Devons, 4th Battalion, 278 ; 5th Battalion, 272, 353, 363, 364, 407, 408, 412 ; 10th Battalion, 50, 155, 156, 289, 290, 445

Suffolk, 4th Battalion, 92 ; 5th Battalion, 92, 102, 268, 297, 298, 305, 413

Somerset L.I., 1st Battalion, 5, 8, 12, 22, 23, 31, 32, 36, 64, 67, 211, 212, 214, 247, 325, 337, 339, 343, 365, 392, 393 ; 2nd Battalion, 117 ; 2/4th Battalion, 409 ; 5th Battalion, 271

E. Yorkshire, 2nd Battalion, 294

Bedfordshire, 5th Battalion, 307

R. Irish, 2nd Battalion, 321 ; 5th Battalion, 52, 142 ; 6th Battalion, 184

Lancashire Fusiliers, 1st Battalion, 73, 345 ; 2nd Battalion, 27, 67, 330

R. Welsh Fusiliers, 2nd Battalion, 197

South Wales Borderers, 2nd Battalion, 76, 260, 261

K.O.S.B., 1st Battalion, 84, 85, 87, 258, 259, 261, 382, 385, 431

R. Inniskilling Fusiliers, 2nd Battalion, 32

Gloucestershire, 2nd Battalion, 153, 419, 421

Worcestershire, 4th Battalion, 42, 72, 73, 76, 77, 79, 80, 85, 87, 95, 96, 171, 172, 176, 193, 194, 216, 236, 248, 249, 253, 254, 255, 259, 335, 337, 367, 369, 379, 380, 384, 386 ; 2/8th Battalion, 437 ; 9th Battalion, 403

E. Lancashire, 1st Battalion, 5, 12, 14, 20, 133, 170, 171, 195, 203, 211, 212, 247, 310 ; 6th Battalion, 97, 98

[1] This index does not include mentions of the regiments from which attached officers or drafts came, or to which Hampshire officers were posted, but only of units with which the various battalions of the Hampshire co-operated.

E. Surrey, 6th Battalion, 442 ; 12th Battalion, 185, 226, 231, 239, 323, 369, 370

D.C.L.I., 2nd Battalion, 153, 288, 422 ; 8th Battalion, 50, 156, 290, 296, 408, 422, 423, 445

Duke of Wellington's, 2nd Battalion, 343, 349 ; 2/4th Battalion, 364, 376 ; 1/5th Battalion, 356, 360, 375, 376, 390, 394

Border, 1st Battalion, 88 ; 15th Battalion, 352

R. Sussex, 1st Battalion, 117 ; 11th Battalion, 54, 180, 199, 229 ; 12th Battalion, 54, 139, 197 ; 13th Battalion, 54, 139, 229

HAMPSHIRE :
1st Battalion (37th Foot) mobilized, 3–4 ; passage to France, 4 ; journey to front, 5 ; at Le Cateau, 5–12 ; in retreat from Mons, 13–18 ; at the Marne, 19–22 ; at the Aisne, 22–26 ; transfer to Flanders, 26–27 ; in advance to Lys, 27–29 ; defence of Ploegsteert Wood, 29–34 ; trench warfare, winter 1914–15, 35–40 ; transfer to Ypres, 56 ; in Second Ypres, 56–65 ; at the International Trench, 66, 67 ; transfer to Third Army, 68, 128 ; on Ancre, August 1915–June 1916, 128–131 and 133–134 ; in attack on Beaumont Hamel (July 1st, 1916), 169–172 ; transferred to Ypres, 173 ; in Ypres Salient, 174–175 ; back to the Somme, 188 ; in attack near Lesbœufs (October 1916), 195–197 ; in winter, 1916–17, 202–204 ; to Third Army, March 1917, 204 ; in battle of Arras (Fampoux and Roeux), 211–215, 219–222 ; during summer 1917, 243–245 ; in ' Third Ypres ', 247–248 ; during the winter 1917–1918, 309–310 ; defence of Arras (March 29th, 1918), 327–331 ; in battle of Lys (April 1918), 337–340 ; capture of Pacaut Wood, 342–343 ; during summer, 1918, 347–349, 359 , in attack on Drocourt-Quéant Line; 364–366, 373–374 ; in battle of Selle, 38, (October 1918) 389, 391, 392, 393 ; after the Armistice, 429, 438, 439

2nd Battalion (67th Foot), at outbreak of war, 41 ; return home, 42 ; posted to Twenty-Ninth Division, 42 ; departure for Gallipoli, 69 ; in Gallipoli campaign, VI–IX ; in landing at Cape Helles, 70–76 ; in first advance on Krithia, 77–83 ; attack on June 4th, 84–89 ; Lt. Moor's V.C., 87 ; in attack of August 6th, 94–96 ; transferred to Suvla, 103 ; at evacuation of Suvla, 110–111 ; at evacuation of Cape

Helles, 114–116 ; in Egypt, 136 ; transferred to France, 136; on Western Front, 137–138 ; in attack on Beaumont Hamel (July 1st, 1916), 171, 172, 173 ; transferred to Ypres, 175 ; in Ypres Salient, 173, 175, 176 ; back to Somme, 188 ; in attack near Gueudecourt (October 12th and 18th), 192–195 ; during winter 1916–1917, 204–205 ; in battle of Arras (Monchy to Preux), 215–219, 222–223 ; during summer of 1917, 233–234 ; in Third Ypres, 234–237, 246, 248–250 ; at Langemarck (August 16th), 234–236 ; at Poelcappelle (October 9th), 248–250 ; in Cambrai operations (November 20th–December 5th), XX ; during winter 1917–1918, 311, 312, 313 ; in battle of Lys (April 1918), 334–337, 340, 341 ; during summer 1918, 350–351 ; in Lys Salient (August–September 1918), 360, 361, 367, 368 ; in Flanders advance (Sept.–Oct. 1918), 378–388 ; in final advance across Scheldt (Nov. 1918), 395, 396 ; in advance to Rhine, 430 ; on the Rhine, 430, 431 ; return home, 431 ; reconstituted for North Russia, 431 ; to North Russia, 431–434 ; reconstituted, 434–439

Depot, 3, 4, 42, 44, 429, 438

3rd Battalion, (Hampshire Militia to 1881, 3rd, Militia, Battalion to 1907, then Special Reserve.) Mobilized 3 ; in Isle of Wight, 43–45 ; to Gosport (January 1915), 51 ; draft-finding duties, 38, 42, 51, 52, 83, 93, 103, 104, 107, 109, 111, 128 ; move to Catterick, 438 ; absorbed into 1st Battalion, 439

4th (T.F.) Battalion, mobilized, 4, 45, 46 ; forms 2nd Line, 46 ; volunteers for India, 46 ; voyage to India, 47 ; in India, 47, 117 ; ordered to Mesopotamia, 118, X (Ahwaz operations, 120 ; Euphrates operations, 120–122 ; action at Nasiriya, 123, 124 ; H.Q. to Kut al Amara, 126) ; XII, (in defence of Kut, 157–159 ; relief operations, 166, Ib ; attack on El Hanna (Jan. 21st, 1916), 162–164 ; combined with 5th Buffs, 164 ; resume separate formation, 166 ; posted to 14th Indian Division, 167). XXII, (recapture of Kut operations, 274–278 ; passage of Shumran Bend, 277–281 ; advance to and occupation of Baghdad, 281–283 ; in Diala valley, 283–286.) XXXI (advance into Persia, 397–399 ; action at Resht (July 16th), 401 ; detachment at Baku, 402 ; detachment in Trans-

Caspia, 402 ; action at Kuflan Kuh, 403) ; return home, 437, 439–440

2/4th (T.F.) Battalion, formed, 46 ; volunteers for India, 47 ; in India, 117, 126, 167 ; drafts to 1/4th, 127, 167 ; ordered to Palestine, 270, 271 ; on Gaza front, 272 ; in ' Third Gaza ', 299–300 ; in pursuit up coast, 301–302 ; in advance on Jerusalem and at Nebi Samwil, 303–305 ; winter operations, 1917–1918, 305–308, 411 ; ordered to France, 346, 353 ; to Sixty-Second Division, 353 ; in battle of the Ardre, 355–358, 361 ; at Sapignies and Vaux Vraucourt, 261–362 ; at Havrincourt, 371–373 ; passage of Scheldt canal (Sept. 28th–Oct. 1st), 375–378 ; passage of the Selle, 389–391 ; in advance to Sambre, 393–394 ; operations in Palestine, December 1917–May 1918, to Berukin, 407–411 ; on the Rhine, 434–476 ; reduced, 436

3/4th (T.F.) Battalion formed, 47 ; drafts from, 127 ; absorbed into 4th Reserve Battalion, 438

4th Reserve Battalion, 438

5th (T.F.) Battalion, mobilized 4, 45 ; forms 2nd line, 46 ; volunteers for India, 46 ; voyage to India, 47 ; in India, 47, 117, 167 ; drafts from, 127, 168, 437 ; in N.W. Frontier operations (1919), 441 ; return home, 441

2/5th (T.F.) Battalion, formed, 46 ; volunteers for India, 47 ; in India, 117, 126, 168 ; drafts from, 127, 168 ; to Palestine, 270, 271 ; on Gaza front, 272 ; in Third Gaza, 299–300 ; in advance up coast, 301–302 ; in advance on Jerusalem, 303–305 ; in operations in Palestine, Dec. 1917–June 1918, 305–308 ; El Arak, Berukin, 407–412 ; reduced (Aug. 1918), 412

3/5th (T.F.) Battalion, formed, 47 ; drafts from, 127, 164 ; absorbed into 4th Reserve Battalion, 438

6th (T.F.) Battalion, 4, 45 ; forms 2nd Line, 46 ; volunteers for India, 46 ; voyage to India, 47 ; in India, 47, 117 ; drafts to 1/4th, 127, 167, 168 ; ordered to Mesopotamia, 285 ; in Seventeenth Indian Division, 286, 404 ; in advance on Mosul, 405, 438 ; return home, 441

2/6th (T.F.) Battalion, formed, 46 ; draft to 2/5th, 47 ; to 1/4th, 164 ; absorbed into 4th Reserve Battalion, 438

7th (T.F.) Battalion, mobilized, 4, 42, 45 ; forms 2nd Line, 46 ; volunteers for India, 46 ; voyage to India, 49 ; in India, 47, 127, 287 ; drafts to 1/4th, 127, 167, 168 ; to Aden, 287, 438, 442, 443 ; return home, 443

2/7th (T.F.) Battalion, formed, 46 ; volunteers for India, 47 ; in India, 47, 127 ; drafts from, 167 ; to Mesopotamia, 285, 286, 287, 406, 438 ; return home, 441

3/7th (T.F.) Battalion, formed, 47 ; drafts from, 127, 164 ; absorbed into 4th Reserve Battalion, 438

8th (T.F.) Battalion (Isle of Wight Rifles), mobilized, 47 ; coast defence duty, 47, 48 ; posted to Fifty-Fourth Division, 92 ; to Gallipoli, 101 ; in Suvla Bay operation, 101–103, 108, 112–114 ; to Egypt, 114, 263 : XXI (First Gaza, 265–266 ; Second Gaza, 267–268) : XXIV (Third Gaza, 297–299) : XXXII (at Megiddo, Sept. 1918, 413–418) ; 439, 443, 444

2/8th (T.F.) Battalion, formed, 48 ; absorbed into 4th Reserve Battalion, 438

3/8th (T.F.) Battalion, 263 ; absorbed into 4th Reserve Battalion, 438

9th (T.F.) Battalion (Cyclists), mobilized, 47 ; forms 2nd Line, 48 ; coast defence duties, 47–48 ; dismounted, 168, 287 ; to Siberia, 444 ; return home, 445

2/9th (T.F.) Battalion (Cyclists), formed, 48 ; disbanded, 438

10th (Service) Battalion, formation ordered, 4, 25, 39, 43 ; training of, in Ireland, 45–50 ; posted to Tenth Division, 50–51 ; to England for final training, 52 ; to Gallipoli, 53, 93 ; VIII (at Chunuk Bair, 97–101 ; at Hill 60, 104–106), 108, 111 ; transferred to Salonica, 112 ; XI at Kosturino, 143–144 ; the Struma, 150–155 ; at Komarjan, 151–152 ; transferred to Twenty-Seventh Division, 153) ; XXIII (at Homondos, 292 ; at Ada and Kispeki, 293) ; XXXIII (attack on Roche Noire Salient, 419–420) ; disbanded, 445

11th (Service) Battalion, formed, 48–50 ; posted to Sixteenth Division as Pioneers, 50, 53, 132 ; to France, 132 ; in Loos sector, 134–136 ; to the Somme, 176–177 ; in attack on Ginchy (Sept. 9th, 1916), 183–184 ; during winter 1916–1917, 205–206 ; in ' Third Ypres ', 224, 232, 233 ; to Third Army, 233 ; in Bullecourt attack (Nov. 29th, 1917), 257–258 ; in winter 1917–1918, 315 ; in the March offensive, 318–324,

325–327, 331–332 ; reduced to training cadre, 345 ; back to England to be reconstituted, 352 ; return to France, 353, 359 ; under Fifth Army, 370, 371, 375, 376 ; after the Armistice, 429, 437

12th (Service) Battalion, formed, 50, 53 ; move to France, 131 ; to Salonica, 132, 141, 145, 155, 156 ; XXIII (in attack at Doiran, 289–291) ; XXXIII (at White Scar Hill, 422–423 ; advance in Bulgaria, 424–425, 429) after the Armistice, 445 ; disbanded, 446

13th (Service) Battalion, formation of, 45, 51 ; becomes 'Second Reserve', 53 ; drafts from, 87, 93, 103–104, 111, 131, 174 ; becomes 34th Training Reserve Battalion, 208

14th (Service) Battalion (1st Portsmouth), formed, 51 ; allotted to Fortieth Division, 54 ; transferred to Thirty-Ninth Division, 54 ; to France, 133, 138 ; in Festubert sector, 138–139, 175–177 ; to the Somme, 177 ; in attack of Sept. 3rd, 1916 (Hamel), 180–182 ; on Ancre Front, 188, 197 ; at the Schwaben Redoubt, 198–201 ; to Flanders, 201 ; during winter 1916–17, 206–208, 228 ; in attack of July 31st, 1917 (Pilckem), 227–231 ; 2/Lt. Hewitt's V.C., 230, 239, 242 ; attack of Sept. 26th, 1917, 242–243 ; during winter 1917–18, 313–315 ; disbanded, 315

15th (Service) Battalion (2nd Portsmouth, later Hampshire Carabiniers), formed, 54 ; allotted to Forty-First Division, 54 ; to France, 133, 139 ; on Ploegsteert sector, 140, 175, 176, 177 ; to the Somme, 184 ; in attack of September 15th, 1916 (Flers), 185–188 ; Gird Trench, 189–190 ; to Flanders, 190 ; during winter 1916–17, 208–209, 225–226 ; at Messines, 226–227 ; at Hollebeke, 231–232 ; in the attack of Sept. 20th, 1916 (Tower Hamlets), 238–241 ; 2/Lt. Moore's V.C., 240 ; absorb, Hampshire Carabiniers, 241 ; to Italy, 315–317 ; return to France, 317 ; in the March offensive, 318, 324–327 ; to Flanders, 344, 345, 351, 352, 359 ; attack of August 9th (La Clytte), 360 ; in attack at Vierstraat (Sept. 4th), 369, 370, 375 ; in Flanders advance (Sept. 23rd–Oct.), 378–388, 396 ; after the Armistice, 434, 435 ; on the Rhine, 435, 436 ; disbanded, 437–446

16th (Local Reserve) Battalion, formed, 139, 179, 208 ; becomes 97th T.R.B., 208

17th (T.F.) Battalion (formerly 'Hampshire Brigade Battalion' and 84th Provisional Battalion), 47, 208, 438

18th (H.S.) Battalion, 208, 438

18th (Garrison) Battalion (numbered June 1918), 208, 229, 438

51st (Young Soldiers') Battalion, 429, 434

52nd (Graduated) Battalion, 435

53rd (Graduated) Battalion, 435

Dorsetshire, 1st Battalion, 436 ; 2nd Battalion, 443 ; 5th Battalion, 436

Black Watch, 2nd Battalion, 163

O.B.L.I., 1st Battalion, 287

Essex, 1st Battalion, 3, 42, 73, 77, 87, 88, 95, 171, 193, 216, 218, 235, 236, 253, 254, 256, 260, 311 ; 2nd Battalion, 329, 330, 365 ; 4th Battalion, 264 ; 5th Battalion, 102 ; 7th Battalion, 112

Sherwood Foresters, 1st Battalion, 42 ; 7th Battalion, 39 ; 17th Battalion, 229

Loyal North Lancashire, 2nd Battalion, 272 ; 6th Battalion, 91

Royal West Kent, 2nd Battalion, 157, 158 ; 11th Battalion, 185, 186, 225, 226, 227, 231, 239

K.O.Y.L.I., 4th Battalion, 389 ; 5th Battalion, 357, 372, 373

K.S.L.I., 2nd Battalion, 131

Middlesex, 3rd Battalion, 418 ; 16th Battalion, 218 ; 20th Battalion, 323 ; 25th Battalion, 444

K.R.R.C. (60th Rifles), 3rd Battalion, 131 ; 17th Battalion, 199 ; 18th Battalion, 185, 189, 190, 239, 323, 387

Wiltshire, 4th Battalion, 271, 412 ; 7th Battalion, 50, 155, 156, 289, 290, 295, 417, 418

Manchester, 10th Battalion, 83

N. Staffordshire, 2nd Battalion, 117, 119

Durham L.I., 9th Battalion, 60

Highland L.I., 10th/11th Battalion, 323

Seaforth Highlanders, 2nd Battalion, 330

Cameron Highlanders, 10th Battalion (Lovat's Scouts), 153, 292, 417

Royal Irish Rifles, 6th Battalion, 52, 92, 97, 98, 99, 151

Connaught Rangers, 5th Battalion, 52, 105, 142, 143, 144, 150, 152 ; 6th Battalion, 184, 257, 258, 321

Argyll & Sutherland Highlanders, 5th Battalion, 90 ; 14th Battalion, 323

Leinster, 2nd Battalion, 341, 367, 368, 369, 384, 386 ; 6th Battalion, 52, 151 ; 7th Battalion, 136, 258

Royal Munster Fusiliers, 1st Battalion, 71–75, 80, 108 ; 7th Battalion, 145

R. Dublin Fusiliers, 1st Battalion, 24,

195, 196 ; 2nd Battalion, 71, 73, 75, 78, 257 ; 6th Battalion, 144, 145 ; 7th Battalion, 144, 145
Rifle Brigade, 1st Battalion, 6, 7, 12, 20, 22, 36, 37, 67, 195, 212, 213, 221, 247, 248, 330, 331, 342, 343, 359, 365, 366, 393 ; 4th Battalion, 421
17th Entrenching Battalion, 315
London Regiment, 2/1st Battalion, 108
29th Composite Battalion, 151, 152, 84th Composite Battalion, 423, 426
' Huffs ', 163, 164
Monmouthshire, 2nd Battalion, 335
Newfoundland Regiment, 108, 109, 171, 193, 216, 218, 235, 248, 249, 253, 254, 312, 335, 337, 341
New Zealand Mt. Rifles, 105
R.A.M.C., 15
INDIAN ARMY
2nd Rajputs (1/7th), 160
6th Jats (1/9th), 163
24th Punjabis (4/14th), 123, 157
26th Punjabis (2/15th), 167, 275, 280
37th Dogras (1/17th), 163
41st Dogras (3/17th), 163

45th Sikhs (3/15th), 286
48th Pioneers (4/2nd Pioneers), 123
58th Rifles (5/13th), 303, 307, 411
62nd Punjabis (1/1st), 167, 276, 277, 278, 280
76th Punjabis (3/1st), 123, 157
82nd Punjabis (5/1st), 167, 275, 276, 280, 281
84th Punjabis (10/1st), 286
107th Pioneers (1/2nd Pioneers), 160
113th Infantry (10/4th), 286, 405
114th Mahrattas (10/5th), 119
1/2nd Gurkhas, 278, 279, 400, 401, 402
2/3rd Gurkhas, 272, 301, 307, 409, 410
3/3d Gurkhas, 271, 304, 410
2/6th Gurkhas, 97
2/7th Gurkhas, 122–124
1/9th Gurkhas, 279
FRENCH
62nd Infanterie, 128
GERMAN
Pomeranian Grenadiers, 24
9th Bavarian, 185
28th Bavarian Ersatz, 240
395th, 240